PERVASIVE DEVELOPMENTAL DISORDERS

Finding a Diagnosis and Getting Help

D0109423

PERVASIVE DEVELOPMENTAL DISORDERS

DISORDERS

Finding a Diagnosis and Getting Help

Mitzi Waltz

Beijing • Cambridge • Farnham • Köln • Paris • Sebastopol • Taipei • Tokyo

Pervasive Developmental Disorders: Finding a Diagnosis and Getting Help
by Mitzi Waltz

Copyright © 1999 Mitzi Waltz. All rights reserved.
Printed in the United States of America.

Published by O'Reilly & Associates, Inc., 101 Morris Street, Sebastopol, CA 95472.

Editor: Linda Lamb

Production Editor: Claire Cloutier LeBlanc

Printing History:

July 1999: First Edition

Library of Congress Cataloging-in-Publication Data:

Waltz, Mitzi, 1962- .
    Pervasive Developmental Disorders: finding a diagnosis and
getting help / Mitzi Waltz. — 1st ed.
        p. cm. — (Patient-centered guides)
    Includes bibliographical references and index.
    ISBN 1-56592-530-0 (pbk.)
    1. Developmental disabilities—Popular works. 2. Developmentally disabled
children—Services for. 3. Parents of exceptional children. I. Title. II. Series.
    RJ506.D47 W34 1999
    616.85'88—dc21
                                                    99-23708
                                                    CIP

For Ian

Table of Contents

Preface

WHEN IAN WAS TWO, he communicated with grunts, shrieks, and only occasionally, sounds that resembled words. He insisted on watching the same videos over and over. Eye contact was hard to get, but if he wanted your attention *now*, he would literally grab your head and turn your face toward his own. He was a very cuddly, loving child at home, but seemed to shy away from intense sensations everywhere else. A trip to the grocery store was overwhelming; a visit with the dentist was impossible. His moods were mercurial, with quick laughter and equally quick temper tantrums. He was clumsy, constantly banging into furniture and falling, often with no sign of pain.

We loved our beautiful little boy, but we knew something was not quite right.

Starting with his well-baby checkup at the age of six months, we expressed concerns about his development. The answer was always "Give him time—babies develop at their own rate. He's so big and healthy, and cute, too!" If you're reading this book, you've probably heard that one before. It's the answer an overanxious parent with a late bloomer needs to hear, but for many others, it's false reassurance.

When Ian was almost three, we were finally able to schedule a speech and hearing assessment at a nearby teaching hospital. His hearing was just fine, but our developmental concerns were justified, the speech pathologist said. She collared a doctor in the corridor and asked him to take a look at Ian's shambling gait. "Looks like mild cerebral palsy to me," he said. "You should give Early Intervention a call." Then he walked away.

We were devastated.

Early Intervention, a service of the public schools for children with disabilities, provided Ian with an hour and a half of special-education preschool three days a week. He received some speech therapy, which did seem to help jump-start his speech. He also got occupational therapy and physical therapy services. His muscles, previously hypotonic (weak and floppy), got a little stronger. The occupational therapist helped him handle sounds, touches, and other sensations better.

Meanwhile, we read everything we could find about cerebral palsy. Some things fit—the speech delay, the gait—but other things didn't. For one thing, Ian's behavior was becoming increasingly obsessional and repetitive. There was nothing in the CP literature about toddlers who could watch a ceiling fan rotate for an hour. He was a real handful to manage, too, always into something and yet paying little attention to much of what went on around him. He went through periods where he made odd sounds or movements, and his tantrums were downright scary.

It took six years to finally get a real diagnosis for Ian, and when it came, it didn't explain much. He didn't have cerebral palsy after all. The new label, pervasive developmental disorder, not otherwise specified (PDD-NOS), was accompanied by names for his unusual behaviors, labels like chronic tic disorder or Tourette syndrome, obsessive-compulsive disorder, and attention deficit hyperactivity disorder.

There was a certain relief in finally having an explanation of sorts for our son's differences, but now a new set of questions kept us up at night: What did PDD-NOS mean? Had we done something to cause Ian's problems? Was there treatment? Could he get better or had the delay in diagnosis ruined his chances? What would his life be like?

Now we know that at least a quarter of a million families in the US alone are faced with the same dilemma. Experts estimate that one out of every 1,000 children has a pervasive developmental disorder—and the number appears to be growing. Of these children, one-third will be diagnosed with the best-known of the PDDs: autistic disorder, usually called autism. But the great majority do not meet the diagnostic criteria for autism, and may not be able to benefit from (or qualify for) therapeutic and educational programs designed for autistic children.

We devoured literature and medical studies devoted to the pervasive developmental disorders, including the many books available about autism or written by high-functioning autistic adults such as animal scientist Temple Grandin and Australian author Donna Williams. We learned a lot, but still yearned for a book that would cover the majority of children affected with PDDs: those diagnosed with PDD-NOS, atypical PDD, autistic spectrum disorder (ASD), or autistic tendencies. And so this book came to be.

A few notes about the text

The intention of this book is to bring together all the basic information needed by parents of a child diagnosed with these disorders, adults with PDDs who want to gain more insight and self-help skills, and professionals working with individuals who have PDDs. The first two chapters provide a broad overview of the entire pervasive developmental disorders family, with special attention to PDD-NOS and atypical PDD. Subsequent chapters cover diagnosis, treatment, insurance, school, family issues, money and management ideas, and building a support system.

The final chapter of this book provides an inside look at PDD-NOS and atypical PDD, with personal narratives from both children and adults with PDDs about how they see the world, what they need from family, professionals, and friends, and how they cope with these challenging disorders. Their perspective is unique and, in our opinion, crucially important.

Several appendices provide extensive resource lists, including books, Web sites, organizations, research centers, medications and supplements, and diagnostic tools. A glossary of acronyms is included as well.

Although PDDs are more common in males than females, they are not exclusive to one gender. We've tried to alternate between pronouns when talking about patients.

We've done our best to provide accurate information about resources in the English-speaking world, including North America, the United Kingdom, the Republic of Ireland, Australia, and New Zealand. PDDs are a universal phenomenon, however, and occur in all races and nationalities. Readers in other parts of the world may be able to find current data about local resources (including information available in languages other than English) on the World Wide Web. Many useful Web sites are available in Appendix A, *Resources*, and Appendix B, *Support and Advocacy*. Simply because we are writing in the US, some information will be skewed toward American readers. Most, however, will be useful to all.

Throughout the text we present information from the latest medical research. This information is not intended as medical advice. Please consult your physician before changing, stopping, or starting any medical treatment. Some of the health information provided comes from small studies or is controversial in nature. We don't endorse any particular medical or therapeutic approach to PDDs, and we encourage readers to carefully examine any claims made by healthcare facilities, pharmaceutical firms, supplement manufacturers, therapists, and others before implementing new treatments.

We also bring you the words of other parents and patients throughout the book, whose quotes are offset from the rest of the text and presented in italics. In many cases the names and other identifying details have been changed at their request.

Acknowledgments

There are many people who deserve credit for helping this book come to be. Our first thanks go to the many parents and patients who took the time to answer our questions. Your replies opened our eyes to many issues we hadn't considered, and guided the structure and content of this book. We hope that the questions you asked us in return have been fully answered in the text—and we hope this book will be helpful to you in your daily lives.

Dr. Stephen M. Edelson of the Center for the Study of Autism and Dr. Bernard Rimland of the Autism Research Institute have devoted their careers to researching the autistic spectrum and helping children with PDDs. They have also helped us immensely. We are grateful to Dr. Marc Potenza, Dr. Douglas Beer, Dr. Maria A. Pugliese, and Dr. Michael J. Goldberg, among others, for granting us interviews, and to Eric Schopler and Western Psychological Services for allowing us to use an excerpt from the Childhood Autism Rating Scale. Dr. Edelson, Dr. Goldberg, parent/researcher Susan Owens, parent/author Elizabeth Gerlach, and parent/education advocate Sheryl Lilly reviewed the manuscript, helping to correct numerous omissions and errors.

The Autism Society of America and the National Autistic Society (UK) have been excellent sources of current information. Dr. Gene Stubbs, Dr. Benson Schaeffer, Dr. James Schimschock, and Dr. Marv Rosen have also helped us greatly through their research and patient-centered practices.

Kathy Henley, Jane Rake, and others affiliated with the Autistic Children's Activity Program (ACAP) in Portland, Oregon, have provided training and assistance for many, including the author. Our fabulous social worker, Mike Smith, has given us an example of how wraparound services should work, as well as an insider's view of how they really work. Kate Marble, a talented teacher who used her spare time to research ideas that helped our son, showed us that it's caring, not special training, that makes all the difference.

Fay Martinolich's monthly support group meetings for families of autistic-spectrum children in our neighborhood have offered a wonderful discussion forum, a shoulder to lean on, and some great Italian food. Likewise, the Tourette Syndrome Association, the Obsessive-Compulsive Foundation, and Children and Adults with Attention Deficit Disorders (CHADD) have been helpful in bringing issues related to neurobehavioral disorders to the fore, and in funding important research that sheds light on PDDs as well as co-morbid disorders.

Jackie Aron, manager of the Sunrise Tourette email list, has brought together a group of families contending with multiple neurological disorders, including PDDs, and made her list a forum for solid medical information and personal support. Many other Internet-based forums and their participants have been helpful as well, including Ray Kopp's Autism mailing list at St. John's University, the Apraxia-Kids list managed by Sharon Gretz, Elaine Montoya's Strep-n-TS list, Martijn Dekker's list for people with Asperger's syndrome and high-functioning autism, and the Massachusetts General Hospital neurology forums maintained on the Web by John Lester.

Everyone at O'Reilly & Associates has been wonderful to work with. Much-deserved thanks go to Linda Lamb, Carol Wenmoth, Edie Freedman, and all of the extraordinarily professional editing and production staff. I have to thank my agent, Karen Nazor, as well—she always makes my life easier by handling the most difficult details with aplomb.

Of course, Ian has been our greatest teacher, and we continue to learn from him every day.

—Mitzi Waltz

If you would like to comment on this book or offer suggestions for future editions, please send email to *patientguides@oreilly.com*, or write to O'Reilly & Associates, Inc., at 101 Morris St., Sebastopol, CA 95472.

CHAPTER 1

The Medical Facts About PDDs

PERVASIVE DEVELOPMENTAL DISORDER (PDD) is a label of convenience created by psychiatrists. It describes a variety of neurological conditions that adversely affect a person's speech and communication, emotional growth and socialization, and physical capabilities. This book concentrates on PDD-NOS, atypical PDD, and other "unspecified" PDDs. Several other disorders fall into the general category of PDDs, and they may not have identical causes.

All of the pervasive developmental disorders are rooted in a complex combination of genetics, individual brain wiring, and, to a much lesser extent, environmental factors. As of this writing, no genetic test can predict PDDs, and nothing can be done during pregnancy or infancy to prevent them. They are not caused by poor parenting, abuse, or economic deprivation. Although there is no cure, effective treatment is possible in many cases, and promising research is underway.

In this chapter, we explain what's known about PDDs in general, and about PDD-NOS and atypical PDD in particular. We talk about the PDD label and how it is used by physicians, including its role in the frustrating process of diagnosis by elimination. We discuss basic neurology as it relates to this topic, including differences in brain chemistry, structure, and electrical activity that may be involved in PDDs. We also cover genetic and other factors in PDDs, and wind up with a brief discussion of where research is heading.

Not quite right

The person with PDD-NOS or atypical PDD is a puzzle—"not quite right" in ways that are easy to see, but hard to define medically or treat. It's not autism in the classical sense, although autism is also part of the larger diagnostic family called pervasive developmental disorders. It's not mental retardation or emotional disturbance, although its symptoms can mimic these conditions or coexist with them. In fact, although it is considered a psychiatric diagnosis, conditions in the autistic spectrum are not mental illnesses.

Unfortunately, PDDs are not rare. About 1 of every 1,000 children born in the US is diagnosed with a pervasive developmental disorder. Autistic disorder (autism) is the best-known PDD, but PDD-NOS is at least twice as common—and a hundred times more vaguely defined.

> The most frustrating thing about the diagnosis is that Stevie has mild [autistic] traits and is nonverbal, but he does not totally behave in the autistic mold. Therefore he does not fit in with certain parameters outlined by clinicians and school districts. —Roni, adoptive mother of five-year-old Stevie (diagnosed atypical autism)

Parents of a young child with undiagnosed PDD-NOS or atypical PDD may suspect any number of things, from autism to severe allergies. Doctors may be just as befuddled, trying out labels like:

- Atypical
- Pathologically shy or withdrawn
- Severely emotionally disturbed
- Mentally retarded
- Developmentally delayed
- Atypical autism
- Autistic-like
- Autistic tendencies
- Severe communication disorder
- Developmental language disorder
- Apraxia of speech
- Speech and/or gross motor dyspraxia
- Obsessive-compulsive disorder (OCD)
- Central auditory processing deficit (CAPD)
- Severe attention deficit disorder (ADD) or attention deficit hyperactivity disorder (ADHD)
- Atypical or mild cerebral palsy

One or any combination of these terms may be used in an attempt to describe a child—or, eventually, an adult—who tends to be socially inappropriate and emotionally immature, who often seems unaware of his or her surroundings, who may not be able to speak or move quite normally, who has great difficulty with social relationships, and who may behave in obsessive, compulsive, repetitive, or unusual ways.

> *When Jeffrey was four years old, a pediatric neurologist wrote "static encephalopathy." When he was seven years old, another pediatric neurologist wrote "bilateral brain damage with secondary mental retardation." Just this month, I had a PhD in the psychiatric department review Jeff's history, test results, school and medical records, interview him, and interview me. He wrote in his report "typical of autism." That's as close as I am at this time. —Cindy, mother of 15-year-old Jeffrey (diagnosed verbal dyspraxia with autistic-like features)*

Alternatively, a physician may diagnose the child as autistic, even though he or she does not meet all the official criteria for autism. (See Appendix F, *Diagnostic Tools,* for questionnaires used by professionals to diagnose autism and other PDDs.)

The problem with the PDD label

Pervasive developmental disorder is not a very descriptive label, nor is it entirely accurate. The word "pervasive" is misleading, because individuals are usually not affected in every aspect of their lives or every body function. Developmental is a bit of a misnomer as well, since the problem doesn't really lie in how or how fast the person's abilities are manifested. There may be true delays in the emergence of speech, physical capabilities, social relationships, or emotional function. On the other hand, some abilities may never appear at all. Each child with a pervasive developmental disorder is an individual with a unique pattern of symptoms, and this label doesn't really capture that fact.

Dr. Bernard Rimland, one of the most respected researchers in the field of autism, is a vociferous critic of the term. "The PDD designation, along with its cumbersome bureaucratic baggage (i.e., PDD-NOS: not otherwise specified), should be relegated to the Archives of Failed Attempts," he wrote in a 1993 article titled "Plain Talk About PDD and the Diagnosis of Autism."[1] Dr. Rimland recommends ditching the term altogether, and he is probably right—but until the medical establishment can decide on something more appropriate, we're stuck with PDD-NOS, atypical PDD, and all the rest.

> The most frustrating thing about his diagnosis was that it was put to me like it was the end of the world. He'd never do this, or that. And PDD-NOS is not an answer. It's too vague. He fit all the criteria for autism. [PDD-NOS] didn't come with a set of instructions. —Ann, mother of eight-year-old Theron (diagnosed PDD-NOS, psychotic disorder, borderline intellectual functioning)

One possible substitute is "autistic spectrum disorders" (ASDs), a term that is getting increased acceptance in the medical world. In addition, at least some subtypes of PDD probably fall into the newly proposed diagnostic categories of multi-system neurological disorders or regulatory disorders, both championed by Dr. Stanley Greenspan and his allies in the fields of child psychiatry, psychology, and neurology. (You'll find Dr. Greenspan's books, which are excellent source material for both parents and professionals, listed in Appendix A, *Resources*.) These categories haven't won official acceptance yet, but they're a closer fit for many than PDD.

Defining pervasive developmental disorders

Now that you know what PDDs are not, you'll want to know what they *are*. Simply put, the label "pervasive developmental disorder" describes an array of neurological conditions that share some similar characteristics. It appears in the *Diagnostic and Statistical Manual of Mental Disorders* (DSM-IV), the book used by psychiatrists and other physicians to define brain-based medical problems.

Quite honestly, it shouldn't be in the DSM at all. Other neurological disorders, such as epilepsy, are considered medical issues, pure and simple. But for reasons that are unclear, our medical system has chosen to set the brain apart from all other organs of the body. When your heart isn't working properly, you see a medical doctor. When your brain is a bit haywire, the first person you probably see is a counselor, social worker, psychologist, or psychiatrist. Of these, only the psychiatrist is an MD. Many other professionals still seem to believe that, because the brain can think, all of its ailments, too, can be controlled through better thinking.

Research is changing that picture rapidly, however, and it's not a moment too soon. Fifty years ago, when the now-discredited theories of Bruno Bettelheim held sway among doctors who saw patients with PDDs, it was believed that emotionally unavailable parents created autistic children. Parents were encouraged (and sometimes forced) to institutionalize their children with autism or other PDDs. The institutions were unable to do much to help these children, but Bettelheim and other doctors claimed that was because irreparable damage had already been done in infancy.

A few doctors still hold such theories—and if you should happen to encounter one, run away quickly!

The truth is that pervasive developmental disorders are probably caused by a variety of factors working together. Parenting style is simply not one of them, although an abusive or neglectful home environment certainly will take its toll on a child with PDD, as on any other child.

Medical science has not even identified some of the factors that cause PDDs. It's certain that genetic inheritance plays the most prominent role, but only some children in families with a history of autistic spectrum disorders end up with a PDD. Quite possibly, it takes genetic susceptibility plus something else—a particular combination of genes from both parents, an infection, immune system problems, allergies, even drugs or environmental pollution—to cause PDDs.

A crash course in basic neurology

The brain is the most complex and least understood organ in the body. It is the focal point of the central nervous system (CNS), which also includes the nerves of the spine. The CNS receives, processes, and sends billions of signals every day by way of chemicals and electrical impulses. Neurologists (physicians who specialize in studying and treating brain diseases and disorders) are only starting to identify how these chemicals and power surges work, and what we know right now is woefully inadequate for helping when these processes go awry.

Most of the medical information presented in this chapter is derived from studies of people with autism rather than people diagnosed with PDD-NOS or atypical PDD. The findings are believed to apply across the entire spectrum of PDDs, although there may be differences according to the severity of each individual's symptoms. There may also be some special, as yet unknown, factors involved in various PDDs.

Brain structure 101

The brain has several parts, all of which work together to control body functions, produce thought and emotion, and store and retrieve memories (see Figure 1-1). Researchers are not even sure which parts of the central nervous system are affected by PDDs, although a clearer picture is emerging every year thanks to brain-imaging technologies. These include computer tomography (CAT), magnetic resonance imagery (MRI), and single photon emission computed tomography (SPECT or NeuroSPECT) scans.

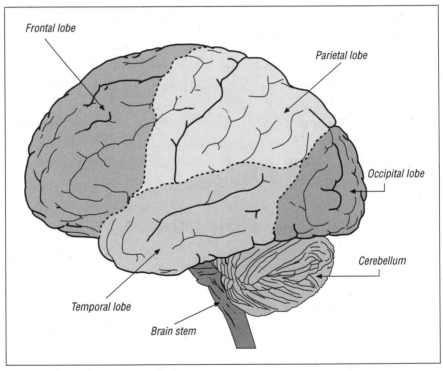

Figure 1-1. Parts of the human brain

Although they can't be used as to diagnose PDDs just yet, brain scans can show where abnormal activity is occurring or whether the brain is structured differently than usual. Tests of cerebrospinal fluid, blood, and urine are also producing hard data.

The brain is mostly made up of two kinds of cells. The first kind, neurons, do the hard work of transmitting all that information. The second kind, glial cells, are twice as numerous as neurons. Glial cells have the less glamorous jobs of making sure the neurons have enough nutrients and other chemicals, repairing the brain if it is injured, and confronting bacteria that try to attack the brain. Obviously, problems with either type of cell could be involved in PDDs, and if one type of cell is affected, that would change how the other type functions as well.

Brain differences in PDDs

Autopsy studies over the past twenty years have indicated some differences at the cell level in people with autism. Neurons in the limbic system of the brain seem to be smaller and closer together, while neurons in other areas of the brain may be larger or smaller than usual. There appears to be a loss of Purkinje cells (a particular type of neuron) in the cerebellum. Some cell differences seem to depend on the age of the person, with brains from autistic children tending to be larger than normal and brains from autistic adults smaller than usual.

One 1997 autopsy study did find brain-stem damage, which would also explain the higher-than-normal number of people with autism who have minor ear malformations. This study was spurred by the observation that, when the dangerous drug Thalidomide was in use, one-third of the children who had been exposed to it between the twentieth and twenty-fourth day in the womb were later diagnosed as autistic. This is the period in which both the brain stem and the ears form.[2]

Researchers are careful to say that certain types of brain damage, such as lesions on the temporal lobe or damage due to infection, can cause "autistic-like" symptoms. One current theory is that the development of some brain cells or structures is slower than normal or never completed in people with PDDs.

Of course, there haven't been very many autopsy studies, since PDDs do not cause death. Very recently, researchers using MRI machines and other high-tech tools have been finding very subtle differences in the brains of living people with autism. The parietal, temporal, and occipital lobes are all reported as being larger in volume than expected, for instance, and there are signs of unusual activity patterns. There may also be differences in the size of the cerebellum.

Although research continues into differences in brain structure, most doctors are more concerned with how the brain actually functions. It's a pretty adaptable organ, after all—with proper medical care, people can recover from strokes, accidents, or illnesses that cause brain damage, because the brain is built to route around problems whenever possible. It seems that where PDDs are concerned, relatively minor structural or chemical differences may be influencing how brain cells communicate with each other, with the CNS, and with the body as a whole.

Neurotransmitters: the brain's telephone system

Neurons are the brain's internal communication centers, but they don't trade messages directly. Neurons have a central cell body with long "arms" called axons, and smaller tentacle-like structures called dendrites (see Figure 1-2). Inside a neuron, all the messages are sent via electrical impulses. Where two neurons meet to swap information, however, there's a small space between them called the synaptic cleft. Electrical impulses have to be translated into neurotransmitters, chemicals that cross the synaptic cleft and are then re-translated into electrical signals on the other side (see Figure 1-3).

Much has been learned about the role of neurotransmitters in PDDs by accident. For example, autistic symptoms improved in some patients when they were taking medicines for something else, such as depression. Now, targeted studies of medications indicate that several kinds of neurotransmitters have something to do with PDDs.

There are many different neurotransmitters running around in the human brain, the CNS, and the gastrointestinal system. They're all site-specific chemicals that can be absorbed only by certain cells and at certain spots. This ensures that the right kinds of messages get through. They are also used and absorbed differently in various areas of the body, and sometimes turned into other kinds of chemicals.

Several neurotransmitters appear to be involved in pervasive developmental disorders, including:

- **Serotonin.** Serotonin, also called 5-hydroxytryptamine or 5-HT, controls sleep, mood, some types of sensory perception, body-temperature regulation, and appetite. It affects the rate at which hormones are released and has something to do with inflammation. Studies have shown that autistic people tend to have increased amounts of serotonin

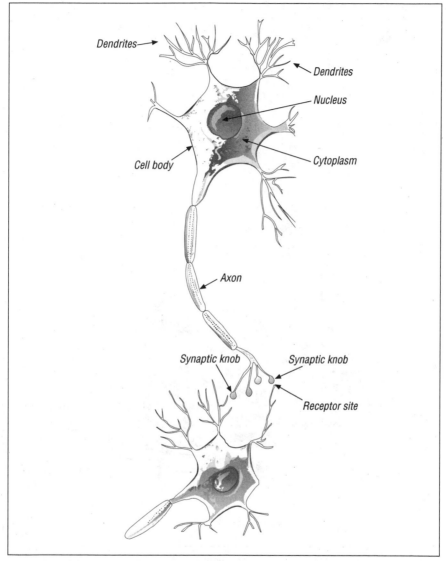

Figure 1-2. The structure of a neuron

in their blood. They may produce, absorb, or metabolize serotonin differently, although studies are still trying to determine how.

- **Dopamine**. Dopamine, sometimes abbreviated as DA, helps control body movements and thought patterns, and also regulates how hormones are released. Although medications that block dopamine have been useful to some people with autism, researchers are not sure why.

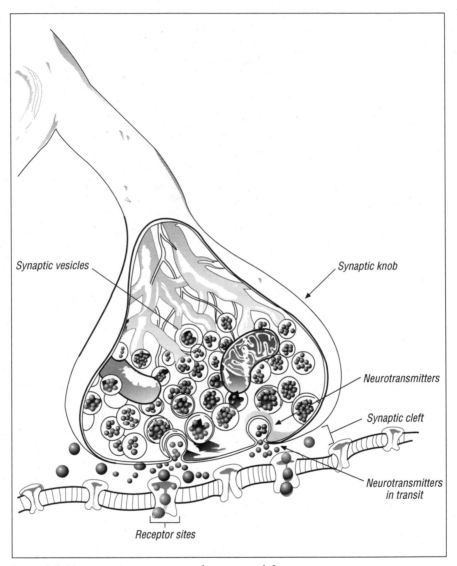

Figure 1-3. *Neurotransmitters crossing the synaptic cleft*

Perhaps there are differences in how these people create or absorb dopamine.

- **Norepinephrine.** Norepinephrine is used by both the CNS and the peripheral sympathetic nervous system (the nerves that communicate with the rest of the body). It governs arousal, the "fight or flight" response, anxiety, and memory. There seem to be small differences in how autistic people make and process norepinephrine.

Medications that change how much of certain neurotransmitters are produced, or how these chemicals are absorbed in the brain, produce changes in PDD symptoms—that's one of the clues that have let researchers know which chemicals have something to do with the condition. These medicines don't cure the underlying disorder, but in some people they can create major improvements in behavior and emotional stability. (See Chapter 5, *Medical Interventions,* and Appendix D, *Medication Reference,* for more information about these medications and how they work.)

Physical activity, exercise, diet, vitamins, and herbal supplements can also affect these neurotransmitters. That's one of the reasons that parents and professionals need to be as careful about choosing alternative treatments as they would be about prescription drugs. (For more information about nonpharmaceutical treatments for PDDs, see Chapter 6, *Therapeutic Interventions,* and Chapter 7, *Other Interventions.*)

Electrical miswiring

The brain's electrical system is intimately intertwined with this chemical messaging system. Problems can occur during the electrical side of the communication process when uncontrolled surges of electricity, called seizures, take place inside the brain. Seizure disorders (epilepsy) are common in people with autism. By young adulthood, between a quarter and a third of autistic people have experienced identifiable physical seizures.

Many more people with PDDs may experience other types of seizures, some of which are hard to recognize, even with sophisticated monitoring equipment. For example, some doctors believe that the inexplicable temper tantrums some people with PDDs have may be related to seizures occurring deep within the frontal lobe.

If seizures are suspected, neurologists usually rely on evidence gathered from an electroencephalogram (EEG). Unfortunately, EEG equipment is not sensitive enough to detect all types of seizures in all parts of the brain. (Chapter 2, *PDD Categories,* and Chapter 5 present more information about the connection between seizures and PDDs, and about how seizure disorders can be treated.)

Genetics and PDDs

There is no genetic screening test available for autism or other PDDs today, but several teams of researchers around the world are searching for genes that contribute to these disorders. In 1997, one group of genetic researchers announced that the first of the three to five genes believed to cause most autistic spectrum disorders had been tentatively located on chromosomes 7 and 16. Much more work remains to be done in this area.

Pervasive developmental disorders do run in families, and the genetic connection is fairly strong, although the pattern of inheritance is unknown. Many parents of children diagnosed with PDDs recognize a little of themselves when they look at their child's symptoms, or can recall close relatives who seem to have been somewhere on the autistic spectrum. The current wisdom is that parents of a child with autism have a 3 to 4.5 percent chance of having a second child with autism, about 50 times the normal risk. Other studies have indicated that a greater number of autistic children's siblings have some degree of autistic tendencies, up to and including PDD-NOS or atypical PDD, than autism per se. In some cases, of course, there are no known relatives with even mild autistic tendencies.

Several genetic disorders are known to be associated directly with autism. Of these, fragile X syndrome (FRAXA) and tuberous sclerosis are probably the most important and most widespread.

Somewhere between 2.5 and 5 percent of people with autism have a fragile site on their X chromosome. These individuals usually have some degree of mental retardation, and their autistic features are a little different from those of others on the spectrum. When neurologists suggest genetic screening for children they suspect may be autistic, what they are usually checking for is FRAXA.

Tuberous sclerosis is a relatively rare disorder (about 1 out of 6,000 people) that affects the brain, the skin, the eyes, and other organs of the body with varying degrees of severity. As many as half of all children diagnosed with tuberous sclerosis have autistic features. Most have epilepsy, and many are mentally retarded. Tuberous sclerosis can be caused by two different genetic defects, one on chromosome 9 and one on chromosome 16. Only one of these genes is necessary to cause the condition, although other genetic factors as yet unknown may determine who develops the disorder. The link between tuberous sclerosis and autism may be physical rather than genetic.

A 1997 study published in the medical journal *Lancet* stated that patients with both tuberous sclerosis and autism or atypical PDD whose brains were imaged had tubers (a tumor-like growth characteristic of tuberous sclerosis) in their temporal lobes, and had more tubers in their brains in general than those patients without autistic features.[3]

Two genetic disorders caused by mutations on chromosome 15, Prader-Willi syndrome and Angelman syndrome, also correlate with autism and other PDDs. These are discussed briefly in Chapter 2.

Several other neurological disorders occur more frequently in people with PDDs and their relatives than in the general population. Affective disorders, particularly depression and bipolar disorder (manic depression), are especially high in these families. Other problems reported more often include ADD/ADHD, phobias and other anxiety disorders, obsessive-compulsive disorder, and Tourette syndrome. All of these conditions are believed to be associated with genetic differences, but the genes have not been definitively identified for any of them. Direct genetic or functional relationships to PDDs may eventually be found, or these links may turn out to be circumstantial.

Genes that are different can cause the brain to develop in ways that are outside the norm, and they also affect how the rest of the body works, including the endocrine (hormonal), metabolic, and immune systems. The late autism researcher Dr. Reed Warren's work suggested that some of the genes connected to autism might be among those that control immune function.

Just as this book went to press, a team of researchers in the UK announced that the first genetic mutation associated with speech and communication disorders, and particularly with apraxia of speech, had been located on chromosome 7, in the same general area as the mutation previously linked to autism.

When researchers finally find all of the genes that contribute to PDDs, it may be possible to develop screening tests—although using such tests will certainly raise ethical issues. It may also be possible to develop some sort of gene therapy that could actually cure PDDs, although today this type of medicine is only in its infancy.

Other factors in PDDs

Most researchers downplay the importance of infections, metabolic disorders, environmental insults, and other factors in full-blown autism. However, some of the most prominent researchers in the field say there is persuasive evidence that neurological differences and genetics alone are not the culprits. In addition, other factors probably do play a role in the development of autistic features in at least some people who don't meet all the criteria for autism, including people diagnosed with PDD-NOS, atypical PDD, and similar disorders.

Among the metabolic disorders known to be associated with autistic features are phenylketonuria (PKU), histidinemia, and Lesch-Nyhan syndrome. In the US, PKU tests are routinely given to newborns. Tests are available for the other two metabolic disorders mentioned, although the link to PDDs is rare enough that physicians are reluctant to order testing without additional evidence.

A number of researchers and parents have noted that gastrointestinal (GI) tract problems, diarrhea, and food allergies are much more common in children with PDDs. Some are trying vitamin supplements, GI tract medications, and special diets in case there is an underlying metabolic disorder involved, with varying degrees of success. Chapter 5 and Chapter 7 detail the current state of these efforts.

> We always knew, because of observing our son, that all of his behavioral difficulties were something metabolic—problems happened right after eating. Jared has a history of heavy antibiotic use. At eleven months old, he had an infected benign tumor on his tongue. He developed a massive staph infection throughout his body, and was on a very strong antibiotic for a full year. All of his developmental problems occurred after that.
> —Amy, mother of seven-year-old Jared (diagnosed PDD-NOS/atypical autism)

One feature that may contribute to autistic spectrum disorders is some degree of immune system dysfunction. It could be that infections affect children born with particular genes more severely. A recent study at NIH, which will be discussed further in Chapter 5, has found a link between obsessive-compulsive disorder and Tourette syndrome (a tic disorder) in some children infected with the same common streptococcus bacteria that causes strep throat or ear infections.[4] The NIH research team thinks this link may extend to some children with PDDs, and hopes to take a closer look at this population soon.

There are also many anecdotal reports of infection during pregnancy with rubella, herpes, Epstein-Barr, cytomegalovirus, HIV, and other agents, followed by the birth of children with PDDs. Other parents have reported that autistic features emerged after an illness in infancy or early childhood, or shortly after vaccination. There's no absolute proof, but it's not right to simply brush off such suspicions. Parents may be on to something, as they so often have been in the past.

A very recent study found correlations between significant levels of antibodies to the measles virus (measles-IgG) or the common human herpes virus (HHV-6-IgG) and/or the presence of antibodies to the person's own myelin basic protein (anti-MBP) and/or neuron-axon filament protein (anti-NAFP) in autistic subjects. Not all people with autistic spectrum disorders have these antibodies, but in those who do, it indicates the possibility of an autoimmune disorder that may be triggered by a virus or vaccine.[5] Dr. Andrew Wakefield's research in the UK has also implicated the measles vaccine in autism.[6] Although preliminary results of his study were recently published in *Lancet*, Wakefield's hypothesis is still considered somewhat controversial.

The only positive aspect of the AIDS crisis is that it has driven scientists to understand as much as possible about the human immune system. What they have learned about immune function, and the medications and other treatments developed to boost immunity, may turn out to be helpful for some people with PDDs.

Finally, there have been a number of reports linking PDDs with environmental insults, ranging from cocaine use during pregnancy to living near centers of industrial pollution. There's no proof, but this may hold true for individual cases. The recent identification of possible geographic PDD clusters raises the ominous possibility that at least some cases of PDD may be caused or exacerbated by unknown environmental or infectious factors. Not enough is known at this time, but you can be sure that dedicated researchers and advocacy groups are trying hard to find out what's behind this phenomenon.

You are not alone

Whatever they are called, pervasive developmental disorders other than autism affect at least a quarter of a million people in the US, one-third of whom are children. According to researchers, there may be as many as twice that number who fit the criteria for PDD-NOS or atypical PDD, but who remain undiagnosed or misdiagnosed. Extrapolate these numbers to get a worldwide figure, and you can see that PDDs are not a minor medical problem.

There are probably other families in your community who are experiencing the same challenges that you face. It can be hard to connect, because the behaviors associated with PDDs can keep families isolated from each other. But even people who live in remote areas of the world can now make contact by joining support groups, subscribing to newsletters, or using the Internet. Chapter 12, *Support*, focuses on building these connections, which are essential for families, people with PDDs, and professionals who work with this population as well.

You can help people with PDDs

Parents are sometimes afraid to ask the $64,000 question: what will happen to my child? Teens and adults with PDDs may feel discouraged about their future in the world as well. At this time there is no sure cure for any form of pervasive developmental disorder, but there are medications, therapies, and educational techniques that can address symptoms and improve the lives of people with PDDs. In some cases, the results can be spectacular—although subtle deficits and differences will probably remain, the properly treated individual can live a rich, enjoyable, and independent life.

> *My hopes for Stevie are that he reaches adulthood and is able to function on his own, make his own decisions, hold down a job, drive a car (which he tries to do now at age five), and have the communications abilities to enable him to do this.* —Roni

As for the residual differences, who wants a world of cookie-cutter humans? People with PDDs are all unique and wonderful individuals, many with special talents to share, and each with a right to be accepted just as they are.

Today, only about one-third of those diagnosed with a pervasive developmental disorder achieve full independence as adults, but that statistic is changing rapidly. Due to accumulating medical knowledge, new types of education programs, and the efforts of determined advocates for children and adults with disabilities, we are going to make the future much brighter for newly diagnosed children—and adults with PDD will also benefit from these developments.

Adults with autism and other PDDs are now working together to improve their status. Through support groups, Web sites, online discussion groups, and self-advocacy work, they are trying to access better medical care, accept their differences, and find opportunities to use their often considerable abilities.

Best of all, current research into the possible causes of PDDs may hold the secret to real healing. Interest in the medical and research communities is growing, as evidenced by the rapid growth of the international Annual PDD Symposium, which held its third session in 1998, the National Institutes of Health's intensive, multiple-site autism research program, increased research grant awards for PDD-related studies around the world, and improved information about these disorders in medical textbooks.

We strongly encourage you to keep abreast of the latest research into autistic spectrum disorders. There probably won't be one big breakthrough, but many small steps can take you to the same destination as a giant leap.

CHAPTER 2

PDD Categories

THIS BOOK BEGAN BY EXPLAINING what the pervasive developmental disorders are as a general diagnostic category. In this chapter, we get down to specifics. If you're trying to make sense of a diagnosis—or if you're wondering whether PDD-NOS, atypical PDD, or something else entirely would be an appropriate label—this chapter can help.

Before making a diagnosis of PDD-NOS or atypical PDD, doctors rule out the specified PDDs. Along with autistic disorder (autism), these include Asperger's syndrome, childhood disintegrative disorder, fragile X syndrome, and Rett syndrome. This chapter describes each of these PDDs in some detail.

Next, we look at other conditions that share some symptoms with the autistic spectrum disorders. These may need to be ruled out before a PDD diagnosis is made, although one of these conditions may coexist with a PDD.

Finally, we provide the latest information about PDD-NOS, atypical PDD, and other unspecified autistic spectrum disorders. We also offer a brief discussion of diagnostic categories under development that may more accurately describe some individuals with PDD-NOS or atypical PDD.

About categories and labels

The diagnostic merry-go-round is incredibly frustrating. It's especially hard to wait for another appointment, another referral, another opinion, when you feel that the opportunity to help a child is slipping away with every passing day.

Doctors understand this frustration, and that's why PDD is described as a spectrum disorder, where individuals may be at any point along a rather broad continuum. Each person with a PDD diagnosis is neurologically impaired in one or more ways, but other systems may be unaffected. The degree of impact can also vary from mild to severe. For example, one person with PDD-NOS may have a severe and persistent speech delay, but only mild social deficits, while another is unable to form social attachments at all, but has developed relatively normal speech patterns by grade school.

Naturally, the descriptions of the specified PDDs are much more cut and dried than the criteria for PDD-NOS and atypical PDD. That's because, for the past twenty years or so, researchers have been painstakingly teasing out the details of these subtypes within the overall category of pervasive developmental disorders. There are surely additional subtypes yet to be discovered—in fact, the Autism Research Institute is currently crunching the numbers on questionnaires returned by parents of children diagnosed with autism or related disorders. ARI hopes to identify some new categories that might make their way into the next DSM. Similar efforts are going on elsewhere. Some of the preliminary concepts now arising are discussed later on in this chapter.

It might seem that categorization doesn't do much for patients in the here and now, but it's actually a very important task. With greater understanding comes clearer diagnosis and, eventually, realistic treatment options. It could be that people with one subtype will respond amazingly well to a particular medication, while others do not. Another subtype may respond to a yeast-free diet. Until the process of categorization is more complete, choosing therapeutic options is a hit-and-miss process.

As you read through these descriptions, you may notice that your child, your patient, or you resemble parts of one of these diagnoses. A child may have the kind of topic fixations you'd expect with Asperger's syndrome, for instance, but also have a significant speech delay. Unless a person meets all of the criteria for one of the specified PDDs, proper practice is to place them in the PDD-NOS or atypical PDD category. (Note: Strategies and medications that work with specific symptoms can often be used across the spectrum, no matter what PDD subtype they were originally developed for. For example, if a child with PDD-NOS is repetitively hitting herself in the head to the point of injury, a behavior more common in "low-functioning" people with autism, the methods used to stop this activity in autistic people might be just the thing to try. Labels are important, but when it comes to treatment, you have to look at the person and his or her actual symptoms, not just the label.)

Finally, a person may start out with one diagnosis, such as PDD-NOS, and end up with another one several years later when new symptoms emerge or old ones disappear. There are many cases in which a very young child diagnosed with autistic disorder later "moved up" to PDD-NOS or atypical PDD or, in a few cases, to no PDD diagnosis at all. Sometimes the first diagnosis was simply wrong, but other times the person has made truly remarkable progress. That's what we're all hoping for, and, with luck, studying these cases can teach us how to reach that goal.

In other patients, autistic symptoms can get worse. This is particularly true when PDD is complicated by severe or untreated seizure activity. In addition, when an individual with PDD suffers neglect or abuse, as has happened to many institutionalized children, a promising future becomes less likely—although it is never too late to try.

One family's experience

One family's long journey toward diagnosis took four years of trekking from doctor to doctor. Seven-year-old Joshua was given the following diagnoses:

- PDD-NOS. "The psychologist who gave this diagnosis said Joshua would probably never be able to live independently," says his mother, Krista.

- Disturbed. "The HMO child psychiatrist who gave this diagnosis had white plastic bags full of sweets all over his office floor," Krista notes, with more than a touch of residual ire in her voice.

- Severe communication disorder, ADHD, and possible Tourette syndrome. "The developmental pediatrician and neuropsychologist at Children's Hospital gave this diagnosis, saying the PDD was wrong, that they'd seen specialized cases like Joshua's enough to know," Krista says.

- Rolandic epilepsy.

- Receptive and expressive language aphasia, central nervous system dysfunction, and ADHD.

In the past four years, Joshua has been through many medication trials, including stimulants, antidepressants, antipsychotics, and other drugs, none of them particularly helpful. He has undergone tests for allergies, metabolic disorders, chromosome abnormalities, hearing problems, and seizures.

Joshua sees a speech therapist, an occupational therapist, an adaptive PE specialist, and a behaviorist, and is taught by a special education teacher. He attends school in a mainstream second-grade class. He has been variously described as intelligent, easily distracted, obsessional, unusual, sweet-natured, and overly emotional.

> *Aside from the extreme attentional problems, the most difficult thing to deal with is his extreme variability. On good days, he does everything well: reads well, talks well, takes disappointment well. On bad days, he can't do anything. He can't talk, he can't read, he can't tolerate frustration, he can't perform at all. Everyone who works with him knows this is a child with a great deal of potential who presents different facets of himself as puzzles that are unresolved and unaccounted for, bewildering.*
> —Krista, mother of seven-year-old Joshua

How do you label a child like Joshua? It isn't enough to enumerate the symptoms and then say, "Let's just think of him as Josh."

As another parent said about his son, Jeremy:

> *What does having [it be] "just Jeremy" do for my son? Are there schools for "just Jeremy"? Is anyone developing medications for "just Jeremy"? I do see him as an individual first—he's my son. But the rest of the world can't and won't. I want to make sure he gets as much help as we can get him.* —George, father of six-year-old Jeremy (diagnosed PDD-NOS)

Specified pervasive developmental disorders

Five specified PDDs are listed here in alphabetical order, not in order of how common they are or their severity. You may also want to see Appendix F, *Diagnostic Tools*, which includes questionnaires and rating scales that professionals use to make a diagnosis.

When faced with a difficult diagnosis, less-experienced professionals sometimes use videos that illustrate typical behaviors associated with each autistic disorder. The wringing hand movements common to Rett syndrome, for example, are much easier to recognize once you've actually seen them. Medical libraries or a local organization for families coping with autism may have a video diagnostic aid available.

Asperger's syndrome

Asperger's syndrome is also called Asperger's disorder, and often abbreviated to AS. Some people with AS call themselves "Aspies" for short.

Asperger's syndrome is characterized by narrow areas of interest and a self-centered way of looking at the world. People with AS are rarely retarded and are often quite intelligent. However, social skills just don't come naturally to them. They don't have noticeable language delays; in fact, many are very early talkers and early readers (a symptom known as hyperlexia). Most do have speech differences, most noticeably a tendency to lecture endlessly on topics of special interest like a pedantic "little professor."

Unlike people with autistic disorder or most other PDDs, people with AS tend not to show large discrepancies between verbal and nonverbal areas of intelligence when they take IQ tests. AS is characterized by strong interests in a limited number of subjects or activities, interests that become full-fledged obsessions.

> Tom has an odd way of walking and moving. He loves to shoot hoops with his older brother, but he's very uncoordinated. He has a passion for insects that borders on the bizarre. Remember the scene in Close Encounters of the Third Kind where the Richard Dreyfuss character just had to build the model of that mountain? That's Tom in full effect. —Serena, mother of nine-year-old Tom

Many people with AS are highly successful in technology careers, such as computer programming and engineering, that both minimize contact with other people and make use of their special interests. Others find their progress hampered by social difficulties, or by co-morbid conditions like depression, which are fairly common in this group.

Autistic disorder

Autistic disorder is what most people think of as autism, and is also called classical autism or Kanner's syndrome. Some people with autism call themselves "Auties" for short.

Autism is a neurological disorder that features marked impairment in social interaction and communication, as well as restricted, repetitive patterns of behavior, activities, or interests. It is often, but not always, accompanied by some degree of mental retardation. When the term "low-functioning autism" is used, retardation is generally present and symptoms are usually more difficult to remedy. High-functioning autism blends into PDD-NOS territory, with autistic traits less prominent and capabilities higher.

> We had suspected that Candy was autistic since she was a baby. When that was confirmed by testing, we found out at the same time that she's moderately mentally retarded. She walks on her toes most of the time and usually avoids eye contact, but she does have relationships with people, on her own terms, anyway. Definitely with us and with her classroom aide.
>
> She is very sensitive to certain sounds, to clothes, and to many other physical sensations. She used to hit her ears over and over because noises drove her crazy, but now she wears headphones and they help. When she was a toddler, her favorite "game" was lining up stuffed animals on her bed for hours on end. If you interrupted, she would tantrum.
>
> She seems to enjoy using a computer at home and at school, and has begun to say a few words. She also tries to communicate in other ways at least some of the time, including using the signs for "potty" and "eat." It's been a tough fight, but we are thrilled with even these small steps. If she can go from nonverbal to verbal, and from no eye contact to limited eye contact with certain people, we know she can do even more. —Lynda, mother of eight-year-old Candy

With intensive help, children with autism can often improve a great deal. Some will make such gains that the diagnosis will no longer apply. Others don't respond to treatment—and no one knows why.

About half of children with autism respond to intensive behavioral intervention, some are helped by medications, and others seem to make progress with special diets, vitamin supplements, or occupational therapy that includes sensory integration work. This indicates that, as with the other PDDs, there is probably no single cause for autism. No single treatment will work for everyone, but with early diagnosis, therapeutic intervention, and lots of love, slow and steady improvement is the norm.

Childhood disintegrative disorder

Childhood disintegrative disorder is a heartbreaking mystery. Most parents notice that something is different about their babies or toddlers, who are later diagnosed with a PDD—not so with this variant, in which the losses occur sometime before five years of age, but after a time of seemingly normal development. Although many of these children can be helped with the same interventions used for autism, studies have shown that many tend to get worse with time instead of better, despite efforts at intensive therapy.

> Until a year ago, Armando had a great sense of humor, a mischievous smile, and a nonstop motor mouth. He spoke in full sentences, had regular conversations with me and his brothers, and played every day. But around last January, something happened. He began to "lose" words, and talked less and less. We would find him rocking in the corner, or hiding under the sofa cushions instead of playing outside. He threw tantrums whenever his routines changed. He no longer speaks, he doesn't want to be held, eye contact has all but disappeared. He doesn't even seem to care that we're here. —Elena, mother of five-year-old Armando

It seems likely that childhood disintegrative disorder has a different cause than other PDDs, although it hasn't been found. It could be caused by some sort of virus, for example, or by undetected seizures that cause brain damage or scramble how the child interprets the world (see "Landau-Kleffner syndrome" later in this chapter).

Fragile X syndrome

Fragile X syndrome is also called Martin-Bell syndrome, and may be abbreviated as FRAXA.

Fragile X syndrome is the most common inherited form of mental retardation, occurring in about 1 in 2,000 males and a smaller percentage of females. It is diagnosed with a genetic test that looks for a break in a particular spot on the X chromosome. About one-third of fragile X boys show PDD-like characteristics. Some meet the full criteria for autism, but most tend toward the milder end of the spectrum.

There is a characteristic fragile X "look" for male patients. Often this clue will help physicians make an early diagnosis. As with autistic disorder, the degree of impairment depends a lot on the degree of mental retardation.

> Benny is mildly retarded, but he gets along okay. He goes to a regular school, and he gets extra help from a reading specialist. His teacher helps him keep on track with an agenda book, a daily homework reminder, and a few other adaptations.

He is an unusual-looking kid. The first thing you notice is his long, horsey face and prominent chin. His jug-ears are set low, and he often sits in postures that other kids can't master. They love watching him in gym class, where he can show off his double-jointedness to full effect.

He does have a habit of repeating what was just said to him, and he talks in a high-pitched, super-fast voice. We're working on that in speech therapy twice a week. —Peter, father of twelve-year-old Benny

Characteristics of fragile X syndrome in boys include prominent or long ears, a long face, delayed speech, macroorchidism (large testes), hyperactivity, tactile defensiveness, and gross motor delays.

Much less is known about girls with fragile X syndrome. Only about half of all females who carry the genetic mutation have symptoms themselves. Of those, half are of normal intelligence, and only one-fourth have an IQ under 70. Few fragile X girls have autistic symptoms, although they tend to be shy and quiet.

Rett syndrome

The cause of Rett syndrome is unknown, although it is probably a genetic disorder. It's not obvious at birth, but usually becomes so between the age of six and eighteen months. The torso and limbs may shake, the gait is wobbly and rigid, and breathing seems difficult, as does eating.

Children with Rett syndrome are always female, although very similar symptoms have been seen in a few boys. They tend to grow slowly and be short, they have a small head (microcephaly), and there is always retardation, generally ranging from severe to profound. About 80 percent of girls with Rett syndrome also have epilepsy.

Girls affected by Rett syndrome always seem to be wringing their hands. While they may start out with social avoidance problems, these tend to lift by the grade-school years.

Kinesha was a quiet but normal baby, but when she was about eleven months old she started to rock and shake her body. She wasn't developing on schedule anymore either. When we took her in and asked her pediatrician about it, she recognized Rett syndrome right away.

*Now she walks stiffly and on tiptoe, she sleeps at odd hours and
never seems to be on schedule, and her hands are always in motion. She
grinds her teeth so often that we had her fitted with a dental guard. She is
profoundly mentally retarded, so much so that potty training is still a long
way away. —Rose, mother of four-year-old Kinesha*

Some girls diagnosed with Rett syndrome do recover some abilities that were
lost. This is rare, however, and may represent yet another PDD subtype. A
1997 study published in *European Child and Adolescent Psychiatry* described
seven girls of Italian descent and one of East Indian heritage who fit this profile. The researchers noted that, despite regaining many abilities, including
making major improvements in speech and socialization, these children
retained many autistic features. Some of the more severe symptoms associated with Rett syndrome, including seizures and microcephaly, were much
rarer in this group.

Other possibilities

There are a few other conditions that doctors like to rule out before making
a PDD diagnosis, or that they may mistake for a PDD.

If speech delay is present, hearing is usually the first thing to be checked,
followed by an examination of the muscles and structures in the mouth and
throat. If everything appears to be in working order, the possibility of a hearing problem or a birth defect that's affecting expressive speech can be discounted.

Children with severe communication disorders sometimes show symptoms
that look a lot like PDD. Many children with developmental verbal dyspraxia, oral-motor apraxia or apraxia of speech, dysphasia, or aphasia have
sensory integration issues or gross motor problems, for example. A speech
and language pathologist is qualified to evaluate and treat speech disorders.

It's important to note that a diagnosis of a communication disorder does not
rule out the possibility of PDD—the two can coexist in one person. Apraxia,
for example, is common in people with fragile X syndrome. This common
misconception has been responsible for denial of services to many children.

In some cases, a doctor may consider selective mutism (previously known as
elective mutism). This is a very rare psychological condition in which a person with the ability to speak chooses not to do so, either as a result of some

great trauma or as an expression of a social phobia. Normally this possibility would be investigated only if parents report that speech was developing normally up to a certain point, then stopped. If the child's background is unknown, as in the case of an adopted child with no speech, selective mutism should also be ruled out. This disorder is treated by skilled and gentle psychotherapy and family therapy if related to trauma, and behavior therapy and medication if related to social phobia.

Alternatively, a diagnosis of mild cerebral palsy may be a better fit. Cerebral palsy is caused by brain damage. In its most severe forms, it affects mobility, but sometimes it affects primarily speech production. These patients may have just a few signs of gross- and fine-motor problems, such as a knock-kneed gait. A neurologist can rule out cerebral palsy with exercises that test how well the brain-body connection is working. Some people with CP have sensory integration problems that can lead to autistic-like behavior.

At one time the terms "autism" and "childhood schizophrenia" were used interchangeably. Today, we know they aren't the same thing at all. It's rare for schizophrenia to emerge during childhood, but it does happen. Schizophrenia is also a neurological disorder. People with this condition have hallucinations and delusions, and tend to have what psychiatrists call "flat affect"— not much personality. Like autistic children, schizophrenic children may shun eye contact and physical contact, have limited social skills, and behave in unusual ways. They may have self-soothing behaviors that look autistic, such as repetitive rocking, and they may develop self-abusive behaviors. Medications are now available that can help most children and adults with schizophrenia.

Some people with autistic features better fit the criteria for childhood or adult bipolar disorder (manic depression), obsessive-compulsive disorder (OCD), Tourette syndrome (TS), or very extreme ADHD. People with these diagnoses sometimes report sensory sensitivities that could make them look autistic (for example, avoidance of eye contact or touch) unless properly treated. Obsessions and compulsions are certainly common across the PDD spectrum. The vocal and physical tics that characterize Tourette syndrome are not that dissimilar from the stereotypic movements and repetitive sounds made by some people with PDDs. Medications, interpersonal or behavior therapy, and adjustments to school programs can usually help people with these problems.

As with communication disorders, the presence of a different neurological disorder does not necessarily rule out the presence of a PDD—many people have more than one. Alphabet-soup diagnoses like ADHD/OCD/TS (known in the literature as TS+), ADHD/OCD/TS/Asperger's syndrome, or apraxia of speech/PDD-NOS/OCD are not that uncommon. There is considerable overlap between these neurological conditions, all of which are more common in families where someone has a PDD than in the general population. Some researchers feel that the autistic spectrum should include OCD, Tourette, and possibly even ADHD—although that idea is still controversial.

Often a patient with suspected PDD will be tested for seizures, both to rule out Landau-Kleffner syndrome (discussed later in this chapter) and to make sure that aggressive or self-injurious behaviors are not due to seizure activity. Seizures can cause brain damage, so it's important to pursue diagnosis and treatment if they are suspected. Some of the signs to look out for are staring spells, times when the child appears to be confused or in a daze, inexplicable falling episodes, and, of course, convulsions that are not associated with a fever. These are called febrile convulsions, and, although they are a serious matter, they do not indicate epilepsy.

Of course, if you have a history of epilepsy or seizures in your family, be sure to let your doctor know.

Some researchers have reported that brain lesions or tumors, or brain abnormalities, such as a missing cerebellum, can cause autistic symptoms. Neurologists can use brain-scanning technology to locate these, and may be able to remove a tumor or lesion surgically. Obviously, abnormalities in brain structure cannot be helped, although some people who are missing parts of their brains go on to function quite well. These causes for autistic symptoms are believed to be very rare.

Rare conditions with autistic-like features

The following disorders are so rare that an otherwise knowledgeable neurologist may never have seen a case—and may therefore miss one when it comes through the door. A very few children said to have PDD-NOS or atypical PDD may actually have one of these disorders. If everything seems to fit, it's worth researching further and asking your doctor about. But as the old medical saw goes, "If you hear hoofbeats, think of horses, not zebras."

Angelman syndrome

Angelman syndrome is a genetic disorder. Most patients also have epilepsy. It's not a subtype of autism, but some people who have it exhibit autistic-like behaviors, including hand-flapping, severe speech problems, attention deficits, and hyperactive behavior. Some are aggressive or self-abusive.

People with Angelman syndrome usually have similar facial features, including a wide, upturned mouth with a thin upper lip, and deep-set eyes. They often have very pale eyes, hair, and skin.

Angelman patients are gregarious and love to laugh. They walk and move stiffly, and most are severely mentally retarded.

Cornelia de Lange syndrome

Also called Brachmann-de Lange syndrome, Cornelia de Lange syndrome may be abbreviated to CdLS or BDLS.

Cornelia de Lange syndrome is a very rare genetic disorder whose hallmarks are developmental delays, a small head that may also be short and wide, a small, broad pug nose, thick arched eyebrows that grow together, and long eyelashes that curl. Many other physical differences may be present, including malformations of major organ systems, webbed toes, and unusual hormone activity.

People with CdLS are usually, but not always, mentally retarded. Like people with autism, they often have stereotypic behaviors (mouthing of hands and objects is especially common), perseverations, and self-injurious behaviors.

Landau-Kleffner syndrome

Landau-Kleffner syndrome is a seizure disorder that results in loss of speech (aphasia) some time after eighteen months of age. It is twice as common in males. It can be hard to diagnose, because the seizures are deep within the brain, occur during sleep, and may not show up on a one-time EEG test. If Landau-Kleffner syndrome is suspected, the physician may order a 24-hour or 48-hour EEG test using a mobile unit.

As with childhood disintegrative disorder, which it resembles, no one is sure what causes Landau-Kleffner syndrome. Some cases are definitely due to a known head trauma, but others are a mystery. Researchers suspect that a virus or immune-system problem may be part of the picture for some patients.

> Brad was diagnosed with a form of cognitive epilepsy called continuous spike wave syndrome, which is a variant of Landau-Kleffner syndrome. He also had an intraventricular hemorrhage at birth with VP shunt placement at one year of age. His hallmarks are atypical PDD, autistic regression, cognitive and neuropsychological regression, and expressive language problems. There are so few cases known about that I have no idea what the future holds. —Kim, mother of seven-year-old Brad

This disorder can sometimes be successfully treated with antiseizure medications and/or corticosteroids. A few doctors try brain surgery, which may be effective in some cases. The later speech was lost, the better the prognosis.

Prader-Willi syndrome

Prader-Willi syndrome is a genetic disorder that sometimes occurs with autism or includes autistic-like features. The main perseverations seen are with food and eating. Sexual characteristics may be underdeveloped, as are the muscles. Most people with Prader-Willi syndrome are mildly retarded and have speech and movement problems. Temper tantrums, skin-picking, and sleep difficulties are also frequently seen.

Medication does not seem to help this population very much. It's likely that there is a metabolic disorder involved that governs how food is absorbed and whether the stomach feels full, but no one has yet discovered how to address the problem. Special diets and behavior modification can be useful for maintaining health, and for improving performance at school and in the community.

Williams syndrome

Williams syndrome is a rare genetic disorder characterized by mild mental retardation. Many people with Williams syndrome exhibit autistic behaviors, including hypersensitivity to sounds, extreme food likes and dislikes, and perseveration. They usually have developmental, gross-motor, and language delays.

These sociable, often quite animated people have cardiovascular abnormalities, high blood pressure, and elevated calcium levels, as well as unique facial features that can be described as "pixie-like," including almond-shaped eyes, perfect oval ears, a broad mouth with full lips, and a narrow face with a small chin.

PDD-NOS and atypical PDD

Now we get to the diagnoses that are the heart of this book: the unspecified PDDs. As noted before, doctors play favorites with terminology, and most are careful to avoid misdiagnosis whenever possible. Accuracy of diagnosis depends on how many patients on the autistic spectrum they've seen, whether or not they keep up to date on research in the PDD field, and how comfortable they are with the admittedly limited DSM-IV criteria.

Some doctors are quick to say "autistic" where another might prefer "atypical," simply because they feel they know it when they see it, or because they don't think "atypical" gives families enough information to plan treatment. Others don't have the background to hazard a guess at all.

"Most pediatricians don't know what autism is," says Dr. Stephen M. Edelson, director of the Center for the Study of Autism in Salem, Oregon. "Many physicians are afraid to use the word 'autism,' but all of the parents I've talked to say they want to know the truth."

As a result, there are many people walking around with a PDD-NOS or atypical PDD diagnosis who probably meet all the criteria for autistic disorder.

There is no hard-and-fast way to differentiate between PDD-NOS and atypical PDD.

PDD, not otherwise specified

This condition is also called PDD-NOS, PDD,NOS, autistic tendencies, autistic-like behavior, or autistic spectrum disorder (ASD).

When someone says their child or patient has PDD, they usually mean that he or she has been diagnosed with PDD-NOS.

The term PDD-NOS is most often used to describe patients who meet some, but not all, of the criteria for autism. Either the person is not impaired in all three areas considered when making a diagnosis of autism (social development, communication, and activities and interests) or the problems are very slight in one or more area.

Often the doctors will use a diagnosis of PDD-NOS simply because the child attempts to communicate, with or without speech, or has a strong bond with his or her parents. This says much about many physicians' lack of knowledge about autism, which does not rule out communication or relationships.

> *Steve did not speak until he was four, and still shuns conversation most of the time. When he does speak, it's often in a whisper. He prefers playing beside other children to playing with them, but in the past year he has started to describe one boy in his small kindergarten classroom as his friend, and to tag along behind him on the playground.*

> *He's a handful, but we have a warm relationship with our son. He does have unusual behaviors and interests, but the level of perseveration and obsession varies. There are times when he seems almost normal— and times when he seems almost unreachable. —Judy, mother of five-year-old Steve*

Obviously, there is a gray area between where PDD-NOS ends and high-functioning autism begins. This is a judgment call for clinicians. The best of them simply call it as they see it, without regard for either the supposed stigma of the autism label or the vagueness of the PDD-NOS label.

Atypical PDD

This condition is also called atypical autism, autistic tendencies, autistic-like behavior, autistic spectrum disorder (ASD), or merely "atypical."

Atypical PDD is most often used to describe a child whose symptoms resemble Asperger's syndrome, but who doesn't meet all the criteria, such as a patient with extreme AS-style obsessions but with a severe speech delay. It is also applied to people who have a mix of normal features and autistic-like behavior. For example, a child may show age-appropriate behavior and skills at most times, but occasionally revert to rocking, tantrum behavior, and have stereotypic movements that are consistent with autism.

> *What do you do when your child stumps the experts? My son still doesn't have a diagnosis because no one, educator or doctor, can find*

anything that really fits. I guess that's why they sometimes just have to call it atypical autism.

The most frustrating part is not knowing what the future holds or even what the true diagnosis is. Some days it seems like it would be easier if he had a condition that was visible at birth or could be determined by blood test. These atypical autisms are largely invisible, and the behavioral symptoms shift constantly. He'll have a good few weeks, and I start to doubt the diagnosis, and think that maybe the social problems are secondary to a language disorder and will disappear as his language improves. Other times it seems like he's from another planet. It's a roller coaster that never ends.

It has been a source of tension in the family because, with my son at least, diagnosis is not clear-cut. He is not classically autistic and is, in fact, very affectionate and related to his family, both immediate and extended. There are those in the family who think nothing is wrong and we are stigmatizing him by seeking help, and others who think he is just poorly disciplined and out of control. —Jennifer, mother of three-year-old Joseph (Asperger's-like and autistic-like features, diagnosis still in progress)

The terms "atypical autism" and "atypical PDD" are used interchangeably by some diagnosticians. It's very likely that these groups represent one or more PDD subtypes that have not yet been fully delineated.

Newer PDD classifications

Many professionals refer to PDD-NOS and atypical PDD as "garbage-can diagnoses," meaning that many different conditions have probably been thrown together under these monikers simply because they have similar symptoms. Currently, researchers are looking for ways to define the unspecified PDDs based either on groups of symptoms or on known or suspected causes.

None of the potential PDD subtypes or alternative diagnoses discussed in this section have made their way into the DSM-IV, but you may still hear these terms from a doctor or an educator who's been checking out the latest research. You might also find these ideas discussed in some of the books and online sites listed in Appendix A, *Resources*, or hear about them in parent support groups.

Dr. Stanley Greenspan is a much-respected child psychiatrist who works with George Washington University Medical School and the Washington Psychoanalytic Institute in Washington, D.C. He directed the National Institute of Mental Health's Clinical Infant Development Program for many years as well, and has authored or edited more than 25 books. Over the past decade or so, Dr. Greenspan's clinical research has focused in on the autistic spectrum disorders and related developmental problems of children. He challenges many long-held notions about PDD-NOS and atypical PDD in his most recent book, *The Child with Special Needs* (Greenspan et al., Addison-Wesley, 1998).

In fact, Dr. Greenspan has joined the crowd in asking for a revamped diagnostic system, one that is more specific and based on the latest research. He has proposed the term "multisystem neurological disorder" (MSD) as an alternative that could be used to describe children who, despite communication difficulties, perseverative behavior, and other characteristics of autism, have the capacity for building social relationships. The term "multisystem" is certainly more accurate than "pervasive" when it comes to expressing the variances between patients. "Neurological" is also much more accurate than "developmental."

Dr. Greenspan has also coined the term "regulatory disorders" to describe children whose basic problems lie in regulating attention, sensation, information processing, and movement. This category would include ADD/ADHD, some conduct disorders, and some children at the milder end of the autistic spectrum. Greenspan and his research team have described five types of regulatory disorders, which they call sensitive/fearful, defiant, self-absorbed, active/craving, and inattentive.

Perhaps the best thing about Greenspan's research is its emphasis on uncovering underlying issues and helping each individual to reach his or her full potential. He is a champion of floor-time play therapy, which will be discussed further in Chapter 6, *Therapeutic Interventions*.

Other classifications in popular use are based on similarities between patients, and may represent subtypes. These terms and concepts are controversial in some circles. These classifications all relate to the concept of autism as an autoimmune or metabolic disorder, an idea for which there is some evidence. They include:

- *Candida*-caused autism, a variant that seems to respond extraordinarily well to diet and medications that inhibit the growth of *candida* yeast in the body

- Allergy-induced autism (sometimes called cerebral allergy), in which autistic symptoms appear to be caused or exacerbated by allergies, and diminish when allergies are treated

- Vaccine-related autism (also called vaccine-related encephalopathy), in which the onset of autistic symptoms appears to be caused by or related to a severe reaction to childhood immunizations, particularly the vaccine for measles, mumps, and rubella (MMR)

UK parents may also hear about pathological demand avoidance syndrome.

A relatively new concept that may include some PDDs and other cognitive disorders, neuro-immune dysfunction syndromes (NIDS), has been proposed by Dr. Michael J. Goldberg. Best known for his work with chronic fatigue immune deficiency syndrome (CFIDS) patients, Dr. Goldberg believes there is a relationship between autism and CFIDS, and with other doctors has founded the NIDS Medical Advisory Board and Research Institute to investigate this possibility.

Diagnostic labels can be vitally important. Incorrect diagnosis can lead to incorrect, or even harmful, medical treatment. Correct diagnosis is the first step toward proper treatment. And because a great deal of information is now available about helping people with various PDDs, correct diagnosis can also lead to greater understanding and acceptance of the differences that come with these labels.

CHAPTER 3

Getting a Diagnosis

PEOPLE WITH PDD-NOS OR ATYPICAL PDD need a medical diagnosis to get therapeutic or educational assistance. This chapter—which will be of most use to
parents, other direct caregivers, and adults who suspect they may have a
pervasive developmental disorder—discusses how to navigate the diagnostic
process. Topics covered include starting within either the medical, Early
Intervention, or school system; choosing an evaluation facility and professionals; what to expect during the diagnostic interviews and testing; and
how to make the process easier and more productive.

Who diagnoses PDDs?

The journey to a diagnosis of PDD-NOS or atypical PDD can begin in several different ways, but for most, it starts in the office of a pediatrician or
general practitioner. For others, a mental-health practitioner (counselor,
social worker, psychiatrist, or psychologist) is the first person contacted.
Some children are referred for help by a day-care worker, a teacher, or other
school personnel. A few, mostly patients who already see a neurologist due
to epilepsy or another known brain disorder, will be diagnosed by a specialist without going through any preliminaries at all.

It's important to note that only a medical doctor can make a medical
diagnosis, although a neuropsychologist (a psychologist with special training
in neurological differences) is also qualified to diagnose autistic spectrum
disorders. School counselors, speech therapists, teachers, and other nonphysicians—including parents—may well be correct when they recognize
symptoms of a pervasive developmental disorder, but they can't officially
make the call. If you suspect that your child, your student, or someone you
care about has a PDD, the most helpful thing you can do is assist him in getting an appropriate diagnosis. For professionals and parents alike, that
means finding a specialist with experience in diagnosing autistic-spectrum
disorders.

Ideally, diagnosis is done by a team of specialists working together (see "The multidisciplinary evaluation" later in this chapter) and is accompanied by a report detailing treatment suggestions and referrals.

Starting with a pediatrician

Usually, the first person to hear the concerns of a young child's parents is a pediatrician. In this age of managed care, the pediatrician takes on more importance than ever. Not only is she the doctor who knows the most about how a particular child's development compares to the norm, but she is almost always the primary care provider (PCP) designated by health insurance plans. She generally serves as a gatekeeper to more advanced care, making referrals to medical and therapeutic specialists as needed.

Note to adults and their caregivers: Everything in the following three sections applies to general practitioners (GPs) as well as to pediatricians, so you'll follow the same procedures with your GP or other primary care provider to obtain diagnostic help for an adult.

In an ideal world, pediatricians would be quick to see the early signs of PDDs and would guide parents toward the best medical resources available. Sometimes that's how it works.

> Elaine's pediatrician recognized developmental problems quite early. He said that she did not speak because she couldn't, not because she didn't want to, and advised me to have her seen by St. Mary's Hospital for Early Intervention. At St. Mary's, Elaine was seen by a neurologist, a speech expert, and countless doctors. They couldn't agree on a label—only the neurologist felt certain that it was PDD-NOS. Luckily, they did agree on recommendations for treatment. —Sarah, mother of two-year-old Elaine (diagnosed PDD-NOS, possible oral-motor apraxia)

Because parents know the most about their child, they play a key role. To assure a proper diagnosis, parents need to make their concerns crystal clear.

That isn't always easy. Many pediatricians complain that parents seem almost apologetic about being in their offices, don't ask enough questions, and don't volunteer important information unless asked. By and large, that's learned behavior, ingrained over a lifetime of rushed appointments with harried doctors.

It's true that the typical sore-throat appointment is a ten-minute affair these days, but when you have greater concerns it's okay to ask for more one-on-one time with the doctor. There's no need to feel guilty, because doctors are accustomed to scheduling longer sessions for some types of appointments. Practitioners should reassure parents about this point.

You're not asking the pediatrician to diagnose PDD-NOS or atypical PDD, you're looking for a referral—but before such a referral can be approved, the doctor must be sure that specialized diagnostic help is required. Ask the pediatrician's office for a consultation appointment of at least 30 minutes (more would be nice).

Why do you need to go beyond the pediatrician? Because while pediatricians are indeed experts in the typical problems of children—croup, the flu, pinworms, diaper rashes, and all the rest—they receive very little training in neurological or psychiatric disorders. In fact, a study by Elizabeth Costello, PhD, associate professor of child and adolescent psychiatry at Duke University, found that a large HMO's pediatricians were able to identify only 17 percent of the children who presented with psychiatric disorders. In addition, that 17 percent tended to be children with the most common problems, including bedwetting and learning disabilities.[1]

Pediatricians also have their own opinions about disability. Some know very little about available services, and assume that only the severely disabled are eligible for assistance.

> We began asking our pediatrician questions about Joseph's language regression at fifteen months, but she ignored our concerns because she felt his skill with letters and numbers precluded any developmental disability. She actually discouraged us from seeking Early Intervention when he was 24 months old. She said we might be uncomfortable since "the other children are more severely impaired." —Jennifer, mother of three-year-old Joseph (Asperger's-like and autistic-like features, diagnosis still in progress)

Prepare in advance to use your consultation appointment as efficiently as possible. Accurate, detailed records are the most important thing parents can contribute at this appointment. These should include the usual "baby book" milestones (first step, first word, etc.) as well as notes about anything unusual parents have observed. Areas the pediatrician is likely to ask about include patient and family medical history, speech, relationships with family members and peers, play patterns, and interests. You may want to consult the diagnostic questionnaires in Appendix F, *Diagnostic Tools,* to see the kinds of questions a doctor might ask.

Keeping a daily diary is an excellent way to prepare for a diagnostic evaluation. Many families have learned a great deal during this process as well. If possible, record activities, diet, and behaviors each day for a period of two weeks or more, with the time and duration of activities and behaviors noted. Not only can this diary provide a very complete picture of the child to a professional, it can also help to identify patterns. Some families have identified food allergies this way, or gotten data they needed to create the most beneficial daily routine for their child.

If the patient has seen other doctors, releases must be signed to have any useful records transferred to the pediatrician. Older children may have school records that would be helpful, and these can also be transferred if a signed release is on file. Transfers always seem to take longer than you would expect, so get releases taken care of early, and make sure records were sent and received. Alternatively, if you have your own copies of these records (and you should), you may photocopy and deliver them yourself.

If possible, your information and the patient's records should be provided to the pediatrician at least a week before the consultation appointment. It should be accompanied by a request that she read the material in advance, and review the patient's medical file before the meeting. The goal is to put your child's case on the pediatrician's front burner, and to ensure that all of the details are fresh in her mind when the consultation appointment takes place.

Parents should also summarize their concerns in writing. The records already mentioned can help you gather your thoughts. You don't have to be an eloquent writer to express what worries you. You can jot down a simple numbered list rather than writing whole paragraphs if you prefer. It may help to compare your child to his or her siblings or to other children in the day-care center, school, or neighborhood. Some parents may want to send their summary of concerns to the doctor in advance; others may prefer to use it as an agenda for discussion during the consultation session.

You may also want to discuss your concerns in advance with an advice nurse or another person, such as a physician's assistant, who works closely with the pediatrician. In large medical practices or HMOs, nurses are an important part of the organization and can be important allies for parents who need referrals to specialists or even just a listening ear.

As you prepare for it, keep in mind that the consultation appointment is only a preliminary step toward your real goal: a multidisciplinary evaluation.

The consultation appointment

A consultation appointment is different from a regular visit to the pediatrician. Unless the doctor happens to notice something of medical concern, there will be no need to do the usual eye, ear, and mouth exam, or to check height and weight. In fact, the appointment may take place in a meeting room or office rather than in an examination room.

When you arrive for the consultation, bring any records you have gathered, copies of your earlier letter (just in case it never reached the doctor), your summary of concerns, and any questions that you want to ask. We suggest bringing a small notebook as well, so you can keep a record of the discussion. If your child tends to be difficult to manage, bring a bag of toys or books that are likely to help keep him calm. Parents may want to choose playthings that will help the doctor see where the child is at developmentally, such as a doll or stuffed animal.

If the consultation seems to be getting off to an awkward start, start the ball rolling by referring to your summary of concerns or your list of questions. Always keep your goal in mind: referral to a diagnostic team. You're there to make a case for this referral, and your observations are the evidence you'll need to convince the pediatrician. Think of yourself as a salesperson, trying to convince a customer. You want to be the one in charge of this meeting, and keeping that image in your mind can help.

Most pediatricians will use the consultation appointment to simply listen, discuss the issues raised, and recommend the next course of action. Some will use a set of standard questions about behavior and development to screen the patient. For children, the Pediatric Symptom Checklist (PSC) is one of the most common screening tools used. It's a list of 35 questions created by Dr. Michael S. Jellinek of Harvard Medical School, and has proven to be about 95 percent effective at catching psychiatric disorders in children.

Checklists and guidelines are great, but there's really no substitute for knowledge and experience. As parents interviewed for this book make painfully clear, some pediatricians are reluctant or unable to recognize PDDs, even when faced with a nonverbal three-year-old who spends the entire consultation appointment screaming or disassembling the doctor's scale. You may hear phrases like "Your child just needs to be disciplined more strictly," "He'll grow out of it," or "Let's wait and see." There are several responses you can make:

- Go back over your evidence, showing that your child is having more than one developmental problem, and explaining how it is affecting her life. If you feel comfortable doing so, you may also want to mention how it is affecting your family life.

- Set a "wait and see" timetable. Ask the pediatrician which important milestones (such as meaningful speech) should be passed within the next three months, and secure a promise that if these goals have not been met, a referral will be made. This approach may be appropriate for very young children whose possible impairments are subtle.

- Ask the reluctant pediatrician for a referral to a developmental pediatrician (see below).

- Go up the chain of command in the healthcare organization, if you are using a managed care or HMO practitioner. In medical groups, there is a board that takes patient complaints under consideration. You can petition the board to approve your referral even if the pediatrician refuses. Usually this is done in writing, not in person.

- Ask the doctor to put his refusal to refer in writing. This may not be something he'd like to commit to paper, so you might end up getting the referral after all.

- If the doctor does put his refusal in writing, you can choose to call your diagnostic facility of choice and set up an appointment with the appropriate evaluation team directly. Be prepared to pay for this visit out-of-pocket. However, if the team confirms your suspicions, you should be able to bill your insurance company for reimbursement due to refusal of an appropriate referral.

- If the pediatrician won't refer, but won't put his refusal in writing either, you can still "self-refer," but it will be harder to get reimbursed. You should send a letter to the pediatrician explaining why you have made this choice over his objections. Send a copy to your insurance company as well. This creates a paper record, allowing you to pursue a claim for improper refusal later on, if warranted.

Referral to a developmental pediatrician, a doctor who specializes in treating the health problems of children with developmental delays or handicaps, presents a less-expensive alternative. For you, seeing another pediatrician may seem like one more hurdle to jump on the way to the diagnostic team. Your reluctant pediatrician, on the other hand, will probably like the idea. If your concerns are valid, the developmental pediatrician can explain the reasons to your regular pediatrician, and can provide information about the best resources available locally for full diagnosis and treatment.

Developmental pediatricians are much more familiar with neurological problems, medications, and current research on disabilities. They tend to work closely with specialists, including neurologists, psychopharmacologists, psychiatrists, and therapists of various types. In fact, you may want to continue seeing the developmental pediatrician on a long-term basis, once the diagnostic process is complete.

Roadblocks to referral

Most doctors in the US share the risks and expenses of caring for special-needs patients, including specialist referrals, with business partners or an HMO group. Doctors who make too many referrals can face financial penalties, even if the extra services were absolutely necessary for the patients' health. Physicians may also feel constrained by directives from insurance companies, which want to minimize expenses. We'll talk more about how the insurance system works in Chapter 8, *Insurance*, but right now it's sufficient to say that the healthcare structure in America can make convincing your pediatrician to send you to an expensive facility a little difficult.

Low-income Americans who are uninsured face the biggest roadblock of all: lack of access to healthcare. They may be able to obtain diagnostic help through the school district (see "Starting with the school district," later in this chapter) or through public Early Intervention programs for preschool children. The school district may also provide some diagnostic and therapeutic assistance, especially in the areas of speech, occupational, and physical therapy that relates to classroom performance. There are also special medical programs available for low-income families and for children with handicapping conditions. Both Chapter 8 and Chapter 11, *Finances,* provide many ideas for getting ongoing medical care for people with PDDs who are not covered by private insurance.

In Canada and Europe, where the single-payer system of nationalized health-care predominates, doctors have a different set of constraints on their ability to make referrals. Resources are focused on providing basic healthcare to everyone, so specialists are rarer and harder to access than in the US. Parents may be forced to pay out-of-pocket to doctors who practice outside the national healthcare scheme. The expenses can be considerable. Some families have been able to gain more timely access with help from a sympathetic social worker or health visitor, or have called on disability advocacy groups for assistance.

In countries where neither the private insurance nor the single-payer model predominates, parents should seek out—and pay for—a specialist directly, without going through a preliminary consultation appointment. Reduced-fee or free help may be available through state-run hospitals and clinics, medical facilities run by religious orders or charities, or individual physicians who are willing to take a case at a lower cost than usual.

Starting with an Early Intervention program

All US states, Canadian provinces, and Australian states have Early Intervention (EI) programs that identify, evaluate, and assist children with developmental disabilities, including PDDs. New Zealand, the UK, and many European countries also have publicly funded programs available for young children. Similar services are available in the more-developed countries of Asia, Central and South America, and Africa.

These programs are not identical, however—in fact, they can differ drastically between states, or even between cities in the same state. Some are very aggressive about reaching out to families, while others have such a low profile that parents may not know they exist until their child is too old to benefit. Some provide screening and referral services only, while others offer (and pay for) full multidisciplinary evaluations. Many provide ongoing direct services, such as speech therapy or Applied Behavioral Analysis (ABA) sessions. Services may be very limited outside major urban areas.

Early Intervention services may be offered in the child's home, at a special disabilities center, in a public school, in a hospital or clinic setting, or at multiple sites. In the British model, which prevails in the UK, New Zealand, and Australia, most services are home-based. According to parents interviewed about Australia's EI services, they are extraordinarily flexible and extensive—perhaps the best available anywhere, at any price. Canada and the US both tend toward a school- or medical facility-based model of EI service, which requires parents to arrange for services and transportation.

When home-based programs are available in the US or Canada, that fact is rarely advertised. However, there are families in the US who receive home-based ABA programs, speech therapy, occupational therapy, and much more for a child with an autistic-spectrum diagnosis, and who pay no or very low charges for as much as 40 hours of direct service per week in their own homes. Needless to say, these are parents who have been willing to try everything possible to meet their children's needs. It's not uncommon to find that children in the same city or county are receiving very different levels of services.

The common denominator in Early Intervention programs seems to be that you either get what they offer, or you get what you demand. Services are in high demand, practitioners are not as well paid as those in the private sector (and therefore more likely to quit suddenly, to refuse additional work, or to be substandard), and waiting lists can be dauntingly long. But smart parents can use EI resources to accomplish a great deal on behalf of their children, or to supplement what they're able to pay for privately.

Some EI programs provide excellent services for young children, and the best of them involve the whole family in finding innovative solutions to behavioral and medical problems. At the very least, EI can put you in touch with community resources. Even families with excellent private insurance should contact their local EI program as early as possible.

For most families, the point of entry for Early Intervention programs is a public health clinic or hospital, or the special education department of their local school district. Call any of these places to find out how to contact your local EI program. Your state or county Health and Human Services Department or Social Services Department may also be able to help you access these services. Depending on local regulations, assistance for people with autistic-spectrum disorders may be coordinated by specialists in behavioral heath or in developmental disabilities. In either case, service coordinators are usually social workers.

You may be assigned a caseworker whose job is to inform you about services, hear and respond to your concerns, and coordinate both evaluations and the provision of direct services. Caseworkers may have 100 or more clients, so you will have to be a bit pushy to get your case on their agenda. In fact, you'll find that most of the work will have to be either done by you or double-checked by you. Most caseworkers you will come into contact with are truly caring and decent people—they're simply overburdened to the extreme.

As with a private pediatrician, your job will be to convince the caseworker or other EI representative that your child needs a multidisciplinary evaluation. The same tactics apply. There is one difference: in most cases, you have a *right* to demand an EI evaluation. Don't be afraid to exercise that right.

The evaluation should be identical to the kind of multidisciplinary evaluation discussed later in this chapter. If the process is under the auspices of the local special education department, it may include additional testing for learning disabilities, reading level, and other school-oriented factors.

Starting with the school district

Sometimes parents of an older child with mild autistic-like features are approached by concerned school personnel. First-time parents may not have known their child needed help, or their earlier questions about the child's development may have been rebuffed. Teachers, aides, school counselors, speech therapists, and other nonphysicians cannot diagnose a child with PDD-NOS, but they can help families access resources—sometimes including medical diagnosis and even treatment.

> *Mikael was not thrilled about spending three days with a school-district evaluation team, but I was. After he had struggled with severe school and social problems for four years, a teacher finally recognized that he was more than just shy. Mikael's fourth-grade teacher had worked with two autistic boys in college. "I don't want to scare you, but he does some very similar things, and he seems to think and learn in the same way they did," she told me. "I know he's not autistic, but he's similar somehow, and finding out more can help me teach him."*

She gave me some information from the district's special education office, and we got in touch with a school psychologist. The psychologist set up classroom observations, interviewed us, and spent some time with Mikael. In the end, her diagnosis was PDD-NOS, and the special education team designed some modifications to help Mikael succeed. She also referred us to a local psychiatrist who had worked with similar children.
—Galena, mother of ten-year-old Mikael (diagnosed PDD-NOS)

Schools take a different approach to PDDs and other disabilities than medical practitioners. Their concern is with how the problem affects educational performance, not what caused it or how to treat it. Chapter 9, *School,* discusses educational services for children with PDD-NOS in detail; this section simply explains how parents can use a school-based evaluation to obtain a diagnosis.

Schools are required to perform a special education evaluation at the request of a school-age child's parents, or at the request of school personnel and with parental permission. To start the process, request a special education assessment in writing (preferable) or over the phone. Let the district know that you expect to receive an assessment plan within fifteen days of its receipt of your referral letter. Keep a copy of this letter and of all correspondence with the district.

In most districts, evaluations are carried out by a team that may include a classroom teacher, a disability specialist, an occupational therapist, a speech and language pathologist (SLP) or speech therapist, a psychologist or psychiatrist, and other personnel. Larger school districts may have one or more autism specialists; major metropolitan areas (as well as state or regional education offices) may have an entire autism team. When you make initial contact with your district, ask if you can speak with one of these specialists.

If the school district requires a doctor's diagnosis as part of the special education evaluation, it must pay for that diagnosis if it has not already been obtained. Districts may work closely with regional education centers, Early Intervention programs, and regional child development centers to set up and perform medical evaluations.

Schools tend to lean heavily on standardized tests. On the positive side, that helps ensure that evaluations are more objective than purely observation-based judgments might be. On the not-so-positive side, no standardized test is purely objective. As a result, US federal law has introduced a number of limits on how schools can use tests to evaluate and place students, and other countries are following suit. These rules include:

- Tests must be selected and administered so as not to be racially, culturally, or sexually discriminatory.

- Tests must be administered in the student's primary language or other mode of communication, such as sign language.

- Tests must be validated for the specific purpose for which they are used.

- Testing must assess specific areas of educational need, rather than producing a single intelligence quotient (IQ) score.

- No single procedure can be used to determine an appropriate educational program for a student.

- When a student has impaired sensory, manual, or speaking skills, the tester must ensure that results accurately reflect the student's aptitude or achievement level rather than the student's impaired skills, unless the test is intended to measure those skills.

- Students must be assessed in all areas related to a suspected disability including, where appropriate, health and development, vision, hearing, gross and fine motor abilities, general ability, academic performance, self-help, orientation and mobility skills, vocational aptitude and interests, and social and emotional status.

- Parents must give informed consent for student evaluation procedures.

State special education regulations may add more items to this list. California, for example, requires that psychological assessments be performed by a credentialed school psychologist who has been specially trained to assess cultural and ethnic factors that may affect diagnosis. States are required to make these rules available to parents, so if you have a concern about testing procedures, call your local or state special education office and request a copy. Federal, state, and local regulations may also be available from disability advocacy groups or on the Internet.

Parents in the UK and other countries should contact their local education authority for information about similar regulations. In general, most countries other than the US make educational policy at a national level.

All tests that the district plans to administer should be listed on your assessment plan and arranged according to areas of function to be tested. If you think one of the tests chosen is inappropriate, don't sign the Consent for Assessment form that comes with this plan until the issue is resolved.

You can ask that specific tests or types of tests (for example, a nonverbal intelligence test) be used. If the district doesn't have a qualified person to administer such a test, it can contract with a community provider at no charge to you.

Choosing an evaluation facility

With most pediatricians, Early Intervention intake workers, and school-district representatives, and in most cases of possible PDD-NOS, it will be clear that something is amiss that deserves expert attention. If so, you may move quickly from discussing your concerns to the next step—choosing a setting and date for the formal team evaluation.

Don't assume that the first person to validate your concerns knows the best place to go. If you've heard information about local facilities, positive or negative, feel free to share it. Ask what the outcome has been for other families referred to this facility, if any. If references are available, check them out. You could schedule tours of one or more facilities before making a choice.

Those who live in rural areas may want to request a referral to a regional child-development center instead of opting for an ad hoc evaluation team made up of local professionals or an inexperienced school-based team. All US states and Canadian provinces maintain such centers, which are usually affiliated with a public medical school or teaching hospital. In the UK, your city or county council should be able to locate the closest facility.

If you can't identify a site that's within a reasonable distance of your home, call the national autism organization in your country or, better yet, contact a nearby state or local chapter. If you're an Internet user, mailing lists (list-serves) and chat sites may be good resources for getting names of and opinions about diagnostic facilities.

If you, your doctor, or the school district needs to do some legwork before choosing an evaluation site, make sure to set a date for finalizing the decision. It shouldn't take more than a week or two to get things set up (usually, it's just a matter of making a couple of phone calls). Write this date down, and ensure that the other party also has it in writing.

If you do agree on an evaluation site at the consultation, make sure that the referral process is initiated immediately. It's an unfortunate fact that many of the best facilities have long waiting lists. A three-month wait is not unusual in the US, and some specialists in the UK are booked up for as long as a year in advance. You want to get your name on that waiting list as soon as possible.

No one should have to wait months, even years, just to get a diagnosis. There are strategies you can use to move up the list at a diagnostic facility:

- Keep on top of the process. You wouldn't believe how often important paperwork, referral forms, and case files are misplaced or never sent. Make sure all of the necessary materials are received.

- Make personal contact with someone at the facility. Nurses, secretaries, even the intake specialist can become your advocate if they know who your child is and why she needs to be seen soon. Be more to the staff than just a name on a list.

- Ask if the facility maintains a cancellation fill-in list. This is a list of patients who are willing to come in on short notice in case of a cancellation. If this option is practical for you, it may save you months of waiting.

Choosing the evaluation team

As good as some experienced practitioners are at recognizing developmental disabilities, it's important to work with a team of professionals. The multidisciplinary approach to diagnosis (also called the team-based model) is widely accepted as the best, most thorough method for diagnosing complex disorders like PDDs.

Each person on the team will have a slightly different perspective and area of expertise, and the group will collectively have more background and experience than any single person in it. Ideally, the team will be personalized to meet the needs of each child. Any number of specialties may be represented, including developmental pediatrics, psychology, psychiatry, neurology, audiology, speech and language pathology, physical therapy, and occupational therapy. Some facilities have one or more clinicians who specialize in autistic-spectrum disorders, and who coordinate all multidisciplinary evaluations in that specialty.

Your list of concerns can help you insist on specialists to be included. If lack of communication tops your list, make sure there's both a speech and language pathologist and an audiologist involved. If seizures are a worry, a neurologist must be part of the team. If obsessive-compulsive behaviors are the most urgent symptom, that's a psychiatric issue. The idea is to cover all of the bases. If your multidisciplinary evaluation is taking place in a school setting, the team may not include a medical doctor. You can request that one be included (back up your request with good reasons, of course). School districts routinely contract with local physicians, psychiatrists, neurologists, and medically oriented testing specialists to provide evaluation services. The school district cannot charge parents for medical testing and diagnosis if the district orders it. Some districts will try to bill your insurance, although parents have successfully challenged this practice.

The evaluation team needs to have a leader. The leader will be your main contact during the evaluation process, so it needs to be someone who has time to talk. Often the team selects whichever clinician has the most expertise as its de facto or official leader—the neurologist or psychiatrist, say—but that's not always ideal. These practitioners can be extraordinarily busy, too busy to discuss the team's findings for hours, too busy to field frantic phone calls two months later, and definitely too busy to give hugs and encouragement. The experience of many parents interviewed for this book indicates that social workers, special education caseworkers, and developmental pediatricians tend to make the best team leaders. They're trained in the interpersonal skills necessary for the job, and they tend to use less medical jargon when talking to families and patients.

In some cases, you may be able to request (or refuse) to have specific people be part of the team. You can use the same resources mentioned previously for finding information about evaluation facilities to get a list of practitioners' names. Personal recommendations from other parents in your situation are an excellent indication of expertise.

One size does not fit all when it comes to diagnosing PDDs. A psychiatrist whose specialty is treating adolescents with depression is probably not an expert on pervasive developmental disorders, and a speech and language pathologist who only works with kids who stutter and lisp may be in over his head. If you have a chance to ask the team members about their experience with PDDs before the evaluation, do so—you may find that one or more is not a good fit for the job.

It's okay to say no. If a team member is rude to you on the phone, makes you feel unwelcome or uncomfortable, or gets poor marks from other families, ask for someone different. With luck, an acceptable replacement will be available.

The multidisciplinary evaluation

Multidisciplinary evaluations take time—lots of it. While some public EI programs claim that a multidisciplinary evaluation can be completed in as little as two hours or a single afternoon, most hospital-based programs take one to two days, or even longer, to do a full evaluation. This provides enough time for clinicians to observe the patient, conduct interviews, administer standardized tests, and compare notes. It's essential that the evaluators make time to talk about what parents have observed over years of being with their child on a daily basis, and to speak with older patients one-on-one.

There are a few questions you may want to ask before the evaluation, just to be prepared (or to help prepare your child). You may want to know how many people will be working with you or your child on each day, including assistants; how long each section of the evaluation process will last; and whether a parent, caregiver, friend, or other advocate may be present during all parts of the procedure.

The typical multidisciplinary evaluation schedule can be exhausting for both parents and patients. Children with PDDs tend to act out or withdraw in new situations anyway, and are not very amenable to being poked and prodded by obnoxious practitioners. This may give the clinicians a chance to see your child at his worst—which could be good or bad, depending on how they use that opportunity. Adults with PDDs tend to have more coping skills, but may need to arrange for a "time out" procedure in advance, just in case the process gets too overwhelming.

A typical day of multidisciplinary evaluation might look like this:

    9:00 to 9:30 a.m.—audiological exam
    10:00 a.m. to 12:00 p.m.—speech and language evaluation
    Break for lunch
    1:00 to 2:00 p.m.—occupational therapy evaluation
    2:15 to 3:00 p.m.—psychiatric observation and interview
    3:15 to 4:00 p.m.—neurological exam

The schedule depends on the patient and the team. Some programs feature a full nutritional or metabolic workup, for example, while a research facility may insist that every patient undergo several basic tests in addition to tests related specifically to PDDs.

Each team member will use some kind of standardized instrument to measure the patient's function against established norms. They may also make use of questionnaires, formal or informal observations in one or more settings, and special equipment.

- Audiology tests may require the patient to wear headphones and point to the location of a sound, or they may involve measuring brain-stem response to sound. With very young children, audiologists will probably have to involve parents in the process. Some audiologists provide computerized reports showing the range of hearing.

- Speech and language pathologists (SLPs) employ flash cards, questions, toys, and games to elicit sounds and speech, then grade the performance in standardized ways. There are a number of standardized tests for gauging speech and communication skills. The SLP should also ask parents many questions about actions, gestures, sounds, and words their child uses to communicate.

- Occupational and physical therapists will ask the patient to try various activities, such as throwing a ball to the tester or walking along a low balance beam. To rate the individual for sensory impairments or problems, OTs should use the Sensory Integration and Praxis Tests (SIPT). Parents or adult patients may answer written or verbal questions.

- Psychiatrists and psychologists use checklists, questionnaires, observations, and conversations to make their diagnoses. They may also administer standardized tests.

- Neurologists employ a battery of simple physical tests that can indicate brain dysfunction and can also call upon an array of high-tech tools. If seizures are suspected or if the facility has a research orientation, an electroencephalogram (EEG) and possibly other types of brain-scanning technology may be brought to bear.

The tests and other measures that schools use to assess children with suspected PDDs may be somewhat different than those used in a medical setting. Interviews with parents are usually the starting point. Checklists or questionnaires may be used in these interviews, including various autism rating scales. Parents will be asked many, many questions about their child's development, abilities, difficulties, and learning style. The records and daily diary discussed earlier in this chapter will prove to be invaluable in the parent interview.

Children may be observed in a classroom or playroom setting, in an office setting, or at home. It's best if the child is observed in more than one place—there are many autistic-spectrum children who never speak at school, but who do use some words at home, for example.

Test instruments

Hundreds of standardized tests, questionnaires, and observation plans are available for rating behaviors, abilities, and other factors that could be related to pervasive developmental disorders. The lists in the next sections provide a little information about some of the most commonly encountered tests, but they are by no means complete.

In the US, most standardized tests are developed by commercial publishers, often in concert with university researchers. There is a great deal of competition between firms that publish tests. In most European and Asian countries, as well as Australia, public schools and medical facilities may be required to use special national assessment tools developed by government bureaus instead of, or in addition to, commercially developed instruments. In the interest of keeping this book's length manageable, these tests have not been listed.

Thankfully, no one will be given all of these tests! The evaluation team members will choose tests that are appropriate for the person's developmental level and that provide the most information about areas of strength and weakness.

If you encounter an unfamiliar test, or if you're not sure how to interpret a test score, don't be embarrassed to ask questions. The results returned by these instruments tend to be nearly incomprehensible unless you've had special training.

Sometimes the results of a test will seem very wrong. Many parents of children with PDD-NOS have been dismayed when their children were rated as retarded on an IQ test, for example, when they appear to have normal or even superior abilities in at least some areas of intellectual function.

Although it's true that parents tend to see their own children in the best light, it's also true that they have more information about the child's capabilities than a tester who has met with the child only once. It's often worthwhile to try a different test that measures roughly the same set of capabilities, but in a different way.

Make sure the testing conditions work for the patient. Nonverbal people will obviously score poorly on a test that requires verbal responses, and people with sensory difficulties may be unable to complete a test given in a noisy ward. You'd be surprised at how often such obvious factors are overlooked by evaluators.

Audiological Tests

Audiological tests are used as part of the "differential diagnosis" process, to make sure that communication and social deficits are not being caused by hearing loss or an auditory processing disorder. Autistic-spectrum disorders can also occur in the deaf or hearing-impaired, and the hearing problem will need to be addressed along with other symptoms to achieve progress.

Some audiological tests can also detect auditory over- or under-sensitivity, which is often an issue in people with PDDs.

Acoustic impedance testing
> This test measures middle-ear function, and can detect the presence of fluid or abnormal structure. The results are presented as a diagram called a tympanogram.

Auditory brainstem response/brain stem evoked response (ABR/BSER)
> For this test, sounds are piped directly into a sleeping patient's ears through headphones. The brain's electrical response to these tones is then measured electronically. It's used most commonly with infants and nonverbal children, and can determine the extent of a hearing loss or auditory processing problem.

Bone conduction
> In this basic audiology test, a device called a bone vibrator is placed behind the ear to determine the softest level heard when bypassing the outer and middle ear to stimulate the inner ear directly.

Comprehensive central auditory processing (CAP) testing
> These tests determine how thoroughly a person processes auditory information. A comprehensive battery might include one or more

central nervous system function tests, such as the ABR, as well as measurements of auditory memory, sequencing, tonal pattern recognition, and information storage.

Conditioned play audiometry (CPA)

This is a basic hearing test for young children, using play activities to check function.

Immittance audiometry

This test is made up of three parts: tympanometry, which checks out how the eardrum moves and the status of the middle and inner ear; acoustic reflex thresholds, which determine if there is a sensorineural or conductive hearing loss; and reflex decay, which determines if there is a hearing loss due to problems in the cochlea or acoustic nerve.

Oral myofunctional evaluation

This observation-based test determines the extent of tongue thrust when making some sounds.

Pure tone testing

Using an electronic device called a pure tone audiometer, the audiologist makes a sound. The child is taught to perform some fun activity when she hears that sound. It measures whether children can discriminate between tones.

Visual response evaluation

For this test, the infant or young child is held on a parent's lap in a quiet test booth. While a test assistant tries to get his attention visually, sounds come through a loudspeaker on the other side. Afterward, a visual cue (such as a light or moving toy) activates next to the loudspeaker. (Also called sound field testing).

Autistic behavior and symptom scales

These tests attempt to screen for or diagnose autistic-spectrum disorders. They may also be used to determine the level and severity of autistic behaviors.

Autism Behavior Checklist of the Autism Screening Instrument for Educational Planning (ABC-ASIEP)

The ABC is a subtest of the longer ASIEP and is used alone or in conjunction with four other ASIEP subtests. It consists of fifty-seven behavior descriptions in five areas, and is used to conduct a structured interview with a parent or other caregiver. The score is presented as a scale indicating the existence and severity of autistic behavior, as contrasted to other disorders. It is less effective with high-functioning forms of autism, such as PDD-NOS and atypical PDD, than with "classical" autism.

Autism Diagnostic Interview-Revised (ADI-R)

Used more in the UK and Europe than in the US, the ADI-R is used to conduct a standardized parent interview. It's based on the World Health Organization's definition of autism. (Also called the Wing scale, after developer Lorna Wing.) Score is expressed as a scale.

Autism Diagnostic Observation Schedule (ADOS)

This is a format for conducting a diagnosis via direct observation of the patient.

Autism Research Institute (ARI) Form E-2: Diagnostic Checklist

This questionnaire is reprinted in its entirety in Appendix F, *Diagnostic Tools*. Parents who send the completed checklist to ARI will receive scaled test results, interpretive information, and information on autistic spectrum disorders at no charge. Form E-2 rates behaviors frequently seen in autism on a scale, and also asks parents to rate the results of any treatments they have tried. It is available in several languages.

An optional ARI questionnaire, Form E-3, asks questions about treatments tried and their results. This is not a diagnostic tool, but part of ARI's efforts to build a large database on autism for research purposes.

Behavior Observation Scale for Autism (BOS)

The BOS checklist is a direct-observation format intended to help evaluators distinguish autistic-spectrum children from normal or mentally retarded patients. Score is expressed as a scale.

Behavior Rating Instrument for Autistic and Other Atypical Children (BRIAC)

This observation-based diagnostic tool looks at the areas of relationship to an adult, communication, drive for mastery, vocalization and expressive speech, sound and speech reception, social responsiveness, and psychobiological development. Additional scales are available for non-verbal and/or hearing impaired children. Scores are expressed as scales.

Childhood Autism Rating Scale (CARS)

The CARS is a direct-observation format for evaluating the behavior of children and adolescents. Results can be scored on two scales, one with a range from "age appropriate" to "severely abnormal," the other with a range from "not autistic" to "mild-moderate autistic" to "severely autistic." An excerpt from the CARS is included in Appendix F.

Gilliam Autism Rating Scale (GARS)

Three GARS subtests cover behaviors and their frequency in the areas of stereotyped behaviors, communication, and social interaction. A third subtest asks parents about developmental disturbances in the child's first three years. Scores are expressed as scales and percentages.

Parent Interviews for Autism (PIA)

This set of questions for parents is frequently used when diagnosing younger or nonverbal children.

Behavioral, psychiatric, and neuropsychiatric tests

Some of these tests are highly clinical instruments used for differential diagnosis (for example, to distinguish autism from childhood schizophrenia), and also to diagnose co-morbid disorders, such as depression, bipolar disorder, and ADHD. Others are more subjective and are used by teachers and other nonphysicians to rank behavior problems or uncover emotional difficulties.

Like the Rorschach blot interpretation test, which is rarely used anymore, tests for emotional disturbance that ask patients to draw and interpret what they've drawn are highly subjective. These so-called projective tests have little use in diagnosing autistic-spectrum disorders, but are routinely administered nonetheless, especially in school settings. Drawing-based tests don't make proper allowances for the fine- and gross-motor issues that are common in PDD-NOS and atypical PDD, among other things. These tests should never be used as the sole measure of emotional disturbance.

Aberrant Behavior Checklist (ABC)

One of the most popular behavioral checklists, the ABC also has a good reputation for accuracy. Versions are available for children and adults, and it is set up to account for mental retardation when assessing behavior problems in the home, school, or workplace. Scores are expressed as scales in the areas of irritability and agitation, lethargy and social withdrawal, stereotypic behavior, hyperactivity and noncompliance, and inappropriate speech.

Achenbach Child Behavior Checklist (CBC)

The CBC is available in versions for girls and boys of various ages. Six different inventories are used, including a parent report, teacher report, youth report (if practical), and structured direct observation report. It looks at the child's behaviors in several areas, including withdrawal, anxiety, etc. The results are classified as clinically significant or normal.

Attention Deficit Disorders Evaluation Scale

Versions of this questionnaire about behaviors linked with ADD/ADHD are available for parents to fill out at home or in a clinical setting, as well as for direct use with older children and adults. Scores are expressed as a scale.

Behavior Assessment System for Children (BASC)

This set of tests includes a teacher rating scale, parent rating scale, and self-report of personality. The BASC attempts to measure both problem and adaptive behaviors, as well as behaviors linked to ADD/ADHD. Scores are expressed as a scale keyed to a norm.

Conner's Rating Scales (CRS)

Parent and teacher versions of this scale-based test are available, which is intended to uncover behaviors linked to ADD/ADHD, conduct disorders, learning disabilities, psychosomatic complaints, and anxiety, among other conditions. Scores are plotted graphically.

Draw-a-Person

This a projective psychological screening procedure in which the patient is asked to draw three human figures: a man, a woman, and himself. The drawing is then rated on a scale, with differences in ratings according to gender and age. Ratings are subjective interpretations, not objective measures.

House-Tree-Person Projective Drawing Technique

In this projective test, the patient is asked to draw a house, a tree, and a person, and then is asked a series of questions about these drawings. Sometimes these drawings are separate, sometimes they are done on a single page. Ratings are subjective interpretations, not objective measures.

Kinetic Family Drawing System for Family and School

In this projective test, the patient draws her family doing something or her class doing something. Then the patient is asked questions about what's going on in the drawing. Ratings are subjective interpretations, not objective measures.

Luria-Nebraska Neuropsychological Battery (LNNB)
Luria-Nebraska Neuropsychological Battery—Children's Revision (LNNB-CR)
The LNNB-CR contains 11 scales with a total of 149 test items, which are intended to measure motor skills, rhythm, tactile, visual, receptive speech, expressive language, writing, reading, arithmetic, memory, and intelligence. Each test item is scored on a scale, and a total scale for all items is also derived. The adult LNNB also tests the maturation level of the frontal lobe tertiary zones.

Pediatric Symptom Checklist (PSC)
A simple questionnaire about behavioral symptoms, the PSC is commonly used as a screening tool by pediatricians. Score is expressed as a scale.

Psychiatric Assessment Schedule for Adults with Developmental Disability (PAS-ADD)
Used primarily in the UK, this is a self-reporting questionnaire used to assess psychiatric state in people with developmental delay, learning disability, neurobiological disorders, or senility, among other conditions. Score is expressed as a scale.

Reitan-Indiana Neuropsychological Test Battery (RINTB)
Reitan-Indiana Neuropsychological Test Battery for Children (RINTBC)
Halstead-Reitan Neuropsychological Test Battery for Children (HNTBC)
These may be the most widely used neuropsychological tests, and are intended to look for signs of brain damage. The RINTBC contains the following tests: Category, Tactile Performance, Finger Oscillation, Sensory-Perceptual Measures, Aphasia Screening, Grip Strength, Lateral Dominance Examination, Color Form, Progressive Figures, Matching Pictures, Target, Individual Performance, and Marching. The HNTBC adds the Seashore Rhythm Test, Speech Sounds Perception, Finger-Tip Number Writing Perception, and Trail-Making, but omits some other tests. The RINTB is very similar. Results are usually expressed as a scale (the Neuropsychological Deficit Scale or the Halstead Impairment Index). Additional information about right-left dominance or performance patterns may also be derived.

Vineland Adaptive Behavior Scales

These tests measure personal and social skills from birth to adulthood, using a semi-structured interview with a parent or other caregiver. Versions are available for children of all ages and for low-functioning adults. Social and behavioral maturity in four major areas—communication, daily living skills, socialization, and motor skills—is assessed. Responses are rated on a 100-point scale for each area, and a composite score is also provided. Scores can be translated into developmental or mental ages.

Intelligence, developmental, and academic tests

Intelligence is a tricky concept, especially since repeated studies have shown that children's IQs can and do change when they are measured differently, or when the child is taught differently and then retested. Most IQ tests also carry some cultural, racial, language, and/or gender bias, although testing companies are certainly trying to create better tests. However, because this bias has inappropriately placed nonhandicapped students from ethnic minorities into special education in the past, it is no longer legal to use IQ tests alone as an evaluation tool in US schools.

As a result of misuse, IQ testing is beginning to fall out of favor. It has been supplanted in some school districts by tests that measure adaptive behavior, which can be loosely described as how well and how quickly a person can come up with a solution to a problem and carry it out. These provide a more realistic measure of "intelligence" as most people think of it, as opposed to measuring cultural knowledge.

Developmental tests rank the individual's development against the norm, often resulting in a "mental age" or "developmental age" score. Some of the tests listed in the "Behavior, psychiatric, or neuropsychiatric tests" section in this chapter also chart a patient's developmental stages.

Academic testing is a must during the special education evaluation process. It's also used with older patients to provide clues about undiscovered learning disabilities or to design adult learning programs. Some clinicians like to compare the results of these three types of tests, a practice that provides a picture of actual achievement against the background of supposed innate capability.

Sometimes a local, state, or national academic test is used to rate a child by grade level instead of one of the commercial tests listed.

Although many IQ tests are in use today, you are most likely to encounter one of the Weschler Scales, also called a WISC.

Adaptive Behavior Inventory for Children (ABIC)
This standardized measure of adaptive behavior uses a questionnaire format, with a parent or other caregiver providing the answers. It includes subtests called Family, Community, Peer Relations, Nonacademic School Roles, Earner/Consumer, and Self-Maintenance. Used with the WISC-III IQ test and a special grading scale, ABIC is part of the System of Multicultural Pluralistic Assessment used by some districts to make more sensitive assessments of racial minority children. Results are expressed on a scale.

Battelle Developmental Inventory
This test ranks children's self-adaptive skills (self-feeding, dressing, etc.) as a percentage of his chronological age. The score may be expressed as a percentage, such as "between 40 percent and 55 percent of his/her chronological age," or as a single-number standard deviation.

Cattell Scales
This test rates the person's developmental level. The score is expressed as a Mental Age (MA).

Children's Memory Scale (CMS)
The CMS test is intended to provide a complete picture of a child or adolescent's cognitive ability, and is often used with children who have acquired or innate neurological problems. Areas screened in six subtests include verbal and visual memory; short-delay and long-delay memory; recall, recognition, and working memory; learning characteristics; and attentional functions. It rates skills in all areas and links them to an IQ score.

Developmental Assessment Screening Inventory II (DASI-II)
This screening and assessment tool for preschool children does not rely heavily on verbal or language-based skills. Its scores rate the patient's developmental level.

Developmental Profile II
This developmental skill inventory for children up to nine years old (or older people whose developmental levels fall within that range) is based on an interview with a parent or other caregiver. It covers physical, self-help, social-emotional, communication, and academic skills. Scores are

provided as an individual profile depicting the functional developmental age level in each area.

Kaufman Assessment Battery for Children (Kaufman-ABC)

A nonverbal IQ test, the Kaufman-ABC measures cognitive intellectual abilities in children aged two-and-a-half to twelve. It's one of the best tests for use with nonverbal children without significant fine-motor problems. Scaled scores are provided for overall ability (the mental processing composite) and for simultaneous and sequential processing.

Learning Potential Assessment Device (LPAD)

This test of cognitive function uses different assumptions from some of the other IQ tests, and was designed for use primarily with learning disabled or developmentally disabled children. It provides several scaled scores, with interesting ideas about interpreting and using them.

Leiter International Performance Scale—Revised (Leiter-R)

This nonverbal IQ test has puzzle-type problems only covering the areas of visual, spatial, and (in a few cases) language-based reasoning. It produces scaled results.

Peabody Developmental and Motor Scales (PDMS)

These tests use activities, such as threading beads or catching a ball, to gauge the level of physical development, as well as motor capabilities and coordination. They can be used to test large groups of children. Scores are expressed on a scale interpreted as an age level, so raw numbers may be followed by notations like "below age level by five percentiles" or "above age level."

Peabody Individual Achievement Test (PIAT)

These short tests measure performance in reading, writing, spelling, and math. Scores are expressed as a grade level.

Stanford-Binet Intelligence Test Fourth Edition (S-B IV)

An intelligence test sometimes used with young or nonverbal children, although not preferred by most clinicians. The score is expressed as an IQ number or as a scale.

Test of Nonverbal Intelligence 3 (TONI-3)

This short, nonverbal IQ test for children over five presents a series of increasingly difficult problem-solving tasks, such as locating the missing part of a figure. The score is expressed as an IQ number or age equivalent.

Vineland Adaptive Behavior Scales
> A standardized measure of adaptive behavior, the Vineland scale tests problem-solving and cognitive skills. Scores are presented as a scale, IQ-style number, or age equivalent.

Weschler Preschool and Prima Scale of Intelligence (WPPSI)
Weschler Intelligence Scale for Children-Revised (WISC-R)
Weschler Intelligence Scale for Children-Third Edition (WISC-III)
Weschler Adult Intelligence Scale (WAIS-R)
> All of the Weschler Scales are intelligence tests that use age-appropriate word-based activities and mechanical, puzzle-like activities to test problem-solving skills. They return scores for verbal IQ and performance IQ, which may be broken down into several categories. This test is probably the most frequently used IQ test for diagnosing autistic-spectrum disorders, because a significant discrepancy between verbal and performance IQ is considered symptomatic of PDDs.

Wide Range of Assessment Test—Revision 3 (WRAT 3)
> This standardized test determines academic level in reading, writing, spelling, and math. Scores are expressed as raw numbers or grade level equivalents.

Woodcock-Johnson Psycho Educational Battery—Revised (WJPEB-R, WJ-R)
> An individual test of educational achievement in reading, writing, spelling, and math, the WJ-R has many subtests that can be given as a group or separately. Standard scores are derived that compare the test-taker against US norms and that can also be expressed as an age or grade-level equivalency. One popular subtest, the Scales of Independent Behavior-Revised (SIB-R/Woodcock, Johnson Battery, Part IV), is a standardized measure of adaptive behavior. SIB-R scores are raw numbers similar to IQ scores, but may be shown as a grade or age equivalency.

Occupational therapy tests, including sensory integration

Occupational therapists for children usually evaluate life or school-related skills, such as the ability to hold a pencil and write. OTs for adults may look at life skills or work-related skills. Much of this evaluation will be based on direct observation rather than standardized instruments. For example, the OT might ask the patient for a handwriting sample, or watch her perform typical daily tasks such as opening a door.

Sensory integration (SI) evaluations determine how well the body's sensory systems process information and how they regulate sensation and movement. These tests are usually administered by an OT. The majority of school OTs will use informal, observational measures to look at SI issues.

Developmental Test of Visual-Motor Integration (Berry-Buktenica Test)
This test consists of geometric figures, arranged in order of increasing difficulty, which children have to copy. It works well with kids who have short attention spans. Scores are expressed as a raw number and can be translated into a percentile.

Bruiniks-Oseretsky Test of Motor Proficiency
In this standardized test of gross- and fine-motor proficiency, the tester asks the patient to try a number of simple physical activities and puzzle-like tests, including running, walking on a balance beam, and catching a ball. Results are scored, and then scaled from "much below average" on up.

McCarthy Scales
This simple set of tests rates arm and leg coordination. The raw score is scaled to a percentile.

Sensory Integration and Praxis Tests (SIPT)
Combining standardized testing, parent interviews, and structured observations, the SIPT examines how the child responds to sensory stimulation. It collects information related to posture, balance, coordination, eye movements and play. This battery of tests takes from one-and-a-half to three hours, and is too long and difficult for most children under age six. The SIPT test was developed by Sensory Integration International, and can be legally administered only by an SII-certified evaluator. Results are expressed numerically, and usually also in a narrative report.

Southern California Sensory Integration Test (SCSIT)
This earlier version of the SIPT test is still in use by some OTs. Results are expressed numerically, and usually also in a narrative report.

Speech and language tests

These tests are usually administered by speech and language pathologists (SLPs). Pervasive developmental disorders can coexist with speech and communication disorders, or one can be mistaken for the other. Comprehensive speech and language testing is important for designing treatment plans, no matter what the eventual diagnosis is. Standardized, qualitative measures like the ones listed here are usually accompanied by informal observations and attempts at conversation (qualitative assessments). These are intended to find out how the person uses speech in a more natural setting, and may be presented in the report under the heading "language sample analysis" or something similar.

Along with test scores and a language sample, the speech and language evaluation will probably include observations made by the SLP about issues such as vocal tone (nasal or otherwise unusual voice qualities), stuttering and other fluency problems observed, and any abnormalities seen in the physical structures used to produce speech.

It is possible to do speech and language testing with nonverbal people. In these cases, the examiner looks at other forms of functional communication, including the use of gestures, formal sign language, pictures, and augmentative communication devices.

Standardized tests help the SLP rate various components of speech and language, including the domains of pragmatics (rules that govern the use of functional language to communicate), semantics (the rules that govern language content, including word meaning and word order), syntax (grammatical rules), morphology (rules governing the formation of words from smaller parts), and phonology (rules associated with a particular language's sound system).

Comprehensive testing will look for problems in both expressive and receptive speech, and also for discrepancies between the two. Tests you may encounter include:

Assessment Link between Phonology and Articulation Test (ALPHA)
> This verbal test assesses speech sound production skills. The tester notes pronunciation and other errors as the patient says common words. Results are returned as a raw score, percentile, performance rank (from "profound disability" on up), and scaled against a norm.

Boston Naming Test
> This test assesses expressive vocabulary knowledge, as well as the ability to recall and retrieve word labels. Results are returned as both a raw score and an age equivalency.

Clinical Evaluation of Language Fundamentals—3 (CELF-3)
This is a standardized test of basic communication capabilities. Results are expressed as a raw score, which can be interpreted further with help from the test guide.

Hiskev-Nebraska Test of Learning Aptitude
Developed for assessing the communication capabilities of deaf children, this nonverbal test is also useful for some autistic-spectrum children who do not speak. Directions are pantomimed.

Mayo Test for Apraxia of Speech and Oral Apraxia—Children's Battery
This checklist helps SLPs assess motor speech skills, such as the ability to blow, move the lips, and make other movements that generate sound.

Peabody Picture Vocabulary Test—Revised (PPVT-R)
This standardized test measures receptive vocabulary knowledge. Scores are returned as raw numbers, percentile, and age equivalent, and can be interpreted further.

Preschool Language Scale
This test for children under seven requires picture-identification skills, and assesses receptive as well as expressive speech. Scores are expressed as a scale, and can be translated into a language age.

Sequenced Inventory of Communication Development (SICD-R)
Generally used as a screening tool, the SICD-R works with children of all developmental levels. Kids like it because it employs a box of miniature real objects, such as a tiny basket and a little car, to elicit speech or signs of recognition. The test instructions include hints for assessing autistic, hyperactive, and other "difficult" children. Subtests in three areas of receptive speech (awareness, discrimination, and understanding) and five areas of expressive speech (imitation, initiation, response, verbal output, and articulation) can be given together or separately. Scores are scaled against a norm.

Test of Language Competence (TLC)
This test for school-age children assesses an individual's understanding of semantics, syntax, and pragmatics in communication. It's said to be especially good at picking up the subtle deficits in understanding figurative or abstract language that are common in people with PDDs. Scaled scores compare the test-taker to a norm.

Test of Language Development—2 Primary (TOLD-2)

This rather laborious test for children ages four through nine assesses both receptive and expressive language, including vocabulary, phonology, syntax, and semantics. A composite score is generated, as are scores for each of several subtests.

Test of Language Development—2 Intermediate (TOLD-2)

Similar to the Primary TOLD-2 test, this is for older school-age children. It covers more-advanced language use and includes subtests on sentence combining, vocabulary, word ordering, generals, grammatical comprehension, and malapropisms. A composite score is generated, as are scores for each of several subtests.

Making the most of test time

Environmental factors have an impact on test scores, so test-givers should do their best to make the evaluation a pleasant experience. Proper lighting, good sound, comfortable seating arrangements, a low level of visual or auditory distractions, and many other factors can improve performance. Needless to say, the corner of a noisy classroom or an echoing gymnasium is not an ideal testing environment for anyone.

Despite the team's best efforts, your evaluation experience may not be very enjoyable. It's stressful to take the tests, there may be long waits between tests, and nerves soon start to fray. The situation will really deteriorate if the person being tested hits the sensory-overload threshold. For people with severe sensory issues, be sure to build in extra time to relax and calm down between tests, or even during long tests. The more prepared parents, patients, and evaluation team members are, the better it will be.

It's essential that the team leader have all medical, social, and school (if applicable) files needed at hand, permitting team members to get background information quickly.

Parents need to receive a schedule for the evaluation in advance, allowing them to prepare the child for this sequence of unfamiliar events. Finally, parents should pack a big bag of tricks to help their child participate as much as possible. Most kids get balky and uncooperative well before lunch, but the promise of carrying along a favorite toy or getting a treat can make a big difference. Small snacks, such as M&Ms or crackers, may also prove useful for reinforcing good behavior. Some children perform more readily when held in a parent's lap or when the parent is in the same room. Some, however, act out more when the parent is present. If the latter occurs, it's no indictment of parenting skills—it probably just means that, when alone with a tester, the child feels more inhibited.

Sometimes neither parents nor testers are successful at gaining a child's cooperation. One of the hallmarks of PDDs is "shutting down" when overwhelmed, so this should be no surprise. It's a good idea to talk to the team leader in advance about what will happen if an evaluation can't be finished due to noncompliance. Don't let the team simply blow off part of the evaluation because it's "too hard on the child." Brainstorm some solutions to the problem instead, such as breaking the process down into small parts with play or rest in between.

Histories

Narrative histories, written either by the patient, a caregiver, or a practitioner as a result of interviews, are also an important element in most multidisciplinary evaluations.

- A developmental history talks about when and how the person met common developmental milestones, such as walking, talking, and tying shoes. For adults, the developmental history may get into social-emotional development issues as well.

- A family history includes information about current family structure, such as who lives in the home and who the patient is closest to. In addition, someone on the team will probably ask a long list of questions about psychiatric problems and developmental disorders experienced by other people in the extended family. Because autistic-spectrum conditions have a definite genetic background, these questions are very necessary.

- A complete medical history collects information about all medical conditions, not just psychiatric diagnoses. It should include lists of current and past medications, treatments, and hospitalizations.

- Sometimes a school team will prepare a school history, which concentrates on how well a child has done in school academically and socially. It will generally include information about any significant behavior, learning, or interpersonal problems observed over the years.

- A social history tries to put the patient's life in context, and may include aspects of any of the other reports. Social histories tend to read like a brief biography, starting out with the circumstances of birth and touching on developmental milestones, problems and accomplishments of childhood, family structure and stresses, and socioeconomic, ethnic, religious, and other cultural issues, if relevant.

The evaluation report

The evaluation process itself doesn't mean much to the parent or patient who's seeking answers. It's the result of the evaluation—the finished report—that puts it all together.

This report should not be made up of raw scores. All of the actual data collected should be included, but it must be accompanied by explanations of what the scores mean in real-life situations, including both home and school (or work) environments.

The report should be as jargon-free and understandable as possible. If it doesn't make sense to you, ask that it be rewritten or, at the very least, explained verbally. In the case of Early Intervention or special education evaluations in the US, the report must be translated into the parent's or patient's primary language, if it is not English.

To be truly useful, the report should also include recommendations for addressing those areas of weakness and difficulty uncovered, and for building on areas of strength. It should include specific service recommendations, not just vague statements like "George's sensory defensiveness should be addressed." For example, George's report could instead suggest specific types of sensory integration therapy, note the goals of that therapy, and list local sources of occupational therapy services.

In areas where direct EI services are offered, the report may include a complete list of all services available, or just those that the evaluation team thinks would be useful to your child. Remember, other services (and particularly home-based services) may be available but not listed. Typical offerings include special preschool classes, speech therapy, occupational therapy, and parent training.

The report should offer a very clear picture of where the individual functions right now in all important areas, including communication, socialization, physical skills, and academic or work skills as applicable. This picture will be the baseline against which future therapies and interventions will be measured, so accuracy is a must. If you disagree with any part of the assessment, speak up.

Parents will probably need to fill out a release form to get their own copy of the full evaluation report. When you receive it, check it over to make sure everything's there. Evaluators will soon be moving on to look at other people, so ask any questions as soon as you can.

Parents and patients may supply a copy of this report to anyone they choose, either by delivering it personally or by signing a release/request form. Pediatricians, therapists, classroom teachers, the special education department, and others may be on your list of people to receive the report. However, you are not required to provide the report to anyone else.

You may need to follow up personally to ensure that the report is delivered to the parties of your choice. Paperwork seems to have a way of getting lost.

In most countries, special education (SE) evaluations and Early Intervention evaluations have a legal aspect in addition to their diagnostic purpose: they include a determination of eligibility for public services. In the US, an SE evaluation report must meet a number of specific federal criteria:

- It must state whether the student needs special education and related services.

- It must clearly state the basis for making this determination.

- Relevant behavior noted during observation of the student in an appropriate setting must be described.

- The relationship of that behavior to the student's academic and social functioning must be described.

- It must summarize any educationally relevant health, developmental, and medical findings.

- For students with learning disabilities, it must state whether there is a discrepancy between achievement and ability that cannot be corrected without special education and related services.

- It must include a determination concerning the effects of environmental, cultural, or economic disadvantage, where appropriate.

- It must state if there is a need for specialized services, materials, and equipment for the student with a low-incidence disability. (Note: The autistic-spectrum disorders are considered low-incidence disabilities under current education law, despite their actual prevalence.)

In other countries, the results of an SE or EI evaluation may be more or less binding, and different formats and data may be required in the final report. School officials or disability advocates should be able to help you find out about pertinent regulations and requirements.

About adult diagnosis

PDD-NOS and atypical PDD were not widely used diagnoses twenty or even ten years ago. Accordingly, there are many adults and teenagers who fit the profile but have never been diagnosed, or who have so far gone through life with a misdiagnosis of a psychiatric condition, mild mental retardation, minimal brain dysfunction (MBD is the old term for ADD/ADHD-like conditions), severe ADD, apraxia or dyspraxia of speech, or another inappropriate label.

Adults presenting with undiagnosed PDDs have frequently been frustrated for years in their attempts to receive help. They may have been mistreated by family members and peers, they have often been unsuccessful in school and work, and they may have been given large doses of useless or even harmful medications in the past. As a result, some rarely see a physician or psychiatrist unless they are in acute crisis. Others may present with constant physical complaints (not necessarily psychosomatic, although they may be dismissed as such), but keep the other issues under wraps.

Many suffer from more-noticeable co-morbid disorders, particularly depression and obsessive-compulsive disorder. Often, it's these problems that will bring an adult patient into the doctor's office, not the sensory difficulties and processing problems that have been with him for life. Practitioners savvy enough to recognize the symptoms of a PDD may be able to effect great change in the life of an adult patient.

Unfortunately, most of the diagnostic tools commonly used to pinpoint autistic-spectrum disorders are geared toward use with children. Physicians may be able to access a patient's childhood records and make a post-facto diagnosis based on the data they contain. Alternatively, they can use one of the autism rating scales (asking the patient to answer based on his entire life, not simply current experiences) in conjunction with adult IQ testing and other measures, such as the SIPT test for measuring sensory integration dysfunction. Of course, many adults will not be able to answer the rating-scale questions about infancy and toddlerhood, and memories can be faulty. If the patient provides permission and a family member is available, an interview with a parent or older sibling may be able to clarify things.

Literate adults tend to self-diagnose, and may even bring the book that "finally explained why I'm the way I am" in to the doctor. Practitioners working with patients who might be particularly sensitive to being mislabeled again may want to suggest that patients look at books written by autistic-spectrum adults as a way of gently explaining about PDDs. Books by Donna Williams and Temple Grandin, among others, can be a real eye-opener. Other adults may prefer a "just the facts" approach to these personal accounts. Practitioners might refer them to a book like this one or provide short, printed summaries about PDD-NOS and atypical PDDs, explaining how they are diagnosed and treated.

Nonliterate adults with PDDs also deserve a sensitive and thoughtful approach, of course. Working with an occupational therapist who is knowledgeable about sensory integration issues can be very helpful. Practitioners or family members may be able to read printed materials to the patient, and can facilitate as much discussion as possible. Patients may need to bring a family member, friend, advocate, or sign-language interpreter to the consultation and evaluation sessions. Practitioners should encourage them to do so.

For practitioners, it's important to recognize how intrusive the diagnostic process for PDDs can be. Most adults do not like to answer questions about embarrassing subjects, such as toileting, obsessive-compulsive behavior, social difficulties, or bad school experiences. It's one thing to volunteer such information to a trusted friend or counselor; it's quite another to respond to a cold questionnaire offered by an unfamiliar professional. It may take time to build a relationship that allows for this kind of probing.

Adult patients need to be an equal partner in the diagnostic team, just as parents should be when a child is diagnosed. If you are an adult who suspects that you might have a PDD, do your best to compile the same records of childhood milestones and difficulties that a parent might bring to a child's evaluation. You may want to get help from a disability advocate if getting these records is difficult.

Note for adults seeking diagnosis: If you have sensory issues that have made getting healthcare difficult in the past, such as an extreme sensitivity to flickering fluorescent lights or medical smells, it's okay to ask that the consultation appointment take place in a setting that won't be too stressful. In some cases, public health providers (particularly social workers) will even make house calls. It may put your mind at ease to know that many types of therapy for PDDs, including occupational therapy and speech therapy, can be done in your home or another non-clinical setting. Good therapists can give you "homework" to do on your own as well.

You can choose to bring a family member, friend, advocate, or interpreter to the consultation appointment, and to any evaluation and testing appointments. This is a good idea if communication is an issue or if you tend to get intimidated by doctors.

Writing down your concerns and questions in advance is definitely an excellent plan. You may even want to send them to the physician or evaluation team in advance of your appointment.

About misdiagnosis

Reluctant pediatricians aren't the only problem you may face on the way to diagnosis. Misdiagnosis is common, as is attribution of PDD symptoms to another known health condition, to medication, or to psychiatric or family problems. This often prevents patients from seeking the help of a specialist when it's needed.

> *Brad did not receive a diagnosis until he was seven years old, when his neurologist at a university hospital clinic made the call. Until then, his difficulties had been chalked up to side-effects of his epilepsy medication, or after-effects of a hemorrhage he suffered at birth.* —Kim, mother of seven-year-old Brad (diagnosed Landau-Kleffner syndrome)

If you or your child has other known health problems, be sure to list them in your pre-consultation letter—and explain why you don't think they're the cause of the problems you're investigating. The physician may not agree, but stick to your guns about getting a formal assessment. Tell the doctor that when the diagnostic team's members take a look, they can make a better judgment about the various factors involved.

Nicole was diagnosed a year ago by a psychologist at a regional child development center. At first, the diagnosis was "expressive/receptive language delay," but as the doctor learned more about Nicole, he changed it to "mild autism, high-functioning." She had previously been labeled as having a language disorder by the school district's Early Intervention assessors. I felt valuable time was lost for Nicole by that misdiagnosis.
—*Robin, mother of five-year-old Nicole (diagnosed autistic disorder)*

Misdiagnosis seems to be most common when families rely on a single professional, particularly when that person's training is in special education, psychology, or speech therapy alone, or when a physician has little experience with or interest in developmental disabilities.

Parents also need to know that doctors' answers generally reflect their area of expertise. Psychiatrists are rarely in the know about gastroenterology or immunology, and vice versa, even though problems in one physical system can affect another. If you ask questions of the wrong professional, you can pretty much expect to hear a negative answer, or to hear that some other specialty's perspective on PDDs is bunk.

What to do if you don't agree

You don't have to agree with the evaluation team's diagnosis, or its recommendations. Before you fire off an angry letter, however, go over the report with your spouse, a trusted friend, or a disability advocate so you can make sure you understand what they're saying, and that the problem is not just a difference in perspective or terminology.

Chapter 9, *School,* goes over the legal procedure for appealing a special education evaluation, including choice or denial of therapies. Insurance companies, universal medical care schemes, and medical facilities all have formal appeal boards. Appeal procedures are built into the managed-care/HMO system as well, although they aren't carved in stone (or widely known). Just as with a doctor you pay privately, you can always ask for a second opinion. It may be hard to get the insurance company to spring for more than one multidisciplinary evaluation, however, so your next visit might be with a neuropsychologist, neurologist, or specialized psychiatrist only.

You'll want to make any appeal or request for a second opinion in writing, and keep copies of this and all other correspondence with your doctor, HMO, or insurance company.

Occasionally, there are strong disagreements between team members. Under normal conditions, they work hard to iron these out before writing their report, so parents and patients are none the wiser. However, sometimes these disagreements pop up in the conclusions or recommendations section, or a dissenting opinion may even be attached to the final document.

Unless the dissenter seems to be way out in left field and therefore easily ignored, this puts the patient or parent in a bad situation. You don't want to be drawn into a dispute between the evaluators. You may need to call in a referee, in the form of a medical review board or a practitioner who can reassess the patient and issue a second opinion.

The diagnostic process can be full of fear and worry, but no matter what the verdict turns out to be, most parents and patients are relieved to finally have a name for what's wrong. Plain talk can hurt at first, but a sugar-coated diagnosis has never helped someone get needed services.

> *I personally despise the diagnosis—I call it "Perverse Diagnostic Denial, Not Otherwise Specified." Doctors are too afraid to use the "A word," they think they might break our hearts. They don't realize that our hearts were broken long before we took this child to the doctor for evaluation. We need a firm diagnosis of autism. There are more benefits and programs for those given a correct and definitive diagnosis. —Sally, mother of five-year-old Dhylan (diagnosed PDD-NOS with autistic features)*

No matter how depressing the test scores or reports may seem, keep in mind that they measure only where the patient is today. There is hope, there is help, and things will get better.

That's what the next three chapters of this book are all about.

CHAPTER 4

Getting Started

IN THIS CHAPTER, WE TALK ABOUT HOW YOU CAN MOVE from the shock of a PDD diagnosis to actively helping the person affected. We include many quotes from patients and families who have good advice to share. Their main message: You can't let a diagnosis paralyze you, nor can you let it take over your relationship with your child or your family's life. We'll discuss dealing with difficult emotions, setting goals, and creating your own plan to meet those goals.

Note for adults with PDD and their caregivers: Whenever possible, adult patients should set their own goals and make their own plans to meet them. Some may need assistance with tasks like carrying out research, making official phone calls, and handling extensive paperwork. If you are an adult with a PDD and resources are hard to find in your community, the ideas discussed in this otherwise parent-oriented chapter may be helpful. In addition, adult-oriented support groups and the Internet can put you in touch with local or nationally known professionals and help you meet supportive people.

Professionals who work with PDD patients should find the information in this chapter useful for guiding patients and their families through the difficult post-diagnosis period and for helping them make and carry out plans.

Changing dreams

Coming to terms with a child's permanent disability is like grieving. All people go into the job of parenthood with hopes, dreams, and plans. Even before a baby is born, mothers and fathers fantasize about cheering at soccer games, enjoying family vacations together, watching their progeny graduate from college.

A PDD-NOS or atypical PDD diagnosis changes those dreams. It's as if that child you dreamed about has actually died, or been stolen away and replaced by another. Families go through all the stages of fear, sadness, anger, and acceptance that make up the grieving process before they can finally deal with the diagnosis and move on.

Fear

After a diagnosis, the first emotion that sweeps over most parents is absolute fear and panic. For some people, it's such an overwhelming feeling that they go numb inside, unable to cope with the frightening level of intensity.

> It's been three months since the diagnosis, and I'm only now able to say the letters "PDD-NOS." I can't talk about it with anyone, not even [my wife] ... in fact, she's been yelling at me a lot, saying that I must not care, because she's carrying the whole load right now. The truth is that I care too much, and I just don't know what to do. I don't know if my boy is going to be okay, I don't know if I'm going to be okay, I don't know if this marriage is going to be okay. Some days I want to run away. I keep wishing this was a dream, and I'm going to wake up and everything will be normal again. And then I wake up, and it's so not-normal, and there's nobody among our old friends or at work who I can talk to about it.
> —Peter, father of three-year-old Morgan (diagnosed PDD-NOS)

Some people feel like they need permission to scream, cry, and say the angry, hurt words that want to come out. If your partner seems to have shut down, maybe the best thing you can do is grant that permission—and get out of the way! People do cope differently. It's just a fact of life.

Make time to sit down and talk with your partner, a close friend or relative, a trusted clergy member, or a counselor. Just getting your feelings out in the open can lift your burden perceptibly.

It may be hard to find someone to talk to about these issues, especially if you are a single parent or your relationship is already stressed. Support groups (see Chapter 12, *Support*) were created for exactly this purpose. You might also try pouring your feelings out in a journal.

No matter how you choose to do it, expressing fears lets them out. Once they are no longer a secret, you can examine them, see which ones are realistic and which are not, and make a plan of action to address them. As long as they are held inside, you're expending your energy to keep them pushed down—and it never works.

Here are some of the worries expressed by parents who were interviewed for this book. You may recognize your own worst fears in their statements:

> *I am fearful that he will never progress past early school level. He probably gains two months for each year of age (currently tests at about age three level, except for speech, which is worse). This will eventually slow down. If he isn't helped within two years, he will be institutionalized or our family will dissolve.* —Joe, father of seven-year-old Kyle (diagnosed PDD-NOS with autistic features)

· · · · ·

> *My fears are that he will be unable to defend himself, and that my daughter will have to give up certain things to care for him.* —Holly, mother of three-year-old Max (diagnosed PDD-NOS)

· · · · ·

> *When I think of Doug as an adult, it really scares me. Each day that he gets older, so do I, and I'm finding that he's getting to be so strong. I know Doug is going to be a big boy, probably near six feet tall. Sometimes now I can hardly handle Doug when he's upset, especially in public, and my worst fear is that I'm going to have to find someplace else for Doug to live. I do know that when Doug enters puberty it is going to be the big turning point. Either he is going to mellow or get more aggressive. And I'm seeing him starting to get more aggressive.* —Debbie, mother of eleven-year-old Doug (diagnosed fragile X syndrome)

· · · · ·

> *My fear is that his life will always be stressful and difficult, that he will be alone.* —Julie, mother of four-year-old Sean (diagnosed PDD-NOS)

· · · · ·

> *I am so scared that my son will never know the joys of having a family or friends. I also worry that he won't ever be able to support himself.* —Kim, mother of seven-year-old Brad (diagnosed atypical PDD and continuous spike-wave epilepsy, a variant of Landau-Kleffner syndrome)

Some parents will find that their fear turns into uncontrollable, immobilizing panic or that their crying won't stop. Depression is not an abnormal response to this diagnosis; in fact, you should expect to feel depressed at times. If it goes on too long or is too difficult to cope with, see your doctor. Medical treatment and counseling can help.

Relief

Particularly if the PDD diagnosis was a long time coming, your first reaction may be a happy one. That's something that outsiders will find hard to comprehend.

> We had been to six doctors with Lisa before someone took the time to find out what was really wrong. We got told all kinds of things, some of which are really incredible, like that it couldn't be autism because it only occurs in boys, or it doesn't exist in black children. The first five doctors we saw were all quick to label her as mentally retarded, and just as quickly they said she wasn't like any other retarded child they had seen because she could read, but was not potty trained and rarely spoke. There seemed to be a lot of suspicion about us as parents, assumptions that Monica had done drugs when she was carrying her or that we were abusive. It was such a relief when we found [our current psychiatrist], both of us just broke down and cried in her office when she explained about atypical PDD. —Jamal, father of seven-year-old Lisa (diagnosed atypical PDD)

Newly diagnosed adults are particularly likely to experience the relief reaction. Patients who have spent years in near-useless therapy, who have been prescribed the wrong psychiatric medications, or who have struggled with difficulties in school, work, and life for a long time are in need of information and answers. When they come, it's as if the clouds have parted.

> I was so happy, I felt like I was floating. For the first time in my life, a doctor had said something to me besides "you're crazy." It gave me hope. —Bill, age 43 (diagnosed Asperger's syndrome)

Bewilderment

When it comes to PDD-NOS, atypical PDD, "autistic tendencies," and similar vague labels, post-diagnostic feelings of relief may be short-lived, however. If you run from the doctor's office to the nearest library, bookstore, or

Internet site in search of information, you will usually come up dry. Many doctors do not even explain that pervasive developmental disorders and autistic spectrum disorders are one and the same, leaving families to search through books on developmental disabilities rather than books on autism.

> It is frustrating not knowing what PDD means, and then dealing with the stigma of autism. And then you discover this is not a diagnosis, but merely a label for those whose symptoms are alike. There are many causes of PDD/autism—why so few labels? —Joe, father of seven-year-old Kyle

A label is not the same thing as an explanation. Even with cancer, an illness whose actual cause is rarely known, there is an explanation available about what's going on in the body and how treatments are supposed to change the situation. Your doctor can explain what a cancer cell is, how it grows, and how it can be destroyed with radiation or chemotherapy. This information may be frightening, but it at least gives patients and families a handle on what's happening.

With autistic spectrum disorders, there's no such surety. For now, there's no tissue biopsy, brain scan, or blood test that can show the presence or extent of the condition. Treatment options are scattershot, often seemingly based on guesswork, chance, and luck. It's hard to explain PDDs to your family and friends, not to mention curious strangers.

> People do ask what's wrong with Ian, and I have said a lot of different things. Children are very quick to ask, actually, which is kind of embarrassing to him. I usually explain that he couldn't talk until he was almost three, so he's still learning. Kids seem to accept that, and not to assume that it means he's retarded. To adults I've said, "He's wired differently," and that's probably closest to the truth. I've said he's "mildly autistic," whatever that means. I've said, "He has some neurological problems." I always try to add that he's really smart, especially if he's standing right there. If he was retarded as well as having PDD-NOS, I wonder how I would handle these questions? I know he hates it when people notice that he's different.

Guilt

Guilt is a killer. It poisons relationships, prevents forward movement, and can result in a downward spiral of recrimination, self-blame, even self-hatred. It is in no way productive. It is, however, a very common reaction to any type of neurological diagnosis.

> *I'm stuck in this stupid guilt trip, going over and over everything that I might have done wrong when I was pregnant. I've even blamed my husband—we think the genes were inherited from his side of the family, because he also has a nephew with autism—and then felt horribly guilty for doing it. I can't even begin to tell you how many times I've woken up in the middle of the night, obsessing over having smoked pot in college (eight years before our son was even conceived), having one glass of champagne at a wedding during my pregnancy, allowing Tommy to have his immunizations. Intellectually, I know I didn't cause his problems, but deep down, I can't shake the feeling that I did. —Elizabeth, mother of four-year-old Tommy (diagnosed PDD-NOS)*

Guilt may be the most paralyzing emotion of all. If you can't move beyond this, do not hesitate to seek professional help from a counselor or psychologist, preferably one who has experience with families affected by disability.

Guilt feelings are one thing you have in common with every parent whose child is less than perfect. Both Western and Asian cultures tend to give parents all of the blame for their children's faults, even for medical problems that are beyond anyone's control. It's terribly unhealthy to allow this bias to affect you. It's simply unrealistic. In families where one child has a PDD, most other children do not, despite being raised by the same people in the same environment.

Perhaps the worst guilt hits when you read an article or medical study that indicates a cause for autistic spectrum disorders over which you actually did have some control. Studies that have linked autism and the MMR (measles-mumps-rubella) vaccine are a perfect example of research that makes parents beat up on themselves. Just remember that, as of this writing, all current research on the causes of PDDs is in its preliminary stages, and it's not fair to berate yourself over a hypothesis. Besides, when you chose to immunize your child, adopt a vegetarian diet during pregnancy, give your toddler milk, or whatever past action you fear may have caused harm, you did so with the intention of protecting him, not hurting him. No parent can be held responsible for ill effects that could not have been predicted.

Certainly no one should feel guilty over being the bearer of "bad genes." If guilt feelings in this area are carrying over into your decisions about having more children, you should see a genetic counselor to assess the likelihood of having a second child with a PDD. Genetic counseling services are available at most major hospitals, and referrals are often available through support and advocacy agencies.

If it makes you feel any better, the same families that appear to have a higher risk of having children with autism also appear to have a higher chance of producing artists and geniuses.

Anger

Guilt has a tendency to segue into anger, especially for parents of older children. If the diagnosis comes after your child is no longer eligible for Early Intervention services, or if your child has already suffered ostracism, punishment, or improper medical treatment, you really do have a right to be mad.

> John is fourteen years old, and was diagnosed with atypical PDD last summer. If you knew how many doctors we've seen, and how many times he has been suspended from school, punished, shamed, and made fun of, you would understand why I am mad! I have spent most of his life taking him to doctors. Why didn't someone have the decency to agree with me that his problems went way beyond ADHD, and help us do something? He has missed out on so many opportunities, and arguments over his "bad behavior" were what led to my divorce. There are some teachers I would literally like to strangle for the harm they did to my son. And what can we do now? It seems like all the good programs are for toddlers.
> —Renée, mother of fourteen-year-old John (diagnosed atypical PDD and ADHD)

If you're feeling uncomfortable about the rage bubbling up within you, you may be surprised to hear that it can actually be a productive emotion. Most people, particularly women, try hard to suppress feelings of anger. Hateful words and actions can certainly be damaging forces. However, anger is often the best fuel for action.

Newly diagnosed patients who are adolescents or adults frequently react with anger. Often it's directed at their parents, who they feel should have known, should have sought more information, or should have reacted differently to their symptoms. Older patients frequently fear that they'll never fit in, that their whole life will be a series of failures, that they may be too "disabled" to ever achieve their dreams. These fears produce an anger that's rooted in frustration.

At least one anger-producing misconception can be put to rest: it's never too late for appropriate therapies, lifestyle changes, and medications to improve a person's life. While it's true that starting early is best, you can only begin where you are. Take that anger and make it work for you. Let it be the armor you wear as you weather battles with the school system, the medical system, and people who just don't understand.

From reaction to action

People sometimes talk about the stages described above as if they're something you work through once, then move on from. It's not like that. Feelings of depression, anger, guilt, and more will keep recurring through the years. On the positive side, after the post-diagnosis "nightmare" period, these flare-ups of emotion eventually blend into the rhythms of daily life. They'll be balanced by more enjoyable emotions and activities. Before long, you'll have changed your schedule, your daily goals, and many other factors in your life to accommodate caring for someone with a PDD. It's not going to be easy, but at some point hence you'll realize that all of this seems normal now.

There's no special trick to getting from here to there, but purposeful, goal-oriented activity is usually what helps people move on.

Setting goals

PDDs affect so many aspects of a person's life that it's hard to prioritize which areas of function should be addressed first. It's also hard to generalize about people with PDDs—one may have excellent verbal skills but need targeted work on social skills, while another may be struggling with toilet training and basic communications skills.

The following goals have been pulled from parent interviews, the author's personal experiences, individualized family service plans (IFSPs) and individualized education plans (IEPs), treatment plans, and other sources. In each category are lists of goals for people with varying levels of ability and proficiency. You may want to use these lists as a menu for creating your own list of goals, which may differ from these suggestions.

Remember to prioritize your list. Priorities should be patient-driven whenever practical. A general guideline for setting priorities is to start at the top of the list below, and work your way down:

1. Health and safety

2. Communication

3. Social

4. Academic/vocational

Some might question putting "social skills" before academic and vocational issues, but in truth, without the ability to be marginally appropriate in the social situations of school and work, there is little likelihood of applying academic and vocational skills. However, social, academic, and vocational skills are often learned in concert with one another. In fact, all of these categories overlap to some extent—once learned, communication skills are the bedrock for socialization and academics, for example.

Please note that many goals on these lists apply to caregivers, not to patients. Parents, too, must learn new skills to make it easier for those in their care to progress.

Always start with the most simple goals possible. Take your cue from these necessarily general lists, but make your list specific—for example, "reduce spitting in class" is a more workable goal than "make John stop spitting."

This is part of the approach used in applied behavioral analysis (ABA), which breaks down desired or problematic behavior into discrete skills and works on each one with intense drills. The ABA approach has a proven track record, although other training methods may be more appropriate for some children and some skills. The ABA approach is probably best for basic skills, such as eye contact, that form the building blocks of higher-level skills. Chapter 6, *Therapeutic Interventions*, discusses ABA and similar programs in greater detail.

Health and safety goals

These are the most basic goals: the ones that assure safety, basic health, and personal hygiene. For some, special teaching materials may be available that are geared to the needs of people with disabilities and their families. For others, you may be on your own when it comes to designing a program.

- Seizure control
- Proper nutrition
- Allergy testing, if indicated
- Obtaining basic medical care (not necessarily related to disability) for patient and for caregivers
- Obtaining expert medical care (neurological, psychiatric, etc.)
- Creating a crisis plan in case of a behavioral/mental health emergency
- Medication management, with special attention to monitoring effectiveness, side effects, and interactions
- Writing a school treatment plan, if warranted
- Reducing tantrums/rage behaviors
- Ensuring that the patient is not physically or sexually abused
- Ensuring that the patient does not abuse or injure others by biting, hitting, kicking, pushing, throwing, etc.
- Learning about "good" and "bad" touches
- Learning parenting and disciplinary skills that are effective and nonviolent
- Extinguishing self-abusive behavior
- Protection from self-abusive behavior with helmet, pads or other devices
- Improving awareness of pain and other sensations
- Installing and using child-safety devices in the home to prevent accidents
- Preventing the patient from running away by installing and using fences, locks, alarms, and other security devices
- Learning safety rules for crossing the street, playing, and home activities
- Learning to say, write, or otherwise tell (by pointing to an ID bracelet, for example) name, address, and phone number

- Toilet training

- Learning menstrual health and self-care skills

- Learning about sexual health and safety

- Avoiding drugs and alcohol

- Learning about prescription drug interactions with alcohol and street drugs, and avoiding abuse, misuse, and theft of prescription drugs

- Basic health-related self-care skills, including washing and other sanitary habits

- Advanced self-care skills, such as choosing a nutritious diet, cooking, laundry, basic repairs and mending, and housework

- Medical self-management, including learning about medications and medication interactions, talking to doctors about symptoms, and monitoring coexisting health problems like diabetes or asthma

Communication goals

For many of these goals, progress will be measured by the patient's ability to maintain a communication activity over ever-increasing lengths of time. For example, it could take months of structured work to get eye contact when requested, even with a tangible reward, such as a small treat. Once that goal has been met, you might move on to exercises that lengthen the amount of eye contact. Finally, you might gradually replace the tangible reward with a smile or hug.

Many books about speech disorders claim that there is a "window of opportunity" for learning to speak, and that it closes around the age of seven. While it is certainly easier for most people to learn to speak (or otherwise communicate) during this time period, it's also true that parts of the brain can always be retrained. Just as adults can learn to speak again after a stroke, some nonverbal children can and do surprise us by gaining speech at a late age. Many adults who have never been able to communicate can, with help from an expert or appropriate medical intervention, learn to use gestures, signs, devices, and even words at an advanced age.

Experienced speech and language pathologists say that the "total communication" approach works best. It entails using and rewarding all forms of communication that a person is capable of, including gestures, behaviors, sign language, augmentative communication devices, sounds, and words.

Chapter 6 provides more detailed information about working on speech and communication skills.

- Eye contact
- Attention
- Ability to be peacefully redirected to a new activity
- Pointing
- Use of picture-based communication book
- Sound production (not necessarily for communication)
- Use of basic sounds or gestures to communicate needs
- Improved oral motor function for apraxic/dyspraxic children
- Reducing echolalia and palilalia
- Use of basic sign language (American Sign Language or other)
- Use of simple augmentative communication devices
- Use of simple, single words
- Use of two-word combinations
- Use of simple sentences
- Use of fluent sign language (ASL or other)
- Use of full-featured augmentative communication device
- Therapy for stuttering, cluttering, and other speech patterns
- "Floor-time" interactions aimed at opening and closing circles of communication
- Improving quality of speaking voice
- Improving the "flow" of speech (prosody), or reducing odd speech patterns
- Using a variety of facial expressions
- Understanding common facial expressions
- Decoding "body language"
- Understanding and using high-level speech, including idioms, analogies and slang

Social goals

Most kids seem to pick up social skills by osmosis, but those with PDDs do not. Social skills must be explicitly taught, and reinforced over and over. For some children, successful social interactions or play may be their own reward, while for others, they will not. Most children on the autistic spectrum are confused by the complexity of the social scene, prefer to interact according to their own rules, and may appear socially "clueless." Flexibility can be learned, however, if the topic is approached in a spirit of fun—and if you are relentless in encouraging it.

Remember that many people prefer one-to-one relationships or solitary pursuits over group activities. Some people will never find team sports, clubs, dances, or even shopping at the mall enjoyable, and that's okay. Encourage activities that can be solitary or shared with just one friend, such as bowling, swimming, running, working out, art, model-building, carpentry, working on cars or machines, sewing, cooking, card games, puzzles, and computing. One good friend can be more valuable than a crowd of acquaintances.

Adolescents and adults with PDDs may seem to have skipped their lessons on grooming, dressing, manners, and social behavior. In truth, few schools or families provide actual lessons on these topics—and this is a population that wants them. Books on etiquette and comportment may be much-appreciated gifts, if they are given with kindness. Activities that provide specific information about proper social interactions, such as religious training, Scouting, special classes, even theater classes, can be very beneficial.

- Eye contact
- Attention to another person's play activity
- Parallel play
- Learning to handle and process appropriate social touch and gaze
- Reducing impulsivity
- Reducing inappropriate touch or gaze habits
- Reducing the intensity and frequency of repetitive behaviors or obsessive-compulsive activity
- One-on-one play with, and directed by, an adult
- One-on-one play with peer, directed by an adult
- One-on-one play with peer, closely supervised by an adult

- One-on-one play with peer, loosely supervised by an adult
- Group social activities, directed by an adult
- Play activities "supervised" by older or more advanced peers (or siblings)
- Finding playgroup opportunities
- Understanding and practicing the concepts of taking turns and sharing
- Building basic conversational skills
- Finding and cultivating interests or activities that the patient can share with peers
- Giving and receiving compliments
- Role-playing or discussing hypothetical social situations
- Communicating online
- Joining clubs or affinity groups with peers, such as Scouting or religious organizations
- Religious and ethical education
- Involving the extended family in care and support of people with PDDs
- Learning the rules of playground games
- Learning sports, board games, dancing, and other social activities
- Improving personal hygiene and dress for social reasons
- Initiating social interactions
- Handling teasing and negative attention
- Gaining emotional flexibility, the ability to handle changing situations
- Learning about and using humor and jokes
- Understanding how other people feel, and using it to anticipate their reactions
- Friendships, including both formal, arranged "friendship clubs" and self-chosen friends
- Learning to avoid being misled, abused, or taken advantage of by friends and acquaintances
- Learning the "rules" of workplace social relationships
- Dating and marriage

Academic and vocational goals

In the academic area, your goal should be the best performance that your child is comfortably capable of. Your expectations should be at grade level unless the presence of mental retardation or learning disabilities puts the child at a disadvantage. Even with these added factors, don't assume that the person cannot learn—it may simply be necessary to try another method of teaching.

As students with PDDs enter high school, parents need to make sure that they are earning enough credits to graduate. This is not always the case for students in self-contained special education programs, some of which operate on the assumption that special education students will not be going on to college, so graduation per se is unimportant. A so-called "IEP diploma" is even less compelling to college admissions officers than a General Equivalency Diploma. On the other hand, SE students can have up to four additional years to complete their graduation requirements. Summer school, classes at the local community college, correspondence courses, and classes delivered via television, radio, or the Internet have saved many a diploma.

A new issue in some areas of the US is a trend toward test-based graduation. Some states that have instituted tests as part of their graduation process or for a special, higher-level diploma have refused to allow accommodations to special education students. Without a doubt, this practice is illegal—but you may not have time to challenge it in court if graduation day looms near. If accommodations are refused, protest loudly, but also pursue any resources or special tutoring that could help your child pass the test.

Today, quite a few people who had a childhood diagnosis of high-functioning autism, Asperger's syndrome, PDD-NOS, or atypical PDD attend trade school, community college, four-year college programs, and graduate school. They are entitled to special education assistance through age 22, and should be able to access services for the disabled at all publicly funded institutions. These services may include academic counseling, tutoring, mental-health care, peer mentoring programs, and other supports to improve their chances of success.

Another area where students with PDD may need enrichment is education for daily living skills. Laundromat 101, Borrowing the Car for Beginners, and Balancing the Checkbook are all "classes" that parents must teach. Try to build in flexibility as you teach these topics, as many autistic spectrum individuals learn how to do something like washing the dishes one way (such as in your sink, with the blue soap), but can't seem to generalize the skill to a new situation (such as in their new apartment's sink, with the pink soap). Chapter 9, *School*, covers more specific education issues. Possible academic and vocational goals include:

- Assessment and testing for Early Intervention
- Assessment and testing for special education
- Testing to determine current academic levels
- Testing to determine learning style (visual, auditory, etc.)
- Testing for learning disabilities
- IQ testing, if indicated
- Creating a curriculum to address deficits
- Writing an IFSP or IEP
- Addressing sensory issues in the classroom, such as loud noises or poor lighting
- Learning to recognize letters and numbers
- Learning to read simple words
- Learning to read at an intermediate level
- Advanced reading skills
- Understanding difficult literary concepts, including metaphors and fantasy
- Keyboarding skills
- Printing, typing and/or writing letters
- Printing, typing and/or writing words and sentences
- Learning basic mathematical concepts
- Intermediate math skills
- Advanced math skills
- "Kitchen science" activities
- Structured science activities and basic scientific concepts
- Intermediate scientific knowledge
- Advanced scientific exploration

- Computer basics
- Intermediate computing skills
- Advanced computing skills, including programming and graphics for those interested
- Learning to use the library and reference materials
- Shopping and home economics
- Money management
- Learning to read maps
- Learning to use public transportation
- Learning to ride a bicycle
- Learning to drive
- School-to-work transition planning
- Vocational aptitude and interest testing
- Exploring career ideas, including internships and other kinds of work experiences
- Identifying and working with mentors in fields of interest, job shadowing
- Signing up for vocational assistance programs
- Paid or unpaid employment utilizing a job coach
- Paid or unpaid employment with regular supervision only
- College placement testing (PSAT, SAT, ACT, A levels and O levels, national exams, etc.)
- Identifying resources for success in higher education, including tutors, disability assistance programs, scholarships, classroom assistance, test and coursework modification, etc.
- Trade school
- Community college
- Four-year or longer university programs

Other goals

This category is here because some goals are multifaceted, or don't quite fit into the other lists. These include:

- Planning and setting up a home ABA program to address multiple areas
- Obtaining funding for ABA, therapy, or private school
- Finding transportation or scheduling help to manage therapy and medical appointments
- Finding community resources for respite care
- Finding community resources for day care or after-school care
- Organizing medical and school records
- Setting up "house rules" and consequences to make living together easier
- Reinforcing desirable behaviors with praise and rewards
- Finding new rewards and incentives
- Limiting television and/or computer time, if it has become a problem
- Finding family activities that everyone can enjoy
- Making time for parents to be alone, or alone together
- Working with partner to ensure that you have mutual goals and agree on plans to meet them
- Setting aside special time for siblings to get the attention they need
- Finding support resources for siblings
- Signing up for AFDC, Social Security Disability Income, and Medicaid (or equivalent social support programs, for those outside the US) if needed
- Planning related to financial and inheritance issues
- Researching supported living options and getting on waiting lists
- Researching residential living options and getting on waiting lists
- Researching independent living options, with or without support or supervision
- Advocating for yourself or for other people with PDDs
- Coordinating support for other families

Creating a plan

Now that you have a list of goals, prioritize them. You simply can't achieve everything at once. Break each major project down into small parts. When you match these parts to specific resources, timetables, and activities, you have a plan of action.

Even though it's a pain, planning is incredibly important to both your success and your peace of mind. Plans give you concrete tasks to attend to, and as the details fall into place, you'll see that things can and will get better. Plans give you a regained sense of control.

Your plan might resemble the kind of individualized education plan discussed in Chapter 9, *School*, or it might look like a schedule. Look at least three months ahead with specifics (big goals can go on up to adulthood and beyond).

Here's one part of a plan written for a seven-year-old boy with PDD-NOS:

Goal: Reducing rage behaviors

Activities:

1. Try to identify rage triggers, and eliminate when possible.

2. Work on redirection skills.

3. Possible medication change, explore this with psychiatrist.

4. Work on learning self-soothing behaviors (OT can help with this).

5. Set up "quiet area" in room to go to when agitated.

6. Look into possible link to eating and sleeping habits—changes? Appointment with allergist?

7. Ask about other parents' coping strategies at next support group meeting.

As you can see, each item on the activities list looks at a different way to address the problem. Maybe one will be the obvious solution, maybe it will take all of them together—or maybe the beleaguered parent will still be at his wits' end when that meeting in item No. 7 rolls around. The important thing is that the parent has identified things to do and named people who can help. The next step, setting a timetable, is almost automatic.

Making your plan happen

Whether you're a parent, a therapist, a teacher, or an adult with PDD, you will need help, as the example above makes clear. You can pay for help, you can rely on family and friends, or you can look into free or low-cost community resources and official support groups.

As you look at your first plan, you'll probably notice some areas where extra hands and hearts will be crucial: for example, running a home ABA program for thirty hours per week is not a job for one. Finding community resources can be an uphill struggle, but even in the smallest of towns there are good people who can help. If trained professionals are not an option, go to the folks who have the most spare time and energy: teenagers, college students, and senior citizens. Some families have found unexpected gems at the retirement home or the junior high school.

In big cities, the resources are usually there for the plucking. The problem is finding out about them. Programs change rapidly, and sometimes people from one program don't like a different one. When parents or adult patients put their heads together, however, resource lists seem to magically materialize and grow. Chapter 12, *Support*, offers more concrete suggestions on diving into the local talent pool.

> *It's like pulling teeth to find community resources. Each person gives you little bits and pieces, but no one has a whole local resources guide. I will eventually, and I will give it to the ASA and a few others to distribute it. Maybe I'll put it on the Web!* —Holly, mother of three-year-old Max

If you have persistent problems with follow-through, chances are you've bitten off more than you can chew. Try easier goals and smaller steps at first. You may also need to reward *yourself* for attaining goals, especially if the end result is not its own reward.

Some parents may also need to deal with clinical depression, anxiety, marital conflict, or other personal problems before they can handle intense activity on their child's behalf. If that's the case, do what you need to do to be effective and capable, and try to find someone to fill in for you in the meantime.

Keep your eyes on the prize

Today's goal may be as small as maintaining eye contact for two minutes, but never let go of the big picture. Striving for the best future, even saying out loud that you're working toward a cure when that's supposed to be an impossibility, is what makes today's minuscule, difficult steps manageable.

You may have let go of some very specific dreams for your child upon accepting this diagnosis, but certain goals are universal to all parents, and for all children. Here are some personal hopes that four parents of children with PDD-NOS or atypical PDD would like to share with you:

> *I pay for Sarah's prepaid college tuition every month. It will be paid off in a year! I want her to function and live a normal adult life.* —*Elaine, mother of three-year-old Sarah (diagnosed PDD-NOS and oral-motor apraxia)*

· · · · ·

> *I would love for Dhylan to have the rights of life, liberty, and the pursuit of happiness. I would love for him to be accepted by his peers, to marry, and to live independently. I would love to see him live up to his potential, and for others to allow him this privilege. I dream the same dreams for him as I do for my other seven children. If we don't set our goals high, we fail him.* —*Sally, mother of four-year-old Dhylan (diagnosed PDD-NOS with autistic features)*

· · · · ·

> *I would like to see Jesse go to college one day, be successful in a career, and have a faith in God.* —*Dorthy, mother of five-year-old Jesse (diagnosed PDD-NOS with autistic tendencies)*

· · · · ·

> *My hopes are that he will be able to have a career that takes advantage of his amazing talents, much like [autistic animal-behavior expert] Temple Grandin.* —*Jennifer, mother of three-year-old Joseph (Asperger's-like and autistic-like features, diagnosis still in progress)*

Are these parents foolish to dream of marriage, college, a normal adult life for their children with pervasive developmental disorders? No. Dreams are not the same thing as expectations: they are an expression of your hopes, and they should always be about the possible, not the merely probable.

If someone tries to dash your dreams with unkind words, keep moving forward. More is learned about autistic spectrum disorders every day, so no one can tell you with any certainty what your child's life will be like ten, twenty, or thirty years from now. Your child may not reach all of the goals you set, but your dogged determination and hard work will ensure that he gets just as far as he can go.

And that's all that any parent can do.

CHAPTER 5

Medical Interventions

THE MEDICAL APPROACH TO TREATING pervasive developmental disorders may include physical and mental health assessment, the use of seizure control strategies, including antiseizure medications, prescribing medications to address specific symptoms, case and medication management, and referrals to other treatment providers.

In this chapter, we discuss how doctors and psychiatrists currently treat PDD-NOS, atypical PDD, and similar disorders. We list most of the medications commonly used. This chapter also covers medical tests and treatments that appear to help some people with PDDs by strengthening the immune system. Special diets and supplements that can complement these efforts are discussed further in Chapter 7, *Other Interventions*.

Assessment and testing

If you have prepared a plan of action that prioritizes your areas of concern, as described in Chapter 4, *Getting Started*, this plan will be very helpful to the physician who will be prescribing and managing medication. Your first visit will probably be dedicated to assessment. Bring your plan and any recent evaluations. Also bring a list of past medications, therapies, diets, and supplements that includes dosages, dates used, and effects, if any.

Just as there is no "magic bullet" medicine that can cure PDDs, no medical treatment currently available can treat all of the troublesome symptoms associated with these disorders. Responsible doctors take a top-down approach. Medication is prescribed only for symptoms causing the most distress, preferably after nondrug alternatives have been tried or in concert with such treatments.

At your first assessment appointment with a physician who treats autistic spectrum disorders, you might receive a list like this one:

Interventions Prior to Using Medication

1. Education

2. Behavior modification (ABA)

3. Speech therapy

4. Sensory integration (SI) therapy, including deep pressure, skin brushing, vestibular stimulation

5. Relaxation therapy

6. Structured teaching (TEACCH)

7. Auditory integration training

8. Vitamin B6 plus magnesium

9. Dimethylglycine (DMG)

10. Allergy evaluation, including food sensitivities

11. Casein-free and gluten-free diet

12. Social stories

These terms may sound like Greek to you now, but all of the techniques listed can play an important part in helping people with PDD-NOS or atypical PDD. Some of these approaches are covered in Chapter 6, *Therapeutic Interventions*; Chapter 7; or Chapter 9, *School*. We bring them to your attention now, however, because it's important to look at the roots of problem behaviors before medicating.

Even the most distressing problems, such as head-banging and other forms of self-injurious behavior (SIB), may be a form of communication. In fact, head-banging is often associated with ear infections, and may go away if the underlying infection is treated rather than the behavior. Likewise, hyperactivity in some children is related to an unresponsive sensory system, and can be ameliorated with sensory integration therapy as well as with stimulant medications. Unlike Ritalin, sensory integration has no side effects to worry about. The functional behavioral analysis techniques described in Chapter 6 can help you find the roots of problem behaviors and give you the tools you need to address them. Sometimes those tools are medical, sometimes not.

The assessment process should be followed by a discussion of strategies, including both the medical strategies discussed in this chapter and non-medical alternatives. This strategic plan should also consider seemingly unrelated health issues. Many people have found that what appeared to be a purely psychiatric symptom actually had roots in mundane physical problems.

> My son experiences auditory hallucinations, but after one and a half days on antibiotics, the voices are nearly gone. He is feeling great, and was able to participate normally in classes today.

> Who would have thought... an outer ear infection leading to voices! Which makes me really, really wonder—if ulcers are now known to be caused by bacteria in most cases, how many people classified with "mental" illnesses might show significant improvement if they went through a round or two of antibiotics? And what if I had taken him directly to the psychiatrist to deal with the voices, rather than the pediatrician, who looked in his ear? He would have sat across the desk from the doctor, who would have advised increasing the dosage of the psychiatric drugs.

> I know this can't be the answer for everybody. But how many people are being evaluated on the basis of their "mental" symptoms, without their "physical" symptoms being considered simultaneously? —Lynn, mother of ten-year-old Richard

Help your doctor by answering questions as completely as possible during the assessment and strategic planning process. Ask whether medical testing, a metabolic workup, genetic screening, an immune-system test battery, or allergy testing should be pursued, based on the symptoms you have seen.

If your doctor isn't sure how to proceed, the *DAN! Clinical Options Manual* may be helpful. See the section "PDD-related studies" later in this chapter for more information on DAN!

If your doctor seems to be interested only in prescribing medications, or if follow-up is not handled well, find another physician.

Blood tests and EKGs

Many of the medications currently in use for PDD symptoms can have dangerous side effects if improperly prescribed. In some cases, liver or heart function should be tested first. Liver function is assessed with a blood test that checks the level of certain enzymes, while heart function is usually assayed with a regular blood-pressure test, a physical exam, and an electro-cardiogram (EKG).

The EKG can be done in the doctor's office, and since it uses wires that stick on the chest with an adhesive patch or gooey substance, it doesn't hurt at all. You have to lie still, however, so it's a tough test for hyperactive children. Appendix D, *Medication Reference*, includes information about most tests needed when using common psychiatric medicines. You may also want to check the package insert, if any, or a medication reference book.

With some medications, such as the antispasmodic drug Depakote, regular blood tests will be required. These tests check physical functions or make sure the medication has reached its therapeutic level (the dosage at which it is effective without causing harm). These medications should be avoided by patients who do not have regular access to quality lab facilities, such as those living in remote areas, unless all other alternatives have been explored.

For those who can drop into a doctor's office for a blood draw once a month, however, monitoring soon becomes part of your regular routine. Good phlebotomists (blood-draw specialists) do not cause bruising or more than a twinge of pain when they do their job, unless the patient bruises very easily or has a low pain threshold. If this is the case, let the phlebotomist know—she may have a better way to obtain the sample.

For obvious reasons, children don't relish blood draws. Stickers, treats, and other rewards for bravery can help. Blood tests are especially tough on children who are sensory-defensive. An occupational therapist may be able to help you with techniques for desensitizing the area from which blood will need to be drawn. Numbing ointments can also help.

Seizures and seizure-detection tests

Seizures are the result of nerve cells that fire off abnormal electrical charges. They have many causes, and there is more than one type of seizure. There are three general classifications of seizures, two of which can be broken down into subcategories. These are:

- Generalized seizures, which affect the whole brain.
    - Absence seizures are sometimes called *petit mal* seizures, although this term may be applied to other types of "mild" seizures as well. These brief events are characterized by blank staring and sometimes small, repetitive movements (automatisms).

- Myoclonic seizures are jerking movements of muscles or muscle groups.

- Atonic seizures, also called drop attacks, are seizures in which the body has a sudden loss of muscle tone and cannot stand or sit upright.

- Tonic/clonic seizures, formerly called *grand mal* seizures, are the best-known and most obvious type of seizure. The body is rigid during the tonic phase, and jerks during the clonic phase. Tonic/clonic seizures are often followed by a "foggy" feeling, headaches, or sleep.

• Partial seizures, also called focal or local seizures, which affect only part of the brain.

- Simple partial seizures, in which one part of the body, or several body parts on one side only, may twitch uncontrollably. Alternatively, the person may see, hear, or smell things that are not there, or have a sudden flood of emotions. The person may feel confused and unsure of where they are. They will, however, be conscious.

- Complex partial seizures are like a simple partial seizure, but with loss of consciousness. The person may walk, talk, or move around, but won't remember doing so afterward.

• *Status epilepticus*, a dangerous and possibly life-threatening condition in which multiple seizures occur one after another, without regained consciousness in between. Patients in the throes of *status epilepticus* need to be transported to the closest emergency room. Thankfully, this type of seizure is very rare.

Seizures may be present from infancy or begin later in life. The onset of puberty is a particularly likely time for seizures to begin, possibly because of increased hormonal activity in the brain. No matter when they occur, seizures can have a profound impact on the course and severity of a pervasive developmental disorder.

> One has a better idea of a person's prognosis when he or she reaches puberty. It is estimated that 20 to 25 percent experience seizures for the first time around puberty. This can range from grand mal seizures to

subclinical seizures. I have known a few individuals who were not treated for these seizures, and they went from high-functioning to low-functioning. —Dr. Stephen M. Edelson, director, Center for the Study of Autism

Diagnosis of seizure disorders

If seizures of any type are suspected, you may be referred to a neurologist or other specialist. The primary test for seizure activity is the electroencephalogram (EEG), which records electrical activity in the brain. Electrical impulses are detected by electrodes placed on the patient's scalp and carried to the EEG machine by wires. A printer attached to this device prints out this activity in wavy lines. EEG technicians can see where abnormal activity is taking place by looking at this graph.

Most EEGs take one or two hours. The EEG technician may try to get a reading asleep, at rest, wide awake, during deep breathing exercises, and while a light is flashing. The test is not painful at all, and some little kids think it's "cool," in a Frankenstein's laboratory kind of way.

If the short EEG is inconclusive, the doctor may order a sleep-deprived EEG. As the name indicates, the patient needs to be awake but bone-tired for this test. Parents can take turns keeping a child up all through the night, then bring him to the test site first thing in the morning. You can imagine how much fun this will be with a willful, cranky child! Movie marathons, midnight bowling, and shopping trips to the all-night convenience store are among the carrots that have kept some young ones (and many sleepy adults as well) awake through the night. The idea is for the exhausted patient to drop into a deep sleep right away, and it usually works.

But even this procedure may not show clear evidence of seizures. In cases where the doctor still suspects seizure activity, she may order 24-, 36-, or 48-hour EEG monitoring. This procedure can be done at home with a portable EEG unit or in a hospital setting. The portable units are certainly more convenient, but they're rather cumbersome, and wires have a tendency to come loose. If they do, the test must be redone.

Other types of brain scans are available, but they are also much more expensive than EEGs. These include magnetic resonance imagery (MRI), single photon emission computed tomography (SPECT, also called NeuroSPECT), and positron emission tomography (PET) scans. An MRI can actually show physical changes that are associated with seizure activity; SPECT scans can show cerebral blood flow, which may be a helpful clue to areas where neural activity is abnormally high or low; and PET images can show changes in cerebral metabolism.

Temporal lobe epilepsy, usually now called complex partial seizure disorder, is hard to diagnose. People with temporal lobe epilepsy experience odd states of mind rather than the easier-to-recognize physical seizures that result from activity in the parts of the brain that govern movement. During a temporal lobe seizure, the person's environment may suddenly seem "unreal," for example. Objects and sounds may take on a hallucinatory quality. Strong emotions, such as fear or disgust, may come on in a rush, and with no relationship to reality. Actual auditory and visual hallucinations may occur, often similar to the classic migraine aura or epileptic aura that brings visions of patterns and colors, or creates the sensation of smelling or tasting something that's not there. Some patients describe an internal sensation that "flows up" from their stomach to their head as a seizure begins.

Still more difficult to detect are electrical malfunctions that may occur deep within the brain. Physicians believe these occur in some people, but diagnosis of hidden events is hit-and-miss: it would be surprising if one just happened to occur while an expensive brain scan (or even an EEG) is taking place.

Coping with seizures

Seizures can occur in anyone as a result of fever or injury, so every parent and caregiver should know what to do. Here are the six basic steps:

1. Move the person to the floor and make sure anything nearby that could cause injury is moved.

2. Turn the person on her side to prevent choking. *Never* put an object in the person's mouth, as there's no chance that he will swallow his tongue.

3. Loosen any tight clothing.

4. Stay with the person until the seizure ends.

5. Help the person get comfortable as they recover from the seizure.

6. If a seizure lasts more than five minutes, or if seizures continue to follow each other during a ten-minute period, call for emergency medical care and wait with the person until it arrives.

Some medications and herbal supplements may lower the seizure threshold, causing seizures in patients who have not experienced them before or worsening seizure activity in those who have epilepsy. Be sure to tell your doctor if seizures have happened before, or if they occur during medication or supplement use.

Medication tips

Ask for the results of any screening tests, medical tests, and therapeutic blood levels, as well as for copies of prescriptions and other information collected as part of the assessment and follow-up care process. A physician's assistant or nurse should be able to help you read these records and interpret test results.

Many patients and families have caught potentially harmful errors by examining this paperwork. Common mistakes include drugs prescribed in different doses than the physician intended, misinterpreted blood tests, and blood samples assessed with the wrong test.

> I was cutting my son's pills today to put them in his weekly pill holder, and something looked odd. I called the pharmacy, and they sent someone to pick up the pills and take them back. When the delivery man came back, I noticed that indeed the Clonidine pills looked normal now. I called the pharmacist. "Sure enough," he said, "right medicine, wrong strength." Please remember, if it looks odd, ask. And also remember to look. —Karen, mother of eight-year-old Louis

Keep track of unusual symptoms that could be medication side effects, and immediately report any that are of concern. Most people remember to do this when a prescription is new, but grow lax in their observations over time. That's a mistake, because little information is available on the long-term use of many psychiatric drugs. "The first data that's collected is the short-term efficacy and side effects," explains Dr. Marc Potenza, a Fellow at Yale University's Department of Psychiatry who has researched and written about medications for PDDs. Dr. Potenza adds that drug studies rarely monitor the effects over time, because longitudinal studies are expensive and time-consuming, and they aren't required to gain official approval for a drug.

In other words, patients who use a medication during its first ten or twenty years on the market *are* the longitudinal test group.

Dosage details

Selecting the correct dosage for a patient is more of an art than a science. Doctors who are unfamiliar with a particular medication usually follow manufacturer-provided guidelines on dosage according to the patient's weight and/or age. These guidelines, however, should be just that—guides to keep doses within safe and effective levels.

Each person's body chemistry is different, and people with neurological disorders can have rather unusual responses to many medications. Most people are familiar with the "Ritalin paradox": many hyperactive children calm down when given a stimulant that would energize a normal child. Hyperactive children who also have a diagnosis in the PDD family, however, tend to respond very differently to stimulants than other hyperactive children. People with PDDs may have exquisite sensitivity to medications or require larger doses than would normally be used. This makes life very difficult for those who want to be careful medication consumers.

One of the most common complaints is that doctors don't take simple steps to lessen the chance of medication difficulties. Dosages are often too high to start with, or medications are increased to the full therapeutic dose over just a few days. For many patients, this strategy ensures difficult side effects and makes noncompliance (abandonment of the medication) more likely. Gradual titration (increase in dosage) over a period of weeks can make all the difference, although this strategy has its own drawback: patients are less likely to see dramatic, positive effects right away.

Sometimes, when a medication doesn't seem to be working, the dose actually needs to be *lower*, not higher. This effect has occurred with the selective seratonin re-uptake inhibitor (SSRI) antidepressants in particular. It could be that a low dose of these drugs helps to balance brain chemistry, while a higher dose actually throws it out of whack in the opposite direction.

It doesn't help that drugs often come in one size only. Even a single 25-milligram pill may be too much for some patients to start with. Surprisingly, many doctors are unaware of options that can help in such cases:

- A number of psychiatric medications, including Prozac, Haldol, and Risperdol, are available in liquid form. Liquids can be measured out in tiny doses and increased very gradually. Incidentally, liquid medications can be easily administered to children with swallowing problems, or those who refuse pills. You may even be able to mix them with food or drinks (check with your pharmacist first).

- Some medications can be broken into fractions. Pill splitters are available at most pharmacies for just this purpose. Make sure that it's okay to split a medication before you go this route, however: time-release medications and some pills with special coatings will not work properly when broken. Generally speaking, if there's an indented line down the middle of the pill, you can definitely split it. Otherwise, ask your pharmacist or call the manufacturer's customer hotline.

- Some medications that are too small or unwieldy to split can be crushed and divided into equal parts. Again, ask your pharmacist before doing this. Tiny mortar and pestle sets can be found at health-food or cooking shops. Obviously, it's difficult to get precise doses with crushed pills.

Some medications come in patch form. Tempting though it may be, don't try cutting these patches to get a smaller dose or to move up to a larger dose gradually. Doing so will keep the medication from being absorbed properly.

Compounding pharmacies can make medications to order in their own lab—for example, such pharmacies can make a liquid version of a substance normally available in tablet form only. These pharmacies are especially helpful to individuals with allergy problems. Many pills and syrups contain common allergens, including eggs, soy, corn, and dyes. If a hypoallergenic version isn't available from the manufacturer, seek out a compounding pharmacy. If there isn't one where you live, several allow patients with valid prescriptions to order over the Internet. Just use a search engine like Alta Vista (*http://www.altavista.com/*) or Lycos (*http://www.lycos.com/*) to search for the term "compounding pharmacy." As always with Internet-based or mail-order businesses, check references before you pay for goods or services.

Be careful to follow medication instructions about eating or drinking. Also, avoid taking medications with grapefruit juice—it may sound nutty, but grapefruit juice can prevent the breakdown of certain medications.

Withdrawal procedures

If a person with PDDs is on medication but still having great difficulty, a physician may ask that all medication be withdrawn to get a baseline look at which symptoms are being caused by the disorder, and which are due to over-, under-, or mismedication. This process can be exceptionally trying for patients and families if it is not managed well. There are very few medications that can be stopped cold without causing distress—and with some, such as Clonadine, stopping suddenly can be life-threatening.

Ask your doctor if there are any symptoms you might expect during the withdrawal period. She might be able to recommend over-the-counter or dietary remedies for likely problems, such as diarrhea or nausea. With children, nonmedication strategies should be decided on in advance to deal with problem behaviors that may occur as drugs are tapered off.

Gradual withdrawal is almost always the best approach. Patients should be carefully monitored for signs of trouble. In some cases, medication withdrawal may need to take place in a hospital setting.

About "breakthrough drugs"

It seems that every year some compound is touted as a wonderful new treatment for autistic-spectrum disorders, often based on only a few cases in which it seemed beneficial. Such reports usually result in a stampede of parents and patients, all desperate to try the new drug. Unfortunately, several medications that have been tested for use in autism have eventually been found wanting. Some of these showed much promise initially. Accordingly, it's important to avoid jumping the gun when you hear about new drugs. The list of medication dead ends to date includes:

- **Fenfluramine hydrochloride.** Sold under many brand names, including Pondimin, this amphetamine was the "Fen" in the dangerous and discredited weight-loss drug Fen-Phen. It has been removed from the market in the US.

- **Imipramine.** Also known as Tofranil, this tricyclic antidepressant didn't work well for autistic patients in studies.

- **Methysergide.** Sold as Sansert, an antimigraine medication, methysergide is derived from the ergot fungus.

- **Lysergic acid diethylamide.** Better known by its street name, LSD, this ergot-based compound has been shown to affect the serotonin system. Despite that silly film *Tommy*, its effects were not very useful for autistic symptoms in lab tests.

While a few patients may have experienced positive effects from some of these drugs, they are no longer recommended for use. These abandoned "breakthroughs" should be remembered whenever a new miracle drug is reported. It's better to stick with the tried and true until clinical trials have been completed, and even then, caution should be your watchword.

Medications

Although the US Food and Drug Administration has never approved a drug for the treatment of autism or PDDs, most of the medical treatments currently available for PDDs are drugs. Drugs are prescribed to address specific PDD symptoms, such as difficulty in focusing, hyperactivity, self-abusive behavior, depression, anxiety, and uncontrollable aggression. This section discusses the major types of drugs currently used and explains why they work for at least some people with PDDs. Appendix D provides detailed information about these medications, which are listed by both brand name and generic name whenever possible.

Sometimes medications that have not been formally approved by government regulators are available under "compassionate use" laws, including medications that normally would be available overseas. These laws rarely apply to PDDs. Some unapproved drugs may be made available to participants in human research trials. It is sometimes possible—if not absolutely legal—for a physician in one country to prescribe a medication available only overseas, and for patients to then have the prescription filled at an overseas pharmacy.

Note for non-US readers: Most of the brand names provided in this chapter are those used in the US. Brand names and formulations may vary in other countries, and some drugs may not be available elsewhere. Conversely, there may be new medications approved for use in Asia or Europe that have not made it to North America yet. If you're curious about an unfamiliar medication, look it up by its generic name to find the names of non-US equivalents, or ask your doctor whether something similar is available where you live.

Most of the drugs used for PDDs have an effect on the neurotransmitters, particularly serotonin and dopamine. They include antidepressants, anti-spasmodics, neuroleptics and atypical neuroleptics, and stimulants, among others. Unless otherwise noted below, most of these medications have not been specifically tested on people with autistic spectrum disorders.

You might wonder why medications have not been created specifically for autistic symptoms. Truthfully, with the past decade's explosion of drugs that work on the neurotransmitter system, researchers have barely completed preliminary research on medicines already discovered that might help people with PDDs. "Investigation is still warranted into the drugs that we *do* have available to see in which clinical population drugs are going to be effective," says Dr. Potenza. "There have been significant advances in regards to our abilities to target specific symptoms," he added, but more research is needed. It's likely that the next decade will bring psychiatric medications that target specific neurotransmitters more precisely, improving the quality of medical treatment and reducing side effects.

The National Alliance for the Mentally Ill is one of the best resources for information on new drugs for neurological disorders. Its Web site *(http:// www.nami.org/)* often has reviews of new drugs and previews of medications that are undergoing clinical trials.

Antidepressants

Some people with PDDs are clinically depressed, but that's not the only reason these drugs are increasingly used in autistic spectrum disorders. Low levels of serotonin, or problems in regulating the amount of or use of serotonin, are believed to be one of the root causes of autistic symptoms. Various antidepressants may also affect the production or use of other neurotransmitters. And these drugs do not affect the brain alone: the same neurotransmitters are also involved, if not always so directly, in carrying regulatory messages to the immune system and the gastrointestinal tract. They can even change the way a person perceives pain. Properly used, antidepressants can create global changes.

Today's antidepressants are much more advanced than those used just a decade ago, but they're still a blunt instrument for attacking brain dysfunction. There are several different types, and within each group related medications may function quite differently. That's why you shouldn't write off a whole family of drugs just because one was a disaster. A slightly different medication may turn out to be infinitely preferable.

All of the antidepressants should be used with care. Check package inserts and pharmacy information sheets to avoid interactions with other medications. Be sure to tell your doctor about any over-the-counter drugs you use, even aspirin, herbal medicines, or supplements.

Selective serotonin re-uptake inhibitors (SSRIs)

The brain is chock-full of serotonin receptors, tiny sites that bind with serotonin molecules to move chemical impulses through the brain. The SSRIs block certain receptors from absorbing serotonin. Researchers believe this results in lowered or raised levels of serotonin in specific areas of the brain. Over time, SSRIs may cause changes in brain chemistry, hopefully in the direction of improved neurotransmitter balance. SSRIs may also cause actual changes in brain structure with prolonged use. There are also receptor sites elsewhere in the central and peripheral nervous systems, so SSRIs can have an impact on saliva production, appetite, digestion, skin sensitivity, and many other functions.

Five drugs are currently considered to be part of the SSRI family:

- fluoxetine (Prozac)

- fluvoxamine (Luvox)

- paroxetine (Paxil)

- sertraline (Zoloft)

- citalopram (Celexa)

These medications are not identical in either their chemical composition or their effects on the brain. Prozac and Zoloft tend to have an energizing and focusing effect as well as reducing depression, for example, while Paxil may calm anxious or agitated patients who are also depressed.

Each SSRI has major or minor side effects of its own—see Appendix D for details. For adults, sexual dysfunction is often the greatest concern.

There are two serious side effects you should be aware of when starting to use SSRIs or increasing SSRI dosage. First, SSRIs can trigger manic episodes in some people with bipolar disorder ("manic depression"). Manic episodes may be characterized by nonstop talking ("pressured speech"); grandiose thoughts, speech, and actions; paranoia; lack of need for sleep; flight of ideas; uncharacteristically risky behavior; and hyperactive movements. This effect is most often seen when SSRIs are used to treat depression in a person who actually has bipolar disorder rather than simple, unipolar depression. An acute manic episode can be dangerous to the patient's health, not because of any physical effect, but due to the impulsive, extreme behavior that may occur during the episode.

Second, people who use SSRIs in overly high doses—or mix them with other medications that potentiate (increase) their effects, including herbal remedies like St. John's wort—run the risk of serotonin syndrome. When the brain has too much serotonin, patients may experience shivers, headaches, diarrhea, profuse sweating, confusion, and a "jumpy" feeling that's intensely uncomfortable. If this happens, stop taking the SSRI immediately and see your doctor without delay. In extreme cases, serotonin syndrome can be fatal, although no fatalities have yet been reported from the combination of an SSRI and St. John's wort.

Tricyclic antidepressants

Before Prozac became famous, the tricyclic antidepressants were the wonder drugs for depression and obsessive-compulsive disorder (OCD). They are still the best choice for some patients, although today doctors will usually try an SSRI or two first. There are several tricyclic antidepressants, many of which combine more than one active drug:

- amitriptyline (Elavil)
- amitriptyline/perphenazine (Etrafon, Triavil)
- amitriptyline/chlordiazepoxide (Limbitrol)
- amoxapine (Asendin)
- clomipramine (Anafranil)
- desipramine (Norpramin)
- doxepin (Sinequan)
- imipramine (Tofranil)
- nortriptyline (Avenytl, Pamelor)
- protriptyline (Vivactil)
- trimipramine (Surmontil)

Of these, only clomipramine and nortriptyline are used with any regularity by people with autistic-spectrum disorders. Clomipramine is particularly helpful for treating obsessive-compulsive behaviors. Along with treating depression and OCD, these tricyclics may help with nighttime bedwetting, appetite, sleep, alertness, anxiety, and hyperactivity.

The tricyclic antidepressants work by inhibiting the uptake of various neurotransmitters at adrenergic nerve terminals, resulting in an increase of monoamine neurotransmission.

These drugs require regular monitoring for heart problems and other potentially serious side effects. They can lower the seizure threshold. As with the SSRIs, there is a danger of sending people with bipolar disorder into a manic phase. Some patients also complain of excessive weight gain.

Two serious side effects are associated with some tricyclics. The first is neuroleptic malignant syndrome (NMS). This potentially fatal condition is characterized by rigid muscle movements, fever, irregular pulse and heartbeat, rapid heartbeat, irregular blood pressure, heavy sweating, and strange states of mind. Discontinue the medication immediately and call your doctor if these symptoms occur. In extreme cases, the patient may need emergency care at a hospital. Physicians should report episodes of NMS to the Neuroleptic Malignant Syndrome Information Service (http://www.nmsis.org/), which has set up a registry to help researchers reduce the incidence of this problem.

Tricyclics may also carry a risk of tardive dyskinesia, an irreversible muscle movement disorder more usually associated with long-term use of the older neuroleptic drugs, such as Haldol. Twenty to thirty percent of long-term neuroleptic users eventually develop this disorder, which is characterized by twisting motions of the hands and feet, and smacking or chewing movements of the mouth. It is hoped that some new medications may help patients prevent or treat this permanent side effect. Some physicians recommend that people who take drugs that carry a risk for TD also take Vitamin E supplements, which appear to stave off the disorder in some people.

MAO inhibitors

Three monoamineoxidase inhibitors (MAOIs) are currently available in the US. These medications address depression by inhibiting the metabolization of the neurotransmitters serotonin, norepinephrine, and dopamine:

- moclobemide (Aurorex)

- phenelzine (Nardil)

- tranylcypromine sulfate (Parnate)

MAOIs are rarely prescribed for people with PDDs, and are not used to treat depression as often as they once were. MAOIs can have unpleasant and even life-threatening interactions with many other drugs, including common over-the-counter medications. People taking MAOIs must also follow a special diet, because these medications interact with many foods. The list of proscribed foods includes chocolate, aged cheeses, beer, and many more.

If you or someone you care for is taking a MAOI, check for warning labels on everything, and familiarize yourself thoroughly with the dietary restrictions. MAOIs can also produce hallucinations and have been abused by some drug users to get this effect.

Buproprion

The drug buproprion (Wellbutrin, Zyban) is a unique aminoketone antidepressant. It appears to have mild effects on serotonin, dopamine, and norepinephrine, and it also seems to be a mild general CNS stimulant. It may help with symptoms of depression and ADHD.

Lithium

Lithium carbonate and lithium citrate (Eskalith, Lithane, Lithobid, Lithonate, Lithotabs) are different from all other antidepressants, because they can control bipolar disorder. Made from a naturally occurring salt, lithium is probably the oldest psychiatric remedy on earth. Natural lithium springs were frequented by Native Americans and ancient Europeans alike.

Lithium users need to have blood tests at regular intervals to monitor heart and kidney function, and to make sure the dose is at a therapeutic level. When this drug is taken with a neuroleptic, doses and side effects must be watched very carefully. There is a danger of encephalopathic syndrome with this combination. Encephalopathic syndrome's symptoms mimic those of neuroleptic malignant syndrome, of which it may be a variant. Lithium can be toxic in doses that are not much higher than the therapeutic dose. Despite these cautions, for most patients who experience extreme mood swings, lithium is well-tolerated and provides relief.

Mirtazapine

Described by its manufacturer as a Noradrenergic and Specific Serotonergic Antidepressant (NaSSA), mirtazapine (Remeron) affects the neurotransmitter noradrenaline as well as some serotonin receptors. It has both energizing and anti-anxiety effects. It may have ill effects on white blood cell counts in some people, depressing the immune system. If you experience fever, aches, sore throat, or infections, call your doctor.

Nefazodone

Nefazodone (Serzone), another unique antidepressant, blocks the uptake of serotonin and norepinephrine in the brain. It also increases the levels of two natural antihistamines in the bloodstream.

Reboxetine

Reboxetine, marketed under the brand name Edronax in the UK, is a brand-new antidepressant classified as a non-tricyclic selective norepinephrine re-uptake inhibitor (selective NRI).

Venlafaxine

The antidepressant venlafaxine (Effexor, Effexor XR) is also in its own category. It limits absorption of at least three neurotransmitters: serotonin, norepinephrine, and dopamine. Some people who have not tolerated SSRIs well have had better results with Effexor.

"Natural" antidepressants

St. John's wort, an herbal supplement billed as a "natural" antidepressant, has been in the news lately. Herbal medications and supplements are covered in more detail in Chapter 7 and in Appendix E, *Supplement Reference*, but it's important to know that some natural substances may act on the neurotransmitter system like prescription antidepressants. St. John's wort is one with a very real track record in European clinical trials, and as mentioned above, lithium salts also occur in nature. Inositol, a component of lecithin, also has a growing track record.

Based on reported effects and clinical trials, St. John's wort appears to combine aspects of the SSRIs and the MAOIs. For that reason, it should be taken with the same care and caution as these types of prescription drugs. There have been anecdotal reports of patients with manic episodes attributed to St. John's wort, or (more rarely) with unpleasant food or medicine interactions like those that can occur when taking MAOIs. There have been documented instances of serotonin syndrome associated with St. John's wort, generally when a patient taking a prescription antidepressant "supplemented" it with this herbal remedy. Recent reports implicate this herb in temporary nerve damage, which can occur if the patient stays in the sun too long. Melatonin, a supplement used to regulate sleep, may also affect serotonin. Be sure to tell your doctor about *any* supplements, herbal medications, or folk remedies you add to your medication regimen.

Perhaps one of the most important natural antidepressants is sleep. Researchers speculate that at least some of the positive effects attributed to antidepressants are actually due to their sleep-inducing powers. Lack of adequate sleep is a powerful depressant, and sleep disturbances are often the first sign of impending depression. People with PDDs frequently have unusual sleep schedules, sleep disturbances, or full-fledged sleep disorders. Medications, exercise, relaxation techniques, and scheduling adjustments can help you get control over these problems. Proper sleep can make a huge difference, and it's best if you can achieve it without drugs.

Daily activities can be powerful mood-enhancers as well, from eating a healthful diet to cultivating interests that occupy the troubled mind. Scheduling, even right down to fifteen-minute blocks, can provide daily motivation and the reward of purposeful activity. This is precisely the approach to depression used by the best institutions for the mentally ill, in concert with medication and "talk therapy." You can take these preemptive steps to keep your general physical and mental health in balance, and they may enhance your immune system functions as well.

> I think that you should try to find things that are fun for you, like work and school, a class that you really look forward to. That will help you, because you'll have a reason to go to sleep at bedtime. And eat breakfast, it really helps! —KayCee, age 16 (diagnosed OCD and bipolar disorder)

Anti-anxiety drugs

Most of the drugs prescribed for anxiety are in the benzodiazepine family of tranquilizers. Some of these medications may also help to prevent seizures and ease depression. They include:

- alprazolam (Xanax)
- chlordiazepoxide (Librium)
- clonazepam (Klonopin)
- clorazepate (Tranxene)
- diazepam (Valium)
- lorazepam (Ativan)
- oxazepam (Serax)
- prazepam (Centrax)

Doctors try to avoid prescribing tranquilizers for long-term use. These drugs slow down CNS activity, they often don't mix well with some other medications, and they can be addictive. However, for patients with severe anxiety, benzodiazepine tranquilizers can be very effective. Some people can take these on an "as-needed" basis, avoiding medication dependency.

Buspirone (BuSpar) is a nonbenzodiazepine anti-anxiety drug and tranquilizer. Because it doesn't carry the addiction risk of a benzodiazepine, it may be preferable for some people. Four small studies have shown that BuSpar may be useful for reducing aggressive behavior, hyperactivity, and stereotypic movements in people with autistic symptoms. However, anecdotal reports indicate that some patients find this medication difficult to tolerate.

Buspirone is available as a transdermal patch as well as a pill. The patch has been tested for use in children and was found to address hyperactivity in some with less of a "rebound effect" (see the section "Stimulants," later in this chapter) than amphetamines like Ritalin.

Sometimes BuSpar is added to an SSRI to prolong its effectiveness.

Antispasmodic medications

Although seizures are not part of the DSM-IV definition of pervasive developmental disorders, many people with PDDs have seizures, and seizures can have a deleterious effect on neurological function. In some cases, seizures may be the root cause of a PDD, as in the case of Landau-Kleffner syndrome.

> *Kyle was on Depakote for seizure control [from] ages five to seven. This controlled seizures. One seizure, in which he was nonresponsive for twenty or thirty seconds, caused our son to lose all expressive language for a week. Other symptoms of minor seizures included rapid eye movements back and forth for two to four seconds, followed by laughter or crying. These were controlled by Depakote, which may have helped preserve gains made by taking prednisone. —Joe, father of seven-year-old Kyle (diagnosed PDD-NOS with autistic features)*

For that reason—and also because seizures can be intensely uncomfortable, embarrassing, and dangerous for patients—seizure control is often the first line of business when they occur with PDDs. Commonly used antispasmodic (seizure-control) medications include:

- carmazepine (Tegretol)
- clonazepam (Klonopin)
- ethosuximide (Zarontin)
- ethotoin (Peganone)
- fosphenytoin (Cerebyx)
- gabapentin (Neurontin)
- lamotrigine (Lamictal)
- mephenytoin (Mesantoin)
- phenobarbital (Luminol, Solfoton)
- phenytoin (Dilantin)
- primidone (Mysoline)
- toiramate (Topamax)
- valproic acid (Depakene) and divalproex sodium (Depakote, Depakote Sprinkles)

Tegretol and Depakote are probably the anticonvulsants used most commonly in people with PDDs, mostly because there is quite a bit of information available about how these drugs work in concert with other psychiatric medications.

Phenobarbital can be addictive, and at too-high doses can produce an effect that looks like alcohol intoxication. For these reasons, it is rarely used anymore, except in low doses or as part of a combination that includes a newer antispasmodic.

Antispasmodics are often prescribed in combinations, as two can be more effective together than one. However, mixing drugs can increase the risk of side effects. Monotherapy (treatment with a single drug) is believed to be the best choice whenever possible.

Some forms of epilepsy may also be treated with a combination of steroids, such as prednisone, and antispasmodics. Steroids tend to cause weight gain and mood swings, and they suppress the immune system. Unless nothing else works, steroids should be avoided.

Gabapentin (Neurontin)

This relatively new anticonvulsant has been getting rave reviews from patients. It appears to have fewer side effects than the rest, and can be used as an adjunct to these and other drugs. Not only does it provide seizure control, but it also helps level the mood swings experienced by some patients with bipolar disorder or severe episodic aggression.

Other ways to address seizures

Adolescent and adult patients with seizures can often make lifestyle changes that reduce the number or severity of episodes. One of the most important of these is becoming aware of environmental triggers. Avoiding discos with strobe lights, certain types of carnival rides, and uncontrolled stress, for example, can be helpful. Learning relaxation techniques, such as meditation or biofeedback, is another good step.

Some people with seizure disorders have reported beneficial effects from special diets and supplements, particularly from vitamin B6, and the supplements lecithin and DMG. These claims have been partially substantiated in small studies. One intervention that can definitely help in extreme cases is the ketogenic diet. This high-fat, low-protein, low-carbohydrate regimen has proved very useful for some young children with epilepsy, although it's a less than pleasant experience for the patient and should *never* be undertaken without medical supervision.

In a very few cases, seizure disorders cannot be controlled with medication, diet, or other efforts. Surgery may be considered. A new procedure involves implanting a small device called a vagus nerve stimulator in the chest.

People with uncontrolled epilepsy must take steps to prevent harm during a seizure. They may need to wear a helmet, change their surroundings, or avoid driving a car.

Antispasmodic drugs for aggression or SIB

Physicians may also prescribe antispasmodic medications, particularly Depakote (and now Neurontin), to treat uncontrolled aggressive or self-injurious behavior (SIB) rather than seizures per se. Sometimes this approach works, perhaps because the aggressive episodes are set off by seizures deep in the brain. These subclinical seizures may be affecting areas of the brain that control behavioral inhibition, emotion, or the "fight or flight" response. It's also possible that some antispasmodics have other, as yet unknown, effects on brain chemistry.

Stimulants

The stimulant drugs have a generally energizing effect on the "normal" brain and body, but in many hyperactive individuals they appear to even out brain activity, calming the person down and allowing them to focus their attention more appropriately. It's believed that these drugs increase how much dopamine and norepinephrine are released from the sympathetic nervous system, and inhibit uptake of these neurotransmitters by the caudate nucleus. They also increase the flow of blood to all parts of the brain.

Stimulants are the drugs most frequently prescribed to children with PDDs, despite the fact that no studies of stimulant use have been done in this population. In fact, the Autism Research Institute's database indicates that many autistic-spectrum patients have bad reactions to stimulants, including increased hyperactivity, aggression, and stereotypic behaviors or tics. Out of 2,788 families who replied to a survey question about Ritalin, 45 percent reported that it made their autistic children's behavior much worse.

Some researchers believe that stimulant use can cause brain damage. Certainly this is sometimes the case with illegal amphetamines. Ritalin has been in use for ADHD for quite some time now, but there still isn't much information available on the effects of long-term use.

Stimulants may be appropriate for some people with PDDs, however. If you choose to try them, start with a small dose and titrate very slowly for the best effect.

> Miles has been on Ritalin since the age of five. It has enabled him to learn in a classroom environment, and to reduce the incidence of unsafe behaviors. We tried Dexedrine for about three months; it depressed Miles's mood significantly. —Amy, mother of seven-year-old Miles (diagnosed PDD-NOS and ADHD)

Some people (including quite a few doctors) swear that the brand-name Ritalin is superior to its generic counterpart. It may be worth trying the brand-name version if the generic didn't work well.

Stimulants that may be prescribed for symptoms of PDDs include:

- dextroamphetimine sulfate (Das, Dexampex, Dexedrine, Dexedrine Spansules, Dextrostat, Ferndex, Oxydess)
- dextroamphetimine/amphetamine (Adderall)
- methamphetamine (MTH)
- methylphenidate hydrochloride (Ritalin)
- pemoline (Cyclert)

These drugs work pretty much the same way, but for different lengths of time and with varying danger of the dreaded "rebound effect." This phenomenon's symptoms range from manic-like euphoria to depression or aggression.

The rebound effect can be rather nasty, but it's easily solved with careful dosing. Ritalin is the shortest-acting stimulant, and therefore the one with which the greatest amount of rebound trouble occurs. Doctors often ask that it be given at two-and-a-half to three-hour intervals, with half of a regular dose at bedtime to permit better sleep. A sustained-release version of Ritalin (Ritalin SR) is available, but gets low marks from patients when used alone. Dexedrine has a longer life (four to six hours), and the Dexedrine Spansule formulation can maintain its beneficial effects for up to eight hours.

Adderall is not as well-known as Ritalin, but it may be a better choice for many patients. It time-releases different amphetamine compounds smoothly over several hours, resulting in less chance of rebound.

Cyclert has a long action period, but is rarely used unless all of the others have failed to have positive effects. Regular liver monitoring is a must with this drug.

Stimulants and tic disorders

There is a persistent myth that stimulants can cause tic disorders, including Tourette syndrome. Studies indicate that this is not so: many children diagnosed with ADHD before the school years will go on to evidence signs of a tic disorder later on, often around the age of seven, regardless of whether stimulants are used or not. The two conditions appear to be related, and often occur in the same families or the same individuals. Stimulants are often prescribed around the age of five, hence the appearance of a "cause and effect" relationship between stimulants and tics.

It is possible that stimulants cause tics to appear sooner than they would have otherwise or that they make tics worse. Many people with Tourette syndrome avoid stimulants because they have found this to be the case for them.

Note for non-US readers: Stimulants are not used as widely in Europe as they are in the US for conditions other than narcolepsy. Patients in the UK and France may experience particular difficulty in obtaining any prescription medication for hyperactivity, regardless of how severe the problem is. Persistence—and seeking out a doctor who specializes in treating ADD/ADHD or who has experience in using stimulants with PDD patients—seems to be the key.

Stimulants and addiction

Ritalin and similar stimulants are now among the medications most frequently prescribed to children in the US. Many parents fear that this widespread use of amphetamines could lead to addiction to street drugs later on.

Dr. Maria A. Pugliese, a board-certified psychiatrist with added qualifications in addiction psychiatry at Pennsylvania Hospital and the Malvern Institute, says their fears are largely unfounded. "The biggest risk of addiction in children with ADD/ADHD comes from their genetic inheritance, not from their exposure to stimulant medication," says Dr. Pugliese. "There is a large crossover between families with ADD/ADHD and families with addictive disorders."

The greatest danger of prescription stimulant abuse occurs in junior high, when friends, siblings, or even parents may poach the patient's pills to get an illicit high.

"There are many safeguards built into the system to protect the public from stimulant abuse," Dr. Pugliese notes. "All stimulants except Cyclert are Schedule II drugs, meaning they must be written prescriptions, not phone-ins; they must be filled within 72 hours of being written, and there are no refills allowed without a new prescription. There are no indications that the stimulants that are prescribed for children with ADD/ADHD are addictive by themselves in therapeutic doses."

Parents need to make sure that proper safeguards are in place when medications are stored at home and at school. There have been many cases of theft or accidental use, sometimes with tragic results.

As for the fear that kids given stimulants or other psychiatric medications will come to think pills are the answer to all ills, Dr. Pugliese says education is the answer—and it works. "Children come to learn quite early the difference between medications and 'drugs,' because of schools' drug education and awareness programs," she says. "By the end of elementary school they are able to say the medication is 'good' and 'helps you get better,' and that 'drugs' are 'bad for you' and 'make your life sad.'" In addition, she notes, "If they have a serious psychiatric illness, they are much less likely to develop an addiction problem as an adult if their psychiatric illness is well-treated in childhood."

Over-the-counter stimulants

Some patients and parents have experimented with over-the-counter stimulants, particularly phenylpropanolamine (PPA). PPA is present in "diet pills," usually in combination with caffeine. PPA is also found in a number of common medicines, especially cold remedies. While benefits have been reported anecdotally, these medications can be dangerous if misused or mixed with other drugs. They are certainly not advised for anyone with a heart condition or whose heart function has never been tested.

Side effects reported include high blood pressure, nausea, restlessness, anxiety, insomnia, irritability, and hallucinations. There have been cases of death, generally due to heart attack, from OTC stimulants based on PPA, ephedrine (or the herb ephedra, also called ma huang, from which it is made), or even caffeine. If you insist on using these stimulants, tell your doctor, and monitor side effects carefully.

Neuroleptics

The neuroleptics are also known by the slightly scarier name antipsychotics. These medications are used to treat a wide variety of serious mental illnesses, but they are certainly not limited to the treatment of outright psychosis. Most of these medications affect dopamine production or absorption; some also work on serotonin or other neurotransmitters.

The very first neuroleptics were discovered in the 1950s and 1960s, and represented the first major breakthrough in medical treatment for mental illness. However, the excitement was short-lived when the results of long-term use and overdose were discovered. Many of these older medications are still prescribed for people with PDDs today, however. They include:

- chlorpromazine (Thorazine)
- diphenylbutylpiperdine (Pimozide or Orap)
- fluphenazine (Prolixin, Prolixin Decanoate)
- haloperidol (Haldol, Haldol Decanoate)
- loxapine (Loxitane)
- mesoridazine (Serentil)
- molindone (Moban)
- perphenazine (Trilafon)
- prochlorperazine (Compazine)
- thioridazine (Mellaril)
- thiothixene (Navane)
- trifluoperazine (Stelazine)
- triflupromazine (Vesprin)

Although for some patients they may be the only viable choice, knowledgeable physicians no longer use these older neuroleptics first. The atypical neuroleptics are infinitely preferable, if anything this strong is needed at all.

People involved in the care of institutionalized patients have noted that the older neuroleptics are used more often in these settings than one might think, possibly as a way to control patients in understaffed or poorly run facilities. Psychiatric nurses derisively refer to this approach as "using a chemical straitjacket." If you care for an institutionalized person, the potential for misuse or overuse of neuroleptics is something you should be on the lookout for.

The so-called atypical neuroleptics are recent discoveries. They blend functionality against schizophrenia, psychosis, self-injurious behavior, painful tics, and other major mental-health symptoms with far fewer side effects and dangers than their ancestors. Patients currently taking older neuroleptics should definitely ask their physician about making a switch. The atypical neuroleptic family includes:

- clozapine (Clozaril)
- olanzapine (Zyprexa)
- risperidone (Risperdal)
- quetiapine (Seroquel)
- ziprasidone (Zeldox)

Of these, risperidone and olanzapine have gotten the most attention for their beneficial effects on some people with PDDs. The two are similar in that they both target serotonin and dopamine receptors, but there are subtle differences. Perhaps they each block different receptors. Several recent studies have pronounced these two medications to be reasonably effective for problems ranging from Tourette syndrome with rage attacks to severe autistic behaviors.

Side effects to watch out for with all neuroleptic drugs include agranulocytosis (a dramatic drop in white blood cell count), neuroleptic malignant syndrome and tardive dyskinesia (see the section "Tricyclic antidepressants," earlier in the chapter), and withdrawal dyskinesias (temporary episodes with symptoms similar to tardive dyskinesia, which occur when the medication is stopped).

Neuroleptics may also cause extrapyramidal side effects (EPS). Physical symptoms include tremor, slurred speech, akathesia (an intensely uncomfortable itchy, jumpy sensation that may make the patient move around incessantly), and dystonia (uncontrollable muscle contractions). Emotional symptoms include anxiety, distress, paranoia, and bradyphrenia (slow thought processes). These are serious problems, the kind that understandably make patients want to stop taking their medicine. Careful medication choice and dosage adjustment should reduce these problems, and complimentary adjustments to diet, vitamins, supplements, and relaxation techniques may also help.

Excessive weight gain is also a common problem with both older and atypical neuroleptics.

Other medications

A few medications that don't fit into one of the categories above have proved useful for some people with PDD-NOS or atypical PDD, or are currently being investigated.

Antihypertension medications

Foremost among these are two drugs more commonly used to treat high blood pressure:

- catapres (Clonadine)
- guanfacine (Tenex)

These drugs act on the nervous system to dilate blood vessels, presumably increasing the flow of blood in the brain as well as in the rest of the body.

Clonadine or Tenex are often used to curb hyperactivity when stimulants don't work or can't be combined with other medications. Both may also help curb aggression.

Clonadine is available in pill or patch form, although only the pill is available as a less-expensive generic. Patients generally prefer the patch. It's easier to use, and pill users tend to experience sleepy "crashes" as the medication is first absorbed in the bloodstream. The crash effect can interfere with school or work.

The Clonadine pill was definitely a wash. Our son was out like a light by 10 a.m., and napped for well over an hour. We saw great improvements in his ability to pay attention, stay on task in class, and clamp down on his own inappropriate, impulsive behavior, but we had to go to the patch instead so he wouldn't sleep through first grade. The patch tends to fall off before it should, but it's a much smoother medication.

When using the Clonadine patch, place it on a part of the body where it's likely to stay and be properly absorbed. Adults usually prefer the upper arm. For children, hard-to-reach areas on the back work well. The foam-like overlays packaged with this medication don't work very well, so you may have to buy your own overlay bandages to get the patch to stick. Clonadine users report that the best overlay is the transparent film dressing Tegaderm, although it's expensive. They haven't worked for everyone, but the extra-large semitransparent "Tattoos" bandages made by Nexcare often do a good job at a lower cost.

Both Clonadine and Tenex can affect heart function and blood pressure, so regular monitoring is a must. Neither medication can be stopped suddenly, due to the risk of a dangerous drop in blood pressure.

Opioid blockers

These medications are most often used as part of a comprehensive detoxification program for addiction to drugs and alcohol, but some doctors feel they may have a role in addressing some symptoms of PDDs. The opioid antagonist naltrexone (ReVia, Trexan, or NTX) has been used by autistic children in several studies, with mixed results. A subgroup of people with autism are definitely helped by this drug, and it appears to be especially effective in cases of SIB.

Nicotine

Recent studies have shown that nicotine can potentiate (increase the efficiency of) neuroleptics, and may have other beneficial effects. This does not mean that people with PDDs should take up smoking! Quite the contrary: smoking has serious health risks, and doesn't deliver a controlled dose of this potent drug. The nicotine patch is preferred.

People with PDDs who *do* smoke or chew tobacco need to be aware that nicotine use can affect the potency of psychiatric medications, and should take precautions accordingly.

Welcome to the medical merry-go-round

Some people with PDDs have been on an incredible array of medications. The side effects can be as bad as the symptoms the drug was intended to alleviate—or you may just get lucky and find the perfect fit. "Med trials" are indeed trying, especially when it's hard to find something that works.

Medicines that we tried for hyperactivity:

- *Ritalin, Ritalin ER—no calming effect.*
- *Dexedrine, Dexedrine Spansules—extreme increase of hyperactivity.*
- *Cyclert—hallucinations.*
- *Dextrostat—increased attention span, less hyperactivity.*

Medications that we tried for impulsivity, aggression:

- *Tegretol, Navane, Desipramine, Clonazapam, Lithium, Mellaril, Tenex, Paxil, and Zoloft hyped him up; we also tried Stelazine, Trazodone, Pamelor, and probably many more I can't recall. None of these meds had any effectiveness.*
- *Wellbutrin caused grand mal seizures, Wellbutrin SR did not.*
- *Depakote levels his moods fairly well.*
- *Risperdal reduced auditory hallucinations well, Seroquel and Zyprexa had no effect.*
- *Prozac seems to stop some of the whining and complaining.*
- *DDAVP nasal spray stops the bedwetting, as did Imipramine for several years until immunity was built up.*

—Ann, mother of eight-year-old Theron (diagnosed with PDD-NOS, psychotic disorder, borderline intellectual functioning)

It's very important to keep careful records of all the medications you've tried, including information about whether it was a brand name or generic formula, starting dose, dose titration, length and regularity of use, beneficial effects, and not-so-beneficial effects. You or your doctor may find some surprises when you look back over these records.

Frequently medications that are rejected were never given a fair trial in the first place. Either they were started at too high a dose, causing unpleasant side effects, or they were given in combination with another drug that strengthened or weakened the new medication's effects. As noted in the section "Dosage details," earlier in the chapter, sometimes problems with medications are actually allergic reactions to a dye or filler in the pill.

"Slow and steady" should be the words you live by when trying new medications. Start low, and gradually increase the dose. Keep notes. Research the possibility of interactions with other medications—no doctor can be aware of all interaction possibilities. Research resources include inexpensive books, such as *The Pill Book,*[1] Internet pharmacology sites, your pharmacist, and package inserts. If you have access to a copy of the *Physicians' Desk Reference* (PDR), all the better.

Case and medication management

One of the most difficult dilemmas faced by people with PDDs and their caregivers is obtaining adequate case management and medication management services. Ideally, one person can provide advice on both medications and other treatment options, handle referrals to speech therapists and other providers, make sure appointments and services are scheduled and delivered, and oversee the treatment process in a holistic manner.

Unfortunately, this ideal situation appears to be rare. Often patients and parents must see several different doctors, who may not agree with each other or even read each other's reports. This can lead to medication interactions at worst, and lack of information about other treatment options at best. Of all the parent complaints heard while researching this book, the need for informed case-management services came through the clearest.

> I felt like I was having a nervous breakdown when he was two and I was doing research; again when I got the reports at age seven and was trying to get speech and OT and special education; and now I feel that way again, fighting with [service provider], trying to be a "case manager"

for my son, and figuring out what tests he needs, what specialist I should consult next, to satisfy them and get his eligibility. And now, I'm fighting with the school district too!

In my dreams, one person would be assigned to manage the child's needs, from early identification through diagnosis. This person could help parents and child through the system to get the medical, psychological, educational, recreational, vocational, and independent living skills and services they need to become functioning, productive citizens, or help them be placed appropriately for their needs.

This person could be a government employee, with power to dictate to the local school districts, to any private insurer, to any state or federal agency, to get the evaluations, the reports, the funding, etc., and to get help for the family, too. —Cindy, mother of fifteen-year-old Jeffrey (diagnosed verbal dyspraxia with "autistic-like" features)

Families dealing with autistic spectrum disorders are under a lot of stress, and adding a second job in case management and medication research to their load is more than some can bear. There are options, although you'll probably have to squawk to gain access. Case-management services may be available through:

- HMOs and managed care groups
- Health insurance companies
- Psychiatrists
- Behavioral health clinics
- Government agencies in charge of mental health or medical care (in the US, start at the county level)
- Private charitable organizations for the disabled, such as Easter Seals
- Special school-based programs that arrange for "wraparound" services in addition to educational planning

Some families actually hire someone to do case management and planning, and bring this person to their meetings with doctors, school officials, and therapists as a sort of consultant.

No matter where you find a case manager, you may have to spend a great deal of time educating him or her.

I find that I often know more than my son's teachers, doctors, and case coordinator about hyperlexia and atypical autism—not a very confidence-building feeling. Perhaps there should be regional specialists in atypical autism who not only coordinate care, but put the parents in contact with each other. —Jennifer, mother of three-year-old Joseph (Asperger's-like and autistic-like features, diagnosis still in progress)

The key to getting someone to help manage your case is *asking*. You may have to ask rather insistently, particularly if you're dealing with an HMO or managed care group. Be sure to remind bureaucrats that well-managed cases cost less in the long run, because patients improve more, and do so quicker. Good case management now will mean less need for expensive adult services later on.

Referrals to other treatment providers

Referrals are another hot-button issue. Obtaining speech therapy, occupational therapy, physical therapy, allergy testing, metabolic screening, EEGs and EKGs, and other specialist services is often more of a headache than it should be.

Psychiatric medications are a specialty in and of themselves. Managed care practices sometimes discourage pediatricians and general practitioners from referring patients to a psychopharmacologist (psychiatric medication specialist) or psychiatrist for medication management. You may have to fight to put someone experienced at the helm of your personal treatment plan.

It took two years to even get someone to listen. I was dismissed time and again as a nervous mother. I finally had to let Jesse loose in the doctor's office to get a referral. —Dorthy, mother of five-year-old Jesse (diagnosed PDD-NOS with autistic tendencies)

As a patient or parent, you'll have to make your wishes crystal clear. You may have to petition an HMO or insurance-company board for permission to use or extend your use of these services. You may need to write letters, make many phone calls, even contact government agencies to get needed specialist care. Your best hope is finding someone in the organization you're petitioning who will walk you through the necessary steps.

Unless you have a case manager, you'll need to keep track of specialist services yourself. Make sure appointments are scheduled when they should be, that test results get to the other members of the treatment team, and that direct services are actually delivered and meet the patient's needs.

PDDs and the immune system

Doctors are beginning to experiment with doing more than merely treating the symptoms of pervasive developmental disorders, based on indications that at least some subtypes of PDD are due to underlying immune-system or metabolic dysfunction, an autoimmune disorder, or even an infectious disease. Although we'll look at these concepts separately, it's probably not a case of "one or the other." All of these factors, along with genetic predisposition, are intimately connected.

It helps to think of the central nervous system (CNS), the immune system (including the lymphatic network, which runs throughout the body), and the gastrointestinal tract as a holistic entity. All three are controlled by the same complex stew of hormones, neurotransmitters, and nutrients. When one system is not up to par, the other two will also be affected. In the case of serious illness, the impact can be global.

Indeed, both personal and family medical histories of people with pervasive developmental disorders indicate that disturbances in all parts of this triad occur more frequently than in the general population. This appears to indicate a genetic predisposition to autoimmune disorders or to immune-system dysfunction.

The tendency in medical research is to study each physical process separately. Thanks to the advances in immunology that have occurred due to the AIDS tragedy, however, more clinicians are seeing interconnections and interactions between these three systems as significant. AIDS destroys the immune system, creates abnormalities in nutrient absorption and appetite that can lead to wasting syndrome, and eventually effects the CNS, with many patients experiencing dementia and other neurological problems. Physicians have had to work on all of these fronts to bring AIDS patients back to health. That they are succeeding in many cases shows the value of this approach in the worst of circumstances, and makes it likely that similar successes can be realized in other illnesses that have pervasive effects.

It's unfortunate that as of this writing there is a schism between some autism researchers who have an autoimmune bent and those interested in the possibility of an underlying metabolic disorder. Since PDDs appear to be multifactorial in origin, it would be far better for these camps to work together—and it would be better still if both groups could work in concert with mainstream pharmacological and genetic researchers.

PANDAS

Research that may bear fruit for people with PDDs is now occurring on a number of fronts. One of the first breakthroughs was the Pediatric Autoimmune Neuropsychiatric Disorder Associated with Streptococcus (PANDAS) project, steered by the National Institute of Mental Health's Dr. Susan Swedo. Dr. Swedo's group has identified a bacteria-triggered autoimmune response as the trigger in some cases of childhood neuropsychiatric illness.[2] One of the researchers' most interesting findings was that there is a blood marker, B lymphocyte antigen D8/17, associated with PANDAS. This could permit the development of a diagnostic blood test.

According to the PANDAS hypothesis, when some children are exposed to the common group A beta-hemolytic streptococcus bacteria, the same bacteria that causes strep throat, they develop antibodies that mistakenly attack the basal ganglia in the brain as well as the strep bacteria. These patients present with symptoms consistent with obsessive-compulsive disorder (OCD) and/or Tourette syndrome (TS). PANDAS researchers have also found that some children already diagnosed with OCD or TS have symptom flare-ups when they contract strep infections, although this may occur with other illnesses as well.

Although the initial NIMH study targeted OCD and TS only, it raised interesting possibilities for the diagnosis and treatment of PDDs. First, both OCD and TS appear to have a genetic or medical link with PDDs, appearing fairly often in the same families. Second, both conditions are frequently secondary diagnoses in people who have a primary diagnosis of autism or another PDD. Finally, researchers note that subtle social deficits, sensory integration problems, and other symptoms that might otherwise be attributed to PDDs also occur in some children with TS and OCD.

So it came as no surprise to some observers when a research team at the Seaver Autism Research Center announced in early 1999 that the B lymphocyte antigen D8/17 marker was also found in 78 percent of the autistic children studied, and that its presence correlated strongly with severity of compulsive behaviors.

Many parents interviewed for this book reported that their children with PDD-NOS or atypical PDD have had chronic, recurring strep throat and/or strep-related ear infections. Some have reported obvious increases in stereotypic movements or tics, obsessive-compulsive behavior, aggression, withdrawal, and other "autistic-like" symptoms during these infections.

> *My seven-year-old son was absolutely off the wall—aggressive, obsessive, and having his first bout of complex, full-body tics, which involved making a yipping sound while whacking himself in the groin area. His facial tics got so bad that his chin was chapped from licking it. He was grinding and clicking his teeth, picking his nose compulsively until it bled. It was the pits! On a hunch, I took him in for a strep throat swab. It was negative, but I convinced his pediatrician to send him for a strep blood titer. It came back at 886, over four times the normal level of strep antibodies. His psychiatrist was very interested, especially when his symptoms subsided incredibly quickly when we started a course of antibiotics. When he had similar behavior problems four months later, we did the throat swab and the titer again. This time the throat test was positive and the titer level was 633. He is now taking prophylactic antibiotics, and we're exploring the possibility of IVIG therapy.*

"We feel [the PANDAS subtype] possibly represents a homogeneous subgroup of childhood-onset neuropsychiatric disorders, and I know our group is pretty much concentrating on continuing to do PANDAS-related research," says Dr. Douglas Beer, a research fellow at Rhode Island Hospital's Pediatric Neuropsychiatry Clinic. "PANDAS may represent a significant paradigm shift in terms of investigations into childhood neuropsychiatric illness. Of course, we wonder as well about other etiologic factors that may be out there."

PDD-related studies

Beer and his colleagues at NIMH are not alone in their speculation. Closer to the topic of pervasive developmental disorders, a number of recent studies—in particular, research performed by Dr. V. K. Singh, the late Dr. Reed Warren, and Dr. Gene Stubbs—have looked for immune-system abnormalities and PDDs. Researchers have discovered antibodies to neuronal and glial filament proteins circulating in the blood of autistic patients.[3] These antibodies could damage or destroy parts of the nervous system's communications mechanism.

The evidence suggests that some people with autism have immune systems that are attacking their own myelin. Myelin is the substance covering the spinal cord and nerves, and is necessary for conduction of messages by the nervous system.

Dr. Bernard Rimland (founder of the Autism Society of America and the first medical researcher in the US to seriously debate the concept of autism as a psychological disorder) and Dr. Stephen M. Edelson, both tireless advocates for autism research, have stressed the idea of an autoimmune or immune-system dysfunction connection for years. In 1995, Dr. Rimland's Autism Research Institute was instrumental in getting doctors from all over the world to attend the first annual Defeat Autism Now! (DAN!) conference. Conference participants have since released the *DAN! Clinical Options Manual*,[4] which can be used as a reference by any doctor.

A list of DAN! Doctors[5] is also available from the Autism Research Institute. The DAN! doctors tend to favor dietary interventions, supplements, ABA, and other non-pharmaceutical approaches to PDDs. Individual practitioners may differ in how closely they hew to this formula, prescribing drugs or not, as needed by individual patients.

Possible viral connections

The DAN! doctors are not alone in their enthusiasm for immunology research. It was the focus of Dr. Reed Warren's multiple-site studies, for example.

Dr. John Martin has been particularly active in ferreting out possible connections between neurological disorders and a newly identified viral agent he calls the "stealth virus." Martin says that this virus most closely resembles the form of cytomegalovirus found in the African green monkey, and notes that the live polio vaccine may be a transmission vector, as it is grown using kidney tissue from these animals.

Parents of children with PDDs have brought another viral marker to the fore: the high prevalence of otitis media (ear infections)—and particularly otitis media that does not respond to antibiotics—in this population. Otitis media is usually caused by bacteria, especially those in the streptococcus family. At least 6 percent of cases are viral in origin, and these cannot be cured with antibiotics. Some children with PDDs have had more than twenty ear infections treated with antibiotics to no avail, a practice that could encourage the spread of "superviruses" and the growth of *Candida albicans* yeast as well.

A group organized by Tarzana, California, pediatrician and researcher Dr. Michael J. Goldberg, the Neuro-Immune Dysfunction Syndromes (NIDS) Medical Research Advisory Board (*http://www.neuroimmunedr.com/*), has recently pledged to create its own treatment protocol for some forms of autistic spectrum disorders, and to begin testing it with patients by 1999. Dr. Goldberg says he wants to look at possible environmental insults to the immune system, viral or retroviral causes, and other possibilities. "I'll bluntly say that we're looking at an *illness* affecting a lot of these kids," says Dr. Goldberg. "We're looking at a whole group of children where, with the right trigger—be it an immunization, a virus, or strep—you kick off a whole range of neuroimmune problems."

Dr. Goldberg says he has found surprising similarities between the brain activity observed using the NeuroSPECT scan in adults with chronic fatigue immune deficiency syndrome (CFIDS) and children diagnosed with PDD-NOS or atypical PDD. "I think [prognosis] depends on the age of onset," he says. "With CFIDS, these are adults with mature brains, and then their brains start playing tricks on them. But when you're looking at kids, the brain is still evolving. If you shut it down, you're going to 'lose' those children." In other words, immune-system impairments in people with PDDs, perhaps complicated by opportunistic infections, are skewing the normal developmental process. The end result is autistic symptoms.

Many researchers suspect that a virus, bacteria, or other infectious agent is at the root of some cases of autistic spectrum disorders, not just a contributing factor. Dr. Goldberg has noted that the antibodies to neuron-axon filament proteins, found in the blood of 67 percent of autistic patients in Dr. Warren's 1993 study, are also characteristic of the so-called "slow viruses," Kuru and Creutzfeldt-Jakob disease. This is a highly controversial theory. These rare illnesses are currently attributed to newly identified infectious particles called prions, which are actually neither viruses nor bacteria.

More prosaic agents have also been suggested as triggers, including herpato-form viruses, of which there are many with demonstrated neurological activity. Herpes viruses have been shown to exacerbate some cases of other neurological disorders, including Tourette syndrome, and treatment of presumed herpes infection with antiviral medications has reduced neurological symptoms in some patients with PDDs.

Immunization issues

There's a great deal of controversy over whether common childhood immunizations can be implicated in at least some cases of autism. Vaccines seem to have almost surely been the trigger for some people. In these cases, post-vaccine encephalitis (inflammation of the brain) was medically diagnosed, followed by autistic-like behavior. Sometimes this reaction is erroneously referred to as "vaccine allergy." (Note that it is possible, though very rare, to be allergic to some component in a vaccine, such as traces of the egg albumin in which many vaccines are grown.)

In some patients, blood-test results indicate an unusual response to childhood immunizations. Titers may reveal higher-than-normal amounts of antibodies to illnesses the person was immunized against in the past, as though a low-level infection began then and never quite left. Conversely, titers may show nothing at all, as though the person was never immunized. British researcher Dr. Andrew Wakefield has published a very interesting study on the potential link between the MMR vaccine, GI tract problems, and autism.[6] His research is continuing, and follow-up data is expected in 1999.

> *I think the diagnosis of PDD and autism is a simple way of ignoring the problem and not seeking the real cause. In our son's case, his immune system is out of whack. [He has] very high pertussis and polio titers.*
> —*Joe, father of seven-year-old Kyle*

At the same time, it seems evident that if the MMR vaccine, or any other vaccine, could cause PDD-like neurological symptoms, infection with the actual diseases they were intended to prevent could do similar damage.

Vaccinations are not always a good idea for people whose immune systems have been compromised. If you fear that this may be the case for you or your child, it couldn't hurt to check out immune function with one or more of the tests mentioned in the section "Diagnosing immune-system-linked PDDs," later in this chapter.

People whose immune systems are in good shape have little to fear from routine immunizations. Others should consult with their physician, or perhaps a specialist, to measure the risks of having or forgoing these shots.

Allergies

Some cases of autistic spectrum disorders appear to be linked to (or just exacerbated by) severe allergies. Some patients have made spectacular progress by simply changing their diet and removing allergens from their environment.

Allergies are a type of immune disorder. When you have an allergy, your immune system kicks into hyperdrive while it tries to rid itself of the perceived toxin, making you feel awful in the process. Common signs of allergies include skin rashes, including eczema; runny noses that are not related to colds or viral infections; and puffiness or swelling of the face or of areas that came in contact with the allergen. Swelling of any sort is a potentially dangerous reaction, because if it spreads to the throat, it can be difficult to breathe. Uncommon signs of allergies, according to some (but not all) allergists, can include behavior disturbances.

The concept of allergy-caused autism got a lot of publicity when Mary Callahan's book *Fighting for Tony* was published in 1987. Callahan, a registered nurse, used a combination of a dairy-free diet, floor-time strategies to increase attention and socialization, special education, and dogged determination to end her young son's severe "autistic-like" behaviors. It may well be that so-called cerebral allergies (reactions to foods and other substances that affect brain chemistry) represent a subtype of autistic spectrum disorders. Dr. Doris J. Rapp's *Is This Your Child? Discovering and Treating Unrecognized Allergies in Children and Adults* (William Morrow & Co., 1992) provides quite a bit of observational information about allergies and behavior problems.

However, as noted in the section that follows, "Metabolic disorders," some people absorb the proteins found in milk products or gluten into the bloodstream before they have been thoroughly digested. This is not an actual *allergy*, but it can cause surprisingly severe reactions.

People with PDDs can have allergies without one medical problem causing the other. It's important that this and other aspects of routine health care be dealt with. Tackling allergy problems, particularly serious or asthmatic allergic reactions, has improved function in some children and adults with PDDs simply by boosting general health and physical comfort.

You may have to search for an allergist who is familiar with the possible links between allergies and PDDs. Allergists can perform tests, recommend treatments, and provide good suggestions for reducing allergens in your diet and environment.

Do be careful to find a reputable provider—this is one area of medicine where crackpots still seem to roam free, according to several parents interviewed for this book. The best practitioners are usually board certified in their specialty, and do not propose that allergies are the root cause of all the patient's problems.

Be extra-careful about mixing OTC or prescription allergy medications with psychiatric meds, though, and watch out for behavioral side effects. Asthma inhalers and antihistamines make some patients feel nervous or "foggy" and can increase hyperactivity. Steroids and the steroid inhalers used for some forms of asthma are especially likely to have an impact on behavior. If the medication is needed, use it (steroid inhalers, for example, can prevent mild asthma from progressing and stave off lung damage). Just be aware that it may cause some unusual symptoms and that these should go away once the course of medication has ended.

Metabolic disorders

The story of phenylketonuria (PKU) is inspiring. A group of parents was so angered by the lack of medical research into their infants' unexplained mental and physical decline that it forced researchers to find a solution. The culprit turned out to be difficulty in processing a protein called phenylalanine. In people with PKU, this protein is not converted to amino acid tyrosine. Instead, phenylalanine builds up in the bloodstream, eventually causing brain damage, mental retardation, and neurological symptoms. Today most babies are screened for PKU, and children can be safeguarded by following a special diet. In fact, you may have noticed labels on diet soda and other items that warn phenylketonurics to avoid the product.

What had been a mysterious attacker of young brains turned out to be a treatable metabolic disorder. Metabolic disorders are differences in how the body breaks down or uses food and other substances. Some are fairly common, and not all that serious—lactose intolerance in adults is more uncomfortable than life-threatening, for example, and can be easily addressed.

Some people with PDDs may have metabolic disorders that are unrelated to their autistic-spectrum diagnosis, while in other cases, a metabolic disorder may be a very important piece of the puzzle. Others do not appear to have any metabolic differences from the general population at all.

Some parents and adult patients have had success with interventions that manipulate the balance of nutrients, minerals, and fatty acids. This can be a complex project, but for a few, the results have been worth it.

> Jared had **Candida** yeast, and a leaky gut problem, including severe diarrhea, for four years. We tried all the mainstream stuff first, but none of the mainstream doctors had a clue. He had severe problems with malnutrition and malabsorption. He has been so sick from his inability to take in and absorb nutrients.
>
> In just the last three months, with manipulation of some essential fatty acids on our own, we've seen astounding, astounding changes in our child's behavior. We started playing around with them, trying organic canola oil, almond oil, coconut butter... we've achieved the best balance we can find without the test results. For example, Jared needed a .3 Clonadine patch, now he's down to a .1 patch. I had a child with drastically elevated liver enzymes and toxic hepatitis in March, and Dr. Kane showed us the way to get rid of this problem. —Amy, mother of seven-year-old Jared (diagnosed PDD-NOS, "atypical autism")

Amy has worked closely with Dr. Patricia Kane, a Melville, New Jersey, biochemist involved with the DAN! project. One helpful tool in Dr. Kane's arsenal is a very thorough blood test interpretation from Carbon Based Corporation (*http://www.carbon.com/*)—the "test results" Amy was waiting for at this writing. You'll need to get your doctor on board for this one, as CBC does not do the blood draw itself, but the lengthy report that CBC returns has been very informative for those patients who turn out to have metabolic problems.

Sulfation chemistry

The underlying metabolic process is complex. Some people with PDDs appear to be short on sulfate, the essential substrate of a sulfotransferase enzyme called phenolsulfotransferase (PST), which breaks down phenols and amines. The PST enzyme transfers a sulfate ion from the enzyme Phosphoadenylyl sulfate (PAPS) to a phenolic compound, which should then detoxify the phenolic compound and prepare it for removal from the body. If the PAPS enzyme is short on sulfate, or if the body didn't have enough magnesium available to build the PAPS molecule in the first place, this process is short-circuited. As a result, toxic phenolic compounds build up in the body.

Sulfate is also essential for a number of other detoxification processes, including activating and deactivating certain hormones and neurotransmitters. Other sulfotransferases have the job of maintaining the integrity of the gut wall by surrounding cell surfaces with sulfated sugars attached to a protein core. These are called glycosaminoglycans (GAGs) or mucopolysaccharides. GAGs are released when inflammation occurs.

Dr. Rosemary Waring, a UK biochemist, is doing pioneering work on the sulfation chemistry differences found in people with PDDs. Her research currently indicates that supplementation with sulfation agents, such as MSM and N-acetyl cysteine, may be helpful. Parents and patients should also be careful to avoid medications and environmental triggers that overwork the sulfation system, including Tylenol, sulfa-based antibiotics, and exposure to toxic chemicals.

Leaky gut and opiates

Protein particles form amino-acid chains called peptides as they are digested. Doctors used to believe that the GI tract could not be permeated by large items, such as peptides. According to recent research, however, peptides can escape the GI tract when there is inflammation and damage to the gut wall—for example, when the GAGs are released due to inflammation, or when the gut is overcolonized by *Candida albicans*. This is referred to as the "leaky gut" phenomenon.

Once in the bloodstream, these peptides can make their way into the brain via "leaky" regions in the area postrema and the nucleus of the tractus solitarius. Opiates are also peptides. Sometimes the brain may be fooled into thinking these peptides are natural opiates (or hormones, or neurotransmitters), mistakenly allowing them to bind to sites in the brain. Opiates have many important functions in the body, including modulating various brain functions.

Alternatively, the immune system may decide to attack both these "foreign invaders" and the brain chemicals that they mimic.

Some people with PDDs seem to have an extreme difficulty in handling the protein casein, which is found in all milk products, and/or gluten, the protein found in wheat and some other grains. The peptides produced by breaking down these proteins are particularly similar to opiates. Quite a few patients have experienced improvements in behavior, attention, and general ability when one or both of these proteins was eliminated from the diets.

In some cases of pervasive developmental disorders, there is a diagnosis of actual celiac disease (sometimes called celiac sprue). This is a serious form of malabsorption resulting from inflammation of the small intestine's lining. Inflammation can be caused or exacerbated by an overgrowth of *Candida* yeast (see the section "*Candida* yeast and PDDs," which follows), or can result from the use of antibiotics, operations, autoimmune activity, or other factors. Celiac disease is characterized by difficulties with digesting many everyday foods, followed by chronic diarrhea or unusual stools.

Candida yeast and PDDs

Overgrowth of the ubiquitous *Candida albicans* is a persistent problem for many people, especially those who have taken a lot of antibiotics and those with impaired immune systems, including people with AIDS. It's normal for some *Candida* to be in your system, but when there's way too much of this fungal organism, it's a sure sign that your body's self-righting system is awry. Too much *Candida* can lead to yeast infections of the skin, the mucous membranes in the mouth ("thrush"), and the GI tract, as well as vaginal yeast infections and diaper rash. Some people with autistic-spectrum disorders have experienced relief from some symptoms by treating this yeast overgrowth.

This doesn't mean that *Candida* overgrowth causes autism, however—if it did, autistic behavior would probably be seen in women with chronic vaginal yeast infections, just to give one example. Beware of any doctor who tries to pin the blame for PDDs on yeast overgrowth alone. It's a symptom of underlying dysfunction, and should certainly be treated. It's an opportunistic beastie that can make symptoms worse, but there's no evidence that *Candida* yeast can actually be a causative agent.

Or is there? In a few cases, treatment for *Candida* overgrowth appears to have made a major difference. If the problem can be documented, it's worth a try to eliminate it.

Diagnosing immune-system-linked PDDs

Many neurologists and psychiatrists try to dissuade people from looking for the root causes of neuropsychiatric disorders. They may be aware that a connection is possible, but they also know that thoroughly investigated treatment options are few. There is some wisdom in this approach, especially since interventions like ABA, floor-time play therapy, sensory integration, and psychiatric medication work, and work well, for many patients.

However, as research into pervasive developmental disorders continues, more parents and patients are willing to spend the time and money on a search for specific causes (and, by extension, specific treatments). Be aware that the money and time you spend will be largely your own—it's difficult to get insurance companies to pay for immunological testing, unless your physician is very savvy about his requests for tests.

Testing for autoimmune disorders generally begins with the blood. There are a number of individual tests and panels of tests that are used by immunologists, rheumatologists, and other doctors. Because every person with PDDs is unique, you'll need to discuss test options with your physician. Here are some of the tests that physicians might use:

- Blood count. Depleted white blood cells indicate that there is a virus or other infection active somewhere in the body.

- Sedimentation rate. This test measures how quickly the red cells separate from the serum in a test tube. With normal inflammatory or autoimmune diseases, they separate quickly. Some clinicians have reported a very low "sed rate" in 35 to 40 percent of children with PDDs, indicating that a contradictory type of autoimmune reaction could be taking place.

- General chemistry panel. Generally abbreviated as "Chem," and followed by a number that indicates how many tests were performed (Chem-16, Chem-25, etc.) The basic Chem panel checks levels of glucose (blood sugar), blood urea nitrogen (BUN), creatinine, and electrolytes (including sodium and potassium).

- Immune panel test. This general screen may include a search for antibodies, mitogen, antigen, and lymphocyte surface markers, and blood tests for various specific immune-dysfunction markers.

- Anti-neuronal antibody (ANA) screen. The ANA looks for antibodies to brain tissue in the bloodstream. Their presence is a general indicator for a variety of autoimmune disorders, such as lupus. Note that the anti-nuclear antibody test, also abbreviated as ANA, may also be ordered. This test is part of the screening procedure for several autoimmune inflammatory diseases.

- Tests that look for unusual levels of specific viral antibodies, perhaps including those associated with the Epstein-Barr virus, other human herpes viruses (HHV6, HHV7, HHV8, HSV-1, HSV-2), chronic mononucleosis syndrome (CMS), cytomegalovirus (CMV), rubella (German measles), and, if PANDAS is suspected, titers for group A beta-hemolytic streptococcus (ASO or ASLO). Some may order the antiDNAase B titer as well, although the current view is that this test won't tell you much.

- Tests to check for immunoglobulin G (IgG) subclass abnormalities (IgG1, IgG2, IgG3, IgG4), which are found in patients with increased susceptibility to viral or bacterial infections due to a compromised immune system, autoimmune diseases, and immune-mediated neurological disorders. It's possible to plot the distributions of IgG subtypes against patterns associated with specific viruses or conditions.

- Amino acid profile. Markers for an impaired immune system include low amounts of the amino acids lysine and arginine.

- NeuroSPECT. This brain scan shows the diffusion of blood through the brain, indicating areas of low and high activity. In some people with PDDs, findings include low activity in the temporal lobe and sometimes in other regions of the brain.

- Allergy tests. These can include the common skin test (mostly for environmental allergens), the RAST test (generally used for food sensitivities), and more-precise tests of blood, stool, or urine samples.

- Tests for celiac disease. These may include blood tests for IgG and IgA gliadin antibodies (IgA AGA, which is the most specific of these two tests); IgA reticulin antibodies (IgA ARA, R1 type, a highly specific test); and IgA endomysial antibodies (EmA).

- Tests for *Candida albicans*. Possibilities include microscopic stool exams, or blood serum or urine D-arabinitol (a *Candida* metabolite) levels. Although not definitive, elevated immunoglobulin M (IgM) levels suggest active or recent infection. IgG antibodies may be present long after the *Candida* is cured, so they don't necessarily mean anything. Remember, it is normal to find some *Candida* in the body. Only severely elevated findings should be a cause for concern.

- Coloscopy. For serious GI-tract problems, this invasive test is performed by a gastroenterologist.

A multifaceted immune panel can turn up many small pieces of evidence that, taken together, indicate a compromised immune system. Findings that may mean trouble for patients with PDDs include elevated CD4 and CD8 counts, or very low CD8 counts; low levels of natural killer (NK) cells; and elevated numbers of B cells (the cells that produce antibodies to disease).

Treating immune-system-linked PDDs

The primary goal in treating immune-system dysfunction that may be related to PDDs is to clear away any problem that may be obscuring your view, in addition to promoting the patient's general physical well-being. It's not unlike looking for a baseline by withdrawing psychiatric medications, as described earlier in this chapter: clearing up these problems lets you see what's immune-related, what's purely neurological (based on brain damage or dysfunction), and what's emotional or behavioral.

The National Institutes of Mental Health's preliminary treatment protocol for PANDAS provides some suggestions as to how other autoimmune-linked neuropsychiatric disorders might be addressed. These treatment options are also being studied for use in a wide variety of other neurological disorders, including myasthenia gravis, paraproteinemic neuropathy, and multiple sclerosis. No reputable physician claims that these disorders can be *cured* with any of these treatments, although studies do indicate improvement in many patients.

PANDAS treatment options currently include:

- Intravenous immunoglobulin (IVIG) infusion
- Plasmapheresis (therapeutic plasma exchange, or TPE)
- Prophylactic antibiotics (particularly amoxicillin) to prevent reinfection with strep
- Immunosuppression

All four of these treatments are controversial, and each carries significant risks.

IVIG transfusion

Intravenous immunoglobulin G (IVIG, sometimes also called IVGG) is made from blood taken from thousands of human donors. It has been used to treat immunological disorders since 1980 and is similar to the substance RHogam that some Rh-negative women take during pregnancy.

IVIG is administered via a transfusion, which can take several hours and takes place in a medical facility.

IVIG is expensive and difficult to obtain, so difficult that even NIMH has not been able to arrange for a steady supply for its PANDAS project. In addition, IVIG is not absolutely safe.

Since IVIG is a blood product, there is a risk of blood-borne infection, even though the plasma donors whose blood is used are screened. When IVIG first became available for use in clinical studies, several people contracted hepatitis B or hepatitis C. A solvent/detergent viral inactivation step was then added to the preparation process, which is now believed to be effective against hepatitis A, B, and C, as well as HIV-1 and HIV-2, HTLV-1, HBV, and HCV viruses. This process is used in three commercial IVIG preparations: Venoglobulin S, Polygam, and Gammagard. Batches of IVIG in these preparations are also "DNA fingerprinted" to look for other viruses and traces of viruses.

As of this writing, however, there have been official warnings about so-called "stealth viruses" that may be present in IVIG (according to the National Institutes of Health, there are probably hundreds of obscure viruses, some of which may be relatively benign, and some of which may cause harm). Certain lots of IVIG have been taken off the market because some of the original plasma donors went on to develop Creutzfeldt-Jakob disease, an extremely rare and deadly neurological disorder related to bovine spongiform encephalopathy ("mad cow disease"). There isn't a commonly used test to screen plasma for this disease just yet, so the US Food and Drug Administration has increased its scrutiny of IVIG production and sale. The status of IVIG safety in other countries is unknown.

There is also a risk of non-disease-related side effects from IVIG therapy, including heart attacks due to increased serum viscosity (stickier blood), infection from IV lines, nephrotic syndrome, low blood pressure, and meningitis.

No one is exactly sure why IVIG appears to work against some neuroimmune illnesses. Possibilities that researchers have suggested include:

- IVIG decreases the toxic effects of natural killer (NK) cells.

- IVIG binds to autoimmune antibodies.

- IVIG binds to B-cell surface immunoglobulin, blocking the action of autoimmune antibodies.

- IVIG makes T-suppresser cells work harder, resulting in fewer B-cell autoimmune antibodies being produced.

- IVIG binds to complement, limiting the amount of complement available to bind to autoimmune antibodies. Complement is a substance in the blood that assists the immune system.

- IVIG use in high doses triggers a feedback-based inhibition of antibody production.

A few autism researchers and clinicians have been exploring the use of IVIG, and have gotten encouraging results in some cases. A series of multisite trials is underway as of this writing. The dangers mentioned above have slowed this activity down, however, as has the shrinking supply of screened IVIG.

Plasmapheresis

Therapeutic plasmapheresis (TPE) is an invasive procedure for removing toxins, metabolic substances, and certain parts of blood plasma that may cause disease, including complement and antibodies. The patient's blood is removed, the plasma is separated out, and the remaining blood elements are combined with a plasma replacement and put back into the patient. Currently, between 10,000 and 15,000 patients with neurological disorders are treated with TPE in the US each year. Response rates in the range of 50 percent have been reported, depending on the condition treated.

Plasma exchange takes place in a medical facility and is usually repeated several times over a period of weeks for maximum effectiveness. It rarely produces permanent improvement, although the initial response may make successful pharmaceutical treatment possible.

As with IVIG, there is a possibility of infection at the IV insertion sites. Both serious and fatal reactions have been reported, primarily cardiac and respiratory arrest. The risk of such reactions is probably higher if human plasma is used as the replacement fluid, as it could transmit a new infection.

Its potential for complications makes physicians leery of using plasmapheresis, unless it is absolutely necessary. If this option is chosen, attention to detail is very important, particularly when it comes to mixing the replacement solution.

Prophylactic antibiotic therapy

Prophylactic antibiotic therapy is the long-term use of antibiotics to prevent infection. It is the standard treatment for rheumatic fever with Sydenham's Chorea, a condition that appears to be related to PANDAS. While prophylactic antibiotic use may be appropriate for PANDAS, it may do more harm than good for many people with PDDs. Antibiotics can cause *Candida* overgrowth, which has itself been implicated as a potential contributing factor in some cases of autistic spectrum disorders.

If antibiotics need to be used, they should be accompanied by probiotics, such as acidophilus, to rebuild friendly intestinal fauna. Your physician can suggest supplements and dietary changes to minimize any detrimental impact from antibiotics.

Immunosuppression

In other autoimmune conditions, suppression of the immune response with drugs is a common strategy. Obviously, the primary danger here is that resistance to dangerous diseases could be dampened. This would not normally be supported in cases where a compromised immune system is already a possibility.

Immune-system modulators

AIDS research has resulted in many new medications that could be called "immune system stimulants" or "immune system modulators." The majority of these drugs have side effects that make them undesirable for use, except for patients faced with a life-threatening immune deficiency. Others may deserve a trial for treating immune-system-linked PDDs. As the saying goes, "your mileage may vary" with these medications and supplements.

A few of the immune modulators currently used by some patients are:

- Kutapressin, a porcine liver extract comprised of very small proteins or polypeptides. Kutapressin inhibits human herpes viruses (its best-known use is as a medication for herpes zoster, or shingles) and reduces inflammation. It is given in intramuscular injections, can be rather expensive since the supply is currently limited, and may not be a long-term solution for herpes infection.

- Dimethylglycine (DMG) is a vitamin-like supplement that appears to give a mild boost to the immune system, possibly by boosting the number of natural killer (NK) cells. DMG has a fairly long track record as a treatment for autistic symptoms, including some success in clinical trials. According to ARI's Dr. Rimland, "Many parents have reported that, within a few days of starting DMG, the child's behavior improved noticeably, better eye contact was seen, frustration tolerance increased, the child's speech improved, or more interest and ability in speaking was observed."[7]

- Inosine pranobex (Isoprinosine), an older antiviral, is also active against human herpes virus and other infections. It is a relatively weak immune modulator.

- Acyclovir (Zovirax) is a potent antiviral that works against several human herpes viruses, Epstein-Barr virus, herpes zoster, varicella (chicken pox), cytomegalovirus, and other viruses.

- Foscarnet, another antiherpes drug (unfortunately, rather toxic).

- Ampligen, a nucleic acid (NA) compound that apparently heightens production of the body's own immunological and antiviral agents, such as interferon. It is expensive, is administered via intravenous infusion, and is not available to all patients or in all countries.

- SSRIs. These antidepressants were discussed in greater detail earlier in this chapter. They may affect neurotransmitters in ways that not only address depression and other neurological disorders, but that also directly or indirectly regulate the gastrointestinal and immune systems. When used for this purpose, they are often given at very low doses.

Stevie has been on DMG and SuperNuThera [a B6/magnesium for-mula] for almost 200 days. The biggest improvement has been his immune system: fewer runny noses, ear infections, and colds. He began to speak a few words, but no miracle in the speech department. Calmed him down some and I believe helped improve eye contact. Hard to pinpoint that one, because the more he began to feel comfortable with me and trust me, the better the eye contact and behavior. —Roni, foster parent, and soon to be adoptive mother, of five-year-old Stevie (diagnosed "atypical autism")

When immune modulators are employed to improve the function of people with PDDs, they are not used in the same ways or at the same doses as in fatal immune-system diseases, such as AIDS. The goal is to normalize the patient's system, not hit it with "big guns" that provoke an overwhelming reaction.

Secretin

This hormone has been in the news lately, due to positive preliminary study results indicating that administration of secretin may reduce autistic behavior in some patients. Secretin is normally produced when acid stimulates the mucosa of the duodenum, increasing the secretion of bicarbonate ions by the pancreas. It also acts on the peripheral nervous system to slow down stomach activity, presumably giving food more time to digest. In addition, secretin does appear to have some activity in the brain. It is approved for use in the US to diagnose certain gastrointestinal disorders.

Secretin treatment for autistic spectrum disorders is very new, and its mechanism and usefulness is unknown. Since autistic-like symptoms are not characteristic of conditions that include a known deficiency of secretin, it's somewhat surprising that this therapy has initially gotten good results in some patients. It is possible that one subtype of pervasive developmental disorders—perhaps one hitherto unidentified—does respond to secretin. At first glance, secretin seems most likely to work with patients who have GI tract problems in addition to an autistic spectrum disorder.

Secretin is normally administered by infusion (slow injection), and most families who reported positive results did repeated infusions. Some doctors and parents have been quietly experimenting with other methods for using secretin, including oral administration and devising methods to administer secretin through the surface of the skin.

Further investigation is warranted before choosing this treatment option. Victoria and Gary Beck, a couple whose autistic son had an overwhelmingly excellent response to secretin, produced a short book on the topic in late 1998. Called *Unlocking the Potential of Secretin*, this was the only major piece of printed information available on this treatment at press time—although final study results may be published as early as 1999. The Becks' book is available through the Autism Research Institute, which is also collecting data from parents and doctors who are experimenting with secretin. Dr. Rimland has promised to keep the public informed through a new Web site, *http://www.secretin.com/*, and through his *Autism Research Review International* newsletter.

Regularly updated information is also available from the Autism Research Unit in the UK, directed by Paul Shattock (*http://osiris.sunderland.ac.uk/autism/sec.htm*). The National Institutes of Health maintain some information about secretin studies at *http://www.nih.gov/nichd/html/secretin.htm*. Several scientific studies of secretin are currently underway, including multisite, double-blind (or double-blind crossover) studies.

Some doctors have expressed concerns about secretin treatment as it is currently done. First, the secretin that most families have used is porcine (pig) secretin from Ferring Pharmaceuticals, Inc. It is not an exact match for human secretin. Synthetic human secretin is available, but not yet in common use. Second, some parents have reported doing secretin infusions at home or in clinic offices that were without resuscitation equipment. Generally speaking, this is not a good idea due to the riskiness of any intravenous procedure. The proper dose and administration schedule for secretin as a treatment for PDDs have also not been established.

As this book went to press, secretin was the hottest topic in the world of autism research. Rumors were swirling, most of them false. For example, some parents were informed that the substance was no longer being made, or that there was a shortage. There was a temporary shortage, but it was soon ameliorated. Others were told that the US Food and Drug Administration had banned secretin, or that secretin had been linked to serious adverse effects—including death—in some autistic children. There have been some reports of adverse effects, but there have not been any deaths or life-threatening effects. The FDA has specifically permitted Ferring to increase the secretin supply in the US as long as it does not actively promote it as a treatment for autism.

Sadly, con artists have also gotten involved. Some outfits claiming to sell secretin by mail order or over the Internet have proved to be shams, and products of unknown provenance are being sold as equivalent to the Ferring formulation.

Hospitals and clinics have become aware that parents of children with PDDs may be seeking secretin as a treatment rather than as a diagnostic tool. Unfortunately, this has led some facilities to refuse to administer secretin to such children for GI disorder tests—even in cases where the child has long-standing gastrointestinal problems. If this happens to you, you will probably need to appeal the ban. (Of course, if treatment rather than diagnosis actually was your goal, you could simply seek another source).

Pepcid AC

Pepcid AC (famotedine) is one of several H2 blockers commonly used to treat acid reflux and other common stomach complaints. As a histamine type 2-receptor antagonist, famotidine competitively inhibits the binding of histamine to HA-receptors on the gastric basolateral membrane of parietal cells, reducing the secretion of gastric acid. It may help to heal the gastric mucous membranes and protect them from irritants. It is known to have an effect on the CNS, although the exact mechanism has not been extensively studied.

Pepcid AC is available as an over-the-counter medication. In one study, it was found to help some autistic children who had social deficits. However, it may increase the growth of *Candida* yeasts, which thrive when there is less gastric acid in the digestive system.

You should tell your doctor if you plan to use Pepcid or another H2-blocker, such as cimetidine (Tagamet) or ranitidine (Zantac), whether your intended purpose is addressing autistic symptoms or reducing GI distress.

Incidentally, cimetidine was recently shown to have some antiviral activity as well as efficacy for GI tract problems, and the same may hold true for other H2 blockers.

Antifungals

Medications commonly used to reduce an overgrowth of *Candida albicans* and other yeasts include:

- nystatin (Mycostatin, Nilstat)
- fluconazole (Diflucan)

- itraconazole (Sporanox)

- ketoconazole (Nizoral)

- miconazole (Monistat)

- terbinafine (Lamisil)

These drugs may kill not only *Candida*, but also other harmful fungi, including dermophytes, aspergillus, and cryptococcus. Miconazole preparations and Lamisil tablets are used to treat topical fungal infections, such as diaper rash, athlete's foot, and vaginal infections.

Diet can also be a powerful tool against *Candida*. People who have chronic yeast infections may choose to avoid sugars and many carbohydrates, which seem to make the problem worse. We'll talk more about dietary recommendations in Chapter 7.

Coexisting conditions

People with pervasive developmental disorders have a higher risk of developing a number of coexisting (co-morbid) neurobiological conditions. Some of these disorders may, in fact, represent other facets of the autistic spectrum. They certainly exist more often in families that have an autistic member, leading researchers to believe that there is a genetic link. Common co-morbid disorders include:

- ADD/ADHD

- Depression (both unipolar and bipolar)

- Obsessive-compulsive disorder

- Tourette syndrome

Some medications can have positive effects on both autistic symptoms and co-morbid disorders. However, sometimes patients and parents are faced with hard choices. Reactions and contraindications between medications and other treatment options may require you to prioritize treatment of one condition over another.

Surgery and PDDs

No, there's not an operation that can cure PDDs. However, people with PDD may need surgery for other reasons, and there are a few things you should know.

First, the surgeon, anesthetist, and others taking part in the operation will need some basic information about the diagnosis and any unusual behaviors they may see. For example, if a child has difficulty making eye contact, lack of eye contact should not be considered a sign that the anesthetic is taking effect.

Second, if possible, a parent or other familiar person should accompany the patient during initial anesthesia and meet the patient in the recovery room. Building as much predictability into the process of surgery as possible is a good idea. Familiar clothing, toys, and foods in the hospital can also go a long way toward making the stay comfortable.

Finally, some people with PDD have unusual reactions to anesthetics. Be sure to share any salient information with the anesthetist, including the names and dosages of all drugs, herbal remedies, and supplements the patient uses.

Dental care and PDDs

Dental care is a nightmare for many people with PDDs. Sensory hypersensitivity can turn a routine cleaning into a torture session, and serious dental work can be additionally complicated by unusual reactions to anesthesia.

However, the dentist is a more important part of your medical treatment plan than you might think. Your dentist may be the first professional to notice certain types of health problems. Vitamin deficiencies and dietary problems tend to show up in the mouth first, with certain types of dental caries patterns, receding gums, bleeding, and other symptoms. The dentist may also be the first to notice signs of infection or disease.

Finding and working with a dentist can be difficult. United Cerebral Palsy (UCP), the ARC, and other large organizations that work with people who have other disabilities can help. Dental problems are characteristic of many disabilities, from Down's syndrome to CP. These groups usually have referral lists of sympathetic dentists.

There are a few special dental problems that can occur with PDDs. Tooth grinding and clenching are all-too-common habits. Medication (particularly antidepressants) can help. However, sometimes these behaviors are occurring due to the sensation of dry mouth that these very medications create. A plastic dental guard can be prescribed, made by the dentist, or sometimes even purchased over the counter. These are especially useful for nighttime tooth-grinders. Without intervention, tooth grinding and clenching can lead to loss of enamel, chipped teeth, jaw pain, or loss of teeth.

Dental decay can also have behavioral effects, including self-injurious behavior. Infections in the mouth are among the most painful around, and the most likely to cause general unpleasantness in the body. They can make eating painful, too, so think of tooth trouble when foods are suddenly refused.

Vision care and PDDs

People with PDDs do have a higher incidence of eye problems, including strabismus (crossed eyes), photophobia (extreme sensitivity to light), Duane syndrome, abnormal retinal activity, reliance on peripheral vision, tunnel vision, and stereotypic behaviors that involve the eyes, such as flicking fingers in front of the eyes repetitively or fixating on patterns of light and shadow. Even the most "behavioral-looking" of these symptoms, such as "stims" that involve the eyes, are medical symptoms. No one knows how much of the common difficulty with sustained eye contact seen in some people with PDDs is due to eye sensitivity or physical difficulty with focusing, for example.

Some high-functioning autistic adults have described experiences with visual disturbances, ranging from difficulties in processing and making sense of what they see, to "seeing" sounds. Some of these effects resemble those experienced with certain hallucinogenic drugs. Not only can visual disturbances make the world seem like a scary place, they can interfere with learning to read, write, and do math on paper.

Regular vision care is a must, and the best provider will be one familiar with autistic spectrum disorders. If possible, find a behavioral optometrist—an eye doctor who understands the interplay between vision problems and behavior. These optometrists may recommend vision therapy via exercises or the use of prismatic lenses. Again, groups like UCP, the ARC, or local autism advocacy organizations can be a great resource for finding a sympathetic and resourceful optometrist. The College of Optometrists for Vision Development (619-425-6191) and the Optometric Extension Program (714-250-8070) also provide referrals to behavioral optometrists.

Another vision-related problem is a real hassle for many parents: some children with PDDs have more than the usual trouble with maintaining their contacts or glasses. These expensive items may be broken, scratched, or lost with maddening regularity. First, make it clear that these items are very important and, if you think it will make a difference to how the child thinks of them, very expensive! Make sure that the glasses fit well, and are at the correct strength, and that the child likes the style. Ask if there's a problem with glasses-smashing bullies at school (an all-too-common pest). You may want to try sports glasses, which come with a built-in strap and are practically indestructible. Most opticians have these in stock, or they can be special-ordered. Otherwise, attaching a cool-looking sports strap of the sort used with hip sunglasses may keep them hanging around at least a little longer.

Some people with PDDs, including author Donna Williams, claim that special colored lenses have helped them reduce visual processing problems. The Irlen Institute (*http://www.irlen.com/,* or see Appendix A, *Resources*) developed such lenses, and many eye specialists do recommend them, although they are rather expensive.

It should be noted that the Irlen system and the prismatic lenses used by some behavioral optometrists do not have universal support in the eye-care field—in fact, the American Academy of Pediatrics, the American Association for Pediatric Ophthalmology and Strabismus, and the American Academy of Ophthalmology issued a joint statement in 1992 disavowing the use of colored lenses and prismatic lenses to treat neurological problems.

In some cases, adults with PDDs may want to consider eye surgery to address nearsightedness if broken or lost glasses are a persistent problem.

Coping with self-injurious behavior

As mentioned earlier in this chapter, self-injurious behavior (SIB) needs to be viewed as a medical issue, not a behavior problem. Just as SIB can result from untreated medical problems, including the dental and eye problems just mentioned, it can cause medical problems. Sad to say, children have put out their own eyes, caused permanent scarring, and damaged their bodies in any number of ways through SIB.

SIB is a form of communication. It can be a way of saying "I hurt," especially for nonverbal children or those who have a very hard time being understood with words. It may also be a way of stimulating an underactive dopamine system, one that feels little sensation normally and perceives sensations that would be painful to someone else as almost pleasant. It's essential to examine SIB carefully to find the cause of the problem. The behavior analysis techniques in Chapter 6 can help.

Behavior modification (ABA or other forms) has great effectiveness against SIB. Even if you don't subscribe to this approach as a general treatment for PDDs, make it part of your plan for dealing with SIB if it crops up. In addition, if you eschew pharmaceutical medication as a general treatment, please consider it if your child is in danger of harming himself or others. Naltrexone (ReVia), an opiate blocker, has been very helpful for some people with SIB.

Until SIB has been dealt with medically or behaviorally, take careful steps to minimize any damage. Helmets and other protective devices are available by prescription, through hospitals, and from mail-order catalogs to safeguard the head, eyes, genitalia, and other body parts that may be at risk. You may also need to take some rather extreme "childproofing" measures to keep potentially dangerous items safely stowed. Chapter 10, *Family*, shares ideas that other families have used to keep their children or adult relatives with PDDs safe at home and in the community.

Alternative medicine

Many people see alternative medical practitioners instead of, or in addition to, a traditional MD or GP. These specialists—including naturopaths, homeopathic physicians, chiropractors, practitioners of Asian and Ayurvedic medicine, and acupuncturists—may have different ideas about treating PDDs than those presented in this chapter.

Be sure to check the credentials of your alternative practitioners, and use the same cautions with herbal and homeopathic remedies, vitamins, acupuncture, and other treatments that they may suggest as you would with Western medicine. Look for hard evidence that a treatment is effective for the symptom you want to treat before trying it. There may be much of value in these approaches for some patients with PDDs, but not all alternative therapies are appropriate for all patients.

If you use alternative medicine as well as Western approaches, be sure that all of your healthcare practitioners know what you're doing. If you can, get them to talk to each other. It's certainly not universal, but many Western doctors are gaining a great deal of respect for the track record of their alternative counterparts in treating chronic illness.

Be careful about the herbal remedies you try, too. In the US, supplements are not regulated for content or potency. For example, the *Los Angeles Times* commissioned independent lab analysis of ten major brands of St. John's wort in 1998. Three proved to be less than half as potent as their labels claimed, and four others were less than 90 percent potent.[8] Until there are firm standards, either voluntary or government-imposed, consumers must educate themselves well.

Chapter 7, *Therapeutic Interventions*, discusses a number of specific alternative therapies.

Research

Since the false psychological explanation for pervasive developmental disorders has only recently been wiped away in most English-speaking countries (and is *still* in vogue in some parts of the world), there has not been enough scientific research done on the topic of treatments or cures for these disorders. As the number of diagnoses rise, this may change…but perhaps not soon enough for today's patients.

> Is there a more common disease which is treated as an "orphan disease" than autism? I don't think so. You would think the way pediatricians view autism that it would be extremely rare, but it's more common than childhood cancer, muscular dystrophy, and cystic fibrosis combined. Yet there are many centers of excellence for the treatment of childhood cancer (St. Jude's is just one). Every Labor Day weekend, Jerry Lewis has a huge telethon for muscular dystrophy—everyone in the US knows about "Jerry's Kids." The Cystic Fibrosis Foundation has many big fundraising events throughout the year.
>
> And yet, our kids go through life virtually untreated and unaided by everyone except us—the parents. No one seems to care about our kids.

Maybe the sight of a kid stimming his brains out is not as appealing as one in a wheelchair or one who has lost his hair from chemotherapy.

Why do we parents have to fight for the smallest of diagnostic tests that might help our children?

Here's another one that's really got me angry. Why will insurance companies pay for Viagra and not pay for autism treatment? Surely a child's chance at a reasonably normal existence is more important than erections! —Dr. Amy Holmes, mother to three-year-old Mike (diagnosed with autism)

Objective markers—genes, blood markers, or other ways to provide an indisputable medical diagnosis for PDDs—are at the top of any researcher's wish list. Some of the genes believed to be associated with autism were discovered by a multicenter team of American geneticists in 1997 and by another multicenter team of British scientists in 1998. Work is continuing to refine this information. It's important to note that these researchers have found a group of intersecting genes, not a single gene. This buttresses the concept of autistic spectrum disorders as multifactorial in origin and makes it unlikely that diagnosis will be accomplished with a simple blood test. It is a step forward, however, and may eventually create new treatment options.

Individual and family studies are another important area for research. The Autism Research Institute's database may prove to be an extraordinarily valuable tool, once the data have been fully interpreted. The information in this database is derived from parents' responses to ARI's Form E-2 questionnaire, which is reprinted in Appendix F, *Diagnostic Tools*, and to a second ARI questionnaire on treatment responses. Another database effort, the Autism Genetic Resource Exchange (AGRE) project, is actively looking for multiplex families to study. A multiplex family has two or more close relatives with an autistic spectrum disorder. Genetic data on the first 100 families in AGRE's database is slated for release in 1999. This step will allow multiple labs to use heavy-duty computers and a wide variety of study methods to seek out patterns.

Pharmaceutical research, including investigating existing medicines for use in PDDs, is also a must. New drugs take a long time to develop, so pharmaceutical manufacturers need to feel the pressure from patients and families to get started soon. We can put our energies into supporting research through advocacy groups, particularly the autism research organizations listed in

Appendix C, *Research and Testing Facilities*, by making direct donations to research projects; and by lobbying both government health agencies and the pharmaceutical industry to step up the pace of research.

Another necessary task is disseminating current and future research findings to clinicians around the world. The Internet has proven to be a good tool, but it's not enough. Journal publication, conferences, and government efforts are needed to prevent children and adults from going without treatment, or being subjected to unnecessary or even harmful therapies. In many countries, young children with autism are still routinely banished to orphanages or mental hospitals, where they receive no treatment to speak of.

And even in the developed world, children with PDDs are often "banished" from the medical care they need by the improper classification of these disorders as psychiatric conditions or incurable developmental disorders. These misconceptions may limit the amount and type of health care received. The classification and insurance fight has just begun, as Chapter 8, *Insurance*, will make clear.

Despite it all, pervasive developmental disorders are becoming less of a puzzle as the twentieth century reaches an end. Medical treatment is a real possibility for an increasingly large number of children. When coupled with educational, behavioral, and other interventions, the rate of success is promising.

CHAPTER 6

Therapeutic Interventions

THE MOST IMPORTANT ROLE OF MEDICATION in a well-conceived treatment program may be to help the patient be available for, and capable of, interpersonal therapeutic interventions. Many types of therapy can be useful to individuals with pervasive developmental disorders, and unlike most of the medical interventions available today, these methods can create permanent change.

In this chapter, we'll discuss most well-known therapies used by and for people with autistic spectrum disorders, and offer any evidence available about effectiveness for people with PDD-NOS or atypical PDD.

Therapeutic interventions that may be recommended by physicians or schools (or that you may hear about in the press) include:

- Applied behavior analysis (ABA, "the Lovaas method")
- Animal-assisted therapy
- Auditory integration training (AIT)
- Augmentative communication
- Behavior modification programs other than ABA
- Dance, music, or art therapy
- Floor-time play therapy ("the Greenspan method")
- The HANDLE Institute approach
- The Linwood method
- Occupational therapy
- The Options Institute method ("Son-Rise")
- Physical therapy

- Pivotal response training (PRT)
- Play therapy
- Relaxation techniques
- Psychoanalysis or counseling (talk therapy)
- Sensory integration (SI)
- Speech therapy

Therapeutic choices

For most people with PDDs, no single approach is best. Parents, professionals, and adult patients can combine approaches, taking what's best and most applicable to the individual from each. There's no need to be a slave to one method.

However, proponents of some methods may be very attached to their favorites and may downplay the merits of competing ideas. This can make it hard for you to judge various programs objectively. One thing is certain: if someone tells you, "This is the *only* way to help people with autistic spectrum disorders," that person is probably more interested in the program itself than in the person who might benefit from it.

Just as you should beware of zealotry on behalf of one approach, watch out for "one size fits all" programs. Therapeutic programs, whether they involve speech therapy, counseling, or ABA, must be *individualized*. Even when a program brings together groups of children or adults, such as a social-skills club, each person in the group should have his or her own goals, and each may require different teaching methods.

Applied behavior analysis
(ABA, the Lovaas method)

Dr. O. Ivar Lovaas is a pioneering clinician in the treatment of autism. Working at the University of California at Los Angeles (UCLA), Dr. Lovaas developed an intensive intervention system for autism based on principles borrowed from behavioral modification. ABA is sometimes called discrete trial training, because it is structured around short drills called discrete trials.

The details of ABA are considerably more complex than the brief description that follows. Be sure to consult other resources before you devise or implement a program. Basically, ABA consists of five steps:

1. Observe the behavior that you want to change, replace, or initiate. Take a baseline measurement of where the child is right now. Behavior is charted, as are its antecedents (for example, what led up to the behavior, where it occurred, and when it occurred).

2. If it is a behavior that you want to change or replace, make a hypothesis about what the behavior might be intended to communicate, then design an intervention based on that hypothesis. Your goal must be a positive goal, not a negative one (e.g., "Jimmy will make eye contact when requested," not, "Jimmy will stop avoiding eye contact"). Break this goal down into small steps and design a separate, progressive drill to address each one in turn.

3. If it is a behavior you want to initiate, make a goal and break it down into its smallest components. Each component should be addressed in a separate, progressive drill. Dr. Lovaas recommends starting with speech skills for the first few months and following with drills for social-interaction skills.

4. Apply the intervention, using positive reinforcement for each instance of desired behavior. Since drills are short and repetitive, the rewards must be small and frequent. Small pieces of food, hugs, play activities, and verbal praise have all been employed as reinforcers. The reinforcer must be something the child really wants. Some practitioners use negative reinforcers (aversives) when undesired behaviors occur. Whether you choose to do so is a matter of philosophy and, perhaps, what works best with your specific child. Although Dr. Lovaas's early experiments included the use of mild electric shock and other physical aversives, these are no longer employed in his program.

5. Assess the effectiveness of the intervention, and adjust it if necessary.

In 1987, Dr. Lovaas's team reported good outcomes in 47 percent of the children who completed his program, based on a well-designed study. Since then, hundreds of ABA practitioners have been trained, and thousands of parents have applied Lovaas's methods themselves. ABA techniques have been carefully honed by practitioners, many of whom now report that better than half of the children they work with experience good results.

What constitutes "good results?" For Lovaas, it was approaching normal functioning, including being capable of self-care and mainstream education. For some parents, ABA has been a truly incredible experience. Catherine Maurice, mother of two children diagnosed as autistic, details the miracles wrought by a well-designed, firmly implemented home ABA program in her book, *Let Me Hear Your Voice* (Fawcett Books, 1994). Both of her children are now mainstreamed and, she says, no longer meet the criteria for autistic disorder. Most parents who implement ABA programs do not have the dramatic results reported by Maurice and some other parents. However, it's safe to say that ABA *does* work, and work well, for a very significant number of children.

> *ABA is the most effective of the therapies we have tried. I believe that ABA is also the stepping-stone to being able to accept and benefit from other therapies.* —Holly, *mother of three-year-old Max (diagnosed PDD-NOS, apraxia of speech)*

Lovaas and other ABA experts recommend a very intensive program when working with children who have a diagnosis of autistic disorder. Forty hours per week of one-on-one, structured intervention is the standard. Lovaas's own research (which has been replicated by others) has shown that neither ten hours per week nor twenty hours per week is "enough." Please note, however, that his clinical research was done primarily with moderately to severely autistic children. For children with PDD-NOS or atypical PDD, who may already have some of the basic skills that ABA practitioners work many months to initiate with more severely affected children, mixing a smaller amount of ABA work with other interventions *may* be sufficient. This has been the case for some families who have tried a modified ABA approach, but it has *not* been clinically tested. Many families whose children have a PDD-NOS, atypical PDD, or similar diagnosis choose to follow Lovaas's recommendations to the letter, providing 30 to 40 hours per week of ABA work.

Catherine Maurice recently edited an ABA manual that gets rave reviews from many families, *Behavioral Intervention for Young Children with Autism* (Pro-Ed, 1996). Dr. Lovaas's *Teaching Developmentally Disabled Children: The ME Book* (Pro-Ed, 1981) is also considered a classic for teaching ABA concepts, although parts are somewhat outdated. He is said to be working on a new version as this book goes to press. Videotapes are available from Pro-Ed that show the techniques described in *The ME Book* in action.

There is an Internet mailing list for parents and professionals using ABA techniques, the Me List (see Appendix A, *Resources*). On the Web, Damian Porcari's excellent Recovery Zone site *(http://pages.prodigy.net/damianporcari/recovery.htm)* can lead you to additional resources, including information about insurance coverage for ABA programs, a list of credentialed practitioners, and specific instructions for setting up a home ABA program. The Lovaas Institute for Early Intervention *(http://www.lovaas.com/)* also has many links to practitioners, including ABA-friendly programs in Spain, Iceland, Norway, and the UK. There are now several "Lovaas replication sites" in the US, programs whose practitioners and methods duplicate those used in the original UCLA program.

> *I have a home program based on discrete trials geared around speech. Behavior modification works great with Elaine, as it does with all people. We all work for rewards.* —Sarah, mother of three-year-old Elaine (diagnosed PDD-NOS, possible oral-motor apraxia of speech)

Family participation is very important to an ABA program, although these techniques can be applied in school or residential settings as well. Most families using ABA techniques run a home-based program relying on themselves, other family members, community volunteers, students, and sometimes paid practitioners. Training in ABA techniques is often available at state or regional autism conferences, or through firms that specialize in training parents and providing trained paraprofessionals for home ABA programs.

Dr. Lovaas has noted that follow-up is also very important when using ABA programs. When children have made sufficient gains in social skills to be in school or preschool, he strongly encourages full inclusion in a mainstream classroom, supplemented by continuing instruction in social skills for use in group situations.

Some school districts and Early Intervention programs do support and fund ABA programs. Because ABA has been clinically proven to work, parents in the US and Canada have gone to court to force school districts to pay for and implement ABA programs. Many have succeeded.

ABA drawbacks

No program is perfect, and ABA certainly has its detractors. The most common criticism you may hear is one based on lack of knowledge. Quite a few teachers and other professionals still think that ABA programs rely on aversives to get compliance. As noted above, this is no longer the case.

Others (including some adults with high-functioning autism) decry ABA as being much like animal training, encouraging children to develop robot-like behavior in exchange for bits of food. Parents who have actually implemented ABA programs reply quite strongly that nothing could be further from the truth. The goal of ABA is not Pavlovian response, but the emergence of skills that build the individual's ability to respond naturally, expressing their own needs and ideas.

You may also hear that ABA is only for preschool children or for those with severe autistic behaviors. This is certainly not the case.

Some parents do not turn out to be good ABA practitioners. It takes a lot of stamina and dedication. If a parent is struggling with depression or physical illness, it can be especially difficult. Sharing the duties with your partner, other family members, volunteers, or paid helpers can lighten the load. Parents doing ABA certainly need to take special care of their own physical and mental health, and will need to arrange for at least some time off—time for an occasional dinner out, an evening class, or a quiet walk in the park.

Finally, the time commitment required to implement 30 to 40 hours of ABA is considerable. Lovaas requires families entering his program to commit one parent to working nearly full-time with their child—something that's not always easy in this age of single-parent and two-earner families. Many parents have made considerable sacrifices, both personal and professional, to make ABA work. Not every family has the ability to make that choice. And if you are paying for ABA specialists to work with your child daily, the cost can be very high.

Similar programs

Lovaas was the first to report good results from a well-designed, well-documented study of intensive intervention with a large number of autistic children. Other clinicians offer quite different programs that nevertheless use some similar methods.

Martin A. Kozloff developed a program that also used behavior modification techniques, but in a less stringent manner than Lovaas's ABA program. Kozloff's approach also includes motivators for parents to encourage them to complete training sessions, and intensive counseling work with families. As described in his books *Reaching the Autistic Child: A Parent Training Program* (Research Press, 1973) and *A Program for Families of Children with Learning and Behavior Problems* (John Wiley and Sons, 1979), Kozloff's program might be well-suited for families experiencing significant internal stress, or whose parenting skills need work. If implemented as written, it should provide a particularly supportive structure to help parents help their children, although some aspects might be seen as coercive or blaming. We are not aware of any programs currently using the Kozloff approach.

Pivotal Response Training (PRT), described later in this chapter, also shares some characteristics with ABA.

Dr. Stanley Greenspan's "floor-time play therapy" program, described below, also relies on one-to-one interactions that build basic communication and social skills. Like ABA, it has been clinically successful with many autistic-spectrum children.

Some families may prefer the less regimented approach of PRT or floor-time, or may want to mix and match.

Animal-assisted therapy

Quite a few autistic-spectrum individuals report a feeling of special empathy with animals. Clinicians like Dr. Oliver Sacks (the author of *Awakenings* and other popular books on neurology) have even speculated that, for these people, their extra depth of understanding could be a unique form of intelligence. It can also be a springboard to skills needed for human interaction.

Most people are aware of the therapeutic potential of pet ownership. A strong bond with a cat, dog, or other animal can help a person develop as a compassionate human being. Because animals communicate without words, nonverbal children and those with auditory sensitivities sometimes prefer their company to that of noisy, jabbering humans. Some animals are also natural experts at therapeutic touch, cuddling or nuzzling just when it's most needed. The simple act of stroking a pet can calm a racing heartbeat or a troubled mind.

This knowledge is applied by professionals working in the field of animal-assisted therapy. Programs include therapeutic horseback riding (hippotherapy), bringing animals to visit children in schools, homes, or residential centers, and even "dolphin therapy," whose proponents claim that interacting with these intelligent marine mammals offers benefits for people with PDDs.

Parents and adults with PDDs should be careful of animal-assisted therapy programs that charge a lot of money or make extravagant claims. Pets, including school pets as well as animals kept at home, are a great idea for those individuals who are not likely to injure an animal. Not all people with PDDs like animals, and certain animals (such as high-strung breeds and those likely to bite) are unsuited for the job.

People with PDDs who experience seizures may be able to gain yet another benefit from canine company. Some dogs can be trained to recognize seizures and provide assistance to people who live alone. The Epilepsy International Web site (*http://www.epilepsy-international.com/*) has more information about seizure dogs, as do most local epilepsy support associations.

Auditory integration training (AIT)

Extreme sensitivity to sound and other stimuli may be responsible for the autistic behaviors of some people. In one survey, as many as 65 percent reported painful sensitivity to everyday sounds. Loud, sudden noises, or sounds in certain frequencies, can be excruciating.

Based on principles first developed by French hearing specialist Guy Bérard, AIT involves listening to particular sounds through earphones to retrain the hearing mechanism. The process is somewhat time-consuming. A second AIT-style therapy is called the Tomatis method.

AIT is the topic of one interesting book, *The Sound of a Miracle,* by Annabel Stehli. Stehli tells the story of her autistic daughter Georgie's success with Dr. Bérard's auditory training methods. To date, Georgie's story is probably the most dramatic recovery with AIT alone. AIT has been a contributing factor to improved function in many autistic-spectrum individuals, however.

Quite a few audiologists and other professionals currently offer AIT. For more information, contact the Society for Auditory Integration Training (*http://www.sait.org/*) or the Autism Research Institute, which has sponsored several studies of the method and can provide a list of all known AIT practitioners. Or see the Autism Society of America's Web page on the topic (*http://www.autism-society.org/packages/auditory.html*), which includes a number of informative articles and a smaller list of practitioners maintained by the Georgianna Foundation.

In an interesting twist, it may soon be possible to do a general (but perhaps still effective) AIT program at home. A CD series called EASe, for Electronic Auditory Stimulation effect, has been developed by Vision Audio Inc. *(http:// www.vision-audio.com/)*. You can listen to the EASe CDs using good-quality home equipment, following a prescribed course. No research results on this product are yet available, but it could provide some help for those without access to a full-fledged AIT program. The EASe CDs have been purchased by a number of autism support groups, so you may be able to borrow them from one in your area.

Similar software products are already available for retraining the brain's auditory processing mechanism. These do not reduce sound sensitivity, but help the individual differentiate the sounds of speech from one another. Perhaps the best-known product is FastForward, developed by Scientific Learning Corporation *(http://www.scientificlearning.com/)*. FastForward is based on the research of Dr. Paula Tallal and Dr. Mike Merzenich (Dr. Merzenich was also a codeveloper of the cochlear implant for deafness), and was rigorously tested at Rutgers University for use in speech and auditory processing disorders. It uses video-game techniques to bring users through a series of exercises said to increase temporal processing (acoustics) and language processing.

During clinical trials, FastForward was administrated to a group of children with pervasive developmental disorders, most of whom were diagnosed as autistic. Compared to children with attention deficit disorder (ADD) and central auditory processing disorder (CAPD) alone, the children with PDDs made the most impressive gains. The PDD group started out more impaired than the other two groups, but more than doubled its auditory performance in an eight-week trial. However, the auditory and language skills of the ADD and CAPD groups moved into the low end of the "normal" range after treatment, while those of the PDD group were still classified as impaired. This difference may be due to disparities within the PDD group, however—since autistic spectrum disorders have multiple causes, some children may have excellent progress with FastForward or similar programs, while others will experience no gains at all.

The FastForward software is available to clinicians only, and these purchasers must be trained to use it properly before they can obtain it. A list of licensed clinicians (mostly speech therapists and audiologists) is available from SLC. The program is time-consuming, and many clinicians charge $1,000 or more to administer it over a period of weeks. Some school districts have also purchased the software.

If you are interested in using FastForward, you might want to purchase a tape of a speech by SLPs Karen Supel and Christina Rogers called "Using FastForward with Children with PDD." It is available from the Autism Society of America, which sponsored Rogers and Supel's presentation at its 1998 conference.

A less advanced program called Earobics from Cognitive Concepts Inc. (*http://www.cogcon.com/*) can be purchased for home use and is much less expensive. You might try Earobics first and move on up to FastForward if this approach seems to be beneficial.

Augmentative and alternative communication

Most school districts and medical facilities have specialists in augmentative and alternative communication (AAC), sometimes also called assistive technology. These people are experts in implementing forms of communication for the nonverbal or speech-impaired, methods and devices that can open up new possibilities.

If you've ever seen British physicist Stephen Hawking "talk" with the assistance of his computer, you know what the very finest augmentative communication devices can do. There are a wide variety of products available—and in some cases, the cost (which can be considerable) can be covered by private insurance, government medical plans, or your school district.

Tons of information about these devices, including a list of companies that make them, is available online at *http://www.asel.udel.edu/at-online/technology/aac/*. Some products cost less than $100 US and produce a limited vocabulary of words. You may even be able to find a computer-like "toy" at a local toy store that can do rough sound synthesis of a few letters together or of simple words. Other devices are programmable: parents or clinicians can choose or record the desired words ("potty," "go," "drink," etc.) and map them to an appropriate picture on a keyboard or a screen. At the high end, AAC devices can help a brilliant scientist like Hawking deliver a complete and erudite lecture.

Augmentative communication actually predates the computer age, however. Before machines could synthesize sound, nonverbal people were able to use drawings to let others know their thoughts and needs. Schools often use the PECS (Picture Exchange Communication System) to help young children with severe speech disorders communicate. Developed by Lori Frost and Andrew Bondy, PECS uses specially designed pictures to symbolize words and concepts.

PECS and similar commercial products are available for use at home, school, and work. Parents and professionals working with young children can also create their own customized picture books. These are a great way to stimulate "conversation" with a nonverbal child by offering acceptable choices in the form of pictures.

Health concerns aside, many parents swear by the picture menus available at fast-food restaurants like McDonald's. Children tend to be enthusiastic about getting a desired food or drink by pointing to a picture. You can extend this practice by creating "menus" of your own, using PECS or similar drawings, pictures cut from magazines, or photographs. You might create a menu of food choices at home, clothes to wear to school, or activity choices.

Homemade picture books can also be used to schedule activities. By putting pictures in order, perhaps with a ring binder, children can truly visualize the day's plans.

Always include the written and spoken word when using picture-based AAC systems. Some children will never be verbally proficient, but seeing and hearing words with pictures of the items or activities they represent helps them make essential associations needed to develop their communication skills as fully as possible. For children who do make some attempts at speech, gradually insist that they approximate the word's sound rather than just point at the picture.

You may have heard of facilitated communication (FC), a form of AAC in which a trained aide helps a nonverbal person type by supporting his hand. Unfortunately, scientific studies have shown that the words and ideas generated almost always arise with the aide, not the person being assisted. Reputable researchers have gone so far as to call FC a fraud and to accuse its boosters of giving families false hope. We'll talk more about that toward the end of this chapter.

However, there are a very few instances in which a previously nonverbal person has learned to type independently after starting with FC-style supported typing. We urge extreme caution with this approach, unless a medical exam by a physician, physical therapist, or occupational therapist has verified that the person in question has an orthopedic handicap. Even then, it would be wiser to seek the help of an occupational therapist or an AAC professional. Occupational therapy can help build the muscles needed for typing, and some OTs and physical therapists can recommend splints that could be helpful. A wide variety of systems for typing are available that work well for people with limited hand strength or poor muscle control.

Behavior modification programs other than ABA

In its broadest sense, "behavior modification" includes any system of controlling behavior by means of rewards and punishments. Ever since the work of psychologist B.F. Skinner became widely known, behavior modification techniques have been used in some institutions, prisons, and schools.

These programs can be highly effective, but there was a notable lack of success with the autistic population until the advent of specially targeted ABA techniques. Part of the problem was poor understanding about autism and related disorders. In many cases, people with PDDs who were institutionalized or placed in residential schools were punished for such "willful" acts as not speaking, making repetitive motions, or having self-abusive behavior. Because those in charge of these behavior modification programs did not know the characteristics of PDDs and did not look at behavior as a form of communication, these patients frequently regressed rather than ending their behaviors.

If a school or residential center that you are considering employs behavior modification, make sure the staff has a thorough understanding of autistic spectrum disorders and ABA-style techniques. Even the simplest behavior modification ideas, such as "token economies" or other reward systems, will need to be individualized to meet the needs of people with PDDs.

One area where behavior modification techniques can be helpful is in designing a plan for home discipline. Parents who are frustrated with behaviors can apply these techniques, even with older children or adults in homecare. Training or a behavior consultant may be available through social service agencies.

Doug is getting what's called wrap-around services. This is where a therapeutic support staff person comes to the house, and we target certain behaviors to try and get Doug to stop doing them. The behavior is whatever Doug seems to be doing for a certain time, such as throwing things when he's upset, or things like getting him to sit at the table and eat his meals. —Debbie, mother of eleven-year-old Doug (diagnosed PDD with fragile X syndrome and sensory integration disorder)

As with ABA, behavior modification programs for people with PDDs usually work best when incentives, not aversives, are employed.

Dance, music, or art therapy

There is no proof that dance, music, or art therapy has curative value for people with PDDs, but these activities often draw out hidden talents and bring a sense of joy and accomplishment.

Each also builds important skills. Dance, for example, teaches a sense of rhythm, relies on counting and imitative skills, and can help people develop their sense of balance. Music has mathematical underpinnings, and art can be an alternative form of communication even as it builds fine-motor skills and imagination.

Well-trained dance, music, and art therapists are aware of what they're teaching along with the activity, but integration into mainstream or adapted classes in these subjects can also be enriching.

Some autistic-spectrum people have "splinter skills" in one of these areas, and are able to develop their talents for personal enrichment or as a career.

Floor-time play therapy ("the Greenspan method")

Dr. Stanley Greenspan of George Washington University and the Washington Psychoanalytic Institute is the primary proponent of a relationship-based, interactive, individualized form of therapy that he calls the "floor-time" approach. It utilizes developmental principles to help children build social, emotional, and communication skills from the ground up.

Floor-time interactions are less like ABA drills and more like play, even when they carry the same content and intention. The parent or other therapist tries to engage the child's attention, and rewards the engagement when it occurs.

Floor-time is a one-on-one experience that involves getting right down to the child's level to encourage interaction…by any playful means necessary. If a child tends to line up miniature toy cars in endless lines, for example, Dad might try to find out what happens when car No. 3 in the line drives away noisily. If a child babbles the same sound over and over, Mom might try joining in with a silly look on her face, then varying the tune and the movements. If one strategy doesn't work, you try another. As interaction increases and the child begins to initiate activity, the parent follows the child's lead, always trying to keep attention focused on interaction and communication.

Greenspan suggests that floor-time principles be made the basis for Early Intervention and school programs for children with PDDs, and that they be used by other types of therapists who need to engage the child for their purposes. He recommends that parents or their assistants complete between six and ten twenty- to thirty-minute floor-time sessions every day.

> One-on-one teaching has worked very well. I have been using
> Greenspan's floor-time model at home with [Joseph] with great success.
> He is even beginning to use some imaginative play. Any method that is
> visual rather than auditory also works well. —Jennifer, mother of three-
> year-old Joseph (diagnosis still in progress, suspected atypical PDD)

Greenspan reports in his most recent book, The Child with Special Needs (Addison-Wesley, 1998), that 58 percent of the children with PDD-NOS or autism who participated in his program for two or more years showed "good to outstanding" outcomes, as measured by no longer scoring in the autistic range on the Childhood Autism Rating Scale (CARS) and also based on observation. About 24 percent made a "medium" level of progress, described as having lost many "autistic" behaviors (perseveration, self-absorption, self-stimulation), but having continued difficulty with symbolic communication. Only 17 percent continued to have fairly serious problems, despite whatever small gains they may have made in the program. These judgments were based on file review of 200 cases, formal testing, and videotaped observations over a period of years.

Greenspan reported that the most successful children were those who fell on the low end of the CARS scale before intervention, i.e., those more likely to be labeled PDD-NOS or atypical PDD rather than autistic disorder. This indicates that the floor-time approach may be especially useful for these children, some of whose higher-level abilities and needs don't seem to fit with the ABA approach.

Somewhat controversially, Greenspan also reported that, while a comparison group of children in ABA-style programs for over thirty hours per week made significant gains over those receiving "traditional" (school-based Early Intervention and perhaps medication) interventions, most continued to have significant difficulty with higher-level, spontaneous thought and action. However, Greenspan has since noted publicly that the ABA approach can work very well with some children (including those with the most severe autistic characteristics) and that parents and practitioners should judge each model according to its merits for the individual patient.

Greenspan's program is not much like the psychoanalytic model of play therapy described later in this chapter, but like ABA, it does have some cousins:

- Filial therapy, in which parents take turns initiating structured interactions with their child, is certainly similar.

- Some institutions and day-treatment centers are based on the concept of milieu therapy, where all interactions between staff and patient, patient and patient, or patient and parent are seen as potentially therapeutic.

These approaches are less structured than the floor-time model and could be incorporated with it, particularly for older children.

The Options Institute's method described later in this chapter also has similarities, although it is considerably more intensive.

The HANDLE Institute approach

The Seattle-based HANDLE Institute, founded and directed by Judith Bluestone, works with children and adults who have neurological problems or injuries, including PDDs. The acronym HANDLE stands for "Holistic Approach to Neuro-Development and Learning Efficiency."

HANDLE conducts a rather comprehensive two-part diagnostic interview, including structured observation, after which a series of simple exercises is recommended. These provide what Bluestone calls "gentle enhancement" to retrain and rebuild the nervous system. Videotapes are made at the initial visit and at any follow-up visits to help parents or adult patients assess progress.

The exercises themselves appear to be based on sound principles. Some are similar to exercises used in sensory integration or other occupational therapy programs.

Some parents have reported that they found HANDLE's promotional materials too boosterish for their taste, but others who did try the program praised the individualized approach. These parents said the exercises were easy to fit into their family life and, most importantly, helpful.

There have not been scientific studies of the HANDLE method to date. There is a great deal of anecdotal evidence that the HANDLE Institute's methods can help at least some people with PDDs improve their ability to function. There are other centers and clinics that advertise similar services, but HANDLE has one major advantage: its services are primarily in the area of evaluation and program design. The exercises themselves are performed at home. As a result, it is considerably less expensive than some other therapeutic resources.

As of this writing, HANDLE-trained providers are practicing in Seattle, Austin (Texas), and a few other US cities.

The Linwood method

The Linwood method was developed by Jeanne Simons, director of one of the first high-quality residential programs for autistic children in the US, Linwood Children's Center. Founded in 1955, Linwood took what would be called a milieu therapy approach today—every interaction and event was part of a holistic therapeutic process.

Simons describes her program in *The Hidden Child: The Linwood Method for Reaching the Autistic Child* (Simons, Woodbine House, 1987). The title—and the time period in which Simons's work was done—might lead you to believe that her approach was psychoanalytical, but it actually had more in common with the sensory integration, behavior-modification, and floor-time approaches used today. Children's behavior was observed, and the caretakers worked hard to find and address the motivations for disturbing or dangerous behaviors. Sometimes they found a psychological cause, as in the case of one boy who developed a fixation with people's birthdays when his parents had changed his own "official" birth date due to his small size, to avoid comment from nosey neighbors. More often, the problem was sensory or developmental in nature, and staff members worked out surprisingly thoughtful programs to address these deficits.

Although Simons's book was written to address the needs of residential centers and schools, her careful observations and suggestions can be useful to parents as well. Her chapter on language has some particularly excellent ideas, especially for devising conversation-skills training programs for older children.

If you are considering residential placement, a school that follows Linwood's approach (along with more-modern medical, occupational, and physical therapy ideas) would no doubt be an excellent choice.

Occupational therapy

Occupational therapy (OT) builds fine- and gross-motor skills with special exercises, and also works to ameliorate deficits in the body's sensory systems. Both school special-education departments and hospital rehabilitation centers provide OT assessments and treatment. Private occupational therapists may work out of a doctor's office or clinic, or practice independently. Some will deliver services in the home, particularly for very young children or those with mobility impairments.

Schools and medical centers tend to have different goals for OT. At school, the goals are typically educational: developing correct pencil grasp, for example, or working on the sense of balance to permit inclusion in physical activities. At a medical center, therapists work with people who have brain injuries or birth defects, as well as with people who have neurological problems. Their goals are usually broader, and their repertoire of skills is often (but not always) wider. The two approaches should be seen as complimentary.

> *Jesse sees an OT two times a week for about 45 minutes each time, in conjunction with a speech therapist. His OT is currently helping him with life skills—face washing, buttoning shirts, eating with a fork. —Dorthy, mother of five-year-old Jesse (diagnosed PDD-NOS with autistic tendencies)*

There are many OT techniques, including sensory integration, which is described in greater detail below. Each patient's program should be individualized, based on thorough assessment. Some OT exercises are "occupational" indeed, such as working on pencil grasp by writing out letters using instruments of various sizes and shapes. Others utilize small pieces of equipment, such as an elastic band for building up the arm muscles. Some exercises rely on large equipment, ranging from huge "therapy balls" to swings attached to the ceiling. Children may toss bean bags while swinging, walk on a balance beam, or scoot along on a roller board to build specific muscle groups and sensory skills.

When it's done right, OT is lots of fun. A talented occupational therapist who enjoys children probably has more motivational tricks up his or her sleeve than any other practitioner you'll come into contact with.

> Our son received OT at preschool until being home-schooled this year. The OT helped him learn to suck on a straw, put on clothes, etc. She also worked on calming him, using brushing and vestibular motion. Our son liked this person more than other therapists. —Joe, father of seven-year-old Kyle (diagnosed PDD-NOS with autistic features)

The best occupational therapists see teachers, parents, and especially patients as part of the team. They can teach you home activities for building specific muscles or skills, for self-relaxation, or for handling episodes of sensory overload.

Note to adults with PDDs: Occupational therapy can be easily adapted to meet the needs of both children and adults—in fact, adult patients who attend sessions at a local rehabilitation center will find they have plenty of grown-up company. The equipment used with adults is similar, but sometimes the OTs will encourage more repetition and drill with adults than they might with children. If you feel your abilities are being overtaxed, let the therapist know. Since you're there to work on deficits that have been with you for many years rather than for post-accident or post-stroke care, there's no rush.

The Options Institute method ("Son-Rise")

Barry Neil Kaufman's books, *Son-Rise* (Warner Books, 1976) and *Son-Rise: The Miracle Continues* (H.J. Kramer, 1995), are documentaries of the grueling process he and his wife, Samahria Lyte Kaufman, underwent to help their severely autistic son, Raun. Kaufman literally locked himself in a room with his son for hours on end for almost three years, observing Raun, following his lead when he could perceive an initiative, and trying to "bring him back to the world."

Raun Kaufman is grown now and has graduated from college. The Kaufmans remain heavily involved in the treatment of autism, however, through the Options Institute *(http://www.option.org/sonrise.html)* in Sheffield, Massachusetts. Satellite centers have recently opened in Holland and the UK.

Although the Options program is quite expensive, some parents say it has been helpful. Its primary principles are unconditional love and acceptance.

> *The Options Institute taught us how to interact with a nonverbal*
> *child and gave advice on coping. Our son responds well to the Options*
> *approach, which lets the child direct activity and encourages speech and*
> *interaction. We suspect our Options training has helped our son be non-*
> *self-injurious. —Joe, father of seven-year-old Kyle*

The Son-Rise program is somewhat controversial in the autism community, both because of its price tag and because of its philosophy. Few parents can go to the extremes that Barry Kaufman did with Raun, no matter how admirable and successful, and not everyone is comfortable with his ideas about autism and how to treat it. For those who feel inspired by Kaufman's ideals, the Options Institute holds week-long parent training programs on a regular basis, as well as seminars, individual sessions, and program design assistance.

Physical therapy (PT)

Physical therapists are trained to work in schools, hospital rehabilitation centers, and private practice. Some, particularly those working in Early Intervention, may deliver services in your home. PTs use equipment and exercises to help people overcome mobility impairments or handle the effects of accident or injury. Most PTs work primarily on gross-motor issues: problems involving the major muscles and their movements, such as crawling, walking, and bending. They can also devise exercises that reduce chronic pain from injury, overstress of muscles, or birth defects.

Many autistic-spectrum people will never need the services of a physical therapist, but some do. PTs can help you find solutions to gait problems, low muscle tone, strength deficits, and related issues.

As with occupational therapy, physical therapy at school and in a medical setting may look quite different. PTs in Early Intervention programs often have access to large equipment, such as slant boards, scooters, and walking bars; PTs working in regular K–12 schools may not. Hospital- and clinic-based programs are usually equipment-rich. Not all problems require fancy equipment, however, and a talented PT can get a lot done without it.

Whether the work is done in school, in a clinical setting, or at home, it's important to work toward clear goals. The exercises can be difficult at times, although PT has the potential for being fun if you're working with a gifted practitioner. Regular progress reports are a must, and should be written in language that the parent or adult patient can understand. For nonverbal or very young patients, practitioners should work out a system in advance for indicating that something hurts.

Pivotal response training (PRT)

Pivotal response training, like ABA, is based on discrete trials. Unlike most traditional ABA programs, these trials take place in a more natural play setting. In this way, it has similarities to Dr. Greenspan's floor-time program— one might say that it melds elements of both of these proven approaches.

PRT was developed by Robert L. Koegel and Laura Schreibman. As of this writing, the efficacy of PRT is still under investigation. Clinicians at the University of California at San Diego's Autism Research Laboratory (*http://www-psy.ucsd.edu/~cwhalen/lab.html*) have received NIMH funding to work with children and their parents using either PRT or an ABA-style discrete trials method. Some information is available now, including a parent training manual and a Web site (*http://www-psy.ucsd.edu/~cwhalen/prt.html*).

PRT is similar to an older teaching method called Natural Language Paradigm.

Play therapy

For children, play is a mode of communication and a vehicle for working out ideas about social roles, fears, and relationships. Counselors working with young children often use hand puppets, stuffed animals, dolls, and sand tables with small figurines to encourage them to "talk" about what's on their minds by playing.

Since one of the hallmarks of pervasive developmental disorders is circum-scribed, repetitive, unimaginative play, traditional play therapy would seem to be an unlikely treatment. However, some therapists still rely on it, usually with predictably uneven results, or none at all. The book *Dibs: In Search of Self* (Ballantine, reissued 1990) by play-therapy pioneer Virginia M. Axline has been unfortunately influential. Widely read by psychology students, the book never mentions that the child "Dibs" is obviously on the autistic spec-trum. Instead, the parents are blamed for his "emotional disturbance," and he must be saved by his dedicated therapist.

Traditional play therapy may be worthwhile for working with nonverbal children who have had life traumas in addition to PDDs, because to a well-trained therapist it can provide clues and an avenue for communication. Unless it is incorporated into a structured program, such as the floor-time program described previously, it is unlikely to be useful in general.

Psychoanalysis or counseling (talk therapy)

Long-term psychoanalysis is out of vogue these days, although it can help some adults understand how they think. There's nothing wrong with a little self-understanding, but it doesn't really have a role to play in the treatment of PDDs.

Cognitive-behavioral therapy (so-called short-term therapy) can be useful to adolescents and adults who are dealing with personality or self-esteem prob-lems, or with life crises. Again, it is not useful for treating PDDs per se.

Finally, family counseling or therapy is frequently a part of school or residen-tial-center programs for treating pervasive developmental disorders. Efficacy depends on the skills, background, and knowledge of the therapist, as well as on what goals counseling or therapy is intended to meet. As discussed in Chapter 10, *Family*, raising a child with a PDD, taking care of an adult with a PDD, or being an adult with a PDD can be stressful situations. Family ther-apy sessions can give all family members a chance to unload their negative feelings on a professional instead of each other, to learn new coping skills, and to gain valuable knowledge about helping the affected individual while avoiding burnout.

Relaxation techniques

People with PDDs report that their bodies sometimes send them misleading signals, failing to warn them when they are in true danger or, worse yet, kicking in the "fight or flight" adrenaline response for no good reason. This can be a disturbing feeling, and it's even harder for young children to cope with. Self-stimulatory behaviors, such as hand-flapping or rocking, can be a reaction to these tense and unpleasant sensations.

Many programs working with autistic-spectrum people teach relaxation techniques. These range from high-tech (biofeedback) to old-fashioned (meditation or prayer). Deep breathing, counting, using a device like author Temple Grandin's "Hug Machine," exercises in guided imagery, self-hypnosis—these are all effective for some individuals.

Because having the ability to self-calm is so essential, parents, practitioners, and adults with PDDs should make an effort to include some kind of relaxation training in their therapeutic programming. What works best will depend entirely on the individual.

Sensory integration and auditory integration training can help tune down the over-amped arousal system once and for all.

Sensory integration (SI)

The theories behind sensory integration (SI) were first developed by an occupational therapist and researcher, Jean Ayres. In the US and Canada, many OTs are at least familiar with the principles of SI, although, technically, to practice it one must have completed special training and attained a certificate from Sensory Integration International (http://home.earthlink.net/~sensoryint/). SII will provide parents with a list of trained therapists and evaluators.

In the UK, the treatment methods recommended by Madeleine Portwood (http://web.ukonline.co.uk/members/madeleine.portwood/index.htm) for children with developmental dyspraxia are very similar to SI. Portwood is an educational psychologist with the Durham County Council, and the author of *Developmental Dyspraxia: A Practical Manual for Parents and Professionals* (Educational Psychology Service, 1996).

Sensory integration work is based on the idea that people with motor or sensory problems have difficulty processing the information their body receives through the various senses. Just as auditory integration training attempts to desensitize the sense of hearing, SI exercises are intended to reduce sensory disturbances related to touch, movement, and gravity. These disturbances can occur in any or all of the following areas:

- **Processing**. How quickly (or if) the sensation reaches the central nervous system to be interpreted.

- **Analysis**. How the person interprets the sensation.

- **Organization**. How the person responds to their analysis of the situation.

- **Memory**. How (or if) the person remembers similar sensations and proper responses from the past.

Note to teens and adults with PDDs: Like other forms of occupational therapy, sensory integration work can easily be adapted to meet the needs of adolescents and adults. Some adults may be more comfortable doing an SI-style program of their own design in privacy, while others might want to see an SI specialist in a clinic or hospital.

Adults with sensory-system dysfunction have often devised all sorts of ways to reduce their exposure to difficult or painful sensations, although this avoidance leads to increased isolation. We know of adults with PDDs who have installed expensive soundproofing in their homes, who buy only soft cotton clothing, and whose "picky" eating habits have more to do with avoiding unpleasant textures than with taste. These coping strategies are admirable, but anyone who truly wants to break out of old life patterns without experiencing the discomfort of the past can look to SI techniques for help.

Disturbances can occur in either the traditional five senses (sight, hearing, smell, taste, and touch) or in less well-known senses—senses that actually have a greater effect on gross-motor development. SI exercises generally work on the latter. These "whole body" senses are:

- **Tactile**. Based in the system created by the entire skin surface and the nerves that serve it, this sense processes information taken in via all types of touch.

- **Proprioceptive.** Based in the muscles, ligaments, joints, and the nerves that serve them, this sense processes information about where the body and its various parts are in space.

- **Vestibular.** Based mostly in the inner ear, which acts as a sort of internal carpenter's level, this sense processes information about how the body interacts with gravity as it moves and attempts to retain its balance.

Most of us never think about these senses, unless they are suddenly disordered in some way, such as from an inner-ear infection, a dizziness-producing carnival ride, or a leg that "falls asleep" and causes stumbling. For many people with PDDs, however, dysfunction in these sensory systems is the norm—in fact, for many it is this very sensory dysfunction that is the most pervasive part of the disorder and that may lead to its most disabling effects. Many behaviors commonly thought of as "autistic," including toe-walking, hand-flapping, and rocking, can be attempts to deal with sensory integration dysfunction.

Infants and young children learn to interpret the world around them through their senses. If the information comes in all wrong or cannot be processed properly, the world is a confusing place. Imagine trying to pay attention to your mother's lullaby if it sounded like an electric drill, or trying to play with a toy when your clothing was causing intense discomfort. The tactile, proprioceptive, and vestibular senses are our most elemental ways to relate to the environment—they're with us from the earliest nervous-system development in the womb. Problems in this area are fundamental, because they interfere with the ability to learn the basic skills that are the building blocks for all others.

Luckily, sensory integration work can help most people with PDDs get better control of the information they take in. Please consult an occupational therapist who is trained in SI techniques if possible, or at least explore further by reading some of the SI-related books listed in Appendix A. *The Out-of-Sync Child* (Perigee, 1998), by Carol Stock Kranowitz, while not aimed at the more intense SI problems experienced by autistic-spectrum people, is another widely available source of information. It is an adequate guide to starting a home-based sensory integration program when you can't find professional help.

For Ian, sensory integration was the key to progress in all other areas. He was sensory defensive sometimes, and that made it hard for him to be in his Early Intervention class, where there was a lot of touching. He was undersensitive to touch at other times and had low muscle tone, as evidenced by W-sitting, slack posture, and lack of strength. We did brushing and joint compression; the school OT added working on a balance beam and other equipment. It made a big difference in his life. He was just more comfortable in his body. We continue to use SI activities for calming and to continue that beneficial process.

SI activities are usually quite simple. Special equipment is not a must, although some parents have used swings, hammocks, and small items that can be obtained from catalogs (see Appendix A). The following lists offer a few examples of typical SI activities that may be done at home.

For tactile-sensitivity problems (under- or oversensitivity):

- The so-called Wilbarger brushing technique is based on the use of firm strokes with a soft surgical brush (available inexpensively from medical-supply stores) on the back, arms, and legs. Brushing is interspersed with joint compression, in which the elbows, arm sockets, knees, and hip joints are pushed together firmly several times in succession. It's hard to explain this practice in print—it's really something you should be taught in person.

- Handling materials with a variety of textures, such as wet or dry sand, shaving cream, dry beans, and water. Children can be encouraged to play with the materials, even put them on their arms, legs, or face if appropriate.

- Deep-pressure massage or hugs.

- Making a "kid burrito" by rolling the child up tightly in a blanket, or a "kid sandwich" by (carefully) squishing the child between two gymnastic mats or sofa cushions.

- Parents and other caregivers should also avoid introducing people with tactile oversensitivity to unnecessary unpleasant sensations. Clothing problems are very common in this group, with tags and scratchy materials being frequent offenders. Incidentally, tactile undersensitivity is a common cause of hyperactive behavior.

For proprioceptive problems:

- Swinging (clinics often use a big therapy swing that lets the person swing in a prone position).

- Jumping on a small trampoline.

- The joint-compression technique mentioned above.

For vestibular problems:

- Walking on a balance beam.

- Balancing on a large "therapy ball" as it moves.

- OT work aimed at strengthening and developing gross-motor skills (people with vestibular problems tend to have low muscle tone).

- Exercises that encourage "crossing the midline": using the left hand and arm on the right side of the body, and vice versa. Examples include some kinds of dancing, and rocking from side to side.

- Stair climbing.

Most of these exercises actually work on more than one sense at once. Activities can be combined and varied to keep SI work fun—and most children *do* think it's fun! Adults with long-term sensory issues may have a hard time getting started with an SI program, especially since some of the activities may seem childish or silly.

One special area of concern is oral tactile dysfunction. For years, parents have told their physicians that their children with PDDs had strange, limited food preferences. Many prefer bland, smooth foods, and self-select from only a few favorites: peanut butter, white bread, and applesauce only, for example. Although sometimes food preferences may have their roots in allergy issues (some allergists say that the foods we crave tend to be the very ones we are allergic to), if texture appears to be the primary issue, the problem is more likely to be oral tactile defensiveness. OTs can work to desensitize the nerves in the mouth, helping these children to gradually tolerate more textures and broaden their diet.

Sensory integration differences extend to eating habits. Some people with PDDs will stuff their mouths to the bursting point, for instance, and may not notice when food gets on their faces or hands. The issue here is tactile undersensitivity, and that can also be addressed by an OT.

Most speech therapists are also knowledgeable about sensitivity problems in the mouth and throat, and may be able to help.

In addition to exercises that reduce sensory defensiveness, or that help the undersensitive patient integrate and process sensations, clinicians recommend making a sensory diet part of daily activities at home and at school. This means integrating soothing sensory experiences into daily activities at a regular interval. These activities could include:

- Slow, repetitive rhythmic movements, such as T'ai Chi, water aerobics, or using a rocking chair.

- Firm pressure on the skin, from hugs, compression devices, or another source.

- "Heavy work," such as moving furniture, carrying heavy bags, or lifting weights.

- Activities done upside down, such as headstands or tumbling.

Speech therapy

Speech delay and/or dysfunction is considered to be a primary symptom of autistic spectrum disorders. The issue is usually lack of speech due to an apparent inability to understand speech as a vehicle for symbolic communication.

This does not mean that a person on the spectrum cannot also be affected by another common speech disorder. In fact, they are far more common in people with PDDs than they are in the general population. Speech disorders come in many flavors. The descriptive terms you will see most often are:

- **Aphasia**. Difficulty in using oral language (expressive aphasia) or aural language (receptive aphasia). Can be characterized by pauses in speech or seeming to be "deaf" at times. Aphasia is usually associated with brain injury.

- **Stuttering**. Getting stuck on a sound, usually a single letter or syllable at the beginning of a word, and repeating it.

- **Cluttering**. Getting stuck on a complex sound, such as a word or phrase, and repeating it. Also characterized by a fast, fluctuating rate of speech.

- **Verbal dyspraxia.** Disordered speech due to underlying problems with muscle control. Also called developmental dyspraxia of speech.
- **Oral-motor apraxia.** Lack of speech, or disordered speech, due to underlying problems with muscle control.

Technically, apraxia refers to the absence of speech, while dyspraxia refers to disordered speech. In the UK and some other countries, that's how these terms are used. In the US and Canada, however, the terms are used almost interchangeably, leading to much confusion. Be sure to ask what any diagnosis you or your child receives is actually intended to mean.

With a nonverbal child, simply producing sounds that have communicative intent is the initial goal of speech therapy. As children become verbal, oral-motor problems, stuttering, and such may emerge. Speech therapy should be tailored to fit the child and the problem. Stuttering, for example, can often be remedied in weekly group sessions with homework. Oral-motor apraxia is a much more demanding condition, requiring intense, frequent sessions.

Language disorders

Even children who speak, and speak well, can have language problems. Pragmatic language deficits—difficulty using language in context, such as in a conversation—are common in people with PDDs. The person's grammar, syntax, and conversational gambits may be limited, pedantic (as in Asperger's syndrome), or unusual. The rate, volume, and rhythm of speech may be odd. Perseveration (frequent repetition of words or sentences, or getting stuck on topics) is not uncommon. The voice itself may be unusually raspy, hoarse, whispery, loud, or otherwise unusual. Speech therapists can address these problems, sometimes in individual sessions, sometimes in a group situation where the social aspects of language can be pointed out and practiced.

Two special language disorders are found primarily in people with autistic-spectrum disorders, and are also common in people with Tourette syndrome. These are:

- **Echolalia.** The persistent repetition of words or phrases just heard. Some books on speech disorders still say that echolalia is "meaningless," but it can have communicative intent. For many young children with

PDDs, echolalia is the first or only speech to emerge before intervention is tried.

- **Palilalia.** Repetition of your own words or thoughts (similar to perseveration, but with more of a compulsive quality).

A third language disorder, coprolalia, is experienced by about one-tenth of all people diagnosed with Tourette syndrome, usually as a transitory phase. Coprolalia is the inadvertent blurting of obscene or derogatory language, usually unrelated or only tangentially related to the situation at hand. Some people with PDDs occasionally evidence coprolalia, with or without a co-morbid diagnosis of Tourette. The most common methods for dealing with coprolalia are substituting an inoffensive but similar word for the offending term (saying "fudge" or "ship" instead of the similar obscene word, for example), holding back the urge until the vocal tic can be released in private, or using medication that reduces tics. It's important that parents and professionals understand that coprolalia is a tic—a behavior that occurs because of a short-circuit in the impulse-control system, not a truly volitional act. It is as difficult to control as an eye-blinking or finger-tapping tic, and it should not be punished. Coprolalia causes extreme embarrassment, and most people who experience it are willing to try almost anything to make it disappear.

Speech therapy methods

Methods used by speech therapists (and by parents and teachers) depend on the problem at hand and differ depending on the setting. For oral-motor apraxia, for example, speech therapists in medical centers may work "inside the mouth" using popsicle sticks, fingers, whistles, straws, and other items to help the child gain control over the muscles of the mouth, tongue, and throat. SLPs at school are less likely to do so, but may combine sound drills with adding speech activities to the child's regular classroom program.

For most children with severe communication disorders, one-to-one treatment is essential. Some districts try to cut corners by delivering speech therapy in a group setting. This works well for less serious problems or for speech pragmatics, but is not sufficient for nonverbal, apraxic, or severely dyspraxic children.

There are all sorts of ways to encourage the production of speech, and they can be integrated into ABA, floor-time, or other types of therapeutic systems. Perhaps the best reference available is *Teach Me Language* (SKF Books,

1997), by Sabrina Freeman and Lorelei Dake. Freeman and Dake mix speech and language concepts tailored to the specific needs of autistic-spectrum children with ABA teaching techniques, and their suggestions can easily be incorporated into home and school programs.

When doing speech therapy with children (and particularly with those who have PDDs), motivation can be a roadblock. Smart SLPs use speech games, flash cards, toys, hand puppets, and reinforcers of all sorts to keep sessions on track and encourage children to work harder. These aids are available to parents as well through catalogs (see Appendix A) or sometimes directly from the SLP. Songs and rhythm work well with some people.

> Our son has severe oral-motor apraxia. One thing he simply could not do is breathe through his nose, which caused prosody problems when he tried to talk and breathe through this mouth at the same time. After many frustrating speech sessions, his SLP found the perfect solution! She purchased a package of plastic "nose flutes," which whistle when you blow through your nose with your mouth closed. It took him a week to get the first sound out of one, but it was a fun challenge. One of the first things we noticed was less snoring, because he started breathing through his nose most of the time while sleeping.

Your child may get homework, often in the form of worksheets with sounds to attempt. Ask the SLP how to make these drills more fun. Adults in speech therapy may have homework too, sometimes drills, sometimes mouth exercises with a mirror.

Total communication

The best approach to working with nonverbal, barely verbal, or apraxic children and adults is what some speech therapists call "total communication." It involves not only relying on oral language to build communication skills, but also introducing gestures, sign language, and other visual communication systems even as you do speech therapy. A person who cannot communicate is cut off from others, and it has been conclusively shown that visual communication systems use the same brain circuits as oral communication does. In other words, using visual communication may help build up these weak circuits, laying the groundwork for oral speech. The goal of the SLP in this situation is to help the person transition from the visual to the verbal, first by making the connection between the two, and then by doing traditional speech work. Most experts in helping people with communication disorders endorse the total communication approach.

> *There is research that teaching speech and sign language at the same time will increase the likelihood that the child will speak. Unfortunately, many behavior therapists teach only speech because they feel that sign language will become a crutch, and the child will rely on signs rather than speaking. There is no evidence to support this notion.*

> *Interestingly, when a person talks or uses sign language, the same area of the brain is activated. Thus, the procedure of teaching speech and sign language simultaneously may, in fact, be stimulating two neurological pathways that activate the same area of the brain. —Dr. Stephen M. Edelson, director, Center for the Study of Autism*

Even Dr. Lovaas, who has long pushed a speech-only approach, is beginning to come around to the total communication point of view. If children in an intensive ABA program still have not initiated speech after a long time, he now recommends using PECS symbols or something similar to jump-start communication, according to parents.

Speech and behavior

There is a strong link between speech problems and distressing behavior, as many parents can attest. The frustration of not being understood can build up to produce tantrums. It makes a person feel isolated, and it can make him more vulnerable to abuse.

Interestingly, poor communication abilities are cited by social scientists as one of the three factors most likely to lead to violent behavior in children, adolescents, or adults (the other two: male gender and abuse). Case studies of autistic-spectrum disorders have shown that the development of speech correlates strongly with better outcomes.

Don't let these facts frighten you—let them motivate you. Don't let anyone tell you that a person is too old for speech therapy, unable to behave well enough to benefit from speech therapy, not intelligent enough for speech therapy, or simply a "late talker." Communication is the key to everything else.

When his own brother and mother don't understand his speech, when he can't tell a story or explain a need, that must be so frustrating! And does he feel sad? Or lonely? Or depressed? I don't know. He doesn't have the expressive language to tell me. —Cindy, mother of 15-year-old Jeffrey (diagnosed verbal dyspraxia with "autistic-like" features)

When a child is experiencing behavior problems, communication problems are often at the root. It should be the first area addressed when searching for a solution. Behavior is communication, and for those who have difficulty expressing themselves with words, it can be the only form of communication available. We need to pay attention.

Who delivers, who pays?

If you have read this chapter, you've probably noticed that the most demonstrably effective interventions rely on one-to-one interaction for several hours every day. Parents, grandparents, even teenage or adult siblings can be trained to do much of this work, but it is exhausting. And many important interventions, such as speech therapy, do require college-trained therapists.

Indeed, one of the biggest issues around therapeutic interventions is who delivers them … and who pays for them. Insurance companies often refuse to provide anything, while schools tend to do as little as possible—and increasingly try to bill the parents' insurance for whatever they do deliver! Often families end up spending thousands of dollars for therapy delivered by private practitioners, when either their health insurance or the school system should have paid for it.

You should start your search with your local Early Intervention program or school district. In the US, Canada, and most of Europe, these entities are charged with providing at least some assistance at no charge to the parents. Some programs in the US and Canada *do* pay for home-based ABA or similar intensive therapies for young children. It works, and the growing consensus among advocates for autistic-spectrum children is that intensive, full-time programs should be the norm for all young children diagnosed with a pervasive developmental disorder. Making that a reality will probably require government edicts or court cases.

In the meantime, parents whose budgets cannot bear the weight of paying for ABA, speech, OT, and groceries at the same time must find other resources. The first place to look is inward. Parents and other family members know their children better than anyone else. They understand what motivates them, what annoys them, what sparks a tantrum, and what special skills they have. Parents are the true experts, but they often labor under a burden of self-doubt, fearing that they don't have the skills or energy to teach. Perhaps the most valuable investment is in training that provides you with the actual skills you need and with the self-confidence required to exercise them.

Parent training for ABA, floor-time play therapy, and similar programs is not always easy to find locally. You may have to attend an autism conference, or travel to a center that specializes in training practitioners and parents. Appendix B, *Support and Advocacy,* lists a number of resources that can help you get started. Books can also be used as self-training aids for those who don't have access to classes. Online resources can put you in touch with people who have experience in various types of therapy.

Once parents have been trained, they can train others. These others can be paid, but many families have found volunteers who were more than willing to help out with a home-based program for a few hours each week. They've stood before their religious congregations to ask for help, contacted local high schools and colleges in search of willing students, put up notices on community bulletin boards, and contacted organizations like Volunteers of America or Easter Seals. College students, especially those who need to complete a certain number of hours for a practicum requirement, are an especially excellent resource. Some senior citizens also have the time, patience, and desire to help that make a great volunteer.

It's been estimated that a 40-hour-per-week ABA program for a child with autistic disorder can cost as much as $30,000 to $60,000. Parents whose children have PDD-NOS or atypical PDD can expect to pay less. But some families have successfully provided intensive, one-on-one therapeutic interventions—even for children who are severely autistic—using only their own labor and assistance from unpaid volunteers. Chapter 11, *Finances,* provides some additional ideas in this vein. Two parents interviewed for this book have done so despite having very low incomes, including one subsisting on disability benefit in the UK.

Professionals in the field caution parents against courting bankruptcy to provide high-priced help. Sometimes the most important interventions are those that cost the least. In a recent presentation to families, Dr. Stanley

Greenspan noted that "a really good teenage babysitter, one who will play and interact with your child for a couple of hours, not just watch TV, can sometimes be a better investment than another hour of speech therapy."

As noted at the beginning of this section, schools and insurance companies may try to pass the burden off to each other. In 1997 and 1998, a number of parents in the US were asked for the first time to provide health-insurance billing information to their school districts, which then tried to use this data to extract payment from insurance companies for speech therapy and other services provided by the school district. Because the special education laws specify quite clearly that schools are to provide a *free* and appropriate public education ("FAPE"), we suspect that this practice skirts the law. A number of families have successfully refused to provide this information for any purpose other than ensuring its availability in case emergency medical care is needed during school hours. To our knowledge, no one has yet taken a US school district to court over this issue, but it is likely to happen in the near future.

Why would you want to resist such requests? Other than the legal issue noted above, this practice can block your access to therapies provided in a medical setting. Most health insurers place a limit on the amount of therapeutic services an insured patient can receive. Since schools and medical facilities take different, and yet complimentary, approaches to speech, occupational, and physical therapy, you don't want to lose the opportunity to use both. If your insurer insists on calling PDDs "mental disorders," as so many still do, you may lose access to family therapy and other benefits because the school district has charged the insurer for counseling or social-work services.

In addition, as we will discuss in detail in Chapter 8, *Insurance*, you may not want to share your child's educational diagnosis with your health insurer. Many companies do discriminate against people with autistic-spectrum disorders, refusing them services that are provided to people with other diagnoses.

Some professionals do applaud the practice of school districts billing private insurance, arguing that insurers may be more willing to provide their own services if they will otherwise be forced to pay for school-provided services whose quality and outcome they cannot control.

Evaluating programs and practitioners

Families and adult patients can choose from many therapeutic models, as this chapter makes abundantly clear. Your decision should be based on how comfortable you feel with a particular approach, the provider's reputation, and whether it fits the patient's needs.

Other parents and patients are your best resources for vetting programs and practitioners. Ask around at meetings of autism support groups, and seek out information about patients like you or your child in particular. You can even ask in online forums, although we encourage you to request that all responses be made directly to you rather than to the entire mailing list. Some practitioners take part in these lists, too. Local service agencies, such as Disability Services offices or advocacy organizations, may be able to give you an opinion. Special education case managers are often familiar with private programs in the area.

One thing you should never do is rely on the program itself for references. Almost every method attempted with autistic-spectrum children has produced a "success story" or two, even those that are generally considered to be discredited. If these are the only voices you hear, you aren't getting the full picture.

If a program claims to have documented proof of its efficacy, ask to see the studies themselves, not just their purported results. Sometimes results have been misinterpreted, and sometimes studies are so poorly constructed that the results are meaningless. If you're not sure about a study, take it to your physician or another knowledgeable advisor for a second opinion.

Evaluating practitioners

As you choose speech therapists and others to work with your child, be aware that even the most recent textbooks may have provided them with misinformation about autistic-spectrum disorders. For example, the ninth edition of *Speech Correction: An Introduction to Speech Pathology and Audiology,* by Charles Van Riper and Robert L. Erickson (Allyn and Bacon, 1996), one of the most popular speech textbooks in current US use, classes autism under "emotional problems," describes autistic children as "strange...not of this world," and fails to so much as mention PDD-NOS, atypical PDD, Asperger's syndrome, or that there is a spectrum of autistic disorders at all.

If a therapist has been miseducated, it's not really fair to blame her. But it certainly is a hassle to have to educate professionals year after year, as so many parents have to do. If the professional is resistant to new information, don't delay in finding someone else. In a school setting this can be difficult, and in rural areas you may have no alternative choices.

When bringing volunteers or paid aides for a home program onboard, make sure you feel comfortable with the person's approach, demeanor, willingness to listen, and work ethic. Pay attention to your intuition. If someone makes you feel uncomfortable, they are likely to have a similar effect on your child. Some parents have chosen to do criminal background checks on prospective aides.

Evaluating results

You can't evaluate results of a particular therapy if baseline data was not collected before it began, so that's an essential step. You should receive a report summarizing the results of a baseline evaluation before the therapist gets started. If you see something that doesn't ring true, bring it up now. Sometimes people perform differently in a clinical setting or with strangers than they do at home, and that's information the therapist can use.

You also need to keep some sort of record of the interventions you're trying. We strongly recommend keeping a journal that tracks medications, therapy appointments, changes in diet, vitamins, and everything else you do (see Chapter 11), but it can be time-consuming. At the very least, ensure that services are actually being delivered—not always an easy task with school-based programs—and ask the therapist how he will evaluate the effectiveness of his work.

If standardized tests are to be used as a measure of progress, make sure appropriate instruments are used, that you get a copy of the results, and that they are adequately explained.

Whenever possible, change or add therapeutic interventions just as you would medications: one at a time. It's hard to tell what change is responsible for an advance if you have made many at once.

> I really didn't know what to look for when I was in the Part-H program [an Early Intervention program]. I was willing to stick with the first speech person, and I really wish I had changed before Elaine turned three.

I wanted to at least give her a fair try… [but] after six months I looked for another SLP—much better results! —Sarah, mother of three-year-old Elaine

If you are truly dissatisfied with a therapeutic intervention after you've given it several months, talk to your practitioner. It could be that progress is occurring, but at a more subtle level than expected. It could also be that this is not the right intervention for this patient or that this practitioner is not the right person to work with this patient.

Spotting a scam

Whenever people are desperate, you will find someone looking to take advantage of their desperation. These con artists can be hard to spot. Some sport the initials "MD" after their names, some have published books, others have the ability to make you feel warm and fuzzy inside as you listen to their spiel. They will promise you the moon, but they can't deliver.

The field of autistic spectrum disorders has been home to many a false prophet. Not all have been strictly venal: perhaps a therapy worked for one child, and they were sure it would for all. Perhaps an idea seemed as though it *should* work, and they truly wanted it to. Others are simply charlatans, well aware that they're selling snake oil. How can you avoid being taken in?

First, educate yourself about any therapy that you're considering. If you're told that it's backed by research, ask to see the published research. Real medical researchers publish their work in reputable journals, according to their profession (medicine, occupational therapy, speech therapy, etc.). Check out a practitioner's credentials. Letters after a name can stand for a lot of things, not all of them useful. Some people add them just to fool you, like a certain US practitioner we've heard of who follows his name with the misleading letters "PhC" (meaning PhD candidate)… and has done so for a decade.

Learn the buzzwords used in a particular therapy, so you can sound knowledgeable when you ask questions. Con artists tend to dress up their wares in a lot of fancy terminology, in an effort to make it sound scientific or up-to-the-minute. People who do have something genuinely new to offer are usually happy to attempt a layperson's-level explanation. If you're told it's too complex or mysterious to explain, a red flag should go up in your mind.

Nothing is ever so new that it has no relationship to what has gone before. Ask the practitioner to contrast his approach to mainstream methods, such as ABA or sensory integration.

Dr. Lovaas is widely admired by grateful families, and rightly so, but no one hangs on his every word. He's a good doctor, a good researcher, and an important guy in the field of autism, not a guru. That's as it should be. Watch out for therapies that seem to be hitched to a cult of personality. Some therapies do have such leaders: people who refuse to be questioned, who encourage parents to spend huge sums of money just to bask in their presence, and who accuse those who criticize them of something close to heresy.

These ersatz gurus will tell you that their method is the only method and discourage you from seeking any other kind of help for your child. Often they'll use coercive methods to bring you into their orbit and cult-like techniques to keep you there. Some may even threaten to reveal privileged information about you if you leave. Others may claim that the patient will surely regress, and the blame will all be on you.

Money can be another red-flag issue. Doctors and therapists deserve to get paid, but the cost of treatment should be in proportion to the cost of similar therapies. If speech therapy costs $50 per hour but "Therapy X" costs $500 per hour, it doesn't necessarily mean that "Therapy X" is that much better. Most reputable therapists are in the field of treating patients with PDDs because they care. They want to make an adequate living, but they aren't expecting to live a lavish lifestyle on other people's misery. Ask about costs. If the answer sounds like mumbo-jumbo instead of a truthful accounting of expenses, find the door.

Be especially careful of any method that claims to *cure* PDDs. People do get better with proper intervention. They function better in the world, they feel happier, they're able to enjoy the benefits of being a relational person. A stranger might never know that they once carried the label of PDD-NOS, atypical PDD, or autism. But subtle differences always remain, and any therapist who claims she can make a patient absolutely "normal" is shading the truth at least a little.

If you'd like an inside look at the issue of false therapies, the books *Facilitated Communication—A Passion to Believe: Autism and the Facilitated Communication Phenomenon* (Westview Press, 1998), by Diane Twachtman-Cullen, and *No Time for Jello* (Brookline Books, 1989), by Berneen Bratt, are recommended reading. The first takes the Facilitated Communication phenomenon to task, the second tackles the Doman-Delacato/Institutes for the Achievement of Human Potential "patterning" program. As these books make clear, smart people can be taken in, including idealistic young therapists who themselves end up bamboozled into the wrong camp.

Perhaps the most important thing you can do to protect yourself or your child from therapy scams is to trust your own intuition. If it feels wrong, it probably is.

Don't call it therapy

Most children develop their gross- and fine-motor skills, their social capabilities, and their speech in the course of everyday activities. People with PDDs can also enjoy the therapeutic potential of typical activities.

Young children may not seem to be enjoying an activity at first, perhaps opting out of the action. Try to work up to it in small steps. For example, if your child shows an interest in collecting cards, introduce a card album, show her how to slip the cards into the pockets, and back away. Save the activities of trading cards with other kids, playing collectable card games, going to card stores, and attending card shows for other days.

Here are just a few of the fun activities that build important skills. Every kid should have these experiences. Whatever you do, don't call it therapy (even though it is).

- Playing card games and board games
- Swimming
- Playing on the playground, at the park, or in your yard
- Reading aloud (or silently), with an accent on the "what-ifs" of factual books and on fantasy
- Nursery rhymes, jump rope jingles, and hand games
- Simple group games like London Bridge and freeze tag (see books on "New Games" for some cooperative play possibilities for groups)
- Using costumes and props for imaginative play
- Starting and maintaining collections of rocks, stamps, cards, or toys

- Building models and playing with construction toys
- Turning off the television and video games in favor of relating to one another
- Getting messy outdoors or in the kitchen

Finally, while therapy, medical appointments, taking pills, and eating special meals may be part of your child's life or your own, they shouldn't be the totality of it. Therapies should enhance life. Make time for relaxation, play, hugs, Saturday morning cartoons, and just watching the clouds go by. These moments work a sort of magic too, and they aren't to be missed.

CHAPTER 7

Other Interventions

SINCE MEDICAL SCIENCE HASN'T CAUGHT UP TO addressing the causes of pervasive developmental disorders just yet, many people with PDDs experiment with alternative medicine: herbal supplements, vitamins, chiropractic, homeopathy, acupuncture, and other nonmainstream interventions. This chapter lists and defines most of the alternative treatments that you may hear about, explains how to evaluate the claims of alternative medical practitioners and supplement boosters, and tells you how to do your own carefully controlled "clinical trials" of alternative therapies.

As with the medical and therapeutic interventions discussed in the preceding two chapters, parents and patients need to exercise caution with these remedies. If a substance or treatment has actual effects on the patient (not all of them will, of course), its use should be taken as seriously as a pharmaceutical medication that produces a similar effect. Appendix E, *Supplement Reference*, provides more detailed information about these products.

There is no absolute proof that any of these therapies or programs will help a specific child, but anecdotal evidence—and in a few cases, clinical trials—indicate that some individuals with PDDs may experience significant improvements.

> *At the age of ten months, my daughter was described by the psychologist as follows:*
>
> *"This little girl has a very short, fleeting attention span. She gaze-averts, and makes only intermittent and relatively unmeaningful eye contact. She is a very hypotonic baby ... intermittently unresponsive to sound, and is more responsive to inanimate than vocal input. She appears vacuous, and had many staring episodes which were suggestive of a possible underlying seizure disorder. She flaps her hands, shakes her head, and does some other self-stimulating behaviors in a repetitive manner ... "*

Her BSID II mental age was four months; motor age, five months. On the Gesell, at 42 weeks old, she ranged from a high score of 24 weeks on fine motor to a low of 13 weeks on personal/social. Very erratic.

I only repeat all this because inevitably, there will be those who respond to our success with skepticism about her initial diagnosis. And since the CHAT [CHecklist for Autism in Toddlers] is the earliest diagnostic tool I know of, at 18 months of age, you have every right to do so. However, if Miranda was headed for a confirmed diagnosis of an autistic spectrum disorder at a later date, I truly believe that in her case we have stopped or mediated the metabolic problems that were causing her symptoms, and perhaps prevented irreversible CNS damage.

We started DMG and then Super Nu-Thera first, and got better sleep patterns, more eye contact, and increased babbling. With her history of ear infections, we decided to have Dr. Shaw's test done, and actually started the anti-yeast diet, probiotics, and MCT oil while awaiting the results. Eventually, we added Nystatin. After a two-week nightmare die-off period, the effects were like a fog had lifted from Miranda. Prolonged, meaningful, deep gazes into Mommy's eyes, dissolving into fits of giggles at funny faces, awareness of and interest in her environment, and finally, sitting unassisted.

The test came back with 18 levels high, some extremely so. Several were fungal metabolites, so we were vigilant about the diet, Nystatin, and supplements. We still see regression when Miranda has fruit, and had a terrible regression and actual fungal diaper rash when we tried rice milk (too much sugar). Miranda also had the gluten/casein peptides test done. She showed high IaG, an indicator of gut permeability, and gliadomorphin, but not casomorphine. At the time, she was still breastfed and I was avoiding dairy, so we opted to go both gluten-free and casein-free since the peptides are so similar.

Jump to the present. Miranda is 13 months old. Current interventions: gluten- and casein-free diet and anti-yeast diet, MCT oil, DMG, and Super Nu-Thera, choline/inositol, and just started MSM. She drinks DariFree spiked with EFAs and rice protein powder. She is also in Early Intervention, getting PT, OT, and sensory integration, and tons of intensive interaction and floor-time with a dash of ABA from Mom.

She's a clingy, cuddly, snuggly, affectionate child now. She imitates funny faces and sounds, claps when you say "Yaaaay!" She crawls around the house looking for me and calling "Mamamamamama," gets into all the cupboards, pulls up to stand on the furniture, drinks from a sippy cup. She passed the seven- to ten-month-old competencies in every area of her latest assessment (the IDA) and passed the eleven- to thirteen-month-old competencies for social/emotional development.

Believe me, we have a long way to go—I still worry about language development, her sensory issues, and when my little "doughgirl" will ever have enough muscle tone to actually walk, but she's here, in our world, instead of that foggy one she used to be lost in, and we continue to be amazed and delighted at her progress.

Of course these same interventions won't help everyone, but I encourage you all to continue to be dedicated detectives. Find out the "why?" behind each treatment option, and look at your child's history to see if [he or she] might benefit. Sift, study, analyze, ask, try, compare, and never give up! —Maria, mother of one-year-old Miranda (tentatively diagnosed as autistic at ten months old)

These therapies are not effective for everyone, perhaps not even for most people with a pervasive developmental disorder.

We had problems, and small improvement. [We tried] zinc and a host of other minerals, such as calcium—no real help at all. Immunological testing showed nothing. Allergy testing showed environmental allergies to grass, leaf molds, and ragweed. No food allergies. —Kim, mother of seven-year-old Brad (diagnosed Landau-Kleffner syndrome)

General holistic/alternative treatment systems

In the UK, the Queen herself sees a homeopathic physician. Many insurance plans cover chiropractic adjustments, at least for back trouble. And the oldest medical systems—India's Ayurvedic medicine, Chinese herbalism, and the folk medicine of native peoples around the world—undoubtedly feature some time-tested remedies that Western medicine could adopt to its benefit. Following are brief descriptions of the most common alternative medicine systems.

Acupuncture

Developed in China, acupuncture is based on the concept of chi, an energy force that is believed to course through the human body. If your chi is blocked, acupuncture theory states, illness results. Acupuncturists use tiny needles inserted into the skin to undo these blockages. Modern acupuncturists generally use disposable needles to ensure sterility. Some also employ heat, (noninvasive) lasers, magnetic devices, or electrical stimulation.

You don't have to believe in the chi concept to enjoy the benefits of acupuncture. Even the alternative medicine skeptics at the National Institutes of Health have been forced to admit that it does seem to have benefits for some conditions, including chronic pain, and as an adjunct to other methods in the treatment of drug addiction (in fact, NIH is currently funding several studies on acupuncture). Western doctors think that the needles influence the body's production of natural opioid chemicals and neurotransmitters.

For people with PDDs, the areas of most interest regarding acupuncture are its potential effects on the GI tract and the nervous system. Reputable research indicates that properly applied acupuncture treatments may help heal nerve damage and that they can help regulate gastrointestinal functions. If you can find a good acupuncturist, it might be a worthwhile adjunct to other types of medical care.

Chiropractic

Chiropractors make adjustments to the spine and related body structures. Their work in this area does seem to be useful to some people with back pain, and the International Chiropractic Pediatric Association reports that chiropractic adjustments brought about "positive behavior changes" in about half of the children with autism treated in a 1987 study.[1]

Some parents have reported that their chiropractors have offered to treat their children with autism or other developmental disabilities at low or no cost. Results have been very variable—some children cannot tolerate the sensory experience of being "adjusted," others seem to enjoy it.

Naturopathy

Naturopaths are licensed to practice medicine in some countries, and also in some US states and Canadian provinces. They use the designation ND rather than MD. Naturopaths vary in their personal philosophy about Western medicine. Some will refer patients for ailments they feel are out of their league; others prefer to rely only on nutritional and natural medicine.

For parents and patients who prefer herbal remedies and nutritional interventions, a properly trained naturopath can be a good choice. Be careful whom you choose. In the US, some people calling themselves naturopaths have not completed an accredited program. Properly licensed naturopaths receive medical training roughly comparable to traditional medical school, although with a different emphasis.

For information about finding a licensed naturopath in the US or Canada, contact the American Association of Naturopathic Physicians (http:// www.naturopathic.org/) or the Canadian Naturopathic Association (http:// www.naturopathic.org/canada/Canada.Assoc.List.html).

Homeopathy

Homeopathy is based on the principle that remedies containing infinitesimal amounts of substances that could cause the medical condition being treated can instead prod the immune system into action against the condition. Homeopathy is a fairly mainstream medical practice in the UK.

In the US and Canada, homeopathic physicians are not licensed to practice medicine. However, some MDs and NDs do recommend homeopathic treatments, and a few homeopaths are fully licensed practitioners. For information about homeopaths in North America (or, interestingly, India), see the National Center for Homeopathy (http://www.homeopathic.org/).

For autism, the homeopathic remedies mentioned most often by parents who prefer this approach—Bufo, Bufo rana, Bufo cinereus, Bufo vulgaris, and Rana bufo—contain small amounts of the toxin made by the bufo toad. Oddly enough, one presentation at the 1998 DAN! conference noted that a substance very much like this toxin had been isolated from the blood of some autistic children (not children who were taking these remedies, it should be noted).

Orthomolecular medicine

The most famous proponent of orthomolecular medicine was its late founder, Dr. Linus Pauling. Better known for receiving the 1954 Nobel Prize for Chemistry and the 1962 Nobel Prize for Peace, Pauling spent most of his later life studying and publicizing the effects of megadoses of vitamins, particularly vitamin C. Many of Dr. Pauling's more extravagant claims have not been substantiated, but his reputation as a scientist forced the medical establishment to take his ideas seriously.

Some MDs are firm believers in orthomolecular medicine, and Pauling's principles underlie many of the megadose vitamin concoctions in health-food stores. Since large doses of vitamins can have side effects as well as potential benefits, be sure to discuss what you should expect with your doctor if he wants to try an orthomolecular approach. You shouldn't do megadose vitamin therapy without consulting a physician or a competent nutritionist.

Osteopathy

Osteopaths operate somewhat like chiropractors, adjusting the musculoskeletal system to effect improvement. In the UK, licensed osteopaths participate in the National Health scheme. They are licensed to practice medicine in all US states, and use the initials DO (Doctor of Osteopathy) instead of MD.

One area of osteopathy-related treatment, craniosacral therapy, is often recommended for children with neurological challenges, including autistic spectrum disorders. Although it was developed by osteopath John Upledger, craniosacral therapy is practiced by trained members of other professions, including some occupational therapists and physical therapists. Upledger includes some accounts of beneficial use of this therapy for people with autism in his book *Your Inner Physician and You: Craniosacral Therapy and Somatoemotional Release* (North Atlantic Books, 1997).

Ayurvedic and other traditional medicine

Indigenous peoples everywhere have medical systems that use herbal remedies. Two of these, India's Ayurveda and traditional Chinese medicine, have been systematized and studied to a great extent. The Ayurvedic medicine concept revolves around a life-force called "prana," while Chinese traditionalists talk about chi, as mentioned in the section on acupuncture.

Ayurvedic practitioners will give you an exam and then tell you which "type" you are in their diagnostic system. Then they'll suggest an appropriate diet, lifestyle adjustments, and probably therapeutic meditation. They may also have various suggestions about cleaning out your digestive tract.

Chinese traditional practitioners take a very similar approach, although their dietary recommendations tend to be less strict than a typical Ayurvedic plan.

There is a vast array of Ayurvedic and Chinese herbal remedies available, most of which have not been tested by Western researchers. Some of these concoctions are probably quite effective, while others could be dangerous to your health. If possible, try to find out exactly which herbs are in a remedy and check out their effects. For example, the popular Chinese herb Ma Huang is a common ingredient in traditional "nerve tonics." It is also a powerful central nervous system stimulant and should be taken with caution.

As far as we can tell from a review of the literature in English, no medical researcher has ever surveyed or studied traditional herbal remedies for autistic spectrum disorders, although some parents have tried them. It would be an interesting pursuit, and hopefully someone will do so. One Ayurvedic remedy, forskolin, has recently piqued a great deal of interest among research-minded parents. See Appendix E for more information.

Vitamins

Vitamins are actually considered a first-line approach to autism by many physicians. There is clear and compelling clinical evidence that at least some people with PDDs can benefit from taking additional B6, and the evidence for beneficial effects from some other vitamins is also reliable. The Autism Research Institute (ARI) has been an early and vocal booster of this approach, and has funded some of the research as well. People interested in pursuing vitamin therapy for autistic spectrum disorders would be well advised to contact ARI for the most recent information in this area.

In this section, only those effects that are believed to be relevant to autistic spectrum disorders are mentioned. Vitamins and other supplements may have many other health benefits as well. As always, approach these options with caution, and inform your primary care physician when you add vitamins to your personal healthcare prescription.

The B vitamin family

The B vitamin family includes:

- **Vitamin B1** (thiamin) is needed to fight stress and metabolize glucose into energy. It is sometimes found to be low in autistic subjects. Severe thiamin deficiency is called beri-beri, a potentially fatal condition whose symptoms include pain, weakness, nausea, constipation, and neurological problems.

- **Vitamin B2** (riboflavin) takes part in the conversion of tryptophan, and the synthesis of your body's own anti-inflammatory substances, the corticosteroids. If you follow a vegetarian diet, you probably should add vitamin B2 to your diet as a matter of course. Three medications sometimes used for PDD symptoms—chlorpromazine, imipramine, and amitriptyline—inhibit the body's use of riboflavin. This effect may also hold true for Anafranil, and perhaps other antidepressants. Those using these medications should supplement B2, particularly if they are following a gluten-free diet (in the US and some other countries, breads and other baked goods made with white flour are routinely enriched with vitamin B2).

- **Vitamin B3** (niacin) is believed to reduce inflammation and help the body cope with stress. It is also needed to help red blood cells carry oxygen and to build tissue, including nerve tissue. Severe niacin deficiency is called pellagra, characterized by scaly, inflamed skin; a swollen red tongue; GI tract irritation; and severe neurological problems. A small group of patients misdiagnosed as schizophrenic recover when supplemented with niacin—in fact, this effect was what gave doctors treating autism (then considered to be the same as childhood schizophrenia) the idea of giving the B vitamins a try. If you take antiseizure medicines, however, niacin may potentiate them.

- **Vitamin B5** (pantothenic acid) is necessary for normal antibody production and metabolism. B5 deficiency is rare in people eating a typical Western diet, but when volunteers in one study were given a deliberately deficient diet they developed neurological and GI tract problems.

- **Vitamin B6** (pyridoxine) is needed to process protein, essential fatty acids, and stored starches. It also influences the production of neurotransmitters, particularly norepinephrine, dopamine, and serotonin. Deficiency markers include dry skin, nausea, depression, and neurological symptoms, including seizures. If you choose to supplement with more than 50 mg of B6 per day, as the ARI recommends, you should do so under a doctor's supervision because it can be dangerous at very large doses for some patients. If you feel a tingling sensation in your hands or feet, stop taking B6 and contact your doctor. B6 must be given with magnesium.

- B12 (cobalamin) can be deficient in people who are not making a normal amount of digestive enzymes, such as those with GI tract disorders. It is also needed to build the myelin sheath that protects nerve fibers. Deficiency symptoms include pernicious anemia and depression. People with PDDs who test positive for auto-antibodies to myelin protein should probably supplement with vitamin B12, and others may want to do so as well. One study of autistic children found evidence of B12 deficiency in all subjects.

- Folic acid is required for your body to process the other B vitamins. It also plays a role in producing white blood cells and other immune-system components, in converting amino acids into proteins, and in building the nervous system. Deficiency markers include slow growth in children, depression, and megaloblastic anemia. The seizure medication Dilantin competes with folic acid in the GI tract and in the brain, so people who take Dilantin should consult with a physician about folic acid.

When B vitamin supplementation works, the results can range from minor to major. It is one of several interventions with a good success rate among older patients, as the story below eloquently attests.

> Nathaniel turned twenty in July. It seems like just yesterday that I was trying to imagine what it would be like when he grew up. The first studies on the effects of nutrition in autism were done about the time Nat was born. We heard about them, and even half-heartedly tried some nutritional things, but without any valid research to back it up we gave up almost before we started. Everyone thought we were crazy. We had no support. There was no Internet. The great thing is that it does exist now, the research is there, and we are learning that it is never too late.
>
> Nathaniel was doing okay for many years. When he started having some problems, we started looking for answers. We have had an incredible year. In the spring I talked to Dr. Rimland and decided that we should find a DAN! doctor (another thing that didn't exist twenty years ago). In the meantime, we started Nathaniel on B6 and worked him up to 1000 milligrams a day. It blew us away! He was a different person. We began to have conversations with him...for the first time in his life.
>
> We finally found a DAN! doctor an eight-hour drive away. The doctor decided to take him off of the vitamins for a couple of weeks so that he

*could do tests (we did everything but Secretin). During the time that he
was off the vitamins we saw a gradual loss of awareness, communication,
and self-help skills… it was frightening. His new doctor decided to put
him on different supplementation after he got the test results back. He
lowered the B6 to 500 mg and put him on a complete regimen of other
things, which included SBOs, enzymes, niacin, super multiples, and
CoQ10. At first I was apprehensive, because it seemed like he wasn't
making the gains that he had been on the high dose of B6, but now he has
started to surpass where he was in early July. He is calling people by
name, initiating thoughts of his own, expressing his desires.*

*It's incredible to see this kind of thing in a small child. Imagine what
it's like to watch it in someone twenty years old. We're kind of in shock.
It's a combination of joy and amazement, and guilt that we didn't do it
sooner. We had no idea that something like this could happen.*

*Do all that you can… do all of the tests… spare no expense. This
nutritional stuff is real. We're watching miracles right before our eyes. It's
never too late, but the sooner the better! —Rebecca, mother of twenty-
year-old Nathaniel*

B-vitamin deficiencies may develop in any person during periods of extreme
stress. The B vitamins are water-soluble and are not stored up in any large
quantity, so deficiency can materialize fairly quickly.

B6 is the B vitamin shown to help most in autism, as evidenced by eighteen
studies of its use in this population. It's important to start the dosage of B6
low, and titrate it up slowly. Your doctor can help you make a dosage plan
and monitor side effects. Side effects reported include hyperactivity, nausea,
increased sensitivity to sound, bed-wetting, and diarrhea. A few children
become quite wild and aggressive when just starting B6. If any of these side
effects occurs, cut back the dosage temporarily, and make sure the vitamin is
accompanied with the correct amount of magnesium.

Many people who are taking B6 for PDDs use a multiple-B supplement.
These are readily available. Super Nu-Thera, a brand-name multivitamin
made by Kirkman Sales (http://www.kirkmansales.com/), has become very
popular with parents of autistic-spectrum children because it combines the B
vitamins at the doses recommended by ARI with other nutrients that are
believed to be helpful. Kirkman also sells DMG (described later in this chapter) and folic acid supplements in the ARI-recommended formulations.

Antioxidants

Antioxidants scavenge the bloodstream for particles called free radicals. Free radicals wreak havoc by damaging cells and causing inflammation of tissues. If autistic spectrum disorders have an autoimmune cause, it stands to reason that antioxidants could be important for keeping the patient's immune system in balance. They include:

- **Vitamin A** (retinol) has antioxidant properties and also helps maintain the mucous lining of the intestines. People with celiac disease have a hard time getting enough A, and often experience a deficiency of this vitamin.

- **Vitamin C** (ascorbic acid) has shown benefits for some people with autism in megadoses.[2] Actual vitamin C deficiency, known as scurvy, is mighty rare these days. One population in which it does occur, however, is people who start using megadoses of C and then suddenly stop. The acidic nature of ascorbic acid can also contribute to kidney stones. (The buffered form, calcium ascorbate, is more easily tolerated.) As the cautions mentioned here indicate, megadoses of C shouldn't be taken without consulting your physician first. If you do choose to take large doses of vitamin C, research indicates that you should accompany it with vitamin E.

- **Vitamin E** (alpha tocopherol) is believed to be important for proper immune-system functioning. People who take antipsychotics, atypical antipsychotics, tricyclic antidepressants, or other medications that carry a known risk for tardive dyskensia should *definitely* supplement them with vitamin E. It appears to have protective and symptom-reduction qualities regarding this movement disorder.

- **Beta carotene** is a nutrient related to vitamin A, and is found in dark green leafy vegetables and yellow-orange vegetables. It's best to get it through the diet rather than from a supplement.

- **Coenzyme Q10** (CoQ10, ubiquinone) is a vitamin-like antioxidant, one of the strongest available. It's part of the cellular process that uses fats, sugars, and amino acids to produce the energy molecule ATP. It is said to boost immune-system function and help heal GI tract problems, including gastric ulcers. It does appear to have some benefit for women with breast cancer (although this claim is based on a very small study), and has been helpful to some children with inborn metabolic disorders, although other claims you may see in magazine articles or on the Internet are as yet unsubstantiated. It is most popular in Japan, where it is widely touted as a cancer preventative.

- **Glutathione peroxidase** is an antioxidant peptide manufactured by the body itself. You need to have enough selenium, vitamin C, and vitamin E to make it. There's no need to supplement directly with glutathione itself.

- **Selenium** deficiency occurs in some people with celiac disease and other autoimmune disorders, so if you or your child experiences GI tract problems, you may want to use a supplement of this mineral, preferably in its easily absorbed, chelated form (L-selenomethionane). The cooperation of vitamin E and selenium produces the antioxidant peptide glutathione peroxidase.

- **Zinc** deficiency occurs in some people with celiac disease, so if you or your child experiences GI tract problems, you may want to use a supplement of this mineral in its easiest-to-absorb, chelated form (zinc aspartate or zinc picolinate).

- **Proanthocyanidins** (OPCs, Pycogenol, grapeseed oil) are the active ingredients in several naturally occurring antioxidant compounds. Grapeseed oil is just what its name indicates, while Pycogenol is a brand-name formulation derived from maritime pine bark. Both have been tried by people with PDDs and other neurological disorders, sometimes with beneficial effects for seizure control, reduced aggression, and improved immune-system function.

- **Cat's claw** is another herbal antioxidant, this one from the Peruvian rainforest. No information about its use by people with PDDs is available at this time.

Vitamin cautions

Vitamins A and D are fat-soluble, so they are stored in the body's fat cells for later use. Having a little socked away for a rainy day is probably okay, but if you take too much, hypervitaminosis may develop.

Symptoms of hypervitaminosis A include orangeish, itchy skin, loss of appetite, increased fatigue, and hard, painful swellings on the arms, legs, or back of the head. Symptoms of hypervitaminosis D include hypercalcemia, osteoporosis, and kidney problems.

Don't overdo it with any fat-soluble vitamin, and also be careful with fish-oil supplements (and cod liver oil), which are high in both vitamins A and D.

Parents and patients with PDDs who plan to pursue vitamin therapies should purchase a basic guide to vitamins and minerals that includes information about toxicity symptoms. Some people metabolize vitamins and minerals differently and may be more or less susceptible to potential toxic effects. Along with your doctor's guidance, a good reference book can help you avoid problems.

Also, take vitamin company sales pitches and dosage recommendations with a grain of salt. The testimonials these companies produce are intended to sell their products, not to help you develop a treatment plan. Consult a physician or a professional nutritionist who does not sell supplements for unbiased, individualized advice.

Dietary supplements and herbs

Dietary supplements and herbal remedies are big business these days, thanks to articles and books touting the benefits of everything from garlic to herbal antidepressants. Here are some that you may hear about in relation to pervasive developmental disorders.

Minerals

Several minerals are essential for optimal health. Some are also necessary for utilizing certain vitamins.

- **Calcium** is important for the regulation of impulses in the nervous system and for neurotransmitter production. However, excessive levels of calcium (hypercalcinuria) can result in stupor and have been reported to occur naturally in some autistic people.

- **Magnesium** lowers blood pressure and is also important for the regulation of impulses in the nervous system and neurotransmitter production. If you are supplementing with vitamin B6, you will need to add magnesium as well.

- **Iron** (ferrous sulfate) deficiency in infants can inhibit mental and motor-skills development. Most children do not need an iron supplement, however, and too much iron can cause digestive and elimination problems. Adult women and some older adults may need to add a small amount of iron to their diet in supplement form.

Enzymes and sulfates

Enzymes are produced in the human digestive tract to digest various types of food. Protease acts on protein, amylase on carbohydrates, lipase on fats, pectinase on pectins (found in some fruits and other foods), and cellulase on fiber.

Other enzymes are produced to detoxify the body. One study, and some subsequent clinical research, has shown that many people with autism have lower than normal detoxification enzyme activity.[3] This activity, which relies on a steady supply of sulfate, is essential for maintaining the GI tract's mucous membrane and for moving toxins out of the body through hydrolation. If the mucous membrane in the gut is in good shape, the brain will be protected from a buildup of phenolic compounds, which can interfere with neurotransmission. If it is not, nervous-system problems can ensue.[4]

Some people with a documented sulfation problem take the enzyme methyl-sulphonyl-methane (MSM, or sulfur), which they believe may help them produce the sulfate. It is hard to digest, however. In addition, commercially available MSM is derived from dimethylsulfoxide (DMSO), a substance that has been touted as a boon for so many conditions that one might rightfully be cautious about trying a derivative.

Others have added the amino acid N-Acetyl-Cysteine (NAC), which is also said to have antispasmodic qualities. Another recommendation is taking frequent Epsom salts (hydrated magnesium sulfate) baths. Neither of these approaches is proven to work, but the baths are certainly relaxing and harmless, and some patients do seem to improve as a result. For those who would like to try the Epsom salts approach, one parent who achieved positive results with her child (reduced oppositional behavior and improved language skills) recommends using one and a half to two cups of Epsom salts per daily bath. "Sulfur (Epsom salts) improved socialization," says Holly, mother of three-year-old Max (diagnosed PDD-NOS).

Researchers have noted that dairy and gluten digestion difficulties would be expected in people with low sulfation, lending credence to the gluten-free/casein-free diet approach for these individuals.

Food items that are high in phenols might also be removed from the diet with beneficial results. Among the many phenols are tannin, which gives tea and persimmons their tang; quercitin, found in green beans and rhubarb; and coumarin, found in cabbage, radishes, and spinach. Other items high in phenols include apples, grapes, avocados, and other fruits; some artificial food colorings; many spices, such as cloves and sassafras; some preservatives, particularly the ubiquitous BHA and BHT; some herbs used in antioxidant compounds and teas, including grapeseed oil and comfrey tea; chocolate, coffee, and red wine.

Phenols are also used in many manufacturing processes, cleaning products, insecticides, plastics, and chemical compounds. These products and their fumes should be avoided by people with extreme sensitivity to phenols.

Essential fatty acids

The essential fatty acid (EFA) linoleic acid and its derivatives, including gammalinolenic acid (GLA), dihomogamma-linolenic acid (DGLA), and arachidonic acid (AA), are also called omega-6 fatty acids. These substances come from animal fats and some plants. Another type of EFAs, omega-3 fatty acids, are found almost exclusively in fish oils. As the "essential" in their name implies, these substances are needed to build cells and also to support the body's anti-inflammatory response. They are the "good" polyunsaturated fats that improve cardiovascular health when substituted for the "bad" saturated fats.

The heart and blood vessels aren't the only beneficiaries of EFAs, however. People with autoimmune diseases that involve the nervous system say EFAs are very helpful in reducing symptoms, and there is some research to back them up. EFAs appear to help the GI tract resist and repair damage, probably by restoring the lipid cells. Recent research in psychiatry has even found that omega-3 fatty acids can act as a mood stabilizer for some people with bipolar disorder. Researchers believe that a proper balance between omega-3 and omega-6 fatty acids is also important for optimal health.

- **Evening primrose oil** (EPO) is one of the best EFA sources around, and has become a very popular supplement as a result. Other plant sources for omega-6 fatty acids include borage oil, flax-seed oil, and black current seed oil. The omega-6 fatty acids in evening primrose oil have been reported to lower the threshold for frontal-lobe seizures, however, so people who have seizures should exercise caution. All are available as gelatin caps.

- **Efamol** and **Efalex** are brand-name EFA supplements made by Efamol Neutriceuticals, Inc. Efalex was specifically created to treat developmental dyspraxia in the UK and is widely touted as a supplement for people with ADD or ADHD as well. Efalex contains a mix of omega-3 fish oil, omega-6 EPO and thyme oil, and vitamin E. Efamol, marketed as a treatment for PMS, combines EPO; vitamins B6, C, and E; niacin zinc and magnesium. Both of these commercial EFA supplements are now available in the US and Canada as well, and can be purchased by mail order. Unlike many supplements manufacturers, Efamol adheres to strict standards and also sponsors reputable research.

- EicoPro, made by Eicotec, Inc., is another brand-name EFA supplement you may hear about. It combines omega-3 fish oils and omega-6 linoleic acid. Eicotec is another supplements manufacturer known for its high manufacturing standards.

- Monolaurin is made by the body from lauric acid, another medium-chain fatty acid that is found in abundance in coconuts and some other foods, including human breast milk. It is known to have antibacterial and antiviral properties. Monolaurin may be the active ingredient in colostrum, the "pre-milk" all mammals produce to jump-start a new-born's immune system. Cow colostrum is actually available in supplement form in some areas.

- NutriVene-D is a supplement, created for people with Down's syndrome, that mixes EFAs, vitamins, and other substances.

It's great if you can get your EFAs in food. Low-fat diets are part of the reason some people, especially those who are trying to lose weight, may not get enough. Many cold-pressed salad oils, including safflower, sunflower, corn, and canola oils, do contain EFA. When these oils are processed with heat, however, it may destroy or change the fatty acids. Oily fish are another great source, although, again, cooking may be a problem (and not everyone is a sushi fan).

It is possible to have lab tests done that can discern EFA levels.

> *Our son's essential fatty acids were abnormal. Some were too high and others too low. His iron and copper levels were high. Supplements include evening primrose oil, laktoferron, many vitamins, etc. Our son's supplements cost about $250 per month. —Joe, father of seven-year-old Kyle (diagnosed PDD-NOS with autistic features)*

Diabetics may experience adverse effects from too much EFA, and should consult their physician before supplementing with EFA products.

DMG

Dimethylglycine (DMG, calcium pangamate, pangamic acid, "vitamin B15") is a naturally occurring amino acid that may help some people with autistic spectrum disorders with speech production, increased stress tolerance, seizure reduction, and immune-system strengthening. Studies have been done in Russia and Korea with positive results for between half and 80 percent of the children given DMG, although they were not double-blind studies. New research results about the efficacy of DMG for people with autism are expected to be released soon.

> We have only used DMG for speech, and B6/magnesium. We are seeing improvements in both Nicole's articulation and in her ability to put sentences together. She has gained quite a few new words, and is attempting to place them in short sentences, whereas before she only used single words and more of a pull-and-point method. She definitely is trying harder to "say the words!" —Robin, mother of five-year-old Nicole (diagnosed mild autism)

DMG changes the way your body uses folic acid, so you may need to supplement it with that vitamin. Increased hyperactivity may result from a lack of folic acid when taking DMG.

Melatonin

Melatonin (MLT) is produced by the pineal gland and is responsible for helping the body maintain sleep and other biochemical rhythms. Studies have shown a deficiency or aberrant production of this hormone in autistic subjects,[5] and indeed, at least half of all people with autism have sleep disorders. Melatonin supplements given about half an hour before bed may be useful for addressing these problems. The effect may not be lasting, however. "Using melatonin for sleep worked awesome at first; now it is iffy," says Lesley, mother of three-year-old Danielle (diagnosed PDD-NOS).

Probiotics

As the name indicates, probiotics are intended to counteract the harmful affects of antibiotics. As most people who have taken a course of penicillin know, these valuable medications can cause digestive distress even as they heal infection. Probiotics are substances that attempt to restore the friendly intestinal cultures that help us digest our food. Among other things, these cultures (and other probiotics) keep the growth of *Candida albicans* yeast in balance.

Commercial probiotic supplements may combine a number of substances, sometimes including digestive enzymes as well as helpful bacteria, garlic, and the like.

- **Lactobacillus acidophilus, Bifidobacterium bifidum,** and **Lactobacillus bulgaricus** are friendly bacteria more familiar to most of us as the "active cultures" found in some yogurts. Yogurt itself is a good probiotic for those who eat dairy products.

- **Soil-based organisms** (SBOs) are microbes found in organic soils that are believed to help the body produce important enzymes. Some people believe that modern food-processing techniques have left people deficient in these, so they take SBO supplements. These are increasingly added to probiotic supplements. No information about benefits of use by people with PDDs is available at this time.

- **Garlic** is said to be active against yeast in the digestive tract. You can swallow whole cloves raw or take it in a supplement.

- **Caprylic acid** is a fatty acid said to be active against yeast in the digestive tract. Medium chain triglycerides (MCT oil, also called caprylic/capric triglycerides) are a liquid source of caprylic acid.

- **Biotin**, a vitamin related to the Bs, is normally produced by friendly bacteria in the digestive tract. Replenishing these flora should ensure enough biotin, but some people do choose to take it directly.

Octocosanol

Octocosanol, usually derived from wheat germ, is supposed to increase stamina, reduce cholesterol, and address neuromuscular deficits. It appears on some lists of supplements that may reduce autistic symptoms, but its method of action is unknown, and it doesn't seem to have much of a track record with parents.

Lecithin

Lecithin (phosphatidyl choline) is a phospholipid found mostly in high-fat foods. It is much ballyhooed for its ability to improve memory and brain processes. Lecithin is necessary for normal brain development; however, double-blind studies of patients with Alzheimer's disease did not substantiate claims that it can help people recover lost brain function.

However, it's possible that increased amounts of lecithin may be one of the keys to the ketogenic diet's success in some cases of hard-to-treat epilepsy. Some people with epilepsy have also reported reduced number and severity of seizures from taking lecithin as a supplement. It is possible that extra lecithin might be needed to rebuild damaged myelin protein.

There's no hard evidence that lecithin is a good idea for people with autism, but it does not appear to cause harm, and there are some logical reasons to think it might help—especially for patients who have seizures or who test positive for anti-MBP, the autoimmune agent believed to destroy myelin basic protein.

Lecithin is oil-based, and it gets rancid easily. It should be refrigerated. Lecithin capsules are available, but many people prefer the soft lecithin granules. These are a nice addition to fruit-juice smoothies, adding a thicker texture.

Choline is one of the active ingredients in lecithin. It is needed by the brain for processes related to memory, learning, and mental alertness, as well as for the manufacture of cell membranes and the neurotransmitter acetylcholine.

Inosital is one of the active ingredients in lecithin. It may help in cases of nerve damage and is required by the neurotransmitters serotonin and acetylcholine. Clinical studies have indicated that inositol supplements may be helpful for some people with obsessive-compulsive disorder,[6] depression, and panic disorder.[7] Benefits specific to autistic spectrum disorders have not been officially documented.

Herbal neurological remedies

Quite a few herbs have been used to treat neurological disorders through the ages. These substances are referred to as nervines, and some may prove useful for treating specific symptoms associated with autistic spectrum disorders. Of all the herbal remedies, this group of plant extracts are among the strongest, and the most likely to cause serious side effects.

- **Aloe vera gel** is sometimes recommended for GI tract problems. It's a traditional remedy for ulcers. It has anti-inflammatory (steroidal), hormonal, antioxidant, laxative, and other effects. Many people find it hard to take internally.

- **Black cohosh** (Cimicifuga racemosa, squaw root), a nervous system depressant and sedative, is often used by people with autoimmune conditions for its anti-inflammatory effects. Its active ingredient appears to bind to estrogen receptor sites, so it may cause hormonal activity.

- **Chamomile** is a mild but effective sedative traditionally used to treat sleep disorders or stomach upsets.

- **Damiana** is a traditional remedy for depression.

- **Gingko biloba**, an extract of the gingko tree, is advertised as an herb to improve memory. There is some clinical evidence for this claim. It is an antioxidant, and is prescribed in Germany for treatment of dementia. It is believed to increase blood flow to the brain.

- **Gotu kola** is a stimulant sometimes recommended for depression.

- **Licorice** is not just for candy or sore throats—it boosts hormone production, including hormones active in the GI tract and brain.

- **Passion flower** is recommended by some herbalists for depression, anxiety, and seizure disorders.

- **Sarsaparilla**, like licorice, seems to affect hormone production as well as settling the stomach and calming the nerves.

- **Skullcap**, an antispasmodic and sedative, is found in both European and Ayurvedic herbals. It has traditionally been used to treat tic disorders and muscle spasms, as well as seizure disorders, insomnia, and anxiety.

- **St. John's wort** (hypericum) has gained popularity as an herbal antidepressant. It has the backing of a decent amount of research, but, as noted in Chapter 5, *Medical Interventions*, those choosing to use this remedy should follow the same precautions as with SSRIs and MAOIs, two families of pharmaceutical antidepressants. It can cause increased sensitivity to light. It is available by prescription in Germany, where it is the most widely used antidepressant.

- **Valerian** is a strong herbal sedative. It should not be given to young children.

Herbal antibiotics

Several herbs appear to have antiseptic, antiviral, antifungal, or antibiotic properties. Obviously, if these substances are active, they should be used carefully and sparingly, despite the claims of certain manufacturers who encourage daily use for disease prevention. Those who prefer herbal remedies might want to try cat's claw and grapeseed oil, both mentioned in the previous section on antioxidants, or one of the following:

- **Bitter melon** (momordica charantia), an antiviral from the Chinese herbal pharmacopoeia, is the plant from which the active ingredient in some protease inhibitors (the powerful drugs used to combat AIDS) is derived.

- **Echinacea purpurea**, another herbal antiseptic, also dilates blood vessels and is said to have antispasmodic qualities as well.

- **Goldenseal**, an alkaloid isoquinoline derivative related to the minor opium alkaloids. Its active ingredient, hydrastine, elevates blood pressure. This is a very strong herb with antiseptic properties when taken internally or applied topically in powder or salve form. It acts on the mucous membranes of the GI tract when taken internally.

- SPV-30, derived from the European boxwood tree, is a fairly new item in this category. It apparently includes some antiviral and steroidal (anti-inflammatory) compounds, and has become very popular among people with AIDS as an alternative to pharmaceutical antivirals.

Sphingolin

Sphingolin is a glandular supplement made from cow spinal-corn myelin, repackaged in pill form. Some practitioners recommend it for children who have tested positive for myelin sheath proteins in the bloodstream. It is used by quite a number of people with multiple sclerosis and other neurological disorders that involve demyelinization.

Although anecdotal reports indicate that some people with PDDs have had symptom reductions when taking sphingolin, there could be a hidden problem with this supplement. It could contain particles that cause the deadly neurological disorder spongiform encephalopathy, "mad cow disease." It is not available in the UK for this very reason—and there's no reason to believe that this disease exists only in UK cattle or UK humans.

Evaluating supplement claims

No matter what kind of alternative practitioner or therapy you choose, it's just as important to be a smart consumer in this area as it is with traditional medicine. Unfortunately, it can be more difficult. Medications with approval from the FDA or similar government bodies undergo rigorous testing. Study results and detailed information about these compounds are available in numerous books, online, or directly from the manufacturers.

With "natural" remedies, that's not always the case. It seems like every week another paperback book appears making wild claims for a "new" antioxidant compound, herbal medication, or holistic therapy. The online bookstore Amazon.com lists nearly twenty titles about St. John's wort alone! These books—not to mention magazine articles, Web sites, and semi-informed friends—sometimes wrap conjecture up in a thin veneer of science. They may reference studies that are misinterpreted, that appeared in disreputable journals, or that were so poorly designed or biased that no journal would publish them.

Supplement salespeople, and particularly those who take part in multilevel marketing schemes, seem to have taken lessons from their predecessors in the days of the traveling medicine show. They have little to lose by making outrageous claims for their products and much to gain financially. Here are just a few of the unsupported claims found in a single five-minute sweep of supplement-sales sites on the Internet:

- "Glutathione slows the aging clock, prevents disease and increases life."

- "Pycogenol...dramatically relieves ADD/ADHD, improves skin smoothness and elasticity, reduces prostate inflammation and other inflammatory conditions, reduces diabetic retinopathy and neuropathy, improves circulation and enhances cell vitality..." [and, according to this site, cures almost anything else that might ail you!]

- "Sage and bee pollen nourish the brain."

- "Soybean lecithin has been found to clean out veins and arteries—dissolve the gooey sludge cholesterol—and thus increase circulation, relieve heart, vein and artery problems. It has cured many diabetics—cured brain clots, strokes, paralyzed legs, hands and arms!"

Take the time to browse your local health-food or vitamin store's shelves, and you'll probably spot a number of products that are deceptively advertised. Some companies try to deceive you with "sound-alike" names, packaging that mimics other products, or suggestive names that hint at cures. Other colorful bottles of pills contain substances that can't actually be absorbed by the body in oral form—for example, "DNA" (deoxyribonucleic acid, the building block of human genetic material) graces the shelves of some shops. One site for a manufacturer of this useless "supplement" claims that "it is the key element in the reprogramming and stimulation of lazy cells to avoid, improve, or correct problems in the respiratory, digestive, nervous, or glandular systems." It also notes that this "DNA" is extracted from fetal cells. Other brands are apparently nothing but capsules of brewer's yeast.

As the previous section on vitamins and supplements indicates, some other supplements provide end products of internal procedures, such as glutathione, instead of the precursors needed for the body to make a sufficient supply on its own, such as vitamin E. This approach may not work. When in doubt, consult with your doctor or a competent nutritionist.

How can you assess supplement claims? Start by relying primarily on reputable reference books for your basic information, rather than on advertisements or the popular press. Watch out for any product whose salespeople claim it will "cure" anything. Supplements and vitamins may enhance health and promote wellness, but they rarely effect cures. Be wary of universal usefulness claims. The worst offenders in supplement advertising tout their wares as cure-alls for a multitude of unrelated conditions in an effort to make the most sales.

There are a few other sales pitches that should make you wary. If a product's literature references the myth of the long-lived Hunzas, someone's trying to pull the wool over your eyes. This tale of hardy Russian mountain folk who supposedly all live to be well over 100 years old was refuted long ago by reputable researchers. If it's a natural substance but a particular company claims to be the only one to know the secret of its usefulness, that really doesn't make much sense. Be especially cautious when sales pitches are written in pseudoscientific language that doesn't hold up under close examination with a dictionary. This is a popular ploy. For example, one product that has occasionally been peddled to parents of children with PDDs claims to "support cellular communication through a dietary supplement of monosaccharides needed for glycoconjugate synthesis." Translated into plain English, this product is a sugar pill.

Even when you have seen the science behind a vitamin or supplement treatment, there's still the problem of quality and purity. It's almost impossible for consumers to know for sure that a tablet or powder contains the substances advertised at the strength and purity promised. Whenever possible, do business with reputable manufacturers that back up their products with potency guarantees or standards. In most European countries, potency is governed by government standards; in the US, it's a matter of corporate choice.

"Natural" does not mean "harmless." Vitamins and supplements can have the power to heal, and the power to harm. Be sure to work closely with your physician or a nutritionist if you're using anything more complex than a daily multivitamin.

Diet

Parents have long observed that their children with autism have disturbances in their eating, digestion, and elimination habits. Researchers have noted a relationship between autistic spectrum disorders and celiac disease, chronic diarrhea or constipation, and general GI tract problems. These are sometimes attributed to severely self-restricted diets, *Candida* yeast overgrowth, food allergies, or problems with metabolizing the proteins gluten or casein. Tests are available to help you pinpoint the cause of GI tract distress (see Chapter 5 for more details).

If this is the case for you or your child, a nutritionist with expertise in addressing GI tract problems via dietary changes will be able to help. Effective medical treatments are also available.

Casein-free and gluten-free (CF/GF) diets

Quite a number of children and adults with PDDs have experienced relief from GI tract troubles, and sometimes from autistic symptoms as well, by removing casein, gluten, or both from their diets. One theory is that milk and the gluten-containing grains are fairly recent additions to the human table. Perhaps some people's digestive systems are a little old-fashioned, and work better without these foods. Scientists espousing the opiate excess theory of autistic spectrum disorders say that peptides derived from these foods mimic opioid chemicals, slowing down digestion even more, causing a lack of alertness and increased physical sluggishness, and producing a variety of changes in brain chemistry. Some people seem to have a literal addiction to these opioids, including children who refuse all foods but dairy and gluten-containing starches.

Casein is the easier protein to avoid. It is present only in milk and milk byproducts, so you must rule out milk, cream, buttermilk, butter, sour cream, yogurt, and cheese. You also have to watch out for milk derivatives, which are hiding in many places. For example, check the ingredients label on that soy cheese: almost all varieties are made with casein or caseinate. Ditto for most margarines, which may contain casein, lactose (milk sugar), whey, dry nonfat milk, yogurt, or buttermilk. Cookies, soups, breads, potato chips, and many other supermarket foods may contain milk byproducts.

If you aren't allergic to soy products, there are many excellent substitutes available for casein-containing foods. Soy milk fortified with calcium and vitamins is widely available now, and there are also casein-free soy cheeses and soy yogurts. Tofu substitutes nicely when you want the creaminess of cheese or sour cream in a recipe, and a couple of manufacturers produce dairy-free sour cream, cream cheese, and frozen desserts. Check out vegetarian or vegan (no animal products, including dairy) cookbooks for some ideas on cooking without casein, and keep an eye out for packaged foods that are labeled "vegan."

Gluten is a bit harder to avoid. It is the protein found in wheat, spelt, oats, rye, triticale, and barley. Bread is the staff of life, so how can you avoid gluten? Choose other grains instead. Nonglutenous grains include corn, rice, wild rice, buckwheat, millet, quinoa, teff, and more. As with casein, gluten can be hiding in common supermarket items. Look out for malt, grain starches, textured vegetable protein (TVP), hydrolyzed vegetable protein (HVP), and vinegar, among other items. Sometimes TVP and HVP are made from soybeans, but not always.

There are some commercial gluten-free products on the market, including baking mixes, rice flour, cornmeal, baked goods, frozen waffles, breakfast cereals, and more.

Parents report that children who *do* respond to a CF and/or GF diet tend to exhibit clingy, whiny, irritable behavior when just starting out. Some may go on a hunger strike, refusing to eat at all. This stage will pass. More positive results that you may see are a newfound ability to be toilet trained, willingness to try a wider variety of foods, and more normal bowel movements.

Some parents also report that long-standing skin problems have cleared up on the diet, and that children who wandered aimlessly or even made escape attempts reduce these behaviors.

One of the great questions about CF/GF diets is how long you need to stay on them. The usual recommendation for a trial of the diet is three months to a year, after which it can be safely abandoned if no positive benefits have been seen. If it does seem to be working, one school of thought says that once the gut is healed (assuming that casein and gluten peptides are only escaping into the bloodstream due to GI tract damage), these foods can return to the diet in moderation. Others say it should be a lifelong project, as the sensitivities will not go away. Your best guideline is the results you get. If going casein- and/or gluten-free seems to help, and if regression or behavior problems occur when these proteins are added back to the diet, stick with the strict diet. Some people may want to use urine tests to determine whether the peptides have disappeared.

Lisa Lewis, the parent of a child with PDD-NOS, has written an excellent book on the topic of CF/GF diets and PDD called *Special Diets for Special Kids* (Future Horizons, 1998). She also maintains two Web sites (*http://members.aol.com/lisas156/index.htm* and *http://www.autismNDI.com/*). There is more information about CF/GF diets in books written for people with celiac disease. These individuals must also avoid gluten, and many eschew dairy foods as well.

Two other sites of interest are maintained by Don Wiss: the Gluten-Free Page (*http://www.panix.com/~donwiss/*) and the No Milk Page (*http://www.panix.com/~nomilk/*).

Anti-*Candida* diets

"Don't feed the yeast beast!" is the war cry of the anti-*Candida* dieter. If objective medical tests have shown that you or your child have a significant overgrowth of *Candida* yeast, you may want to adopt some dietary changes that will discourage the yeast from multiplying. Remember that some *Candida* yeast is normal. Overgrowth causes the most trouble for people with serious immune-system conditions, such as AIDS.

Fermented or moldy foods, yeasty foods, and sugars are the main items to be avoided. Fermented or moldy foods include cheese, alcohol, brine pickles, tempeh, soy sauce, vinegar, dried fruits, nut butters, honey, and others.

Yeasty foods include all glutenous grains and all yeasty products, including yeast-containing baked goods, brewer's yeast ("nutritional yeast"), and beer.

It's also suggested that citrus and acid fruits, such as grapefruit, oranges, lemons, limes, pineapple, and tomatoes, be avoided for the first month of an anti-*Candida* diet. In fact, many such diet plans are completely free of fruit. All of them are as sugar-free as possible. Finally, anti-*Candida* diets should contain plenty of roughage for fiber.

Most books on *Candida* overgrowth suggest starting with an allergy elimination/reintroduction diet, and then following a rotation diet. They often suggest paying attention to environmental sources of mold as well, such as damp basements, carpets, and old furnace filters.

Anti-*Candida* diets are gluten-free, and many people avoid dairy foods as well. For more information, see the many books available on *Candida albicans* or this *Candida* Web site (*http://www.panix.com/~candida/*).

Feingold diet

The Feingold diet, promoted by Dr. Ben Feingold in the '70s and '80s, gained prominence as a possible treatment for hyperactivity in children. Feingold recommended avoiding synthetic flavorings and food colors, certain preservatives, and sometimes other additives. Interestingly, many foods forbidden on the Feingold diet are those high in phenolic compounds.

The Feingold Association is a group formed to support families using the diet plan. Its useful *Pure Facts* newsletter lists commercial foods that meet (or do not meet) the restrictions. The Feingold Association also supports "The IA-USA Extended Feingold Program for Autism/PDD and Milk & Wheat Allergies," which combines the original plan with CF/GF restrictions. There is a membership charge to join this group, which can provide meal plans, food lists, information about doctors and nutritionists who support the diet, and contacts with other parents using the diet.

Clinical testing has not proven Dr. Feingold's claims true, but some parents have reported improvements. Generally speaking, the original Feingold diet did not carry any health risks. The autism/PDD diet plan was not available for free inspection at press time. If you want to know more about the Feingold diets, see the Feingold Association Web site (*http://www.feingold.org/indexx.html*).

Elimination/reintroduction diet for food allergies

Diets to detect and eliminate food allergies should be carried out under the aegis of an allergist or other knowledgeable physician. Most start patients out with an elimination diet, taking out all of the most common allergens: dairy products, eggs, all gluten-containing grains, corn, citrus fruits, bananas, nuts (especially peanuts), soy, and vegetables from the nightshade family (tomatoes, eggplant, potatoes, and peppers). Obviously, if you already know of or suspect an allergy to another food, this item should be eliminated as well. Most people stay on this very restricted diet for at least four weeks—some doctors recommend an elimination diet for as long as six months.

Next comes the reintroduction process: Reintroduce one previously eliminated food at a time. Eat it at every meal. If you suffer no ill effects, you aren't allergic to that food and it can be added back to the regular diet.

If you do seem to have an allergic reaction to a food, eliminate it again for several weeks and then reintroduce it once more. You may need to follow this last step several times to make sure you know which food is causing the possible allergic reaction or intolerance problem.

Rotation diet for food allergies

Once you have identified definite food allergies or food sensitivities, allergists usually recommend following a rotation diet. This plan requires that you eat different foods each day in a four-day period to decrease the likelihood of developing new allergies. People with mild food sensitivities may find that they can eventually tolerate foods that once caused them distress when they follow a rotation diet, but reintroducing these foods should be done very carefully.

The ketogenic diet

This diet plan is a nutritionist's nightmare: it includes almost no starches or sugars. Instead, you consume one gram of protein for every four grams of fat. The body is then forced to burn fat for energy, rather than carbohydrates, and it will produce waste products called ketones. The ketones somehow suppress seizure activity.

Obviously, this is not a healthy, balanced diet. It is used as a last-ditch effort to manage seizures that cannot be controlled with medication. Under no circumstances should this diet be tried on your own, without medical supervision. Not only is it potentially dangerous, it's pretty hard to make it appetizing. A medical center that specializes in epilepsy treatment should be able to provide guidance and expert nutritional advice if this option is recommended for you or your child.

Blood-type diet

For some reason, quite a few parents of autistic spectrum children have been intrigued with the "blood-type diet," as taken from the book *Eat Right 4 Your Type* (Putnam, 1997), by Dr. Peter J. D'Adamo, a naturopath. His diet for people with blood type O is gluten-free, the plan for blood type A is casein-free. The science behind it may be iffy, but if you're interested, Dr. D'Adamo has a Web site with additional information about his diet plan (*http://www.dadamo.com/*). If nothing else, this site features quite a bit of information about supermarket foods that fit these diet plans, as well as some recipes.

The "caveman" diet

Also called the hunter-gatherer diet, the Paleolithic diet, and other descriptive names, this one permits no foods introduced with the move to agriculture in the Neolithic period of human history. That means no grains, no gluten, no dairy, no beans or other legumes, no refined sugar, etc. Obviously, this diet is heavy on meat, fruits and vegetables, nuts, and oils made from seeds and nuts. The PaleoDiet Web site (*http://www.PaleoDiet.com/*) is a good resource if you're curious, and a number of popular books have been published on this topic.

By necessity this diet is casein- and gluten-free. It's probably a reasonably healthy choice, although many physicians counsel their patients to eat less meat these days. If the meat is lean and not treated with preservatives, and if you like it, why not, unless otherwise indicated? Potential benefits for people with PDDs would presumably be similar to those of the GF/CF option.

Immune-boosting diets

Many popular diet books claim that their particular regimen will boost your immune system function. Generally speaking, however, these claims have not been proven. A healthy, balanced diet should be sufficient for the average person.

But what about people with known or suspected immune-system dysfunction, including some people with PDDs? Immune-boosting claims have been made (and sometimes substantiated in limited clinical research) for a wide variety of foods, including red wine, tofu, miso (fermented soybean paste), kale, and yams. You might want to research some of these options and incorporate them into your diet plan. As long as these foods are eaten in moderation, they certainly can't hurt.

Allergy treatments

Allergies also have an impact on dietary choices. About 5 percent of all children have food allergies, but the rate of both food allergies and food sensitivities among people with autistic spectrum disorders appears to be higher. The most common causes of food allergy are milk, eggs, peanuts, soy, nuts, fish, and shellfish.

The most common tests for food allergies are the skin-prick test and the radioallergosorbent test (RAST). Of the two, the RAST is preferred for young children and anyone with eczema. It is also more specific, although the skin test may actually be more sensitive. The RAST is a blood test that measures the level of immunoglobulin E (IgE) antibodies to specific foods. If there are no IgE antibodies present in the blood, the person does not have food allergies.

Make sure your allergist knows what medications the patient takes before the RAST is administered. Antihistamines, steroids, and some other medicines can skew the results by inhibiting the inflammatory response.

The only sure treatment for food allergies is food avoidance. There are desensitization shots available for other types of allergens, such as pollens, but this therapy is only in its formative stages for food allergies. Some allergists are willing to try so-called neutralization shots or sublingual drops, also called low-dose immunotherapy. The efficacy of these is not proven, although some clinical trials have been very promising.

Severe allergic reactions are rare, but those at risk must be extra-careful about reading labels and should always carry an emergency kit. Your allergist can help you put this together. People who have both asthma and allergies have a higher risk of dangerous allergic reactions. Food sensitivity reactions can sometimes be cut short with a simple dose of baking soda, or commercial preparations containing bicarbonate of soda, such as Alka-Seltzer.

Allergies to food colorings and additives are relatively rare, although some people may have unusual (but not allergic per se) reactions to these substances.

Eye therapies

Do the eyes have it? Of all the areas that parents and patients may choose to investigate, eye-related procedures are among the most hotly contested. Little hard research has been done. Accordingly, you should assess claims carefully.

Irlen lenses

As noted in Chapter 5, the use of colored lenses like those developed by the Irlen Institute is highly controversial as a treatment for autism, although some patients and parents have reported benefits. Glasses with colored lenses are used to remediate visual perception problems (the Irlen people call it scotopic sensitivity). Many people with autism do report visual perceptual problems, such as tunnel vision, reliance on peripheral vision, or difficulty in telling foreground from background.

Vision therapy

Also called eye training, visual training, behavioral optometry, and a host of other names, vision therapy is delivered by some optometrists and ophthalmologists. Eye exercises, and sometimes prismatic lenses, are used to address obvious eye defects such as "lazy eye" and crossed eyes. Some practitioners use these same rehabilitative methods to treat visual processing deficits that may have behavioral consequences.

As mentioned in Chapter 5, some people with PDDs have reported a reduction in symptoms due to vision therapy. For more information, see the Children with Special Needs Web site (http://www.children-special-needs.org/) and the Center for the Study of Autism's visual training section (http://www.autism.org/visual.html).

Rapid eye therapy (RET)

With this therapy, the patient blinks rapidly to simulate the movements of the eye during REM sleep, while the practitioner moves a wand back and forth. According to RET believers (including Ranae Johnson, author of a memoir of life with her autistic son called *Winter's Flower*), this activity stimulates the limbic system, pituitary gland, and pineal gland. There does not seem to be any hard evidence for this therapy's efficacy in autistic spectrum disorders.

Iridology

Iridologists believe you can diagnose illnesses by looking at the irises of the eye. The eyes may be windows on the soul, but generally speaking, the irises alone can tell you nothing about autism. Despite persistent reports of parents taking their children to iridologists to find out about underlying conditions, there is currently no evidence that this procedure (or any therapy suggested by iridologists) is at all useful for autistic spectrum disorders.

Bodywork

The general label of "bodywork" applies to many types of therapeutic touch. When performed by a trained practitioner, none of the common bodywork methodologies listed here should be harmful. They can relax the patient, and may increase flexibility and range of movement. Some bodywork boosters make more extravagant claims for their work, such as neurological or even spiritual benefits. Don't accept such claims at face value—ask to see any studies that a practitioner refers to, and do your own research before choosing either a method or a practitioner.

- **Acupressure** is similar to acupuncture, which is discussed briefly at the beginning of this chapter. Instead of using needles, acupressure employs touch on specific sites on the body. The pressure may be light or firm. Like acupuncture, acupressure does have a track record in helping with chronic pain and some other disorders. Its efficacy for autistic symptoms is unknown.

- **Massage** comes in many forms, including Swedish, Shiatsu (which resembles acupressure in some ways), and more. It's relaxing and enjoyable, and one study at the University of Miami School of Medicine's Touch Research Institute showed that autistic toddlers who received a thirty-minute massage two times a week for five weeks showed social-ization and imitation improvement by objective measures, as compared with a control group of children who were held by a teacher while play-ing instead.[8]

- **The Feldenkrais method**, developed by Moshe Feldenkrais, concen-trates on rebuilding sensory and movement systems, particularly through unlearning poor movement patterns. A number of Feldenkrais practitioners work with children who have neurological problems, including autism. The therapy is gentle, and some children have experi-enced gross-motor, fine-motor, sensory, and relational improvement—as have some autistic-spectrum adults. A variant called Feldenkrais for Children with Neurological Disorders (FCND) is specially geared toward this population. FCND practitioners have had additional training. For more information, see the Movement Educators Web site (*http://www.movement-educators.com/children.html*).

- **Craniosacral therapy**, discussed earlier in this chapter along with oste-opathy, involves delicately manipulating the plates of the skull and the "cranial tides" of the body. Some may question the scientific basis of craniosacral work, but it is gentle, noninvasive, and has been reported as helpful by parents of many children with neurological problems, includ-ing autism. Adults with PDDs may also enjoy this approach. Most cran-iosacral therapists employ a certain amount of "talk therapy" along with the bodywork, which may or may not appeal to you. For more informa-tion, see the Craniosacral Therapy Web site (*http://www.craniosac-ral.co.uk/*).

- **The Alexander Technique** is used by practitioners to help patients streamline and increase the gracefulness of their movements. Patients try new, more balanced movement patterns. Since self-awareness is an important part of this approach, the Alexander Technique is probably more applicable to adults with PDDs (especially those who have signifi-cant problems with clumsiness) than to children. For more information, see the Alexander Technique Web site (*http://www.alexandertech-nique.com/*).

There are many other bodywork methods, but the five listed above are the ones you are most likely to hear about in relation to autistic spectrum disorders.

For any bodywork method, including those not mentioned here, be sure to check the practitioner's credentials and make sure you feel comfortable with both the person and the methodology. All of the modalities listed here have accrediting bodies in most Western countries. Generally speaking, accredited, well-trained practitioners are more likely to do beneficial work than self-trained or nonaccredited practitioners.

Parents of children with PDDs, partners of adults with PDDs, and practitioners of related disciplines such as occupational therapy and physical therapy may want to get some training in one of these methods themselves. If you happen to be near a massage school or a training center for another bodywork method, inexpensive classes may be available. Some schools also operate free or low-cost clinics that allow students to practice on live patients under close supervision.

Multifaceted approaches

There are so many possible alternative medicine approaches to treating PDD symptoms that it's hard to choose a starting point. As the story that opened this chapter indicates, most families and patients end up trying several different options.

For example, the Centre for the Study of Complimentary Medicine in Manchester, England, has a treatment protocol for autism that includes PST testing, and a low-salicylate diet if PST levels are low; herbal and homeopathic medications to repair problems in the GI tract and liver; probiotics; DMG; and vitamin supplements, among other interventions. The CSCM also recommends using applied behavior analysis, and pharmaceuticals are prescribed if indicated.

DAN!

The Defeat Autism Now! (DAN!) protocol ("Clinical Assessment Options for Children with Autism and Related Disorders: A Biomedical Approach," available from the Autism Research Institute) is similarly inclusive, with more than 40 pages of information about nonpharmaceutical treatments that participating doctors may choose from. DAN! doctors have attended at least one of the yearly DAN! conferences sponsored by ARI since 1995. They are not necessarily recommended or approved by ARI, however.

Each doctor using the DAN! protocol has his or her own biases and preferences. Some eschew pharmaceuticals entirely; others practice complimentary medicine, mixing both alternative and medical therapies. Some may simply be interested in the latest research, and continue to use primarily traditional treatments. For more information about DAN!, including a list of practitioners, see its Web site (*http://www.autism.com/ari/dan.html*).

Evaluating alternative interventions

Desperate to find something that works to ameliorate difficult symptoms, parents and adult patients tend to pile on the interventions. That makes it hard to tell when something really is working—or if it would work without interference from some other remedy!

To get the clearest picture possible of any alternative interventions, you must introduce them independent of each other, and independent of pharmaceuticals or therapeutic interventions. Obviously, this will often be impractical—you wouldn't stop speech therapy to see if DMG might help with speech, for example.

Barring the one-thing-at-a-time scenario, keep careful, *daily* records of supplements and dietary changes you introduce, when they are given and in what amounts, what brands you used, and any visible effects that you observe. If after four to six weeks you have not seen improvements with a supplement, it's unlikely that it will be of benefit. Dietary changes, bodywork, and other interventions may take much longer to bear fruit.

Remember that many parents report initial problems with supplements and dietary changes, and some children may be resistant to bodywork at first as well. Don't gloss over dangerous side effects, but expect to weather some behavior problems for a couple of weeks.

If you can convince your physician to make alternative therapies part of his prescription, you're in luck. Some actively oppose them, and that may force you to find a new doctor. Whatever you do, don't operate behind your doctor's back in any significant way. If you're philosophically incompatible, you should simply part ways—but you need a medical expert on your team.

CHAPTER 8

Insurance

AS THE PREVIOUS CHAPTERS HAVE MADE CLEAR, pervasive developmental disorders are not easily treated with medications alone. One-on-one therapeutic intervention, and often major lifestyle changes such as special diets, should be part of a well-rounded treatment plan. Treatment will be a long-term affair. Unfortunately for patients and their families, paying for this amount of healthcare is expensive. Insurance should help, as it does for other major medical expenses, but as we shall see, that's not always the case.

You don't have to have health insurance for this chapter to be useful. We'll cover private insurance, including HMOs and other forms of managed care, national health plans, and alternatives to health insurance as well. We'll describe typical insurance roadblocks and show you how to get around them. We'll begin by talking about health insurance in the US, but the systems of other English-speaking countries are also addressed.

An insurance company's perspective on PDDs

First, you need to know what you're up against. PacifiCare Health Systems, Inc., headquartered in Santa Ana, California, offers health plans in fourteen US states and on the island of Guam. As major US insurance companies go, it is fairly typical—not the worst, not the best. Dr. Ellen Betts, clinical supervisor for western region outpatient services for PacifiCare Behavioral Health, Inc., provided very clear insights into the way insurance companies and managed care entities look at PDDs.

"Because there is no recognized cure for pervasive developmental disorders, direct treatment is no longer included in the benefits," she says. "The qualifier is that we know there are some interventions that contribute to a higher quality of life. There are medications that are prescribed to help with symptoms, and we would reimburse a psychiatrist to help with some of the medication issues. We would not cover any kind of psychological testing to rule in or rule out a PDD. That's primarily because that kind of testing is usually available through the school system or regional centers." Most major insurers take a similar position, although a few will not fund any interventions at all.

Dr. Betts says she is aware that funding for school-based programs and regional centers has been cut back significantly in recent years. "It's become a gaping hole between [insurance companies and public resources], and an increasing societal problem," she observes.

After reading the last few chapters of this book, you're probably surprised to learn that insurance companies feel free to ignore the proven, long-term clinical track record of ABA, floor-time play therapy, and other interventions for PDDs—interventions with better success rates than many treatments for cancer and heart disease that are routinely covered by insurance. "Thus far, that is still not recognized per se by the insurance companies," says Betts, about ABA in particular. "They would probably put that in the category of 'experimental treatments.'"

PacifiCare does make long-term therapeutic services available for schizophrenia and other neurobiological disorders, however, including full and partial hospitalization programs. "The rationale behind that is that, with the proper medication and proper compliance, as well as whatever rehabilitation services are available, a person with schizophrenia could be a productive, tax-paying member of society," said Dr. Betts. "That's not applicable to pervasive developmental disorders."

It should be noted here that the prognosis for schizophrenia is not terribly different from that of PDDs: only one-fourth are expected to experience complete remission, while one-tenth will probably commit suicide. Of the remainder, most will continue through life with mild to moderate symptoms, while the rest struggle with severe, chronic schizophrenia. It should also be noted that a great many people with PDDs are "productive, tax-paying members of society"—some of whom are probably reading this book!

As for legislative efforts, Dr. Betts notes that when California legislators first proposed a state mental health parity law, autism was included in the list of covered diagnoses—but was later removed from the listed conditions to make the law more financially palatable. "I do think that with the mental health parity laws being passed state by state, it will have an exceedingly major impact on the industry," she adds.

Dr. Betts did have some pointers for parents whose children have a disability that their insurance company classifies as psychiatric or "behavioral." The most difficult companies to deal with will be those that have a "carve-out" for mental healthcare, she cautions. This means insurance companies and HMO-style plans that do not provide mental healthcare themselves, but instead refer patients to an outside provider. "When they outsource for mental health benefits, that imposes a risk for individuals with those diagnoses to fall between the cracks. You can end up in these protracted debates between the major medical carrier and the mental health carrier. When you have a totally integrated HMO, like Kaiser, you could have a very different experience," she adds. Neurobiological disorders like PDDs are a gray area, because they are medically based illnesses with psychiatric symptoms. Your insurer, your HMO, and any outside mental-health providers may argue with each other about what kind of care is needed, who should deliver it, and who will pay for it. Meanwhile, you may go without any care at all.

Dr. Betts says that, like most clinical specialists, she is well aware that doctors try to get around insurance restrictions by giving the patient an alternative primary diagnosis that is covered, and perhaps adding PDD-NOS or atypical PDD as the secondary or tertiary diagnosis. Then physicians can say they are actually treating the covered diagnosis.

One bright spot in insurance company practice is a move toward integrated case management, says Dr. Betts. PacifiCare, for example, is instituting a new program called the Assertive Case Management model. "Managed care entities are backing off on micromanagement of mental healthcare, and concentrating on severe mental illness," she says. "[Our] new clinical model will… take a holistic social services approach. That means coordinating care with child protective services, social welfare agencies, the school system, parents, clergy, social workers, and others." This model will include weekly contact between patient or parent and a permanent case manager.

Insurance companies show their feelings about autistic spectrum disorders in many ways. For example, PacifiCare's health education office does not have written material available for parents of children with autism or related disorders, nor does it provide educational materials for adult patients in this class, as it does for patients with Alzheimer's, breast cancer, and other conditions. This is the case with almost all major insurers and HMOs. Despite the increasing prevalence of these disorders, they haven't put much thought into how they might better respond, or how families can be supported with accurate and timely information.

When you choose an insurance company or HMO, do your best to assess its attitude toward PDDs in advance. You may be surprised at what you learn.

The coverage question

In the US and other countries where private medical insurance is the norm, the insurance system can be hard to deal with under the best of circumstances. Each company in the industry offers multiple plans with various rates and benefits, and there's no central oversight. And as Dr. Betts explained, patients with PDDs and their families are often hit with an unpleasant post-diagnostic surprise: many insurance plans specifically refuse to cover autism, pervasive developmental disorders, any mental or neurological disorder, or any condition they deem "developmental" or "incurable."

> *We do not have any insurance coverage. We are getting by with the bare minimum healthcare. Due to this situation we have never taken Nicole to a developmental specialist or neurologist, though we would like to.* —Robin, mother of five-year-old Nicole (diagnosed mild autism)

Others cover these conditions in a substandard way. For example, they may cover only short-term therapy programs. They may refuse coverage for necessary speech therapy, occupational therapy, or physical therapy. They may have no qualified "in-plan" practitioners but refuse to make outside referrals, or they may call PDD-NOS or atypical PDD a mental health issue rather than a medical problem, and limit coverage accordingly.

It's mostly about money, but to some extent it's also about outdated medical notions. Take, for example, the words developmental disorder. What this term really means is a medical condition that skews the process of normal child development. Doctors use it as a euphemism for mental retardation, and also to describe a wide variety of neurological, metabolic, and chromosomal disorders that emerge in childhood. Insurance companies, however, seem to think that developmental disorders are temporary conditions that the child will grow out of. Accordingly, this term is commonly found on lists of conditions excluded from coverage.

The idea that pervasive developmental disorders are incurable, and therefore not worthy of treatment, also persists, as Dr. Betts's comments made abundantly clear. If your insurance company tries this tactic, tell it that its position makes no sense, since the same standard is not applied to other conditions. For ammunition, you might ask the company what coverage is provided for children born with spina bifida. Spina bifida is a birth defect of the neural tube. It is incurable, but thanks to modern medical technology, children with spina bifida can now live long and productive lives. Most will need multiple operations and physical therapy, and many will need a wheelchair or other orthopedic equipment. Few insurance companies have the gall to refuse coverage for this incurable, but treatable, condition. Asthma, epilepsy, and diabetes are even more common conditions that are incurable, but treatable.

You can buttress your arguments by bringing copies or abstracts of pertinent medical studies, information from the National Institutes of Health or other official government sources, or books like this one with you when you argue your case for coverage.

PDDs are eminently treatable. There are many medically validated treatments available, including medications for specific symptoms, speech therapy, occupational therapy, ABA, floor-time play therapy, and in some cases nutritional or metabolic interventions. The success rate of early intervention using either ABA or floor-time techniques alone exceeds that of many medical treatments for other conditions that your insurance would probably cover without question. If you add more interventions to the picture, the chances of a good outcome will most likely be even brighter.

Treatment and the law

In the US, both case law and state legislation may support parents who say that treatment for autism and related disorders should be covered by their health insurance. For example, the 1988 case *Kunin v. Benefit Trust Life Insurance Co.*, which was settled in the federal court in California and later affirmed by the United States Court of Appeals for the Ninth Circuit, established that, because autism has organic causes, it is not a mental illness and so cannot be used as a basis for denying or limiting insurance benefits. Cases in other states have affirmed this conclusion in relation to other neurological disorders.

Christopher Angelo, a consumer and plaintiff's trial attorney with the Los Angeles firm Mazursky, Schwartz, and Angelo, is all too familiar with the insurance problems experienced by people with autistic spectrum disorders. Angelo is the father of an autistic son, and also the author of the Autism Society of America's booklet, *For Our Children: A Lawyer's Guide to Insurance Coverage and a Parent's Call to Organize.*

About 90 to 95 percent of insurance companies refuse outright to cover treatment for pervasive developmental disorders, according to Angelo, although most will cover the cost of the initial diagnosis. Their refusal is rarely legal, and never ethical, he adds. Parents need to know this and take steps to successfully appeal such blanket denials of care. Begin by asking for a copy of the denial of coverage or services in writing. Make sure that the reason you were given verbally is also the reason given in this written denial.

Your next stop is the insurance company's own documents. You'll need a copy of the health plan's master policy (See "Managing managed care," later in this chapter). Somewhere in its fine print you will probably find a provision stating that, if any of the company's policies are unenforceable based on state law, they cannot be asserted. Most insurance company claims adjusters know very little about state insurance law. Your job is to educate yourself, and then educate them.

Now you need to find out what your state says about pervasive developmental disorders and autism. The answer may be found in actual legislation. For example, Angelo notes, California's state legislature has specifically declared that as illnesses with organic causes, PDDs, bipolar disorder, schizophrenia, and many other "mental illnesses" are to be considered medical conditions under the law. Your state may have similar laws or public policies on the books, possibly within state mental health parity laws or in laws protecting the disabled against discrimination. Your state's insurance commission— every state has its own, there's no federal insurance commission—will also have policy statements. Remember, actual state law trumps policy statements every time. State laws may be more restrictive than federal regulations, in which case the state prevails. If state laws are less restrictive than federal mandates, the federal government prevails.

Your state's chapter of the Autism Society of America or other disability advocacy organizations may already have the information you need on hand. The ARC (Association of Retarded Citizens) is one of the largest and best-organized advocacy groups and may be able to help you right away. Nonprofit disability law services, some of which are listed in Appendix B, *Support and Advocacy*, are another good resource.

If no one seems to know the status of insurance law and PDDs in your state, you'll have to start researching on your own. If you have Internet access, state laws, some public policies, and possibly insurance commission decisions may be available online. You could also call your state representative's office and ask a staff member to research this issue for you. Insurance commission staff members should also be able to help you.

What you learn may be quite enlightening. For Angelo, research into applicable state laws led to a high-profile case, *Broughton v. CIGNA*. Angelo said he hopes this case will ensure that all US parents and patients have a right to appeal arbitrary and illegal healthcare restrictions in court. "If I continue to win Broughton, HMOs and insurance companies will have to change their practices not only statewide but nationwide," he said. The Broughton case, currently in litigation, may indeed yield the landmark decision that thwarted healthcare consumers have been waiting for.

Angelo's innovative case hinges on laws against discriminatory business practices that most US states adopted after civic unrest rocked several major cities in 1967. In California, this law is called the Consumer Legal Remedies Act. It prevents consumers from signing away their right to sue for relief in court when they are discriminated against by a business. Disability is a protected class under law, as are race, sex, and age. Many insurance companies say consumers can't force them to cover certain conditions, and push unhappy customers into internal appeals procedures and then arbitration instead of court. Under the Consumer Legal Remedies Act and similar state laws, this practice appears to be illegal.

If you can show your insurance company that it is trying to assert a provision that violates a state mandate, it should back down and provide treatment.

Legal arguments of the sort needed to secure coverage can be hard for a layperson to craft. Advocacy groups may be able to help you write a well-written and persuasive letter of appeal on legal grounds.

Incidentally, Angelo adds, formal arbitration is rarely a viable solution. "Arbitration is a stacked deck," he says. "Arbitrators on average get paid $400,000 per year by healthcare plans, which only continue to use those arbitrators on stipulation. If it gets one arbitration decision it doesn't like, it stops using that arbitrator." Consumers are also unable to recover their costs in arbitration, which can range upwards of $50,000. Most consumer-law cases in the courts are taken by lawyers who work on contingency, so it's hard to secure legal help for an arbitration.

The mental health exemption

If the company provides some treatment for PDDs, but only as part of a limited mental health or nervous disorders benefit, you can also challenge that limitation. It's easy to show that autistic spectrum disorders are biologically based, so you may be able to get out from under the mental health limit altogether.

One piece of information to gather in advance is how the company treats acquired nervous-system disorders, such as stroke, brain tumors, or traumatic brain injuries. If your insurance covers long-term care for these conditions, most states mandate equal benefits for patients with biologically based brain disorders.

Incidentally, a neurologist may be your best witness. Most people with PDDs have concrete signs of neurological dysfunction, which can't be written off as simply psychological. Some parents have successfully asserted that their child is the victim of an acquired brain disorder, based on the child having developed normally and then regressed; on a documented reaction to a vaccine, medication, or environmental toxin; or on the basis of tests that show anti-myelin antibodies or other substances in the blood.

And, as Angelo noted, some states specifically exempt PDDs from mental health limits.

The educational services exemption

After blanket denial of coverage, says Angelo, the second most frequent insurance roadblock is the educational services exclusion. "They'll say, 'We don't have to pay to teach your child how to speak, because that's education,'" he explains. "However, if a teacher wants to be a speech therapist, it requires a healthcare license in all fifty states, not just a teaching credential."

> I have insurance, but as of yet I have not been able to get coverage
> for any speech therapy. I am now spending approximately $250 a week
> [for a speech-centered home ABA program]. That does not include

anything that I purchase for her learning, that's just payroll. —Sarah, mother of two-year-old Elaine (diagnosed PDD-NOS)

Angelo encourages parents to work with their Early Intervention providers and school systems to force health insurers to pay for speech therapy, physical therapy, occupational therapy, home-and-hospital programs, and other services that must legally be delivered by healthcare professionals. He feels that schools should bill parents' health insurance for these services and sue if the insurer refuses to pay.

He notes that school districts, state healthcare programs, and the federal government are logical allies in the fight to force insurers to do their share. "When insurers won't pay, the consumer then goes to overworked, underfunded taxpayer programs, like Social Security Disability, Medicare, the schools, regional centers, etc., to try to get funding for speech, OT, recreational therapy, partial hospitalization programs, and more, all of which should have been covered by the healthcare system. As soon as healthcare companies realize that passing the buck wrongfully to school districts and other public programs will cost them, they will start training their claims adjusters in state law," he says.

For now, however, Angelo's last bit of advice may be problematic for parents. Only in the past two years or so have major school districts begun to attempt billing insurers for services provided in school settings. Many parents rightfully fear that denial of payment will lead to denial of services by the school district—it is illegal, but lack of funds is one of the most frequent excuses given for refusal of needed special education services. Parents who have been persistent enough to get therapeutic services from both the school district and their insurance company are afraid that their services will be cut in half, not augmented. And since schools and medical facilities generally have very different approaches to therapeutic interventions (see Chapter 6, *Therapeutic Interventions*, for more information on this topic), this could be detrimental in other ways.

You can sometimes challenge denial of therapeutic services by explaining that speech or other therapeutic goals are essential activities of everyday life, useful not only in school but for functioning in the larger world. This "essential activities of everyday life" rationale is what people with orthopedic disabilities use to get the therapies they need covered by insurance.

Getting coverage for new treatments

All insurance plans bar coverage for experimental treatments. Some do have a "compassionate care" exception, which comes into play when regular treatments have been tried unsuccessfully and the plan's medical advisors agree that the experimental treatment could be workable. This exception is generally available only to people with life-threatening illnesses.

So what do you do to pay for promising new treatments for PDDs, such as Secretin, IVIG, or auditory integration training? You either pay out of pocket or you work closely with your physician to get around the experimental treatment exclusion.

> The HMOs won't cover any experimental tests. I switched this year to a dual medical plan where we can go out of the HMO. The insurance will pay 70 percent and we pay 30 percent. This allowed us to get tests done we knew might help find a cause (titers, allergies, yeast), and we found a flexible out-of-plan MD.

> We are very frustrated with trying to find the right specialists and having to battle our son's primary care physician for a referral. —Joe, father of seven-year-old Kyle (diagnosed PDD-NOS with autistic features)

"Creative coding" is the term doctors use to describe billing the insurer or managed care entity for something that's not quite what was actually delivered. For example, an audiologist might be willing to bill for AIT, which the insurance company probably would not pay for, as something else that the insurer would pay for.

Creative coding is not exactly ethical, and it may not be desirable, either. Providers who do it take tremendous risks, and parents or patients for whom it is done must remember that they can't discuss these services with the rest of the healthcare team for fear of exposing the deception. That said, the practice seems to be increasingly common. It is not infrequently used to ensure treatment for people with PDDs by managed care companies or insurers that normally do not cover autistic spectrum disorders.

For immunological or GI-tract-related treatments, physicians may choose to bill their services as treatments for immune-system dysfunction, GI tract, or nutritional problems alone, with no mention of PDDs. Unlike creative coding, this probably will not get the physician in trouble if they have documented evidence of the conditions they are treating.

Your physician may have to prepare a "letter of medical necessity" to support your treatment request—or this task may fall to you. This letter must include:

- The diagnosis for which the service or equipment is needed

- The specific symptom or function that the service or equipment will treat or help

- A full description of the service or equipment and how it will help the patient

- If the service or equipment is new or experimental, supporting evidence (medical studies, journal articles, etc.)

- If there are less expensive or traditionally used alternatives to the new or experimental service or equipment, well-supported reasons that these alternatives are not appropriate for this patient

Make smart insurance choices

If you have more than one insurance plan to choose from, your best bet is a plan that has an out-of-network clause. These plans allow you choose your own providers if you can't find the right professional within the plan. You will generally pay more for these out-of-plan visits, but you won't have to run the referral gauntlet as often. As PacifiCare's Dr. Betts noted, integrated HMOs that offer both medical and mental healthcare may offer similar advantages to their customers, although not all customers agree.

> We had no insurance years ago, and I paid for some things out-of-pocket. Now I have him covered with Kaiser. It's a struggle to get them to care, to get to a specialist, to get them to take me seriously. I am trying to get chromosome studies and an MRI. It will be a challenge, I am sure.
> —Cindy, mother of fifteen-year-old Jeffrey (diagnosed verbal dyspraxia with "autistic-like" features)

If your employer does not offer insurance that covers speech therapy, mental healthcare, out-of-network providers, or other needed services, this is something that employees can take up with the human resources department (or, in small companies, the boss). When the cost is spread over a group, these additional benefits may not be very expensive.

Although many healthcare consumers think federal oversight might be the solution, so far federal law has done more harm than good. Many HMOs are protected from individual customers' lawsuits by federal law, although there are ways to get around this exemption.

Insurance for families or individuals affected by any long-term disability is very hard to get in the private market. It's available, but premium costs can be extraordinarily high. If you anticipate leaving a job that provides you with health insurance for one that does not, be sure to look into participating in a COBRA plan. (COBRA is the Consolidated Omnibus Budget Reconciliation Act of 1985.) COBRA plans allow you to continue your coverage after leaving employment. You will pay the full rate, including the contribution previously made by your employer, but it will still be less than what you'd pay as an individual customer.

Maintaining continuous coverage is critical to avoid being locked out of healthcare due to pre-existing conditions. If a COBRA plan is not available, other lower-cost possibilities include group plans offered by trade associations, unions, clubs, and other organizations. You may also want to look into public health insurance options, which are discussed later in this chapter.

Appendix A, *Resources*, lists several books and publications that can help you in your quest to secure insurance coverage and appropriate healthcare services for a person with a disability. For managed care issues, you may want to visit the Web site maintained by MCARE, the National Clearinghouse on Managed Care and Long-Term Supports and Services for People with Developmental Disabilities and Their Families (*http://www.mcare.net/*). The National Coalition of Mental Health Professionals and Consumers also maintains a useful site (*http://www.NoManagedCare.org/*).

The Mental Health Parity Act and you

The federal Mental Health Parity Act was passed with much fanfare in 1996 and went into effect at the beginning of 1998. Many people now believe that all insurance plans in the US must cover mental healthcare at the same level as they do physical healthcare. This is a misconception. This law affects only employer-sponsored group insurance plans that wish to offer mental health coverage. They are not required to do so. Additionally, if such coverage raises the company's premium cost by more than 1 percent, they need not comply with the law. Companies with fewer than 50 employees are also exempted.

The Mental Health Parity Act raises the annual or lifetime cap on mental healthcare in the plans that it covers, but it does not prevent insurance companies from limiting access or recovering costs in other ways. They may, for example, legally restrict the number of visits you can make to a mental health provider, raise the co-payment required for such visits, or raise your deductible for mental healthcare.

In 1997, twelve states—Arkansas, Colorado, Connecticut, Indiana, Maine, Maryland, Minnesota, New Hampshire, North Carolina, Rhode Island, Texas, and Vermont—passed their own, more restrictive, mental health parity laws. As noted previously, these laws supersede the federal regulations. Eleven other states have parity laws that are equal to the federal act, and others have less-restrictive parity laws. Of the twelve with tighter restrictions, all of the laws are written in ways that should require coverage for PDDs. Colorado, Connecticut, Maine, New Hampshire, Rhode Island, and Texas specifically require coverage for autistic spectrum disorders and other "biologically based" mental illnesses. For parents and patients living in these states, this is a step in the right direction, although it remains to be seen how these laws will be enforced and what steps some insurers may take to evade responsibility.

Managing managed care

Once you have health insurance, you will almost surely find yourself dealing with the dominant trend in medical care today: managed care. The managed care concept has some consumer-friendly components. In most health maintenance organizations (HMOs) and other managed care entities, providers and provider groups earn more if their patients stay healthy. An emphasis on preventive care and timely intervention can work to the benefit of many patients. Patients with long-term disabilities, however, may be perceived as obstacles in the way of profits.

There are four basic rules for managing your insurance affairs when you're dealing with an HMO or other managed care organization:

1. Make yourself knowledgeable
2. Document everything
3. Make your providers into allies
4. Appeal

Make yourself knowledgeable

Informed insurance consumers are a rarity. Most people look at the glossy plan brochure and the provider list, but unless something goes wrong, that's about as much as they want to know. If you or your child has a disability, however, that's not enough. As mentioned earlier in this chapter, you'll need a copy of the firm's master policy, the document that specifies what is and isn't covered.

To get this hefty document, call your employer's human resources office (for employer-provided insurance or COBRA plans administered by a former employer) or the insurance company's customer relations office (for health insurance that you buy directly from the insurer). Read it. It will be tough going, but the results will be worthwhile. If you need help interpreting this document, disability advocacy organizations and related sites on the Web can help.

Document everything

Keep copies of all your bills, reports, evaluations, test results, and other medical records. You'll also want to keep records of when and how your insurance payments were made. This information will be essential if a dispute with your healthcare provider or insurer arises.

You'll also need to document personal conversations and phone calls. You needn't tape-record these, although when a dispute is in progress this can be a good idea (make sure to let the other party know that you are recording, of course). Simply note the date and time of your call or chat, whom you spoke with, and what was said or decided.

Referral forms are especially important. Most managed care firms send a copy to both the patient and the provider. This document usually has a referral number on it. Be sure to bring your referral form when you first see a new provider. If the provider has not received his or her copy of the form, your copy and the referral number can ensure that you'll still be seen. Without it, you may be turned away.

Make your providers into allies

Money is a motivator for doctors and other healthcare providers, but most of them also care about helping their patients. Your providers are the most powerful allies you have. Give them information about PDD-NOS and atypical PDD, and make sure they know you or your child's case well. Let them know how important their help is. They have the power to write referrals, to recommend and approve treatments, and to advocate on your behalf within the managed care organization.

Don't rely on your providers completely, however. They have many patients, some of whose needs will likely take precedence over yours. A life-or-death emergency, a large caseload, or, in certain cases, a very important golf game may cause paperwork or meetings on your behalf to be overlooked temporarily or even forgotten. Another staff member, such as a nurse or office assistant, may be able to keep your provider on track, but you will have to be persistently involved as well. Make sure that you return calls, provide accurate information, and keep the provider's needs in mind. For example, if you have information about a new treatment that you want to give to your doctor, summarize it on one page, and attach the relevant studies or journal articles. The doctor can then quickly scan the basics in her office, and read the rest when time permits.

Appeal

Would you believe that 70 percent of insurance coverage and claims denials are never appealed? It's true. Most healthcare consumers are so discouraged by the initial denial that they don't pursue it further.

However, all insurance companies and managed care entities have an internal appeal process, and it is worth your while to be part of the persistent 30 percent. The appeals process should be explained in the master plan. If it is not, call the company's customer service office or your employer's human resources department for information.

A grievance or appeal is not the same thing as a complaint. Companies can ignore complaints at their leisure, as they do not require a legal response. Grievances and appeals do, and healthcare consumers are entitled to have matters presented in this way addressed. Grievances should be made in writing and clearly marked "grievance" at the top of the document.

When you file a formal grievance, the managed care entity will convene a grievance committee made up of people not involved in your problem. This committee will meet to consider the matter, usually within 30 days of receiving your written complaint. Particularly in HMOs, where the committee is usually made up mostly of physicians, your medical arguments may fall upon receptive ears.

It's unlikely that you will be personally present at an insurance company or HMO appeal. You can send written material to support your appeal, such as medical studies that support your position. It's best if your physician or care provider also writes a letter of support, explaining why he or she supports your request for a specific service.

Some companies have more than one level of grievance resolution, so if you are denied at first, ask if you can appeal the committee's decision to a higher body. You may have the right to appear in person at this higher-level hearing, to bring an outside representative (such as a disability advocate, outside medical expert, or healthcare lawyer), and to question the medical practitioners involved. In other words, if a second-level procedure is available, it will be more like a trial or arbitration hearing than an informal discussion.

If you are still denied, you may be able to pursue the matter with your state's Department of Health or Insurance Commission. If your managed care plan is part of a public insurance program (for example, if you receive state medical benefits and have been required to join an HMO to receive care), you may also have an appeals avenue through another state agency, such as your welfare office.

Semi-sneaky tips

Some people are better at managing managed care than others. The following suggestions may be a little shady, but they have worked for certain managed care customers:

- Subvert voicemail and phone queues. If you are continually routed into a voicemail system and your calls are never returned, or if you are left on hold forever, don't passively accept it. Start punching buttons when you are stuck in voicemail or on hold, in hope of reaching a real person. If you get an operator, ask for administration (claims and marketing never seem to have enough people to answer the phone). Nicely ask them to transfer you directly to an appropriate person who can help, not to the department in general. The old "Gosh, I just keep getting lost and cut off in your phone system" ploy may do the trick.

- Whenever you speak to someone at your HMO, especially if it's a claims representative, ask for her full name and direct phone line or phone extension. It makes the person feel more accountable for resolving your problem, because she knows you'll call her back directly.

- If you can't get help from a claims or customer service representative, ask for his supervisor. If you're told that he isn't available, get the supervisor's full name, direct phone line, and mailing address. Simply asking for this information sometimes makes missing supervisors magically appear.

- Use humor when you can. It defuses situations that are starting to get ugly, and humanizes you to distant healthcare company employees.

- Be ready to explain why your request is urgent, and to do so in terms that low-level employees can understand. For example, if receiving a certain treatment now could mean avoiding expensive hospitalization later, that's an argument that even junior assistant accountants can comprehend.

- Whatever you do, stay calm. If you yell at managed care people, they'll dismiss you as a loony. That doesn't mean being unemotional. Sometimes you can successfully make a personal appeal. You can act confused instead of angry when you are denied assistance for no good reason. You may also want to make it clear that you're gathering information in a way that indicates legal action—for instance, asking how to spell names and asking where official documents should be sent.

National healthcare

Some US families have even more serious health insurance problems: they just can't get any. If this ever-growing group includes you, publicly funded options include Medicaid, state programs for low-income residents or residents with disabilities, and county health programs.

Outside the US, universal publicly funded coverage is the norm in Canada, Australia, New Zealand, some Asian countries, and most of Europe—but that doesn't mean that treatment for PDDs is necessarily provided or provided well. Mental healthcare varies considerably based on location, access to specialists, and medical philosophy.

Government healthcare plans in the US

The US government does supply low-cost health insurance to some citizens through the Medicare and Medicaid programs. It also has healthcare plans for those in current military service (Tricare) and, through the Veterans Administration, for former military personnel. Some states have their own healthcare plans as well, including Hawaii and, to a lesser extent, Oregon. These plans make innovative use of budgets that combine state funding with federal Medicaid payments.

Medicaid

Medicaid is the federal insurance program for those who are not senior citizens. It will pay for doctor and hospital bills, six prescription medications per month, physical, occupational or speech therapy, and adaptive equipment. If you are old enough to receive regular Social Security, or if you receive Social Security survivor's benefits, you or your child should be eligible for healthcare benefits as well through Medicaid or, for seniors, Medicare. Some people on either Medicaid or a state plan will be asked to join a managed care group.

Disabled adults and children who qualify for Supplemental Security Income (SSI) also qualify for healthcare coverage via the federal Medicaid plan. SSI is normally available only to people with serious health impairments and either low family income (for children) or limited ability to earn a living (for adults). Chapter 11, *Finances*, explains more about applying for SSI, which is a special part of the Social Security program.

Too much family income may not always bar a disabled child from qualifying for SSI and Medicaid. In some cases, family income will reduce the amount of SSI received to as low as one dollar per month, but the beneficiary will get full medical coverage. Parents may need to apply for a "Katie Beckett waiver." Katie Beckett was a severely handicapped child whose parents wanted to care for her at home, but government regulations would only cover her care in an expensive hospital setting. Her family, which could not bear the full cost of at-home care but had an income too high to qualify for SSI, successfully lobbied for a program that would allow seriously handicapped children to qualify for Medicaid coverage.

Applying for a Katie Beckett waiver

The waiver program is administered at a state level. Some states have severely limited the number of Katie Beckett waivers they will allow. You must apply for SSI and be turned down to qualify. When you are denied SSI, ask for a written proof of denial. Next, contact your county Child and Family Services department and ask for a Medicaid worker. Schedule an appointment with this person to apply for a Katie Beckett waiver.

This appointment will be long, and the questions will be intrusive, so be prepared. You will need copious documentation, including:

- Your SSI rejection letter
- Your child's birth certificate and Social Security number
- Proof of income (check stubs, or a statement provided by Child and Family Services for your employer to sign, and possibly income tax forms)
- Names, addresses, and phone numbers of all physicians who have examined your child
- Bank account and safety deposit box numbers, and amounts in these accounts
- List of other assets and their value, including your house and car
- A DMA6 medical report and physician referral form signed by the doctor who knows your child best (CFS will provide you with these forms)

If you have a caseworker with your county's Developmental Disabilities or Mental Health offices, or if you regularly work with someone at a regional center or in an Early Intervention program, this person may be able to help you navigate the SSI, Medicaid, and Katie Beckett waiver process.

If you have specific problems with accessing appropriate medical benefits under Medicaid, Medicare, or allied state health plans, talk to a disability advocacy attorney or consult the Health Law Project (you can call them at (800) 274-3258).

The problem with Medicaid and state health plans

Coverage is a fine thing, but what happens when no one will accept you as a patient? This is the situation faced by millions of Americans who have government-provided healthcare. You may find yourself limited to over-crowded, understaffed, and possibly inadequate county health clinics or public hospitals, and to those providers willing to work for cut-rate fees. Medicaid and its cousins don't pay healthcare providers as much as private insurers do, and there's no law that says a given provider must take this type of insurance or similar payments from public agencies.

> We have no insurance. We are relying on Early Intervention and special education. We are supposed to be starting OT for sensory integration soon. The funding was approved three weeks ago, but the state agency cannot find a local provider that is willing to accept the rates that they are required to pay. He is only eligible for this funding source for another three months, so I hope and pray they will be able to get this started soon.
> —Jennifer, mother of three-year-old Joseph (diagnosis in progress, possible PDD-NOS)

You may also be disrespected by healthcare providers. For example, a few years ago only a single oral surgeon was willing to accept patients with Medi-Cal, the California state insurance plan for welfare recipients, in one particular county. This doctor would not give firm appointments to his Medi-Cal clients. Instead, they were forced to wait in his office until a private-pay patient failed to show up for an appointment. He was verbally abusive with Medi-Cal patients, and his work was so substandard that several patients filed injury claims. But if you had Medi-Cal in that county, he was the only game in town—and he knew it. Patients complained to their Medi-Cal caseworkers, but they had little recourse without another provider to go to instead.

Health Canada

In Canada, the Canada Health Act ensures coverage for all Canadian citizens and for noncitizens who need emergency care. Healthcare regulations are the same nationwide, although providers can be hard to find in the less-populated northern provinces.

To initiate an evaluation for PDD-NOS or atypical PDD, parents might go through the school system or talk to their child's pediatrician. Adults would first see their primary care physician. The pediatrician or family doctor would then make a referral to an appropriate specialist.

> Our family doctor referred us to a specialist pediatrician, who specialized in emotional problems in children. She assessed D'Arcy carefully and then referred us on to the area mental health clinic, where D'Arcy was seen by (and still sees) a psychiatrist. The psychiatrist arranged for necessary tests (EEG, CAT scan, MRI) and arranged for D'Arcy to meet regularly for about a year with a counseling psychologist. —Rae, mother of thirteen-year-old D'Arcy

A wide variety of specialists are available through the Canadian health system, which is called Health Canada/Santé Canada. Many of the best are affiliated with university hospitals. Waiting lists are a reality, but parents report that calls and letters (especially if they come from the pediatrician or family doctor as well as the patient or patient's family) can often open up opportunities quicker than usual.

If no qualified providers are available in rural areas, public assistance programs may be available to help a patient get expert care in the closest city. This help may include covering transportation costs, housing the patient (and a parent, if the patient is a child) during evaluation and treatment, and providing regular consultations later on with a pediatrician or family doctor who's closer to home. In practice, however, families faced with severe disabilities in rural Canada sometimes have great difficulty in obtaining adequate care.

Therapeutic services, such as speech therapy, may be delivered in a medical or school setting. There isn't much coordination between the school and healthcare systems, according to Canadian parents.

Parents also report that privatization and other changes are starting to limit their access to healthcare. Some families are starting to carry private insurance to ensure timely and frequent access to care providers.

Canadians in border areas may wish to consult with specialists in the US. Except in rare (and pre-approved) cases, these visits will not be covered by Health Canada.

ABA and similar intensive programs may, in some cases, be funded by Health Canada. These techniques are gaining in popularity, and trained practitioners are available in urban areas. Coordinating public funding for home delivery of such services can be a chore, but some families have succeeded.

National Health in the UK

The National Health system in Britain and Scotland has undergone tremendous upheaval over the past three decades. All services were once free to UK citizens, while private-pay physicians were strictly for the wealthy. Public services have since been sharply curtailed, and co-payments have been introduced. Nevertheless, services for people with autistic spectrum disorders are probably better now than they were in the past, when grim government boarding schools and then institutionalization were the norm.

Parents who want to have a child assessed for PDD-NOS or atypical PDD may begin with their health visitor, pediatrician, a psychiatrist or psychologist, a Child Development Centre, or a local or specialist child and family guidance clinic. Adult patients will probably want to access a specialist through their general practitioner (GP). Referrals to specialists are notoriously difficult to obtain, even for private-pay patients.

> It is very difficult for some parents to reach a specialist [due to] long waiting lists, not being able to get the referral in the first place, not knowing where the specialists are, etc. When the child does get a diagnosis, their GP is always informed of the outcome. —Denise Cunningham of the UK's National Autistic Society

The National Autistic Society (NAS) was set up precisely to help parents and adult patients navigate the National Health and educational system in the UK. It publishes excellent materials, runs more than 50 schools and care centers, and sponsors the NAS Network, which can help parents and patients obtain direct care and other services they need. Local autism societies are also active in bringing parents and adult patients together around healthcare issues.

Since healthcare practitioners are an important part of the Statement of Special Needs ("statementing") procedure for getting Early Intervention and special education services, it may be quite practical to pursue both a medical diagnosis and statementing at the same time.

ABA and other intensive programs are becoming more prevalent in the UK, although they are not normally available as in-home programs with public funding. Trained practitioners are likely to be available in urban areas. Some schools for autistic-spectrum children offer ABA-like interventions as part of their school programs. Social Services departments are responsible for helping parents with home needs and for creating a coordinated service plan.

Medicare in Australia

Medicare, the Australian health plan, pays 85 percent of all doctor's fees. It also qualifies Australian citizens for free treatment in any public hospital. Many general practitioners and pediatricians "bulk-bill": they charge the government directly for all of their patient visits and let the 15 percent co-payment slide. Specialists usually won't bulk-bill. Once a certain cost level has been reached, Medicare pays 100 percent of the bill.

Patients can see the physician of their choice without getting a preliminary referral, but many specialists have long waiting lists.

A number of programs have been set up to identify and help Australian children with developmental disabilities at an early age. Parents say that medical professionals are sometimes less than savvy about neurological disorders in general, but if you can make contact with one who is, services are available.

> If a child has really obvious problems, such as clear autistic behavior, lack of language, or a physical disability, this would possibly be picked up by the Infant Welfare Service (a free service where mothers can take their toddlers to be weighed, vaccinated, screened for hearing loss, etc). The Infant Welfare Centres are run by trained nurses who are supposed to guide and advise mothers during the first few years of their child's life. This service has been progressively cut back in recent years. Some of the

Centres are fantastic, others mediocre, even bad. It all depends on the nursing staff, really.

Less obvious problems would not be picked up at this level. The tendency would be for the nurse to reassure the mother that the child will "grow out of it," "is going through a stage," "all children follow somewhat different developmental trajectories," etc.

In the past, the government used to provide a free screening for all children at age four, and again at around age six. This would be conducted in kindergartens, some day-care centers, and in schools. This was mainly a medical screening, but basic developmental and behavioral differences were sometimes picked up at this stage. Nowadays the screening is no longer universal... either the parent or teacher/child-care worker has to request it. Many children who would benefit from intervention thus slip through the net.

In Australia, some pediatricians specialize in behavioral issues (the specialty of "ambulatory pediatrics"), and at the present time children with neurological issues end up being sent to one of these. Neurologists and psychiatrists are not involved in the care of children, except in cases of clear physical signs (e.g., epilepsy) or adolescent depression. —Kerry, *mother of twelve-year-old Kim*

Services such as speech therapy, occupational therapy, and physical therapy may be delivered at home, in a school, or in a clinical setting. Parents in rural areas may have difficulty getting access to qualified practitioners, although the emergency healthcare system for rural Australia is enviable. In some situations, parents or patients in very rural areas may be able to access professionals for advice or "virtual consultations" over the Internet, telephone, or even radio.

Some prescription medications are not covered by Medicaid, and there is a sliding-scale co-payment for those that are.

ABA and other intensive programs for people with PDDs are still fairly new in Australia, although US- or UK-trained providers may be available in major cities.

New Zealand

About 75 percent of all healthcare in New Zealand is publicly funded. Care is delivered through private physicians who accept payment from the public health system. Treatment at public hospitals is fully covered for all New Zealand citizens, and also for Australians and UK citizens living and working in New Zealand.

Healthcare and disability services are both provided through a central Health Authority, which has for the past few years been making special efforts to improve the delivery of mental health, child health, and minority-group care. To start an assessment for PDD-NOS or atypical PDD, parents or adult patients should first talk to their pediatrician or family physician about a specialist referral. Self-referral is also possible.

Urban patients may have access to group practices centered around Crown (public) hospitals, which often have excellent specialists. Maori patients may access healthcare and assessments through medical clinics centered around traditional *iwi* (tribal) structures if they prefer.

About 40 percent of the population in New Zealand carries private insurance, primarily for hospitalization or long-term geriatric care only. This insurance is helpful when you need elective surgery and want to avoid waiting lists at public hospitals. It is not needed or required to access speech therapy, occupational therapy, physical therapy, psychiatric care, or other direct health or disability services.

As in Australia, ABA and other intensive programs for people with PDDs are novel. Patients and their families complain that waiting lists for assessments and major medical treatments can be excessive. Until recently, patients on waiting lists were not given a firm date for their visits, and were expected to be available immediately should an opening occur. A more reliable booking system was instituted in 1998.

For patients in need of temporary or permanent residential care, volunteer organizations (particularly churches) are heavily involved in running long-term care facilities in New Zealand. These facilities are usually free of charge to the patient or family, although some are reimbursed by public health.

Privatization is a growing trend in New Zealand. Public hospitals and their allied clinics have been recreated as public-private corporations. However, the government still provides most of the funding and regulations for health-care.

Alternatives to insurance

No matter where you live, there are alternatives to expensive medical care. Those who don't have insurance, or whose insurance is inadequate, will want to investigate these resources.

In some cases, creative private-pay arrangements may be possible. Parents have traded services or products for care, and others have arranged payment plans or reduced fees based on financial need. The larger the provider, the more likely it is to have a system in place for providing income-based fees. Hospitals and major clinics may have social workers on staff who can help you make financial arrangements. On the other hand, small practices are more likely to agree to barter arrangements.

ABA and similar intensive programs can be delivered by parents themselves, perhaps with some paid help and some from volunteers. Special education students, ABA providers in training, and community volunteers can often be recruited to help with discrete trials for a few hours a week, giving parents time to rest or work.

> Our insurance refused to play for Rory's out of school speech and occupational therapy. We receive assistance from a United Way program, and some grant funds from the state Department of Mental Retardation. As far as medical tests, etc., the insurance was no problem. —Charlotte, mother of four-year-old Rory (diagnosed PDD-NOS)

Sources of free or low-cost healthcare or therapeutic services may include:

- Public health clinics, including school-based health clinics
- Public hospitals
- Hospitals and clinics run by religious or charitable orders, especially the Shriners Children's Hospitals
- Charitable institutions associated with religious denominations, such Catholic Charities, the Jewish Aid Society, or the Salvation Army
- Medical schools, and associated teaching hospitals and clinics
- Nursing schools

- College special education programs (for speech, OT, and PT)
- Scottish Rite fraternal order (for speech and hearing)
- Easter Seals
- United Cerebral Palsy
- Urban League
- United Way (an umbrella fund-raising organization for many programs, can often give referrals)
- Children's Home Society
- Grant programs, both public and private

In the UK, special resources outside of National Health include:

- National Autistic Society
- Aidis Trust (for augmentative communication assistance)
- Camphill Communities (a charitable rural residential program)
- Mind (the National Association for Mental Health)
- Community Trust associations for autism, particularly the Tarka Home Trust (for a complete list of these organizations, as well as local autism societies, see *http://www.caritasdata.co.uk/ind_c181.htm*)
- The New Masonic Samaritan Fund (for members and families of Masons)
- Samaritans and other charitable groups

Medical savings accounts

This is a new healthcare payment option in the US that may have benefits for some children and adults with PDDs. A medical savings account (MSA) allows families to put away a certain amount of money specifically for healthcare costs. This income will then be exempted from federal (and in some cases state) income taxes. Unused funds continue to gain tax-free interest. These accounts can be used to pay for insurance deductibles, co-payments, prescriptions, and medical services not covered by insurance.

Families faced with paying out-of-pocket for an expensive ABA program or an augmentative communication device might be able to use an MSA to reduce their expenses by an impressive percentage. You'll need to check the regulations of the specific MSA plan to see what expenses will qualify.

Changing the rules

Advocating for changes in the insurance system or your national healthcare system is a big job. Unless you want to make it your life mission, it's probably too big for any one patient or parent. But by working together—and by working with healthcare providers, most of whom are just as dismayed with the current state of medical care—individuals can accomplish a lot.

Advocacy organizations can be the point of contact between healthcare consumers, insurers, HMOs, and public health. The Autism Society of America does not do any direct outreach to insurance companies, according to development and public affairs coordinator Caroline Ketchum. "It's too big an undertaking, since each state has an insurance commissioner," she said. Effective action in the US will probably be at the state level. There's a need for education, for public advocacy, for legislative action, and even for legal action. Parents and patients can and should be involved in these efforts.

There's also a backlash brewing in the ranks of providers. For example, the Washington, D.C.-based American Psychological Association (APA) has filed suit against Aetna US Healthcare. Inc., and related managed care entities in California, alleging that the company engaged in false advertising when they claimed to offer "prompt, accessible mental health treatment services." The APA has further alleged that Aetna put hidden caps on its already limited mental health benefits, disregarded what practitioners had to say about medical treatment of their patients, and deliberately delayed referrals.

"Despite the managed care industry's argument to the contrary, it's typically the managed care company that determines and controls the treatment of patients, not the doctor," said Russ Newman, Ph.D., J.D., executive director for professional practice for the American Psychological Association, in an APA press release. "And the financial bottom line, not patient need, is usually the controlling factor."

All of us—parents, patients, and practitioners—want to see improvements in healthcare and in how it's delivered. By working closely with our allies in the public, private, and volunteer sectors, we can make it happen. Even insurance companies and managed care entities can be brought on board if they can be shown the positive benefit of better-functioning patients, who require less emergency care, less hospitalization, and fewer expensive medications. Alternative models for delivery of care are evolving, and with hard work these new systems can be both more humane and more cost-efficient.

CHAPTER 9

School

IN THE US, FEDERAL LAW MANDATES THAT ALL CHILDREN receive a free and appropriate education (FAPE), regardless of disability. That means providing, free of charge, special education programs, speech therapy, occupational therapy, physical therapy, psychiatric services, augmentative communication techniques and devices, and other interventions as needed to help the child learn. So why are families around the country angry about how their children with PDDs are being (mis)educated, pulling their children out of public schools in frustration or taking their local school district to court? Simply put, law and reality collide daily in the schoolhouse.

This chapter will offer the latest information about appropriate school placements for children with PDD-NOS or atypical PDD under the latest version of IDEA, the federal law governing special education. We'll present the voices of parents and students about classrooms that work. And for those faced with an inappropriate placement, we'll provide a primer on special education law, including appealing improper placement and service decisions on up to due process (the internal appeals system used by public schools) and/or the court system.

Lack of adequate funding, lack of information about educating children with autistic spectrum disorders, and many other factors are at work here, and these are certainly not unique to the US. School issues in the rest of the English-speaking world are covered separately in this chapter as well.

Early Intervention

The first educational placement for a young child with PDD-NOS or atypical PDD will usually be made through an Early Intervention program. EI service offerings vary widely. They should, however, be determined by the child's needs, not just what happens to be available or customary in your area.

The document that spells out these needs and the services that will be provided to meet them is the Individual Family Service Plan (IFSP), which should be based on comprehensive evaluation of the child (see Chapter 3, *Getting a Diagnosis*). This document should be created at an IFSP meeting, which you will be invited to attend and contribute to. Although it's a good idea for both parents and practitioners to write down their ideas for goals and interventions in advance, the IFSP itself should not be written in advance and simply handed to the parents to sign.

The first page of the IFSP is for basic information on the child and on the team members present at the IFSP meeting, including contact information for each of them. It also summarizes the services to be provided, who will provide them, how often they will be provided, and where they will be delivered. The details of these services will be entered on the pages for goals and objectives later in the IFSP. Accordingly, this section should not be filled in until the goals and objectives have been set. They will dictate which services and how much of them will be required for your child. Your cover page should be similar to the one shown in Figure 9-1.

One or more pages of the IFSP summarize the evaluation of your child. These pages should cover medical information, psychiatric diagnosis, and the results of hearing, vision, and developmental screening. This information is entered on forms similar to the one shown in Figure 9-2.

Finally, the IFSP lists specific goals and objectives for the EI team to meet, and explains how this will be done. These goals will be developed by the team at the IFSP meeting. You are part of this team. You can bring your own goals to IFSP meetings, and you should make sure that your ideas are taken seriously by the rest of the team.

There will usually be goals in the areas of cognition, fine- and gross-motor development, communication, social skills, and self-help skills. Chapter 4, *Getting Started*, lists many general goals that may give you some good ideas. Most of these are long-term goals.

It's good to keep these overall goals in mind as you develop the IFSP, but you'll want to break them down into small, manageable steps in the final document. For example, you might have the long-term goal "Billy will learn

Individual Family Service Plan (IFSP)

Child: _____ Birthdate: _____ Meeting Date: _____

Parent(s)/Guardian: _____ Home Phone: _____ Date Eligibility Established: _____

Work Phone: _____ Address: _____ Review Date: _____

Annual Review: _____

IFSP Coordinator/Agency: _____ Transition Plan? ☐ Yes ☐ No

Resident School District: _____ 12-Month Services? ☐ Yes ☐ No

Team Members in Attendance: Name/Role/Phone

_____

_____

_____

Team Members Not in Attendance: Name/Role/Phone

_____

_____

_____

Extent of participation with non-disabled peers: _____

Summary of Services

Service/Method	How Often?	Where?	Who Will Do This?	Who Will Pay?	Start Date	Stop Date

I (We) have had the opportunity to participate in the development of this IFSP. Signature(s): _____

Figure 9-1. An IFSP sample cover page

Current Developmental Information Summary

Child's Name: _____ Date: _____

Child's Strengths and Interests: _____

_____

_____

Sources of Information in Developing This IFSP: _____

Pertinent Medical Information: _____

_____

_____

Hearing Screening: _____

_____

_____

Vision Screening: _____

_____

_____

Present Skill Levels

Cognitive: _____

_____

Communication: _____

_____

Social: _____

_____

Fine Motor: _____

_____

Gross Motor: _____

_____

_____

Self-Care: _____

_____

_____

Figure 9-2. A current developmental information form

to say his name." To meet this goal, the team might put steps into the IFSP such as:

1. Billy will understand the concept of names.

2. Billy will associate his name with himself.

3. Billy will produce the sounds in his name.

4. Billy will say his name.

5. Billy will say his name when he sees a picture or mirror image of himself.

6. Billy will use his name in response to the question, "What is your name?"

Figure 9-3 shows a sample IFSP page for goals and objectives. Your EI program may use different forms, but they should include space for all of the items shown. Each goal item should include information on what services will be provided, how progress will be measured, and who will deliver the services needed.The IFSP can also include services needed by the whole family to help you care for your child. For example, these services might include parent education classes, the services of a behavior expert who can help you with home discipline problems, or assistance in finding and accessing community resources.

EI placements

Ideally, the IFSP will dictate the proper placement. EI placements commonly used for autistic spectrum children include:

- **Home-based services.** Programs in this category can range from sending an SLP or parent consultant into the home once a week to implementing a 40-hour-per-week applied behavior analysis program with extensive wrap-around services. For very young children with severe impairments, such as extreme sensory sensitivity, home-based services often make the most sense. Home-based programs may include direct therapeutic and educational services, training and supervision for parents and volunteers working with the child, and assistance with medical procedures and care needed to allow education to take place.

- **Direct services.** This category includes all types of professional services, such as speech therapy, occupational therapy, physical therapy, and psychological therapy, that are delivered independent of each other in a

Child's Goals and Objectives

Child: _____ Date: _____ Developmental Area: _____

What we want to happen (long-term goal): _____

Who will work on it? _____ Who will keep track of progress? _____

How We Will Do It (Short-Term Objectives and Criteria)	Evaluation Procedures and Schedule	Family Resources/ Other Resources	Start Date	Review	Annual Review

Figure 9-3. A sample IFSP page for goals and objectives

school (but not as part of a preschool program), clinic, or other setting outside the home. For example, the IFSP might specify that your child is to receive one hour of speech therapy three times per week at the university's speech clinic, or physical therapy for 45 minutes twice a week at a clinic. These services may be delivered by professionals or facilities under contract with Early Intervention, or by practitioners working directly for the EI program.

- **School-based services.** This category includes all services delivered as part of a public or private preschool program at the school site. Therapeutic services may be integrated into a special or typical preschool program, or may be delivered as pull-out services for which your child leaves the class for one-on-one or small-group work.

A primarily home-based program goes the furthest to build a strong relationship between the child and his parents, which will be the building block for all later social interactions. It takes place in a familiar, non-distracting environment that has probably already been made appropriate for the child's sensory needs. It eliminates lost time and problems related to transporting a preschool child to school (many EI programs actually bus infants and toddlers across town). It also provides the best stage for intensive, one-on-one intervention using applied behavior analysis, floor-time play therapy, and similar techniques.

It is also extraordinarily difficult to get approval for. One tool that may help you win this battle is a thorough and accurate financial appraisal that compares the cost of an intensive home-based program in the early years to twelve years of aide services, residential placement, or private placement.

Early Intervention classrooms

For many children with a diagnosis of PDD-NOS or atypical PDD, a preschool setting with other children is considered the best placement. That's because one of the hallmarks of these disorders is differences in how the patient relates to others, plays, and learns. Spending time with other children in a structured setting can be very beneficial for developing more age-appropriate social skills.

Of course, an autistic spectrum child should never simply be plopped down in a room full of screaming three-year-olds and left to fend for herself on the grounds that it's "therapeutic." Attention must be paid to your child's special needs, deficits, strengths, sensory issues, and so on.

EI preschools come in four major flavors:

- **Regular preschool classroom, with or without special support.** Also called a full integration setting or mainstreaming, this might be a Head Start or similar preschool classroom. Your child would attend preschool with therapeutic services, classroom adaptations, and personal support, such as an aide, as needed. These services, adaptations, and supports must be written into the IFSP.

- **Supported integrated preschool classroom.** Also called a reverse integration setting, because it's the nondisabled students who are integrated into a special program rather than the other way around. This is a specially created preschool setting that brings together a small group of children with disabilities and children without disabilities. Therapeutic services, classroom adaptations, and personal support are provided to each child with a disability according to his IFSP. Children in a supported integrated classroom may have a variety of different disabilities, such as developmental delay, Down's syndrome, or cerebral palsy. Often autistic spectrum children are placed with children who have various speech and language disabilities, such as cleft palate, stuttering, and apraxia. Some supported integrated classrooms mix only children with PDDs and normally developing children. In these cases, the severity of autistic behavior may range from severe to mild.

- **Special preschool classroom.** This is a specially created preschool setting for children with disabilities only. The children may have a mix of various disabilities, or all may be somewhere on the autistic spectrum. The classroom may be part of a larger school with other types of classrooms.

- **Special preschool.** This is an entire preschool program created specifically to work with children who have disabilities. It may be within a larger school program that also educates school-age children. It may be owned and run by a public school district, or it may be a private school that contracts with the Early Intervention program to provide services. If it is private, EI and/or the school district should pay the full cost of tuition if it is judged to be the most appropriate setting for your child.

There are positive aspects to each of these typical settings. For children who can handle full, supported inclusion in a regular preschool classroom, there are ample opportunities to model behavior and speech on that of typically developing peers.

Supported integrated classrooms offer similar benefits, with a daily program and structure that's more geared toward the child with special needs.

Special classrooms and schools generally have the most services, but provide few opportunities to interact with nondisabled peers. Your child's needs, abilities, and difficulties will dictate the right placement, as there is no workable one-size-fits-all approach. Here are some families' experiences with Early Intervention—and one student's fond memories:

> *Early Intervention has been a positive experience. I feel these people truly care, and I have been approached for additional services rather than having to ask for services.* —Shayna, mother of three-year-old Max (diagnosed multisystem developmental disorder)

· · · · ·

> *My son has had good Early Intervention services, which I feel is the key to his wonderful progress. He started school when he was three years old. It is a full-time program at a school for autistic children. It is a marvelous school, and it has benefited him enormously. They use the TEACCH program, and have a very good student-to-teacher ratio: about two students to one teacher. They have a very structured day.*
>
> *If I had a magic wand, I would create schools for autistic children in every city, and the education would continue through high school. I dread putting him in the public school system—he learns so differently.* —Sally, mother of four-year-old Dhylan (diagnosed PDD-NOS with autistic features)

· · · · ·

> *Max received very inappropriate center-based EI for a short period, upon which he started exhibiting self-injurious behavior [SIB] and was taken out. The SIB stopped right afterwards. Now he receives in-home, one-to-one Early Intervention and ABA services. The ABA is the most helpful of everything. He receives occupational therapy three times per week. This has effectively stopped feces smearing, and it helps with calming and balancing. Since movement gives him speech, it helps generally.*
>
> *In-home EI is only as good as the provider. Mine is marginal, but certainly better than the criminal-type behavior at the EI center.* —Holly, mother of three-year-old Max (diagnosed PDD-NOS)

· · · · ·

Danielle is in an integrated preschool; they are wonderful with her. She is inconsistent with everything, so finding the right teaching style is difficult, though. Still, she seems really content and happy with her life. —Lesley, mother of three-year-old Danielle (diagnosed PDD-NOS)

• • • • •

I liked the teachers and my friend Linneus at Rice School [site of his supported integrated Early Intervention preschool]. I learned my ABCs. I did the sand table and the water table. I loved the water table and I still do! I hated circle time, it was so boring. —Seven-year-old Ian (diagnosed PDD-NOS, Tourette syndrome, obsessive-compulsive disorder, ADHD)

The right placement will be indicated by the goals in your IFSP, and it can make a huge difference. Unfortunately, what many parents get from their school district is strictly an effort to fit their child into an existing program, with perhaps an offer to adapt the program slightly. Sometimes this approach works very well. Other times, it's absolutely inappropriate.

You may be told that only a few hours of preschool or a type of therapy are available to any child due to budget constraints, staff limitations, or other reasons. This information is incorrect. Legally, the only factor that should limit your child's access to services is her actual needs. If the EI program is having a hard time financially, it needs to find additional resources.

If a program is suggested that doesn't make sense to you given the goals and objectives in your child's IFSP, you can advocate for a better placement.

Jesse's "Early Intervention program" was putting him in preschool for two years. That was two half-days a week at first, then upgraded to four half-days a week. While his teacher and the aides were wonderful, I really felt that he needed more time and was not given it. This year looks to be the same, with the exception that he will now be in school five half-days a week. —Dorthy, mother of five-year-old Jesse (diagnosed PDD-NOS with autistic tendencies, ADHD)

• • • • •

Although Joseph is now receiving a very good program, it took over nine months of fighting to get it, and now Early Intervention is almost over. The providers didn't seem to know what to do with my son because he didn't fit any of their preconceived categories. They also did not want to provide anywhere near the level of intensity that he needed. For example, speech therapy was only provided after we filed for a due process hearing. On a more positive note, he has gone from single words to three- to four-word communicative sentences in just over three months of therapy. But I do wonder how much more he would be talking if he had nine months of intensive therapy behind him instead of only three. —Jennifer, mother of three-year-old Joseph (diagnosis in progress, possible PDD-NOS)

As explained in the sections on ABA and floor-time play therapy in Chapter 6, *Therapeutic Interventions*, intensive intervention is the key to helping children with autistic spectrum disorders reach their full potential. What the EI program won't offer, you'll have to do on your own, while advocating at the same time for a more appropriate level of public services. It's a tough balancing act.

Other educational settings for young children

A fourth type of setting, the diagnostic classroom, may be a joint project of the school system and a regional center or medical facility. These classrooms are used for long-term medical or psychiatric observation and evaluation of children whose behavior and abilities don't seem to fit the profile of any typical diagnosis. This is not a permanent placement, but if your child's case is especially unusual, she may stay in the diagnostic classroom for quite some time.

A very few young children with PDD-NOS or atypical PDD will be placed in a day treatment or residential setting. Day treatment centers are generally for children with very difficult behaviors (such as SIB or aggression toward other children), or coexisting psychiatric or medical problems, that make even a self-contained classroom inappropriate at this time. Good day treatment centers provide medical and psychiatric support, specially trained staff, a very secure environment, and intensive intervention. However, very few day treatment centers have experience working with young autistic spectrum children—most have until recently specialized in school-age children, and in the treatment of behavior disorders. At the end of the school day, children in day treatment go home to their families.

Residential schools offer educational programming and 24-hour care for the child. For obvious reasons, residential schools are rarely considered as a placement for a preschool child. The very few exceptions are children with very severe health or behavior problems whose parents are unable or unwilling to care for them at home, and those who cannot obtain services in any other setting—for example, an isolated family living in rural Alaska, where school-age children are generally either home-schooled or sent to boarding schools.

If the issue is the family itself rather than the family's location, as in cases of abuse, neglect, or abandonment, child services authorities will generally pursue a long-term placement in therapeutic foster care. These are homes where the foster parents have been trained to work with children who have special needs (in some states, a college degree in social work, psychiatry, special education, or a related discipline is required in addition to the foster care agency's own training program) and are willing to provide full-time, family-style care for these children. In some cases, parental rights will be terminated and the child will be placed for adoption.

Therapeutic foster homes are also an option for families who are simply unable to handle the stress of caring for a child with PDDs—for example, a teenage single parent, a parent with mental illness, mental retardation, or physical disability, a parent who is currently homeless or in recovery for substance abuse, or a family that already has many children or that already has one or more children with a serious disability. Most counties try to help these types of families with home-based services, but sometimes placement in a therapeutic foster home is a good option. In these cases, the foster parents and birth parents will work as a team to meet the child's personal and educational needs, with eventual family reunification as another goal. Permanent placement would generally not be part of the plan.

Monitoring progress in EI

Most IFSPs are fairly lengthy, with two or more pages of goals. That can make monitoring progress hard for parents and teachers alike. It's important to talk informally as often as you can, rather than waiting three months or longer for a formal review to take place. Your child may meet some goals quickly, and these sections should be revised right away. Other goals may seem impossible to reach. These goals may need to be broken up into even smaller steps, or the team may need to come up with different teaching methods.

Using a communications notebook or daily report form works well for many families. A communications notebook can be a spiral-bound notebook or notepad that goes to and from school every day with the child. Both teachers and parents can write notes in this notebook. For example, you might let the teacher know that Jennie slept poorly last night and ran a slight fever. The teacher might let you know that Jennie did very well in speech today, is working on naming colors, and had a normal temperature when the school nurse checked it at noon.

Both problems and successes should be written into the notebook. Too often, communications notebooks are used as gripe books, and parents get the inaccurate idea that their children are performing poorly overall instead of just in certain areas. Parents also may forget to let teachers know about successes at home that could have an impact on the classroom, such as the emergence of new words or skills.

All of your child's goals and objectives will be revised as needed at IFSP review meetings. These are held at least once during the school year. If you think one is needed sooner, you can call the team together yourself.

If your child is in a residential setting, you may need to designate someone else to be your compliance monitor. A caseworker from the local Early Intervention program's staff, or someone from the county's Child Services, Developmental Delay, or Mental Health department, may be able to take on this responsibility. Some parents have chosen to pay an independent advocate. Of course, you should still get regular reports by mail or telephone and attend meetings in person with the staff and your child whenever possible.

Transition from EI to school

Children in Early Intervention are transitioned into the district's special education program around three years of age, although in some areas the transition comes when they are judged ready to enter kindergarten (if available) or first grade. At this time, your child will be reevaluated—this time for special education eligibility (see Chapter 3). This eligibility determination is made by a committee of specialists in most areas, which may be called the multidisciplinary team (M-team), eligibility committee, child study team, or a similar name. You should have input during the eligibility process.

The eligibility team will decide if your child has a condition that qualifies him for special education. Exact language differs between states, but typical qualifying categories include:

- Autism
- Hearing impaired (deafness)
- Visually impaired
- Both hearing impaired and visually impaired (deaf-blindness)
- Speech and language impaired
- Mentally retarded/developmentally delayed
- Multihandicapped
- Severely orthopedically impaired
- Other health impaired (OHI)
- Seriously emotionally disturbed (SED)
- Severely and profoundly disabled
- Specific learning disability
- Traumatic brain injury

Check your state's special education regulations for the list of labels used in your state.

The condition that causes the most impairment in school-related activities will usually be called the primary handicapping condition, and any others that coexist with it will be called secondary handicapping conditions. For example, a child might be considered eligible for special education under the primary condition deaf/blind, with autism as a secondary criterion. In this case, the child would also qualify under the term multihandicapped, if available.

Although the eligibility committee will take your child's medical diagnosis and the opinions of Early Intervention evaluators into account, these categories are defined by the school district or state Department of Education in terms of education, not medicine. If your child has a medical diagnosis from a psychiatrist, neurologist, or other physician of PDD-NOS, atypical PDD, atypical autism, or even autistic disorder, the committee can still decide that your child does not meet the educational definition of autism. This means that the committee feels your child does not need special services to take advantage of educational opportunities.

In fact, one of the stickiest educational issues related to PDDs involves the label "autism." Children with an educational diagnosis of autism, no matter how "high functioning" they may be, are automatically entitled to special education services, but children labeled as having related disorders may not be entitled to the same level of services, no matter how impaired they are. That's not to say that districts are giving autistic students enough help, either—in fact, court battles are underway in almost every state over unavailable, inadequate, or even harmful special education services.

You have a right to appeal the eligibility team's decision about the autism label or any other issue. If its decision prevents your child from receiving special education eligibility or needed services, you should do so. It is helpful to prepare a list of ways your child's neurological problems affect his ability to be educated without the added help of special education services.

Other categories under which a child with PDD-NOS or atypical PDD may qualify for services are:

- Speech and language impaired, if speech is delayed or unusual
- Other health impaired, if the child has a known autoimmune condition that contributes to autistic symptoms, or has a co-diagnosis of obsessive-compulsive disorder, Tourette syndrome, or ADD/ADHD
- Developmentally delayed
- Traumatic brain injury, if the child's autistic symptoms are known to be due to infection or injury to the brain
- Seriously emotionally disturbed (SED), especially if the child has a co-diagnosis of depression, bipolar disorder, etc.

Using the SED label on autistic spectrum kids is controversial, and obviously not proper. However, in certain school districts it is used as a label of convenience to obtain special placements, such as day treatment or residential slots, that are not available without it.

You may still receive some services through an Early Intervention program while your child is under an IEP with the school district. For example, US regional centers supply many parents of older children with special supplies, including diapers and nutritional items, and may be a source for respite care providers.

Special education

The special education evaluation forms the basis of a document that will soon become your close companion: your child's individualized education plan (IEP). Like the IFSP used in Early Intervention programs, the IEP describes your child's strengths and weaknesses, sets out goals and objectives, and details how these can be met within the context of the school system. Unlike the IFSP, the IEP is almost entirely about what will happen within school walls. There will be little information about services from outside programs or parents, unless the IEP team agrees to include it.

The IEP is created in a meeting of the IEP team, which has a minimum of three members: a representative of the school district, a teacher, and a parent. The district may send more than one representative. If your child has more than one teacher, or if direct service providers such as her speech therapist would like to attend, they can all be present. If it is your child's first IEP and first assessment, one team member is required by federal law to have experience with and knowledge of the child's suspected or known disabilities. You may want to check this person's credentials in advance. The "autism specialists" employed by some school districts can have as little as one college course on the topic of autism, or even no qualifications other than the title itself.

Both parents are encouraged to participate in the IEP process. Parents can also bring anyone else they would like: grandparents or other relatives, a friend, an after-school caretaker, a disability advocate, or a lawyer, for example. The child himself can also be at the IEP meeting if the parents would like—however, it's a good idea to bring a sitter with a young child to avoid disruptions. You want to be able to give the IEP process your full attention, and that's hard if you're also trying to keep a child out of trouble.

Districts are trying to involve middle school and high school students in the IEP process more often, and this is probably a good trend. You may want to discuss the meeting with your child and elicit her suggestions in advance. Some adolescents prefer to write up their suggestions rather than (or in addition to) attending the meeting. As with young children, be sure someone is available to take care of your child if she tends to be disruptive, or that you've brought a book or game in case the meeting gets boring. It's not beneficial to force an unwilling child to take part in the meeting.

Usually the IEP meeting is held at a school or a district office. However, you can request another location for the meeting if it is necessary—for example, if your child is on homebound instruction or has severe behavior problems that make caring for him impossible away from the controlled environment of home at this time. The meeting date and time should also be convenient to you (and, of course, to the other team members).

Your first IEP meeting should begin with a presentation of your child's strengths and weaknesses. This may be merely a form listing test scores and milestones, or it can include verbal reports of observations by team members—including you. You can use this time to tell the team a little more about your child, her likes and dislikes, her abilities, and the worries that have brought you all together for this meeting. Even if you're repeating information that the team members already know, this kind of storytelling humanizes your child and yourself. You'll want to keep it brief, though, so you may want to use a short outline and even practice in advance. Five or ten minutes seems about right, although you may find that you need more time. If you can keep your written description to one or two pages, that would be good.

This kind of information may also be entered on an evaluation or record summary form.

The meat of the IEP is the cover sheet, usually called the accommodations page, and the goals and objectives pages. Your district may have its own bureaucratic names for these pages, such as a "G3" or an "eval sheet." If team members start throwing around terms you don't understand, be sure to speak up! If the wrong forms are filled out or if important paperwork is left undone, you may not have an acceptable IEP at the end of the meeting.

Parents tend to focus on the goals and objectives pages, and often overlook the accommodations page. That's a *big* mistake. The goals and objectives are all about what your child will do, and if they are not accomplished, there's no one who can be truly held accountable but your child. The accommodations page, however, is about what the school district will do: what services it will provide or pay for, what kind of classroom setting your child will be in, and any other special education help that the district promises to provide. This is where really important promises are made. Figure 9-4 shows a sample accommodations page.

Student's Name: _____ Birthdate: _____ Grade: _____ PPS ID#: _____

Home School: _____ Attending School: _____ IEP Meeting Date: _____

IEP Manager: _____ Position: _____ Projected Review Date: _____

Specially Designed Instruction

	Service Time	Date of Initiation	Anticipated Duration
☐ Adapted PE	___	___	___
☐ Independent Living	___	___	___
☐ Language Arts	___	___	___
☐ Mathematics	___	___	___
☐ Motor	___	___	___
☐ Recreation/Leisure	___	___	___
☐ Self Management	___	___	___
☐ Social/Behavioral	___	___	___
☐ Speech/Language	___	___	___
☐ Vocational/Career Ed	___	___	___

Related Services Necessary

	Service Time	Date of Initiation	Anticipated Duration
☐ Audiology	___	___	___
☐ Counseling/Interv.	___	___	___
☐ Health Care	___	___	___
☐ Occ. Therapy	___	___	___
☐ Physical Therapy	___	___	___
☐ Transportation	___	___	___
☐ _____	___	___	___
☐ _____	___	___	___
☐ _____	___	___	___
☐ _____	___	___	___
☐ _____	___	___	___

Regular PE ☐ Yes ☐ No

Attends Home School ☐ Yes ☐ No
If no, explain: _____

Extent of participation in general education classes/activities: _____

Modifications and/or supplementary aids and services: _____

High School Students Only

Projected Diploma: ☐ Standard

☐ Modified ☐ Certificate

Credits earned to date: _____

Passed PALT/GST:

Math ☐ Yes ☐ No

Reading ☐ Yes ☐ No

Pre-Requirement Completed ☐ Yes ☐ No

Individual Transition Plan Completed/Updated ☐ Yes ☐ No

Social Security Number: _____

Participants in Individualized Education Program

Parent/Guardian/Surrogate: _____

_____

Teacher: _____

District Representative: _____

Student: _____

Other: _____

Other: _____

Figure 9-4. A sample accommodations page

Accommodations that your child may need include:

- Specific type of classroom
- Other specific types of environments, such as the availability of a "resource room" for certain subjects, mainstreaming for certain subjects, or an area for time-outs or self-calming
- Changes to the classroom environment to accommodate your child's sensory difficulties
- Specific learning materials or methods
- A personal educational assistant, aide, or "shadow"—not a monitoring aide who simply helps with behavior control, but an inclusion or instructional aide
- Therapeutic services and their frequency
- Adaptive communications equipment or procedures
- Other classroom equipment needed to help your child learn, such as a microphone or sound field system to help the child with auditory processing problems, a slanted work surface, or pencils with an orthopedic grip

The accommodations page should not already be filled out when the IEP meeting begins, as the goals and objectives should dictate what accommodations will be needed. Beware: Saying that your child will do something costs the district nothing, but promising that the district will do something has a price tag attached. Be prepared to hear phrases like "I don't want to commit the district to that" over and over—and to methodically show that the accommodations you're asking for are the only way the goals and objectives the team has set can be met. With few exceptions, district representatives see their role in the IEP as being the gatekeeper. This role may be interpreted as spending as little money as possible, or ensuring that children are matched with services that meet their needs, depending on the person, the district, and the situation. Most district representatives struggle to balance these two goals. As your child's advocate, your job is to persuade the representative to tip the scales in your child's favor.

As with the IFSP, you'll be working backward when you fill out the goals and objectives pages. You'll begin with big goals—"Katie will learn how to read," for example—and break them down into developmentally appropriate steps that can be accomplished in the classroom. The classroom teacher(s) and direct service providers should be the experts at this task. Often each of these team members will send or bring a list of goals and objectives already broken down for the whole IEP team to discuss. This saves a lot of time, and allows everyone to concentrate on the pros and cons of their ideas rather than having to actually come up with the ideas themselves at the meeting. You may choose to meet one-on-one with these team members to talk over IEP ideas before the big meeting.

As in an IFSP, there may be goals in the areas of cognition (problem-solving and pre-academic skills, such as knowing the names of colors), fine- and gross-motor development, communication, social skills, and self-help skills. There will also be academic goals. Chapter 4 lists many general goals that may give you some good ideas. Most of these are long-term goals. They will be detailed on a form similar to the one shown in Figure 9-5.

Academic goals

Academic goals are often the center of controversy in an IEP meeting. Schools do not want to guarantee that a student will learn certain material; in many cases, they don't even want to promise that they'll try to teach it. And if an autistic spectrum child happens to have certain academic skills that are close to being age-appropriate, appropriate for his age, or even superior, it is very hard to have anything written into the IEP about maintaining or developing these skills further. Special education services are about addressing deficits, say the educators. (One exception to this rule is the state of Massachusetts, which has regulations requiring school districts to "maximize the potential" of disabled students.)

Parents, however, know from experience that whatever gifts or islands of competence their child may have are essential to his well-being and educational success. The child who can read well but does not speak needs to continue to develop that reading skill, as it may be his only mode of communication for now. The child with a special gift for mathematics may be offering the teacher a way to impart other lessons, from the rules of grammar to the rules of playground basketball. Parents and experienced, caring teachers can often show the rest of the team why IEP goals based on strengths can be as important as those based on deficits.

Generally speaking, children in special education programs should be educated to the same standards as all other students whenever that is possible.

Individualized Education Program Goals and Objectives

Page: _____ of: _____

Student's Name: _____ ID Number: _____ Date: _____

Home School: _____ Attending School: _____ Grade: _____ Birthdate:____

Skill Area: _____

Present Level of Educational Performance (including test data, remedial areas, etc.): _____

_____

_____

Annual Goal: _____

√ If Objective Carried Over	Short-Term Objectives	Criteria	Evaluation Procedure(s)	Schedules

Figure 9-5. A sample IEP goals and objectives page

They should also work with the same curriculum and objectives. For example, if third graders in your district are normally required to present a ten-minute oral report about state history, a child with a severe speech impairment that prevents an oral report from being fully understood should be allowed to present a visual report, to have her written report read out loud by a helper, or to use an augmentative communication device to deliver the report. A child with mild mental retardation might present an oral report with a simpler format or shorter length, according to his abilities.

As a parent, you'll want to talk to your child's teacher about the academic curriculum in use in your child's school and in the district itself. Make sure that your child is being instructed in the skills, concepts, and facts needed to proceed in school.

In some states, children are required to meet certain benchmark standards to move on to the next grade level or to complete high school. High school diplomas are discussed further in the section "Graduation," later in this chapter, but you may be able to include a provision in your child's IEP regarding how any standardized achievement tests of this type will be handled. This may range from exempting the child from the testing requirement to insisting that the school provide extra academic help and/or test-taking accommodations to allow the student her best chance of doing well on the test.

Social opportunities

Another area that is often left out of IEP plans is opportunities for socialization and enrichment (see the section "Social skills training," later in the chapter). Again, you may be told that this is not part of special education. Because the primary deficit in autistic spectrum disorders is precisely in the area of socialization, however, this is emphatically *not* true where your child is concerned. The best place for children to learn appropriate social skills is in supervised activities with peers, and most schools make a plethora of these available to their students.

> At my school now I would like to have play time always. I wish they had a Greek myths club after school. I am going to start going to Cub Scouts soon. —Seven-year-old Ian (diagnosed PDD-NOS, Tourette syndrome, obsessive-compulsive disorder, ADHD)

• • • • •

An after-school program has been wonderful for Miles. He loves science, and they really stress sciences in this program. It has helped him with socialization also. —Ann, mother of seven-year-old Miles (diagnosed PDD-NOS and ADHD)

In fact, under the Americans with Disabilities Act (ADA), all children with disabilities have the right to be involved in all school activities and clubs, not just classroom-based educational activities. This includes band, chess club, chorus, sports, camping trips, field trips, and any other activities of interest to your child that are school-sponsored or school-affiliated. If your child will need accommodations or support to take advantage of these activities, the IEP is where these should be listed. If you do not have an IEP, a 504 plan (see later in this chapter) can be used.

Socialization opportunities may also be through nonaffiliated community programs. You can write support for these activities in the IEP as well.

Signing the IEP... or not

When the IEP is complete, the accommodations page will include a list of each promise, information about where and when it will be met, and the name of the person responsible for delivering or ensuring the delivery of the service or accommodation. If the complete IEP is acceptable to everyone present, this is probably also where all team members will sign on the dotted line.

You do not have to sign the IEP if it is not acceptable. This fact can't be emphasized enough! If the meeting has ended and you don't feel comfortable with the IEP as it is, you have the right to take home the current document and think about it (or discuss it with your spouse or an advocate) before you sign. You also have the right to set another IEP meeting, and another, and another, until it is truly complete. Don't hinder the process unnecessarily, of course, but also don't let yourself be steamrolled by the district. The IEP is about your child's needs, not the district's needs.

Needless to say, you should never sign a blank or unfinished IEP: it's a bit like signing a blank check. Certain school districts ask IEP meeting participants to sign an approval sheet before even talking about the IEP. Others are in the habit of taking notes for a prospective IEP and asking parents to sign an approval form at the end of the meeting, even though the goals, objectives, and accommodations have not been entered on an actual IEP form.

This is not okay. If they insist that you sign a piece of paper, make sure to add next to your name that you are signing because you were present, but that you have not agreed to a final document.

If your child already has an IEP in place from the previous year, this IEP will stay in place until the new one is finalized and signed. If your child does not, you may need to come to a partial agreement with the district while the IEP is worked out.

If the process has become contentious, be sure to bring an advocate to the next meeting. A good advocate can help smooth out the bumps in the IEP process while preserving your child's access to a free and appropriate education.

Classrooms that work

There are as many educational techniques and settings that work for kids with PDD-NOS or atypical PDD as there are children with these diagnoses. There are some settings that have a marked record of success, however, and that parents would love to see replicated.

Some characteristics of a successful classroom include:

- Caring, informed personnel
- Adequate ratio of children to classroom personnel
- Good rapport between classroom personnel, specialists, and parents
- Availability of appropriate teaching materials
- Individualized educational programming for each child with a disability
- Opportunities for interaction between children with PDDs and their normally developing peers
- Consideration for the sensory differences of autistic spectrum individuals

Most of these items take more time than money, and they can be implemented in a variety of settings. Two factors govern the choice of setting: the most appropriate educational program and the least restrictive environment (LRE). Typical special education settings include, in order of their restrictiveness:

- **Regular classroom, with or without special support.** Also called a full integration setting or mainstreaming, this is a regular classroom with nondisabled students. Your child would attend school with therapeutic services, classroom adaptations, and personal support, such as an aide, as needed. These services, adaptations, and supports must be written into the IEP.

- **Supported integrated classroom.** Also called a reverse integration setting because the nondisabled students are being integrated into a special program rather than the other way around. This is a specially created school setting that brings together a group of children with disabilities and children without disabilities. Therapeutic services, classroom adaptations, and personal support are provided to each child with a disability better according to his IEP. Children in a supported integrated classroom may have a variety of disabilities, such as developmental delay, Down's syndrome, or cerebral palsy. Often autistic spectrum children are placed with children who have different speech and language disabilities, such as cleft palate, stuttering, and apraxia. Some supported integrated classrooms exist that mix only children with PDDs and normally developing children. In these cases, the level of autistic behavior may range from severe to mild.

- **Special school classroom.** This is a specially created school setting for children with disabilities only. The children may have a mix of various disabilities, or all may be somewhere on the autistic spectrum. The classroom may be part of a larger school with other types of classrooms. Most districts have a range of classrooms available. There may be life skills classes geared toward teaching children toileting, speech, and movement; classes for students with communications disorders; classes for children with behavior problems; and classes for students who are primarily developmentally delayed. It matters less what the class is called than what the teacher's philosophy and practices are.

- **Special school.** This is an entire school program created specifically to work with children who have disabilities. It may be owned and run by a public school district, or it may be a private school that contracts with the school district to provide services. If it is private, the school district should pay the full cost of tuition if it is judged to be the most appropriate setting for your child.

- **Home-based program.** Home-based programs are, as the name implies, delivered entirely or almost entirely in the student's home. Tutors approved by the district use appropriate curriculum to meet the IEP's requirements. Therapeutic services may be delivered in the home, or the student may travel to a clinical or school setting if possible and appropriate. For some older students on home instruction, tutors may choose to meet and work with their charges in a public library or another especially resource-rich location.

- **Hospital-based or residential care setting.** For special education students who are hospitalized or who have been placed in residential care for any reason, delivery of a free and appropriate public education according to their IEP is still mandatory.

In between these options are combination settings created to meet a student's specific needs. For example, a student with PDD-NOS and severe anxiety might be able to handle a half-day full inclusion program in the morning, then have home-based instruction for other subjects in the afternoon. Another child might be placed in a special class for everything but art and music classes, which he would attend with normally developing peers.

Each child's needs are different, and they will likely change as your child progresses through school. The setting(s) listed in your child's IEP will be reviewed every year (or more often at your request) to ensure that the educational program is still meeting his needs and that he is still in the least restrictive setting. Whenever possible, the current movement in US schools is toward full inclusion. This may or may not be appropriate for your child. If a less restrictive setting is proposed by the district, be open-minded enough to check it out, but don't say yes unless you're sure it's right. Inquire about supports, such as personal or classroom aides, that can be added to make inclusive settings more realistic.

Here are the experiences of several families in finding an appropriate setting for their school-aged children:

> *Kyle was home-schooled this year using a modified Options Method program. We had our volunteers go from 10:00 to 2:00, so it was hard on my wife, who had to work with him all the other hours. —Joe, father of seven-year-old Kyle (diagnosed PDD-NOS with autistic features, language disorder, ADHD)*

· · · · ·

Ian spent the last year and a half in a private day treatment program paid for by the school district. At first, we thought it would be awful because it was geared strictly toward SED kids. They had never had a child like Ian before. We had to work hard to ensure that his needs were met, but we had a cooperative, caring, wonderful teacher who went out of her way for him. We also had an excellent speech therapist, although there was no equipment for OT, PT, or adaptive physical education. The program was far from perfect due to high staff turnover and other factors, but since Ian was a "runner," the high security level was essential. It gave him a chance to stabilize after a horrible experience in a public-school "behavioral" kindergarten, get a real diagnosis, and go through some difficult medication trials in a safe environment.

· · · · ·

My son attends a regular elementary school and has been mainstreamed in the past with only reading and math in special education. However, due to problems last school year he will be in a self-contained special education class receiving all classes with a private tutor who has been hired exclusively for him. —Ann, mother of eight-year-old Theron (diagnosed PDD-NOS, psychotic disorder, borderline intellectual functioning)

· · · · ·

Doug goes to a regular elementary school, but is placed in a special life skills classroom. We are currently using the TEACCH method, and it's working very well with Doug. Also, the speech teacher started to introduce the PICS system to Doug at the end of the school year, and plans to continue with that when school starts again. —Debbie, mother of eleven-year-old Doug (diagnosed PDD with fragile X syndrome and sensory integration disorder)

· · · · ·

Mainstream "full inclusion" type classes with the promise of modification and support were a disaster. Confined, modified environments (special day class with one teacher and an aide, one room, small class size) worked best. —Cindy, mother of fifteen-year-old Jeffrey (diagnosed verbal dyspraxia with "autistic-like" features)

· · · · ·

*Brad attends a regular, K–5 elementary school. The small group
approach works best with Brad. The ideal situation would be for him to be
home-schooled, due to distractions at school. If he is in a crowded classroom, he will zone out due to sensory overload.*

*I would say that as far as teaching styles go, it is best for Brad's
teacher to be strict and extremely structured. He is doing better than ever,
because his teacher is having the kids sit down at their desks and do their
work quietly. The disorganization of center-based learning, where a child
learns with others at, let's say, a reading or math center, was disastrous.*
—Kim, *mother of seven-year-old Brad (diagnosed Landau-Kleffner syndrome)*

The TEACCH method

TEACCH (*http://www.unc.edu/depts/teacch/*) stands for Treatment and Education of Autistic and Related Communication Handicapped CHildren. Developed by Eric Schopler in the early 1970s, it's a special system for educating
autistic spectrum children that was developed at the School of Psychiatry at
the University of North Carolina in Chapel Hill. It has since been adopted
whole or adapted for use, by schools around the country. It is a highly structured program that integrates individualized classroom methods, services
delivered by outside community organizations, and support services for
families.

The part of the TEACCH program most frequently implemented outside of
North Carolina is structured teaching. This approach hinges on careful classroom design, scheduling, and the use of predictable teaching methods in a
systematic way.

TEACCH has contributed many logical, workable ideas to the knowledge
base on educating people with autism. Nevertheless, it sometimes comes in
for criticism. The antipathy between adherents of the ABA approach and
TEACCH fans sometimes reaches a violently angry level. Certain TEACCH
people have accused ABA proponents of forcing people with PDDs to fit into
a "normal" mold against their will, and of creating robotic rote thinkers with
their repetitive drills. For their own part, ABA fans have accused TEACCH of
having low expectations for autistic people and allowing school districts to
base their programming on price rather than effectiveness.

The truth probably lies in neither camp. Certain personalities involved on
both sides have allowed their personal differences to become a vendetta,

which certainly doesn't serve children. It would be far more logical to look at these approaches, and all other educational methods, in relationship to each child with a pervasive developmental disorder. TEACCH methods, ABA, a combination of the two, or neither may be the best approach for a specific child.

General classroom tips

When education majors are instructed in pedagogical technique, they're given this classroom model: control, curriculum, motivation, setting.

In other words, a good teacher starts by maintaining control of the classroom, develops and/or provides an appropriate curriculum, motivates her students to do the work, and ensures that they have a good environment to do it in—in that order.

Autistic spectrum children's needs can turn this whole paradigm on its head. They often will be uncontrollable unless the setting is correct, they won't pay attention to the curriculum unless properly motivated, and the curriculum itself (along with setting and motivation) is the key to maintaining control.

It can take a while for teachers to figure this out, especially teachers in newly integrated classrooms who have never had a student with PDD-NOS or atypical PDD before. In the meantime, chaos ensues and everyone will probably blame the child, the IEP, or the parents. See if your district can provide a regular consult service from a teacher experienced in working with autistic spectrum children. This person can observe the situation, then give the frazzled teacher some good ideas for turning it around.

One area where parents, teachers, and students can work closely together is developing a system for classwork and homework. Options range from using a single notebook with sections for each subject to color-coded schemes. Students with PDDs benefit greatly from homework checklists and other visual memory aids, including checklists broken down to show when parts of a long project, such as a book report, should be completed. They may need verbal reminders and increased oversight as well to successfully complete and turn in assignments.

Social skills training

In the effort to tackle basic skills and then academic skills, social skills are sometimes left in the lurch. Schools are the primary social venue for children, but many schools are unsure how to fit social skills into their curriculum. Community organizations that convey the social graces to "normal" children, such as Scouting and religious youth groups, may be unprepared to deal with a child whose social skills are far behind his peers. And even children who interact well with their siblings may not be able to carry these skills over easily to socializing with unfamiliar children and adults.

Not surprisingly, many children and adults with PDDs find themselves ostracized due to barbaric manners, inability to tackle the back-and-forth of playground conversation, and difficulty in reading common social cues. It's not their fault—these skills do not come naturally to people on the autistic spectrum, and parents are usually so busy teaching other essentials that messy eating habits and such are the least of their worries. But for the person without positive social skills, true inclusion in the workplace and community will be elusive.

Note to adults with PDDs: Some people might be surprised to learn that many adults with PDDs are avid readers of books about etiquette, protocol, and body language. These books spell out the things that everyone else seems to know. Others take courses in psychology or anthropology, or tackle self-help books that promise to teach readers how to be successful in work, life, and love. Depending on the book or course, this can be a good approach for many adults.

Some systems have pitfalls, however: one adult we know took up neurolinguistic programming (NLP), which promises to teach practitioners the secrets of influencing others through verbal and nonverbal communication. Communication had always been difficult for him, and he often felt that he was ineffective and misunderstood. Although he progressed through his courses well, his acquaintances found his efforts to be rather transparent and, ultimately, manipulative. As always, *caveat emptor*!

There are many skill areas to work on, including:

- Maintaining appropriate eye contact
- Maintaining appropriate body space
- Developing a sense of empathy for others
- Giving and receiving complements
- Sharing interests and other strategies for making friends

- Decoding facial expressions and body language
- Using facial expressions and body language
- Learning conversational techniques, including openers and closers
- Determining whether a topic is appropriate for discussion
- Learning table manners
- Understanding rules for community activities, such as riding the bus or going to a movie
- Understanding dating and sexual etiquette
- Learning grooming techniques and expectations
- Interacting with authority figures
- Using observation to determine appropriate behavior, dress, and manners in a new social situation

Developing and using self-calming techniques can be one of the most important social skills your child will ever learn. These techniques help your child develop a self-righting mechanism of sorts, preventing embarrassing meltdowns that lead to ostracism.

Many schools are implementing variations on the theme of friendship clubs or social-skills clubs. These are small, adult-supervised groups of children brought together to help one or more children in the group learn appropriate social behavior. The adult—and eventually the other children—acts as a social-skills coach.

One of the best mechanisms for teaching appropriate social behavior is the use of social stories, a special kind of storytelling originally developed by educator Carol Gray. Social stories provide the child with a narrative about events that are going to happen or that should happen. They are short, easy to remember, and can be told over and over to help the child internalize what's expected. Here's a sample of a social story:

James Is a Good Bus Rider

When James gets ready for school in the morning, he has his coat and backpack ready before the school bus arrives.

When the bus comes, he gives his mom a hug and gets on the bus right away.

James sits in the seat right behind the driver as soon as he gets on the bus. He puts on his seat belt. Then he puts his backpack on his lap.

Sometimes James talks to his friends when he is riding the bus. They talk quietly.

Sometimes James draws pictures or looks at a book while he is riding the bus. He makes sure that his paper, crayons, and books are in his backpack when the bus gets to school.

If someone bothers James on the bus, he can ask the bus driver for help.

When the bus gets to school, James is the first to get off the bus. He waits with Mr. Smith until all of the children have gotten off the bus, and then they walk to class in a line.

You'll notice that the story is about all the good things that James does, or should do, on the bus. It isn't a list of "don'ts," no matter how tempting it might be to add a line like "James doesn't hit or bite the other children on the bus."

"Sometimes" lines like the ones in the example above can be very important for autistic spectrum children, who have a tendency to get stuck in very specific routines. These lines introduce and emphasize the idea of flexibility: sometimes we do X, and sometimes we do Y.

Some parents and teachers like to set social stories to music, which can make them even easier to remember. Others have made them into picture books with illustrations or photographs. For example, James might be asked to act out his bus social story while a teacher or parent takes some instant photos. Then the book can be written out one line to a page, with an illustration for each line.

Thick paper and lamination can be used to protect social stories that children want to carry with them.

Social stories can work well for people of all ages, even teenagers and adults.

Social-skills work may actually be harder today than it was 50 years ago, despite everything we've learned about behavior and human development. The rules of society are in flux everywhere, and children may not see the lessons of the home or classroom reinforced in everyday life. For children who tend to take rules very seriously, this can make life quite difficult. The playground may be full of inappropriate language and behavior, diners at fast-food restaurants wolf their food down sloppily as though no one is looking, rudeness abounds on the television, and the freeway is full of drivers who break the rules.

Interestingly, school district officials often comment that the most well-behaved children they meet when visiting schools are in the special education classes, where standards are explicitly spelled out and enforced for all students.

Monitoring progress

Once you have an educational program in place, your next job is playing spy and enforcer. You can't rely totally on the school or the school district to monitor your child's progress or to ensure compliance with his IEP. Keep a copy of this document and other important notes at hand, and check them against any communications notebooks, progress reports, report cards, or other information that comes home from the school or that your child tells you about activities, therapies, and results.

Of course you'll want to attend all official meetings, but make a point of just dropping by occasionally on the pretext of bringing your child her coat or having paperwork due at the school office. If you can volunteer an hour a week or so in the school (not necessarily in your child's classroom), even better.

If the school is not complying with the IEP, start by talking to the teacher and work your way up. Most compliance problems can be addressed at the classroom level.

One area that can be especially difficult is monitoring the delivery of therapeutic services. It seems like a relatively simple task, but parents across the country report that their school district refuses to provide any type of checklist that parents can see to make sure their child is receiving the services listed in the IEP. If your child is verbal, just ask. If she isn't, that should clinch your need for this essential information.

Another problem area is the administration of medication at school. Some parents have reported refusal to deliver medication at the appointed time, mysteriously missing pills (especially Ritalin and other amphetamines), and missed or mistaken doses. Most self-contained classrooms have many children who take scheduled medications, and they tend to have processes in place. The worst medication problems seem to occur in full inclusion settings, especially if the student is not capable of monitoring medication delivery himself. You may need to insist on a daily checklist, and increase your own monitoring efforts.

If your IEP includes academic goals, see if there are standardized ways to monitor progress. Too often parents are told that their child is participating well and learning, and then discover that he has not gained new skills or has actually regressed when an objective measure is used.

Be sure to praise your child's teacher and service providers when your child makes progress, even if it's small. People who feel appreciated work harder. Besides, we need to encourage the good guys!

Extended school year services

If your child needs to have a consistent educational and therapeutic program year round, most school districts will only provide services during summer vacations and other long breaks if you can document his need for extended school year (ESY) services. This requires special attention to monitoring how your child copes with breaks in the school routine. Teachers and service providers can help you amass the evidence you need to show that your child loses skills or regresses behaviorally after being out of school for more than a weekend. During breaks from school, keep your own log of behaviors and regressions, if any.

Some parents have also been able to qualify their children for ESY services by showing that services available during the summer satisfy parts of the IEP not addressed adequately during the school year. For example, a student might be able to get ESY funding approved for a special summer program geared toward teaching social skills or independent living skills to autistic spectrum individuals.

Dealing with behavioral dilemmas

Due to recent episodes of violence, many US schools are taking a hard line on verbal threats, aggressive or assaultive behavior, and even on the presence of students with behavioral, emotional, or neurological disorders in schools. In some cases, this campaign has crossed over from prudent caution to violating the rights of special education students. For example, some districts have announced that all assaults (a category that includes hitting, biting, and even playground pushing) will result in police being called to actually arrest the student. Students have been suspended or threatened with expulsion for angrily saying things like "I wish this school would burn down" or even for singing that traditional student song that begins with the line "Mine eyes have seen the glory of the burning of the school," which has probably been part of American childhood folklore for 100 years.

According to IDEA, students with disabilities are subject to discipline for infractions of school rules just like all other students—unless the problem is a result of the disability. For example, it would be unfair to suspend a child with Tourette syndrome for having a spitting tic, even though spitting would normally be a rule violation. Likewise, it would be wrong to expel or arrest a student for biting a classroom aide if his assaultive behaviors were related to a pervasive developmental disorder.

At the same time, schools do have a duty to protect other students, faculty, and staff. Case law has upheld the idea that if a student cannot be safely maintained in a less restrictive setting, the district has the right to place the student in a more restrictive setting. The devil is in the details, of course. Parents in these situations find they carry the burden of proving that the district did not do all it could to keep the student in the least restrictive setting.

If you or the school suspects that your child's misbehavior is the result of her disability, a functional behavior assessment (FBA) and a functional intervention plan (FIP) are the correct response. The FBA should include:

- A clear description of the problem behavior, including the pattern or sequence of behavior observed

- Time and place when the behavior occurs (setting and antecedents)

- The current consequences attached to the behavior

- A hypothesis about the cause and effect of the behavior

- Direct observation data

The FIP should derive from the FBA and consist of guidelines for modifying the student's environment to eliminate or improve behavior, as well as ideas for teaching the student positive alternative behavior. Creating a workable FIP may require trying several hypotheses about the behavior and then testing different interventions. This procedure should be followed whenever a special education student has a long-lasting behavior problem or has any behavior problem that puts him in danger of suspension, expulsion, or arrest.

For example, in the situation cited earlier where a child has a spitting tic, the FIP could include several ideas for handling the problem. The child could go to the bathroom to spit, use a trash can, or spit into a handkerchief. Adults could see if stress is leading to increased ticcing and then reduce stress or try a different medication for tic reduction. For the child who bites, the FBA could be used to find out why the child is doing so, and the FIP could provide ways to prevent the behavior.

Suspension and expulsion

If a student covered by an IEP is suspended for more than ten days in one school year or is expelled, the district is responsible for finding an appropriate alternative educational setting immediately and continuing to implement the IEP. Suspension of a disabled student for more than ten days requires parental permission or a court order. The district is also required to do an FBA and create a FIP if this has not already been done, or to take a new look at the existing FIP in light of the incident.

Suspensions of longer than ten days constitute a change of placement, and that means that an IEP meeting must be called immediately. IDEA does not spell out exactly how this procedure should work, so districts may not have a plan in place to deal with these emergency placements. Parents have reported that many school districts respond by putting the student on home-bound instruction until a new placement can be found. This may or may not be acceptable. Delivery of therapeutic services may be a problem on home-bound instruction. Parents will probably have to get involved to prevent the search process from dragging on too long.

For the purpose of these protections, the category of disabled students includes not only those with a special education IEP or other formal agreement with the district, but also those students whose parents have requested special education assessment or written a letter of concern about the child to school personnel (if the parent is illiterate or cannot write, a verbal inquiry will suffice) before the incident occurred, students whose behavior and performance should have indicated a disability to any objective observer, and children about whom district personnel have expressed concern before the incident.

Expulsion is an even more serious matter. Parents must be informed in writing about the district's intention to seek expulsion, and this document must include clear reasons for this action, evidence, and information about the child's procedural rights. There must be an assessment before expulsion can take place, and parents must also be informed of this in writing. Only if all safeguards are provided and all procedures are followed can a disabled student be expelled.

And expulsion for a disabled student does not mean the same thing as it does for a garden-variety miscreant, who may simply be kicked out to rot in front of the TV at home. It's more like a forced change of placement. By expelling the student, the district has determined that the current placement is not working. It must then find an appropriate placement, which means revisiting the IEP.

504 plans

Some children with PDD-NOS or atypical PDD may not qualify for special education services, based on the district's evaluation. You should probably appeal the evaluation, but while you wait for the appeals process to move forward, your child is still eligible for some special services under Section 504 of the Rehabilitation Act of 1973. These services and accommodations are written into a document colloquially known as a 504 plan.

In fact, some special education advocates recommend that parents request a 504 evaluation at the same time they start the IEP process. This can mean asking the 504 coordinator to attend your IEP meetings. It may confuse your district, because it isn't a common practice, but it will save time in obtaining some services and accommodations if services are denied under IDEA and the parents have to appeal.

Unlike special education eligibility, Section 504 eligibility is not based on having a certain type of disability. Instead, it is based on:

1. Having a physical or mental impairment that substantially limits a major life activity, such as learning (note that, in contrast to IDEA regulations, learning is not the only activity that applies: 504 plans can cover other major life activities, such as breathing, walking, and socialization).

2. Having a record of such an impairment, such as a medical diagnosis.

3. Being regarded as having such an impairment.

A 504 plan can put many helpful procedures in place, ranging from medication delivery to exemption from timed tests to the provision of a classroom aide. 504 plans are usually not accorded the status of an IEP by teachers and school administrators, but they have equal legal weight. In fact, 504 plans have a certain advantage, because you can appeal them at a state level without going through several district procedures first, as you must with a due process complaint.

One thing that a 504 plan can be very good for is ensuring that certain procedures are followed in case your child has a difficult behavior episode at school. Many children with PDDs who have progressed well enough to be in a full inclusion setting still experience an occasional meltdown. These episodes of anxiety, rage, or unusual behavior may occur in response to stress, fear, teasing, illness, missed medications, or even from eating a food that the child is sensitive to. You can develop a response plan in advance and put it in place via a 504 plan, ensuring that it is there just in case. Other excellent uses for a 504 plan include medication arrangements, planning for communication between home and school, classroom accommodations, requiring certain organization systems for homework and books, requiring in-services or special training for personnel, ensuring socialization opportunities, and bringing in outside agencies as part of your education team.

If you apply for 504 status and are still denied services, appeal this decision to your state's Office of Civil Rights (OCR). If your child has a medical diagnosis of PDD-NOS or atypical PDD, a 504 plan is the very least he qualifies for. Even students with mild ADHD or occasional asthma attacks qualify for services under a 504 plan. Under no circumstances should your child be denied this limited protection, no matter how "high-functioning" he may be.

Taking on the school system

What can you do when the school district refuses your child a free and appropriate public education? Your options include:

- Sitting back and letting it happen (obviously not recommended)
- Advocating for your child within the classroom and the IEP process

- Bringing in an expert to help you advocate for your child

- Requesting a due process hearing

- Organizing with other parents to advocate for a group of students with similar problems

- Working with other advocates at a legislative level

- Going to court

Most school problems can be worked out with the teacher or within the IEP system. While some school districts have a well-deserved reputation for venality, most are simply hampered by a lack of resources and knowledge. These are areas where an informed parent can make a difference. You can snow them under with information about educational possibilities, and you can let them know that the resource problem is something to take up with government funding sources, not to penalize children with.

Bringing in an expert can do much to tip the scales in your favor, however. All over the country educational advocates and self-styled IEP experts are becoming available. Some of these people work for disability advocacy organizations or disability law firms. Others are freelance practitioners. Some are parents of children with disabilities who have turned their avocation into a vocation.

You may have to pay for expert services. Services can include researching programs available in your area, connecting you with appropriate resources, helping you write a better IEP, and advocating for your child at IEP meetings and due process hearings.

Due process

The words "due process" are guaranteed to strike fear into the hearts of school district bureaucrats—in fact, some parents have gotten a lot of mileage out of conspicuously placing a folder marked "Due Process" on the table during IEP meetings.

Due process usually refers to a due process hearing: an internal appeals procedure used by school districts to determine whether or not special education procedures have been handled properly—in other words, whether the child and his family have been given access to the processes that they are due under the law.

The due process hearing will hinge on whether the district has followed federal and state-mandated procedures for evaluating a child for special education and setting up a program for that child. Violations can include small things, like notifying parents of a meeting over the phone rather in writing, or major issues, like using untrained or incompetent personnel to evaluate children or deliberately denying needed services to save money.

Issues that tend to end up in due process include disagreements over evaluations or educational labels, provision of inadequate therapeutic services, placement in inappropriate educational settings, noncompliance with the IEP, lack of extended school year services when appropriate, and poor transition planning.

Obviously, every due process case is unique. Each state also has its own due process system. Regulations that all of these systems have in common are:

- Parents must initiate a due process hearing in writing.

- The hearing must take place in a timely fashion.

- Hearings are presided over by an impartial person who does not work for the district.

- Children have the right to stay in the current placement until after the hearing (this is called the "stay put" rule).

- Parents can attend due process hearings and advocate for their child.

- Parents can hire an educational advocate or lawyer to represent them at the due process hearing.

- If the parents use a lawyer and they win, they are entitled to have their legal fees paid by the district.

Due process hearings resemble a court hearing before a judge. Both sides will be asked to argue their case and present evidence on their behalf. Both sides can call on experts or submit documents to buttress their statements. However, experienced advocates know that, despite the veneer of impartiality, if it comes down to your word against the district's on educational or placement issues, the district will probably have an edge.

Some districts offer a less formal procedure, arbitration, also called mediation. In an arbitration hearing, both parties agree in advance to comply with the arbitrator's ruling. You can't recover your legal fees in arbitration, and your rights are not spelled out in the law. Be very cautious before agreeing to waive your right to a due process hearing in favor of arbitration. You can pursue mediation while waiting for your due process hearing. That way, if mediation works, you're done, and if it doesn't, everything is in motion for your due process proceeding.

Public advocacy

Parents may discover that they have a great deal of company in their disgruntlement. Some problems in special education are systemic, and as such, they require changes at the top. Parents in several states have banded together effectively to get better services for their autistic spectrum children. The organization Families for Early Autism Treatment (FEAT), for example, works to make ABA programs and similar intensive interventions a part of state and provincial Early Intervention programs.

You may choose to form your own organization, join an existing group covering PDD-related issues, or work with a larger group of special education parents. If you're looking for potential allies, see the list of organizations in Appendix B, *Support and Advocacy*. You may also find allies in teacher's unions and organizations, regular parents associations, and elsewhere in your community.

If you're not the kind of person who enjoys conflict, advocacy and due process can be very draining. School districts count on endless meetings, criticism of your parenting skills, and constant references to their superior knowledge about your child to wear down your defenses. You must always stay on guard, and yet be open to logical compromises and the possibility of beneficial alliances. It's not easy, but it's necessary.

> *I'm the mother, I know what my child needs! Sometimes my husband is just too easy—he would let people just have their way as not to have any type of conflict. But I want what my daughter has coming to her, and I want it now. I'm her strongest supporter. I will not let the school system push me around! —Sarah, mother of two-year-old Elaine (diagnosed PDD-NOS, possible oral-motor apraxia)*

Going to court

Due process is bad enough. Going to court is absolutely, positively your last recourse. It's something you do only when nothing else works, not even marching on a school board meeting with a bunch of disgruntled parents.

Going to court is time-consuming, exhausting, and expensive. The outcome is uncertain, and while the case drags on, your child may be languishing in an inappropriate setting. Sometimes it just has to happen, though, as the now-infamous 1994 case *W.B. v. Matula* makes clear.

In this case, a New Jersey kindergartner identified as E.J. was refused appropriate assessment for special education services, given a grossly inappropriate placement, and punished for actions and conditions related to his disability. He was later refused appropriate interventions based on an incomplete evaluation, from which some documents were withheld from the parents. E.J. was later diagnosed with severe neurological impairments, including Tourette syndrome, obsessive-compulsive disorder, ADHD, and specific learning disabilities (he also had marked symptoms of a pervasive developmental disorder, although this was not diagnosed). E.J.'s mother filed for a due process hearing and won at that level, but the district refused to comply with the edicts of its own due process hearing officer.

As a result, E.J.'s mother was forced to obtain evaluations and diagnostic help at her own expense, provide her increasingly emotionally disturbed child with psychiatric care at her own expense, and watch her child regress due to improper educational placement and procedures. Eventually she won a second due process hearing, after which she sued the district for violations of federal education law and on Constitutional grounds under the Fourteenth Amendment, which entitles all citizens to equal protection under the law. To the consternation of school districts everywhere, she won her case, which included a substantial financial judgment.

Since the Matula case, school districts have been put on notice that parents of special-needs children can successfully pursue them beyond the due process hearing. Besides the federal education laws and Constitutional grounds used in the Matula case, parents may be able to ask the courts for redress under state education laws or even contract law. There are few legal precedents as yet, but as in the area of health insurance and autism, the number of successful legal challenges is growing.

Private schools

As noted earlier in this chapter, school districts sometimes contract with private schools and programs to provide services that they do not. These programs are usually not religious in nature (there are a few exceptions, such as residential programs that are affiliated with a religious denomination), and they must be willing to comply with district regulations.

Sometimes parents have good reasons to opt for private school placement directly, at their own cost. Perhaps daily religious instruction is very important to you, or your child's siblings already attend a private school. Luckily, choosing a private school does not automatically disqualify your child from publicly funded Early Intervention and special education services.

To receive these services, you will have to have your child evaluated and qualified within the public system. Then you'll use the IFSP or IEP to determine which services will be delivered, where they will be delivered, and by whom. This can get sticky, depending on your state or local district. Some districts are so cautious about maintaining separation of church and state that if several children in a parochial school need speech therapy, they will send a "speech van" to park outside the school, then have children receive speech therapy in the van rather than allowing a public employee to help children inside the walls of a parochial school. Other districts have no qualms about sending employees to private school sites.

Unlike a public school, your private school itself will not be required to fulfill any academic promises made in an IEP. The IEP is a contract between you and the school district only. However, enlightened private schools that wish to better serve students with disabilities are well aware of how valuable the ideas in a well-written IEP can be. Some parochial and private schools encourage teachers to be part of the IEP process. In some cases, these private school representatives have entered their own goals into the IEP, usually under the aegis of the parent. Private schools that accept any form of public funding may be subject to additional regulations. Many are also subject to the Americans with Disabilities Act.

Not everyone has a rosy private school experience. The school that served your other children well may be horribly wrong for a child with a pervasive developmental disorder. Educational programming for PDD-NOS and atypical PDD requires a certain level of knowledge and flexibility that not all schools have, public or private. You can advocate until you're blue in the face, but in the end, private schools do not *have* to take your child.

Home-schooling

Educating your children at home is legal in most US states. Each state has its own regulations about who can home-school, what (if anything) must be taught, and how (or if) children's learning will be tested. If these regulations include standardized testing, exceptions to the testing requirements for disabled children are usually not written into the law. You will want to be very careful about doing baseline testing and documenting reasons that a child may not do well on standardized tests, if they are required.

Eligible home-schooled children are entitled to Early Intervention and special education services. These services may be delivered in the child's home, at a neutral site, or in a nearby school or clinic.

Some districts have programs to help home-schooling parents create good programs for children with disabilities, while others actively oppose the practice of home-schooling special education students and go out of their way to make it difficult. In most states, home-schoolers can take part in extracurricular activities at their neighborhood public school, or even take some classes while doing the bulk of their schoolwork at home.

For children with social deficits, it's important to set up socialization opportunities if you are home-schooling. Many home-schooling families share teaching duties with other parents, bringing several children together for certain lessons or activities.

If you are *forced* to home-school your child because your district cannot or will not provide a free and appropriate educational placement, you may be eligible to be paid to teach your child. This has been the case for certain parents in very rural areas, as well as for parents in more populated districts that could not provide a safe setting for a child with assaultive behaviors or a tendency to run away.

Transition planning

Transition planning should begin in the early years of high school, when the student's peers are beginning to gain work skills and amass credits toward high school graduation. Special education students have a right to also be prepared for graduation, higher education, and work in ways that fit their needs. For most, extra support will be needed to make the transition from high school to adulthood go smoothly. The transition plan should address high school graduation, higher education, and work skills and opportunities. It may also include helping the young adult apply for public assistance, supported housing, and other necessary benefits; learn how to self-manage his medical and psychiatric care; and gain life skills such as budgeting, banking, driving, and cooking.

Graduation

Many students with PDD-NOS or atypical PDDs will be headed for a regular high school diploma. This usually requires passing a certain number of specified courses. If the student needs changes in the graduation requirements—for example, a speech-impaired student faced with a foreign language requirement might ask that the requirement be waived, or might ask that fluency in sign language be allowed to substitute for foreign language proficiency—now's the time to arrange for these changes.

Some students will need extra coursework to make it through high school, such as special instruction in keyboarding or study skills. These abilities will also help with higher education or work later on.

Some students will not be able to earn a regular diploma. A special form of graduation called an IEP diploma is also available. If a student earns an IEP diploma, that means he has completed all of the objectives set out in his IEP for graduation.

A General Equivalency Diploma, which is earned by passing an examination, may be an option for some other students.

Students who are headed for college may want or need to go beyond the basic high school diploma. If your state has a special diploma for advanced students, such as Oregon's Certificate of Advanced Mastery or New York's Regents Diploma, check early on about any accommodations that may be needed for the examination or portfolio process for these credentials. Some states (including Oregon, as of this writing, but not New York) have refused to permit accommodations. This is patently illegal and will surely be successfully challenged. If you don't want to be the one to bring the challenge, ask instead for special tutoring in advance of the test.

In the UK, Australia, New Zealand, and Ireland, special help may be available to help teens pass their level exams, including modified exams in some cases. Talk to your LEA or education department for more information about options in your area.

Work

Preparing for the world of work means gaining appropriate skills, such as typing, filing, driving, filling out forms, using tools, cooking, or lifting. These skills may be gained in school-based vocational-technical classes, in classes taken at a community college or vocational school while the student is still in high school, in a union- or employer-sponsored apprenticeship program, via job shadowing arrangements or internships, or on the job. Vocational planning is mandatory for special education students in the US by age sixteen, and should really be undertaken much earlier.

Transition-to-work services may include moving into the public vocational rehabilitation system, which trains and places adults with disabilities into jobs. However, in many states the vocational rehabilitation system is severely overloaded, with wait times for placement ranging from three months to as much as three years. Typical opportunities range from "sheltered workshop" jobs (splitting kindling wood, sorting recyclables, light assembly work) under direct supervision, to supported placement in the community as grocery clerks, office helpers, chip-fabrication plant workers, and the like. Often the person works with a job coach, a person who helps him learn work skills and how to handle workplace stresses. In some cases, the job coach actually comes to work with the person for awhile.

School districts may sponsor their own supported work opportunities, such as learning how to run an espresso coffee cart or working in a student-run horticultural business. Many schools have vocational programs that give students a chance to have a mentor in their chosen field, and that may include actual work experience with local employers.

Some public and private agencies may also be able to help with job training and placement, such as the state employment department, the Opportunities Industrialization Commission (OIC), and the Private Industry Council (PIC). Goodwill Industries also operates a job placement service in many larger cities.

Students with disabilities should receive appropriate vocational counseling, including aptitude testing, discussion of their interests and abilities, and information about work possibilities. Parents need to ensure that students are not shunted into dead-end positions that will leave them financially vulnerable as adults.

Higher education

Students planning to attend trade school, a two-year community college program, or a four-year (or longer) college program need information far in advance on which high school courses will be required for entry. This is especially important for those students with disabilities who carry a lighter course load, as they may need to make up some credits in summer school or via correspondence courses.

Transition programs should address the move from high school to trade school, community college, or a four-year college program. Students are eligible for publicly funded education and/or services until age 22 if needed. Tuition in some programs may be covered for some students, in full or in part. Special education services and help for students with learning disabilities are available on campus and in the dorms at many colleges.

It's against the law to deny admission to students based on disabilities; of course, other admission criteria generally must be met. Public universities and community colleges may waive some admission criteria for disabled students on a case-by-case basis if the student can show that they are capable of college-level work. For example, if a student's poor hand coordination made getting a high score on the SAT difficult, but the student will have a classroom aide available at college to make up for this problem in class, she might be admitted despite the low score. Standardized test requirements might also be set aside if high school grades or the student's work portfolio look good.

Schools that normally require all freshmen to live on campus may waive this requirement for a student with special needs. If living at home is not an option, a group home or supervised apartment near campus might be. Before your child leaves for college in another city, make sure that you have secured safe and appropriate housing, found competent local professionals to provide ongoing care, and rehearsed daily life activities like grocery shopping and visiting the laundromat. You'll also want to work out a crisis plan with your child, just in case things go wrong. She will want to know who to call and where to go.

Education in Canada

The Canadian special education process is very similar to that used in the US. Provincial guidelines are set down by the national Ministry of Education and governed by the Education Act, but most decisions are made at the regional, district, or school level. Evaluations are done by a team that may include a school district psychologist, a behavior specialist, a special education teacher, other school or district personnel, and in some cases a parent, although the latter is not required by law as it is in the US.

Children between the ages of six and twenty-two may qualify for special education assistance under the Designated Disabled Program (DDP), the Special Needs Program (SNP), or the Targeted Behaviour Program (TBP), depending on the labels they receive in evaluation.

The evaluation is used as a basis for an IEP. Almost identical to the US document of the same name, the IEP is usually updated yearly or more frequently if needed. A formal review is required every three years.

> We have IEPs, but they don't have quite the same clout here that they appear to have under the US legislation. What you have to trumpet here is the legal requirement, under human rights legislation, that disability be "accommodated." For us, the school counselor is being very helpful, as is the district behavior specialist. I'm doing some research at the moment on the actual legal requirements so that I know just how much I can demand. I've found the most effective resource is to be a pleasant, informed, persistent, somewhat annoying pest. —Rae, mother of thirteen-year-old D'Arcy

A full range of placement options is available for Canadian students, from home-based instruction to full inclusion. Partial inclusion is increasingly common, as is supported mainstreaming. Students from rural or poorly served areas may be sent to a residential school, or funding may be provided for room and board to allow the student to attend a day program outside of her home area.

If disputes arise between the school or the district and the parents, there is a School Division Decision Review Process available for adjudicating them. The concept known as due process in the US is usually referred to as fundamental justice in Canada.

Education in the UK

When a child in the UK is judged eligible for special education services, he is said to be statemented. This term refers to an IEP-like document called a

Statement of Special Educational Needs, or Record of Needs. This document is developed at the council level by the Local Educational Authority (LEA), and lists the services that a statemented child needs. Usually the team that creates the statement includes an educational psychologist, a teacher, and the parents. It may also include the family's health visitor or other personnel, such as a speech therapist, physiotherapist, occupational therapist, or child development specialist. Each child's statement is reviewed and updated annually. Disability advocates strongly urge parents to get expert help with the statementing process.

Your LEA can limit services according to its budget, even if those services are listed as necessary on your child's statement. Service availability varies widely between LEAs. Some therapeutic services, such as speech therapy, may also be available through National Health.

School placements in the UK run the gamut from residential schools to specialist schools to full inclusion in mainstream schools. There are more residential options available than in the US system due to the English tradition of public schools (American readers may be confused by this term: in the UK, "public schools" are privately owned and run, while government schools are those run by the LEAs).

Schools working with statemented students operate under a government Code of Practice that is analogous to, but much weaker than, the federal IDEA in the US. Parents and disability advocates can insist that LEAs follow this code when devising programs for statemented students, and have access to a formal appeals process.

The UK government has recently taken steps toward improving Early Intervention offerings. Currently, EI services are not mandated by law, although they are available in many areas.

Parents report that home-schooling a child with a disability is particularly hard in some parts of the UK. Regular inspection by an educational welfare officer is required, and some of these bureaucrats are not very knowledgeable about disabilities. Parents should be prepared to document their child's educational experiences and learning progress.

The Autism UK Web site (*http://www.autism-uk.ed.ac.uk/*) provides many pointers for parents.

Education in Australia

Australia's system is paradoxically looser and yet more accommodating to students with disabilities of all sorts. There is only a thin legal framework for the provision of special education services, but in the urban areas, where most Australians live, these services are apparently no harder to obtain than they are in the UK.

Early Intervention services are usually readily available in urban areas for children age six and under, including EI services specifically for autistic students. To obtain an EI evaluation, parents should contact the Specialist Children's Services Team at their local Department of Human Services.

Placement options for older children include residential schools (including placement in residential schools located in the UK, for some students), Special Schools for children with moderate to severe developmental delay or autistic spectrum disorder, special classrooms for disabled children within regular schools, and the full range of mainstreaming options. "Mix and match" placements that allow students to be mainstreamed for just part of the day are still rare, however. For students in rural areas, there is a Traveling Teacher service focused on autism and other disabilities.

There are federal regulations regarding special education, but most of the regulatory action takes place through each state's Department of Education, Training, and Employment (DETS, formerly called the Department of Education and Children's Services), or at a local or school level. The DETS in each state provides information, parent services, assistive technology, augmentative communication, special curricula, and many more services for students with disabilities.

The Autism Victoria Web site (*http://avoca.vicnet.net.au/~autism/*) offers links to a number of excellent education-related resources throughout Australia.

> We don't have anything like IEPs, and I think that there are some
> cultural factors involved in the way disability is approached here. I've
> been trying to put my finger on just what it is… I think it has to do with
> the fact that Australian society is less "harsh" than American society.
> There's a bit more sense of cooperation and caring for the underdog. People don't talk as much about "rights," don't sue each other very often, etc.
> (though it is happening more). Perhaps there has been less need to label
> kids because there is somewhat less tendency to isolate and discriminate.

*I'm not saying that there aren't huge problems for kids with differ-
ences (especially subtle differences which aren't at all obvious); however, I
think that people here tend to expect to talk things through with schools
and teachers and make informal arrangements. There's an expectation of
reasonableness, in many cases. I get to know teachers on a personal level
and explain about Kim's differences. On the one hand we have less
bureaucratization of services and more individual innovation, on the
other hand we have less services altogether.   —Kerry, mother of twelve-
year-old Kim*

Education in New Zealand

Students who qualify for special education services in New Zealand are
called "section nined" (old terminology) or "qualified for the Ongoing
Resourcing Scheme" (ORS). ORS qualification is currently reserved for those
children whose impairment is judged to be "high" or "very high," with the
most resources going to the latter group. As of this writing, special education services for early childhood centers and home-based programs are not
funded. Nevertheless, some young children with PDDs receive Early Intervention services through special arrangement, in a clinical setting, or in
home-based programs.

The Ministry of Education sets up qualifying guidelines for early childhood
and school-age special education services. The Autistic Association of New
Zealand (*http://www.autism.org.nz/*) provides parent education, expert evaluation services, educational and vocational advocacy, and other direct services.

Recent news reports indicate that limited local resources and a move to push
for full inclusion under the Special Education 2000 program has eliminated
many special education resources that were once available in New Zealand's
schools. Autistic spectrum children are said to be highly represented in the
large group that is now being denied ORS funding.

School placements include a few special schools, attached special education
units within regular schools, and a range of inclusion options in mainstream
settings. Some students are in residential settings. Under Special Education
2000, many more schools will have a resource-room-like arrangement rather
than self-contained special education units.

Lifespan services for autistic spectrum individuals in New Zealand have been getting a closer look since the death of an autistic girl in 1997. Seventeen-year-old Casey Albury was killed by her mother, who cracked under the strain of caring for her without the availability of respite or other needed services.

Changing educational paradigms

No matter where you go in the world, there's one similarity in the nature of educational services for children and adults with PDDs: an increasing emphasis on intensive intervention early in life and a wider spectrum of services for older children and adults as well.

At the same time, most school systems are struggling with budget restrictions. How these conflicting forces will affect educational service offerings for children with PDD-NOS and atypical PDD remains to be seen.

CHAPTER 10

Family

THERE'S A COMMON MYTH THAT A CHILD'S DISABILITY brings a family together, but divorce rates are actually twice as high in families dealing with disability or serious illness as they are in the rest of the population. The attention and effort required to care for a "difficult" child tears apart parents, siblings, extended families, and friendships. People often need help to work through the blame, guilt, sorrow, and fear that get in the way of healthy relationships. The extra stress also serves to magnify the normal difficulties that family relationships face. Working together and staying together is difficult enough that many do not succeed.

In this chapter, we look at typical issues that families face when a member has a pervasive developmental disorder, and we discuss coping strategies that have worked for other families. We explore how to keep talking, how to accept a partner who has a different approach, finding time for each other and for other children, and caring for older relatives when you are also responsible for a child with PDD.

We'll also provide creative solutions to common problems of daily family life—solutions that have worked for real families.

Most of the material in this chapter applies to parents or to professionals who work directly with families. Some adult patients may also find it useful for figuring out their own family dynamics, and as they consider whether to have children of their own.

Welcome to Holland?

There's a parable about accepting children with disabilities that regularly makes the rounds of support-group newsletters and Internet discussion groups. Written by Emily Perl Kingsley, "Welcome to Holland" (Kingsley, 1987) talks about the experience of planning a trip to Italy but accidentally ending up in Holland, which doesn't have the Colosseum or Michelangelo's

David, but does have lovely tulips and Rembrandt. Holland is different, but it's good in its own way—just like your child with a disability.

While many parents have found this fable comforting, others feel patronized by well-meaning advice and reading material that encourages them to simply accept their lot.

> I look at that "Welcome to Holland" pap piece and think, "What the hell do they mean? Try 'Welcome to Bosnia'!" —Krista, mother of seven-year-old Joshua

When you are encouraged to accept your lot, even to see it as a gift, it can make you think you don't have the right to be mad—but you do. No one deserves to have these disorders, and no one deserves to have their lives turned upside down by caring for someone else who does. On one level, you do have to accept the situation. On another, you cannot, and must not if you are to have the energy and determination to help your child.

You may feel surprisingly angry if you're told that God or nature has chosen you for the "special" duty of parenting a child with a disability. People usually mean these words as a compliment, but they can add to internal feelings of being trapped in a role you never asked for, and to feelings of inadequacy.

And as Krista's comments above indicate, a PDD diagnosis can turn family life into a battlefield. Looking at the carnage through rose-colored glasses isn't always an option.

Family strife

Mary Callahan's book *Fighting for Tony* is a fine portrait of how a PDD diagnosis can affect a family. Whether you agree with Callahan's theories about the causes of her son's autistic behavior or not, her description of a marriage's disintegration under pressure will be sadly familiar to many parents of children with PDDs. As her son's mysterious illness pitched the Callahans into repeated battles with doctors, the school system, and each other, a solid and loving relationship was destroyed by the pressure. This true story has a happy ending—not only did Callahan "recover" her son, she and her husband eventually recovered their marriage.

Another poignant portrait of autism's effects on the family is *Family Pictures*, a novel by Sue Miller. Later made into a very affecting TV movie, *Family*

Pictures chronicles the dramatic impact of an autistic son on his affluent Northeastern family.

Both Callahan's real-life account and its fictional counterpart demonstrate the same point: the word "pervasive" in pervasive developmental disorders describes the impact of these conditions on the people around the patient, as well as on the patient himself.

> *My marriage has definitely suffered, also my relationship with my older daughters. I find it difficult to keep it all in perspective.* —Lesley, *mother of three-year-old Danielle (diagnosed PDD-NOS)*

Every family is different, but there are a few problems that many have in common. These include:

- Differences over discipline
- Inability to handle problem behaviors
- Withdrawal by one parent, or by one or more siblings
- Overinvolvement by one parent
- Burnout
- Resentment
- "Genetic blame"
- Parental neuropsychiatric problems
- Breakdown of extended family relationships
- Community isolation
- Financial problems related to disability
- Sibling rivalry compounded by behavior problems

Discipline

Perhaps the number one problem in any family with children is differences of opinion about what constitutes appropriate discipline. These are only compounded when a child has a neuropsychiatric disability. The behavior problems are bigger, and solving them is more difficult. Conflicts between parents become more likely.

Uncontrollable tantrums or rages in an eight-year-old, self-injurious behavior, assaultive or destructive behavior, and communication problems between parent and nonverbal child were not dealt with by Dr. Benjamin Spock or Penelope Leach. Grandparents and friends haven't a clue. The usual strategies may not work at all.

In particular, spanking and other forms of corporal punishment often seem to feed the parent-child conflagration. For one thing, autistic-spectrum people often have unusual perceptions of pain. There's a danger that getting through to the child with a smack on the behind won't work, and parents may then be tempted to go too far with physical punishment. In addition, hitting can reinforce a child's assaultive or self-injurious behaviors. For these reasons, parents are strongly advised by almost every expert in autistic-spectrum disorders to find alternative methods of discipline.

And therein lies the rub.

With "normal" children, rules, reasoning, brief time-outs, and an occasional docked allowance will usually suffice. What do you do when the child can't follow your reasoning or puts up a wall that you can't get through? This is a struggle for any parent, and when two parents are at odds it only gets worse.

It's very common for one partner to have a lower tolerance threshold, or a smaller repertoire of effective, nonviolent discipline strategies. This is where the arguments begin. One parent lets a behavior go, while the other is hugely annoyed by it and eventually blows up. One parent spanks, and the other rushes to comfort the child. One parent gives a time-out, and the other adds a second punishment because that doesn't seem like enough.

> My husband and I had trouble for several years because he did not want to admit that our son had a problem. It was just too much for him to face. He felt that strict discipline would overcome the hyperactivity and the short attention span. Finally, after my son regressed to the point that he didn't want to be touched and couldn't find his way around, [my husband] came to the party. —Kim, mother of seven-year-old Brad (diagnosed atypical PDD, cognitive epilepsy/Landau-Kleffner syndrome)

Differences over discipline are often deep-seated. Most of what we know about raising well-behaved children we learned from our parents, for better or for worse. Chances are that not only were your parents imperfect disciplinarians at best, but also weren't raising children with PDDs. Techniques that worked on you as a youngster may be totally inappropriate for your child.

The first key to resolving discipline disagreements is making a compact between parents. Behavior experts who have worked with families affected by a wide variety of neuropsychiatric disorders agree that this compact should include, at minimum, the following points:

- The best discipline is positive, so parents must rely on providing incentives for desirable behavior before using punishment to control undesirable behavior. The "token economy" schemes used in many classrooms can be successfully adapted for home use, for example. Parents should also learn about alternative strategies for addressing the roots of problem behavior, such as relaxation techniques.

- Punishment must fit the crime. Whenever possible, the only punishment should be experiencing the natural and logical consequences of an undesirable action. For example, if Joe bites his friend Jane, Jane will go home. If Joe pours his juice on the table, Joe has to clean it up and does not get another glass of juice.

- Parents must agree on basic guidelines for stopping undesirable behavior, such as whether physical punishment is ever acceptable, what form discipline will take, and under what circumstances it will be meted out.

- If physical punishment is ever to be used, it should be a last resort and used in a controlled fashion.

- Accordingly, parents must come up with a common set of effective disciplinary measures for undesirable behavior. These may include loss of allowance or privileges, addition of chores or other responsibilities, time-outs, and, for older children, grounding.

- Parents must agree to avoid calling the child (or each other) hurtful names or using other verbal abuse.

- Parents need to support each other in the effort to remain calm during behavior problems. If a parent is losing control, he or she should feel free to turn the situation over to the other partner long enough to take a "parental time-out."

- Parents must not, however, give one partner the permanent role of disciplinarian. The old "wait 'til Daddy gets home" scenario lets one parent off the hook, and encourages children to be fearful and manipulative. For children with neurological problems, delayed discipline can be particularly confusing.

- If an undesirable behavior happens repeatedly, and neither incentives nor disincentives seem to curb it, parents should agree to look closer for hidden causes. The behavior analysis techniques discussed in Chapter 6, *Therapeutic Interventions*, can be very useful in this regard.

- Most importantly, parents must present a united front, even when they don't actually agree. Arguments over discipline should not occur in front of the child. If Mom thinks Joe needs a time-out for throwing blocks, but Dad thinks a reprimand is sufficient, Dad can let her know how he feels while Joe is in time-out. Next time it happens, they'll be in full agreement about the proper consequence for throwing things.

Parents do need to remember that people with PDDs may respond to discipline unevenly. A child who has rages that arise out of seizures or other neurological events may not be able to gain self-control at these times, but can do so when the behavior is a garden-variety temper tantrum. People with PDDs may perform acts compulsively and be unable to control these actions by force of will alone. Interventions may have to include protective devices, security measures like those discussed in the section "Tips for daily life," later in the chapter, and medication.

The bottom line is that you know your child. To be effective, the discipline plan you create must be individualized, and must be flexible enough to take into account the child's mental and neurological realities.

Finding help

These skills do not come naturally, so the second key to defusing the behavior time bomb is finding expert assistance. Behavior modification professionals, ABA practitioners, family therapists who are knowledgeable about neuropsychiatric disorders, and others can help. Usually the professional should observe the child interacting with parents and siblings at home, preferably more than once.

These professionals can help with both an overall behavior plan, much like those used in schools (see Chapter 9, *School*) and with specific suggestions. The best experts can be available on a long-term basis, providing parents with someone to call when they run out of ideas or patience. A good family therapist can be of particular help when parents do not agree about appropriate rules and discipline (see the section "Family therapy," later in the chapter).

Your special education case manager, government mental health or developmental disabilities department, psychiatrist, or ABA provider should be able to help you find professional help for behavior management.

About time-outs

For most children, time-outs are an effective way to gain the child's attention, make it clear that a behavior is undesirable, and attach a consequence to a behavior that doesn't have built-in natural and logical consequences. For some children with PDDs, they are very effective.

For others, they are not. Children who are severely socially withdrawn may actually find time-outs to be reinforcing. For these children, ABA and behavior modification techniques are a better choice.

You may want to modify your time-out procedure to take your child's special needs into account. For children who have trouble with time concepts, for example, a timer or stopwatch can help. Children who are often given time-outs to deal with frustrated, aggressive behavior may need a space with pillows or foam bats they can safely bang around. Some families have cleared out a closet for a time-out space, removing the clothes bar and any other potentially dangerous items and adding a punching bag, beanbag chair, and other items that can help a child work out angry feelings.

Parenting classes

Parenting classes may or may not be useful. Parent Effectiveness Training, Positive Parenting, and similar courses are designed for children whose responses fit the predictable pattern. When a child has PDD, his response to a particular incentive or disciplinary measure may not fit the mold. For example, a child may not be able to grasp the concept of natural and logical consequences until a much later age than expected. As noted earlier, corporal punishment may be ineffective or counterproductive. Reasoning with a grade-school child who has a PDD may be a useless exercise. The incentives that motivate "normal" children may be of little interest.

> My son's day treatment center required parents to attend a weekly
> skill-building group. I'm sure it was valuable for some of the families, but
> it just gave me a regular reminder of how far out of the mainstream we
> were. When I asked my first question, it was about how to handle a child
> in an out-of-control rage. The teacher asked me to explain what I meant.

When I started talking about a child who turns bright red, falls to the floor, bites anything in reach, and can't be calmed for as long as two hours, she blanched and said, "Gee, I don't know ... maybe you should ask a psychiatrist." The psychiatrist, of course, had suggested that I bring up the issue in my parenting class.

We never have gotten a good answer. We definitely need parenting skills that are different from what worked with our daughter. Who can tell us what we should be doing?

Sometimes parenting classes geared to the special needs of families with disabled children are available through local hospitals, Early Intervention or special education programs, or disability support groups. Depending on the instructor's skill level and approach, these can be very valuable.

A number of good books on parenting the special-needs child are listed in Appendix A, *Resources*.

Problem behaviors

What do you do when your child has a behavior that you (or your partner) simply can't handle? Echolalia, weird noises, constant humming, headbanging, pestering the pets—whatever it is that makes you flip your lid, your child with PDD-NOS or atypical PDD will probably find it.

If it appears to be something neurological that you'll just have to live with for a while, try dealing with your reaction rather than the behavior. Try ear plugs, a Walkman with headphones, asking your partner if you can go for a walk for fifteen minutes ... whatever it takes to keep you sane. Likewise, if your partner is the one being driven up the wall, be willing to take over for a while and let him avoid the annoyance.

Alternatively, change the situation to avoid the annoying behavior. If your child's fine-motor problems lead to atrocious eating habits that turn your stomach, have a kids' table and an adults' table at dinnertime, or two different dinner times. Or serve the child foods that are harder to make a horrible mess with. Try relaxing your standards a bit—Martha Stewart does not have an autistic-spectrum child at home, so you really shouldn't try to compete with her in the creative housekeeping department. Get a sitter instead of taking the child with a PDD to a fancy restaurant, or choose restaurants where being messy is no big deal.

Be creative in your solutions, and don't worry about whether your family's way of coping is "normal" or not. Go grocery shopping at midnight, order clothes from catalogs, put a lock on the refrigerator, set up a cot in your room for your child who has night terrors. If it works for you and harms no one, it's all right.

> *Our son is almost eight, and he still sleeps in our bed almost every night. I brought this up hesitantly in my email chat group, and found out that we are far from the only parents who allow this. He seems to need the extra contact, and he sleeps through the night consistently.*

Withdrawal and overinvolvement

A pattern often in seen in families with a disabled child is one parent who stays as remote from the situation as possible while another's involvement borders on obsession. The withdrawn parent may be just as concerned, but either doesn't have the coping skills or has delegated responsibility to the more-involved partner. Generally—but not always—fathers tend to withdraw, and mothers tend to jump in with both feet.

> *My relationship with my husband is changed due to his (and most males', I'm finding) lack of whatever it takes to deal with this disability. —Holly, mother of three-year-old Max (diagnosed PDD-NOS and apraxia of speech)*

This situation is not healthy for either parent, nor does it really benefit the child. Parents need to keep the lines of communication open, even when job responsibilities and schedule conflicts force one partner to be more directly involved in activities like in-home ABA training, attending school meetings, or talking with doctors.

Set up a time each week to talk about events and, perhaps more importantly, feelings and frustrations. Try to find ways to keep the parent who has a tendency to pull back actively involved. Perhaps that parent can take part in some rambunctious play time while the other fixes dinner, or can take on a special weekend activity, such as Scouting, team sports, or a hobby. The trick is to actually *schedule* these activities and make sure that they happen. It's a rare pair of parents who are absolutely fifty-fifty in their involvement, but for the sake of their partnership, the most-involved parent needs to know that there will be regularly scheduled break times ahead.

Burnout and respite

What happens when break time doesn't happen? Burnout. No matter how much you love your child, there will be a day when your batteries just quit. Single parents, and couples who have a very unbalanced system of sharing responsibility for their child with a PDD, are at high risk.

Anyone who's ever had a horrible job knows the symptoms of impending burnout. You start feeling hopeless, numb, resentful, and angry, all at the same time. You may get physically ill, suffering from an increase in headaches, stomachaches, bowel complaints, and fatigue. You start fantasizing about running away.

Sadly, some parents really do run away—away from their share of responsibilities, away from their marriage, even away from their child.

> *His father simply saw him as flawed, and never became involved in searching for an answer or diagnosis. He abandoned me, Kevin, and his younger brother Jonah when the boys were seven and five, respectively. After I fought through the courts for support, he surfaced for occasional visits, but lives out of town. He never asks what is wrong with his son, and isn't careful with him when they are out in public. Jonah, who is thirteen now, "parents" his brother when the three of them are together.* —Cindy, *mother of fifteen-year-old Jeffrey (diagnosed verbal dyspraxia with "autistic-like" features)*

Don't let this happen to you or your partner. It's okay to say that you're overwhelmed. Only then can you look for a way to remedy the situation. If you have trouble doing it on your own, a good family counselor can help you set up a schedule that gives you some time off to clear your head, take a class, or just enjoy a quiet cup of tea or a game of golf. Usually it doesn't take much to lift the burden of your day-in, day-out duties—but you do have to ask.

Like Jeffrey's father, some parents deal with feelings of guilt, embarrassment, and shame with denial. These feelings are anything but easy to work out—particularly for men (or women) who have trouble articulating their emotions. A little understanding can go a long way.

Single parents, and couples who want their time off to be time together, should access respite-care services if they are available. Respite providers are trained to care for disabled youth and adults for the afternoon, overnight, or even during a family vacation.

> Dhylan is very hard to manage at times, and therefore we don't go out without him (kind of like the American Express card). We just applied for respite care and are hoping we get it. A break is so important. —Sally, mother of four-year-old Dhylan (diagnosed PDD-NOS with autistic features)

Respite care may be available at no or low cost through community agencies, public or private. A county caseworker or local disability organization should be able to put you in touch with respite resources in your area.

As an alternative, perhaps you can set up an informal respite arrangement with one or more parents of children with disabilities in your area. For young children, play-group co-ops can be a great idea, and they're one that many parents are already familiar with. The same concept can work with older kids and even adults cared for at home too, and can be extended to cover overnight care and occasionally longer visits.

If you have the financial resources, of course, you could hire someone with appropriate training to provide respite services in your home on occasion. If a nearby college has a special education degree program, students may be able to earn extra credit and gain valuable experience, as well as earning some money, by caring for your child.

Summer day-camp programs, overnight camps, "parents' night out" programs, and other options are also available for giving yourself some much-needed time off. It's not a selfish thing to do at all; in fact, avoiding burnout is an essential part of being a good parent for a child with PDDs. The sanity you save may be your own!

Resentment

Resentment is an ever-present emotion in families affected by disabilities. Unfortunately, it usually festers away in private, only surfacing when an argument crosses the line of civility. It's hard not to feel resentment when this diagnosis can take so much away from your life: free time, undisturbed sleep, quiet mealtimes, the ability to go places with your old friends and their "normal" children, community approval, financial security…the list goes on.

My husband has had to put off finishing school and finding a career in order to stay with my son during the day. He feels some resentment towards that, but now we have the common goal of our son to keep us warm. —Shayna, mother of three-year-old Max (diagnosed multisystem developmental disorder)

Resentment is the result of feeling like you're not getting a fair shake, so it's important that any suffering that's being done for the child's sake is validated by other family members. No one should feel like a silent martyr (and with any luck, no one will act like one either).

Siblings may harbor more resentment toward their disabled sister or brother than they're willing to admit. We'll discuss this in the "Siblings" section later in this chapter.

Genetic blame

Family problems are often compounded by the red herring of "genetic blame": whose crummy genes caused this PDD problem, anyway? You would be surprised at how often this unspoken issue underlies arguments that only appear to be about disciplinary methods or parenting style. When it finally comes out into the open, watch out!

Parents and relatives all need to know that PDDs are neither rare nor exclusively found in your respective families. You could not have predicted that your child would have this diagnosis, not even if you had discussed every unusual relative in your respective family trees before procreating. Nor could a professional genetic counselor have been of much use.

It may also be useful to remind each other about what's *good* in your genetic heritage or your partner's. The same side that passed on the genes for PDDs probably also passed on many wonderful characteristics, which hopefully your child will also share.

Also, make an agreement with your partner early on that if your parents or other family members try to start a genetic blame conversation, you will nip it in the bud immediately.

Parental neuropsychiatric problems

There are real parenting issues that have to do with genetic heritage. PDDs are, at least in part, inherited disorders. It is not uncommon for one or both parents to have neurological difficulties of their own, and these may make it even harder to raise a child with a PDD.

It's been said by some professionals that a few of Bruno Bettelheim's "cold and distant" mothers of autistic children may have actually been suffering from mild forms of autism themselves. Certainly, parents of children with PDDs have a slightly higher incidence of depression and other mental disorders, as well as a higher incidence of health problems in general, perhaps related to an underlying immune-system dysfunction. Some of this may be genetically based, although some may derive from being in a difficult situation.

It's best to be open about these problems with your medical provider. Medical care and counseling for your own neuropsychiatric problems can help you feel better, and that alone will make you a better parent. You will be more available to your child, more patient, and less easily stressed.

Unfortunately, it isn't always to your advantage to let state or school authorities know if you are experiencing mental or physical problems. There are many people in social services and education who have negative attitudes about parents with psychiatric or neurological diagnoses. They may not take you seriously when you discuss your child's needs, and in some cases you may even be in danger of losing your children (see the section "Noncustodial parents," later in this chapter).

Siblings

When a child is in crisis, the everyday problems of her brothers and sisters seem to recede into the background. Reactions differ. Siblings may become superachievers to get their share of the attention—or they may seek negative pursuits, for the same reason.

Resentment is also a natural reaction when another child in the family takes more attention and more financial resources than you do.

> Our child's siblings are wonderful with him, however, they do sometimes feel that he gets away with more. But so far we have been able to talk this out with them. —Julie, mother of four-year-old Sean (diagnosed PDD-NOS)

Problems faced by the siblings of disabled children are beginning to get more attention. Books are available that discuss typical reactions. One of the best is *Views from Our Shoes: Growing up with a Brother or Sister with Special Needs* (Meyer, Woodbine House, 1997). It's an excellent guide to sibling issues, and it's written from the children's point of view.

Chat groups and workshops can also help. You may be able to get your other children involved in SibShops, which are part of a Seattle-based sibling-support project. SibShops and similar workshops give siblings a chance to meet other kids their age who share their situation. With a little help from adult facilitators, these workshops can help siblings talk about their feelings and fears. Friendships are frequently a nice side effect.

You can find an international directory of sibling support groups, including SibShops, at *http://www.chmc.org/departmt/sibsupp/sibshopdirectory_map.htm*. This site also has links to a variety of online and offline resources for siblings.

The behaviors of people with PDD-NOS or atypical PDD can be difficult for siblings to deal with. If your child has behaviors that are aggressive or assaultive, dealing with these is the first order of business. It's not fair for your other children to be at risk for actual harm. If you need this kind of help, call a behavioral professional immediately.

You may need to take special steps to safeguard the personal property of your other children, and to ensure that they have a quiet place to get away from your disabled child's tantrums, loud noises, or intrusive behaviors. Some of the solutions are not things that most parents would normally want to do. Possibilities include putting a keyed lock on a child's door, situating children's bedrooms as far apart in your home as possible, and providing niceties like a telephone, television, computer, or stereo in the child's room (or in a lockable family room) to permit their uninterrupted use. You'll have to set rules for the use of these devices that prevents the sibling from withdrawing into couch-potato land, of course.

It goes without saying that a fair share of your time is far more important than possessions, space, or even privacy. It's essential to make some special time for your other children. Some parents have a meal out, go to a movie, or enjoy an activity with their other children each week, and swear by the results. Ensure that your other children can find time to talk with you about school, friends, ideas, and concerns, without interruptions from your child with a PDD. You may need to be flexible about bedtimes one night each week, allowing another child to stay up just a bit later than usual to enjoy some one-on-one time with you. Another way to carve out time is to wake one child up a bit early once a week for a cup of cocoa and some quiet talk.

Your extended family may be able to help by taking up some of the slack. Grandparents, aunts and uncles, or older cousins may be available to take on some minor duties, such as transporting another child to soccer practice twice a week. Some grandparents may even be willing to fund enrichment activities or excursions together.

Many parents have special friends or neighbors who might be willing to get more involved, if you ask—this system can work out very well if you can recruit the parents of a sibling's friends. Family friends, and other trusted adults in the community, can act as mentors and advisors, and help your other children pursue personal interests.

Most siblings do have worries and questions about PDDs, and they may be afraid to talk to you about their fears. Children are exquisitely sensitive to family stress, and they don't want to burden you with more. It's essential for their well-being that these issues be put on the table, though. Common fears include wondering if their sibling is going to die from his illness, worries about possibly dangerous medication, feeling different from other children who don't have a disabled sibling, being teased because of their sibling's odd behaviors, and fear that their parents are unconcerned with their needs because of the other child's demands.

Quality information is the key. There are some films available that can help you start the conversation. *What's Eating Gilbert Grape?*, starring Johnny Depp and Leonardo DiCaprio, is a particularly good one, as is the Dustin Hoffman-Tom Cruise film *Rain Man*, although both portray individuals with more severe forms of autism. Short videos for siblings may be available through disability advocacy organizations as well.

Children's books on autism, of which there are quite a few, may be more frightening than reassuring to siblings of children with PDD-NOS or atypical PDD. They may fear that their brother or sister will become "worse," like the child in the story, or they may not identify their sibling with the more severely autistic child at all. Teens may find books by high-functioning autistic writers like Donna Williams or Temple Grandin interesting and informative.

Adolescent and adult siblings may resent the very real impact on their future of having a brother or sister with a disability. As Joe's quote in the section

"Financial problems," later in this chapter, illustrates, siblings may lose out on a lot, including opportunities for higher education, participation in community sports leagues, music and dance lessons, having a car, or (as explored to tragi-comic effect in *Rain Man*) receiving an inheritance.

They may also fear that as their parents age, they will be expected to take on increasing responsibilities for their sibling—and this is not an unreasonable worry. You may indeed need to pass on guardianship at some point. This is something that should be discussed and understood as early as possible.

As siblings approach the teen years, where family conflicts can get especially difficult, parents will need to ensure that each child has activities that give him a chance to shine on his own. School activities, religious youth groups, and volunteer organizations can be good choices if money is tight due to medical bills.

Quite a few parents interviewed for this book report that their children have become fierce advocates for their brother or sister with a PDD. Some have even chosen careers in medicine, teaching, or psychology due to the influence of their sibling's struggles.

Other parents noted that siblings have been therapeutically important, particularly when it comes to helping their child with a PDD learn language and social skills. Children can insist on interaction in ways that adults can't seem to get away with. Basically, they know how to make it *fun*—and we should always let them know how much we appreciate their efforts.

Lack of family support

If it takes a village to raise a child, some extended families of autistic-spectrum children don't see themselves as part of that village.

> *As far as the extended family, most of them act like Doug doesn't even exist. That's mainly on Doug's father side of the family. On my side, Doug is just kind of "there," nobody really does much with him. I don't have much help or support from them.* —Debbie, mother of eleven-year-old Doug (diagnosed PDD, fragile X syndrome, and sensory integration disorder)

You ought to be able to turn to your own parents and other relatives for support and encouragement, but it isn't always possible. Many families of people with PDDs find that their child is passed over for family activities, such as invitations to grandmother's house for Christmas or trips to the mall with siblings. Some family members even neglect to send birthday cards.

Sometimes the problem is simply a deep-seated prejudice against disabled people, and you can't do much about that. Often it's related to a lack of adequate information about the child.

> *It has been a source of tension in the family because, with my son at least, diagnosis is not clear-cut. He is not classically autistic and is, in fact, very affectionate and related to his family, both immediate and extended. There are those in the family who think nothing is wrong and say we are stigmatizing him by seeking help. There are others who think he is just poorly disciplined and out of control.* —Jennifer, mother of three-year-old Joseph (diagnosed atypical PDD)

It might make you feel uncomfortable to do so, but you can share evaluations from your child's school or doctor with the family member(s) who seem to question the disability's existence. Some parents have even brought a grandparent along for a psychiatrist or doctor visit, with hopes that hearing the diagnosis from an expert in a white coat will help it be accepted at last. You might want to discuss this possibility with one of your most accessible professionals, perhaps asking that they deliver some suggestions for helping your child along with information about the disability.

Community isolation

All it takes is one embarrassing episode in the checkout line or at the public park to make the average parent want to crawl under a rock. Every time the worst happens, the impulse to withdraw from public life is amplified.

> *We cannot do anything with him, except go for car rides (this calms him), walk with him (he needs the motion), and bring him to the playground. He prevents people from talking to each other with his noise and disruptions. He is not communicative, he is hyperactive, and he makes weird noises. We cannot even bring him out to eat. We try to shop in the early morning when the stores are empty.* —Joe, father of seven-year-old Kyle (diagnosed PDD with autistic features)

One of the most difficult areas for family members of people with PDD-NOS or atypical PDD is dealing with rude or clueless remarks from strangers. Children with PDDs are rarely beneficiaries of the sympathy factor. There's no wheelchair or leg brace to signal "this is a disabled child," so onlookers may assume that they're witnessing willful misbehavior. Some are quite vocal about letting parents know it, which can do a number on your self-esteem.

Some people carry cards explaining the problem that they can give to busybodies. Others have a canned speech for these situations, such as "My daughter has a neurological problem that can cause [insert the unusual behavior of the moment here]. I'm sure you understand."

You may be tempted to add, "In other words, she's disabled. What's *your* excuse?" although it's probably not a good idea. You may also be tempted to avoid the problem altogether by disappearing from public view. But isolation is a breeding ground for depression, and it does a child with social deficits no favors, either. Chapter 13, *Living with PDDs*, goes into some detail about ways that children with PDDs can break out of their isolation. But what about parents?

It's sadly true that the friends you had before your child's problems became evident may fall away. You'll have to be the judge of whether the cause is fear, prejudice, dislike of your child, or simply the fact that you have less free time to spend with friends than you used to. Disability support groups are frequently a source for new, and potentially rewarding, friendships. On the other hand, you may struggle mightily to hold onto friendships that have no relationship to PDDs, just to avoid having your child's disability permeate every aspect of your life.

As for being included in community activities, such as attending civic events or religious services, you will probably have to turn educator to make a place for your family. Some religious bodies do have formal programs for including people with disabilities in services and religious life. Check at the national, regional, or diocese level to find out what's available. Religious life is one area that many parents interviewed for this book cited as an island of acceptance in the larger community.

Other interest groups, from car clubs to the Grange to volunteer organizations, may also be able to find room for you, either with your entire family or as an individual participant. Be direct: ask how your child (or your hectic schedule) can be accommodated.

In the US, the Americans with Disabilities Act (ADA) was passed specifically to ensure that people with disabilities have equal access to community life and facilities. If your child's condition is causing discrimination against your entire family, the ADA covers you, too. The European Community charter and some European countries have similar regulations—and legality aside, full inclusion is certainly the ideal that people everywhere should aspire to. Don't be afraid to assert the natural right that you, your child, and your family have to participate in everyday life whenever possible.

Financial problems

PDDs can be a financial drain, and that's a family strain. Chapter 8, *Insurance*, and Chapter 11, *Finances*, cover specific strategies for keeping the wolves at bay. But parents do cite money woes as a major source of family stress.

> We've spent about $11,000 out-of-pocket in four years! We had to recently use our home-equity line of credit to pay for this, and haven't been able to save money for our older son's college (we have four kids, ages seventeen through seven). We rarely can afford nice vacations, music lessons for the other children, etc. I drive a car with 200,000 miles on it because we cannot afford a replacement. —Joe, father of Kyle

As this father's words indicate, money problems are about more than a low bank account balance. Other family members may miss out on important opportunities or do without some material things. Unless the situation is thoroughly and regularly discussed with them, they may not understand why the person with PDD's needs are costing so much, and why they are a family priority.

Social services programs are both a source of assistance and a source of financial difficulty for many families. Job choices and saving money for future needs may be jeopardized by these programs' earning and property rules. Parents who want to take advantage of these services and still meet their responsibilities to their other children (not to mention to themselves) may need specialized financial planning, as discussed in Chapters 11 and 13.

Family therapy

Finding professional help for family problems isn't always easy when a person with a PDD is part of the equation, because few family therapists know much about neurological disorders. The wrong therapist can cause irreparable harm by once again blaming the parents for the disorder, looking around for nonexistent sexual abuse, or inflaming feelings of guilt or resentment in one partner.

> *The last thing we needed was for the therapist to goad us into a fight during the session. We are dealing with an incredible amount of stress. At the end of the hour, he got to leave. We got to go home steaming, our problems still unresolved. When we hadn't gotten around to talking about making any positive changes after three sessions, we decided to call it quits.*

Parents interviewed for this book cited many negative experiences with traditional models of family therapy, particularly when sessions were conducted by inexperienced or "old-school" personnel. Parents of autistic-spectrum adults interviewed for this book had particularly heinous tales to tell from the "bad old days." But in the hands of a competent, experienced professional, family therapy can be a positive growth experience for people dealing with PDDs.

> *My main sources of strength are the autism newslist on the Net and the other parents at therapy.* —Dorthy, *mother of five-year-old Jesse (diagnosed PDD-NOS with autistic tendencies)*

According to parents who have tried family therapy, there are two models that seem to get the best results: "whole family" approaches that may include working separately with parents, siblings, and the patient, then bringing everyone together on a regular basis to hash out interpersonal issues; and group therapy sessions that involve several parents. The latter can provide families who are new to the diagnosis with a built-in support system, and participants in well-run groups report a growing sense of confidence as they, too, are able to pass knowledge on to others.

The focus of either approach should be less on "fixing" dysfunctional family systems than on empowering family members with new coping skills and providing a safe place to work out conflicts. Some therapeutic groups for parents operate more like parenting classes, with speakers invited in to discuss various topics of concern to the group.

Separation and divorce

As noted in this chapter's introduction, marriages suffer when a child is disabled. The legal aspects are beyond the scope of this book, but it is important that parents of a child with PDD-NOS or atypical PDD who do choose to end their relationship take the child's special needs into account.

Issues may include:

- Custody arrangements that allow both parents access to the child and respite. These arrangements may constrain the parents from living too distant from each other, which can be a difficult situation.

- Financial settlements that take into account the added expenditures needed to care for a disabled child, possibly including extended alimony for a stay-at-home parent.

- Financial arrangements to ensure that both parents will be responsible for the child's needs after the age of eighteen (most divorce decrees only cover support until the age of legal majority).

- Written agreements about which parent will pay for medical bills, tuition, therapy, and other expenses related to the disability, and to ensure that health-insurance coverage is maintained.

- Special agreements may be needed if the divorce is due to abuse, neglect, or substance abuse by one parent, in order to protect the child.

There's very little good that can be said about families splitting up, unless it's for reasons of safety. Parents should simply do their best to ensure that each partner's relationship with the child(ren) is maintained. Professional help, either in the form of social-worker aid or family counseling, is strongly advised.

Single parents

Couple problems are plenty of trouble, but it's trouble that those going it alone sometimes wish they had. No matter how ineffectual one half of a couple is, your partner is still an adult sounding board and a shoulder to cry on.

Single parents also face increased financial pressure, and have a terrible time getting meetings with school districts, doctors, and other helpers to fit into their schedule. Voicemail, pagers, email, and fax machines can be the single parent's best friends. You may also try to fit several appointments (school, psychiatrist, and pediatrician, for example) into one day off work. If your child has a low tolerance level, however, the results may not be great.

Some therapists do offer evening and weekend hours, and school districts can often be convinced to hold early-morning meetings. You may need to work with an advocate who can represent you at meetings. A friend, relative, sitter, or professional hired specifically for the purpose may be able to take your child to medical appointments.

And don't forget to take some time out for you—if you can find it! There's nothing like a child with a PDD to stop any semblance of a post-breakup love life. The time commitment alone may take you away from the dating world for years, and explaining what your home life is like could turn off a potential mate.

> *Theron's behavior problems keep me from finding a partner to share my life with, as his father left six years ago. His two younger brothers have many of the same problems, though not the same diagnoses, so my attention is divided fairly equally amongst them, none for me! —Ann, mother of eight-year-old Theron (diagnosed PDD-NOS, psychotic disorder, borderline intellectual functioning)*

Single parents have more reason than any others to seek allies in their extended family or community. Respite care and quality after-school care are absolute necessities. Foster grandparents programs, Big Brothers, Scouting, religious institutions, and parent groups can all be part of your web of support.

Multigenerational living

If you're part of the "sandwich generation"—caring for children and aging parents at once—your family also faces extra stress.

Older relatives in the home can be a wonderful addition to your life, but if they have many medical needs of their own or can't handle the behaviors of your child with a PDD, the situation will eventually explode.

An extra pair of hands is a must in these situations. In the US, Canada, Britain, Australia, and most parts of Europe, home health aides are available for frail or disabled elderly people, even when they are cared for by their children. Private social-service agencies and religious institutions may also be able to provide assistance.

Housekeeping help may give you more time for the important stuff, if you can afford it. Again, volunteer help or public assistance may be available in this area. Contact your government department for services to the elderly for more information, and be sure to explain that you have the extra burden of caring for a disabled child.

As with siblings, you may need to take special care to ensure that older relatives are safe from aggressive or assaultive behaviors, and that they can secure their possessions and peace of mind. Locks, latches, intercoms, and soundproofing can help in some situations.

Noncustodial parents

In some countries, and in some US states, parents are told that they must give up legal custody of their child to the state if he needs publicly funded residential services. Disability advocacy organizations, many of which are listed in Appendix B, *Support and Advocacy*, can help you sort through various options.

Giving up custody need not mean having no input. However, some programs are so unused to parental involvement that they aren't sure how to include family members in the lives of their institutionalized clients. Set up a meeting to discuss the ways you can help your child, activities you want to continue to share and, if applicable, issues related to financial management and personal safety.

Although full independence is every parent's goal, some adults with PDDs do continue to need help and oversight long after the age of 18 or 21—and retaining a close relationship with one's parents is valuable in and of itself. Custody issues can get in the way here, however. Once your child has reached the age of majority, you don't have the right to determine her medical care or to control any other aspect of her personal life. You may find yourself shut out of important decisions about housing, food, medical care, education, and vocational choices. If your child is able to handle these choices alone, that's great, even if you don't always agree with her decisions. For many families, the problems occur when the adult child's friends, therapists, or professionals with various programs start calling the plays. You may not be sure that your adult child is in agreement with these decisions, and sometimes these individuals will deliberately try to prevent you from having access to the decision-making process. Your input can help ensure your child's safety and keep his personal needs met. You may need to take legal steps to make sure that you stay in the picture. Chapter 13 discusses in greater detail how to work with transition services and adult programs.

Divorce can also prevent parents from retaining full custody. Both parents' level of personal and financial involvement should be written into the divorce settlement. If the settlement is unsatisfactory, or you are being prevented from involvement in your child's life, you will need legal help to assert your custodial rights.

Medical care is a frequent sticking point. If parents disagree about the right medical approach (for example, if one is totally opposed to using medications and the other is not, or if one prefers a traditional approach while the other is into alternative therapies), they may need to use the services of a counselor or arbitrator to work things out. Alternatively, parents may be able to agree on a practitioner or program, and simply agree that both will abide by the recommendations of this third party.

Worst of all is the situation of having your children forcibly taken from you. This has happened to parents of children with neurological disorders when uninformed social workers thought the child's behavior resulted from abuse, especially when the disorder had not been diagnosed before the action took place. Parental neuropsychiatric problems are often a complicating factor in such cases. Of course, families of people with PDDs are not immune to abuse, neglect, or parental substance-abuse problems, either.

If you feel that you are at risk of losing custody of your child to the state or to an ex-spouse, do not delay in seeking legal (and medical) support. Disability advocacy organizations may be able to provide you with advice and, in some cases, legal assistance.

Adoption and foster care

Although hard numbers are not available due to confidentiality laws, it's well known that childhood disability is a major factor in adoption and foster care placements by natural parents. Some simply don't have the knowledge or resources to take care of a child with a potentially lifelong disability. Tragically, these children are among the hardest to place. Parents who step up for this duty deserve a medal and may need special support.

> *Stevie was originally diagnosed as deaf, which is why I got him, as I sign. He was three and a half years old when first diagnosed with autism.*

I'm in the process of adopting him. His deprivation was so severe we aren't sure just how much is the autism and how much is the deprivation.

Unfortunately, Early Intervention wasn't an option in his case. All diagnosis, progress, services, schooling, etc., started 21 months ago, when he came to live with me.

Finding community resources has been the biggest thorn in my side. We are hooked up with a regional center that tends to pass the buck to the foster agency or school district until the adoption is final. Our FFA [foster family agency] has not been helpful in any way. No backup, no help finding babysitting services, it all falls on me. I'm not complaining, honest, I wouldn't trade my life now with Stevie for anything!

As I am raising Stevie as a single mother, I can tell you that I have depleted most of my savings and live hand-to-mouth many months. Even though I receive a monthly stipend for him, it hardly covers the cost of shoes! It's a great struggle, but I have great faith and trust in a Higher Power... if I didn't, I couldn't survive. —Roni, foster parent, and soon to be adoptive mother, of five-year-old Stevie (diagnosed atypical autism)

Some foster-care and adoption agencies that work with special-needs children have more to offer than Roni's. Private agencies for the disabled could help those that do not, but communication between the public and private sectors is apparently difficult. Parent support groups and disability advocacy groups can sometimes provide a bridge between the two.

Some parents of children with PDDs may have to place their children in a therapeutic foster home, either temporarily or permanently. This type of foster-care arrangement is set up to provide specially trained round-the-clock caregivers for medically fragile or disabled children who cannot be cared for at home. Typical reasons for placement may include assaultive or aggressive behavior that endangers parents or siblings; a parent's disability, incarceration, or death; or difficult medical issues, such as tube feeding.

With temporary foster-care placements, the goal is usually to wait out or find a solution for the situation that led to placement. Natural parents must stay as involved as possible—it's very important to attend all meetings and therapy sessions when your child is in foster care, even if the placement was voluntary. Lack of participation can lead to the termination of parental rights in some cases.

Natural parents also need to maintain oversight of the child's medical, educational, and personal needs during the foster-care placement. Foster-care arrangements vary in quality, ranging from homes you wish you had grown up in to the worst of abusive environments. Most therapeutic foster parents are quite good, however.

If the foster placement is in another city, you may need to secure assistance to make regular visits, or send an advocate to make visits for you. Regular communication by mail, email, and/or telephone with your child should be assured when distance is an issue.

It's sad that in the US, foster-care placement is sometimes chosen as a way to ensure the delivery of essential services to children. Foster parents merit a stipend to pay for the cost of the child's care, and the child receives publicly funded healthcare and mental health services. In a better world, natural parents could receive the special training provided to therapeutic foster parents, as well as the subsidies and services they need to care for their difficult children. In all of the nations of Europe, and in many other parts of the world, parents of disabled children are guaranteed financial assistance, healthcare for their child, and other services.

Tips for daily life

There are a lot of things about raising a child with PDD-NOS or atypical PDD that teachers, therapists, and doctors don't know much about. The way you live will change, like it or not.

The good news is that the behaviors that cause these changes usually don't last forever: the child who this week broke wineglasses just to hear them smash will probably not be tossing them two years from now. But if you want to avoid rushing from disaster to disaster, you must have a proactive parenting style. Avoid conflict, redirect behavior, and always be on the lookout for an alternative solution to behavior problems.

Here's some advice culled from many parents on handling typical trouble spots:

Haircuts

If you can figure out what it is about haircuts that drives your child wild, then remove that particular trigger. You may then be able to get the job done at a regular barbershop or salon, with modifications. Common problems and solutions include:

- **Sensitivity to barbershop or salon odors.** If this is the case, look for an old-fashioned barbershop that eschews smelly shampoos, or buy a home haircutting kit. Unscented products are often available, but you may have to buy them yourself and bring them in, or request them in advance.

- **Sensitivity to the sound of buzzing clippers or snapping scissors.** Some people can tolerate one but not the other. There are also old-fashioned hand razors for cutting hair, but it's hard to find a barber who can wield one with precision. Call around! You might also try ear plugs, or a Walkman playing a favorite tape over headphones. Your barber will happily work around headphones if it keeps the child in the chair. You might also choose to accept a longer hairstyle, if grooming is not a problem.

- **Sensory sensitivity in general.** Try brushing the head and hair frequently with a medium-soft hairbrush. This may desensitize the area in time. You may be able to have your child sit in your lap during a haircut; a tight hug may calm him down. Again, home haircuts may be your best bet. Make sure you or your professional uses a neck strip and a cape to keep hair off the skin and clothes, and clean up with a soft brush and/or a blow dryer set on cool. Parents whose children are of African descent may have a particularly hard time with sensory issues when it comes to hair care. Braided styles are the most convenient when it comes to grooming, but take a long time to achieve and involve a lot of pulling. Straightening chemicals and pressing are no picnic either. Short, natural styles may be the easiest to manage.

- **Extreme hyperactivity.** One false move in the barber's chair can result in inadvertent punk-rock 'dos. Many parents swear by cutting hair while the child is fast asleep. Scissors work best for this operation. Keep a brush and comb handy, and work slowly. You may want to use a plastic bowl on the head to get an even length or, for longer styles, hair tape (available at beauty supply stores and many drugstores or chemists).

Toenail and fingernail clipping/cleaning

may be an exaggerated fear of being cut, a desire to not lose a part of one-
or the metallic clicking of the clippers, but many children with PDDs

hate this grooming task. It's best if kids learn to do it for themselves as early as possible, although those with fine-motor problems may find it difficult.

Curved toenail clippers are larger and easier to operate than smaller finger-nail clippers, and can do both jobs passably.

This is another job that parents can do while a child is asleep.

Bathing

This is a problem area with teenagers more often than it is with young children, according to parents. You may have to institute a schedule, or even allow gym-class showers to suffice during the school year.

Even for older kids, tub toys, soap "paints," bubble bath, or other items may allow you to get them in and out of a warm tub once a week.

Contrary to popular belief, it's not necessary to bathe children daily unless there are special medical or sanitary reasons to do so. Use a washcloth to zap any particularly grungy areas daily, and schedule an unavoidable bath time for one or more days each week. A flexible shower hose can be very useful for washing the hair of children who are afraid of the big shower.

Some kids who won't go near a bathtub will go swimming, which usually comes with the added bonus of a mandatory shower. In a pinch, you can see if they'll run through a lawn sprinkler in a pair of shorts. The novelty of pools and sprinklers sometimes trumps fear of getting wet.

Clothing

What do you do with a child who strips off his clothes at every opportunity? First, you try to find out why. The most common reason is sensory sensitivity, so first talk to an occupational therapist about instituting a program of sensory integration therapy.

In the meantime, see what you can do to make staying clothed more comfortable. Verbal children may be able to explain what they don't like about wearing clothes. Common problems include chafing waistbands, itchy fabrics, "new clothes" smells, and annoying tags. Kids who can't stand regular waistbands can often handle elastic-waist pants and shorts, especially those made with soft fabrics, such as sweatpants. Others can wear only overalls or coveralls with ease—and these have the added bonus of being harder to remove.

For children who wear diapers, the diaper itself may be the problem. Check for and treat any actual diaper rash (incidentally, diaper rash can be caused by a yeast infection on the skin, which may indicate a larger problem with yeast overgrowth—see Chapter 5, *Medical Interventions*). Experiment with different types of cloth diapers, various brands of disposables, and larger diapers if tightness around the waist and legs is an issue.

Over the diaper or training pants, sweatpants, overalls (especially the ones with snaps along the inseam), coveralls, and jumpsuits work well. Some parents actually stitch down the overall straps each morning, or replace easy-open fasteners with something more complex. It's possible to open overalls and coveralls for larger children along the inseam and add unobtrusive snaps or Velcro for easy toileting without complete clothes removal.

Some children who tend to remove all their clothing in the bathroom are simply taking extreme steps to prevent getting their clothes dirty. Careful work on toileting technique and rewards for good performance can help. Some may also want to have wet wipes available to improve their after-toilet cleanup, and thereby avoid dirtying their clothes. Wipes can be purchased in small, discreet containers that fit well in a purse or backpack.

Catalogs that carry special clothing for children with disabilities are listed in Appendix A. Many items in these catalogs are especially good for older children who have toileting problems, or for children with orthopedic impairments in addition to PDD-NOS or atypical PDD.

Shirts and dresses that button up the back are also hard to remove.

Many people with sensory problems prefer soft fabrics, such as cotton jersey or terrycloth, over stiff fabrics like denim. If this is the case with your child, go shopping with that in mind. It can help to wash new clothing a few times before wearing it, to remove that stiff feeling as well as any unfamiliar smells.

And speaking of smells, if an aversion to clothing crops up suddenly, make sure you haven't just changed your detergent or fabric softener. There may be a smell or allergy issue going on.

Remove tags from inside of garments as needed.

One solution that will save you money and hassles is purchasing used clothes instead of new ones. These presoftened garments may already feel "just right." Again, they may need to be washed a few times to take away any bothersome scents.

Decorating for autism

The homes of most young children with autistic-spectrum disorders have a certain uniformity. After a few incidents of shattered heirlooms and leaning towers of furniture, accessible areas tend to get a makeover in the direction of a simple, stripped-down look. Baby gates, locked doors, childproofing devices, and the like abound.

When shopping for new furniture, pay extra attention to sturdy, easy-to-clean pieces. You may want to use sticky-back Velcro or foam to secure a few knick-knacks, but it's best to relegate the family china and precious ornaments to an inaccessible room or a locked (and hard to overturn or shake) china cabinet.

Bunk beds and other furnishings that invite acrobatics may not be a good idea for your child. Then again, they might, if your child tends to be unresponsive to her environment, but gets excited about climbing up to an upper bunk or bouncing on a springy mattress.

Likewise, shelves that could be used as steps up to precipitous locations should be removed or very securely anchored.

> *Even though he couldn't walk yet, Ian kept using our dining room chairs to climb up onto the table. Several times he made his way up there in seconds, knocking items onto the floor and risking a fall of several feet. We solved the problem by chaining the dining room chairs to the wall, one in each corner. It made visitors scratch their heads when they saw us do it, but to use the chairs at the table, we just unhooked them.*

Some children seem to have a compulsion to move furniture around, often using it to build ramps up to places they shouldn't be. Solutions include:

- Removing wheels or plastic sliders from furniture legs
- Choosing very heavy furnishings
- Weighting or blocking the movement of furniture with heavy concrete blocks hidden beneath stuffed couches and chairs
- Literally attaching furniture to walls or floor with hook-and-eye fasteners or other hardware

For the early years at least, it's good if you can learn to appreciate thrift-store chic. You'll feel a lot worse if your child picks holes in a $1,000 couch than if he damages a $75 sofa from a garage sale. Slipcovers are a good idea for protecting nice fabrics.

If you want to have one or more nice rooms, either lock them or be prepared to stand guard at all times. Experienced parents can attest that the latter option is not worth it—you definitely have better things to do with your days than worrying about stains on your Persian rugs. There will probably be a time when you can enjoy some of the finer things again, but now may not be that time.

Childproofing dangerous items

Most parents of crawling babies and toddlers take pains to remove hazards from their reach. You may need to continue and even expand this program with a child who has PDD. Funding may be available through government developmental-delay or mental health departments or private agencies to help cover the expense of these modifications. Several catalogs with commercial childproofing solutions are listed in Appendix A, *Resources*.

Items that can pose dangers include:

- **Exposed electrical outlets**. A variety of plugs and covers are available for these.

- **Exposed electrical wiring and extension cords**. Obviously, any exposed wires should be walled off somehow. Extension cords can either be eliminated by adding additional wall outlets or stapled to the wall. Rubber channels are available for making them inaccessible; these can usually be found at office supply stores.

- **Electric fans**. Box fans are less dangerous, but little fingers may still fit in. Experiment with fan placement. You might consider using ceiling fans, swamp coolers, or air conditioning instead in hot weather.

- **Stove burners**. Burner covers can eliminate the attraction of fire or glowing coils, but can also cause burns if touched when hot. Some parents remove the knobs from their stove, place a barrier in front of the stove, add a disconnect valve for the gas behind the stove or unplug it when not in use, or add locking doors to the kitchen.

- **Matches, lighters, and combustibles**. Lock these up, and watch out for guests who carelessly leave lighters or matches on tables.

- Household cleaning supplies, paints, solvents, and other chemicals. A securely locked cabinet is a must if your child tastes and smells everything. Some young autistic children have incurred serious brain damage by repeatedly sniffing gasoline, glue, or other solvents. Of course, these items are sometimes abused as drugs by adolescents and teens.

- Medications, including herbal remedies and vitamins. Most people are unaware that aspirin and Tylenol top the list of medication overdose causes—in other words, keep everything that's medicine out of reach. Securely locked bathroom cabinets can work, but storing medications in the bathroom is actually not that great an idea due to the moisture level. You might install a similar cabinet in another room or use a simple lockbox. Small cash boxes work well and are available at office supply stores for a reasonable price. For convenience's sake, you may wish to keep one week's medications, supplements, and vitamins counted out in a plastic pill box, then keep the pill box in your purse or another more secure location. Be especially wary about leaving chewable medications and vitamins within reach.

- Houseplants. A few are out-and-out poisonous, but heavy pots coupled with tantalizing fronds and tendrils can lead to hurt heads and major messes. Use ceiling hooks to hang trailing plants well out of the way, or try using sticky-back Velcro or foam to secure pots to a flat surface.

- Cigarettes. You would think they'd taste too horrible to eat, but some kids will do it. Tobacco can be quite dangerous when eaten. Keep cigarettes, cigars, chewing tobacco, and full ashtrays under wraps.

- Alcohol. It's dangerous to mix even a little with many of the medications used for PDDs, and it has plenty of inherent dangers of its own. If you like to keep a selection of liquor, wine, or beer at home, you might consider a locked liquor cabinet, or keeping a separate refrigerator in a locked garage or basement.

- Cat litter boxes. Cat feces carry disease and should not be handled by pregnant women or anyone with immune-system problems. The covered boxes may or may not be less attractive to marauding children. Protect the room where the cat box is with a baby gate, or add a cat door to a locked door.

- Stairs and stair banisters. Baby gates or locked doors at the top and/or bottom of stairs may be enough. If the stairs need to be available to your child, make sure that any slats and banisters are too closely spaced for heads or bodies to slip through. If they aren't, you could add more slats or change the banister's style or position. Another solution is blocking access with a net, piece of fabric, or sheet of wood. Commercial stair nets are available that tie securely to open banisters and slats in a stairwell.

- **Guns and other weapons**. These do not belong in the homes of children with neurological disorders, particularly teenagers. The combination of a high potential for depression and easy access to lethal force is very dangerous, and younger children with PDDs may be at risk simply due to their impulsivity. As some recent, tragic cases have shown, storing guns in a locked box under the parents' bed or in a gun cabinet does not guarantee safety around determined teens. If you enjoy shooting sports or hunting, see if you can store your guns at a shooting range or hunt club.

- **Knives**. Sharp knives are common household tools, of course, but they also pose dangers. A drawer latch may be sufficient for keeping kitchen knives out of reach, or you may need to install a keyed lock on the knife drawer. Watch out for knives and other sharp kitchen tools that may be left in the sink, on countertops, or in the dishwasher.

- **Glass, including glass items and windows**. Some children seem to enjoy the sound of broken glass. This may necessitate using window treatments that can be locked down or even boarding up some windows. Cutting a piece of foam to fit within the interior window well is an inexpensive solution that has worked for some parents. Replacing the glass in picture frames with unbreakable plastic may save accidents.

- **Window-blind cords**. These present a danger of hanging if the child puts her head inside the loop. Simply cut through the loop. For persistent offenders, you may want to cut the cords very short as well.

Take a walk through your house with your child's size and interests in mind. If you can notice and remove potential problems before your child sees them, you've done well.

Safety precautions

Some autistic-spectrum children seem to have a Houdini-like ability to escape their rooms, homes, and yards. This would be an amazing talent if it didn't cause families so much fear and heartache. In the film *What's Eating*

Gilbert Grape?, an autistic boy runs away repeatedly to climb a nearby electrical tower, with near-tragic results. The recent thriller *Mercury Rising* presented another autistic character with no fear of heights, trains, or traffic.

Incidents of harm to autistic individuals are depressingly common. At least two autistic children in the US have died in drowning accidents after escaping from their homes in recent years A third spent several harrowing days alone in the Florida Everglades before being rescued—an experience that the nonverbal child's pictures indicated may have included an encounter with an alligator.

The parents of all three of these children had spent considerable time and expense to secure their homes—all it took was a second for the child to slip out of view. If escapes are a problem for your family, please consider using the services of a professional security consultant. You may be able to get help from government developmental-delay or mental health agencies or from private agencies, to find and even pay for these services. Most of us would not normally wish to turn our homes into fortresses, but in some cases it's the most caring thing a parent can do. It could very well save a life.

Security options that parents have tried, with varying degrees of success, include:

- Installing key locks or doorknobs with twist-locks facing outward on bedroom doors can keep a child securely in his room at night. Obviously, toileting could be a problem with this solution. An intercom or buzzer to summon parents can solve this problem (as could a chamber pot, for those willing to try it).

- Latch-style locks, hook-and-eye hardware, or chain-locks installed at the top of interior doors can limit access to certain rooms, or keep a child in one room. Of course, these can be foiled easily when a child gets taller, becomes strong enough to force the door, or figures out how to stand on a chair.

- Double- or triple-bolt security doors can slow down a would-be escapee, and some types can be unlocked only from the inside with a key. While expensive, they are tremendously jimmy-proof. Keep the keys well hidden, of course—on your person, if need be. Fire regulations may require that an exterior-lock key be secured in a fire-box or stored at the nearest fire station in case of emergency.

- Windows can be nailed or latched shut.

- Bars can also be placed on windows, as many homeowners in urban areas already do. Like key locks, these can be a fire hazard. A security consultant, or perhaps your local fire department, may be able to come up with ideas. Some types of bars have interior latches.

- Alarms are available that will warn you if a nocturnal roamer is approaching a door or window. Other types only sound when the door or window is actually opened. Depending on your child's speed, the latter may not give you enough response time.

- Obviously, fences and gates are a good idea for backyards. Some types are less easily scaled than others. Although it might seem cruel, in extreme cases a child's safety could be secured by using electric fencing (usually this involves a single "live" wire at the top of a tall fence). Electric fencing kits are available at some hardware stores or at farm-supply stores.

- Key locks are more secure than latches for gates.

- Electronic locks of various types are another option, including remote-control and keypad varieties. These can be used for garage doors, gates, or exterior doors.

In some cities, the local police department is sensitive to the needs and special problems of the disabled. Officers may be available to provide information about keeping your child or adult patient safe and secure, whether he lives in your home, in an institution or group home, or independently in the community.

Some also have special classes to teach self-defense skills to disabled adults.

Some police departments also keep a registry of disabled people whose behavior could be a hazard to their own safety or whose behavior could be misinterpreted as threatening. If your child is an escape artist, has behaviors that could look like drunkenness or drug use to an uninformed observer, uses threatening words or gestures when afraid, or is extremely trusting of strangers, avail yourself of this service if possible.

People with PDDs can have a bracelet or necklace made with their home phone number, an emergency medical contact number, or the phone number of a service that can inform the caller about their diagnosis. Legends you might want to have engraved on this item include:

- Nonverbal

- Speech-impaired

- Multiple medications

- Medications include ... (list)

- Epilepsy (or other medical condition)

Members of the general public, and even some safety officials, may not know the word "autistic." They are even more unlikely to know what pervasive developmental disorder or PDD means.

If this section has conjured up visions of a nightmarish life with your child, please remember that most people with PDDs do not experience severe problems in the home that cannot be helped with therapeutic, medical, or educational interventions. However, as experienced parents can tell you, once one problem behavior is extinguished it invariably seems to be replaced by a new one. Parents always need to keep on their toes, and it can be exhausting. Take time occasionally to look at the positive side of life with PDDs. There is humor, joy, and sweetness to be found and appreciated along with the challenges.

CHAPTER 11

Finances

THIS CHAPTER DEALS WITH THE TREMENDOUSLY IMPORTANT ISSUES of time and money, two closely related things that no one ever has enough of. We will discuss record-keeping methods that can save you time and that also ensure continuity and appropriateness of care. We'll also discuss government and private sources of direct assistance, other financial resources, and financial planning for the future.

Record keeping

Time is money, and there's no worse waste of both than losing that all-important referral slip or medical report. File every single piece of paper you get from your doctors, therapists, insurance company, service agencies, and school. This includes assessments, evaluations, diagnostic reports, report cards, test results, IFSPs, IEPs, etc. Be especially sure to save copies of your own correspondence. You can be sure that you'll need it later, if only to impress some recalcitrant official with the depth of your organizational abilities.

A portable plastic file box with a handle can be a real boon. You can carry this box to IEP or other meetings easily and have absolutely everything right at hand. Put your documents in labeled folders or large envelopes. Typical sections include Educational, Financial, Medical, Psychological, and Social/Recreational. If an item fits two categories, file it in one folder and make a note on the outside of the other folder about where it is.

Try to file items as they are received. It's much more difficult to go through a whole pile of documents that have been tossed together.

These folders can also help you keep track of relevant articles, photocopies, and computer printouts.

Daily record keeping

It sounds time consuming to keep daily records, but it can be essential for monitoring the effect of dietary changes, medications, vitamins, or supplements. It's also important for assessing behavior patterns and sleep problems.

The easiest thing to do is use a small notebook or daily planner specifically for this purpose. This journal can also be used to keep track of medical, therapy, and school appointments.

It's more precise to bind a year's worth of photocopied pages with important items prelisted to jog your memory or to create a customized electronic journal on your home or notebook computer. Items that you may want to include on your journal pages, either as fill-in-the-blank listings or check-boxes, include:

- Medications taken, with time and dose
- Vitamins and supplements taken, with time and dose
- Food and drink taken, with time and rough amount
- Observable reactions to any of the above
- Elimination (time, amount, characteristics, etc., as needed)
- Any medical or emotional problems observed, with comments
- ABA or floor-time sessions completed, with comments
- Therapy appointments, with comments
- Medical appointments, with comments
- Recreational activities, with comments
- Self-care activities, with comments

Depending on the individual, there may be many other items to add to this list—or far fewer may suffice.

Other items that you should always have on file include a current profile of your child (strengths, weaknesses, abilities, areas of deficit), a list of current medical or psychiatric concerns, and a list of past concerns and how they were addressed.

Many parents and patients like to jot down a few personal notes in their daily journal as well, when they have the time. You might mention how you're feeling, how your relationships are faring, what stresses you're under—whatever helps you unwind and put the day in perspective.

Be sure to save your journal, even if it's just a list on your computer. You'd be surprised how handy the information you have gathered might be in the future. It will help you take a long-term look at what's working and what isn't. Although it's possible to become a bit obsessive about observing your child's every mood, reaction, and action, all of these things may be clues to her medical condition. Playing detective may give you the key to a breakthrough someday.

School record keeping

It's especially important to save both official and unofficial documents from and about your child's years in Early Intervention programs or school. If your school is out of compliance or has not followed proper procedures with your child, you'll need to have these records at hand. Report cards, IEPs or Statements, notes from meetings with school officials, and test results can help you monitor your child's progress. They'll also help you identify techniques and settings that work best.

Of course, should you ever be forced into a due process hearing or a court battle, these records will prove invaluable.

Direct financial support

Most people dealing with PDDs have plenty of practice when it comes to squeezing a buck. Some, however, are hard put to find a dollar to squeeze. Parents with challenging children and adults with serious difficulties can have trouble securing gainful employment.

There are some programs available that may provide you or your family with direct financial support. The checks will be small, but with careful planning they may allow you to give your child the gift of a home-based intensive program or allow you time to develop a career that meets your needs.

United States

The US stands alone in the civilized world as the only country that would rather pay strangers or an institution to care for a child than provide support for parents to do so themselves. While all Western European nations (and many others) provide family support allowances to encourage one parent to stay home with all young children, the US government has cut support even to single parents, and provides extraordinarily low allowances when they are available.

This policy affects the parents of children with disabilities particularly harshly.

Until recently, single, low-income parents of children with disabilities tended to receive Aid to Families with Dependent Children (AFDC, "welfare") and Social Security Income (SSI). When put together, income from these two programs permitted them to eke out a living well below the poverty line, but with some hope of obtaining adequate housing and food. For many of these families, the most important benefit was access to healthcare, as government health insurance (Medicaid) comes with both AFDC and SSI.

Welfare reform has changed this picture drastically. Many states have recon-figured AFDC as a short-term emergency support program. Most states have imposed stringent limits on AFDC programs, such as limiting assistance to once in a lifetime, insisting that parents work for their grants, or forcing par-ents into job-training schemes geared toward a rapid transition to low-wage employment. In some areas, exceptions are still made for single parents car-ing for disabled children, and AFDC caseworkers may be allowed a certain degree of discretion.

If you have a pervasive developmental disorder or other handicap and are parenting and receiving AFDC, this may work for you or against you. Some parents who have let their caseworker know about a personal neurological problem have been exempted from certain regulations. Others have lost their children. You should see a welfare rights organization or sympathetic social worker before making the decision to tell. They can help you ensure your children's security by approaching the issue correctly.

You can apply for AFDC at your county's Child and Family Services depart-ment. The program is primarily for single parents, but two-parent families are eligible in some areas and under some circumstances. The amount of the monthly grant varies. It is determined by the county government, which administers AFDC programs at the local level. Grants range from around $150 per month in some rural Southern counties to about $650 per month in expensive cities like San Francisco, where a small supplemental housing benefit is factored into the grant.

You'll need to provide very complete documentation to get and retain AFDC benefits on the basis of needing to provide full-time home care for a child. You can expect to have an eligibility review at least every three months, during which all of your documents will be reviewed and you will be re-interviewed. Generally speaking, you cannot have savings or possessions worth over $1,000, although you may own a home and a modest vehicle. You may be forced to sell a car or other valuables before you can receive benefits. Your AFDC grant may be reduced by the amount of other financial assistance you receive. If you find part-time work, your grant will also be reduced by this amount or a portion thereof—some states do have work incentive programs. Court-ordered child-support payments to AFDC recipients are paid to the county rather than directly to the parent, and your grant will be debited for these as well.

You may be eligible for food stamps, "commodities" (free food), and other benefits, such as job training, if you receive AFDC. People leaving AFDC may be eligible for certain short-term benefits, such as subsidized childcare and continued health insurance.

SSI is a federal program that provides a small monthly stipend for children and adults with disabilities that cause marked and severe functional limitations. Benefits range from around $300 to $400 per month for children or for adults living in another person's household to over $600 per month. More importantly for many, SSI recipients are also eligible for Medicaid, a federal health-insurance plan. As with AFDC, your assets and income from other sources will have to be limited, which can bring stress of its own as parents are forced to "spend down" any savings and let careers slide to become or remain eligible.

> *Staying able to get SSI and Medicaid has meant my husband could not get a better job because the pay would knock us out of contention for Medicaid. We don't care about the SSI, we just need Medicaid for therapy and vision coverage.* —Holly, mother of three-year-old Max (diagnosed PDD-NOS and apraxia of speech)

Getting SSI may be one of the most difficult things you'll ever do. You apply at your nearest Social Security office, which can provide you with the paperwork and a current instruction book. You can also do a pre-eligibility screen over the phone (call the national Social Security hotline at 800-772-1213).

The application form is extremely long, and requires copious documentation. SSI caseworkers and medical examiners seem to thrive on placing road-blocks in your way.

The SSI application process has become increasingly adversarial over the past two decades. You may get the distinct impression that the people interviewing you think you or your child is faking a disability—and your impression may be right. The Social Security department will order an Individualized Functional Assessment (IFA), which may include seeing more doctors as well as a review of your medical documentation. Your child may be interviewed and observed by a psychiatrist or medical doctor working for Social Security. You have the right to be present for this interview, although parents report that some doctors seem to want to exclude them from the process.

Most applicants for SSI are rejected on their first try. You do have the right to appeal SSI denial, however—and you should, because a high percentage of appeals succeed. In addition, successful appellants get a lump sum equal to the payments they should have received had their original application been properly approved. This sum can be several thousand dollars, and has helped many families fund things like more secure housing, wheelchairs, and other important needs.

If you need help with SSI (or, for that matter, with AFDC if you are applying primarily because of your own or your child's special needs), contact a disability advocacy agency (see Appendix B, *Support and Advocacy*). This agency can help you through the application process, and most can provide legal assistance if you need to appeal. Additional information about the program is available online (for adults or general information, *http://www.ssa.gov/odhome/* or for children, *http://www.ssas.com/ssikids.html*).

SSI is usually an income-dependent program. If you are working and earn more than the regulations allow, your child will not be eligible for SSI. However, a special income-limit waiver is available to help families who have income but whose children have expensive medical needs. See Chapter 8, *Insurance*, for information on the waiver process.

Some states, large cities, private agencies, and Native American tribes also have income support programs. You may be eligible for one of these. A county social worker or tribal official should be able to help you find out if you qualify.

We receive assistance from a United Way program and some grant funds from the state Department of Mental Retardation. —Charlotte, mother of four-year-old Rory (diagnosed PDD-NOS)

Canada

Welfare is available in Canada for people with disabilities, single parents, and unemployed adults with or without children. The amount of the monthly payment is set at the provincial level. The disability payment varies from a low of about $580 per month in poor provinces like New Brunswick to around $800 per month in more expensive Ontario and British Columbia. Under the Canadian system, payments to parents caring for children, single or otherwise, are higher than those for disabled adults.

To apply for state welfare benefits, visit your nearest Ministry or Department of Social Services. For disability benefits, regulations vary by state. Generally speaking, however, you must be eighteen years of age or older and require, as a direct result of a severe mental or physical impairment:

1. Extensive assistance or supervision in order to perform daily living tasks within a reasonable time, or

2. Unusual and continuous monthly expenditures for transportation, special diets, or other unusual but essential and continuous needs, and

3. Have confirmation from a medical practitioner that the impairment exists and will likely continue for at least two years or longer, or that it is likely to continue for at least one year and then recur.

There are limits on the amount and kinds of savings and other property that a person or family receiving benefits can have.

As in the US, welfare reform is a growing trend in Canada. Some states have introduced mandatory workfare programs for single adults and for some parents on welfare. These provisions generally do not apply to people receiving disability benefits, and parents caring for disabled children may be able to have welfare-to-work requirements waived or deferred.

Canadians who are denied benefits or who have other problems with the benefits agency can appeal its decisions to an independent tribunal.

Some assistance for people with disabilities may also be available at the federal level, or from First Nations (Native Canadian) agencies.

Other direct and indirect income assistance is available, such as subsidized travel and tax benefits. For example, college students with permanent disabilities can have their student loans forgiven, and are also eligible for special grants to pay for a note-taker, transportation, and other education-related expenses.

United Kingdom

In the UK, people with disabilities have access to three major types of direct state benefits. You can apply for these programs at your local Benefits Agency Office.

The Disability Living Allowance (DLA) is for adults or children with a disability. Parents or carers can apply on behalf of a child. Payment ranges from 15 to 35 pounds per week. The DLA forms are relatively complex, so, if possible, find an experienced disability advocate to help you fill them out. Some autism support groups have DLA experts on staff, as may your local council. Adults may be able to do some paid work while receiving DLA.

Parents and others caring for a child who receives DLA can apply for the Attendants Allowance (also called the Carers Allowance) program as well.

Any person over five years old who receives DLA can also get a Mobility Allowance, a small sum of money to help them get to appointments and meet general transportation needs.

Your local council may also have its own benefits scheme. These may be direct payments, such as a supplemental housing benefit or tax offsets. A number of supported work schemes are also available for people with disabilities and adults receiving other forms of public assistance. In some cases, these programs are mandatory.

Students pursuing a college degree may find themselves in a "Catch-22" situation: on some occasions benefits officers have decided that, if they are well enough to go to college, they're well enough to work, and have canceled their benefits. You can appeal these and other unfavorable decisions to a Social Security Appeals Tribunal.

See the report at *http://www.ahead.ie/grants/grants.html#toc* for special information about disability benefits in Northern Ireland.

Republic of Ireland

Disability Allowance and Disability Benefit are available in Ireland, but are far from generous. Both are administered via the Department of Social Welfare. Disabled students can continue to receive these benefits while attending third level courses, although they may lose other types of public assistance, such as rent allowance.

Maintenance Grant (a general benefit for poor families) is not affected by these benefits.

Supported work schemes are available, although your earnings may make you lose your disability benefits. The exception is work that the local welfare officer agrees is "rehabilitative" in nature.

A number of scholarship and grant programs are available to assist students with disabilities. See the report at *http://www.ahead.ie/grants/grants.html#toc* for more information.

Australia

A variety of income support programs are available to Australian citizens, including direct financial assistance for adults with disabilities, parents caring for children with disabilities, single parents, unemployed single adults, youth and students. Programs related specifically to disabled citizens and their families include:

- Disability Support Pension
- Related Wife Pension
- Sickness Allowance
- Mobility Allowance
- Carer Payment
- Child Disability Allowance

Employment programs for people with disabilities are many and varied, including the Supported Wage System (SWS), which brings the earnings of disabled workers in sheltered workshops or other types of supported or low-wage employment closer to the livability range.

Indirect benefits may also be available under the Disability Services Act in the areas of education, work, recreation, and more.

To apply for benefits or disability services, contact your local Department of Family and Community Services.

New Zealand

Direct benefits in New Zealand are similar to those provided in Australia, although the payments have historically been much lower. Domestic Purposes Benefit is for single parents. There are also a number of additional services available to the disabled and their carers, including training schemes, supported employment, and recreational assistance. The social safety net in New Zealand is currently being revamped, but services for people with disabilities are actually expected to expand.

To apply for benefits or services, contact your local Ministry of Social Welfare office, which runs the Income Support program. If you need help with paperwork or appeals, Beneficiary Advisory Services (*http://canterbury.cyberplace.org.nz/community/bas.html*) in Christchurch provides assistance and advocacy, as do a number of disability advocacy groups, particularly the information clearinghouse Disability Information Service (*http://canterbury.cyberplace.co.nz/community/dis.html*).

Indirect financial help

In the US, tax deductions have replaced direct financial assistance to the poor in many cases. Since these benefits are provided but once a year, they are less convenient, but families coping with the high cost of disability care should take advantage of them.

One of the most important tax benefits is the medical deduction available on your federal tax forms. You can write off not only the direct cost of doctors' visits not covered by health insurance, but also your insurance co-payments and deductible, and out-of-pocket expenses for medications, medical devices, in-home healthcare assistants (presumably including ABA therapists), travel costs related to medical care, and at least some expenses related to attending medical or disability conferences and classes. Special deductions for health-insurance premiums are available for self-employed people.

Because medical deductions limit your federal tax liability, they will also reduce your state income taxes (state taxes are usually based on taxable income figures from your federal form). Some states have additional tax-time benefits for the disabled. In Oregon, for example, each disabled child counts as two dependents.

Another important federal tax benefit is the Earned Income Credit (EIC) program. This benefit for the working poor can actually supplement your earnings with a tax rebate, not just a deduction.

Mortgage interest is also tax-deductible, as most people are aware. Since your home is usually not considered an asset when determining eligibility for direct financial assistance, this makes home ownership particularly attractive to disabled adults and to families who expect to provide care for a child with a PDD into adulthood. Some banks and credit unions have special mortgage programs for low- and moderate-income families. Given the strong financial benefits of home ownership, including the opportunity to keep your housing costs from going up in the future, purchasing a house is very advisable.

Very low income families, including adults with PDDs who rely on SSI or fixed-income trusts, may be able to get additional help in reaching the goal of home ownership from organizations like Habitat for Humanity or Franciscan Enterprises.

Help with medications

Low-income patients may be able to get their medications for free just by providing documentation to charitable programs run by pharmaceutical companies. In the US, the Pharmaceutical Manufacturers Association publishes a directory of indigent programs. Doctors can get a copy of the PMA's official guide by calling (800) PMA-INFO. Alternatively, you or your doctor can call the company that makes your medication directly to find out about its indigent patient program:

Pharmaceutical Company	Phone Number
3M Pharmaceuticals	(800) 328-0255
Allergan Prescription	(800) 347-4500
Alza Pharmaceuticals	(415) 962-4243
Amgen, Inc.	(800) 272-9376
Astra U.S.A., Inc.	(800) 488-3247
Berlex	(800) 423-7539
Boehringer Ingleheim	(203) 798-4131
Bristol Myers Squibb	(800) 736-0003

Pharmaceutical Company	Phone Number
Burroughs-Wellcome	(800) 722-9294
Ciba-Geigy Patient Support Program	(800) 257-3273 or (908) 277-5849
Eli-Lilly	(317) 276-2950
Genetech, Inc.	(800) 879-4747
Glaxo, Inc.	(800) 452-7677
Hoechst-Roussel	(800) 776-5463
Hoffman-Larouche	(800) 526-6367
Ici-Stuart	(302) 886-2231
Immunex Corp.	(800) 321-4669
Janssen	(800) 253-3682
Johnson & Johnson	(800) 447-3437
J&J (Janssen)	(908) 524-9409
Knoll	(800) 526-0710
Lederle	(800) 526-7870
Lilly Cares Program	(800) 545-6962
Marion Merrel Dow	(800) 362-7466
McNeil Pharmaceuticals	(800) 682-6532
Merck Human Health	(800) 672-6372
Miles	(800) 998-9180
Ortho Pharmaceuticals	(800) 682-6532
Parke-Davis	(202) 540-2000
Pfizer Indigent Patient Program	(800) 646-4455
Pharmacia, Inc.	(800) 795-9759
Proctor & Gamble	(800) 448-4878
Rhone-Poulenc Rorer	(610) 454-8298
Roche Labs	(800) 285-4484
Roxane Labs	(800) 274-8651
Sandoz	(800) 937-6673
Sanofi Winthrop	(800) 446-6267
Schering Labs	(800) 521-7157
Searle	(800) 542-2526
Serono	(617) 982-9000
SmithKline Access to Care Program	(800) 546-0420 (patient requests) or (215) 751-5722 (physician requests)
Solvay Patient Assistance Program	(800) 788-9277
Survanta Lifeline	(800) 922-3255
Syntex Labs	(800) 822-8255
UpJohn Co.	(800) 242-7014
Wyeth-Ayerst	(703) 706-5933
Zeneca Pharmaceuticals	(800) 456-5678

An organization called the Medicine Program (573-778-1118, *help@themedicineprogram.com*, *http://www.themedicineprogram.com/*) can help you and your doctors ensure that you can sign up with indigent patient programs for medications.

Most of these programs require that you have no insurance coverage for outpatient prescription drugs, that purchasing the medication at its retail price would be a hardship for you due to your income and/or expenses, and that you do not qualify for a government or third-party program that can pay for the prescription.

Another source for free medications is your physician's sample cabinet. All you have to do is ask, and hope that the pharmaceutical representative has paid a recent visit. Samples can help tide you over rough financial patches, but you can't rely on getting them monthly.

In some cases, you can reduce the cost of your monthly medication bill by using a mail-order or online pharmacy (see the section "Mail-order medications," later in this chapter).

Miscellaneous discounts

Don't forget, adults with PDDs, children with PDDs, and sometimes, by extension, their families may be eligible for a variety of discounts and special access programs. For example, the US National Parks Service offers a lifelong pass that gives disabled individuals free entry to all national parks, as well as half-price camping privileges. If the recipient is a child, her family also gets the discount. Disneyland, Disneyworld, and many other theme parks have special perks for people with disabilities, such as not having to wait in line for attractions.

There are a number of programs around the world that help disabled people get access to computers and the Internet. One that offers *free* computers is Minneapolis, Minnesota-based DRAGnet. You can reach them at (612) 378-9796, fax (612) 378-9794, *gille027@tc.umn.edu*.

If you need medical assistance in a location far from home but can't afford the cost of a flight or hotel, here are some resources that may be able to help in the US or Canada:

- AirCare Alliance (referrals for TWA Operations Liftoff and AirLifeLine), (800) 296-1217

- AirLifeLine, (916) 429-2166 or (800) 446-1231

- Corporate Angel (arranges flights on corporate jets for patients), (914) 328-1313

- Miles for Kids in Need, (817) 963-8118

- Continental Care Force, (713) 261-6626

- Wings of Freedom (negotiates with commercial airlines for low-cost tickets), (504) 857-0727

- National Association of Hospitality Houses, (800) 524-9730

Similar corporate programs may be available in Europe, Australia, and New Zealand. Contact the public relations office of your national airline to find out more. You may also be eligible for an emergency travel grant from a social services agency to cover these needs.

Planning for your child's future

As noted in Chapter 9, *School*, transition planning services for teens in special education may include helping them arrange for financial support through SSI, getting young adults into medical insurance programs via Medicaid or state insurance plans, helping young adults manage their own medical and/or psychiatric care, and other services, such as GED assistance, job shadowing, and so on. You can also make your own transition plan. Areas that most families need to work on include:

- Housing, including group homes or other supported housing if needed

- Work or financial assistance

- Higher education

- Healthcare

- Health insurance (see Chapter 8, *Insurance*)

- Case management

- Long-term planning

Start thinking about the future while your child is still young, and revise your expectations as you go. Don't be afraid to have big dreams for your child, as starting early makes them more likely to be realized, no matter how "unrealistic."

> *I hope Jeffrey will be able to live in a supervised rental, with others his age, and be able to take care of his needs with some assistance. I hope he will find meaningful, satisfying work (not hauling trash or sweeping floors!) and be able to earn some of his own money. I hope he develops a physical activity he is able to do on a regular basis, perhaps with others, which will keep him healthy. And most of all, if life gets to be too much for him, I hope he will be able to tell me.* —Cindy, mother of fifteen-year-old Jeffrey (diagnosed verbal dyspraxia with "autistic-like" features)

Housing

Some disabled people in the US are eligible for financial assistance with housing and for housing preference programs through Housing and Urban Development (HUD) programs, including the Section 8 grant program. Section 8 is especially flexible, because the grant you receive each month can be used to reduce the cost of housing you find on the open market. Some charitable organizations and churches also manage low-income housing projects or voucher programs, and may have preferential treatment for people with disabilities.

Subsidized housing ranges from adult foster homes with full-time staff on up to private apartments with no support on site. The wait for housing can be long (three years or more for Section 8 vouchers), so it's important to apply before there's a pressing need. This may mean applying while a teenager is still in high school.

Some subsidized housing is substandard, especially in urban areas where the supply of low-cost units is tight. You'll need to pay special attention to security concerns, such as locking doors and windows, having a personal telephone in case of emergencies, and the safety of the surrounding neighborhood for a person who may be particularly vulnerable to crime. Sanitary conditions may also need work, especially if you are considering an older housing project or a residential hotel. Landlords can be made responsible for bringing units up to code, but they may not respond until the tenant's family or a social services agency gets involved.

If you are or are about to be homeless, you may be able to move to the front of the line for subsidized housing. Contact a social services agency for help in pressing your case quickly, especially if you have children.

Other options are also available. Some of these programs may be covered by long-term care insurance, health insurance, funds placed in trust, or monthly payments made by you or your adult child. They include institutional care, supported farm communities, group homes that stress independent living, and self-managed group homes or co-ops. Your regional autism advocacy group should have a list of subsidized and commercial housing possibilities in your area that are appropriate for people with PDDs, or you can check in with a public or private social services agency.

Note for adults with PDDs: Many, perhaps even most, adults with PDD-NOS or atypical PDD will be able to live largely independent lives if their families and professional helpers lay the groundwork. Adults with PDDs should have full input on any decisions made on their behalf, particularly where an important issue like housing is concerned. If you are dissatisfied with a group home or other living situation, talk it over with your family or a case manager. There are alternatives available, including housing arrangements set up by and for people with disabilities who wish to live as independently as possible in the community.

Services to help you achieve the goal of independent living include housekeeping services, budgeting help, and special transportation arrangements. Don't be afraid to ask: these basic services are generally much less expensive than group homes or other living arrangements with round-the-clock support.

There is a growing trend toward helping disabled adults purchase their own homes. Sometimes grants are available for down payment assistance, along with special loan programs, trust arrangements, and home buying and home ownership training.

In the UK, Ireland, Australia, and New Zealand, your local housing authority or council housing office can help you get on the waiting list and inform you of any preference programs for the disabled and their carers that might move you up the queue faster. Charitable agencies and churches may also have low-income housing programs.

Healthcare

You won't always be there to take your child to medical and therapy appointments, make sure he takes his medications and vitamins, and wrangle with his managed care issues. Parents need to start teaching their children as early as possible about using public transportation or driving, picking up prescriptions and reading their labels, paying medical bills, and knowing where to go for help. Some adults are never able to handle all of these tasks adequately, even though they may be perfectly competent in other areas of their life. These individuals will need support to help them get appropriate medical care. Case management services (see the section that follows) can help, but a personal aide or a self-care advocate may be even better.

You'll also need to identify adult healthcare providers in advance as your child nears the end of adolescence. Young women will need to see a gynecologist, for example, and both boys and girls will be leaving their pediatrician for a general practitioner.

If there will be changes in how your child's healthcare is paid for—for example, if she will be transitioning from private health insurance to Medicaid—you may have to prospect for knowledgeable doctors in an unfamiliar medical bureaucracy.

You can also help your adult child develop methods for keeping track of medications, appointments, dietary restrictions, and the like. Visual charts, calendars, and personal agenda books may be useful if appointments are filled in far in advance.

Case management

You may continue to act as your adult child's "case manager" for many years, or you may wish to give this job to a professional. Case management services can encompass arranging for healthcare, connecting the client with community services, a certain amount of financial management (such as being the client's payee for SSI), and much more.

Case managers can be hired privately or found within government departments or advocacy agencies for the disabled. Some medical facilities provide health case management services for adult disabled patients.

What we opted for was the services of a caseworker with County Mental Health, who will continue to be a resource person for KayCee as

*she transitions to adulthood. He signed her up for a supplemental mental
health insurance program available through the state that will cover any
needs that fall outside of our insurance plan, like mental health inpatient
care or extra therapy sessions. When she reaches the age of eighteen,
she'll be eligible for state health insurance or Medicaid, based on her own
income from work.*

Long-term planning

If you're lucky enough to have an estate left to help your child after your
death, do not put off making arrangements. Because of the laws surrounding public disability benefits, inheriting money could end up being a terrible burden rather than a safety net.

Special trusts, usually called discretionary trusts, can make funds or real
property (such as a home) available to adults with disabilities. These trusts
are set up to keep the recipient eligible for government assistance, publicly
funded health insurance, and subsidized housing. Generally speaking, discretionary trusts require a trustee other than the recipient to be in charge.
Money in a discretionary trust can be used to pay for items other than food,
clothing, and shelter, such as education, phone bills, and recreation, without reducing benefits. If these funds are used for food, clothing, or shelter, a
limited amount can be deducted from the SSI check.

You'll need to consult a financial planner and/or a lawyer with experience in
working on disability issues to set up a discretionary trust.

When you must be self-reliant

Children and adults with PDDs who live in isolated rural areas, or who simply do not have access to appropriate healthcare and education services due
to lack of money, face a serious struggle. They must be largely self-reliant,
using their ingenuity and limited community resources to build support
systems.

It can be done.

DIY treatment

DIY stands for "do it yourself," and that's what many adults and families
affected by pervasive developmental disorders must do. That may mean

going without expensive pharmaceutical interventions and relying instead on diet, vitamins and supplements, and one-on-one help.

Two of the most effective interventions for children with PDD-NOS or atypical PDD, ABA and floor-time play therapy, can be delivered at home by parents and volunteers. No special equipment is required, just time and dedication. Books that explain how to start and run ABA and floor-time programs are available via mail order (see Appendix A, *Resources*).

Obviously, medical and psychiatric care requires expertise that most of us don't have, but even there, resources are available. Bibliotherapy, the time-honored process of getting medical or psychiatric information from self-help books, is what you're doing right now.

You may also be able to get direct help from physicians and therapeutic professionals via mail or telephone. Some are even willing to make themselves available for a "virtual consultation" online. Naturally, it's best to see a doctor or other medical professional in person, but if your location or financial situation prevents that, there may be ways to work things out—it never hurts to ask.

Home-schooling support

If appropriate educational facilities are not available in your area and residential schooling is out of the question, you will probably decide to opt for home-schooling. If you can possibly afford it and access it, get an Internet connection. Online support is available for home-schoolers, particularly on the World Wide Web, that will allow you to offer your child "classes" at home in everything from geography to calculus. Compared to the cost of purchasing books and encyclopedias, the Net is almost always a bargain. Even a simple text-only dial-up account can put you in touch with the latest medical information, and can be accessed with the most basic of computer equipment. Dial-up access (and often Web access as well) may be available at no charge through your public library, a nearby school, or a business or government agency that's willing to provide you with occasional access to its equipment.

Home-schooling support is also available by mail via newsletters, magazines, and parent-to-parent letters.

Books for home-schoolers can be purchased by mail order, although public libraries may have enough of a selection. If you are in a very rural area, you may be able to borrow books from a library at some distance via mail.

Mail-order medications

Lack of a drugstore or a limited budget need not cut you off from medications, either. If you can't get it for free (see the section "Help with medications," earlier in this chapter), there are also cheaper and more convenient ways to fill your prescription.

Online and mail-order pharmacies can fill your prescription and mail it to you, sometimes at a substantial savings. Medications may be available via mail order within your country or from overseas. The latter option can be surprisingly inexpensive and may provide you with access to medications that normally would not be available where you live. Communicating via fax, email, or telephone generally works best with these firms, which can usually send you a three-month supply in each order. Be sure to check for any Customs regulations that might prohibit you from importing medication before ordering, of course, especially if the drug is not approved for use in your country.

Some mail-order and online pharmacies were initially created to serve the market for AIDS medications, but have since expanded to cover a wide selection. Many will accept health insurance if you have a drug benefit—some will actually cover your medication co-payment as part of the deal.

Your doctor may have to fill out some paperwork before you can use these mail-order services. As with any other transaction by mail or over the Internet, you'll want to do as much as you can to check out the company's reputation and quality of service before sending money or using your credit card.

If you are stationed overseas with the US military, contact your Tricare health benefits representative about mail-order arrangements.

Mail-order pharmacies that some parents and patients have worked with successfully include:

CanadaRx
http://www.canadarx.net/

This is a consortium of Canadian pharmacies set up specifically to provide discounted prescriptions to US customers, although Canadians and others can use the service as well. Mail-order arrangements must be made over the Net or directly through one of the consortium members (their addresses are available on the Web site).

Continental Pharmacy
P.O. Box 94863
Cleveland, OH 44101-4863
Phone (216) 459-2010 or (800) 677-4323
Fax (216) 459-2004

Farmacia Rex S.R.L.
Cordoba 2401
Esq. Azcuénaga 1120
Buenos Aires, Argentina
Phone (54-1) 961-0338
Fax (54-1) 962-0153
http://www.todoservicio.com.ar/farmacia.rex/rexmenu.htm

Deeply discounted prices, and they mail anywhere.

GlobalRx
4024 Carrington Lane
Efland, NC 27243
Phone (919) 304-4278 or (800) 526-6447
Fax (919) 304-4405
info@aidsdrugs.com
http://globalrx.com/

Masters Marketing Company, Ltd.
Masters House No. 1
Marlborough Hill
Harrow, Middlesex HA1 1TW
England
Phone (011) 44-181-424-9400
Fax (011) 4481 427 1994

Carries a limited selection of European pharmaceuticals, as well as a few American-made drugs, including Prozac.

No Frills Pharmacy
1510 Harlan Drive
Bellevue, NE 68005
Phone (800) 485-7423
Fax (402) 682-9899
refill@nofrillspharmacy.com
http://www.nofrillspharmacy.com/

Peoples Pharmacy
http://www.peoplesrx.com/

This Austin, Texas-based chain provides Net-only mail-order service and can compound medications as well.

Pharmacy Direct
3 Coal St.
Silverwater, NSW 2128
Australia
Phone (02) 9648-8888 or (1300) 656-245
Fax (02) 9648 8999 or (1300) 656 329
pharmacy@pharmacydirect.com.au
http://www.pharmacydirect.com.au/home.htm

You must have a prescription from an Australian doctor to use this mail-order service.

The Pharmacy Shop (also known as Drugs by Mail)
5007 N. Central
Phoenix, AZ 85012
Phone (602) 274-9956 or (800) 775-6888
Fax (602) 241-0104
sales@drugsbymail.com
http://www.pharmacyshop.com/ or *http://www.drugsbymail.com/*

Preferred Prescription Plan
2201 W. Sample Road, Bldg. 9, Suite 1-A
Pompano Beach, FL 33073
Phone (954) 969-1230 or (800) 881-6325 or
Fax (800) 881-6990
cust-svc@prefrx.com
http://www.prefrx.com/

Stadtlanders Pharmacy
600 Penn Center Blvd.
Pittsburgh, PA 15235-5810
(800) 238-7828
enroll@stadtlander.com
http://stadtlander.com/

Stadtlanders Pharmacy has a stellar reputation in the disability community.

Victoria Apotheke (Victoria Pharmacy)
Bahnhofstrasse 71
Postfach CH-8021
Zurich, Switzerland
Fax (01) 221-2322 (Europe) or (011) 411-221-2322 (US)
Phone (01) 211-2432 (Europe) or (011) 411-211-24 32 (US)
victoriaapotheke@access.ch
http://www.access.ch/victoria_pharmacy

CHAPTER 12

Support

FAMILIES INTERVIEWED FOR THIS BOOK say that feelings of isolation, public disapproval, and the loss of social support that they once enjoyed make dealing with pervasive developmental disorders more difficult than it should be. Parents and adult patients look for support wherever they can find it. Many do go wanting, but in this chapter we explore how you can build a solid support system for a person with PDDs and his or her family.

Breaking out of isolation

When a child is diagnosed with PDD-NOS or atypical PDD, his family has already experienced a period of prediagnosis crisis. The family has usually undergone immense stress and become increasingly isolated. Old friends have fallen away, the family may have stopped attending religious services or participating in community activities, and breaks with the extended family have often occurred. Marriages and sibling relationships have suffered. Once the diagnosis has been made, one of the most important tasks at hand is building a new support system.

This support system is likely to be very different from the old one. When your life is rolling along nicely, you seek out friends and activities for the purpose of mutual enjoyment. When you are in the throes of difficulty, however, you look for a lifeline. The old sources of support may not be adequate anymore. Your new support system is also likely to include some paid professionals—counselors, social workers, psychologists, or psychiatrists—as well as people who are personally involved with autistic-spectrum disorders as parents, adults with PDDs, support group coordinators, and advocates. It can feel pretty strange to pay for support, or to find yourself immersed in a community of people drawn together by a disability. It may not seem natural. It takes some getting used to at first, but it will be worthwhile.

Support groups

Support groups, in person or on the Internet, can help you break through the wall of isolation. Many excellent support resources are available for parents, and there are a few springing up for children or adults with PDDs as well.

Every support group is different, even local groups that are based on a regional or national model. Personalities, style, location, and local issues set the tone for each group. Typical types of support groups include:

- Groups for parents of newly diagnosed children, which may have a professional in a leadership or organizational role. These groups tend to be short-lived or to be an official service made available to a new set of parents each year (for example, as part of an Early Intervention program).

- Parent groups for mutual support and for exchanging information about local resources. These may be organized by parents themselves, or they may be provided by a school or organization. Some groups bring in speakers for each meeting, while others are more informal.

- Parent groups organized around a specific topic or activity, such as groups for parents implementing special diets, families whose children attend the same school, or those pursuing the possibility that their child's PDD was caused by vaccinations.

- Social skills groups for children and teenagers. These groups are usually founded by parents to organize activities that allow their children (and sometimes nondisabled peers or siblings) to get to know each other and enjoy mutual interests. While the children play, adults often find time for informal socializing and support.

- Adult support groups, which may include older teens or other family members as well. Some such groups are purely social, some act as formal information forums, and others get involved in advocacy projects.

- Advocacy groups that take on specific political or educational projects. Most developed nations have a national autism organization of some sort, and many have similar regional and local groups as well. These groups may publish informational materials for parents and professionals, sponsor conferences and classes, provide direct services to parents and people with PDDs, lobby for increased government or private funding for PDD-related services, lobby in favor of medical research, and try to raise the profile of autistic-spectrum disorders.

- Online support groups, which may be open to all comers and unmoderated, open but moderated, or limited to approved members only.

If a group that appeals to you already exists, you can simply join in. If it's strictly a parent- or patient-run enterprise, you can be sure that you'll be expected to lend a hand occasionally. This isn't easy when your life is already full of work and stress, but there are small tasks available in any group that will make you a valuable contributor without taking away too much time from the rest of your life. One thing's for certain: you will get out what you put into any group. If no one's willing to put energy into an organization, it will wither away quickly.

Starting a new group

If there isn't already an organization available that meets your needs, you might consider starting your own. It's easier than you might think.

Typically, new support and advocacy groups arise in periods of crisis. If this is your situation—for example, if adequate educational services are not available in your area for children with PDD-NOS or atypical PDD—the stage is set. To contact other parents who might be interested, you can send flyers home with children in special education classes; publish a notice in the local newspaper; use Internet chat forums to post information; put up flyers around town; ask local religious institutions to let their congregations know about the issue; and ask doctors, psychiatrists, neurologists, and others who work with parents to pass the word. Word of mouth is also a powerful organizing tool.

> We have a really special support group for parents in our neighborhood. It's so informal that it doesn't even have a name. Once a month we meet at an inexpensive Italian restaurant for dinner and talk about our troubles and our triumphs. I also go to meetings of a national support group, but this other one makes me feel the most nurtured. I look forward to those dinners all month.

Some of the best support groups are quite small, made up of just a few families coming together to share their feelings and ideas over a meal or coffee. Even advocacy groups need not be large to have an effect. All it takes is a few people with the time and vision to plan a campaign. Disability advocacy groups can often attract volunteers who don't have a personal connection to the disability. Many organizations and forums exist that help prospective volunteers hook up with groups that need them. Schools are also an excellent source of volunteers, who may even be able to earn credit for their work with your organization.

Keeping your group alive

.No matter how large your group is or what its purpose will be, there are a few issues that will affect it right from the start. These include:

- **Money.** Passing the hat will suffice for coffee and copier fees, but groups that publish newsletters or pamphlets, conduct research, or do major outreach and lobbying efforts will need more secure funding. In some cases, money may be available through a hospital, government health or disabilities department, or private foundation. Some groups are able to tap outside donors or philanthropists. You may want to charge members a small fee to join, hold annual fundraising events, put penny jars at businesses around town, or try other methods to help the group meet its financial goals.

- **Leadership.** Your group may or may not want to have elected officials, but it may be required by law if you choose to have a nonprofit tax status. Generally speaking, members should set the direction of the group and do the work, but sometimes an official spokesperson or a facilitator (someone who keeps discussions on track at meetings) will also be needed. Larger advocacy organizations generally have some paid staff members, but they still rely heavily on volunteers to get things done. Finding and motivating volunteers, tapping new resources, and thinking up ideas for activities takes a special kind of leadership. Leaders are made, not born, and they do require nurturing. Many groups have found that rotating new people through leadership positions prevents burnout, spreads skills throughout the organization, and brings new ideas to the fore.

- **Meeting space.** Support groups may meet in members' homes, in restaurants, or in rented meeting rooms. Others find rooms available at no or low cost at schools; hospitals or clinics; mental health facilities; churches, mosques, or synagogues.

- **Communication.** Phone trees, email lists, Web sites that allow members to post and reply to messages, and printed newsletters are the main ways that support and advocacy groups communicate between meetings. Electronic communication is the least expensive, but printed newsletters have the added advantage of being available for anyone who can read. Many groups use a combination of communication methods. Some support groups don't have communication between meetings at all, other than notes or cards sent out to inform members of when and where the next meeting will be. Some groups have been able to get hospitals or other medical facilities to send out their newsletters or announcements at no or low cost.

- **Information.** The greatest source of information in any support or advocacy group is its members. However, many groups choose to maintain a library of books, videotapes, pamphlets, documents, medical reports, and ideas for the use of all members. Some keep computer databases or files of local resources and problems, perhaps making them available via the Internet. A support group's library can be as simple as a box of books, videos, and file folders brought to each meeting. Members can look at materials during the meeting, make copies if a machine is convenient, or borrow items. Some groups work with a hospital or medical center library to maintain up-to-date files on autistic-spectrum disorders.

Professional support

As the previous section indicated, support groups can be part of a range of professional services provided to parents or to adults with PDDs. These kinds of support groups may be organized by government bodies, schools, or healthcare organizations.

Group therapy

Group therapy is perhaps the most common type of professional support group. In a therapy group, patients or families with a common problem get together with one or more professionals to discuss the difficulties they are experiencing and find solutions. This can be a tremendously empowering experience, especially for those dealing with a new diagnosis.

It's also less expensive than individual therapy, so it's an attractive concept to managed care organizations concerned with mental health or neurological issues. If you'd like to see these kinds of services available in your area, the best way to begin is by contacting a healthcare organization or facility that might be willing to sponsor such a group. Explain what kind of help you and others are looking for, and how it might be provided in a clinical setting. Group therapy sessions may be paid for by your insurance, or each participant might pay a small fee.

Some mental health organizations sponsor support groups as a free or low-cost benefit for their patients. These groups may be able to use meeting space at a clinic after hours, and may get access to resources such as a photocopy machine, postage meter, professional library, or Internet hookup. Often, a counselor, social worker, or other professional facilitates this type of support group. There may be speakers or meetings geared to specific topics, such as discipline, diet, or medication side effects, or each meeting may be a forum for free-form discussion.

Individual support

Not everyone is a candidate for support services in a group setting. Sometimes a family's problems are too overwhelming to make attending or making use of group therapy possible. Other times, parents and patients simply need individual attention. As noted in Chapter 10, *Family*, family therapy and respite services can be essential parts of a well-conceived support system. There are other types of professional support services as well. These include:

- Case management services that help families manage complex medical, educational, and social programs.

- Personal support and informational services delivered by a social worker or counselor.

- Direct support services from professionals who help parents and patients solve specific problems.

Many families have a long-term need for these kinds of services, which can be hard to find and expensive. However, if the professionals involved have the expertise to truly help, they will prevent many problems further on down the line. Volunteer-based groups—such as the ARC, Easter Seals, and Samaritans—may be able to provide referrals for low-cost services; some also supply such services directly at little or no cost. Government services for people with disabilities may also include a social work or case management component.

Autism advocacy groups sometimes have parent-to-parent programs available that match the parents of a newly diagnosed child with an experienced family. Others have crisis intervention help, or even case management services, available at no or low cost. You may have to be a dues-paying member to access these services, although that's not always the case.

Community activities

With everything else they have to contend with, families affected by PDD-NOS or atypical PDD may shy away from participation in community activities. Unfortunately, some that would truly like to be involved in Scouting, sports, religious congregations, or clubs have been shunned due to their child's behavior or, for adults with PDDs, their own differences.

Others have successfully integrated themselves into community activities that interest them. What's their secret? Planning, persistence, and flexibility.

Strategies that families have successfully used include assuring other adults involved in children's activities that they will be present with their child at all times if needed, educating other parents and children, and being careful to choose activities that meet their family's needs without overwhelming their child. For example, some children enjoy the crowds, costumes, and lights of holiday parades, while others would prefer to wrap gifts for the needy with a few quiet volunteers.

Many people with PDDs like being with other people, but not necessarily doing an activity that involves a lot of social interaction. Rather than team sports like football and baseball, they may prefer joining a track, swimming, or martial arts team. Others might enjoy working out at a gym, taking a dance or exercise class, joining in on a cleanup day at a park or beach, having a chess match with a few enthusiasts, hanging out at the video arcade with other teens, or going on a guided nature walk. Many activities can be adapted to fit these preferences.

> *Gymboree [a children's exercise program] has been a Godsend. It is based on sensory and developmental principles, and also provides a natural environment for socialization and parent/child bonding. The teachers know about Joseph's diagnosis and have always been very welcoming.*
> *—Jennifer, mother of three-year-old Joseph (Asperger's-like and autistic-like features, diagnosis still in progress)*

These activities provide opportunities for controlled socialization: people with PDDs can decide how much conversation they want to take part in, how close to others they wish to be physically, and how much activity they can handle. People who are unused to group activities may hang on the periphery for quite some time. Many never progress past the point of engaging in activity with only one or two members of the group. That's fine—you're not trying to create a social butterfly, just to help a child or adult with a PDD find an enjoyable role as part of the larger community.

This kind of socializing may not appeal as much to the parent or caretaker, but respecting the need for personal space and for self-paced involvement is important. You have to remember that social situations may feel different to the person with PDDs. Because he or she may not pick up on cues or know the rules of interaction, social activities can be confusing and fraught with opportunities for mistakes, misunderstandings, and embarrassment. The sensory input involved in noisy activities or crowds may be unbearable. Many people with PDDs are very content to limit their interactions to family and just one or two friends.

> We treat Rory like a regular kid and take him everywhere. His grandparents adore him, especially his maternal grandmother. She has great faith in him and points out that he's a very smart little boy. And he loves her; he never wants to leave when we go to visit her. —Charlotte, mother of four-year-old Rory (diagnosed PDD-NOS)

You may want to seek out community activities set up especially for disabled children or adults. In the US, Special Olympics has an excellent program centered on sports that is very accepting. There are also organized sports leagues specifically for children with disabilities or that integrate them into sports teams with nondisabled children. Challenger leagues for baseball are the best known, but similar groups exist for soccer and other sports.

Public parks and recreation departments may also have staff who can help children and adults with PDDs participate in activities, classes, and trips that they organize. In larger cities, they may also sponsor some special activities for the disabled, ranging from trips to the bowling alley to summer camps.

Religious activities

Activities at your place of worship can be a great venue for socializing and support—assuming that your congregation understands and accepts people with PDDs. Some denominations have disability specialists who can provide education to religious leaders and congregations and who may be able to help activity leaders adapt programs to fit.

Leaders and members of your congregation may also be able to provide help of a more practical sort. Counseling on personal, family, medical, or spiritual matters; volunteers to help with home-based therapy programs; respite care; or even housework and prepared meals when your family is in crisis are all support services that some grateful families have found.

> *Our church family is fairly helpful, given the limited knowledge they have of PDD/autism. My main sources of strength are the St. John's Autism list on the Net and the other parents in our therapy group.*
> *—Dorthy, mother of five-year-old Jesse (diagnosed PDD-NOS with autistic tendencies)*

School activities

As mentioned in Chapter 9, *School*, autistic-spectrum children also have the right to be involved in school clubs and activities, to the extent that they wish to do so. Many young people have become valued members of school track and swim teams, golf and tennis clubs, chess clubs, science clubs, choirs, orchestras, and theater groups, among other activities. If your child needs an aide to be successful in class, she may also need an aide to participate in these activities. Support services that make these activities possible can be written into an IEP or 504 plan.

Children with disabilities should not be excluded from school field trips, either, including overnight trips. Providing support for longer activities can be difficult, and parents may have to attend with their child.

Neighborhood activities

Most children with PDDs are not part of neighborhood street hockey games and sandlot baseball. The political aspects of child's play are anything but simple, and navigating within large groups of fussing, pushy kids is often just too much.

Some children do take a special interest in a child who is different, especially children whose home situation is difficult or who have some minor "differences" of their own. Should you be so lucky as to attract a potential friend like this, take advantage of the opportunity as much as you can.

Matthew and Ian have been friends since they were toddlers. Sometimes their friendship is very one-sided because they are so different, but despite the fights and arguments they still seek each other out. Matthew is the youngest in a large family, and visiting with Ian gives him individual attention. We include him in our family activities whenever we can. He has probably taught Ian more about social skills than anything we or the school has ever done.

· · · · ·

One of the best things we ever did was set up play dates for Alyssa. She usually can't handle the whole gang of little girls on our street at once, and even if she tried to tag along they might leave her behind because she is nonverbal. We've found that if it's just her and one girl, we can set up simple activities that both can enjoy, like stringing bead necklaces or baking cookies. They are learning about Alyssa and coming away from an afternoon at our house with a good feeling about her. So far this year, two girls invited her to their birthday parties and one asked her to go roller-skating. They also wave and say hi when they see her. I can tell by the smile on her face that this makes her happy. —Patti, mother of four-year-old Alyssa (diagnosed atypical PDD, mild mental retardation)

Not all neighborhood relationships are so great. Parents have to go out of their way to educate neighbors about their child with PDD-NOS or atypical PDD, and not everyone will be receptive. Parents whose children have a tendency to scream or break things in a rage or who have other unusual behaviors (such as SIB, stripping off their clothes, or using inappropriate language) have sometimes had to deal with police or child protective services workers called in because their neighbors didn't understand.

And when the parents don't understand or even actively cause trouble, their children are likely to follow suit.

Our relationship with our neighbors is not very good. They allow their children to torment our son, then come running if he fights back. We don't allow him to play outside unsupervised, and there are certain children that we have instructed him to avoid because they are just plain mean!

Friends are important, and your own neighborhood is the most convenient place to find them. Those who live in very rural areas or in areas that are not safe for children to play without direct supervision may have to turn to other resources for finding friends. A playground, indoor park, organized play-group, or children's club can also be the stage for introducing your child to social activities.

Most of the families interviewed for this book indicated that much of their support system is internal. Parents lean on each other; other children in the family learn to take on responsibilities for their sibling with a PDD and help their parents cope; and the extended family ideally gets into the act as well. Despite the difficulties that tend to beset families affected by PDDs (see Chapter 10), once everyone has found a role that fits his or her strengths, much can be accomplished.

> *I'm now divorced...but I also have a daughter who is fourteen. She does lots of things with her brother and is very good at handling him.*
> *—Debbie, mother of eleven-year-old Doug (diagnosed PDD, fragile X syndrome)*

· · · · ·

> *I turn to my husband, who has worked with handicapped children and adults for over fifteen years. He helps me. I turn to family and friends, and to Dhylan's teachers.   —Sally, mother of five-year-old Dhylan (diagnosed PDD-NOS with autistic features)*

Is there a better way?

If parents and adults with PDDs could design the perfect support system, it would be reliable, comprehensive, and adaptable to meet the changing needs of people with PDDs as they move through life's stages.

> *I'd do more than you could imagine. I'd give them local resources, actually answer their questions and not fob them off onto another agency, be a lending library, be an IEP expert, describe the differences between one program and the next. Be a one-stop shopping resource list, but also be available to answer questions that no one thought of at the time.*
> *—Holly, mother of three-year-old Max (diagnosed PDD-NOS with autistic tendencies, apraxia of speech)*

Can this ideal be achieved? Probably not by any one program, but making a "cafeteria plan" of support possibilities available to families and individuals affected by autistic-spectrum disorders would go a long way toward this goal. Creating and maintaining these resources will probably always fall primarily to those who are closest to the problem, but as professionals in healthcare and education become more aware of the value of support groups, institutional support is emerging to help people with PDDs and their caregivers better meet their own needs.

One trend that may help is a move toward giving families who use social services more choices about how to spend "their" dollars. Some programs are experimenting with giving direct grants to families or adults dealing with mental, physical, or developmental disabilities. When recipients have the power to choose services, the range of services available is likely to change in response to demand.

CHAPTER 13

Living with PDDs

CHILDREN DON'T COME WITH GUARANTEES. The popular, bright nine-year-old may be schizophrenic at twenty-five; the fabulous teenage athlete may spend adulthood in a wheelchair. Every parent dreads the cruel twist of fate that could damage their child forever. People with PDDs are far from being "damaged goods," however: they are simply different from the average. As parents, friends, spouses, teachers, and professionals, we need to accept and see the bright side of these differences for the best outcome. As adults with PDDs, we need to use these differences to find the place in life where we fit best.

In this chapter, we'll discuss some of the options available for adults with PDDs. We'll also present a few accounts from the inside, in the words of people with PDDs and those who love them.

Adult life with PDDs

The prognosis for autistic-spectrum disorders used to be dismal, or so parents were told. The future held, at best, living at home and perhaps working a menial job or, at worst, life in an institution. Some families may still be given this erroneous information.

Today, the prognosis depends entirely on what kind of intervention was available in childhood, and what kinds of services are available to help adults live more or less independently. There is a full range of options available for adults with PDD-NOS or atypical PDD, depending on their level of functioning, including:

- **Full inclusion in work, family, and community life, without special supports.** These individuals may need and seek out medication or a therapist, or may continue to take supplements or follow a special diet, but will live entirely independently, work as needed, and marry and raise a family if they so desire.

- **Full inclusion in work, family, and community life, with some special supports.** Along with the minor items mentioned previously, these individuals may need professional case management, more intensive medical or therapeutic interventions on an ongoing basis, and minor assistance with such items as finding and keeping a job, finding housing, etc. You could compare their lives to those of a person with any chronic medical or psychiatric condition: most things are possible with some special help.

- **Inclusion in some areas of work, family, and community life with intensive support.** These individuals may be able to handle work well, but need a supported living situation (an apartment in a supported living facility, placement in a group home, or a living situation with support from family members), case management, and intensive medical and therapeutic interventions, for example.

- **Supported involvement in all spheres of life.** These individuals will need intensive support in all areas of life. This will include a supported living situation, a supported workplace (ranging from assistance with placement and job coaching to a sheltered workshop), or in some cases institutionalization.

Institutionalization for any neurological condition is now exceedingly rare in the US. Most programs that existed 30 years ago have been phased out, and most large state mental institutions have been closed to all but the most difficult cases.

Unfortunately, the system of community-based care that was supposed to have replaced the big institutions in the US was never fully funded. Adults with PDDs and their families will have to spend a great deal of time, and sometimes money, to ensure that needed supports are there. For those who would truly benefit from institutional life, such as autistic-spectrum adults with difficult behaviors who do not have adult family members to care for them, it may be very hard to find an appropriate placement.

There are more residential alternatives in Europe, including "therapeutic communities" in rural settings that could be an excellent alternative for some.

There is a broad middle ground between full inclusion and institutionalization. Possibilities range from complexes where each resident has a private apartment, but social services and medical care are available on-site, to group homes where residents may bunk one or two to a room, eat meals family-style, and have professional staff who act as house parents. Almost all group homes established for autistic-spectrum adults so far cater to the needs of severely autistic people. Parents, professionals, affected adults, and advocacy groups can work together to create new group homes that meet the needs of this population—group homes can be a surprisingly inexpensive alternative to other living arrangements. It's also possible that some adults with PDD-NOS or atypical PDD might qualify for other supported living situations on the basis of an additional psychiatric diagnosis.

Work and PDDs

Those capable of full inclusion will have the usual range of employment options available to them, but will probably want to take advantage of careful aptitude testing and career counseling. Some types of jobs can be excruciating for autistic-spectrum individuals, particularly those that require a great deal of personal interaction and teamwork, or those where the work is performed in a noisy, smelly environment. Accommodations may be necessary to make some types of work bearable, even when the person has a strong interest in the job. For example, one person working as a stocker in a grocery store might want to schedule himself for late-night hours to avoid contact with crowds of loud people. Another stocker might be able to work during the day if she wears earplugs. Often the changes needed are simple and inexpensive. In the US, accommodations for disabled workers are mandated in most workplaces by the Americans with Disabilities Act (ADA).

Quite a few adults with PDDs have been very successful in the research sciences, computer-related pursuits, carpentry, art, and similar jobs that are based primarily on individual skills and efforts. These jobs allow the person to practice their trade in a small office or workshop or alone. Home-based employment at decent pay has become a very real possibility in the 1990s, thanks to the Internet. Of course, skills and interests vary: others with PDDs have enjoyed careers ranging from nursing to farming, from full-time parenting to legal research.

Work can be difficult for anyone with a chronic health condition. Part-time and flexible work schedules can be a boon for those who need to work therapy appointments, medical appointments, and a significant amount of "down time" into their day. This may mean that full-time work is not possible, making supplemental income, such as disability benefits or a trust fund, a necessity.

Transition planning

As discussed in Chapter 9, *School*, transition planning should begin around age 13, with vocational planning mandatory at 16 in the US. Most school-based transition programs address preparation for work and/or higher education, or concentrate on life skills training. That leaves parents and caregivers with the responsibility for setting up an infrastructure that addresses needs such as housing, transportation, and medical care. Ideally, these needs will also be addressed through the IEP process or in the framework of social services support.

It's important for parents and older children to think through post-high-school lifestyles as early as possible, however, so that nothing important is left until the last minute. Examples of chores that can be time consuming include applying for SSI or other income-support programs, teaching a young adult how to use the public transit system independently, and finding good adult healthcare professionals for a teenager who has outgrown her pediatrician.

Adult relationships and PDDs

Some people with PDD-NOS or atypical PDD do have friendships and romantic relationships, marry, and/or have children. This is rarely the case for those individuals diagnosed with autistic disorder. Accordingly, it's essential that explicit instruction be provided to all people with these milder autistic-spectrum diagnoses on meeting and approaching potential friends or romantic interests, appropriate dating behavior, avoiding domestic violence, sexuality (see below), contraception, pregnancy, childbirth, and child-rearing. This is information needed by both sexes, and should be imparted in ways appropriate to the person's age and ability to understand.

Adults with PDDs who have successful adult relationships, including marriage, report that the experience can be rocky. Professional or religious marriage counseling is invaluable, particularly before marriage, when the partners have a chance to work out areas of potential conflict in advance. Some married couples in which one or both partners has a PDD have made a long-term commitment to family therapy for this reason.

Some adults with PDDs need assistance with household upkeep and parenting, which is often provided by their partner or by other family members. Housekeeping services, and ongoing parenting education and support, may also be available through government or private agencies for the disabled. Of course, a housekeeper or nanny can also be privately hired if you have the financial means. As with school and work, adults with PDDs may need to use visual charts and careful scheduling to assure that they meet their home and family responsibilities, from doing housework to making their children's medical appointments.

Incidentally, it's important to initiate early screening for the children of adults with PDDs because of the genetic component of autistic-spectrum disorders. Social enrichment programs, such as a good preschool, can also help to close gaps in learning that young children may experience as a result of their parent's disability.

PDDs and sexuality

Many parents fear that their children with PDDs may be sexually abused or exploited, even as adults. Sadly, this fear is realistic, particularly for those individuals who are nonverbal or institutionalized.

Another concern is more prosaic: will their children be able to navigate the sexual aspects of life, including menstruation, contraception, and adult sexuality? With careful instruction about the physical aspects of sexual function and self-protection, the answer should be yes—but these factors are lacking in the lives of many adults with PDDs.

A nationwide survey on sexual activity in the autistic population of Denmark[1] covered these issues, as well as the problem of public masturbation and other inappropriate sexual behaviors. This survey established that autistic-spectrum individuals have a number of difficulties in the area of sexuality, including naive and socially inappropriate expressions of sexuality, social deficits that make sexual relationships difficult to initiate and maintain, obsessional sexual desire or behavior, and the sexual side-effects of psychiatric drugs.

This survey also noted that the autistic-spectrum patients surveyed had a higher than usual level of "deviant" sexual behavior, which the researchers hypothesized had some relationship to the unnatural conditions under which the population surveyed discovered and learned about sexuality (all were adults living in group homes, and many had been institutionalized since early childhood), and also a possible relationship to the sensory disorders that can be part of autism (e.g., sexual fetishism, in which certain smells or objects are perceived as sexually arousing, was fairly common). As the researchers put it, "sexual behavior or autistic behavior is neither deviant nor disturbed, but rather an expression of social and emotional immaturity. In fact, autistic people develop inappropriate sexual behavior because of their inability to understand social norms and rules, and because of their inability in communicating and establishing reciprocal relationships."

Regarding adults with PDD-NOS and atypical PDD, the Danish researchers' findings on the sexual difficulties of the high-functioning autistics in their survey group were particularly enlightening. They found that frustrated sexual feelings, including an inability to masturbate to a climax and frustrated desires for sexual relationships, correlated strongly with self-abusive behavior. Often this behavior had an obvious connection, such as hitting the genitals.

The message here is one that many parents and professionals will find difficult: some people need explicit instruction on how to enjoy themselves sexually. This is a basic human right, but it's often overlooked in the disabled. We expect that most people will be able to simply "do what comes naturally," ignoring the fact that for some, it does not come naturally at all. There is also a tendency to infantilize adults with disabilities, assuming that they do not experience sexual desire. The services of a professional sex therapist can be engaged to teach techniques if parents or caretakers don't feel comfortable with the task.

There is a surprisingly large amount of literature available on the general topic of disability and sexuality, including information on facilitating appropriate sexual expression in the disabled population, teaching disabled adults about related health and hygiene concerns, and preventing sexual abuse. A number of states, school districts, and agencies have developed instructional materials geared toward various special populations, including mentally retarded, deaf, mentally ill, behaviorally disordered, physically handicapped, and institutionalized youth and adults. At least some of these materials could be useful for adolescents and adults with PDDs. A 1991 bibliography, *Disability, Sexuality, and Abuse*, is referenced in Appendix A, *Resources*.

Accounts from the inside

Over the past dozen years, a number of adults diagnosed with autism have been able to make their voices heard. The reports of Donna Williams (author of *Nobody, Nowhere*; *Somebody, Somewhere*; *Like Color to the Blind*; and other books), Temple Grandin (author of *Emergence: Labeled Autistic*, *Thinking in Pictures*, and other books), Sean Barron (co-author of *There's a Boy in Here*), and others have illuminated the internal experience of pervasive developmental disorders. Their inspiring stories are about courage in the face of difficulty and difference, the voyage of self-discovery, and the search for a meaningful, satisfying life in a world that only gives lip service to celebrating diversity in all its forms. These same themes are part of the lives of thousands of others who have persevered despite (or sometimes because of) PDDs and had their own quiet successes.

Of course, not all life stories are so positive. A generation ago most doctors consigned patients with autism to institutions, and sent people with milder autistic tendencies out into the world with no treatment and little hope. Children and adults diagnosed with PDD-NOS, atypical PDD, and similar conditions today have many more options, but life can still be hard and unpredictable.

Here are some of their stories.

Walking the line

Amy's son Miles is seven, and his differences are not always evident to outsiders. Initially diagnosed with severe ADHD at three and a half, his current diagnosis is PDD-NOS. For Miles, social relationships are probably the most difficult part of childhood to navigate.

> *He knows he is different. He has a few motor stereotypies—arm-flapping is the most conspicuous—that cause him to be teased at school. He has trouble making friends, and he knows it.*

Miles attends second grade in a regular public school classroom, and has pull-out sessions for speech therapy and occupational therapy. Amy credits these two interventions, and particularly sensory integration work, with his success in a mainstream setting. Schoolwork isn't a problem, as long as he's in a very structured environment.

> *Miles is very intelligent, and at the same time he has many communication and social difficulties. Some days, I see him as a research scientist when he grows up... some days, I worry that he will never gain the skills to be independent of me. This highlights the biggest issue for me, that Miles could go either way. With the proper teaching and support, he will do well; without it, he will surely fall through the cracks. He looks "typical," and he dances on that fine line between "our world" and*

"Miles's world" every single day. Hopefully, he will use this precarious position to his advantage someday—I am trying to give him the tools to do that.

Feeling different

Ian is eight and attends school in a self-contained special education class-room. His academic skills mirror his IQ scatter—great at math, struggling with reading but improving, hopeless in PE. He's a talented artist, and is beginning to reach out socially after being a very self-involved toddler and young child.

He recently had a birthday party with four guests. This was the largest social gathering Ian had ever asked for, and he was a little nervous. With structured activities and a short time-frame, the party was a success, and Ian said afterward that it made him feel "like a regular kid."

When he was young, Ian says, he really wasn't interested in other kids. Now it's easier to approach others, but not so easy to make them want to play with him. He's unaware that he comes across as overbearing and bossy, or that his ideas about playing are more rigid than other children's.

Ian is intensely aware of some of his differences, however. His speech delay in particular makes him a target for bullying. "Sometimes [other kids] won't share with me. Sometimes they don't want to be my friend," says Ian.

He doesn't deal well with being teased. Just the other day, neighborhood boys threw mud at him and mimicked his high-pitched scream and arm-flapping as he ran away. When he got home, he buried his head in his mother's lap, saying "Why is everybody so mean to me?"

There's no good answer to that question, and Ian's parents aren't always able to counteract the depression that sets in after incidents of teasing. They are working to build up his resilience by helping him have success in other areas. His drawings are always proudly displayed on the refrigerator, and his skills with math, computers, puzzles, and Lego blocks get lots of praise. They've carefully engineered social situations for him as well, supervising play dates with children who are gentler than the neighborhood bullies.

Ian is not depressed about his future prospects. He fully expects to be in "regular" school for junior high and senior high, and to go on to college. When asked what his plans are when he grows up, he has lots of answers.

I'm going to play basketball, live in Greece, hunt Bigfoot or the Loch Ness monster or aliens. Visit Egypt, Rome, the Himalayas, Scotland, England, and... where did the man in the iron mask live? Oh, yeah, France.

For an eight-year-old boy, those goals are just great.

Side by side

Liz can't tell her own story. At 22 years old, she is still primarily nonverbal. Her 24-year-old sister Donna, however, has stuck by her side ever since her previously rambunctious and talkative three-year-old sister developed encephalitis, which resulted in autistic-like symptoms and epilepsy.

When her little sister got a flu-like illness, Donna wasn't all that worried—but Liz kept getting worse instead of better. When the medical crisis was finally over, major changes were immediately evident. "The first thing I noticed was that she wasn't talking really," Donna says. Liz was also having seizures, and the medications she took to control them made her violent and unpredictable.

Donna's life changed almost as much as her sister's. She took on more responsibility for her two other siblings, since her parents needed to supervise Liz very closely. Her sister's behavior kept her from bringing friends over as well.

> *It was embarrassing. I wouldn't want to bring them home because I didn't know what kind of state she'd be in. One time she threw this metallic toy cymbal across the room like a Frisbee, and it sliced into my friend's face. I became an "outside" kid. I was over at other people's houses all the time.*

On the other hand, Liz's struggle made Donna more sensitive to the disabled.

> *Whenever anybody made fun of someone who was disabled, I'd say "Stop that, my sister's like this." I was always trying to educate people.*

As an adult, she's chosen a career that builds on that desire to help others. She currently works for a local social services agency and works directly with several clients, including a grade-schooler diagnosed with PDD-NOS.

She rides the school bus with him several days a week, helping him handle social interactions and learn appropriate bus behavior.

Liz's path has been different, but she has also found adult pursuits she enjoys. She works part-time on a nearby farm, where she feeds and cares for the animals. She's especially fond of the horses and has learned to ride well. Liz still lives at home with her parents.

Liz communicates with sounds, some ASL signs, her own personal sign language, and expressive body and facial movements. New medications for her seizures have helped minimize her violent episodes.

> She still goes up and down quite a bit, especially around her menstrual cycle. Some days she'll have a lot of seizures and be almost catatonic, but sometimes she's very connected. She understands short, one-word things, but I think sometimes what she hears is kind of jumbled, like it's hard to process so much information at once.

The next step for Liz will probably be placement in a group home, once her parents have found a safe, appropriate place with people she enjoys. She's able to take care of herself in most ways, but may need help in activities for independent living, such as budgeting, and some level of daily supervision. As she gets older, though, her moods are more manageable, and she's able to make her own wishes known. That, along with her supportive family, bodes well for a more independent life as she gets older.

The worth of a label

Twenty-four-year-old Kalen was never told as a child that she had been speculatively diagnosed autistic at age three. She struggled through school with social and organizational difficulties, and finally was identified as "learning disabled" when she was fourteen. Academics weren't a problem; it was everything else: all of the daily interactions with peers and teachers, trying to process convoluted chunks of information, and being teased by her classmates. Things were a mess at home, too, with an abusive family situation adding to her difficulties.

The pieces started to fall together for Kalen in college.

> In college I found that some teaching styles don't work for me. For example, I was taking a literature course in which the instructor had us

break up into small groups during every class. I couldn't process the conversations or deal with the interaction required.

Adult relationships were a puzzle as well. She's now the single parent of a daughter, who is in foster care.

After doing research online, she finally found out about autism, was able to confirm clues from her early childhood, and just over a year ago was given a medical diagnosis of high-functioning autism (HFA).

I have spent a long time trying to figure out what's wrong with me, as well as in therapy for childhood abuse.

On one hand, I am glad I found out I am autistic. It gives me an explanation for what I thought was laziness or not caring. It was also wonderful to find out that I am not the only person like this on the planet... although in a way I would have liked to think I was the only one. On the other hand, laziness and apathy are things that can be overcome, while autism carries with it permanent limitations. It is hard to come to terms with the fact that I have a disability and can't do everything I had always been told I could.

For the past two years, Kalen has attended college part-time, taking courses in calculus, chemistry, physics, English, and philosophy. Although she has not finished every course she started, her grades in completed classes have been quite good. She also has found some community support, both in the city where she lives and online, where she has made many friends.

Last year I lived with an older couple who took care of my practical needs. That was nice, because I am not good at taking care of myself and the housework. It was actually the ideal situation for me: I was responsible for myself and my own money, but I had help with the things I have difficulty with. Those people still have me over for supper once or twice a month, and they fix things around my apartment.

Currently living on permanent disability benefit in her own small apartment, she also has a part-time job building and maintaining a Web site for the local autism society. She is able to see her daughter for just four hours each week, but is appealing this limited access.

My life is pretty boring. I spend most of it on the Internet with the TV on beside me. I am currently taking a life skills course for single parents.

It is extremely difficult for me to deal with the group interaction, espe-
cially the unstructured times of coffee breaks and lunch. I need a lot of
time to decompress in the evenings, and if I don't have that, I fall apart.

She also has gotten engaged to a man in England whom she met online.
They write to each other daily via email, and talk on the phone when possible. She plans to move to England to live with him when she regains full
custody of her daughter. She has two other friends as well, although she says
they don't spend much time together.

Despite her obvious high intelligence, Kalen has no plans to move into a
career due to her social difficulties and some additional health problems.

The stress of having to work in order to live would be more than I
could cope with, and I would end up not working at all. Sorry to be dis-
couraging to parents...I do think that a lot of this could have been reme-
diated if I had proper support as a child and adolescent. I would like to
see a supported living situation for HFA and Asperger's syndrome adults.
I'm working on this with the autism society here, which already has four
homes for lower functioning people. It seems that I am too low function-
ing to get on in the world very well, and too high functioning to get any
help.

For other adults recently given a diagnosis in the autism spectrum, she has
some simple (if tongue-in-cheek) advice:

Don't panic. There are good things about being autistic, and there are
others from the home planet trying to exist here.

Like parent, like child

When five-year-old Nicole was diagnosed with mild autism, her mother was
worried, but not crushed. She had already seen a success story, and he was
sitting right across from her at the dinner table: her husband, Nicole's father.

The reason for my optimism is the fact that my husband was diag-
nosed ADHD, and probably also had high-functioning autism—behavior-
ally, he matched that diagnosis even more than Nicole does.

The three local public schools kicked him out at the tender age of
seven. They did not know what to do with him! He had very supportive
parents who had him tutored from first grade to seventh grade. Through

hard work, perseverance, and many prayers, he did get through school, attending regular mainstreamed junior and senior high.

College was an even more successful experience. He completed senior-level engineering courses, and now runs his own successful business working with computers and doing electronics repairs.

He went much further than his parents expected him to, and started out with many of the same issues as our daughter.

Nicole is already showing signs of her father's fighting spirit.

We attend church regularly, and Nicole seems to enjoy her time there. She also takes swimming lessons at the YMCA and loves that activity as well. I have every reason to believe that with the same spirit of perseverance and support that her father had, Nicole can also be successful in whatever she chooses to conquer in her life.

A final word

Children and adults with autistic-spectrum disorders interviewed for this book report a variety of feelings about their diagnosis. Frustration seems to be a common denominator. Because of the scattered ability profile so common to these conditions, it's hard for them to predict what areas they will succeed in. Sometimes simple tasks turn out to be quite tough, while things that their peers consider complex are a snap.

These contradictions in skill level are difficult for outsiders to understand: how can you explain that you have a full command of advanced calculus, but wear shoes with Velcro closings because you can't tie your own shoelaces? PDDs are "invisible disabilities," and people with PDDs do not always find the world to be a sympathetic place.

Many have also felt the pain of misdiagnosis, being perceived as mentally retarded, stupid, or crazy by people who aren't familiar with autistic-spectrum disorders. These aren't small misunderstandings, either—they can affect education, work, and social relationships intensely.

Childhood abuse, teasing, and other cruel or thoughtless behavior can have a lifelong effect on a person's self-esteem, if not countered by strong support and success in other sectors of life. Parents and caregivers can help by ensuring that people with PDDs discover their areas of greatest competence and have experiences that show them their true self-worth. Whether it's being a Special Olympics champ, succeeding in Girl Scouting, or learning how to build a cool computer from scratch, these experiences buoy up the spirit and can counteract negative messages.

Emotions about this diagnosis will change over time from early childhood, through the teen years, and into adulthood. There will be days and even years that are more difficult than others. There will also be episodes of personal triumph, as new skills are learned and abilities are discovered. As Kalen comments above, there *are* good things about PDDs. Every individual with a diagnosis of PDD-NOS, atypical PDD, or other high-functioning forms of autism has something special to offer. Parents, caretakers, and friends have much to learn about them, and from them.

Resources

THE BOOKS, PAMPHLETS, AND OTHER RESOURCES LISTED HERE can help you further explore areas of interest related to pervasive developmental disorders. We have included addresses for printed materials that are not usually available in stores or libraries. Otherwise, you should be able to find these items in your local library or via interlibrary loan, or be able to purchase them in regular or online bookstores.

Autistic-spectrum disorders

These books are general guides to aspects of autistic-spectrum disorders, some with an emphasis on high-functioning people with PDDs.

Attwood, Tony. *Asperger's Syndrome: A Guide for Parents and Professionals*. London: Jessica Kingsley Publishers, 1998.

Autism Research Institute. *Autism Research Review International (ARRI)*. This informative newsletter summarizes medical study results, and includes reports on traditional and alternative medicine for autistic symptoms. 4182 Adams Avenue, San Diego, CA 92116

Baron-Cohen, Dr. Simon, and Dr. Patrick Bolton. *Autism: The Facts*. Oxford: Oxford University Press, 1995. Somewhat outdated as an introduction to the topic, but has some UK-specific information.

Cohen, Shirley. *Targeting Autism: What We Know, Don't Know, and Can Do to Help Young Children with Autism and Related Disorders*. Berkeley, California: University of California Press, 1998.

Gerlach, Elizabeth. *Autism Treatment Guide*. Eugene, Oregon: Four Leaf Press, 1996. Practical suggestions for addressing autistic symptoms.

Kephart, Beth. *A Slant of Sun: One Child's Courage*. New York: W.W. Norton & Co., 1998. A beautifully written mother's memoir of raising a son with PDD-NOS.

Kozloff, Martin A. *Reaching the Autistic Child: A Parent Training Program*. Cambridge, Massachusetts: Brookline Books, 1998.

Leicestershire County Council and Fosse Health Trust. *Autism: How to Help Your Young Child*. London: National Autistic Society, 1995. Excellent introductory booklet for parents of a newly diagnosed child in the UK.

Schopler, Eric, and Gary B. Mesibov, editors. *High-Functioning Individuals with Autism (Current Issues in Autism)*. New York: Plenum Publishing, 1992.

Siegel, Bryna. *The World of the Autistic Child: Understanding and Treating Autistic Spectrum Disorders*. Oxford: Oxford University Press, 1996.

Sperry, Virginia Walker, and Sally Provence. *Fragile Success: Nine Autistic Children, Childhood to Adulthood.* Hamden, Connecticut: Archon Books, 1995. Fascinating profiles written over a period of years, including one follow-up report by a young man with autistic tendencies who is also profiled as a child.

Tantam, Digby. *A Mind of One's Own: A Guide to the Special Difficulties and Needs of the More Able Person with Autism or Asperger's Syndrome.* London: The National Autism Society, 1991.

Wing, Lorna. *Autistic Spectrum Disorders: A Guide to Diagnosis.* London: National Autistic Society, 1993. This diagnostic guide is also available on tape.

Wing, Lorna. *The Autistic Spectrum: A Guide for Parents and Professionals.* London: Constable & Co., 1996. A UK-centric guide to autistic-spectrum disorders, diagnosis, and treatment.

Books by adults with PDDs

Barron, Sean. *There's a Boy in Here.* New York: Simon & Schuster, 1992.

Gerland, Gunilla. *A Real Person: Life on the Outside.* London: Souvenir Press, 1997.

Grandin, Temple. *Thinking in Pictures, and Other Reports from My Life with Autism.* New York: Vintage Books, 1996.

Grandin, Temple, and Margaret M. Scariano. *Emergence: Labeled Autistic.* New York: Warner Books, 1996.

Williams, Donna. *Nobody, Nowhere: The Extraordinary Autobiography of an Autistic.* New York: Avon Books, 1994. Williams is a very high-functioning autistic woman with other psychiatric difficulties, who grew up in an abusive Australian family. Her story (now three books long) is unusual and very compelling. Soon to be a major motion picture!

Williams, Donna. *Somebody, Somewhere: Breaking Free from the World of Autism.* New York: Times Books, 1995.

Williams, Donna. *Like Color to the Blind: Soul Searching and Soul Finding.* New York: Times Books, 1996.

Children's books about autism and PDDs

One of these can be a good introduction to autistic-spectrum disorders for siblings, young relatives, and classmates. Another good choice for helping young children understand the maddeningly literal thinking patterns common in individuals with PDD-NOS, atypical PDD, and Asperger's syndrome is the *Amelia Bedelia* book series by Peggy Parish.

Amenta, Charles A., III. *Russell Is Extra Special: A Book About Autism.* Washington, D.C.: Magination Press, 1992.

Gartenberg, Zachary M. *Mori's Story: A Book About a Boy with Autism.* Minneapolis: Lerner Publications Co., 1998. Written by a grade-schooler about his brother—and very good.

Gold, Phyllis-Terri. *Please Don't Say Hello.* New York: Human Sciences Press, 1986.

Gottlieb, Eli. *The Boy Who Went Away.* New York: St. Martins Press, 1997.

Katz, Illana, and Dr. Edward Ritvo. *Joey and Sam: A Heartwarming Storybook About Autism, a Family, and a Brother's Love.* Los Angeles: Real Life Story Books, 1993.

Lears, Laurie. *Ian's Walk: A Story About Autism.* Morton, Illinois: Albert Whitman & Co., 1998.

Thompson, Mary. *Andy and His Yellow Frisbee*. Rockville, Maryland: Woodbine House, 1996.

Watson, Esther. *Talking to Angels*. New York: Harcourt Brace, 1996.

Werlin, Nancy. *Are You Alone on Purpose?* New York: Houghton Mifflin, 1996.

Web sites about PDDs

Autism Book List
http://web.syr.edu./~jmwobus/autism/autism-bib.html

Compiled by the manager of the St. John's Autism list, this is an exhaustive compilation of titles, including many that are out of print or in languages other than English.

Autism-PDD Resources Network
http://www.autism-pdd.net/

There's some misleading information on this site, but the links can be useful.

Autism Research Institute
http://www.autism.com/ari/

See the ARI Publications List for a wide variety of ARI pamphlets, papers, books, and videotapes on subjects related to autistic-spectrum disorders.

Autism Society of North Carolina Online Bookstore
http://www.autismsociety-nc.org/cgi-bin/Web_store/web_store.cgi

Good source for books.

Center for the Study of Autism
http://www.autism.org/

Excellent Web site with the latest information, including diet, vitamins, and other alternative therapies. Some non-English information available (Chinese, Italian, Japanese, Korean, Spanish).

Jypsy's Autism Links
http://www.isn.net/~jypsy/autilink.htm

Quite possibly the largest collection of addresses for PDD-related Web sites around the world.

The National Autistic Society
http://www.oneworld.org/autism_uk/publica.html

UK publications on autism and related topics.

NLDline
Nonverbal Learning Disabilities Web site
http://www.NLDline.com

Best source of information on these learning disabilities, which are common among people with PDDs.

O.A.S.I.S.
Online Asperger's Syndrome Information and Support
http://www.udel.edu/bkirby/asperger/

Information Central for issues related to Asperger's syndrome, with much of interest to those affected by PDD-NOS or atypical PDD as well.

PDD Web Site
http://www.geocities.com/HotSprings/9647

Small site devoted to PDD-NOS and related disabilities.

"A Tiger by the Tail"
http://members.aol.com/bertvan/index.htm

A mother's story of raising an autistic child in the bad old days.

General disability

Exceptional Parent
555 Kinderkamack Road
Oradell, NJ 07649-1517
(201) 634-6550
Fax (201) 634-6599

This magazine for parents of children with any disability is an invaluable resource. Most issues are constructed around a theme, such as transition planning, mobility, or special education. The parent-to-parent letters section is especially useful for families trying to identify or find others with a rare disability.

Massachusetts General Hospital Neurology Forums
http://neuro-www.mgh.harvard.edu/

This site features discussion groups (live and bulletin board-style) on almost every known neurological disorder.

PediaNet
http://www.pedianet.com/index.html

An online resource for child development issues. Includes *EParent*, the online version of *Exceptional Parent* (see above).

Healthcare and insurance

American Association on Mental Retardation Publications Center. *Health Care Financing for Severe Developmental Disabilities* (monograph). 444 N. Capitol Street NW, Suite 846, Washington, DC 20001-1512, (202) 287-1968 or (800) 424-3688, Fax (202)-387-2193, *aamr@pmds.com*.

Beckett, Julie. *Health Care Financing: A Guide for Families.* Iowa City: National Maternal and Child Health Resource Center. This overview of the healthcare financing system includes advocacy strategies for families and information about public health insurance in the US. University of Iowa, Iowa City, IA 52242, (319) 335-9073.

The Disability Bookshop. *How to Get Quality Care for a Child with Special Health Needs: A Guide to Health Services and How to Pay for Them.* P.O. Box 129, Vancouver, WA 98666-0129, (206) 694-2462 or (800) 637-2256.

Larson, Georgianna, and Judith Kahn. *Special Needs/Special Solutions: How to Get Quality Care for a Child with Special Health Needs.* St. Paul, MN: Life Line Press, 2500 University Avenue, St. Paul, MN 55141.

McManue, Margaret. *Understanding Your Health Insurance Options: A Guide for Families Who Have Children with Special Needs.* Bethesda, Maryland: ACCH. This guide covers healthcare financing, insurance coverage, and long-term planning. 7910 Woodmont Avenue, Suite 300, Bethesda, MD 20814, (301) 654-6549.

Neville, Kathy. *Strategic Insurance Negotiation: An Introduction to Basic Skills for Families and Community Mental Health Workers.* Boston: Federation for Children with Special Needs. Single copies of this pamphlet are available at no cost. Very helpful if your insurance company insists on forcing you to use the mental health system rather than your regular medical benefits for care. CAPP/NPRC Project, 95 Berkeley Street, Suite 104, Boston, MA 02116.

Oreck, Stephen. *How to Get the Most Money Out of Your Health Insurance (pamphlet).* Medic Publishing Co., P.O. Box 89, Redmond, WA 98073, (206) 881-2883.

Peterson, Robert and David Tenenbaum. *Fighting Back: Health Insurance Denials.* Madison, Wisconsin: Center for Public Representation, Inc. For parents of children with special needs in the US, this book can help you get better coverage and combat claims denials. 121 S. Pinckney Street, Madison, WI 53703, (800) 369-0338.

ASA Health Insurance Package
http://www.autism-society.org/packages/health_insurance.html
Informative Web site about health insurance and autistic-spectrum disorders.

Association of Maternal and Child Health Programs (AMCHP)
1350 Connecticut Avenue NW, Suite 803
Washington, DC 20036
(202) 775-0436

Call AMCHP to locate your state's Children with Special Health Care Needs Program (CSHCN).

National Association of Insurance Commissioners (NAIC)
444 National Capitol Street, N.W., Suite 309
Washington, DC 20001
(202) 624-7790

Call NAIC to locate your state insurance commissioner, who can tell you about health insurance regulations in your state regarding PDDs.

Parenting and siblings

Brill, Marlene Targ. *Keys to Parenting the Child with Autism.* New York: Barron's Hauppauge, 1994.

Gray, David E. *Autism and the Family: Problems, Prospects, and Coping with the Disorder.* Springfield, Illinois: Charles C. Thomas Publishers Ltd., 1998.

Greenspan, Dr. Stanley I., with Jacqueline Salmon. *The Challenging Child.* Reading, Massachusetts: Addison-Wesley, 1995. Introduces Dr. Greenspan's concepts about tailoring interventions to each specific child.

Greenspan, Dr. Stanley I., and Serena Wieder, with Robin Simons. *The Child with Special Needs.* Reading, Massachusetts: Addison-Wesley, 1998. Highly recommended for all parents and professionals working with people who have PDD-NOS or atypical PDD! Greenspan presents details of how (and why) to do floor-time play therapy, and explains how to match it to your child's personality, physical needs, and diagnosis. Includes results of his floor-time play therapy research project with autistic-spectrum children.

Hallowell, Dr. Edward. *Driven to Distraction: Recognizing and Coping with Attention Deficit Disorder from Childhood Through Adulthood.* Reading, Massachusetts: Addison-Wesley, 1994. The classic book on ADD/ADHD. Dr. Hallowell's follow-up book, *Answers to Distraction,* is also quite good.

Hallowell, Dr. Edward. *When You Worry About the Child You Love: Emotional and Learning Problems in Children.* New York: Simon & Schuster, 1996.

Kurcinka, Mary Sheedy. *Raising Your Spirited Child.* New York: Harper Perennial, 1991. Written for parents of nondisabled but "difficult" children, this is nevertheless an excellent parenting guide to have on hand. Covers sensory issues, feeding problems, and more.

Meyer, Donald, and Patricia Vadasy. *Living with a Brother or Sister with Special Needs.* Seattle: University of Washington Press, 1996.

Meyer, Donald, editor. *Views from Our Shoes: Growing up with a Brother or Sister with Special Needs.* Rockville, Maryland: Woodbine House, 1997.

Meyer, Donald, editor. *Uncommon Fathers: Reflections on Raising a Child with a Disability.* Rockville, Maryland: Woodbine House, 1995.

Naseef, Robert A. *Special Children, Challenged Parents: The Struggles and Rewards of Raising a Child with a Disability.* New York: Birch Lane Press, 1997.

Schopler, Eric, editor. *Parent Survival Manual: A Guide to Crisis Resolution in Autism and Related Developmental Disorders.* New York: Plenum Publishing, 1995. Based on the TEACCH model, this book provides concrete suggestions for dealing with specific problems and general issues. A very worthwhile book to have.

Schopler, Eric, and Gary B. Mesibov, editors. *The Effects of Autism on the Family.* New York: Plenum Publishing, 1984. A bit dated, this compilation came out of the 1982 TEACCH conference. It could be very helpful for developing multifaceted programs that involve parents and professionals as partners. Includes well-written papers on sibling issues and dealing with family burnout.

Stehli, Annabel, editor. *Dancing in the Rain: Stories of Exceptional Progress by Parents of Children with Special Needs.* Westport, Connecticut: Georgiana Organization, 1995.

Special education

For information about local school programs, consult both parent groups and advocacy organizations in advance. They can usually tell you about specific schools or programs that have been successful in the past—and warn you away from those that may be detrimental to your child. National autism and disability advocacy groups can also help you locate residential programs and private schools, if these are options that meet your child's needs. The following are general special education resources, including information for parents and about pedagogical techniques.

Anderson, Winifred, Stephen Chitwood, and Dierdre Hayden. *Negotiating the Special Education Maze: A Guide for Parents and Teachers,* 2nd Ed. Rockville, Maryland: Woodbine House, 1990. Well-written and very complete. A new edition with information on the changes wrought in IDEA 97 that was said to be in production at press time.

Cutler, Barbara Coyne. *You, Your Child, and "Special" Education: A Guide to Making the System Work.* Baltimore: Paul H. Brookes Publishing Co., 1993. An uppity guide to fighting the system on your child's behalf.

Dornbush, Marilyn P. and Sheryl K. Pruitt. *Teaching the Tiger: A Handbook for Individuals Involved in the Education of Students with Attention Deficit Disorders, Tourette Syndrome, or Obsessive Compulsive Disorder.* Duarte, California: Hope Press, 1995. This is a *wonderful* book, full of practical suggestions, organizing aids, and ideas for teachers, parents, and students. Very applicable to children with PDD-NOS and atypical PDD.

Fouse, Beth. *Creating a Win-Win IEP for Students with Autism.* Arlington, Texas: Future Horizons, 1996.

Fullerton, Ann, editor. *Higher Functioning Adolescents and Young Adults with Autism: A Teacher's Guide.* Austin, Texas: ProEd, 1996.

Koegel, Robert L. and Lynn Kern Koegel, editors. *Teaching Children with Autism: Strategies for Initiating Positive Interactions and Improving Learning Opportunities.* Baltimore: Paul H. Brookes Publishing Co., 1996.

National Autistic Society. *Schools, Units, and Classes.* London, 1998. List of specialist schools and units (self-contained classrooms) in the UK for children with autism; also includes addresses of county education councils.

Peeters, Theo. *Autism: From Theoretical Understanding to Educational Intervention.* Lewisville, Texas: J.A. Majors Co., 1997. Explains the techniques used by TEACCH.

Powell, Stuart, and Peggy Ahrenhold Gallagher. *Autism and Learning: A Guide to Good Practice.* London: David Fulton Publishers, 1997.

Quill, Kathleen Ann, editor. *Teaching Children with Autism: Strategies to Enhance Communication and Socialization.* Albany, New York: Delmar Publications, 1995.

Simpson, Richard L. and Brenda Myles, editors. *Educating Children and Youth with Autism: Strategies for Effective Practice.* Austin, Texas: ProEd, 1998.

Advocating for the Child
http://www.crosswinds.net/washington-dc/~advocate/

Maintained by the mother of a girl with autism and boys with Tourette syndrome, this site is an all-purpose guide to advocating for your child's educational rights in the US. Information-rich, with great links and lots of inspiration.

California Department of Education
http://www.feat.org/CABP/

Maintained by Families for Early Autism Treatment, Inc., this Web site contains the article "Best Practices for Designing and Delivering Effective Programs for Individuals with Autistic Spectrum Disorders."

Low Incidence Unit Web site
http://curriculum.qed.qld.gov.au/lisc/

Publications and information about special education in Australia for children with PDDs.

Special Education and Disabilities Resources
http://www.educ.drake.edu/rc/sp_ed_top.html

US information and links on special education law, assistive technology, and related topics.

Childproofing

These are just some of the companies that sell child safety devices. Some safety companies also sell products that may be offensive to some readers (i.e., weapons, hidden spy cameras, and the like). We haven't ordered from any of these suppliers, so we cannot offer recommendations.

Canada: National of Canada
P.O. Box 1808
600 Fentons Crest
Swift Current, Saskatchewan
Canada S9H4J8
(306) 773-2914
information@natman.com
http://www.natman.com/newproductchildsafety.htm

Childproofers Online
(314) 962-BABY
info@childproofers.com
http://www.childproofers.com/

ChildProtect Inc.
710 Glenwood Drive
York, PA 17403
(717) 854-5974
support@childprotect.com
http://www.childprotect.com/

National Manufacturing Co.
US: National Manufacturing Co.
P.O. Box 577
Sterling, IL 61081
(815) 625-1320

Safe 'n' Sound Kids
P.O. Box 100-605
Brooklyn, NY 11210-0605
(718) 252-2229 or (888) 252-2229
Fax (718) 258-4217
safetots@aol.com
http://www.safensoundkids.com/

The Safety Store
4115 Irving Street
San Francisco, CA 94122-1220
(415) 661-8500 or (888) 723-3897
Fax (415) 661-8500
http://www.safetystore.com/

Special-needs clothing

These companies (and many others) carry clothing designed for kids who have difficulty with fasteners, people in wheelchairs or with mobility problems, older children and adults with special toileting needs, etc. A few of the catalogs listed include
shoes, which tend to be a problem. Slip-ons or styles with Velcro closures may be
available locally; alternatively, there are a variety of items that can replace regular
laces, including lace-in Velcro closures and curly elastic laces that bounce shut.

Adrian's Closet
29571 Monarch Drive
San Juan Capistrano, CA 92675
(800) 831-2577
Fax (714) 364-4380
http://www.adrianscloset.com/

Disability Scotland Clothing Index
http://dis_scot.gcal.ac.uk/Clothing/ClothingIndex.html

Lists several manufacturers of helmets and special clothing in the UK, including
companies with designs for children.

E-Z Clothes
P.O. Box 213
Tupelo, MS 38802
(800) 320-7889

Personal Touch Health Care Apparel Inc.
P.O. Box S
Brooklyn, NY 11223
(718) 375-1703 or (888) 626-1703
Fax (718) 627-0200
info@nursinghomeapparel.com
http://www.nursinghomeapparel.com/

Clothing in adult sizes only, including styles with easy closures.

Restart Gear
(61) 3 9781 2533
Fax (61) 3 9781 2544
http://findit.cowleys.com.au/clients/restart.htm
Very hip Australian designs for people with disabilities.

Special Clothes
P.O. Box 333
Harwich, MA 02645
(508) 896-7939

Specific therapeutic interventions

Here are some resources related to the interventions discussed in this book. The general PDD Web sites mentioned earlier may also contain useful links to online information.

Diet, vitamins, and allergy-related interventions

The Autism Research Institute's Web site and publications list has a wealth of information on these topics, as do the following resources:

Callahan, Mary. *Fighting for Tony*. New York: Simon & Schuster, 1987. A mother's story of "recovering" her autistic son, whose behavior improved dramatically with dietary changes.

Crook, Dr. William G. *The Yeast Connection Handbook*. Jackson, Tennessee: Professional Books, 1997.

Hagman, Bette. *The Gluten-Free Gourmet: Living Well Without Wheat*. New York: Henry Holt, 1990.

Hagman, Bette. *The Gluten-Free Gourmet Cooks Fast and Healthy: Wheat-Free with Less Fuss and Fat*. New York: Henry Holt, 1996.

Lewis, Lisa. *Special Diets for Special Kids: Implementing a Diet to Improve the Lives of Children with Autism and Related Disorders*. Arlington, Texas: Future Horizons, 1998. Written by the mother of a son diagnosed with PDD-NOS who was helped greatly by dietary intervention.

Meyer, Elisa. *Feeding Your Allergic Child: Happy Food For Happy Kids: 75 Proven Recipes Free of Wheat, Dairy, Corn, and Eggs*. New York: St. Martin's Press, 1997.

Rapp, Dr. Doris. *Is This Your Child?: Discovering and Treating Unrecognized Allergies in Children and Adults*. New York: William Morrow and Co., 1991.

Shaw, Dr. William, et al. *Biological Treatments for Autism and PDD: What's Going On? What Can You Do About It?* Toronto: Sunflower Publications, 1998. An in-depth introduction to biological interventions, including diet and vitamins.

Autism Network for Dietary Intervention (ANDI)
http://members.aol.com/AutismNDI/PAGES/links.htm

Founded by Lisa Lewis and friends, this is an advocacy and information site for diet and vitamins as treatments for PDDs.

Celiac/gluten-free archive
http://www.fastlane.net/homepages/thodge/archive.htm#first

The Non-Dairy Page
http://www.non-dairy.org/

NO-MILK mailing list
LISTSERV@SJUVM.STJOHNS.EDU

To subscribe, send email with the subject: SUB NO-MILK YourFirstName YourLast-Name. Open, unmoderated discussion list for those following a milk/casein/lactose-free diet.

Applied behavior analysis

These books and online resources cover aspects of ABA and ABA-like interventions.

Fouse, Beth. *A Treasure Chest of Behavioral Strategies for Individuals with Autism.* Arlington, Texas: Future Horizons, 1997.

Harris, Sandra L., and Mary Jane Gill-Weiss. *Right from the Start: Behavioral Intervention for Young Children with Autism: A Guide for Parents and Professionals.* Rockville, Maryland: Woodbine House, 1998.

Lovaas, Dr. Ivar, et al. *Teaching Developmentally Disabled Children: The ME Book.* Austin, Texas: Pro-Ed, 1981. An updated version of this book for parents and ABA therapists was under development in 1998.

Luiselli, James K., and Michael J. Cameron, editors. *Antecedent Control: Innovative Approaches to Behavioral Support.* Baltimore: Paul H. Brookes Publishing Co., 1998.

ABA
http://www.geocities.com/Heartland/Plains/1648/

Includes an Internet Relay Chat (IRC) channel devoted to live chat about applied behavioral analysis.

Australian ABA list
aba-aus-subscribe@makelist.com

Maurice, Catherine, Gina Green, and Stephen C. Luce, editors. *Behavioral Intervention for Young Children with Autism.* Austin, Texas: Pro-Ed, 1996.

The Journal of Applied Behavior Analysis (JABA)
Department of Human Development
University of Kansas
Lawrence, KS 66045-2133
(785) 843-0008
jabamlw@idir.net
http://www.envmed.rochester.edu/wwwrap/behavior/jaba/jabahome.htm

The Web site includes a searchable archive of this professional journal for ABA practitioners and researchers.

"Lovaas method"
AOL chat room

Visit between 8:00 and 9:00 p.m. Eastern Standard Time for live chat about ABA.

The Me List
Rallen@indyvax.iup

To subscribe, send email to moderator Ruth Allen. The Me List is a private, archived mailing list on ABA and related topics. Lots of "how to" and "how it worked" information.

The Recovery Zone
http://pages.prodigy.net/damianporcari/recovery.htm

An excellent Web site for those interested in or doing ABA. Includes links to mailing lists, online publications, a list of practitioners, and much more.

Animal-assisted therapy

Dog-Play
http://www.dog-play.com/therapy.html

Web site with many links related to animal-assisted therapy and therapy animals.

Island Dolphin Care
http://www.islanddolphincare.org/

One of several facilities that provide dolphin-assisted therapy.

North American Riding for the Handicapped Association (NARHA)
http://www.narha.org/autism.html

This site provides information on hippotherapy (horse-assisted therapy) for autism and other disorders, as well as referrals to members.

Art therapy

Flowers, Tony. *Reaching Children with Autism through Art: Practical Fun Activities to Enhance Motor Skills and to Improve Tactile and Concept Awareness.* Arlington, Texas: Future Horizons, 1996.

ASAFARI Gallery of Autistic Spectrum Art
http://columbia-pacific.interrain.org/ASAFARI/

This online art gallery is great, and includes some information on art therapy for people with PDDs.

Auditory integration and related therapies

Alvin, Juliette, and Auriel Warwick. *Music Therapy for the Autistic Child.* Oxford: Oxford University Press, 1991.

Berard, Dr. Guy, Simone Monnier-Clay, and Bernard Rimland. *Hearing Equals Behavior.* New Canaan, Connecticut: Keats Publishing, 1993.

National Autistic Society. "A Visit to the Light and Sound Therapy Centre" (pamphlet). London, 1996.

Stehli, Annabel. *The Sound of a Miracle: A Child's Triumph over Autism.* Westport, Connecticut: Georgiana Organization, 1997. A mother's account of her autistic daughter's recovery via auditory integration.

Tomatis, Dr. Alfred. *The Ear and Language.* Ontario: Moulin Publishing, 1996.

Earobics, Earobics Step 2
Cognitive Concepts Inc.
1123 Emerson Street, Suite 202
Evanston, IL 60201
(847) 328-8099 or (888) 328-8199
Fax (847) 328-5881
http://www.earobics.com/

An AI-like software package for home or school use.

EASe (Electronic Auditory Stimulation effect) recordings
Vision Audio Inc.
611 Anchor Drive
Joppa, MD 21085
(888) 213-7858
visionaud@aol.com
http://members.aol.com/visionaud/Vision.htm/ease.htm

Musical recordings specially engineered to have a relaxing effect on people with auditory sensitivities.

Fast ForWard, Fast ForWard Two
Scientific Learning Corp.
1995 University Ave., Suite 400
Berkeley, CA 94704-1074
http://www.scientificlearning.com/

Well-tested software for helping people with speech, language, and auditory processing disorders. For professional use only.

Society for Auditory Integration Training
1040 Commercial Street SE, Suite 306
Salem, OR 97302
http://www.sait.org

Sound Listening and Learning Center (Tomatis Method)
2701 E. Camelback Rd., Suite 205
Phoenix, AZ 85016
(602) 381-0086
Fax (602) 957-6741

Facilitated communication

Twachtman-Cullen, Diane. *A Passion to Believe: Autism and the Facilitated Communication Phenomenon.* Boulder, Colorado: Westview Press, 1998.

Floor-time play therapy and similar interventions

Hewett, David, and Melanie Nind. *Interaction in Action: Reflections on the Use of Intensive Interaction.* London: David Fulton Publishers, 1998.

Greenspan, Dr. Stanley. "Floor Time." This videotape is about using floor-time techniques with typically developing children, but many parents and professionals will find it useful to see the method in action.

VanFleet, Dr. Risë. *Filial Therapy: Strengthening Parent-Child Relationships Through Play.* Sarasota, Florida: Professional Resource Press, 1994.

About Floor Time
http://www.mindspring.com/~dgn/playther.htm

Basic Web site on floor-time concepts and ideas, with a question and answer section.

Family Enhancement and Play Therapy Center
P.O. Box 613
Boiling Springs, PA 17007
(717) 249-4707
Fax (717) 249-9479
http://play-therapy.com/

"Child-Centered Play Therapy with Risë VanFleet, Ph.D." Video on techniques used in child-centered play therapy (CCPT) and filial therapy.

Developmental Stages of Communication
http://www.arabambassador.com/developmental.htm

Basic Web site on floor-time concepts and ideas.

Dr. Stanley Greenspan
http://www.stanleygreenspan.com/

Several of Dr. Stanley Greenspan's books are listed under "Parenting and siblings," earlier in this appendix. *The Child with Special Needs* provides many, many ideas for implementing floor-time techniques. Audiotapes of his lectures on using floor-time techniques and other interventions can be ordered through his Web site.

Mutual Attention and Engagement
http://www.saveachild.com/wieder.html

More on setting up floor-time interactions.

Scholastic Inc.
2931 East McCarty Street
Jefferson City, MO 65101
(573) 659-1687 or (800) 724-6527
Fax (573) 635-5881
http://www.scholastic.com/

Irlen lenses

The Irlen Institute
5380 Village Rd.
Long Beach, CA 90808
(562) 496-2550
Fax (562) 429-8699
Info@Irlen.com
http://www.irlen.com

The Irlen Institute's Web site includes pointers to practitioners who can fit the Irlen system, and a company newsletter, among other resources.

Medical information

See also "Autistic-spectrum disorders" and "Diet, vitamins, and allergy-related interventions," earlier in this appendix.

Baker, Dr. Sidney M. and Jon Pangborn. *Defeat Autism Now! (DAN!) Clinical Options Manual*. San Diego: Autism Research Institute, 1998. Written especially for physicians, this collection of data and suggestions for treating autism and other PDDs is updated regularly with information from the yearly Defeat Autism Now! conference. Parents who don't have access to a DAN! doctor may wish to buy this as a guide for their regular physician, or as a guide for setting up their own treatment plan.

Cohen, Donald J., and Fred R. Volkmar, editors. *Handbook of Autism and Pervasive Developmental Disorders, 2nd Ed.* New York: John Wiley & Sons, 1997. This is the most current collection of research data and papers related to autistic-spectrum disorders. It compares and contrasts studies from around the world. It's in medical language, but not impossible to read. Expensive—check your nearest medical library.

Gillberg, Christopher, and Mary Coleman. *The Biology of the Autistic Syndromes*. Cambridge, England: Cambridge University Press, 1992. Heavy-duty reading—covers brain-imaging studies, genetics, and more. A great deal has been uncovered since 1992, but this book is useful for those who want the hard medical facts.

Medscape
http://www.medscape.com

Searchable, online index to hundreds of medical journals. Many articles are available in full, others as abstracts only.

PubMed
http://www.ncbi.nlm.nih.gov/PubMed/

Free interface for searching the MEDLINE medical database, which can help you find out about studies, medications, and more.

Books about medications

Chapter 5, *Medical Interventions*, and Appendix D, *Medication Reference*, cover most of the commonly used medications for PDD symptoms. However, it's important to educate yourself as well. There are a number of books available that list side effects, cautions, and more regarding medications. The biggest and best is the *Physicians Desk Reference* (PDR), but its price is well out of the average parent's or patient's league. You may, however, find a used but recent copy at a good price.

Those with allergies to food dyes, or to corn, wheat, and other materials used as fillers in pills, may need to consult the manufacturer directly.

British Medical Association and the Royal Pharmaceutical Society of Great Britain. *The British National Formulary (BNF)*. The standard reference for prescribing and dispensing drugs in the UK, updated twice yearly.

Preston, John D., John H. O'Neal, and Mary C. Talaga. *Consumer's Guide to Psychiatric Drugs*. Oakland, California: New Harbinger Publications, 1998.

Silverman, Harold M., editor. *The Pill Book, 8th ed.* New York: Bantam Books, 1998.

Sullivan, Donald. *The American Pharmaceutical Association's Guide to Prescription Drugs*. New York: Signet, 1998.

Web sites about medications

Canadian Drug Product Database
http://www.hc-sc.gc.ca/hpb-dgps/therapeut/htmleng/dpd.html

Dr. Bob's Psychopharmacology Tips
http://uhs.bsd.uchicago.edu/dr-bob/tips/

Excellent information on psychiatric drugs, including things like the MAOI dietary restrictions and common SSRI interactions.

Federal Drug Administration (FDA)
http://www.fda.gov/cder/drug.htm

Official US information on new drugs and generic versions of old drugs, FDA warnings and recalls, etc.

The Internet Drug List
http://www.rxlist.com/

MmedEc Interactive
http://www.pdrnet.com/

Includes link to a Web-accessible version of the PDR.

Pharmaceutical Information Network
http://pharminfo.com/

PharmWeb
http://www.pharmweb.net/

The Royal Pharmaceutical Society's Technical Information Center
http://wrww.rpsgb.org.uk/300.htm

There is a nominal fee for use of the RPS database, but one might be able to have it waived.

RXmed
http://www.rxmed.com/

Occupational therapy

Anderson, Elizabeth, and Pauline Emmons. *Unlocking the Mysteries of Sensory Dysfunction: A Resource for Anyone Who Works with, or Lives with, a Child with Sensory Issues.* Arlington, Texas: Future Horizons, 1996.

Ayres, Jean, and Jeff Robbins. *Sensory Integration and the Child.* Los Angeles: Western Psychological Services, 1983.

Bissel, Julie, et al. *Sensory Motor Handbook: A Guide for Implementing and Modifying Activities in the Classroom.* Torrance, California: Sensory Integration International, 1988.

Kranowitz, Carol Stock. *The Out-of-Sync Child: Recognizing and Coping with Sensory Integration Dysfunction.* New York: Perigee, 1998.

Reisman, Judith E., producer. Video: "Making Contact: Sensory Integration and Autism." 1993.

Reisman, Judith E., producer. Video: "Sensory Processing for Parents: From Roots to Wings." 1996.

Sensory Integration International (SII)
1602 Cabrillo Avenue
Torrance, CA 90501
(310) 320-9986
Fax (310) 320-9934
http://home.earthlink.net/~sensoryint/

Referrals to SII-qualified occupational therapists, books, and other materials for sensory integration.

Secretin

Beck, Victoria, and Gary Beck. *Unlocking the Potential of Secretin.* San Diego: Autism Research Institute, 1998. Short, parent-written book about the successful use of Secretin to treat their autistic son.

ARI's Secretin page
http://www.secretin.com

The Autism Research Institute is collecting data on Secretin trials and results, and will present as much data as possible on this page.

"Autism and Secretin"
http://curry.edschool.virginia.edu/go/cise/ose/information/secretin.html

An online paper by John Wills Lloyd with many links to related data.

The Use of Secretin for the Treatment of Autism
http://osiris.sunderland.ac.uk/autism/sec.htm

This Web site includes the full text of the "Dateline" show that featured Victoria and Gary Beck and their son, references to related journal articles, and regularly updated data. Managed by British researcher Dr. Paul Shattock.

Social skills training

Gray, Carol. *Comic Strip Conversations*. Arlington, Texas: Future Horizons, 1994.

Gray, Carol. *The New Social Stories*. Arlington, Texas: Future Horizons, 1994.

Gray, Carol. *Taming the Recess Jungle: Socially Simplifying Recess for Students with Autism and Related Disorders*. Arlington, Texas: Future Horizons, 1993.

Greenspan, Dr. Stanley I., with Jacqueline Salmon. *Playground Politics: Understanding the Emotional Life of Your School-Age Child*. Reading, Massachusetts: Addison-Wesley, 1993.

Mannix, Darlene. *Social Skills Activities for Special Children*. New York: Prentice Hall, 1993. Teacher's guide with reproducible worksheets.

Simpson, Richard, editor. *Social Skills for Students with Autism, 2nd Ed*. Reston, Virginia: Council for Exceptional Children, 1997.

Speech therapy and communication

Carr, Edward G. *How to Teach Sign Language to Developmentally Disabled Children*. H & H Enterprises, 1981.

Crystal, David, editor. *The Cambridge Encyclopedia of Language*. Cambridge, England: Cambridge University Press, 1987.

Freeman, Sabrina, and Lorelei Dake. *Teach Me Language: A Language Manual for Children with Autism, Asperger's Syndrome, and Related Developmental Disorders*. Langley, British Columbia: SKF Books, 1996. A set of worksheets and forms is also available for use with this guidebook.

Lund, Nancy J. and Judith F. Duchan. *Assessing Children's Language in Naturalistic Contexts, 3rd Ed*. Englewood Cliffs, New Jersey: Prentice Hall, 1993.

Schwartz, Sue, and Joan E. Heller Miller. *The New Language of Toys: Teaching Communication Skills to Special-Needs Children*. Rockville, Maryland: Woodbine House, 1996.

American Speech-Language Hearing Association

10801 Rockville Pike
Rockville, MD 20852
(800) 638-8255 or (301) 897-8682

Offers pamphlet: "Do Your Health Benefits Cover Audiology and Speech-Language Pathology Services?"

Apraxia-Kids mailing list

listserv@listserv.syr.edu
http://liam.avenza.com/~apraxia/

This mailing list covers oral-motor apraxia and related disabilities. The Web site is also superb, especially if you're having trouble getting your insurance to cover speech therapy. To subscribe, send an email with the message: "subscribe apraxia-kids."

Imaginart
(800) 828-1376
Fax (800) 737-1376
imaginart@AOL.com
http://www.imaginart.com

Speech therapy and occupational therapy materials.

Super Duper Publications
Dept. SD 98
P.O. Box 24997
Greenville, SC 29616-2497
(800) 277-8737
Fax (800) 978-7379
custserv@superduperinc.com
http://www.superduperinc.com

Excellent catalog of speech and language learning materials, games, videos, books, and tests; also includes items related to augmentative communication, social skills, and sensorimotor activities.

Transition planning and adult issues

Gray, Carol. *What's Next?...Preparing the Student with Autism or Other Developmental Disabilities for Success in the Community.* Arlington, Texas: Future Horizons, 1992.

Hingsburger, Dave. *Just Say Know! Understanding and Reducing the Risk of Sexual Victimization of People with Developmental Disabilities.* Eastman, Quebec: Diverse City Press, 1995.

Howlin, Patricia. *Autism: Preparing for Adulthood.* London: Routledge, 1997. Transition planning, with special attention to resources and possibilities in the UK.

Morgan, Hugh. *Adults with Autism: A Guide to Theory and Practice.* Cambridge, England: Cambridge University Press, 1996.

Mortlock, John. "The Socio-Sexual Development of People with Autism and Related Learning Disabilities" (pamphlet). London: National Autistic Society, 1993.

Smith, Marcia Datlow, Ronald G. Belcher, and Patricia D. Juhrs. *A Guide to Successful Employment for Individuals with Autism.* Baltimore: Paul H. Brookes Publishing Co., 1995.

Sobsey, Dick, et al., editors. *Disability, Sexuality, and Abuse: An Annotated Bibliography.* Baltimore: Paul H. Brookes Publishing Co., 1991.

Support and Advocacy

National autism/PDD organizations

In addition to the national organizations listed below, there are also many local autism/PDD support groups. We are not able to include all of these groups here, but we have listed local support groups on the web site for this book at *http://www.patientcenters.com/autism.*

Action for Autism
P.O. Box 3678
Defense Colony
New Delhi 110 024
(91) 11-469-0132 or (91) 11-462-0360
Fax (91) 11-469-0132
actaut@nda.vsnl.net.in
http://www.autism-india.org/

English-language advocacy and support group active in India and South Asia.

Asperger's Syndrome Support Network (Australia/New Zealand)
C/O VACCA
P.O. Box 235
Ashburton, Victoria 3147
http://www.vicnet.net.au/vicnet/community/asperger.htm

Asperger Syndrome Education Network of America, Inc. (ASPEN)
P.O. Box 2577
Jacksonville, FL 32203-2577
(904) 745-6741
aspen@cybermax.net
http://www.asperger.org

AUTINET links
http://ireland.iol.ie/~wise/autinet/anflinks.htm

This international site has a long list of links that may lead you to advocacy and support groups in non-English-speaking nations.

Autism in Africa
http://autism-alabama.org/africa/

A small collection of links to sites in South Africa, Botswana, and West African nations, including information in continental and West African French.

Autism Europe (continental Europe)
Avenue E. Van Becelaere 26b, Bte. 21
B-1170 Bruxelles, Belgium
(32-0) 2-675-75-05
Fax (32-0)2-675-72-70
autisme.europe@arcadis.be
http://www.autismeurope.arc.be/

Information available in French, English, and sometimes other languages.

Autism Network International
P.O. Box 448
Syracuse, NY 13210-0448
http://www.students.uiuc.edu/~bordner/ani.html

A self-help and self-advocacy organization for people with autism.

Autism Society of America
7910 Woodmont Avenue, Suite 650
Bethesda, MD 20814-3015
(301) 657-0881 or (800) 3AUTISM
Fax (301) 657-0869
Fax on demand for information (800) 329-0899
http://www.autism-society.org/

Autistic Organization of New Zealand Inc.
P.O. Box 7305
Sydenham, Christchurch, New Zealand
(03) 332 1038
m.s.whitworth@xtra.co.nz
http://www.autism.org.nz/

Irish Society for Autism (Republic of Ireland)
Unity Building
16/17 Lower O'Connell Street
Dublin 1, Republic of Ireland
(071) 744684
Fax (071) 744224
http://osiris.sunderland.ac.uk/autism/irish.html

National Association of Developmental Disabilities Councils
1234 Massachusetts Avenue N.W., Suite 103
Washington, DC 20005
(202) 347-1234
Fax (202) 347-4023
http://www.igc.apc.org/NADDC/index3.html

There are DD Councils in each US state and territory. They work with state legislatures to advocate for disabled citizens, make policy, and start programs.

The National Autistic Society (UK)
393 City Road
London EC1V 1NE
0171 833 2299
nas@mailbox.ulcc.ac.uk
http://www.oneworld.org/autism_uk/

The National Autistic Society in Wales (NASW)
William Knox House
Britannic Way
Llandarcy, Wales
West Glamorgan, SA10 6EL
(01) 792 815915

Parents for the Early Intervention of Autism in Children (PEACH, UK)
School of Education
Brunel University
300 St. Margaret's Road
Twickenham, Middlesex TW1 1PT England
(0181) 891 0121 Ext. 2348
Fax (0181) 891 8209
Peach@clara.net
http://www.peach.uk.com/

The Scottish Society for Autistic Children
SSAC Headquarters
Hilton House
Alloa Business Park
Whins Road
Alloa, FK10 3SA Scotland
(01259) 720044
Fax (01259)720051
ssac@autism-in-scotland.org.uk
http://www.autism-in-scotland.org.uk/

The Society for the Autistically Handicapped (UK)
199/201 Blandford Avenue
Bettering, Northants NN16 9AT United Kingdom
(01) 536 523274
Fax (01) 536 523274
autism@rmplc.co.uk
http://www.rmplc.co.uk/eduweb/sites/autism/index.html

World Autism Organisation (WAO)
Contact c/o Autism Europe, *autisme.europe@arcadis.be*
http://web.syr.edu/~jmwobus/autism/news/world-autism-organization.html

WAO was founded in 1998, and hopes to work with the UN, UNESCO, and other international organizations to improve the lives of people with autism worldwide.

Online support groups

AUT2BHOME
http://www.paulbunyan.net/users/shannon/autism.htm

This Web site can help you join a list for home-schooling families with autistic-spectrum children.

Autism-U.K.
majordomo@lists.ed.ac.uk
http://www.autism-uk.ed.ac.uk/welcome.html

To join, send email with a blank subject line and the message body: subscribe autism-U.K.

Independent Living on the Autistic Spectrum (InLv) list
martijn@inlv.demon.nl
http://www.inlv.demon.nl/

This is an international list primarily for adults with PDDs. To join, send email to Martijn Dekker with a message about why you want to participate in the list.

New Zealand ASD Support Group
Email Kay Harrison at: *TGG@xtra.co.nz*

OzAutism List (Australia and New Zealand)
Email Carolyn Baird at: *cas@attila.apana.org.au*

St. John's AS Support list
asperger-request@maelstrom.stjohns.edu

This is a list for adults with PDD/HFA/AS and parents of children with these conditions. Include a message about why you want to join the list, your name, and your email address.

St. John's Autism list
listserv@maelstrom.stjohns.edu
http://web.syr.edu/~rjkopp/autismlistfaq.html

Sponsored by St. John's University, this is a very active list for parents of children with autism/PDDs and adults with PDDs. More information is available at the Web site. Send email with the message: subscribe autism Firstname Surname

Related conditions

Angelman syndrome

Angelman Syndrome Foundation U.S.A.
414 Plaza Drive, Suite 209
Westmont, IL 60559
(630) 734-9267 or (800) IF-ANGEL
Fax (630) 655-0391
asf@adminsys.com
http://chem-faculty.ucsd.edu/harvey/asfsite/

Canadian Angelman Syndrome Society
P.O. Box 37
Priddis, Alberta TOL 1WO Canada
(403) 931-2415

Cornelia de Lange syndrome

Cornelia de Lange Syndrome Foundation, Inc.
302 West Main Street, Suite 100
Avon, CT 06001
(860) 676-8166
cdlsintl@iconn.net
http://cdlsoutreach.org

Deafness and communication disorders

NIH/National Institute on Deafness and Other Communication Disorders Information Clearinghouse
1 Communication Avenue
Bethesda, MD 20892-3456
(301) 907-8830
NIDCD@AERIE.COM
http://www.nih.gov/nidcd/

Epilepsy

Epilepsy International
info@epiworld.com
http://www.epiworld.com/

This Web site, available in English and Spanish, provides worldwide listings of local and national support, advocacy, and research organizations. It also contains a wealth of information about the diagnosis, treatment, and management of epilepsy.

Fragile X syndrome

The Fragile X Society
53 Winchelsea Lane
Hastings, East Sussex, TN35 4LG England
(44–0) 1424-813147
http://www.fragilex.org.uk/

This group's excellent Web site covers fragile X basics, including resources in the UK.

The National Fragile X Foundation
1441 York Street, Suite 303
Denver, CO 80206
(303) 333-6155 or (800) 688-8765
Fax (303) 333-4369
http://nfxf.org/

Hyperlexia

American Hyperlexia Association
479 Spring Road
Elmhurst, IL 60126
(630) 415-2212
Fax (630) 530-5909
president@hyperlexia.org
http://www.hyperlexia.com/

Canadian Hyperlexia Association
300 John Street, Box 87673
Thornhill, Ontario L3T 7R3 Canada
(905) 886-9163
Fax (905) 886-4624
cha@io.org
http://home.ican.net/~cha/

Landau-Kleffner syndrome

C.A.N.D.L.E.
4414 McCampbell
Montgomery, AL 36106

Friends of Landau-Kleffner Syndrome (FOLKS)
P.O. Box 749
Erith, Kent DA8 3UA United Kingdom
(0870) 847-0707
http://www.bobjanet.demon.co.uk/lks/folks.html

Learning disabilities

Learning Disabilities Association of America (LDA)
4156 Library Road
Pittsburgh, PA 15234
(412) 341-1515
Fax (412) 344-0224
http://www.ldanatl.org/

Mental retardation

The Arc (Association of Retarded Citizens)
500 East Border Street, Suite 300
Arlington, TX 76010
(817) 261-6003
thearc@metronet.com
http://thearc.org/welcome.html

Prader-Willi syndrome

The Prader-Willi Foundation, Inc.
40 Holly Lane
Roslyn Heights, NY 11577
(516) 621-2445
Fax (516) 484-7154
http://www.prader-willi.org/

Prader-Willi Syndrome Association
2510 S. Brentwood Blvd., Suite 220
St. Louis, MO 63144
(800) 926-4797

Ontario Prader-Willi Syndrome Association
1910 Yonge Street, Fourth Floor
Toronto, Ontario M4S 3B2 Canada
(800) 563-1123

Rett syndrome

International Rett Syndrome Association
9121 Piscataway Road
Clinton, MD 20735
(301) 248-7031 or (800) 818-RETT
Fax (301) 856-3336
irsa@rettsyndrome.org
http://www.rettsyndrome.org/

Tuberous sclerosis

National Tuberous Sclerosis Association
8181 Professional Place, Suite 110
Landover, MD 20785-2226
(800) 225-6872
Fax (301) 459-0394
ntsa@ntsa.org
http://www.tsctalk.com/faq.html

TSCTalk mailing list
http://www.tsctalk.com/faq.html

General special needs

Australian Early Intervention Network
c/o CAMHS
Flinders Medical Centre
Bedford Park, South Australia 5042 Australia
Fax (61) 8-8357-5484
AusEinet@flinders.edu.au
http://auseinet.flinders.edu.au/

DisabilityNet
http://www.disabilitynet.co.uk
UK-based disability information site.

Federation for Children with Special Needs
95 Berkeley Street,
Boston, MA 02116
(617) 482 2915
http://www.fcsn.org/hometext.htm
Contact for help locating parents or parent organizations in your area.

Integrated Network of Disability Information and Education
info@indie.ca
http://www.indie.ca/

Information in English and French about disabilities and related topics in Canada, as well as international links.

March of Dimes Birth Defects Foundation
1275 Mamaroneck Avenue
White Plains, NY 10605
(914) 428-7100
resourcecenter@modimes.org
http://www.modimes.org/

Disability Information & Communication Exchange (Australia)
(61) 2 6280 8858
Fax (61) 2 6280 8868
dicenet@dice.org.au
http://www.ozemail.com.au/~ncid/

National Information Center for Children and Youth with Disabilities (NICHCY)
P.O. Box 1492
Washington, DC 20013-1492
(202) 884-8200 or (800) 695-0285
Fax (202) 884-8441
nichcy@aed.org
http://www.nichcy.org/

National Organization for Rare Disorders Inc.(NORD)
P.O. Box 8923
New Fairfield, CT 06812-8923
(203) 746-6518 or (800) 999-6673
TDD (203) 746-6927
Fax (203) 746-6481
orphan@nord-rdb.com
http://www.nord-rdb.com/~orphan/

National Institute of Child Health and Human Development
National Institutes of Health
9000 Rockville Pike, Building 31, Room 2A32, MSC 2425
Bethesda, MD 20892
(301) 496-5133
http://www.nih.gov/nichd/

Parent Educational Advocacy Training Center (PEATC)
10340 Democracy Lane, Suite 206
Fairfax, VA 22030
(703) 691-7826
Fax (703) 691-8148
peatcinc@aol.com
http://members.aol.com/peatcinc/index.htm

The Sibling Support Project
Children's Hospital and Medical Center
P.O. Box 5371, CL-po
Seattle, WA 98105
Contact: Donald Meyer, *dmeyer@chmc.org*
http://www.chmc.org/departmt/sibsupp/

Offers information about the Sibshops support group project and online support lists SibKids and SibNet.

Legal advocacy/SSI help, US

A complete list of state legal referral services and disability advocacy groups is available on the web site for this book at *http://www.patientcenters.com/autism*. For help with Social Security Income, disability rights issues, or violations of special education law, call your state bar association and ask for its pro bono (free legal help) referral service, or contact:

National Association of Protection and Advocacy Systems
900 2nd Street, N.E., Suite 211
Washington, DC 20002
(202) 408-9514

Legal advocacy, UK

England

Disability Access Rights and Advice Service (DARAS)
Unit 303
The Chandlery
50 Westminster Bridge Road
London SE1 7QY England
(03) 45 585 445
Fax (03) 45 585 446
Textphone (03) 45 558 447
dda_daras@deloitte.touche.co.uk
http://www.daras.co.uk/

Disability Law Service
49-51 Bedford Row, 2nd Floor, Room 241
London WC1R 4LR England
http://www.mkurrein.co.uk/work/disdiscm.html

Independent Panel for Special Education Advice (IPSEA)
4 Ancient House Mews
Woodbridge, Suffolk IP12 1DH
(01) 394 382814 (advice) or (01) 394 380518
http://www.indiracc.demon.co.uk/ipsea/parents.htm

JUSTICE
59 Carter Lane
London EC4V 5AQ England
(01) 71 329 5100
(01) 71 329 5055
justice@gn.apc.org

Organization for legal access and human rights issues.

National Disability Council
Caxton House, Level 4
Tothill Street
London SW1H 9NA England
(0171) 273 5636
Fax (0171) 273 5929
Minicom (0171) 273 5579
http://www.open.gov.uk/ndc/ndchome.htm

Rights Now Campaign
c/o RADAR
12 City Forum
250 City Road
London EC1V 8AF England
(01) 71 250 3222

Scotland

Glasgow Association for Mental Health
Melrose House, First Floor
15/23 Cadogan Street
Glasgow, G2 6QQ Scotland
(01) 41-204 22 70
Fax (01) 41-204 27 70
GAMH@colloquium.co.uk
http://users.colloquium.co.uk/~GAMH/

Legal advocacy, Australia

A complete list of contacts for disability-related legal help in Australia can be found on the web site for this book at *http://www.patientcenters.com/autism*. For general information about the Disability Discrimination Act and disability-related legal issues, you may want to start with:

Human Rights and Equal Opportunity Commission
Level 8, Piccadilly Tower
133 Castlereagh Street
Sydney, NSW 2000 Australia
(02) 9284 9600 or (1300) 656 419 (complaints)
TTY (800) 620 241
Fax (02) 9284 9611
http://www.hreoc.gov.au/disability_rights/index.html/

Action Resource Network, Inc.
266 Johnston Street
Abbotsford, Vic. 3067 Australia
(03) 9416-3488 or (800) 808-126 TTY (03) 9416-3491 Fax (03) 9416-3484

Legal advocacy, New Zealand

The Human Rights Commission of New Zealand/Komihana Tikanga Tangata
P.O. Box 6751
Wellesley Street
Auckland, NZ
(0508) 505 809
Fax (09) 375 8611
help@hrc.co.nz
http://www.hrc.co.nz/

Information in English and Maori about the Human Rights Act and related legal matters.

New Zealand CCS, Inc.
P.O. Box 8066
Christchurch, New Zealand
(03) 348-8974
nzccs@lynx.co.nz
http://www.webview.co.nz/ccia/nzccs/ccs_index.htm

Research and Testing Facilities

THE ESTABLISHMENTS AND PRACTITIONERS LISTED IN THIS APPENDIX have been compiled from a variety of sources, including parent recommendations, PDD support groups, and official government healthcare documents. We don't imply endorsement of their medical or therapeutic approaches by including them here.

Autism research facilities

These facilities and organizations are centers of or fundraisers for research into autistic-spectrum disorders. Although they may carry out or fund studies of new treatments, they are generally not sources of ongoing medical care. Their Web sites, publications, and staff may be sources of information on the latest developments, however.

Allergy Induced Autism Support and Research Network
8 Hollie Lucas Road, King's Heath
Birmingham, UK B13 0QL
Fax (44) 0-121 444 6450
aia@kessick.demon.co.uk
http://www.demon.co.uk/charities/AIA/aia.htm

Autism Autoimmunity Project
45 Iroquois Avenue
Lake Hiawatha, NJ 07034
Contact: Ray Gallup, *truegrit@gti.net*
http://www.gti.net/truegrit/

The Doug Flutie, Jr. Foundation for Autism
c/o The Giving Back Fund
230 Congress Street
Boston, MA 02110
(617) 556-2820
Fax (617) 426-5441
http://www.dougflutie.org/

Founded by pro football player Doug Flutie, who is the father of an autistic son, this foundation raises funds to help disadvantaged families pay for treatment and to support research efforts.

The Autism Research Foundation (TARF)
Moss-Rosene Lab, Suite W701
715 Albany Street
Boston, MA 02118
(617) 534-5286
Fax (617) 534-7207
http://ladders.org/tarf/TARF.htm

Autism Research Institute (ARI)
4182 Adams Avenue
San Diego, CA 92116
Fax (619) 563-6840
http://www.autism.org/

Autism Research Unit
School of Health Sciences
University of Sunderland
Sunderland SR2 7EE United Kingdom
(44) 0 191 510 8922
Fax (44) 0 191 567 0420
aru@sunderland.ac.uk
http://osiris.sunderland.ac.uk/autism/ind1.htm

Center for the Study of Autism
P.O. Box 4538
Salem, OR 97302
http://www.autism.org/

The Cure Autism Now (CAN) Foundation
5225 Wilshire Boulevard, Suite 226
Los Angeles, CA 90036
(323) 529-0500
CAN@primenet.com
http://www.canfoundation.org/

Defeat Autism Now! (DAN!)
c/o Autism Research Institute
4182 Adams Avenue
San Diego, CA 92116
Fax (619) 563-6840
http://www.autism.org/dan.html

DAN! holds a yearly medical conference about new autism therapies and research. A list of doctors who attend this conference is available from the organization.

International Autism Consortium
http://www.well.ox.ac.uk/~maestrin/iat.html

This is an international group of researchers who are coordinating studies on the molecular genetics of autism.

Laboratory for Research on the Neuroscience of Autism
8110 La Jolla Shores Drive, Suite 200B
La Jolla, CA 92037
(619) 551-7925
Fax (619) 551-7931
http://nodulus.extern.ucsd.edu/

National Alliance for Autism Research (NAAR)
66 Witherspoon Street, Suite 310
Princeton, NJ 08542
(908) 359-9957
http://www.naar.org/

The Seaver Autism Research Center
Mt. Sinai School of Medicine
Dept. of Psychiatry, Box 1230
One Gustave L. Levy Place
New York, NY 10029
(212) 241-2994
Fax (212) 987-4031

Medical and treatment facilities

We have posted an extensive list (approximately 35 pages) of medical and treatment facilities online at *http://www.patientcenters.com/autism/*. The online list can be freely printed, copied, and shared, as long as its source is cited. The list includes facilities throughout the US, Canada, UK, Ireland, Australia, and New Zealand. The list includes state agencies that can send you to an evaluation center, well-known evaluation and treatment centers, and larger ABA providers.

There are, of course, many private physicians and smaller clinics that have expertise in PDD-NOS and atypical PDD. Your local autism advocacy and support organization is almost always the best source of information about where to go for evaluation and ongoing care, because other families can tell you about their experiences with these and other care providers.

Test facilities and programs

As discussed in Chapter 5, *Medical Interventions*, and Chapter 7, *Other Interventions*, some researchers suspect that allergies, food sensitivities, metabolic disorders, *Candida* yeast overgrowth, viral infection, unusual reactions to immunizations, and other factors may be involved in some cases of PDDs. Ferreting out these causes usually requires obtaining test results on blood, urine, or stool samples. Your physician may not be able (or willing) to do these tests. If this is the case, the facilities listed below have expertise in this area.

Be sure that you have expert medical help in interpreting the test results. The reports you receive may be unintentionally misleading if you don't know what you're looking at. If the results seem inconsistent or strange, you may want to duplicate the tests at another lab. Labs do make mistakes.

Alletess Lab
216 Pleasant Street
P.O. Box 343
Rockland, MA 02370
(617) 871-4426

Alletess does follow-up blood testing for Dr. Cade (see below).

Antibody Assay Labs
1715 E. Wilshire, Suite 715
Santa Ana, CA 92705
(714) 972-9979
Fax (714) 543-2034
http://www.antibodyassay.com/

Urinary peptide tests for casein and gliaden (gluten).

Autism Research Unit
School of Health Sciences
University of Sunderland
Sunderland SR2 7EE United Kingdom
(44) 0 191 510 8922
Fax (44) 0 191 567 0420
aru@sunderland.ac.uk
http://osiris.sunderland.ac.uk/autism/ind1.htm

Dr. Paul Shattock of the Autism Research Unit offers specific types of urinary peptide tests, at no charge, to children and adults with autistic-spectrum disorders.
These can be done by mail. His lab is very small, and there may be a wait. Contact
the unit for further details. He is collecting the data from these tests as part of an
ARU research project. Dr. Shattock has taught the staff at Antibody Assay Labs
(above), a commercial facility in the US, how to duplicate his peptide test technique.

Carbon Based Corp.
920 Incline Way, Suite 2C
Incline Village, NV 89451
(702) 832-8485 or (800) 722-8327
Fax (702) 832-8488
http://www.carbon.com/

CBC does an exhaustive blood test panel and report by mail, recommended by Patricia Kane (see below).

Dr. Robert Cade
University of Florida
Department of Physiology
Gainesville, FL 32611
(352) 392-8952

Pioneering researcher in urinary peptides and autism (and also, believe it or not, the
inventor of Gatorade!). The initial test is free; contact his department for more information.

Dr. William Crook
45 Conrad Drive, Suite 100
Jackson, TN 38305
(901) 660-5027

Dr. Crook, author of *The Yeast Connection*, specializes in testing and treatment of *Candida* yeast-related conditions.

The Great Plains Laboratory/Dr. William Shaw
9335 West 75th Street
Overland Park, KS 66204
(913) 341-8949
Fax (913) 341-6207
williamsha@aol.com
http://www.autism.com/shaw-yeast/

Dr. Shaw, author of *The Biological Basis of Autism and PDD*, provides home test kits and lab analysis for a variety of PDD-related conditions.

Great Smokies Diagnostic Laboratory
63 Zillicoa Street
Asheville, NC 28801
(704) 253-0621 or (800) 522-4762
http://www.gsdl.com/

Provides home sample kits and mail-in lab analysis for *Candida* yeast and other PDD-related health issues.

Immuno Laboratories
1620 West Oakland Park Boulevard
Fort Lauderdale, FL 33311
(800) 231-9197
http://www.immunolabs.com/

Provides home sample kits and mail-in lab analysis for food and other allergies/sensitivities.

Patricia Kane, PhD
P.O. Box 829
South 12th Street
Millville, NJ 08332
(609) 825-2200
Fax (609) 825-2143

Medication Reference

THIS APPENDIX PROVIDES MORE INFORMATION ABOUT MEDICATIONS that may be prescribed to treat specific symptoms in people with PDD-NOS, atypical PDD, or similar conditions. Inclusion in this appendix does not mean that a particular medication is recommended for these disorders—in fact, some of these medications, such as the old-line neuroleptics, are very much out of favor with reputable physicians. That said, it's important to know as much as possible about drugs you may be prescribed or that you may hear about from other parents or patients.

We have listed commonly reported side effects and certain rare but especially dangerous side effects only. Less common and rare side effects may be associated with any medication, and you may experience side effects that no one else has ever had. If you experience unusual symptoms after taking medicine, or after combining more than one medication, call your doctor right away. You may also want to consult the drug reference sheet packaged with your medication by the pharmacy.

The information in this chapter was taken from the *Physician's Desk Reference*, pharmaceutical company literature, and other reputable sources. It should be accurate as of this writing, but new information may emerge. Be sure to personally check out any medications you or your child takes using a detailed medication reference book, such as those listed in Appendix A, *Resources*, to ensure that you are aware of all possible side effects and interactions.

Here are some more important dos and don'ts:

- Do not start or stop taking any prescription medication on your own.
- Be careful to follow dosage, time, and accompaniment ("take with food," etc.) instructions specifically.
- If you are pregnant or breastfeeding, or if you could become pregnant, ask your physician or pharmacist about any side effects specifically related to female reproduction and nursing.
- Men who are actively trying to father a child may also want to ask about male reproductive side effects.
- Be sure to tell both your physician and your pharmacist about all other medications you take, including over-the-counter drugs—even aspirin and cough syrup can cause dangerous side effects when mixed with the wrong medication.
- Inform your doctor about your use of alcohol, tobacco, any illegal drugs, and any vitamins or supplements (other than a regular daily multivitamin).

- If your doctor is unsure how a medication might interact with a supplement, you may need to help him or her find more information about the chemical action of the supplement. Most doctors are not well informed about nutritional supplements or herbal medicines, but many are willing to work with you on these matters.

- If you suspect that you have been given the wrong medication or the wrong dosage, call your pharmacist right away. Such errors do occur, and your pharmacist should be able to either reassure you or fix the problem.

The latest data on medications for PDD symptoms

The following three tables summarize what's currently known about medications that address some symptoms of autism and other PDDs. They were adapted with permission from "New Findings on the Causes and Treatment of Autism," by Dr. Mark Potenza and Dr. Christopher McDougle, a 1997 article published in the medical journal *CNS Spectrums* (Copyright © 1997, Medical Broadcast Limited). They are based on information from the latest studies of human subjects who have autistic-spectrum disorders. You can find out more about these studies by reading the original journal articles about them, all of which are listed in *Notes* at the end of the book.

Table D-1. Drugs with Mixed 5-HT Receptor Agonism/Antagonism Properties in Pervasive Developmental Disorders

Reference	Study Design	N	Age (yrs)	Dosage (mg/day)	Duration (weeks)	Efficacy	Adverse Effects
Buspirone							
Realmuto et al. (1989)[1]	Open-label with blinded comparison to fenfluramine or methylphenidate	4	Range, 9–10 mean 9.3	15	4	Improvement in hyperactivity (2/4), aggression (2/4), & stereotypy (2/4)	None
Ratey et al. (1989)[2]	Open-label	14 (3 with PDDs)	Range, 23–63 (25–38) Mean, 35.3 (32.2)	15–45	26–52 in well-described cases	Improvement in 9/14, with decreases in aggression and ritualistic behavior, and increases in social interactions	None reported
Gedye (1991)[3]	Single-blind, ABAC design, open comparison to serotonin-enhancing diet	1	39	20	10 active	Decrease in aggression (65–76%)	None
Ratey et al. (1991)[4]	Multiple baseline, placebo lead-in, ABC design	6 (1 with PDD)	Range, 18–50 (29) Mean, 28.4 (29)	15–45	9 active	Improvement with decreases in self-injurious behavior and anxiety	None reported
Ricketts et al. (1994)[5]	Open-label	5 (3 w/ PDDs)	Range, 27–45 (27–34) Mean, 34.6 (30)	Range, 30–60 (30–60) Mean, 49.5 (45)	6–33	Decrease in aggression (13%–72%)	None
Trazodone							
Gedye (1991)[3]	Open-label, ABAB design	1	17	50–150	10 active	Decrease in aggression (70%–79%)	None reported

Table D-2. Selective Serotonin Reuptake Inhibitors in Pervasive Developmental Disorders

Reference	Study Design	N	Age (yrs)	Dosage) (mg/day)	Duration (weeks)	Efficacy	Adverse Effects
Clomipramine							
Gordon et al. (1993)[6]	Double-blind crossover	12 vs DMI 12 vs PLA	Range, 6–18 Mean, 9.7	152+/-56	5	CMI>DMI, CMI>PLA for stereotypies, anger, rituals; CMI=DMI>PLA for hyperactivity	Insomnia, constipation, sedation, twitching, EKG changes (N=1), tachycardia (N=2), grand mal seizure
McDougle et al. (1992)[7]	Open-label	5	Range, 13–33 Mean, 25.2	185+/-74	12	4/5 patients showed improved social relatedness and reduced repetitive behavior and aggression	Dry mouth
Garber et al. (1992)[8]	Open-label	11	Range, 10–20 Mean, 15.0	70+/-37	4–52	10/11 patients had >50% reduction in SIB and stereotypies	Hypomania, constipation, sedation, enuresis, aggression
Brasic et al. (1994)[9]	Open-label	5	Range, 6–12 Mean, 9.4	200+/-0.0	8–78	5/5 patients showed reduced adventitious movements and compulsions	None reported
Brodkin et al. (in press, 1997)[10]	Open-label	35	Range, 18–44 Mean, 30.2	139+/-50	12	18/35 patients "much improved" or "very much improved," with reduced repetitive behavior, aggression, and echolalia	Constipation, sedation, weight gain, seizures (N=3)
Sanchez et al. (1996)[11]	Open-label	8	Range, 3.5–8.7 Mean, 6.4	103.6	5	7 patients worse, 1 moderately improved	Urinary retention, constipation, insomnia, sedation, aggression

CGI = Clinical Global Impression Scale; CMI = clomipramine; DMI = desipramine; N = number of subjects; PLA = placebo; SIB = self-injurious behavior.

Table D-2. Selective Serotonin Reuptake Inhibitors in Pervasive Developmental Disorders (continued)

Reference	Study Design	N	Age (yrs)	Dosage (mg/day)	Duration (weeks)	Efficacy	Adverse Effects
Fluvoxamine							
McDougle et al. (1996)[12]	Double-blind parallel groups	30	Range, 18–53 Mean, 30.1	277+/-42	12	8/15 patients "much improved" or "very much improved" on fluvoxamine, 0/15 patients improved on placebo. Reduced repetitive behavior and aggression and improved language usage	Nausea, sedation
Fluoxetine							
Cook et al. (1992)[13]	Open-label	23	Range, 7.0–28.8 Mean, 15.9	28.3	1.5–67	15/23 patients had an improvement of 1 or more on CGI Severity Rating. Reduced rituals and aggression, better eye contact	Agitation, hyperactivity, insomnia, "elated effect," decreased appetite, increased screaming
McDougle et al. (unpublished data)	Open-label	42	Range, 18–39 Mean, 26.1	122+/-61	12	24/42 patients "much improved" or "very much improved." Improvement seen in repetitive behavior and aggression	Agitation, headaches, reduced appetite, sedation, weight gain

CGI = Clinical Global Impression Scale; CMI = clomipramine; DMI = desipramine; N = number of subjects; PLA = placebo; SIB = self-injurious behavior.

Table D-3. "Atypical" Neuroleptics in Pervasive Developmental Disorders

Reference	Study Design	N	Age (yrs)	Dosage (mg/day)	Efficacy	Adverse Effects
Clozapine						
Zuddas et al. (1996)[14]	Open-label	3	Range, 8–12 Mean, 9.33	200–400	Improvements in hyperactivity, SIB, aggression, and communication	Transient sedation, enuresis
Risperidone						
Purdon et al. (1994)[15]	Open-label	2	Range, 29–30 Mean, 29.5	6–8	Improvements in hyperactivity, social interactions, repetitive behaviors	None reported
McDougle et al. (1995)[16]	Open-label	3	Range, 20–44 Mean, 31.67	2–8	Improvements in social relatedness, repetitive thoughts and behaviors, and impulsive aggression	None
Simeon et al. (1995)[17]	Open-label	7 (2 with PDD)	Range, 11–17 Mean, 14.43 (Range, 13–14 Mean 13.50)	1–4	Improvements in social interactions and aggressive behaviors	None (transient sedation at higher doses)
Fisman et al. (1996)[18]	Open-label	1	14	1	Decrease in compulsive avoidances and agitation, and improved attention	None
Demb (1996)[19]	Open-label	3	Range, 5–11 Mean, 7.66	1–3	Decreases in SIB and hyperactivity	Temporary sedation, extrapyramidal side effects, weight gain
Fisman & Steele (1996)[20]	Open-label	14	Range, 9–17 Mean, 12.72	0.75–1.5	Improvement (13/14) with decreases in disruptive behaviors, agitation, anxiety, and repetitive behaviors; and increased social awareness and attention	Initial sedation (5/14), sleep onset insomnia (1/14), rhinorrhea (1/14), and transient headache (1/14)
Hardan et al. (1996)[21]	Open-label	20	Range, 8–17 Mean, 13.35	1.5–10	Improvement (13/20) with decreases in aggression, SIB, impulsivity, hyperactivity, and psychosis	Weight gain (3/20), galactorrhea (2/20 [2/7 girls])

N = number of subjects; SIB = self-injurious behavior.

Table D-3. "Atypical" Neuroleptics in Pervasive Developmental Disorders (continued)

Reference	Study Design	N	Age (yrs)	Dosage (mg/day)	Efficacy	Adverse Effects
Rubin (1997)[22]	Open-label	2	Range, 3.5–5 Mean, 4.25		Improvement with decreases in repetitive and aggressive behaviors, and increased social function	None
Olanzapine						
Rubin (1997)[22]	Open-label	1	17	30	Decrease in pacing and aggression, and stabilization of mood	None

N = number of subjects; SIB = self-injurious behavior.

Medication List

Medications are listed below under the brand name that occurs first in the alphabet. They are also cross-indexed by other brand names and by generic chemical name. Please note that many of these medications are not yet available commercially as low-cost generic drugs, and many may not be available outside the US. Others may be marketed under different brand names outside the US.

Acyclovir

See Zovirax.

Adderall

Generic name: dextroamphetamine/amphetamine

Use: ADD/ADHD.

Action, if known: CNS stimulant.

Side effects: Loss of appetite, weight loss, headache, insomnia, dizziness, increased heart rate, agitation. May increase tic severity in people with an underlying tic disorder.

Known interaction hazards: None known.

Tips: Said to be smoother-acting than many other medications for ADD/ADHD. Vitamin C supplements, citrus juices, citric acid, more than four cans per day of soda pop, or taking this medication with food can reduce its effectiveness. Make sure you drink plenty of water, even if you're not thirsty.

Alprazolam

See Xanax.

Amitriptyline

See Elavil.

Amitriptyline/chlordiazepoxide

See Limbatrol.

Amitriptyline/perphenazine

See Etrafon.

Amoxapine

See Asendin.

Ampligen

Generic name: poly I: poly C12U

Use: Older drug recently retried for AIDS, chronic fatigue syndrome (CFIDS), fibro-myalgia, Hepatitis B and C.

Action, if known: Immune modulator, antiviral. Ampligen is a nucleic acid (NA) compound that apparently heightens production of the body's own immunological and antiviral agents, such as interferon, and boosts natural killer (NK) cell and monocyte activity. It inhibits the growth of viruses and tumor cells.

Side effects: Dizziness, facial flushing.

Known interaction hazards: None known.

Tips: Ampligen may have hazards, actions, and benefits that are as yet unknown (and probably won't be covered by your insurance). It also may not work—its man-ufacturer has been accused of fraud by certain investment firms. However, some patients with CFIDS and other disorders who have obtained it overseas are staunch supporters. Not approved for US use as of this writing.

Anafranil

Generic name: clomipramine

Use: Depression, OCD, obsessive-compulsive behavior, panic disorder, chronic pain, eating disorders, severe PMS.

Action, if known: Tricyclic antidepressant—blocks norepinephrine and serotonin use, works against the hormone acetylcholine. Weak antihistamine properties.

Side effects: Sedation, tremor, seizures, dry mouth, light sensitivity, moodswings in people with diagnosed or undiagnosed bipolar disorder, weight gain. Lowers the sei-zure threshold.

Known interaction hazards: Alcohol, MAOIs, blood pressure medications (includ-ing Clonadine and Tenex), thyroid medication. Potentiated by estrogen, bicarbonate of soda (as in Alka-Seltzer and other OTC remedies), acetazolamide, procainamide, and quinidine. Cimetidine, methylphenidate, Thorazine and similar drugs, oral con-traceptives, nicotine (including cigarettes), charcoal tablets, and estrogen may inter-fere with Anafranil's action in the body.

Tips: Take with food if stomach upset occurs. Take bulk of dose at bedtime to reduce sedation, if so directed.

Asendin

Generic name: amoxapine

Use: Depression, panic disorder, chronic pain, eating disorders, severe PMS.

Action, if known: Tricyclic antidepressant—blocks norepinephrine and serotonin use, works against the hormone acetylcholine.

Side effects: Sedation, tremor, seizures, dry mouth, light sensitivity, moodswings in people with diagnosed or undiagnosed bipolar disorder.

Known interaction hazards: Alcohol, MAOIs, blood pressure medications (including Clonadine and Tenex), thyroid medication. Potentiated by estrogen, bicarbonate of soda (as in Alka-Seltzer and other OTC remedies), acetazolamide, procainamide, and quinidine. Cimetidine, methylphenidate, Thorazine and similar drugs, oral contraceptives, nicotine (including cigarettes), charcoal tablets, and estrogen may interfere with Asendin's action in the body.

Tips: Take with food if stomach upset occurs. Take bulk of dose at bedtime to reduce sedation, if so directed.

Ativan

Generic name: lorazepam

Use: Anti-anxiety, panic disorder, PMS, irritable bowel syndrome.

Action, if known: Benzodiazepine, slows CNS activity.

Side effects: Sleepiness (this usually passes after a week), lethargy, confusion, headache, slurred speech, tremor. Addictive, withdrawal may be difficult.

Known interaction hazards: Alcohol, all tranquilizers (including OTC sleep aids), narcotics, MAOIs, antihistamines (including OTC allergy and cold remedies), antidepressants. Potentiated by cimetidine, SSRIs, Depakene, disulfiram, isoniazid, ketoconazole, metoprolol, probenecid, propoxyphene, propranalol, rifampin, and oral contraceptives. Potentiates digoxin and phenytoin; decreases effect of L-Dopa.

Tips: If you smoke, take theophylline, or use antacids, Ativan may be less effective.

Aurorex, Manerix

Generic name: moclobemide

Use: Depression, anxiety.

Action, if known: A so-called "reversible" MAO inhibitor, Aurorex increases levels of serotonin, norepinephrine, and dopamine in the brain.

Side effects: Headache, insomnia, dizziness, tremor, agitation, nervousness, sedation, anxiety, weakness. Said to be safer and to have fewer side effects than the older MAOIs.

Known interaction hazards: Tricyclic antidepressants, meperidine, cimetidine, other MAOIs, SSRIs, alcohol, anesthetics, amphetamines (including CNS stimulants like Ritalin and OTC cold and allergy remedies containing ephedrine, ephedra, and similar stimulants).

Tips: Not currently available in the US. Aurorex is still a relatively new drug in Canada and Europe. Although it appears to have fewer dangerous interactions with foods and medications than older MAOIs, caution, monitoring of medication doses and interactions, and careful eating are still recommended.

Avenytl, Pamelor

Generic name: nortriptyline

Use: Depression, panic disorder, chronic pain, eating disorders, severe PMS.

Action, if known: Tricyclic antidepressant—blocks norepinephrine and serotonin use, works against the hormone acetylcholine.

Side effects: Sedation, tremor, seizures, dry mouth, light sensitivity, moodswings in people with diagnosed or undiagnosed bipolar disorder.

Known interaction hazards: Alcohol, MAOIs, blood pressure medications (including Clonadine and Tenex), thyroid medication. Potentiated by estrogen, bicarbonate of soda (as in Alka-Seltzer and other OTC remedies), acetazolamide, procainamide, and quinidine. Cimetidine, methylphenidate, Thorazine and similar drugs, oral contraceptives, nicotine (including cigarettes), charcoal tablets, and estrogen may interfere with Aventyl's action in the body.

Tips: Take with food if stomach upset occurs.

Buproprion

See Wellbutrin.

BuSpar

Generic name: buspirone

Use: Anxiety, decreasing emotional lability or moodswing, ADHD, PMS.

Action, if known: Non-benzodiazepine tranquilizer—enhances serotonin transmission, blocks dopamine receptors, increases metabolism of norepinephrine in the brain.

Side effects: Dizziness, nausea, headache, fatigue, jitteriness, tremor, sore muscles, heart palpitations, sweating, possible liver or kidney damage, tardive dyskensia-like movements or tics.

Known interaction hazards: Do not use with MAOIs. Potentiates Haldol and possibly other neuroleptics. Can cause liver inflammation when used with Desyrel. May have other side effects when used with antidepressants or similar drugs.

Tips: Side effects are a frequent problem with BuSpar, especially when taken in combination with other medications, including OTC remedies. The BuSpar patch may be better tolerated and smoother acting than the pill, especially for treatment of ADHD or moodswings. Has been tested with good results in children with PDD-NOS for treatment of anxiety and irritability

Buspirone

See BuSpar.

Carmazepine

See Tegretol.

Catapres

See Clonadine.

Celexa

Generic name: citalopram

Use: Depression.

Action, if known: SSRI—increases the amount of active serotonin in the brain. Has a calming effect.

Side effects: Dry mouth, insomnia or restless sleep, increased sweating, nausea, sexual dysfunction. Lowers the seizure threshold. Can cause moodswings in people with diagnosed or undiagnosed bipolar disorder.

Known interaction hazards: Alcohol. Never take with an MAOI or soon after stopping an MAOI. Use with caution if you take a drug that affects the liver, such as ketoconazole or the macrolides.

Tips: People with liver or kidney disease should be monitored regularly while taking Celexa.

Centrax

Generic name: prazepam

Use: Anti-anxiety, muscle spasm, seizures, panic disorder, irritable bowel syndrome.

Action, if known: Benzodiazepine, slows CNS activity.

Side effects: Sleepiness (this usually passes after a week), lethargy, confusion, headache, slurred speech, tremor. Addictive, withdrawal may be difficult.

Known interaction hazards: Alcohol, all tranquilizers (including OTC sleep aids), narcotics, MAOIs, antihistamines (including OTC allergy and cold remedies), antidepressants. Potentiated by cimetidine, disulfiram, SSRIs, Depakene, disulfiram, isoniazid, ketoconazole, metoprolol, probenecid, propoxyphene, propranalol, rifampin, and oral contraceptives. Potentiates digoxin and phenytoin; decreases effect of L-Dopa.

Tips: Many people should not take Centrax, including people with severe depression, lung disease, liver or kidney disease, sleep apnea, alcoholism, or psychosis. Intended for short-term use. If you smoke, take theophylline, or use antacids, Centrax may be less effective.

Cerebyx

Generic name: fosphenytoin

Use: Seizure disorders.

Action, if known: Hydantoin antispasmodic—inhibits activity in the part of the brain where local-focal [grand mal] seizures begin.

Side effects: Gum growth, confusion, twitching, depression, irritability, and many more, some of which are very serious. Due to the many interaction problems with this drug, discuss it thoroughly with your doctor and pharmacist.

Known interaction hazards: Potentiated by alcohol, aspirin, sulfa drugs, succinimide antiseizure medications, some neuroleptics and antidepressants, and many other drugs. Potentiates lithium, acetaminophen, and many other drugs. Effects are changed by use of calcium, antacids, charcoal tablets, and many prescription drugs.

Tips: Do not use if you have low blood pressure or heart trouble. Keep an eye out for skin rash or bruising, which can be serious warning signs. You may want to supplement with folic acid, which is depleted by Cerebyx. You will need to have regular blood tests while taking this drug. Take with food if stomach upset occurs—but not with high-calcium foods, such as dairy products, sesame seeds, or some nuts. Do not switch brands without telling your doctor.

Chlordiazepoxide

See Librium.

Chlorpromazine

See Thorazine.

Citalopram

See Celexa.

Clomipramine

See Anafranil.

Clonadine

Generic name: catapres

Use: High blood pressure, ADD/ADHD, tics/Tourette syndrome, extreme impulsivity, migraine, drug and alcohol withdrawal aid, ulcerative colitis, childhood growth delay.

Action, if known: Stimulates alpha-adrenergic receptors in brain to widen blood vessels, stimulates similar receptors throughout the body.

Side effects: Dry mouth, dizziness, constipation, sedation, unusually vivid or disturbing dreams, weight gain.

Known interaction hazards: Could interact with other medications for blood pressure.

Tips: Do not use if you have heart trouble, disease of the blood vessels in the brain, or chronic kidney failure. The time-release Clonadine patch is far less sedating than the pills. You can become tolerant of Clonadine, requiring a higher dose. You should have regular eye exams, as Clonadine can affect the retina.

Clonazepam

See Klonopin.

Clorazepate

See Tranxene.

Clozapine

See Clozaril.

Clozaril

Generic name: clozapine

Use: Schizophrenia.

Action, if known: Atypical neuroleptic—works against the hormone acetylcholine, other actions unknown.

Side effects: Sedation, fever (this usually passes), changes in blood pressure or heartbeat, overproduction of saliva, tremor. Major dangers include agranulocytosis (a serious blood condition), seizure, neuroleptic malignant syndrome (NMS), tardive dyskensia.

Known interaction hazards: Alcohol, CNS system depressants, drugs for high blood pressure, tricyclic antidepressants, and similar drugs should be avoided or used with caution. Danger of NMS increases when used with lithium.

Tips: Weekly blood tests are required. Some people of Ashkenazi Jewish descent, women, and people with low white blood-cell counts have a higher risk of agranulocytosis. You may want to supplement with vitamin E, which may protect against tardive dyskensia. People with heart disease, glaucoma, prostate trouble, or liver or kidney disease should be monitored carefully. Smoking cigarettes can affect how quickly your body uses Clozaril.

Compazine

Generic name: prochlorperazine

Use: Psychosis, severe nausea.

Action, if known: Phenothiazine neuroleptic—affects the hypothalamus gland in the brain, which in turn affects metabolism, body temperature, alertness, muscle tone, and hormone production.

Side effects: May suppress the gag reflex. Sedation, depression, light sensitivity, jaundice (this should pass), anemia, changes in blood pressure or heartbeat.

Known interaction hazards: Alcohol, any tranquilizer or CNS depressant (including OTC sleep aids), antacids, lithium, tricyclic antidepressants. Loses effectiveness when you eat or drink items containing caffeine.

Tips: Avoid extreme heat when taking Compazine. You may want to supplement with vitamin E, which may protect against tardive dyskensia.

Cromolyn

See Gastrocom.

Cyclert

Generic name: pemoline

Use: ADD/ADHD, narcolepsy.

Action, if known: CNS stimulant.

Side effects: Irritability, insomnia, appetite changes, depression. Lowers the seizure threshold.

Known interaction hazards: Potentiates other CNS stimulants. May increase tic severity in people with an underlying tic disorder.

Tips: You will need to have liver enzyme tests every six months—those with known liver problems may need to avoid Cyclert. Not recommended for children with psychosis. Has the longest life of the stimulants commonly used for ADHD. Vitamin C supplements, citrus juices, citric acid, more than four cans per day of soda pop, or taking this medication with food can reduce its effectiveness (you can take it with food if stomach upset occurs, but dose may need to be adjusted). Make sure you drink plenty of water, even if you're not thirsty.

Das, Dexampex, Dexedrine, Dexedrine Spansules, Dextrostat, Ferndex, Oxydess

Generic name: dextroamphetamine sulfate

Use: ADD/ADHD.

Action, if known: CNS stimulant.

Side effects: Agitation, restlessness, aggressive behavior, dizziness, insomnia, headache, tremor, dry mouth, change in appetite, weight loss. May raise blood pressure. May increase tic severity in people with an underlying tic disorder.

Known interaction hazards: Do not use with MAOIs. Interacts with tricyclic antidepressants, meperidine, norepinephrine, phenobarbital, phenytoin, propoxyphene, acetazolamide, thiazides, and some GI medications.

Tips: If you are diabetic, discuss your use of insulin and oral antidiabetes drugs with your doctor, as Das may force a change in dosage. Not recommended for children with psychosis. Vitamin C supplements, citrus juices, citric acid, more than four cans per day of soda pop, or taking this medication with food can reduce its effectiveness. Make sure you drink plenty of water, even if you're not thirsty.

Depakene

Generic name: valproic acid

Use: Seizure disorders, bipolar disorder, migraine, panic disorder, rages/aggression.

Action, if known: Antispasmodic—increases the levels of gamma-aminobutyric acid (GABA) in the brain, and increases its absorption. Also stabilizes brain membranes.

Side effects: Nausea, sedation, depression, psychosis, aggression, hyperactivity, changes in blood platelet function.

Known interaction hazards: Do not take with milk, and do not use charcoal tablets. Be careful with alcohol and with any medication that has a tranquilizing or depressant effect. Side effects may increase if you use anticoagulants, including aspirin or nonsteroidal anti-inflammatory drugs, erythromycin, chlorpromazine, cimetidine, or felbamate.

Tips: Watch out for increased bruising or bleeding, an indicator of blood platelet problems. Regular liver tests are a must. Do not crush or chew tablets.

Depakote, Depakote Sprinkles

Generic name: divalproex sodium (valproic acid plus sodium valproate)

Use: Seizure disorders, bipolar disorder, migraine, panic disorder, rages/aggression.

Action, if known: Antispasmodic—increases the levels of gamma-aminobutyric acid (GABA) in the brain, and increases its absorption. Also stabilizes brain membranes.

Side effects: Nausea, sedation, depression, psychosis, aggression, hyperactivity, changes in blood platelet function.

Known interaction hazards: Do not take with milk; do not use charcoal tablets. Be careful with alcohol and with any medication that has a tranquilizing or depressant effect. Side effects may increase if you use anticoagulants, including aspirin or non-steroidal anti-inflammatory drugs, erythromycin, chlorpromazine, cimetidine, or felbamate.

Tips: Watch out for increased bruising or bleeding, an indicator of blood platelet problems. Regular liver tests are a must. Do not crush or chew tablets.

Desipramine

See Norpramin

Desoxyn

Generic name: methamphetamine, MTH

Use: ADD/ADHD, narcolepsy.

Action, if known: CNS stimulant.

Side effects: Agitation, restlessness, aggressive behavior, dizziness, insomnia, headache, tremor. May raise blood pressure. May increase tic severity in people with an underlying tic disorder.

Known interaction hazards: Never use with MAOIs. Effect of Desoxyn may be counteracted by barbiturates, tranquilizers (including OTC sleep aids), and tricyclic antidepressants. Desoxyn may potentiate other CNS stimulants, including caffeine, OTC cold and allergy medications. Potentiated by cetazolamide and sodium bicarbonate. May interact with some GI medications.

Tips: If you are diabetic, discuss your use of insulin and oral anti-diabetes drugs with your doctor, as Desoxyn may force a change in dosage. Not recommended for children with psychosis. Vitamin C supplements, citrus juices, citric acid, more than four cans per day of soda pop, or taking this medication with food can reduce its effectiveness. Make sure you drink plenty of water, even if you're not thirsty. Well known as a drug of abuse, and therefore rarely prescribed in the US.

Dexampex, Dexedrine, Dexedrine Spansules, Dextrostat

See Das.

Dextroamphetamine/amphetamine

See Adderall.

Dextroamphetamine sulfate

See Das.

Diazepam

See Valium.

Diflucan

Generic name: fluconazole

Use: Yeast infections.

Action, if known: Antifungal—inhibits an enzyme that occurs in *Candida albicans* and other yeasts.

Side effects: Some patients report unpleasant "die-off" reactions as yeast in the GI tract are killed.

Known interaction hazards: Potentiates certain drugs for diabetes, causing low blood sugar. Potentiates cyclosporine, phenytoin, theophylline, warfarin, and zidovudine. Potentiated by hydrochlorothiazine. May cause oral contraceptives to be ineffective.

Tips: Call your doctor if you develop a rash while taking Diflucan.

Dilantin

Generic name: phenytoin

Use: Seizure disorders.

Action, if known: Hydantoin antispasmodic—inhibits activity in the part of the brain where tonic-clonic seizures begin.

Side effects: Gum growth, confusion, twitching, depression, irritability, and many more, some of which are very serious. Due to the many interaction problems with this drug, discuss it thoroughly with your doctor and pharmacist.

Known interaction hazards: Potentiated by alcohol, aspirin, sulfa drugs, succinimide antiseizure medications, some neuroleptics and antidepressants, and many other drugs. Potentiates lithium, acetaminophen, and many other drugs. Effects are changed by use of calcium, antacids, charcoal tablets, and many prescription drugs.

Tips: Do not use if you have low blood pressure or heart trouble. Keep an eye out for skin rash or bruising, which can be serious warning signs. You may want to supplement with folic acid, which is depleted by Dilantin. You will need to have regular blood tests while taking this drug. Take with food if stomach upset occurs—but not with high-calcium foods, such as dairy products, sesame seeds, or some nuts. Do not switch brands without telling your doctor.

Diphenylbutylpiperdine

See Pimozide.

Divalproex sodium

See Depakote.

Doxepin

See Sinequan.

Edronax

See Reboxetine.

Effexor, Effexor XR

Generic name: venlafaxine

Use: Depression, especially depression with anxiety.

Action, if known: Antidepressant—limits absorption of at least three neurotransmitters: serotonin, norepinephrine, and dopamine.

Side effects: Blurred vision, sedation, dry mouth, dizziness, tremor, nausea, sexual dysfunction, insomnia. Anecdotal evidence indicates it may cause moodswings in people with diagnosed or undiagnosed bipolar disorder.

Known interaction hazards: Do not take with MAOIs.

Tips: Take with food.

Elavil

Generic name: amitriptyline

Use: Depression, panic disorder, chronic pain, eating disorders, severe PMS.

Action, if known: Tricyclic antidepressant—blocks norepinephrine and serotonin use, works against the hormone acetylcholine.

Side effects: Sedation, tremor, seizures, dry mouth, light sensitivity, moodswings in people with diagnosed or undiagnosed bipolar disorder.

Known interaction hazards: Alcohol, MAOIs, blood pressure medications (including Clonadine and Tenex), thyroid medication. Potentiated by estrogen, bicarbonate of soda (as in Alka-Seltzer and other OTC remedies), acetazolamide, procainamide, and quinidine. Cimetidine, methylphenidate, Thorazine and similar drugs, oral contraceptives, nicotine (including cigarettes), charcoal tablets, and estrogen may interfere with Elavil's action in the body.

Tips: Take with food if stomach upset occurs.

Eskalith, Lithane, Lithobid, Lithonate, Lithotabs

Generic name: lithium (lithium carbonate, lithium citrate)

Use: Bipolar disorder, mood regulation, manic psychosis, PMS, eating disorders, thyroid problems, aggression.

Action, if known: Regulates circuits within the brain, possibly by having an effect on inositol monophosphatase. May also have unknown antiviral action.

Side effects: Hand tremor, excessive thirst and urination, nausea (this should pass), diarrhea, blurred vision. Any of these side effects can be signs of toxicity. Call your doctor if they persist.

Known interaction hazards: Potentiates neuroleptics, danger of encephalopathic syndrome.

Tips: Before starting lithium, have kidney function, thyroid, blood salts, and blood cell counts checked. Lithium users must have heart function, kidney function, thyroid function, and therapeutic level monitored regularly. Lithium can be toxic in doses that are not much higher than the therapeutic dose. If you are allergic to tartrazine dyes, ask your pharmacist if these are used in your lithium product. If side effects are a problem, the slow-release Lithobid version may be more tolerable. People who have diabetes or a family history of diabetes should be very careful with lithium, which may affect the pancreas.

Ethosuximide

See Zarontin.

Ethotoin

See Peganone.

Etrafon, Trilafon, Triavil

Generic name: amitriptyline/perphenazine (Trilafon includes only perphenezine)

Use: Depression, panic disorder, chronic pain, eating disorders, severe PMS.

Action, if known: Neuroleptic with qualities similar to those of a tricyclic antidepressant—blocks norepinephrine and serotonin use, works against the hormone acetylcholine.

Side effects: Sedation, tremor, seizures, dry mouth, light sensitivity, moodswings in people with diagnosed or undiagnosed bipolar disorder. Danger of tardive dyskensia, extrapyramidal side effects, neuroleptic malignant syndrome.

Known interaction hazards: Alcohol, MAOIs, blood pressure medications (including Clonadine and Tenex), thyroid medication. Potentiated by estrogen, bicarbonate of soda (as in Alka-Seltzer and other OTC remedies), acetazolamide, procainamide, and quinidine. Cimetidine, methylphenidate, Thorazine and similar drugs, oral contraceptives, nicotine (including cigarettes), charcoal tablets, and estrogen may interfere with Etrafon's action in the body.

Tips: Avoid extreme heat when taking this drug. Not recommended for use in people with severe depression, lung disease, severe asthma, liver disease. Take with food if stomach upset occurs. You may want to supplement with vitamin E, which may protect against tardive dyskensia.

Ferndex

See Das.

Fluconazole

See Diflucan.

Fluoxetine

See Prozac.

Fluphenazine

See Prolixin.

Fluvoxamine

See Luvox.

Foscavir

Generic name: foscarnet sodium, phosphonoformate trisodium

Use: Infection with human herpes viruses, cytomegalovirus, HIV/AIDS, and other viruses.

Action, if known: Immune modulator—inhibits human herpes viruses, cytomegalovirus.

Side effects: Nausea, tremor, twitchiness, anemia, electrolyte imbalance in the blood. Toxicity risk. Lowers the seizure threshold. Any intravenous procedure can have side effects ranging from mild discomfort to death.

Known interaction hazards: May interact with acyclovir, amphotericin, calcium chloride, calcium folinate, calcium gluconate, co-trimoxazole, diazepam, digoxin, diphenhydramine, dobutamine, droperidol, ganciclovir, Haldol and similar drugs, lorazepam, midazolam, pentamidine, prochlorperazine, promethazine, and vancomycin—your doctor may need to adjust your doses carefully if you take one or more of these drugs.

Tips: You will need to have regular kidney function checks while taking Foscavir. You may want to take a calcium supplement. Make sure to drink extra water. Intravenous procedures should always be done in a setting where resuscitation equipment and trained personnel are available. A topical numbing agent may decrease discomfort from needle insertion.

Fosphenytoin
See Cerebyx.

Gabapentin
See Neurontin.

Gammagard
See Venoglobulin S.

Gastrocom

Generic name: cromolyn

Use: Prevention of allergic reaction to foods.

Action, if known: Prevents mast cells from releasing antihistamines, reducing allergic reactions; may block absorption of allergens.

Side effects: Headache, diarrhea, allergy attacks.

Known interaction hazards: Do not take with food, juice, or milk.

Tips: People with heart, kidney, or liver problems should be monitored when taking Gastrocom. You can take Gastrocom with water, and you may dissolve the contents in hot water to drink it.

Guanfacine
See Tenex.

Habitrol, Nicoderm, Nicotrol, ProStep

Generic name: Nicotine

Use: Aid to stopping smoking; may be prescribed to potentiate neuroleptics or atypical neuroleptics without increasing the actual dose.

Action, if known: Affects many CNS functions, not all actions known. May reduce tics and anxiety in some people.

Side effects: Diarrhea, insomnia, nervousness. Addiction possible.

Known interaction hazards: Caffeine interferes with absorption.

Tips: People with insulin-dependent diabetes, heart problems, liver or kidney disease, high blood pressure, or pheochromocytoma should be carefully monitored when using nicotine in any form (including cigarettes).

Haldol, Haldol Decanoate

Generic name: haloperidol

Use: Psychosis, tics/Tourette syndrome, schizophrenia.

Action, if known: Butyrophenone antipsychotic—affects the hypothalamus gland in the brain, which in turn affects metabolism, body temperature, alertness, muscle tone, and hormone production.

Side effects: Lowers seizure threshold. Sedation, jaundice (this should pass), anemia, changes in blood pressure or heartbeat, dizziness.

Known interaction hazards: Avoid alcohol and other CNS depressants, narcotics, and tranquilizers (including OTC sleep aids). Potentiated by lithium, causing a greater risk of encepholopathic syndrome. Potentiates tricyclic antidepressants. Anticholinergic medications may make Haldol less effective. Risk of tardive dyskensia.

Tips: Do not take if you have low blood pressure, Parkinson's disease, or diseases of the blood, kidneys, or liver. You may want to supplement with vitamin E, which may protect against tardive dyskensia.

Haloperidol

See Haldol.

Imipramine

See Tofranil.

Inosine pranobex

See Isoprinosine.

Inversine

Generic name: mecamylamine HCI

Use: High blood pressure, rage/aggression, aid to stopping smoking.

Action, if known: This older drug, now rarely used for hypertension, blocks nicotine receptors in the brain and relaxes blood vessels.

Side effects: Dizziness, blurred vision, nausea, dry mouth, constipation.

Known interaction hazards: Interacts with sulfa drugs and antibiotics. Potentiated by antacids, bicarbonate of soda, acetazolamide, potassium or sodium citrate, citric acid. Decreases the effects of ambenonium, neostigmine, and pyridostigmine.

Tips: The use of Inversine for rage and aggression in PDDs and related disorders is still experimental, although early research looks promising. Those with bladder, kidney, prostate, or bowel problems will require regular monitoring while taking Inversine. May make glaucoma and heart problems worse.

Isoprinosine, Inosiplex

Generic name: inosine pranobex

Use: Infection with human herpes viruses and other viruses, including cytomegalovirus, Epstein-Barr, varicella, measles, HIV/AIDS, hepatitis.

Action, if known: Immune modulator—inhibits human herpes viruses and other infections by mimicking the effect of hormones produced by the thymus gland.

Side effects: Unknown, although any type of hormone or hormone analogue supplementation can be hazardous.

Known interaction hazards: Unknown

Tips: Relatively new drug in the potential PDD arsenal, effectiveness unknown. Not approved for use in the US.

Itraconazole

See Sporanox.

IVIG

See Venoglobulin S.

Ketoconazole

See Nizoral.

Klonopin

Generic name: clonazepam

Use: Seizure disorders, panic attacks, restless leg syndrome, manic psychosis, schizophrenia, chronic pain, speech problems from Parkinson's disease.

Action, if known: Benzodiazepine, depresses CNS activity.

Side effects: Drowsiness, unusual behavior, difficulty controlling muscles. Addictive, withdrawal may be difficult.

Known interaction hazards: Do not take with Depakene/Depakote. Avoid alcohol, narcotics, tranquilizers, CNS depressants, MAOIs, tricyclic antidepressants, and other antispasmodic drugs, or make sure your use of these is carefully monitored. Do not take with antacids. Potentiates digitoxin. Potentiated by cimetidine, ketoconozole, metoprolol, probenecid, propoxyphene, propranolol, rifampin. Works against the effects of L-Dopa.

Tips: You will need regular blood and liver function tests while taking Klonopin. Smoking may interfere with Klonopin's effectiveness. People tend to build up a tolerance to this drug quickly, so your dose may need to be changed frequently.

Kutapressin

Generic name: kutapressin, KU

Use: Immune modulator, treatment of human herpes viruses, including herpes zoster (shingles).

Action, if known: A porcine (pig) liver extract, kutapressin potentiates bradykinin, inhibits human herpes viruses and Epstein-Barr virus.

Side effects: None known. The fact that it is an animal extract could be problematic for some due to possible antibody crossreactivity or viruses, although there have been no reports of these problems.

Known interaction hazards: None known.

Tips: Kutapressin is administered via intramuscular (IM) injection. A topical numbing agent may decrease discomfort from needle insertion. Most doctors feel that kutapressin's effectiveness has been far outstripped by more recent antivirals.

Lamictal

Generic name: lamotrigine

Use: Seizure disorders, Lennox-Gastaut syndrome in children.

Action, if known: Binds to the hormone melanin. Stabilizes electrical currents within the brain and blocks the release of seizure-stimulating neurotransmitters.

Side effects: Headache, dizziness, nausea, general flu-like feeling, light sensitivity. If you develop a rash, call your doctor immediately as it may be a warning of a serious side effect. May make seizures worse in some people.

Known interaction hazards: Interacts with Depakote/Depakene, carbamazepine, and phenytoin—your doctor will have to monitor doses carefully. Potentiated by anti-folate drugs. Phenobarbital and primidone may lessen its effects.

Tips: Not recommended for use by children. If you have heart, kidney, or liver disease, use only under careful supervision.

Lamisil

Generic name: terbinafine hydrochloride

Use: Treatment of fungal infection of the skin or nails, including Candida.

Action, if known: Kills fungal organisms.

Side effects: Itching or irritated skin from cream; headache, diarrhea, or rash from oral Lamisil.

Known interaction hazards: Potentiated by cimetidine, terfenadine, and rifampin. May counteract cyclosporin. Potentiates the effect of caffeine.

Tips: Do not take with food. People with kidney or liver disease should be carefully monitored when taking Lamisil.

Lamotrigine

See Lamictal.

Librium

Generic name: chlordiazepoxide

Use: Anxiety, panic attacks, irritable bowel syndrome.

Action, if known: Benzodiazepine, depresses CNS activity.

Side effects: Sedation (this should pass), depression, stupor, headache, tremor, dry mouth, sexual dysfunction. Addictive, withdrawal may be difficult.

Known interaction hazards: Avoid other CNS depressants, including alcohol, narcotics, tranquilizers (including OTC sleep aids), MAOIs, antidepressants, and both prescription and OTC antihistamines. Do not take with antacids. Potentiates digoxin and phenytoin; reduces potency of L-Dopa.

Tips: Many people should not take Librium, including people with severe depression, lung disease, liver or kidney disease, sleep apnea, alcoholism, or psychosis. Intended for short-term use. Smoking may reduce the effectiveness of Librium.

Limbitrol

Generic name: amitriptyline/chlordiazepoxide

Use: Depression, panic disorder, chronic pain, eating disorders, severe PMS.

Action, if known: Tricyclic antidepressant—blocks norepinephrine and serotonin use, works against the hormone acetylcholine.

Side effects: Sedation, tremor, seizures, dry mouth, light sensitivity, moodswings in people with diagnosed or undiagnosed bipolar disorder, weight gain. Lowers the seizure threshold.

Known interaction hazards: Alcohol, MAOIs, blood pressure medications (including Clonadine and Tenex), thyroid medication. Potentiated by estrogen, bicarbonate of soda (as in Alka-Seltzer and other OTC remedies), acetazolamide, procainamide, and quinidine. Cimetidine, methylphenidate, Thorazine and similar drugs, oral contraceptives, nicotine (including cigarettes), charcoal tablets, and estrogen may interfere with Limbitrol's action in the body.

Tips: Take with food if stomach upset occurs.

Lithane, Lithobid, Lithonate, Lithotabs

See Eskalith.

Lithium, lithium carbonate, lithium citrate

See Eskalith.

Lorazepam

See Ativan.

Loxipax, loxapine, Loxitane

Generic name: loxapine

Use: Neuroleptic.

Action, if known: Blocks or changes the use of dopamine in several areas of the brain.

Side effects: May suppress the gag or cough reflex. Sedation, depression, light sensitivity, jaundice (this should pass), anemia, changes in blood pressure or heartbeat, dry mouth. Lowers the seizure threshold. Danger of tardive dyskensia.

Known interaction hazards: Alcohol, any tranquilizer or CNS depressant (including OTC sleep aids), antacids, lithium, tricyclic antidepressants.

Tips: You may want to supplement with vitamin E, which may protect against tardive dyskensia.

Luminol, Solfoton

Generic name: phenobarbital

Use: Seizure disorder, insomnia.

Action, if known: Barbiturate—blocks or slows nerve impulses in the brain. Usually used in combination with another drug to control seizures.

Side effects: Drowsiness, slow reflexes, "stoned" feeling, allergy-like symptoms, labored breathing. Call your doctor if any side effect becomes bothersome, or if you develop anemia or jaundice. Addiction risk—taper off dose carefully if stopping.

Known interaction hazards: Alcohol, MAOIs, and Depakote/Depakene all potentiate phenobarbital. Alcohol should be avoided. Neutralized by charcoal, chloramphenicol, and rifampin. Potentiates acetaminophen (Tylenol) and the anesthetic methoxyflurane. Changes the way many other drugs act in the body, including anticoagulants, beta-blockers, oral contraceptives, and corticosteroids. Be sure to go over all medicines you take with your doctor, as doses may need to be adjusted.

Tips: You may want to supplement with vitamin D when taking phenobarbital. People with liver or kidney disease should be monitored when taking this drug.

Luvox

Generic name: fluvoxamine

Use: Depression, OCD.

Action, if known: SSRI—increases the amount of active serotonin in the brain.

Side effects: Headache, insomnia, sleepiness, nervousness, nausea, dry mouth, diarrhea or constipation, sexual dysfunction. Lowers the seizure threshold. Can cause moodswings in people with diagnosed or undiagnosed bipolar disorder.

Known interaction hazards: Never take with an MAOI or soon after stopping an MAOI. Potentiated by tricyclic antidepressants, lithium. Potentiates many medications, including clozapine, diltiazem, methadone, some beta-blockers and antihistamines, Haldol and other neuroleptics.

Tips: Avoid taking this drug if you have liver disease. Cigarette smoking may make Luvox less effective. Luvox does not bind to protein in the body, unlike the other SSRIs, and may have a very different effect in some people.

Manerix

See Aurorex.

Mecamylamine HCI

See Inversine.

Mellaril

Generic name: thioridazine hydrochloride

Use: Psychosis, depression with anxiety, aggression.

Action, if known: Phenothiazine neuroleptic—affects the hypothalamus gland in the brain, which in turn affects metabolism, body temperature, alertness, muscle tone, and hormone production.

Side effects: May suppress the gag or cough reflex. Sedation, depression, light sensitivity, jaundice (this should pass), anemia, changes in blood pressure or heartbeat, dry mouth. Lowers the seizure threshold. Danger of tardive dyskensia.

Known interaction hazards: Alcohol, any tranquilizer or CNS depressant (including OTC sleep aids), antacids, lithium, tricyclic antidepressants. Loses effectiveness when you eat or drink items containing caffeine.

Tips: Avoid extreme heat when taking Mellaril. You may want to supplement with vitamin E, which may protect against tardive dyskensia. Do not take if you have blood, liver, kidney, or heart disease, low blood pressure, or Parkinson's disease. Take with food or juice if stomach upset occurs.

Mephenytoin
See Mesantoin.

Mesantoin

Generic name: mephenytoin

Use: Seizure disorders.

Action, if known: Hydantoin antispasmodic—inhibits activity in the part of the brain where local-focal [grand mal] seizures begin.

Side effects: Gum growth, confusion, twitching, depression, irritability, and many more, some of which are very serious. Due to the many interaction problems with this drug, discuss it thoroughly with your doctor and pharmacist.

Known interaction hazards: Potentiated by alcohol, aspirin, sulfa drugs, succinimide antiseizure medications, some neuroleptics and antidepressants, and many other drugs. Potentiates lithium, acetaminophen, and many other drugs. Effects are changed by use of calcium, antacids, charcoal tablets, and many prescription drugs.

Tips: Do not use if you have low blood pressure or heart trouble. Keep an eye out for skin rash or bruising, which can be serious warning signs. You may want to supplement with folic acid, which is depleted by Mesantoin. You will need to have regular blood tests while taking this drug. Take with food if stomach upset occurs—but not with high-calcium foods, such as dairy products, sesame seeds, or some nuts. Do not switch brands without telling your doctor.

Mesoridazine

See Serentil.

Methamphetamine

See Desoxyn.

Methylphenidate hydrochloride

See Ritalin.

Miconazole

See Monistat.

Mirtazapine

See Remeron.

Moban

Generic name: molindone

Use: Psychosis.

Action, if known: Neuroleptic.

Side effects: Drowsiness, sedation, depression, nausea, dry mouth. Risk of tardive dyskensia.

Known interaction hazards: Alcohol and all other CNS depressants, tranquilizers (including OTC sleep aids), barbiturates, anesthetics, tricyclic antidepressants, lithium. Moban may have negative interactions with many other medications, including other antipsychotics, Asendin, and Cyclert.

Tips: People with liver disease or Parkinson's disease should not take Moban. You may want to supplement with vitamin E, which may protect against tardive dyskensia.

Moclobemide

See Aurorex.

Molindone

See Moban.

Monistat

Generic name: miconazole

Use: Fungal or yeast infections.

Action, if known: Antifungal.

Side effects: Nausea, diarrhea. Some people note uncomfortable "die-off" reactions during the treatment as yeast in the GI tract is killed.

Known interaction hazards: None.

Tips: None.

MTH

See Desoxyn

Mycostatin, Mykinac, Nilstat, Nystex

Generic name: nystatin

Use: Fungal and yeast infections.

Action, if known: Antifungal—chemically binds to the cell membranes of fungi, causing cell contents to leak out. This kills the fungi.

Side effects: Nausea, diarrhea. Some people note uncomfortable "die-off" reactions during the treatment as yeast in the GI tract is killed.

Known interaction hazards: None known

Tips: None

Mykinac

See Mycostatin.

Mysoline

Generic name: primidone

Use: Seizure disorders.

Action, if known: Antispasmodic—controls nerve impulses in the brain.

Side effects: Restlessness, especially in children. Dizziness, drowsiness, rash.

Known interaction hazards: Alcohol and all other CNS depressants, including tranquilizers, narcotics, and OTC sleep aids, allergy drugs, and cold medications. May decrease the effects of corticosteroids, oral contraceptives, and blood-thinning medications. May interact with other antispasmodics, such as Depakote/Depakene. Do not take with MAOIs.

Tips: People with porphyria should not take Mysoline. If you have lung disease (including asthma), kidney disease, or liver disease, you will need to be carefully monitored while taking Mysoline.

Naltrexone

See ReVia.

Nardil

Generic name: phenelzine

Use: Depression that does not respond to SSRIs or tricyclic antidepressants, eating disorders, migraine.

Action, if known: MAO inhibitor—interferes with the action of the enzyme monoamine oxidase (MAO), which normally breaks down neurotransmitters. This increases the amount of norepinephrine and other neurotransmitters stored throughout the CNS.

Side effects: Drowsiness, blurred vision, dizziness, tremor, agitation, uncontrolled muscle movements, loss of appetite, sexual dysfunction, insomnia. Can cause very high blood pressure in some. May aggravate stereotypic movements, palilalia, echolalia, tics.

Known interaction hazards: Never take with an SSRI, guanethidine, dextromethorphan (found in many OTC drugs), another MAOI, or trancypromine sulfate. MAOIs change the affects of many other medications in potentially dangerous ways. Go over all drugs you take carefully with your doctor, including OTC remedies. You will also need to strictly follow a special diet while taking Nardil, which you should discuss thoroughly with your doctor before starting this medication.

Tips: Do not take Nardil if you have high blood pressure; heart, liver, or kidney problems; headaches; or a history of minor or major strokes. Make sure you have exhausted your other antidepressant possibilities before taking an MAOI. Interactions between this drug, other medications, and even foods can be life-threatening. You must still avoid forbidden foods and medicines for two to four weeks after you stop taking Nardil.

Navane

Generic name: thiothixene

Use: Psychosis.

Action, if known: Thiothixene neuroleptic—affects the hypothalamus gland in the brain, which in turn affects metabolism, body temperature, alertness, muscle tone, and hormone production.

Side effects: Sedation, depression, light sensitivity, jaundice (this should pass), anemia, changes in blood pressure or heartbeat. Danger of tardive dyskensia.

Known interaction hazards: Alcohol, any tranquilizer or CNS depressant (including OTC sleep aids), antacids, lithium, tricyclic antidepressants. Do not combine with propranolol. Effect may be reduced by use of anticholinergic medications.

Tips: Avoid extreme heat when taking Navane. You may want to supplement with vitamin E, which may protect against tardive dyskensia. Do not take if you have blood, liver, kidney, or heart disease, low blood pressure, or Parkinson's disease. Take with food or juice if stomach upset occurs.

Nefazodone

See Serzone.

Neurontin

Generic name: gabapentin

Use: Seizure disorders, especially those that do not respond to other drugs; bipolar disorder, rage/aggression.

Action, if known: Antispasmodic—appears to act by binding a specific protein found only on neurons in the CNS. May increase the GABA content of some brain regions.

Side effects: Blurred vision, dizziness, clumsiness, drowsiness, swaying, eye-rolling.

Known interaction hazards: Alcohol and all other CNS depressants, including tranquilizers, OTC medications for colds and allergies, OTC sleep aids, anesthetics, and narcotics. Antacids may counteract the effects of Neurontin.

Tips: People with kidney disease should be carefully monitored while taking Neurontin. Corn is used as a filler in the usual formulation of this drug, causing allergic reactions in some. A new drug under development called Pregabolin is based on Neurontin, but with fewer side effects.

Nicoderm, Nicotrol

See Habitrol.

Nicotine

See Habitrol.

Nilstat

See Mycostatin.

Nitoman, Regulin

Generic name: Tetrabenazine, TDZ

Use: Tardive dyskensia, dystonia, Huntington's Chorea, Tourette syndrome.

Action, if known: Depletes dopamine in nerve endings in the brain.

Side effects: Depression.

Known interaction hazards: May interact with other drugs that affect dopamine production or use.

Tips: Available in Canada, Norway, Sweden, the UK, and Japan, tetrabenazine can be obtained only through compassionate use programs in the US. This is the only drug currently known to help with tardive dyskensia.

Nizoral

Generic name: ketoconazole

Use: Fungal infections (not very effective if the infection is in the nervous system, however).

Action, if known: Invades the outer membrane of fungal cells, destroying them.

Side effects: Headaches, dizziness, drowsiness, nausea, itching. Decreases the level of the hormone testosterone, so men may experience swollen breasts. Also reduces the level of natural steroids in the body, which may depress the immune system. Can cause liver inflammation—call your doctor immediately if you see signs of jaundice or have abdominal pain.

Known interaction hazards: Do not take with antacids or histamine H2 antagonists. Interacts with corticosteroid drugs, cyclosporine, cisapride, some antihistamines, phenytoin, and theophylline.

Tips: Take with food.

Norpramin

Generic name: desipramine

Use: Depression, panic disorder, chronic pain, eating disorders, severe PMS.

Action, if known: Tricyclic antidepressant—blocks norepinephrine and serotonin use, works against the hormone acetylcholine.

Side effects: Sedation, tremor, seizures, dry mouth, light sensitivity, moodswings in people with diagnosed or undiagnosed bipolar disorder, weight gain. Lowers the seizure threshold.

Known interaction hazards: Alcohol, MAOIs, blood pressure medications (including Clonadine and Tenex), thyroid medication. Potentiated by estrogen, bicarbonate of soda (as in Alka-Seltzer and other OTC remedies), acetazolamide, procainamide, and quinidine. Cimetidine, methylphenidate, Thorazine and similar drugs, oral contraceptives, nicotine (including cigarettes), charcoal tablets, and estrogen may interfere with Norpramin's action in the body.

Tips: Take with food if stomach upset occurs.

Nortriptyline

See Aventyl.

Nystatin

See Mycostatin.

Nystex

See Mycostatin.

Olanzapine

See Zyprexa.

Orap, Pimozide

Generic name: diphenylbutylpiperdine

Use: Psychosis, severe tics/Tourette syndrome, schizophrenia.

Action, if known: Neuroleptic—affects the amount and action of dopamine in the brain.

Side effects: Extrapyramidal side effects, such as restlessness and unusual movements. Risk of tardive dyskinesia, neuroleptic malignant syndrome (NMS).

Known interaction hazards: Do not take antihistamines (including OTC cold and allergy remedies) or anticholinergic drugs. Alcohol, other CNS depressants, tranquilizers (including OTC sleep aids). Taking other neuroleptics increases your risk for tardive dyskensia, NMS, extrapyramidal side effects. Taking tricyclic antidepressants and many other medications with heart effects can increase your risk for heart problems with Orap. Your doctor may need to adjust dosages of other medications you take, especially antiseizure drugs.

Tips: You should have an EKG before starting Orap, and regular heart monitoring while taking it. You may want to supplement with vitamin E, which may protect against tardive dyskensia. Orap is considered more risky than some other old-line neuroleptics, not to mention the atypical neuroleptics. Make sure you have exhausted your other options first.

Oxazepam

See Serax.

Oxydess

See Das.

Pamelor

See Aventyl.

Parnate

Generic name: tranylcypromine sulfate

Use: Depression that does not respond to SSRIs or tricyclic antidepressants, eating disorders, migraine.

Action, if known: MAO inhibitor—interferes with the action of the enzyme monoamine oxidase (MAO), which normally breaks down neurotransmitters. This increases the amount of norepinephrine and other neurotransmitters stored throughout the CNS.

Side effects: Drowsiness, blurred vision, dizziness, tremor, agitation, uncontrolled muscle movements, loss of appetite, sexual dysfunction, insomnia. Can cause moodswings in people with diagnosed or undiagnosed bipolar disorder. Can cause very high blood pressure in some. May aggravate stereotypic movements, palilalia, echolalia, tics.

Known interaction hazards: Never take with an SSRI, guanethidine, dextromethorphan (found in many OTC drugs), another MAOI, or trancypromine sulfate. MAOIs change the effects of many other medications in potentially dangerous ways. Go over all drugs you take carefully with your doctor, including OTC remedies. You will also need to strictly follow a special diet while taking Parnate, which you should discuss thoroughly with your doctor before starting this medication.

Tips: Do not take Parnate if you have high blood pressure; heart, liver, or kidney problems; headaches; or a history of minor or major strokes. Make sure you have exhausted your other antidepressant possibilities before taking an MAOI. Interactions between this drug, other medications, and even foods can be life-threatening. You must still avoid forbidden foods and medicines for two to four weeks after you stop taking Parnate.

Paroxetine

See Paxil.

Paxil, Seroxat

Generic name: paroxetine

Use: Depression.

Action, if known: SSRI—increases the amount of active serotonin in the brain. Has a calming effect.

Side effects: Headache, insomnia or restless sleep, dizziness, tremor, nausea, weakness, dizziness, sexual dysfunction, dry mouth. Lowers the seizure threshold. Can cause moodswings in people with diagnosed or undiagnosed bipolar disorder.

Known interaction hazards: Alcohol. Never take with an MAOI or soon after stopping an MAOI. Potentiates warfarin, theophylline, paroxetine, procyclidine. Changes how digoxin and phenytoin act in the body.

Tips: People with liver or kidney disease should be monitored regularly while taking Paxil.

Peganone

Generic name: ethotoin

Use: Seizure disorders.

Action, if known: Hydantoin antispasmodic—inhibits activity in the part of the brain where local-focal [grand mal] seizures begin.

Side effects: Gum growth, confusion, twitching, depression, irritability, and many more, some of which are very serious. Due to the many interaction problems with this drug, discuss it thoroughly with your doctor and pharmacist.

Known interaction hazards: Potentiated by alcohol, aspirin, sulfa drugs, succinimide antiseizure medications, some neuroleptics and antidepressants, and many other drugs. Potentiates lithium, acetaminophen, and many other drugs. Effects are changed by use of calcium, antacids, charcoal tablets, and many prescription drugs.

Tips: Do not use if you have low blood pressure or heart trouble. Keep an eye out for skin rash or bruising, which can be serious warning signs. You may want to supplement with folic acid, which is depleted by Peganone. You will need to have regular blood tests while taking this drug. Take with food if stomach upset occurs—but not with high-calcium foods, such as dairy products, sesame seeds, or some nuts. Do not switch brands without telling your doctor.

Pemoline

See Cyclert.

Pentoxifylline

See Trental.

Perphenazine

See Trilafon.

Phenelzine

See Nardil.

Phenobarbital

See Luminol.

Phenytoin

See Dilantin.

Pimozide

See Orap.

Polygam

See Venoglobulin S.

Prazepam

See Centrax.

Pregabolin

See Neurontin.

Primidone

See Mysoline.

Prochlorperazine

See Compazine.

Prolixin, Prolixin Decanoate

Generic name: fluphenazine

Action, if known: Phenothiazine neuroleptic—affects the hypothalamus gland in the brain, which in turn affects metabolism, body temperature, alertness, muscle tone, and hormone production.

Side effects: May suppress the gag or cough reflex. Sedation, depression, light sensitivity, jaundice (this should pass), anemia, changes in blood pressure or heartbeat. Danger of tardive dyskensia.

Known interaction hazards: Alcohol, any tranquilizer or CNS depressant (including OTC sleep aids), antacids, lithium, tricyclic antidepressants. Loses effectiveness when you eat or drink items containing caffeine.

Tips: Avoid extreme heat when taking Prolixin. You may want to supplement with vitamin E, which may protect against tardive dyskensia. Do not take if you have blood, liver, kidney, or heart disease, low blood pressure, or Parkinson's disease. Take with food or juice if stomach upset occurs

ProStep

See Habitrol.

Protriptyline

See Vivactil.

Prozac

Generic name: fluoxetine

Use: Depression, OCD, eating disorders, ADHD, narcolepsy, migraine/chronic headache, Tourette syndrome, social phobia.

Action, if known: SSRI—increases the amount of active serotonin in the brain. Usually has an energizing effect.

Side effects: Headache, insomnia or restless sleep, dizziness, tremor, nausea, weakness, dizziness, sexual dysfunction, dry mouth, itchy skin and/or rash. May cause change in appetite and weight. Lowers the seizure threshold. Can cause moodswings in people with diagnosed or undiagnosed bipolar disorder.

Known interaction hazards: Alcohol. Never take with an MAOI or soon after stopping an MAOI. Do not take OTC or prescription cold or allergy remedies containing cyproheptadine or dextromethorphan. Potentiated by tricyclic antidepressants. Potentiates lithium, phenytoin, neuroleptic drugs, carbamazepine, and cyclosporine. Reduces effectiveness of BuSpar.

Tips: Prozac has a long life in your body. People with liver or kidney disease should be monitored while taking Prozac.

Quetiapine

See Seroquel.

Reboxetine

Generic name: edronax

Use: Depression—has an energizing effect.

Action, if known: A nontricyclic selective noradrenaline reuptake inhibitor (selective NRI), Reboxetine inhibits the reuptake of norepinephrine by cells, increasing noradrenaline availability in the synaptic cleft.

Side effects: Dry mouth, constipation, insomnia, sweating, heart irregularities, dizziness, urine retention, sexual dysfunction.

Known interaction hazards: Alcohol and other CNS depressants. May interact with SSRIs, tricyclic antidepressants, and MAOIs. May change the way some antispasmodics work. If you take other medications, your doctor may need to adjust doses.

Tips: Reboxetine may counteract some of the interactions associated with MAOIs, and so it may be prescribed in concert with these. This combination should be monitored closely, of course. Not currently available in the US.

Regulin

See Nitomin.

Remeron

Generic name: mirtazapine

Use: Depression, anxiety.

Action, if known: Noradrenergic and specific serotonergic antidepressant (NaSSA)—affects the neurotransmitter noradrenaline as well as some serotonin receptors. Has an energizing effect.

Side effects: Sleepiness, dry mouth, dizziness, weight gain, constipation. Lowers the seizure threshold. Can cause moodswings in people with diagnosed or undiagnosed bipolar disorder. Can depress the immune system, causing a lower white blood cell count.

Known interaction hazards: Never take with an MAOI or soon after stopping an MAOI. Potentiates alcohol, tranquilizers (including OTC sleep aids), and other CNS depressants.

Tips: If you experience fever, aches, sore throat, or infections, call your doctor. Take with food if stomach upset occurs. People with heart, liver, or kidney disease or hypothyroidism should be monitored while taking Remeron.

ReVia

Generic name: naltrexone hydrochloride

Use: Heroin/opioid and alcohol addiction withdrawal aid.

Action, if known: Opioid antagonist—blocks opioid chemicals.

Side effects: Anxiety, nervousness, insomnia, abdominal discomfort, nausea, headache, muscle or joint pain.

Known interaction hazards: Alcohol and all CNS depressants, including anesthetics, narcotics, and sedatives. ReVia may block the effects of these substances until they reach a critical, even deadly, level.

Tips: People with liver problems must be closely monitored while taking ReVia. This drug has been tested for use in autism with mixed results.

Risperdal

Generic name: risperidone

Use: Psychosis, schizophrenia, rage/aggression.

Action, if known: Atypical neuroleptic—affects serotonin and dopamine, raises level of the hormone prolactin.

Side effects: Sedation, headache, runny nose, anxiety, insomnia. Weight gain, especially in children. Danger of neuroleptic malignant syndrome (NMS), tardive dyskensia.

Known interaction hazards: Decreases action of L-Dopa. Interacts with carbamazepine and clozapine. May potentiate or be potentiated by SSRIs.

Tips: You should have an EKG before starting Risperdal and regular heart monitoring while taking it. You may want to supplement with vitamin E, which may protect against tardive dyskensia.

Risperidone

See Risperdal.

Ritalin

Generic name: methylphenidate hydrochloride

Use: ADD/ADHD, narcolepsy, social phobia.

Action, if known: CNS stimulant.

Side effects: Agitation, restlessness, aggressive behavior, dizziness, insomnia, headache, tremor. May raise blood pressure. May increase tic severity in people with an underlying tic disorder.

Known interaction hazards: Alcohol. Potentiated by MAOIs to a high degree. Potentiates tricyclic antidepressants. Reduces action of guanethidine.

Tips: The rebound effect can be bad with Ritalin, which has the shortest life of the stimulants commonly used for ADHD. Some doctors combine Ritalin SR with regular Ritalin for the smoothest effect (SR's action is said to be erratic). Vitamin C supplements, citrus juices, citric acid, more than four cans per day of soda pop, or taking this medication with food can reduce its effectiveness. Make sure you drink plenty of water, even if you're not thirsty. Some patients report different results from generic methylphenidate hydrochloride and brand-name Ritalin.

Secretin

Generic name: secretin

Use: Testing GI tract function, experimental therapy for autism/PDDs.

Action, if known: Secretin is a polypeptide hormone produced in the small intestine to stimulate pancreatic fluid secretion and biliary epithelial excretion, including immunoglobulins. It is known to target receptors in the GI tract and brain, and to affect intracellular cAMP and neurotransmitter production, probably including serotonin. It may break down potentially aggravating peptides, such as those produced in response to gluten and casein.

Side effects: None known from one-time use, but this medication has not been thoroughly tested for repeated use. Some children who have received infusions of secretin have not responded; a few have developed new and difficult symptoms. Parents have reported fever, runny noses, and coughing during the week following infusion. There may be as yet unknown side effects. Some doctors have expressed concern that antibodies in porcine (pig) secretin could cross-react with human secretin, perhaps causing the body to stop producing any of its own secretin, or causing other health problems. Synthetic human secretin might be safer, but has not yet been widely used.

Known interaction hazards: None yet known, although some doctors have advised that supplements, megavitamin therapy, antifungals, antibiotics, and some medications may interfere with the action of secretin.

Tips: Intravenous procedures should always be done in a setting where resuscitation equipment and trained personnel are available. A topical numbing agent may decrease discomfort from needle insertion. Some doctors administering secretin recommend testing for certain antibodies or health conditions before and after infusion. Some also recommend dietary changes and courses of certain medication for several months in advance of trying secretin. This is a very new therapy for autistic-spectrum disorders, so you will want to work closely with your physician.

Special note: It may be possible to increase the body's own production of secretin rather than administering it directly. Substances that may have this effect include phenylpentol, methanol extract of licorice root, plaunotol, and teprenon.

Serax

Generic name: oxazepam

Use: Anxiety, muscle spasm, seizures, panic disorder, irritable bowel syndrome.

Action, if known: Benzodiazepine, slows CNS activity.

Side effects: Sleepiness (this usually passes after a week), lethargy, confusion, headache, slurred speech, tremor. Addictive, withdrawal may be difficult.

Known interaction hazards: Alcohol, all tranquilizers (including OTC sleep aids), narcotics, MAOIs, antihistamines (including OTC allergy and cold remedies), antidepressants. Potentiated by cimetidine, SSRIs, Depakene, disulfiram, isoniazid, ketoconazole, metoprolol, probenecid, propoxyphene, propranalol, rifampin, and oral contraceptives. Potentiates digoxin and phenytoin; decreases effect of L-Dopa.

Tips: Many people should not take Serax, including people with severe depression, lung disease, liver or kidney disease, sleep apnea, alcoholism, or psychosis. Intended for short-term use. If you smoke, take theophylline, or use antacids, Serax may be less effective.

Serentil

Generic name: mesoridazine

Use: Psychosis.

Action, if known: Neuroleptic.

Side effects: Drowsiness, dizziness, sedation, agitation, nausea, changes in appetite, weight gain or loss, sexual dysfunction. Lowers seizure threshold. Risk of tardive dyskensia and extrapyramidal side effects.

Known interaction hazards: Avoid alcohol and all CNS depressants, including tranquilizers, sedatives, OTC sleep aids, narcotics. Potentiates atropine, phosphorus insecticides, quinidine.

Tips: Avoid extreme heat while taking this drug. You will need regular blood tests and eye exams while taking Serentil. Not recommended for people with severe depression, bone marrow depression, liver or heart disease. Those with high blood pressure should be carefully monitored while taking Serentil. You may want to supplement with vitamin E, which may protect against tardive dyskensia.

Seroquel

Generic name: quetiapine

Use: Psychosis, rage/aggression.

Action, if known: Atypical neuroleptic—believed to increase availability of serotonin and dopamine at specific receptors in the brain.

Side effects: Drowsiness, dizziness, sedation, agitation, nausea, changes in appetite, weight gain or loss, sexual dysfunction. Lowers seizure threshold. Danger of neuroleptic malignant syndrome (NMS), extrapyramidal side effects, and tardive dyskensia.

Known interaction hazards: Avoid alcohol and all CNS depressants, including tranquilizers, sedatives, OTC sleep aids, narcotics. Potentiated to a high degree by phenytoin. May interfere with the effects of drugs for high blood pressure. May be potentiated by other drugs, including ketoconazole, erythromycin, clarithromycin, diltiazam, verapamil, and nefazodone.

Tips: Avoid extreme heat while taking this drug. People with liver or kidney problems, heart disease, thyroid problems, or low blood pressure should be monitored while taking Seroquel. You may want to supplement with vitamin E, which may protect against tardive dyskensia.

Seroxat

See Paxil.

Sertraline

See Zoloft.

Serzone

Generic name: nefazodone.

Use: Depression, especially if it occurs with agitation.

Action, if known: Blocks the uptake of serotonin and norepinephrine in the brain, antagonizes some serotonin and noradrenaline receptors, increases the levels of two natural antihistamines in the bloodstream.

Side effects: Sleepiness, dizziness, confusion, dry mouth, nausea, visual disturbances, rash. Lowers the seizure threshold.

Known interaction hazards: Never take with an MAOI, astemizole, propranalol, terfenadine, alprazolam, or triazolam. Potentiates digoxin.

Tips: People with heart or liver trouble should be monitored while taking Serzone.

Sinequan

Generic name: doxepin

Use: Depression, panic disorder, chronic pain, eating disorders, severe PMS.

Action, if known: Tricyclic antidepressant—blocks norepinephrine and serotonin use, works against the hormone acetylcholine.

Side effects: Sedation, tremor, seizures, dry mouth, light sensitivity, moodswings in people with diagnosed or undiagnosed bipolar disorder, weight gain. Lowers the seizure threshold.

Known interaction hazards: Alcohol, MAOIs, blood pressure medications (including Clonadine and Tenex), thyroid medication. Potentiated by estrogen, bicarbonate of soda (as in Alka-Seltzer and other OTC remedies), acetazolamide, procainamide, and quinidine. Cimetidine, methylphenidate, Thorazine and similar drugs, oral contraceptives, nicotine (including cigarettes), charcoal tablets, and estrogen may interfere with Sinequan's action in the body.

Tips: Take with food if stomach upset occurs.

Solfoton

See Luminol.

Sporanox

Generic name: itraconazole

Use: Fungal infections.

Action, if known: Antifungal—inhibits enzymes within fungi living in the body, eventually killing them.

Side effects: Nausea, rash, water retention, sexual dysfunction.

Known interaction hazards: Never take with astemizole or terfenadine. Avoid taking with amlodipine or nefedipine. Potentiates cisapride, digoxin, some medications for diabetes, phenytoin, quinidine, tacrolimus, and warfarin. May be counteracted by cimetidine, ranitidine, famotidine, nazatidine, isoniazid, phenytoin, and rifampin.

Tips: People with liver disease should be monitored while taking Sporanox.

Stelazine, Vesprin

Generic name: trifluoperazine

Action, if known: Phenothiazine neuroleptic—affects the hypothalamus gland in the brain, which in turn affects metabolism, body temperature, alertness, muscle tone, and hormone production. Blocks dopamine receptors in the mesolimbic system, increasing turnover of dopamine.

Side effects: May suppress the gag or cough reflex. Sedation, depression, light sensitivity, jaundice (this should pass), anemia, changes in blood pressure or heartbeat. Danger of tardive dyskensia.

Known interaction hazards: Alcohol, any tranquilizer or CNS depressant (including OTC sleep aids), antacids, lithium, tricyclic antidepressants. Loses effectiveness when you eat or drink items containing caffeine.

Tips: Avoid extreme heat when taking Stelazine. You may want to supplement with vitamin E, which may protect against tardive dyskensia. Do not take if you have blood, liver, kidney, or heart disease, low blood pressure, or Parkinson's disease. If you have thyroid problems, use extreme caution. Take with food or juice if stomach upset occurs.

Surmontil

Generic name: trimipramine

Use: Depression, panic disorder, chronic pain, eating disorders, severe PMS.

Action, if known: Tricyclic antidepressant—blocks norepinephrine and serotonin use, works against the hormone acetylcholine.

Side effects: Sedation, tremor, seizures, dry mouth, light sensitivity, moodswings in people with diagnosed or undiagnosed bipolar disorder, weight gain. Lowers the seizure threshold.

Known interaction hazards: Alcohol, MAOIs, blood pressure medications (including Clonadine and Tenex), thyroid medication. Potentiated by estrogen, bicarbonate of soda (as in Alka-Seltzer and other OTC remedies), acetazolamide, procainamide, and quinidine. Cimetidine, methylphenidate, Thorazine and similar drugs, oral contraceptives, nicotine (including cigarettes), charcoal tablets, and estrogen may interfere with Surmontil's action in the body.

Tips: Take with food if stomach upset occurs.

Tegretol

Generic name: carmazepine

Use: Seizure disorders, nerve pain, bipolar disorder, rage/aggression, aid to drug withdrawal, restless leg syndrome, Sydenham's chorea and similar disorders in children.

Action, if known: Antispasmodic—appears to work by reducing polysynaptic responses, and has other as yet unknown effects.

Side effects: Sleepiness, dizziness, nausea, unusual moods or behavior, headache, retention of water. May cause low white blood cell count. Call your doctor right away if you have flu-like symptoms or other unusual reactions while taking this drug.

Known interaction hazards: Never take with an MAOI. Tegretol is often used in combination with other antispasmodics or lithium, but the dose of Tegretol and drugs used with it must be very carefully adjusted. Tegretol is potentiated by numerous prescription and OTC medications, including many antibiotics, antidepressants, and cimetadine. It also counteracts or changes the effect of many drugs, including Haldol, theophyllin, and acetaminophen. Because these interactions can be very serious, discuss all medications you take—including all OTC remedies—with your doctor before beginning to use Tegretol.

Tips: You should have a white blood cell count done before taking Tegretol and be monitored thereafter. Do not take if you have a history of bone marrow depression. Tegretol can be fatal at fairly low doses, so all patients taking this drug should be carefully monitored, particularly since it interacts with so many other medications.

Tenex

Generic name: guanfacine

Use: High blood pressure, migraines, extreme nausea, heroin withdrawal aid, ADHD/ADD, tic disorders/Tourette syndrome.

Action, if known: Stimulates CNS to widen blood vessels and has other as yet unknown effects.

Side effects: Sleepiness, changes in blood pressure or heart rate, nausea.

Known interaction hazards: Alcohol and other CNS depressants. May be counteracted by stimulants such as Ritalin and many OTC drugs; by estrogen and oral contraceptives; and by indomethacin, ibuprofen, and non-steroidal anti-inflammatory drugs.

Tips: If you take another medication that lowers blood pressure, your doctor will need to adjust your Tenex dose accordingly to prevent problems. Most people take Tenex at bedtime due to its sedating effect.

Terbinafine hydrochloride

See Lamisil.

Tetrabenazine, TDZ

See Nitoman.

Thioridazine

See Mellaril.

Thiothixene

See Navane.

Thorazine

Generic name: chlorpromazine

Use: Psychosis, schizophrenia.

Action, if known: Phenothiazine neuroleptic—affects the hypothalamus gland in the brain, which in turn affects metabolism, body temperature, alertness, muscle tone, and hormone production. Interferes with the action of dopamine in the basal ganglia, mesolimbic area, and medulla. Anticholinergic.

Side effects: May suppress the gag or cough reflex. Sedation, depression, light sensitivity, jaundice (this should pass), anemia, changes in blood pressure or heartbeat, dry mouth. Lowers the seizure threshold. Danger of tardive dyskensia.

Known interaction hazards: Alcohol, any tranquilizer or CNS depressant (including OTC sleep aids), antacids, lithium, tricyclic antidepressants. Loses effectiveness when you eat or drink items containing caffeine.

Tips: Avoid extreme heat when taking Thorazine. You may want to supplement with vitamin E, which may protect against tardive dyskensia. Do not take if you have blood, liver, kidney, or heart disease; low blood pressure; Reye's disease; or Parkinson's disease. Take with food or juice if stomach upset occurs.

Tofranil, Janimine

Generic name: imipramine

Use: Depression, panic disorder, chronic pain, eating disorders, severe PMS.

Action, if known: Tricyclic antidepressant—blocks norepinephrine and serotonin use, works against the hormone acetylcholine.

Side effects: Sedation, tremor, seizures, dry mouth, light sensitivity, moodswings in people with diagnosed or undiagnosed bipolar disorder, weight gain. Lowers the seizure threshold.

Known interaction hazards: Alcohol, MAOIs, blood pressure medications (including Clonadine and Tenex), thyroid medication. Potentiated by estrogen, bicarbonate of soda (as in Alka-Seltzer and other OTC remedies), acetazolamide, procainamide, and quinidine. Cimetidine, methylphenidate, Thorazine and similar drugs, oral contraceptives, nicotine (including cigarettes), charcoal tablets, and estrogen may interfere with Tofranil's action in the body.

Tips: Take with food if stomach upset occurs.

Topamax

Generic name: topiramate

Use: Seizure disorders.

Action, if known: Antispasmodic, mode of action unknown.

Side effects: Slowed speech, thought, and action; sleepiness; tingling in the extremities; nausea; tremor; depression; visual disturbances.

Known interaction hazards: Alcohol and other CNS depressants. Interacts with other antispasmodics, so your doctor may need to adjust dosages. Reduces effectiveness of digoxin and oral contraceptives.

Tips: People with kidney or liver problems should be monitored while taking Topamax.

Topiramate

See Topamax.

Tranxene

Generic name: clorazepate

Use: Anxiety, panic disorder, irritable bowel syndrome.

Action, if known: Benzodiazepine—slows CNS activity.

Side effects: Drowsiness (this should pass), confusion, tremor, dizziness, depression. Addiction danger, withdrawal may be uncomfortable.

Known interaction hazards: Do not take with antacids. Alcohol and other CNS depressants, tranquilizers (including OTC sleep aids), narcotics, barbiturates, MAOIs, antihistamines (including cold and allergy medications), and antidepressants all interact negatively with Tranxene. This drug potentiates digoxin and phenytoin. Potentiated by cometidine, disulfiram, fluoxetine, isoniazid, ketoconazole, metoprolol, probenecid, propoxyphene, propranolol, rifamin, and Depakote/Depakene.

Tips: You should not take Tranxene if you have lung, liver, or kidney disease, psychosis, or depression. Intended for short-term use. Smoking may interfere with the action of Tranxene.

Tranylcypromine sulfate

See Parnate.

Trental

Generic name: pentoxifylline

Use: Reduction of blood viscosity to improve blood flow.

Action, if known: Thins the blood, increasing blood flow to the brain and circulation system.

Side effects: Nausea, dizziness, headache.

Known interaction hazards: Potentiates drugs that lower blood pressure, such as Clonadine. May potentiate warfarin.

Tips: Do not take Trental if you are sensitive to caffeine, or to theophylline and theobromine (the active ingredients in tea). People with kidney disease need to be carefully monitored when taking Trental. Take with food if nausea occurs.

Triavil

See Etrafon.

Trifluoperazine

See Stelazine.

Trilafon

See Etrafon.

Trimipramine

See Surmontil.

Valacyclovir

See Valtrex.

Valium

Generic name: diazepam

Use: Anxiety, muscle spasm, seizures, panic disorder, irritable bowel syndrome.

Action, if known: Benzodiazepine, slows CNS activity.

Side effects: Sleepiness (this usually passes after a week), lethargy, confusion, headache, slurred speech, tremor. Addictive, withdrawal may be difficult.

Known interaction hazards: Alcohol, all tranquilizers (including OTC sleep aids), narcotics, MAOIs, antihistamines (including OTC allergy and cold remedies), antidepressants. Potentiated by cimetidine, SSRIs, Depakote/Depakene, disulfiram, isoniazid, ketoconazole, metoprolol, probenecid, propoxyphene, propranalol, rifampin, and oral contraceptives. Potentiates digoxin and phenytoin; decreases effect of L-Dopa.

Tips: Many people should not take Valium, including people with severe depression, lung disease, liver or kidney disease, sleep apnea, alcoholism, or psychosis. Intended for short-term use. If you smoke, take theophylline, or use antacids, Valium may be less effective.

Valproic acid

See Depakene.

Valtrex

Generic name: valacyclovir hydrochloride

Use: Antiviral, works against herpes zoster and other herpatoform viruses.

Action, if known: Valtrex is converted into the antiviral acyclovir in the liver and intestine. Acyclovir battles the herpes viruses by inhibiting an enzyme they need to reproduce.

Side effects: Headache, bowel complaints, dizziness, nausea, loss of appetite.

Known interaction hazards: Can cause loss of energy and sedation when combined with zidovudine to create AZT. Potentiated by cimetidine and probenecid.

Tips: Valtrex should not be taken by people with serious immune-system suppression, including AIDS.

Venlafaxine

See Effexor.

Venoglobulin S, Polygam, Gammagard

Generic name: intravenous immunoglobulin (IVIG)

Use: Infection with bacteria or viruses that does not respond to other therapies, Kawasaki disease, idiopathic thrombocytopenic purpura, autoimmune disorders, recurrent miscarriage due to autoimmune activity.

Action, if known: Gamma globulin is the component of human blood that contains antibodies. When injected into the body, it provides (presumably temporary) passive immunity to those infections for which it has antibodies, and also decreases the activity of natural killer (NK) cells.

Side effects: Fever, chills, headache, nausea, back pain. Gamma globulin could also contain viruses, despite careful screening. Some lots were withdrawn from the market in 1998 for this reason. Any intravenous procedure can have side effects ranging from mild discomfort to death.

Known interaction hazards: None known.

Tips: Before receiving IVIG, you should have a quantitative immune globulin panel blood test to make sure you do not have this deficiency, which can lead to anaphylactic shock. Drink plenty of water or other liquids before, during, and after your IVIG infusion. Benadryl may help with side effects. Intravenous procedures should always be done in a setting where resuscitation equipment and trained personnel are available. A topical numbing agent may decrease discomfort from needle insertion. Note that as far as we can tell, only the three brands mentioned screen their IVIG for Hepatitis C.

Vesprin

See Stelazine.

Vivactil

Generic name: protriptyline

Use: Depression, panic disorder, chronic pain, eating disorders, severe PMS.

Action, if known: Tricyclic antidepressant—blocks norepinephrine and serotonin use, works against the hormone acetylcholine. More energizing than other tricyclics.

Side effects: Sedation, tremor, seizures, dry mouth, light sensitivity, moodswings in people with diagnosed or undiagnosed bipolar disorder, weight gain. Lowers the seizure threshold.

Known interaction hazards: Alcohol, MAOIs, blood pressure medications (including Clonadine and Tenex), thyroid medication. Potentiated by estrogen, bicarbonate of soda (as in Alka-Seltzer and other OTC remedies), acetazolamide, procainamide, and quinidine. Cimetidine, methylphenidate, Thorazine and similar drugs, oral contraceptives, nicotine (including cigarettes), charcoal tablets, and estrogen may interfere with Vivactil's action in the body.

Tips: Take with food if stomach upset occurs.

Wellbutrin, Wellbutrin SR, Zyban

Generic name: buproprion

Use: depression, ADHD.

Action, if known: Aminoketone antidepressant—appears to have mild effects on serotonin, dopamine, and norepinephrine; mild general CNS stimulant; affects hormonal system; suppresses appetite.

Side effects: High risk of seizures. Restlessness, anxiety, insomnia, heart palpitations, dry mouth, rapid heartbeat or heart palpitations, tremor, headache/migraine headache.

Known interaction hazards: Potentiated by L-Dopa, ritonavir. Effects decreased by carbamazepine. Interacts with MAOIs. Do not use with other drugs (or supplements) that lower the seizure threshold.

Tips: Take with food if stomach upset occurs. Be especially careful to start low, increase dose slowly, and limit dose size to reduce seizure risk.

Xanax

Generic name: alprazolam

Use: Anti-anxiety, panic disorder, PMS, irritable bowel syndrome.

Action, if known: Benzodiazepine, slows CNS activity.

Side effects: Sleepiness (this usually passes after a week), lethargy, confusion, headache, slurred speech, tremor. Addictive, withdrawal may be difficult.

Known interaction hazards: Do not use with alcohol, tranquilizers of any kind (including OTC sleep aids), MAOIs, antihistamines (including OTC allergy and cold medicines), antidepressants, unless under strict medical supervision.

Tips: Many people should not take Xanax, including people with severe depression, sleep apnea, liver or kidney disease, lung disease, alcoholism, or psychosis.

Zarontin

Generic name: ethosuximide

Use: Absence [petit mal] seizure disorders.

Action, if known: Succinimide antispasmodic.

Side effects: Nausea, abdominal pain, changes in appetite, weight loss, drowsiness, headache, dizziness, irritability, insomnia. May lower the seizure threshold in some patients with mixed forms of epilepsy.

Known interaction hazards: Potentiates fosphenytoin, phenytoin, and ethotoin.

Tips: You should have regular liver function and blood tests while taking this drug. May cause systemic lupus erythematosus (a medication-caused form of lupus).

Zeldox

Generic name: ziprasidone

Use: Psychosis, rage/aggression.

Action, if known: Atypical neuroleptic.

Side effects: Drowsiness, dizziness, nausea, lightheadedness.

Known interaction hazards: Not yet known, but probably similar to those of other atypical neuroleptics.

Tips: Regular heart monitoring is advised when taking Zeldox. You may want to supplement with vitamin E, which may protect against tardive dyskensia. This is a very new drug, not yet approved for use in the US.

Ziprasidone

See Zeldox.

Zoloft

Generic name: sertraline

Use: Depression, OCD, obsessive-compulsive behavior

Action, if known: SSRI—increases the amount of active serotonin in the brain. Has an energizing quality.

Side effects: Dry mouth, headache, tremor, diarrhea, nausea, sexual dysfunction. May precipitate a manic episode in people with diagnosed or undiagnosed bipolar disorder. Lowers the seizure threshold.

Known interaction hazards: Alcohol and all other CNS depressants. Never take with an MAOI or soon after stopping an MAOI. Potentiates benzodiazepine drugs, warfarin. Potentiated by cimetidine.

Tips: People with epilepsy, bipolar disorder, liver disease, or kidney disease should be carefully monitored if they take Zoloft. May affect therapeutic level of lithium.

Zovirax

Generic name: acyclovir

Use: Infection with human herpes viruses, Epstein-Barr virus, varicella (chicken pox) and varicella pneumonia, cytomegalovirus, and other viruses.

Action, if known: Immune modulator—inhibits the growth of viruses from within by interfering with reproduction of viral DNA.

Side effects: Sore or bleeding gums, fever, dizziness, headache, digestive trouble, diarrhea, rash, insomnia

Known interaction hazards: Potentiated by oral probenecid, sleepiness when combined with zidovudine.

Tips: Take with food if stomach upset occurs.

Zyban

See Wellbutrin.

Zyprexa

Generic name: olanzapine

Use: Psychosis, rages and aggression in PDDs or Tourette syndrome, tics; also used in cases of hard-to-treat OCD, depression (usually with an antidepressant), or bipolar disorder (usually with a mood stabilizer).

Action, if known: Atypical neuroleptic—blocks uptake of dopamine and serotonin at certain receptors, may have other actions.

Side effects: headache, agitation, dry mouth, hostility, disinhibition, insomnia, slurred speech, neuroleptic malignant syndrome (NMS), tardive dyskensia, dizziness, seizures.

Known interaction hazards: Alcohol. Potentiated by carbamazepine; potentiates medications for high blood pressure (such as Clonadine and Tenex).

Tips: Avoid extreme heat. If you smoke, you may need to take Zyprexa more frequently. You may want to supplement with vitamin E, which may protect against tardive dyskensia.

Supplement Reference

THIS APPENDIX EXPANDS ON WHAT'S KNOWN ABOUT HERBAL REMEDIES, nutritional supplements, some brand-name "natural" remedies or supplements, and a few over-the-counter medications that you may hear about in connection with PDD-NOS or atypical PDD. Because medications have not been proven to cure or reliably treat all cases and symptoms of autistic-spectrum disorders, many people are interested in alternative medicine. We cannot recommend any of the possibilities listed here, but we encourage you to explore those that interest you in concert with your physician, a nutritionist, or other appropriate health professional.

As with medications, doses are specific to the individual, so you will want to consult a knowledgeable health professional or a book. If you choose the latter, try to find the most recent guide you can, preferably one by a reputable physician. Avoid any book that makes outrageous claims for supplements and vitamins. If one of these items were a sure cure for AIDS, cancer, or autism, we would all know it by now.

This appendix doesn't list homeopathic remedies. If you are interested in trying homeopathy, it's best to see a qualified homeopathic practitioner who can help you create a holistic treatment program. It also doesn't list many Asian or Ayurvedic remedies, simply because so little is known about these in the US and Europe at this time. Much information on Chinese herbs can be found at *http://www.rmhiherbal.org/ai/articles.html*, and you can find a brief list of common Ayurvedic remedies, including a number of nervines, at *http://www.niam.com/mediplnt.htm*. It's quite possible that there are some herbal remedies in these ancient pharmacopoeias that could prove useful for symptoms of PDDs, either on their own or as the basis for pharmaceuticals. If you're interested in what the East has to offer, consult a knowledgeable professional.

The information included here was gathered from a wide variety of sources, including standard herbal references, European studies of standardized herbal extracts, clinical data from the US National Institutes of Health's alternative medicine project, the Autism Research Institute's reports on survey results and clinical trials of vitamins and some other substances, and, in some cases, anecdotal reports from natural healthcare practitioners and parents. Since few of these remedies have undergone the intense scientific scrutiny given pharmaceuticals, there is less information available about possible side effects, interactions, and dangers. That does not mean that these "natural" remedies are absolutely safe—in fact, it stands to reason that if they are effective, they could also be dangerous if misused. It's important to work with a practitioner who knows these types of interventions well. If that's not possible, at least be sure to tell your physician about any herbal or nutritional interventions you are trying.

Aloe vera gel

Use: GI tract problems, ulcers.

Action, if known: Nervine, anti-inflammatory (steroidal), hormonal, antioxidant, laxative, and other effects. The active ingredient in aloe vera, allantoin, is also found in cabbage juice and comfrey.

Side effects: Nausea.

Interaction hazards: None known.

Tips: Has a bitter taste, so you may want to dilute it with water or juice.

Alpha tocopherol
See Vitamin E.

Ascorbic acid
See Vitamin C.

Aspirin (acetylsalicylic acid)

Use: Pain, headache.

Action, if known: Aspirin thins the blood, makes compounds called lipoxygenase products, and is classified as a nonsteroidal anti-inflammatory drug (NSAID). It blocks enzymes called COX-1 and COX-2 (cyclooxygenase 1 and cyclooxygenase 2). COX-2 may damage nerve cells, is involved in the process of inflammation and fever, and is also believed to cause cancer and tumors to start growing.

Side effects: Thins the blood, can cause internal bleeding or GI tract irritation if overused.

Interaction hazards: Aspirin is a "hidden" ingredient in many prescription and OTC remedies. Some foods and herbal remedies also contain aspirin-like salicytates. Too much aspirin can cause sudden drops in blood pressure. Too much aspirin also counteracts the effects of buprobenecid, sulfinpyrazone, ACE inhibitors, beta-blockers, and diuretics. Too much aspirin can potentiate methotrexate, propoxyphene hydrochloride (Darvon) and some other narcotics, and Depakote/Depakene.

Tips: Not recommended for use in children due to the risk of Reye's syndrome, a rare complication of chicken pox or influenza B. Do not take if you have (or are at high risk for) stomach ulcers.

Beta carotene

Use: Improving energy metabolism, fighting the physical effects of stress, supporting liver function, protecting skin from the sun, supporting the immune system.

Action, if known: Fat-soluble antioxidant—protects the lipid (fat) layer of cells.

Side effects: Too much can give your skin an orangey color.

Interaction hazards: Counteracted by mineral oil supplements, may interact with nicotine or tobacco products. Although beta carotene is made into vitamin A by the body, it doesn't seem to carry a risk for hypervitaminosis like vitamin A.

Tips: It's best to eat your dark green leafy vegetables and yellow-orange vegetables rather than taking beta carotene supplements. Diets high in beta carotene have been shown to decrease cancer risk in well-designed scientific studies, but studies of beta-carotene supplements have been inconclusive.

Bifidobacterium bifidum

See Probiotics.

Biotin

Use: Water-soluble vitamin with probiotic qualities.

Action, if known: Normally, biotin is produced by the symbiotic bacteria that live in the digestive tract. Lowers blood sugar, may help to alleviate depression.

Side effects: None known.

Interaction hazards: Counteracted by raw egg whites and alcohol. May change your dose requirements for insulin and diabetes medications.

Tips: If you are taking acidopholous or other supplements to maintain a healthy bacterial balance in the GI tract, you should not need to supplement with biotin. You may want to use it if you are taking antibiotics, however. You should take biotin if you are deficient in magnesium.

Bitter melon (Momordica charantia)

Use: Viral infection, stomach ache, colitis, diabetes, high blood pressure. The green leaves and unripe fruit are used.

Action, if known: Antiviral, "herbal antibiotic." Bitter melon is the plant from which the active ingredient in some protease inhibitors is extracted. It may also lower blood sugar and have a beneficial effect on the GI tract.

Side effects: None known, although the strong actions attributed to this plant indicate that it has a high potential for side effects.

Interaction hazards: None known.

Tips: Bitter melon is considered a delicacy in Asia and can often be found in the produce section of Oriental food markets. It is also available canned. It is not known what effect processing may have on its medicinal qualities, however. Not safe for pregnant women, according to some herbalists, because it may have tumor-dissolving capacities that could also endanger the fetus.

Black cohosh (Cimicifuga racemosa, squaw root)

Use: Autoimmune disorders, especially rheumatism; Sydenham's chorea; nerve-related tinnitus; sore throat. The rhizome and root are used.

Action, if known: CNS depressant, sedative, anti-inflammatory.

Side effects: Active ingredient appears to bind to estrogen receptor sites, so it may cause hormonal activity.

Interaction hazards: Do not use with alcohol or other CNS depressants, or with drugs that are not recommended for use with CNS depressants.

Tips: Some multiherb remedies used for seizure disorders contain black cohosh.

Caffeine

Use: Pain relief, especially with aspirin; energizing effect.

Action, if known: CNS stimulant.

Side effects: Jitteriness, stomach acid, increased heart rate, insomnia. In extreme overdose, caffeine can actually kill.

Interaction hazards: May counteract calcium and magnesium. Potentiates some asthma drugs. Potentiates aspirin, and too much aspirin can cause sudden drops in blood pressure. Too much aspirin also counteracts the effects of probenecid, sulfin-pyrazone, ACE inhibitors, beta-blockers, and diuretics. Too much aspirin can potentiate methotrexate and Depakote/Depakene.

Tips: The use of OTC stimulants containing caffeine (such as No-Doz) can cause moodswings in people with diagnosed or undiagnosed bipolar disorder.

Calcium

Use: Preventing bone loss.

Action, if known: Mineral, regulates nervous system impulses and neurotransmitter production, coagulates blood, builds and repairs bone, activates the production of some enzymes and hormones.

Side effects: Excessive levels of calcium (hypocalcinuria) can result in stupor. This has been reported to occur naturally in some autistic people.

Interaction hazards: May be counteracted by corticosteroids, antispasmodics, and thyroid hormone supplements. May be counteracted by spinach and other green leafy vegetables, cocoa, soybeans, phosphates (including soda pop), caffeine, and phytic acid (found in bran and whole grains). May be counteracted or potentiated by antacids. May be potentiated by iron.

Tips: You must have enough vitamin D in the diet or by supplement to utilize calcium. Best taken with a light meal or snack.

Calcium ascorbate

See Vitamin C.

Calcium pangamate

See DMG.

Caprylic acid

Use: Probiotic.

Action, if known: Probiotic—this fatty acid is said to be active against yeast in the digestive tract.

Side effects: Some people report unpleasant "die-off" reactions when taking caprylic acid to combat intestinal yeast infections.

Interaction hazards: None known.

Tips: Medium chain triglycerides (MCT oil, also called caprylic/capric triglycerides) is a liquid source of caprylic acid. Caprylic acid also occurs naturally in coconuts.

Carnitine

Use: Heart trouble, muscle weakness. Also taken to remedy inborn deficiency or to counteract depletion of carnitine from medications or diet.

Action, if known: Transports fats from foods to the mitochondria of cells, which turn them into energy.

Side effects: None known.

Interaction hazards: Depakote and Depakene can deplete your body's supply of carnitine, as does the ketogenic diet.

Tips: You need an adequate supply of vitamin B6 to make your own carnitine from meat and dairy products. Some people may have an inborn carnitine deficiency, which can be discovered through testing. Carnitor is the best-known prescription carnitine supplement.

Carnitor

See Carnitine.

Cat's claw (uncaria tomentosa, una de gato)

Use: Viral infection, diabetes, lupus and other autoimmune disorders, asthma, ulcers, irritable bowel syndrome and related disorders.

Action, if known: Antioxidant, antibiotic, antiviral. Contains four oxindol alkaloids that appear to boost the immune system's ability to destroy foreign cells and to increase the production of white blood cells and other immune-system components. Quinovic acid glycosides in cat's claw appear to have antiviral capabilities. May lower blood pressure.

Side effects: None known, but the strong effects of this herb make it likely that there could be some.

Interaction hazards: None known, but the strong effects of this herb make it likely that there could be some.

Tips: This herb appears to have powerful effects, and should be used with caution.

Chamomile (Matricaria recutita)

Use: Insomnia or sleep disorders, nausea, irritable bowel syndrome.

Action, if known: Sedative, contains volatile oils with antispasmodic and anti-inflammatory effects on the GI tract.

Side effects: Can cause allergic reaction in people who are sensitive to daisies or ragweed.

Interaction hazards: None known.

Tips: Chamomile is safe enough for occasional use by children. It may be taken in capsule form or in the traditional chamomile tea.

Choline (phosphatidyl choline)

Use: Tourette syndrome, bipolar disorder, Alzheimer's disease, tardive dyskensia, memory loss, sleepiness, irritability, insomnia, poor muscle coordination, learning difficulties, liver problems (including alcohol-induced cirrhosis).

Action, if known: Helps in the manufacture of cell membranes, and in the production of the neurotransmitter acetylcholine, which controls the parasympathetic nervous system (including the GI tract), and also has effects within the brain. Promotes metabolism of fats. Reduces the level of "bad" cholesterol.

Side effects: In high doses, nausea, gas, excessive sweating or salivation, fishy body odor.

Interaction hazards: Phenobarbital and methotrexate may counteract choline.

Tips: Choline is one of the active ingredients in lecithin. Normally, your body should produce enough on its own. Also found in eggs, soybeans, cabbage, and many other foods.

Cobalamin

See Vitamin B12.

Coenzyme Q10 (CoQ10, ubiquinone)

Use: Immune disorders, including HIV/AIDS; GI tract problems, including gastric ulcers; gum disease; cancer.

Action, if known: Antioxidant, immune system booster. Part of the cellular process that uses fats, sugars, and amino acids to produce the energy molecule ATP.

Side effects: None known.

Interaction hazards: None known.

Tips: None.

Comfrey (Symphytum officinale, consolida, consound, knitbone, healing herb)

Use: GI tract disorders, ulcers. Usually the root (dried or fresh) is used.

Action, if known: Nervine, anti-inflammatory (steroidal), hormonal, antioxidant, antibiotic, laxative, and other effects. Its active ingredient is allantoin, also found in cabbage juice and aloe vera, and it contains a number of important vitamins.

Side effects: Can cause serious, even fatal, liver damage—not recommended for internal use by the US Food and Drug Administration. Diarrhea; may cause hormonal activity.

Interaction hazards: None known, but the strong action of this herb makes them likely.

Tips: Please note the warning above. Comfrey contains tannin, a bitter-tasting phenol that may aggravate problems in people with low sulfation.

CoQ10

See Coenzyme Q10.

Damiana (Turnera aphrodisiaca)

Use: Depression, high blood pressure.

Action, if known: Mild CNS stimulant, dilates blood vessels, astringent.

Side effects: Nausea.

Interaction hazards: None known.

Tips: As its scientific name indicates, Damiana also has a reputation as an aphrodisiac, probably because it dilates blood vessels.

Dimethylglycine

See DMG.

DMG (dimethylglycine, calcium pangamate, pangamic acid, "vitamin B15")

Use: Autistic-spectrum disorders, communication disorders, heart and liver problems, high cholesterol, diabetes.

Action, if known: Immune modulator—this vitamin-like supplement appears to boost the immune system, possibly by increasing the number of natural killer (NK) cells and white blood cells. Also helps metabolize fats. Some minor antioxidant properties. Reduces lactate levels in muscle tissue, and increases the level of oxygen in the brain. May help reduce the number or severity of seizures in some people. Has been shown in several studies to precipitate or increase speech in nonverbal or communication-disordered children.

Side effects: Increased hyperactivity in some.

Known interaction hazards: None known, although one report indicates that it could interfere with sulfation via Epsom salts.

Tips: DMG is usually found in the body-building/athletics area of a grocery or health food store. The sublingual tablets taste lemony, and dissolve readily under the tongue.

Echinacea (Echinacea purpurea, Echinacea augustifolia, Echinacea pallida)

Use: Viral or bacterial infection, epilepsy.

Action, if known: Antibiotic and antiseptic, may have antispasmodic qualities. Dilates blood vessels. Increases the production of saliva and mucous. Increases production of white blood cells and spleen cells. Activates granulocytes.

Side effects: None known, although it probably should not be used on a long-term basis.

Interaction hazards: Could potentiate or interfere with the action of medications that dilate the blood vessels, or with antispasmodics.

Tips: Not recommended for use by people with autoimmune conditions. Some doctors do not recommend this herb for people with AIDS or tuberculosis, because it may affect T-cell function, although it may also have retrovirus-fighting abilities. Often mixed with goldenseal in herbal remedies for cold and flu.

EFAs

See Essential fatty acids.

Efalex

Use: Brand-name EFA supplement made by Efamol Nutriceuticals Inc. for treating developmental dyspraxia, ADD/ADHD, and related conditions.

Action, if known: See descriptions of essential fatty acids and other Efalex ingredients elsewhere in this appendix.

Side effects: Increased hyperactivity, agitation in some. Evening primrose oil may lower the seizure threshold.

Interaction hazards: None known.

Tips: Efalex contains a mixture of fish oil, evening primrose oil, thyme oil, and vitamin E.

Efamol

Use: Brand-name EFA supplement made by Efamol Nutriceuticals Inc. for treating PMS.

Action, if known: See descriptions of Essential fatty acids and other Efamol ingredients elsewhere in this appendix.

Side effects: Evening primrose oil may lower the seizure threshold.

Interaction hazards: None known.

Tips: Efamol combines evening primrose oil; vitamins B6, C, and E; niacin, zinc, and magnesium.

EicoPro

Use: Brand-name EFA supplement made by Eicotec Inc.

Action, if known: See Essential fatty acids later in this appendix. Linoleic acid is the building block for production of prostaglandins, hormones and related compounds that help regulate the immune system, nervous system, and cardiovascular system.

Side effects: None known.

Interaction hazards: None known.

Tips: EicoPro combines fish oils and linoleic acid.

Ephedra (Ma Huang)

Use: Hyperactivity, asthma.

Action, if known: CNS stimulant—contains ephedrine and pseudoephedrine, which have stimulant effects and are also bronchodilators.

Side effects: Aggression, excessive sweating, increased hyperactivity in some, high blood pressure, heart irregularity, nerve damage, stroke. If misused, ephedra can be fatal.

Interaction hazards: Should not be used with other CNS stimulants. Potentiated by caffeine. See the listings for prescription stimulants for other potential interactions and dangers.

Tips: Ephedra should not be taken by people with high blood pressure, diabetes, glaucoma, heart trouble, or a high danger of stroke. It should not be used on a long-term basis. Ephedra is the building block of ephedrine, and is often used to synthesize the potent and often deadly street drug methamphetamine ("speed," "crank"). It is also a "hidden" ingredient in some OTC drugs for allergies and colds.

Epsom salts (magnesium sulfate)

Use: Hydrated magnesium sulfate—the traditional Epsom salts bath—is an excellent remedy for sore, aching muscles and backache. The magnesium is said to "draw out" inflammatory compounds. Taken internally, it is a potent laxative. Some people with PDDs appear to have positive behavioral effects from Epsom salts baths, including reduced hyperactivity, agitation, and aggression; and increased ability to concentrate.

Action, if known: Epsom salts are sometimes given intravenously in a hospital emergency room to reduce dangerous seizures, especially in eclampsia (a seizure disorder that emerges in pregnancy). It stands to reason, therefore, that they may have gentler antispasmodic effects when taken in other ways.

Side effects: If taken internally, can cause nausea and diarrhea.

Interaction hazards: None known.

Tips: Do not take Epsom salts internally if you have kidney problems.

Essential fatty acids (Omega-3 and Omega-6 fatty acids)

Use: Inflammation, autoimmune conditions of the nervous system, eczema, high blood pressure, hyperactivity, irritable bowel syndrome, arthritis, mood swings. One EFA, gammalinolenic acid (GLA) is available from evening primrose oil, black current seed oil, and other sources. Oil from certain cold-water fish, such as salmon and cod, contains eicospentaenoic acid (EPA) and docosahexaenoic acid (DHA). This is also called Omega-6 fish oil. Lauric acid, another EFA, is found in breast milk, coconuts, and a few other places. Its glycol ester (monolaurin or lauricidin) is available in supplement form.

Action, if known: Normally, linoleic acid is converted to gammalinolenic acid by enzymes, creating hormones and hormone-like substances called prostaglandins. These prostaglandins are involved in regulating the immune system, nervous system, and circulatory system. Lauric acid is known to have antibacterial and antiviral qualities.

Side effects: Evening primrose oil may lower the threshold for frontal-lobe seizures. EPA fish oil can cause fluctuations in blood sugar, so diabetics should use it with caution. Both EPA and DHA (and, to a lesser extent, GLA) thin the blood, and may increase your risk of bleeding or bruising easily.

Interaction hazards: The arachnoidic acid in evening primrose oil may counteract the effects of some antispasmodics, while EPA fish oil could counteract or add to the effects of medications for high or low blood pressure, or drugs that treat heart conditions.

Tips: EFAs are available as gelatin caps or liquids; of course, EPA fish oil can also be obtained by eating cold-water fish. Brand-name EFA supplements include Efalex, Efamol, and EicoPro, among others.

Essiac tea

Use: Cancer, autoimmune disorders.

Action, if known: There are a number of concoctions available under the name "Essiac tea." The original version contained sheep sorrel and burdock root, as well as slippery elm bark and rhubarb. These plants contain lots of vitamins and are said to have anti-inflammatory, astringent, vasodilating, antibiotic, antibacterial, antiviral, and mildly laxative effects. Slippery elm is especially good for assisting the GI tract's mucous membranes.

Side effects: Diarrhea, stomach pain.

Interaction hazards: None known, although sheep sorrel and burdock root are both fairly strong herbs.

Tips: Diabetics and people with a history of kidney stones should not use this tea. You can find some noncommercial information about Essiac tea at *http://essiac-info.org/*, including cautions about scam (and even dangerous) products using the "essiac" name.

Evening primrose oil

See Essential fatty acids.

Feverfew

Use: Migraine, nausea, depression.

Action, if known: One compound found in feverfew, parthenolide, is a serotonin inhibitor. This compound also inhibits leukotrienes and serum proteases.

Side effects: Irritating to the mouth if chewed.

Interaction hazards: None known, although it could be counteracted by medications that have differing effects on serotonin.

Tips: Use only standardized feverfew extract, as the amount of parthenolide varies widely from plant to plant.

Fish oil

See Essential fatty acids.

Flax seed

See Essential fatty acids.

Flowers of sulfur

See MSM.

Folic acid

Use: Depression, anemia, slow growth; needed to make B vitamins available to the body, so it's taken as part of B vitamin formulas for autistic symptoms. Also taken to counteract some of the side effects of methotrexate (Rheumatrex).

Action, if known: Anti-inflammatory, helps to produce white blood cells and other components of the immune system, helps to convert amino acids into proteins, necessary for building and rebuilding the nervous system.

Side effects: None known in proper dose.

Interaction hazards: Dilantin competes with folic acid in the GI tract and in the brain—if you take Dilantin, consult with your physician about how to get around this interaction.

Tips: Folic acid is found in green leafy vegetables, beans, asparagus, citrus fruits and juices, whole grain foods, and liver. However, many doctors (and the March of Dimes, which is campaigning against spina bifida and other birth defects linked to a lack of folic acid in the diet) do recommend taking a supplement.

Forskolin (Coleus forskohili)

Use: Asthma, glaucoma.

Action, if known: Stimulates the production of adenylate cyclase and elevates cyclic adenosine monophosphate (cAMP) levels—cAMP regulates and activates enzymes required for cellular energy transfer. Inhibits production of proteoglycan synthesis, lowers blood pressure by dilating blood vessels, increases the amount of tyrosine hydroxylase, powerful bronchodilating action.

Side effects: This is a strong herb that could have many side effects, particularly on the heart and lungs. Use with caution!

Known interaction hazards: Potentiates antihypertensives, such as Clonadine, and antiasthmatic drugs.

Tips: This is a powerful Ayurvedic herb. It should not be used by people with low blood pressure, heart trouble, prostate cancer (and possibly other types of cancer), or peptic ulcers. People with heart, lung, or circulation problems should use forskolin only under medical supervision.

Gammalinolenic acid

See Essential fatty acids.

Garlic

Use: Immune disorders, high blood pressure.

Action, if known: Probiotic—said to be active against yeast in the digestive tract while protecting helpful flora; may lower blood pressure slightly.

Side effects: "Garlic breath" if eaten, causes stomach discomfort for some.

Interaction hazards: None known.

Tips: Available as a food or a supplement. Incidentally, garlic contains high amounts of the mineral germanium (see below), as does ginseng.

Germanium

Use: Viral infection, immune disorders, cancer, inflammation, high blood pressure.

Action, if known: Stimulates the body to produce its own interferon, lowers blood pressure (probably by dilating blood vessels), inhibits enzymes that reduce endorphin levels, has an anti-inflammatory action.

Side effects: None known.

Interaction hazards: None known, although it could interfere with medications for high or low blood pressure.

Tips: Make sure you buy the sesqui-oxide form of germanium (or get your germanium from food sources or other herbs).

Gingko biloba

Use: Forgetfulness, dementia, depression, Reynaud's disease, tinnitus.

Action, if known: Antioxidant; increases blood flow to the brain; increases uptake of oxygen, glucose, and neurotransmitters by neuronal cells.

Side effects: Stomach or intestinal upset, headache, allergic skin reactions.

Interaction hazards: None known.

Tips: Well-studied and often prescribed in Germany, where it is available as a controlled pharmaceutical, gingko extract is just catching on the US.

Goldenseal (Hydrastis Canadensis L).

Use: Viral or bacterial infection, immune disorders, GI tract problems. Generally the powdered root is used.

Action, if known: Two of the active ingredients in goldenseal, hydrastine and berberine, elevate blood pressure and stimulate circulation. It has antiseptic and antibiotic-like properties, and acts on the mucous membranes of the GI tract when taken internally.

Side effects: Overdose can cause seizures, although mild goldenseal solutions were an old-time remedy for epilepsy.

Interaction hazards: Could interfere with or add to the action of blood-pressure medications, antispasmodics, or antibiotics. People taking opioid blockers like ReVia may not get full benefit from goldenseal (see the "ReVia" section in the previous appendix).

Tips: Goldenseal is an alkaloid isoquinoline derivative related to the minor opium alkaloids. Goldenseal is a powerful herb and should not be taken for long periods of time, by pregnant women, or by people with high blood pressure. It has a strong taste that most people find unpleasant. The best way to take it may be adding a few drops of a tincture (concentrated liquid extract) to a glass of water. Gel caps are the easiest, but may not get the goldenseal to the GI tract as well.

Gotu kola (Centella asiatica)

Use: Depression, fatigue, memory loss, high blood pressure.

Action, if known: CNS stimulant, dilates blood vessels.

Side effects: None known.

Interaction hazards: If you take medication for high blood pressure, talk to your doctor before using this herb.

Tips: Not recommended for use by pregnant women.

Grapeseed oil

See Proanthocyanidins.

Hap Caps

See NutriVene-D.

Inosital

Use: OCD, depression, panic disorder, degenerative and autoimmune disorders of the nervous system (including diabetic neuropathy), liver disease.

Action, if known: Required by the neurotransmitters serotonin and acetylcholine, inositol helps the nerves conduct impulses correctly, possibly by rebuilding the myelin sheath. May also have sedative effects in high doses.

Side effects: None known.

Interaction hazards: Caffeine counteracts inositol.

Tips: Inositol is one of the active ingredients in lecithin. People with PDDs who test positive for anti-myelin antibodies in the blood might want to try inositol.

Iron (ferrous sulfate)

Use: Anemia, restless leg syndrome.

Action, if known: Helps blood carry oxygen.

Side effects: Even a few iron tablets taken by a small child can cause death. Stomach upset, constipation, bowel distress, darkened urine or teeth (this will pass when you stop taking iron). If you have dark, hard, sticky stools and constipation, you are probably taking too much iron.

Interaction hazards: Antacids and tetracycline may counteract iron. Do not take with dairy foods or whole-grain products.

Tips: Children who have not been medically diagnosed with iron-deficiency anemia do not need an iron supplement. Iron accumulates in the body, particularly as you get older, and may cause heart and neurological problems. It's best to get iron through the diet.

Lactobacillus acidophilus, lactobacillus bulgaricus

See Probiotics.

Lauricidin

See Essential fatty acids.

Lecithin (phosphatidyl choline)

Use: Tourette syndrome, bipolar disorder, Alzheimer's disease, tardive dyskensia, memory loss, sleepiness, irritability, insomnia, poor muscle coordination, learning difficulties, liver problems (including alcohol-induced cirrhosis), OCD, depression, panic disorder, degenerative and autoimmune disorders of the nervous system, seizure disorders.

Action, if known: See inositol and choline, earlier in this appendix.

Side effects: None known.

Interaction hazards: Caffeine counteracts the inositol in lecithin.

Tips: A phospholipid found mostly in high-fat foods, lecithin is available in capsules or granules. One of the tastiest ways to take it is by blending the granules into a fresh-fruit smoothie. Lecithin is definitely not a cure for any neurological disorder, but both anecdotal reports and recent studies indicate that it may help in some cases.

Licorice (Glycyrrhiza glabra, among others)

Use: Asthma, coughs, GI tract disorders.

Action, if known: Boosts hormone production, including secretin and other hormones active in the GI tract and brain.

Side effects: None known.

Interaction hazards: None known.

Tips: Medicinal-quality licorice is a lot stronger than the sweet, licorice-flavored candy familiar to the American palate. Children may not like the taste: gel caps, powdered licorice root capsules, or licorice tea might be better tolerated.

Linoleic acid

See Essential fatty acids.

Ma Huang

See Ephedra.

Magnesium

Use: Insomnia, heart problems, muscle pain, high blood pressure. If you are supplementing with B6, you will need to add magnesium as well.

Action, if known: Lowers blood pressure, helps to regulate nerve impulses and neurotransmitter production.

Side effects: Blocks calcium channels. Dilates blood vessels, reducing blood pressure.

Interaction hazards: Fatty foods may interfere with the metabolism of magnesium. Talk to your doctor about taking magnesium if you take pharmaceutical calcium channel blockers.

Tips: Magnesium is part of ARI's recommendations for autistic symptoms.

MCT oil

See Caprylic acid.

Melatonin (MLT)

Use: Insomnia, seasonal affective disorder (SAD), mood swings, regulatory disorders, anxiety, depression.

Action, if known: Melatonin is a hormone made by the pineal gland, which regulates the body's sleep/wake cycles. It is also believed to be important to the immune system and to other parts of the endocrine system, particularly for women.

Side effects: None known, although if too large a dose is taken, you may still be tired in the morning.

Interaction hazards: None known in normal doses.

Tips: Detailed information about the use of melatonin by people with autism is available at *http://www.autism.org/melatonin.html*.

Methyl-sulphonyl-methane

See MSM.

Monolaurin

See Essential fatty acids.

MSB Plus

See NutriVene-D.

MSM (methyl-sulphonyl-methane, sulfur)

Use: Diabetes, joint pain, high cholesterol, dysentery/GI tract dysfunction, yeast infections. There is a theory that some people with PDDs have a metabolic error in how they process sulfur. These individuals may need to supplement with sulfur or a related compound.

Action, if known: Conversion of fats into energy; collagen production; activating and producing enzymes that aid in digestion and in protecting the mucous lining of the GI tract; reducing blood sugar, cholesterol, and blood pressure.

Side effects: Some people are very allergic to sulfur. Others are somewhat sensitive, and may experience sulfurous intestinal gas or burping.

Interaction hazards: None known.

Tips: Sulfur can be gotten in the diet via egg yolks, asparagus, garlic, onions, meat, and beans. An old remedy called "flowers of sulfur" or "sublimed sulfur" may be similar in action.

N-Acetyl-Cysteine (NAC)

Use: Seizure disorders, heavy metal poisoning, aspirin or acetaminophen poisoning, viral infection, movement disorders, degenerative neurological disorders, including multiple sclerosis. NAC is the acetylated version of the sulfur amino acid, l-Cysteine. In the body, it turns into l-Cysteine, which in turn is a precursor to glutathione.

Action, if known: Antioxidant amino acid, increases synthesis of reduced glutathione and slows production of H_2O_2. Enhances the immune system, including T-cell growth and production of interleukin-2. Antibacterial and antiviral action. Appears to have chelating effects that help remove toxic heavy metals from the body.

Side effects: None known, although it seems likely that side effects are possible.

Interaction hazards: May interfere with the absorption of magnesium. People taking NAC will also want to take a magnesium supplement.

Tips: A report on the latest studies on NAC and neurological disorders can be found at *http://dem0nmac.mgh.harvard.edu/neurowebforum/MovementDisordersArticles/NAcetylCysteineReport.html*. This report indicates that encouraging results have been found, although NAC tends to only arrest the progression of these disorders rather than causing improvement.

Niacin

See Vitamin B3.

NutriVene-D

Use: Developed as a nutritional supplement for people with Down's syndrome. Contains A, B, C and other vitamins, inosital, a variety of minerals and amino acids, essential fatty acids, and other ingredients. A "night time" formula is also available that contains L-Tryptophan and other amino acids associated with normalizing sleep patterns.

Action, if known: Antioxidant action, and intervention based on known and possible metabolic defects results from this chromosomal abnormality.

Side effects: See the complete list of NutriVene-D ingredients, and then see side effects for each component.

Interaction hazards: NutriVene-D should be taken under a doctor's supervision.

Tips: Take with food or shortly after a meal. Hap Caps and MSB Plus are two other commercial preparations with a similar yet slightly different profile. Prescription nutritional supplement formulas for people with Down's syndrome or other metabolic disorders can be created with your doctor's help.

Octocosanol

Use: High cholesterol, neuromuscular disorders.

Action, if known: Said to improve energy storage in muscle tissue and improve oxygen utilization.

Side effects: None known.

Interaction hazards: None known.

Tips: Octocosanol is usually derived from wheat germ, so you'll probably want to avoid it if you are avoiding wheat products. Takes nearly a month to start working, according to some sources.

Passionflower (Passiflora incarnata)

Use: Depression, anxiety, seizure disorders, insomnia.

Action, if known: Mild CNS depressant—contains an active ingredient, passiflorine, which appears to have opiate-like properties.

Side effects: Sleepiness.

Interaction hazards: Should not be used with other CNS depressants.

Tips: People with PDDs who are known to have problems with opiate excess might want to avoid taking passionflower.

Pepcid AC (famotidine)

Use: GI tract problems, particularly acid reflux disease ("heartburn"); used to treat social deficits in children with autism with some success in one study at the St. Luke's-Roosevelt Hospital Center in New York City (Linda A. Linday, MD, et al., "Oral famotidine: A potential treatment for children with autism," **Medical Hypotheses** 48, no. 5 [May 1997]: 381–6).

Action, if known: Blocks histamine-2 (H2) receptors, which should reduce inhibitory signals to the brain.

Side effects: Diarrhea; can simply mask the pain of serious GI problems.

Interaction hazards: Antacids interact with a number of medications, and H2 blockers in particular have a number of known interactions with other drugs. Consult your pharmacist before using Pepcid.

Tips: Tagamet and Zantac are two other H2 blockers. They may or may not have similar effectiveness for PDD symptoms in some people.

Phenylalinine

Use: Thyroid conditions, depression, autoimmune conditions, chronic pain.

Action, if known: Amino acid precursor to tyrosine, which is in turn the precursor to epinephrine, norepinephrine, and dopamine. Slows the breakdown of natural endorphins. May slow CNS activity.

Side effects: Drowsiness.

Interaction hazards: None known, but could interact with antidepressants.

Tips: You must have an adequate intake of vitamin C to metabolize phenylalanine. Some people, called phenylketoneurics, have a chromosomal defect that prevents them from tolerating any phenylalanine in the diet, including that found in the artificial sweetener aspartame.

Phenylpropanolamine (PPA)

Use: Diet aid, found in many cold and flu preparations.

Action, if known: Alpha-adrenergic receptor agonist, which shrinks mucousal tissue and constricts blood vessels.

Side effects: Nervousness, insomnia, restlessness, headache, nausea, stomach irritation. Although PPA is often touted as a totally safe drug, it can be dangerous if misused—some street methamphetamine is made with PPA.

Interaction hazards: Should never be taken with MAOIs.

Tips: People with high blood pressure, diabetes, heart disease, peripheral vascular disease, increased intraocular pressure, hyperthyroidism, or prostatic hypertrophy should not take PPA.

Phosphatidyl choline

See Choline.

Proanthocyanidins

Use: Proanthocyanidins are the active ingredients in several naturally occurring antioxidant compounds. The best-known of these, grapeseed oil, is just what its name indicates. Pycogenol is a brand-name formulation derived from maritime pine bark. Both have been tried by people with PDDs and other neurological disorders, sometimes with beneficial effects for seizure control, reduced aggression, and improved immune-system function.

Action, if known: Strong antioxidant activity.

Side effects: Loose stools, increased hyperactivity and/or aggression in some.

Interaction hazards: None known.

Tips: Pycogenol tends to be more expensive than other proanthocyanidins, as it is a trademarked product.

Probiotics

Use: Digestive problems, chronic constipation or diarrhea, irritable bowel syndrome and related disorders, yeast infection, autoimmune disorders.

Action, if known: Probiotics are "friendly" bacteria that flourish in the intestine to help with digestion, or substances that protect these bacteria from depredation by antibiotics or other forces.

Side effects: None known.

Interaction hazards: None known.

Tips: Lactobacillus acidophilus, Bifidobacterium bifidum, and Lactobacillus bulgaricus are friendly bacteria more familiar to most of us as the "active cultures" found in some yogurts. Yogurt itself is a good probiotic for those who eat dairy products.

Pycogenol

See Proanthocyanidins.

Pyridoxine

See Vitamin B6.

Retinol

See Vitamin A.

Riboflavin

See Vitamin B2.

Sarsaparilla (Sarsaparilla officinalis, Sarsaparilla papyracea, Aralia nudicaulis, Smilax ornata)

Use: GI tract disorders, asthma.

Action, if known: Appears to have some action against inflammation.

Side effects: None known.

Interaction hazards: None known

Tips: As the list of scientific names indicates, several different plants have been tagged as "sarsaparilla." All of them have a similar, slightly spicy, taste and seem to have similar actions. Like licorice, sarsaparilla seems to affect hormone production as well as settling the stomach and calming the nerves.

Selenium

Use: GI tract disorders; increased sperm production; selenium deficiency (Keshan disease), which occurs in some people with celiac disease and other autoimmune disorders.

Action, if known: The cooperation of vitamin E and selenium produces the vital antioxidant peptide enzyme selenium-glutathione-peroxidase. Appears to help stimulate the production of antibodies, and may stimulate synthesis of protein.

Side effects: Rash, nausea, fatigue, brittle teeth and hair. Muscle, vision, and heart problems have been observed in animals getting too much selenium, and could occur in humans as well.

Interaction hazards: None known.

Tips: Selenium supplements are a must for people who are fed intravenously or tube-fed. If you or your child experiences GI tract problems, you may want to use a supplement of this mineral, preferably in its easily absorbed chelated form (L-selenomethionane). You can also get it in the diet. It is plentiful in fish, shellfish, red meat, grains, eggs, chicken, liver, garlic, brewer's yeast and wheat germ. Only 50 to 200 micrograms of selenium is needed daily.

Skullcap (Scutellarias)

Use: Tic disorders, muscle spasms, seizure disorders, insomnia, anxiety.

Action, if known: Antispasmodic, sedative—its main active ingredient, Scutellarin, is also available in supplement form.

Side effects: Giddiness, stupor, confusion, twitchiness, heart palpitations.

Interaction hazards: Could interfere with or potentiate antispasmodic medications, or others.

Tips: There are several different plants in the skullcap family, all of which have similar action.

Soil-based organisms (SBOs)

Use: Counteracting the GI tract effects of antibiotics and NSAIDs, immune and autoimmune disorders.

Action, if known: Probiotic—these microbes found in organic soils are believed to help the body produce important enzymes that assist with the digestion of proteins, combat yeast and other unwanted growth in the GI tract, and assist the immune system.

Side effects: None known.

Interaction hazards: None known.

Tips: Some people believe that modern food-processing techniques have left people deficient in Bacillus subtilis and similar organisms, which are "friendly" bacteria outside the better-known class of lacto-bacteria, so they take SBO supplements. This theory is not proven, although at least some SBOs have been known to science as beneficial for many years. This is a fairly new supplement in the US, and much of the promotional literature is outrageous—proceed with caution.

Sphingolin

Use: Multiple sclerosis and other disorders involving demyelination.

Action, if known: Said to help rebuild the myelin sheath. Its method of action, if any, is not known.

Side effects: None known.

Interaction hazards: None known.

Tips: Do not take Sphingolin if you are allergic to beef products. Because it is made from the nervous system of cattle, Sphingolin is illegal in the UK due to the potential for mad cow disease. There could be a risk of this disease outside the UK as well.

SPV-30

Use: Viral or bacterial infection, including HIV/AIDS; immune disorders; tuberculosis; inflammation.

Action, if known: Antiviral, antibiotic, steroidal anti-inflammatory.

Side effects: Stomach cramping, skin rash, diarrhea. If cramps occur, drinking more water seems to help. Some people taking SPV-30 in AIDS studies noted that taking it earlier in the day rather than after dinner prevents a possible side effect of insomnia.

Interaction hazards: None known.

Tips: SPV-30 is derived from active ingredients found in the European boxwood tree (Buxus sempervirens). It has shown great promise as an antiviral in AIDS medication trials in France and the US.

St. John's wort (Hypericum perforatum)

Use: Depression, anxiety.

Action, if known: There are at least ten active ingredients in St. John's wort that have some neurological activity. Its exact method of action is not yet known, but clinical studies have shown it to be an effective treatment for mild to moderate depression.

Side effects: Increased sensitivity to light. Can precipitate mania in people with diagnosed or undiagnosed bipolar disorder.

Interaction hazards: Follow the restrictions in diet and medication indicated for pharmaceutical MAO inhibitors or SSRI antidepressants.

Tips: Hypericin, an extract that separates out one active ingredient from St. John's wort, may or may not be as effective as the whole herb.

Sulfur

See MSM.

Thiamin

See Vitamin B1.

Tryptophan (L-Tryptophan, 5-HTP)

Use: Depression, especially with agitation; insomnia; irritability; anxiety; chronic pain.

Action, if known: Precursor for increased brain levels of serotonin and for the body's production of niacin. The 5-HTP version is also said to contribute to the production of melatonin.

Side effects: Appetite suppression.

Interaction hazards: None known, although one should be cautious about using this amino acid with any drug known to have an effect on serotonin, such as an antidepressant.

Tips: Not recommended for people with autoimmune disorders or asthma, or for pregnant women. Not currently available in US, as a "bad batch" was pulled by the FDA in 1989 and the product was subsequently banned. 5-hydroxy L-tryptophan (5-HTP), a plant-derived type of tryptophan, is available in the US, however, and L-Tryptophan can be purchased via mail order, over the Internet, etc. Those with panic attacks may get good results by combining tryptophan with vitamin B6. Tryptophan can also be obtained by eating pineapple, turkey, chicken, yogurt, bananas, or unripened cheese, preferably with a starch.

Tyrosine (L-Tyrosine)

Use: Anxiety, depression, fatigue, thyroid disorders, allergies, headaches, chronic pain; also used as an aid to drug and alcohol withdrawal.

Action, if known: Amino acid precursor to epinephrine, norepinephrine, and dopamine. The body normally synthesizes tyrosine from phenylalanine.

Side effects: None known.

Interaction hazards: Do not take with an MAOI.

Tips: Take Tyrosine on an empty stomach.

Ubiquinone

See Coenzyme Q10.

Valerian (Valeriana officinalis)

Use: Insomnia, pain.

Action, if known: Sedative, CNS depressant—appears to bind to the same receptors used by the benzodiazepine tranquilizers, although it is much weaker.

Side effects: Some people find valerian stimulating instead of sedating.

Interaction hazards: None known, although it would be wise not to mix this herb with other sedatives or CNS depressants, particularly benzodiazepines.

Tips: Valerian is a strong sedative and should not be given to young children. It has a strong, unpleasant odor and taste that is hard to disguise in food or drink.

Vitamin A (retinol)

Use: Viral or bacterial infection, GI tract disorders.

Action, if known: Antioxidant, helps maintain the mucous lining of the intestines.

Side effects: Vitamin A can be deadly in doses of more than 25,000 units per day. Overdose indicators include headache, blurred vision, chapped lips, dry skin, rash, joint aches and pain, and abdominal tenderness.

Interaction hazards: None known.

Tips: People with celiac disease have a hard time getting enough A, and often experience a deficiency of this vitamin.

Vitamin B1 (thiamin)

Use: Wernicke's syndrome, Korsakoff's psychosis (often seen as a complication of alcoholism), peripheral neuropathy, cardiac disorders. Thiamin levels are sometimes low in autistic people.

Action, if known: Needed for the production of acetylcholine and nucleic acids. Part of the process of impulse initiation in neuronal membranes.

Side effects: None known

Interaction hazards: None known.

Tips: In the diet, thiamin is found in lean pork, legumes, and yeast. However, thiamin in foods is destroyed by cooking.

Vitamin B2 (riboflavin)

Use: Hormonal disorders, jaundice in newborns, depression, inflammation, inborn metabolic disorders.

Action, if known: Takes part in the conversion of tryptophan to serotonin, and in the synthesis of your body's own anti-inflammatory substances, the corticosteroids.

Side effects: None known.

Interaction hazards: Chlorpromazine, imipramine, and amitriptyline inhibit riboflavin, as may some other antidepressants.

Tips: Dietary sources for riboflavin include milk, eggs, ice cream, liver, some lean meats, and green vegetables. In the US and some other countries, breads and other baked goods made with white flour are routinely enriched with riboflavin. If you follow a vegetarian or gluten-free and/or casein-free diet, you probably should add B2 to your diet a matter of course.

Vitamin B3 (niacin, nicotinic acid)

Use: Autistic symptoms, schizophrenia, high cholesterol, deficiency (pellegra).

Action, if known: Believed to reduce inflammation, helps red blood cells carry oxygen. Helps build tissue, including nerve tissue. Raises blood sugar. Necessary for fatty acid and corticosteroid synthesis. Relaxes blood vessels.

Side effects: Flushing (red face), produced by a sudden release of prostaglandins and histamine. Skin rash, agitation. Hypouricemia and liver problems are rarely seen, but possible.

Interaction hazards: May potentiate some antispasmodics.

Tips: Choose "no-flush" (buffered) niacin if flushing bothers you. People with diabetes, gout, or ulcers should not take niacin—although nicotinamide, a closely related enzyme, is under investigation as a treatment for diabetes.

Vitamin B5 (pantothenic acid)

Use: Depression, insomnia, heart problems, fatigue, problems of the peripheral nervous system.

Action, if known: Metabolism of carbohydrates, proteins, and lipids; synthesis of lipids, neurotransmitters, steroid hormones, porphyrins, and hemoglobin. Necessary for normal antibody production.

Side effects: Diarrhea, agitation, hyperactivity.

Interaction hazards: None known.

Tips: Foods that are high in B5 include organ meats, lobster, poultry, soybeans, lentils, split peas, yogurt, avocado, mushrooms, and sweet potato—however, heat destroys pantothenic acid.

Vitamin B6 (pyridoxine)

Use: Seizure disorders.

Action, if known: Metabolism of amino acids, protein, essential fatty acids, stored starches, and neurotransmitters, and glycogen. It also influences the production of neurotransmitters, particularly norepinephrine, dopamine, and serotonin. Pyridoxine binds to steroid hormone receptors and may regulating steroid hormone action. May influence the immune system.

Side effects: Agitation, hyperactivity. If you choose to supplement with more than 50 mg of B6 per day, as the ARI recommends, you should do so under a doctor's supervision because it can be dangerous at very large doses for some patients. If you feel a tingling sensation in your hands or feet, stop taking B6 and contact your doctor.

Interaction hazards: A great number of medications counteract B6—talk to your doctor before supplementing with this vitamin.

Tips: B6 must be given with magnesium, and preferably with other B vitamins, as it increases the metabolism of riboflavin. Food sources include poultry, fish, pork, bananas, and whole grains.

Vitamin B12 (cobalamin)

Use: Depression, anemia; demyelination of spinal cord; demyelination of brain, optic, and peripheral nerves; ADD/ADHD

Action, if known: Helps build the myelin sheath around nerve fibers. Needed for amino acid and fatty acid metabolism.

Side effects: Agitation, hyperactivity.

Interaction hazards: None known.

Tips: B12 can be deficient in people who are not making a normal amount of digestive enzymes, such as those with GI tract disorders. People with PDDs who test positive for auto-antibodies to myelin protein should definitely supplement with B12. Vegetarians and others may want to do so as well, as B12 is found only in meat, eggs, and dairy products. Spirulina, blue-green algae, and some other "vegetarian" B12 supplements contain a form of B12 that cannot be absorbed by humans.

"Vitamin B15"
See DMG.

Vitamin C (ascorbic acid)

Use: Deficiency (scurvy), gum disease, fatigue, degenerative disorders, immune disorders. Has shown benefits for some people with autism in megadoses.

Action, if known: Antioxidant. Necessary for the synthesis of neurotransmitters, steroid hormones, and carnitine. Converts cholesterol to bile acids, and helps with metabolism of tyrosine and metal ions. May enhance the bioavailability of iron.

Side effects: Nausea, abdominal cramps, diarrhea.

Interaction hazards: Potentiates iron.

Tips: Consult your doctor before using megadoses of C, which research indicates should be accompanied by vitamin E. Do not start using megadoses of C and then suddenly stop. The acidic nature of ascorbic acid can also contribute to kidney stones. (The buffered form, calcium ascorbate, is more easily tolerated.) Food sources include citrus fruits, berries, melons, tomatoes, potatoes, green peppers, and leafy green vegetables; vitamin C is easily destroyed by heat and prolonged storage.

Vitamin E (alpha tocopherol)

Use: Immune disorders, heart disease, neurological disorders.

Action, if known: Fat-soluble antioxidant, believed to be important for proper immune-system function. Influences signal transduction pathways. Thins the blood.

Side effects: Thins the blood.

Interaction hazards: Do not take vitamin E with anticoagulant drugs, or if you have a vitamin K deficiency.

Tips: People who take antipsychotics, atypical antipsychotics, tricyclic antidepressants, or other medications that carry a known risk for tardive dyskensia should definitely supplement them with vitamin E. It appears to have protective and symptom-reduction qualities regarding this movement disorder. Vegetables and seed oils, including soybean, safflower, and corn oil sunflower seeds, nuts, whole grains, and wheat germ are all good sources for vitamin E.

Zinc

Use: Viral infection, common colds.

Action, if known: Antiviral action has been proposed, as has the possibility that zinc boosts production of natural interferon.

Side effects: Nausea.

Interaction hazards: Citric acid (as found in orange juice—or even in some commercial zinc lozenges for colds!) may counteract the effects of zinc. Coffee and tea should not be taken at the same time as zinc.

Tips: Deficiency occurs in some people with celiac disease, so if you or your child experiences GI tract problems, you may want to use a supplement of this mineral in its easiest-to-absorb chelated form (zinc aspartate or zinc picolinate).

Diagnostic Tools

FOR THOSE READERS WHO NEED TO KNOW MORE about the symptoms of autistic-spectrum disorders and how these disorders are diagnosed and differentiated, this appendix includes two helpful tools: the Autism Research Institute's Form E-2 Check List, and a sample from the Childhood Autism Rating Scale (CARS).

Form E-2 is a questionnaire for parents of autistic-spectrum children. It was developed by Dr. Bernard Rimland, director of the Autism Research Institute. It's important to understand that Form E-2 is not a diagnostic tool per se. Its purpose is to build a large, detailed database on autism-related symptoms and behaviors. By copying this checklist, filling it out, and mailing it to ARI, you will be assisting with the longest-running research project on the topic of PDDs. Dr. Rimland hopes that your answers will help researchers differentiate between disorders—many of them as yet unnamed and unknown—that fall along the autistic spectrum. By identifying subtypes that go beyond such general categories as PDD-NOS, atypical PDD, or high-functioning autism, researchers may be able to suggest more appropriate treatments for people with PDDs. As of this writing, ARI's database includes information about more than 25,000 cases of autism and autism-like conditions in more than 40 countries.

Form E-2 is also available directly from ARI in French, Spanish, Portuguese, German, Italian, Hebrew, Japanese, Turkish, and Serbo-Croatian, as well as in English.

Completing Form E-2 offers a benefit to you as well as to autism researchers. ARI will send you a brief report explaining what your answers seem to say about your child, including a computerized "score." There is no charge for this service. This report may give you valuable information, but it's not a diagnosis. Form E-2 should not be used to self-diagnose PDDs or to permit or deny entrance to programs or services for people with PDDs.

Please send your copied and completed Form E-2 to:

Autism Research Institute
4182 Adams Avenue
San Diego, CA 92116
Fax (619) 563-6840

Diagnostic Checklist for Behavior-Disturbed Children (Form E-2)

Has this child been diagnosed before?

If so, what was the diagnosis?

Diagnosed by:

Where?

Instructions: You are being asked to fill out this questionnaire concerning your child in order to provide research information which will be helpful in learning more about the causes and types of behavior disturbances in children. Please pick the one answer you think is most accurate for each question. If you want to comment or add something about a question, add it right next to the question, if there is room. Or circle the number of the question, copy the number on the back of the question-naire and write your comment there. Your additional comments are welcome, but even if you do add comments, please mark the printed question as well as you can. Remember, pick just one answer, and mark it with an "X," for each question.

It would be helpful if, on a separate sheet, you would write in any information about the child and his sisters or brothers which you think may be significant. (For example: Twins, living or dead; Behavior problems; IQ scores, if known).

USE AN "X" TO MARK ONE ANSWER FOR EACH QUESTION. DO NOT SKIP MAIN QUESTIONS. SUB-QUESTIONS (NOT ALONG LEFT MARGIN) MAY BE SKIPPED.

1. Present age of child:
   - ❏ 1. Under 3 years old
   - ❏ 2. Between 3 and 4 years old
   - ❏ 3. Between 4 and 5 years old
   - ❏ 4. Between 5 and 6 years old[1]
   - ❏ 5. Over 6 years old (Age:_____ years)[1]

2. Indicate child's sex:
   - ❏ 1. Boy
   - ❏ 2. Girl

3. Indicate child's birth order and number of mother's other children:
   - ❏ 1. Child is an only child
   - ❏ 2. Child is first born of _____ children
   - ❏ 3. Child is last born of _____ children
   - ❏ 4. Child is middle born; _____ children are older and _____ are younger
   - ❏ 5. Foster child, or don't know

4. Were pregnancy and delivery normal?
   - ❏ 1. Pregnancy and delivery both normal
   - ❏ 2. Problems during both pregnancy and delivery
   - ❏ 3. Pregnancy troubled; routine delivery
   - ❏ 4. Pregnancy untroubled; problems during delivery
   - ❏ 5. Don't know

---

[1] This checklist is designed primarily for children 3 to 5 years old. If child is over 5, answer as well as you can by recall of the child's behavior.

5. Was the birth premature (birth weight under 5 lbs)?
   - ❑ 1. Yes (about ____ weeks early; ____ lbs)
   - ❑ 2. No
   - ❑ 3. Don't know

6. Was the child given oxygen in the first week?
   - ❑ 1. Yes
   - ❑ 2. No
   - ❑ 3. Don't know

7. Appearance of child during first few weeks after birth:
   - ❑ 1. Pale, delicate looking
   - ❑ 2. Unusually healthy looking
   - ❑ 3. Average, don't know, or other

8. Unusual conditions of birth and infancy (check only one number in left-hand column):
   - ❑ 1. Unusual conditions
     Indicate which: blindness___ cerebral palsy___ birth injury___ seizures___ blue baby___ very high fever___ jaundice___ other___
   - ❑ 2. Twin birth (identical ____ fraternal ____)
   - ❑ 3. Both 1 and 2
   - ❑ 4. Normal, or don't know

9. Concerning baby's health in first 3 months:
   - ❑ 1. Excellent health, no problems
   - ❑ 2. Respiration (frequent infections ____ other ____)
   - ❑ 3. Skin (rashes ____ infection ____ allergy ____ other ____)
   - ❑ 4. Feeding (learning to suck ____ colic ____ vomiting ____ other ____)
   - ❑ 5. Elimination (diarrhea ____ constipation ____ other ____)
   - ❑ 6. Several of above (indicate which: 2 ____ 3 ____ 4 ____ 5 ____)

10. Has the child been given an electroencephalogram (EEG)?
    - ❑ 1. Yes, it was considered normal
    - ❑ 2. Yes, it was considered borderline
    - ❑ 3. Yes, it was considered abnormal
    - ❑ 4. No, or don't know, or don't know results

11. In the first year, did the child react to bright lights, bright colors, unusual sounds, etc.?
    - ❑ 1. Unusually strong reaction (pleasure ____ dislike ____)
    - ❑ 2. Unusually unresponsive
    - ❑ 3. Average, or don't know

12. Did the child behave normally for a time before his abnormal behavior began?
    - ❑ 1. Never was a period of normal behavior
    - ❑ 2. Normal during first 6 months
    - ❑ 3. Normal during first year
    - ❑ 4. Normal during first 1 1/2 years
    - ❑ 5. Normal during first 2 years
    - ❑ 6. Normal during first 3 years
    - ❑ 7. Normal during first 4–5 years

13. (Age 4–8 months) Did the child reach out or prepare himself to be picked up when mother approached him?
    - ❏ 1. Yes, or I believe so
    - ❏ 2. No, I don't think he did
    - ❏ 3. No, definitely not
    - ❏ 4. Don't know

14. Did the child rock in his crib as a baby?
    - ❏ 1. Yes, quite a lot
    - ❏ 2. Yes, sometimes
    - ❏ 3. No, or very little
    - ❏ 4. Don't know

15. At what age did the child learn to walk alone?
    - ❏ 1. 8–12 months
    - ❏ 2. 13–15 months
    - ❏ 3. 16–18 months
    - ❏ 4. 19–24 months
    - ❏ 5. 25–36 months
    - ❏ 6. 37 months or later, or does not walk alone

16. Which describes the change from crawling to walking?
    - ❏ 1. Normal change from crawling to walking
    - ❏ 2. Little or no crawling, gradual start of walking
    - ❏ 3. Little or no crawling, sudden start of walking
    - ❏ 4. Prolonged crawling, sudden start of walking
    - ❏ 5. Prolonged crawling, gradual start of walking
    - ❏ 6. Other, or don't know

17. During the child's first year, did he seem to be unusually intelligent?
    - ❏ 1. Suspected high intelligence
    - ❏ 2. Suspected average intelligence
    - ❏ 3. Child looked somewhat dull

18. During the child's first 2 years, did he like to be held?
    - ❏ 1. Liked being picked up; enjoyed being held
    - ❏ 2. Limp and passive on being held
    - ❏ 3. You could pick child up and hold it only when and how it preferred
    - ❏ 4. Notably stiff and awkward to hold
    - ❏ 5. Don't know

19. Before age 3, did the child ever imitate another person?
    - ❏ 1. Yes, waved bye-bye
    - ❏ 2. Yes, played pat-a-cake
    - ❏ 3. Yes, other (_____)
    - ❏ 4. Two or more of above (which? 1____2____3____)
    - ❏ 5. No, or not sure

20. Before age 3, did the child have an unusually good memory?
- ❏ 1. Remarkable memory for songs, rhymes, TV commercials, etc., in words
- ❏ 2. Remarkable memory for songs, music (humming only)
- ❏ 3. Remarkable memory for names, places, routes, etc.
- ❏ 4. No evidence for remarkable memory
- ❏ 5. Apparently rather poor memory
- ❏ 6. Both 1 and 3
- ❏ 7. Both 2 and 3

21. Did you ever suspect the child was very nearly deaf?
- ❏ 1. Yes
- ❏ 2. No

22. (Age 2–4) Is child "deaf" to some sounds but hears others?
- ❏ 1. Yes, can be "deaf" to loud sounds, but hear low ones
- ❏ 2. No, this is not true of him

23. (Age 2–4) Does child hold his hands in strange postures?
- ❏ 1. Yes, sometimes or often
- ❏ 2. No

24. (Age 2–4) Does child engage in rhythmic or rocking activity for very long periods of time (like on rocking-horse or chair, jumpchair, swing, etc.)?
- ❏ 1. Yes, this is typical
- ❏ 2. Seldom does this
- ❏ 3. Not true of him

25. (Age 2–4) Does child ever "look through" or "walk through" people, as though they weren't there?
- ❏ 1. Yes, often
- ❏ 2. Yes, I think so
- ❏ 3. No, doesn't do this

26. (Age 2–5) Does child have any unusual cravings for things to eat or chew on?
- ❏ 1. Yes, salt or salty foods
- ❏ 2. Yes, often chews metal objects
- ❏ 3. Yes, other (_____)
- ❏ 4. Yes, more than 2 above (which? _____)
- ❏ 5. No, or not sure

27. (Age 2–4) Does child have certain eating oddities, such as refusing to drink from a transparent container, eating only hot (or cold) food, eating only one or two foods, etc.?
- ❏ 1. Yes, definitely
- ❏ 2. No, or not to any marked degree
- ❏ 3. Don't know

28. Would you describe your child around 3 or 4 as often seeming "in a shell," or so distant and "lost in thought" that you couldn't reach him?
- ❏ 1. Yes, this is a very accurate description
- ❏ 2. Once in awhile he might possibly be like that
- ❏ 3. Not an accurate description

29. (Age 2–5) Is he cuddly?
   - ❏ 1. Definitely, likes to cling to adults
   - ❏ 2. Above average (likes to be held)
   - ❏ 3. No, rather stiff and awkward to hold
   - ❏ 4. Don't know

30. (Age 3–5) Does the child deliberately hit his own head?
   - ❏ 1. Never, or rarely
   - ❏ 2. Yes, usually by slapping it with his hand
   - ❏ 3. Yes, usually by banging it against someone else's legs or head
   - ❏ 4. Yes, usually by hitting walls, floor, furniture, etc.
   - ❏ 5. Several of above (which? 2____3____4____)

31. (Age 3–5) How well physically coordinated is the child (running, walking, balancing, climbing)?
   - ❏ 1. Unusually graceful
   - ❏ 2. About average
   - ❏ 3. Somewhat below average, or poor

32. (Age 3–5) Does the child sometimes whirl himself like a top?
   - ❏ 1. Yes, does this often
   - ❏ 2. Yes, sometimes
   - ❏ 3. Yes, if you start him out
   - ❏ 4. No, he shows no tendency to whirl

33. (Age 3–5) How skillful is the child in doing fine work with his fingers or playing with small objects?
   - ❏ 1. Exceptionally skillful
   - ❏ 2. Average for age
   - ❏ 3. A little awkward, or very awkward
   - ❏ 4. Don't know

34. (Age 3–5) Does the child like to spin things like jar lids, coins, or coasters?
   - ❏ 1. Yes, often and for rather long periods
   - ❏ 2. Very seldom, or never

35. (Age 3–5) Does child show an unusual degree of skill (much better than normal child his age) at any of the following:
   - ❏ 1. Assembling jigsaw or similar puzzles
   - ❏ 2. Arithmetic computation
   - ❏ 3. Can tell day of week a certain date will fall on
   - ❏ 4. Perfect musical pitch
   - ❏ 5. Throwing and/or catching a ball
   - ❏ 6. Other (_____)
   - ❏ 7. More than one of above (which? _____)
   - ❏ 8. No unusual skill, or not sure

36. (Age 3–5) Does the child sometimes jump up and down gleefully when pleased?
   - ❏ 1. Yes, this is typical
   - ❏ 2. No, or rarely

37. (Age 3–5) Does child sometimes line things up in precise evenly spaced rows and insist they not be disturbed?

- ❑ 1. No
- ❑ 2. Yes
- ❑ 3. Not sure

38. (Age 3–5) Does the child refuse to use his hands for an extended period of time?

- ❑ 1. Yes
- ❑ 2. No

39. Was there a time before age 5 when the child strongly insisted on listening to music on records?

- ❑ 1. Yes, insisted on only certain records
- ❑ 2. Yes, but almost any record would do
- ❑ 3. Liked to listen, but didn't demand to
- ❑ 4. No special interest in records

40. (Age 3–5) How interested is the child in mechanical objects such as the stove or vacuum cleaner?

- ❑ 1. Little or no interest
- ❑ 2. Average interest
- ❑ 3. Fascinated by certain mechanical things

41. (Age 3–5) How does the child usually react to being interrupted in what he is doing?

- ❑ 1. Rarely or never gets upset
- ❑ 2. Sometimes gets mildly upset; rarely very upset
- ❑ 3. Typically gets very upset

42. (Age 3–5) Will the child readily accept new articles of clothing (shoes, coats, etc.)?

- ❑ 1. Usually resists new clothes
- ❑ 2. Doesn't seem to mind, or enjoys them

43. (Age 3–5) Is child upset by certain things that are not "right" (like crack in the wall, spot on rug, books leaning in bookcase, broken rung on chair, pipe held and not smoked)?

- ❑ 1. Not especially
- ❑ 2. Yes, such things upset him greatly
- ❑ 3. Not sure

44. (Age 3–5) Does child adopt complicated "rituals" which make him very upset if not followed (like putting many dolls to bed in a certain order, taking exactly the same route between two places, dressing according to a precise pattern, or insisting that only certain words be used in a given situation)?

- ❑ 1. Yes, definitely
- ❑ 2. Not sure
- ❑ 3. No

45. (Age 3–5) Does child get very upset if certain things he is used to are changed (like furniture or toy arrangement, or certain doors which must be left open or shut)?

- ❏ 1. No
- ❏ 2. Yes, definitely
- ❏ 3. Slightly true

46. (Age 3–5) Is the child destructive?

- ❏ 1. Yes, this is definitely a problem
- ❏ 2. Not deliberately or severely destructive
- ❏ 3. Not especially destructive

47. (Age 3–5) Is the child unusually physically pliable (can be led easily; melts into your arms)?

- ❏ 1. Yes
- ❏ 2. Seems normal in this way
- ❏ 3. Definitely not pliable

48. (Age 3–5) Which single description, or combination of two descriptions, best characterizes the child?

- ❏ 1. Hyperactive, constantly moving, changes quickly from one thing to another
- ❏ 2. Watches television quietly for long periods
- ❏ 3. Sits for long periods

For example, stares into space or plays repetitively with objects, without apparent purpose

- ❏ 4. Combination of 1 and 2
- ❏ 5. Combination of 2 and 3
- ❏ 6. Combination of 1 and 3

49. (Age 2–5) Does the child seem to want to be liked?

- ❏ 1. Yes, unusually so
- ❏ 2. Just normally so
- ❏ 3. Indifferent to being liked; happiest when left alone

50. (Age 3–5) Is child sensitive and/or affectionate?

- ❏ 1. Is sensitive to criticism and affectionate
- ❏ 2. Is sensitive to criticism, not affectionate
- ❏ 3. Not sensitive to criticism, is affectionate
- ❏ 4. Not sensitive to criticism nor affectionate

51. (Age 3–5) Is it possible to direct child's attention to an object some distance away or out a window?

- ❏ 1. Yes, no special problem
- ❏ 2. He rarely sees things very far out of reach
- ❏ 3. He examines things with fingers and mouth only

52. (Age 3–5) Do people consider the child especially attractive?
- ❑ 1. Yes, very good-looking child
- ❑ 2. No, just average
- ❑ 3. Faulty in physical appearance

53. (Age 3–5) Does the child look up at people (meet their eyes) when they are talking to him?
- ❑ 1. Never, or rarely
- ❑ 2. Only with parents
- ❑ 3. Usually does

54. (Age 3–5) Does the child take an adult by the wrist to use adult's hand (to open door, get cookies, turn on TV, etc.)?
- ❑ 1. Yes, this is typical
- ❑ 2. Perhaps, or rarely
- ❑ 3. No

55. (Age 3–5) Which set of terms best describes the child?
- ❑ 1. Confused, self-concerned, perplexed, dependent, worried
- ❑ 2. Aloof, indifferent, self-contented, remote

56. (Age 3–5) Is the child extremely fearful?
- ❑ 1. Yes, of strangers or certain people
- ❑ 2. Yes, of certain animals, noises or objects
- ❑ 3. Yes, of 1 and 2 above
- ❑ 4. Only normal fearfulness
- ❑ 5. Seems unusually bold and free of fear
- ❑ 6. Child ignores or is unaware of fearsome objects

57. (Age 3–5) Does he fall or get hurt in running or climbing?
- ❑ 1. Tends toward falling or injury
- ❑ 2. Average in this way
- ❑ 3. Never, or almost never, exposes self to falling
- ❑ 4. Surprisingly safe despite active climbing, swimming, etc.

58. (Age 3–5) Is there a problem in that the child hits, pinches, bites or otherwise injures himself or others?
- ❑ 1. Yes, self only
- ❑ 2. Yes, others only
- ❑ 3. Yes, self and others
- ❑ 4. No, not a problem

59. At what age did the child say his first words (even if later stopped talking)?
- ❑ 1. Has never used words
- ❑ 2. 8–12 months
- ❑ 3. 13–15 months
- ❑ 4. 16–24 months
- ❑ 5. 2 years–3 years
- ❑ 6. 3 years–4 years
- ❑ 7. After 4 years old
- ❑ 8. Don't know

60. On lines below list child's first six words (as well as you can remember them).

_____

_____

61. (Before age 5) Did the child start to talk, then become silent again for a week or more?
   - ❑ 1. Yes, but later talked again (age stopped____ duration____)
   - ❑ 2. Yes, but never started again (age stopped____)
   - ❑ 3. No, continued to talk, or never began talking

62. (Before age 5) Did the child start to talk, then stop, and begin to whisper instead, for a week or more?
   - ❑ 1. Yes, but later talked again (age stopped____ duration____)
   - ❑ 2. Yes, still only whispers (age stopped talking ____)
   - ❑ 3. Now doesn't even whisper (age stopped talking ____ age stopped whispering ____)
   - ❑ 4. No, continued to talk, or never began talking

63. (Age 1–5) How well could the child pronounce his first words when learning to speak, and how well could he pronounce difficult words between 3 and 5?
   - ❑ 1. Too little speech to tell, or other answer
   - ❑ 2. Average or below average pronunciation of first words ("wabbit," etc.), and also poor at 3 to 5
   - ❑ 3. Average or below on first words, unusually good at 3–5
   - ❑ 4. Unusually good on first words, average or below at 3–5
   - ❑ 5. Unusually good on first words, and also at 3–5

64. (Age 3–5) Is the child's vocabulary (the number of things he can name or point to accurately) greatly out of proportion to his ability to "communicate" (to answer questions or tell you something)?
   - ❑ 1. He can point to many objects I name, but doesn't speak or "communicate"
   - ❑ 2. He can accurately name many objects, but not "communicate"
   - ❑ 3. Ability to "communicate" is pretty good—about what you would expect from the number of words he knows
   - ❑ 4. Doesn't use or understand words

65. When the child spoke his first sentences, did he surprise you by using words he had not used individually before?
   - ❑ 1. Yes (Any examples? _____)
   - ❑ 2. No
   - ❑ 3. Not sure
   - ❑ 4. Too little speech to tell

66. How did child refer to himself on first learning to talk?

- ❑ 1. "(John) fall down," or "Baby (or Boy) fall down."
- ❑ 2. "Me fall down," or "I fall down"
- ❑ 3. "(He, Him, She, or Her) fall down"
- ❑ 4. "You fall down"
- ❑ 5. Any combination of 1, 2, and/or 3
- ❑ 6. Combination of 1 and 4
- ❑ 7. No speech or too little speech as yet

67. (Age 3–5) Does child repeat phrases or sentences that he has heard in the past (maybe using a hollow, parrot-like voice), what is said having little or no relation to the situation?

- ❑ 1. Yes, definitely, except voice not hollow or parrot-like
- ❑ 2. Yes, definitely, including peculiar voice tone
- ❑ 3. Not sure
- ❑ 4. No
- ❑ 5. Too little speech to tell

68. (Before age 5) Can the child answer a simple question like "What is your first name?" or "Why did Mommy spank Billy?"

- ❑ 1. Yes, can answer such questions adequately
- ❑ 2. No, uses speech, but can't answer questions
- ❑ 3. Too little speech to tell

69. (Before age 5) Can the child understand what you say to him, judging from his ability to follow instructions or answer you?

- ❑ 1. Yes, understands very well
- ❑ 2. Yes, understands fairly well
- ❑ 3. Understands a little, if you repeat and repeat
- ❑ 4. Very little or no understanding

70. (Before age 5) If the child talks, do you feel he understands what he is saying?

- ❑ 1. Doesn't talk enough to tell
- ❑ 2. No, he is just repeating what he has heard with hardly any understanding
- ❑ 3. Not just repeating—he understands what he is saying, but not well
- ❑ 4. No doubt that he understands what he is saying

71. (Before age 5) Has the child used the word "Yes?"

- ❑ 1. Has used "Yes" fairly often and correctly
- ❑ 2. Seldom has used "Yes," but has used it
- ❑ 3. Has used sentences, but hasn't used word "Yes"
- ❑ 4. Has used a number of other words or phrases, but hasn't used word "Yes"
- ❑ 5. Has no speech, or too little speech to tell

72. (Age 3–5) Does the child typically say "yes" by repeating the same question he has been asked? (Example: You ask "Shall we go for a walk, Honey?" and he indicates he does want to go by saying "Shall we go for a walk, Honey" or "Shall we go for a walk?")

  ❑ 1. Yes, definitely, does not say "Yes" directly
  ❑ 2. No, would say "Yes" or "OK" or similar answer
  ❑ 3. Not sure
  ❑ 4. Too little speech to say

73. (Before age 5) Has the child asked for something by using the same sentence you would use when you offer it to him? (Example: The child wants milk, so he says: "Do you want some milk?" or "You want some milk")

  ❑ 1. Yes, definitely (uses "You" instead of "I")
  ❑ 2. No, would ask differently
  ❑ 3. Not sure
  ❑ 4. Not enough speech to tell

74. (Before age 5) Has the child used the word "I"?

  ❑ 1. Has used "I" fairly often and correctly
  ❑ 2. Seldom has used "I," but has used it correctly
  ❑ 3. Has used sentences, but hasn't used the word "I"
  ❑ 4. Has used a number of words or phrases, but hasn't used the word "I"
  ❑ 5. Has used "I," but only where the word "you" belonged
  ❑ 6. Has no speech, or too little speech to tell

75. (Before age 5) How does the child usually say "No" or refuse something?

  ❑ 1. He would just say "No"
  ❑ 2. He would ignore you
  ❑ 3. He would grunt and wave his arms
  ❑ 4. He would use some rigid meaningful phrase (like "Don't want it!" or "No milk!" or "No walk!")
  ❑ 5. Would use phrase having only private meaning like "Daddy go in car"
  ❑ 6. Other, or too little speech to tell

76. (Before age 5) Has the child used one word or idea as a substitute for another, for a prolonged time? (Example: always says "catsup" to mean "red," or uses "penny" for "drawer" after seeing pennies in a desk drawer)

  ❑ 1. Yes, definitely
  ❑ 2. No
  ❑ 3. Not sure
  ❑ 4. Too little speech to tell

77. Knowing what you do now, at what age do you think you could have first detected the child's abnormal behavior? That is, when did detectable abnormal behavior actually begin? (Under "A," indicate when you might have; under "B" when you did.) '

	A	B
❑ 1. In first 3 months		
❑ 2. 4–6 months		
❑ 3. 7–12 months		
❑ 4. 13–24 months		
❑ 5. 2 years–3 years		
❑ 6. 3 years–4 years		
❑ 7. After 4th year		

78 & 78. Parents' highest educational level

77. (Father)	78. (Mother)	
		1. Did not graduate high school
		2. High school graduate
		3. Post high school tech. training
		4. Some college
		5. College graduate
		6. Some graduate work
		7. Graduate degree ( )

79. Indicate the child's nearest blood relatives, including parents, who have been in a mental hospital or who were known to have been seriously mentally ill or retarded. Consider parents, siblings, grandparents, uncles and aunts.

If none, check here:

Relationship	Diagnosis, if known (Schizophrenia, Depressive, Other)
1.	
2.	
3.	
4.	
5.	

Form E2, Part 2

Please answer the following questions by writing "1" if *Very True*, "2" if *True* and "3" if *False* on the line preceding the question. Except for the first two questions, which pertain to the child before age 2, answer "Very True" (1) or "True" (2) if the statement described the child any time before his 10th birthday. If the statement is not particularly true of the child before age 10, answer "False" (3). Remember: 1 = Very True, 2 = True, 3 = False.

80. ___ Before age 2, arched back and bent head back, when held

81. ___ Before age 2, struggled against being held

82. ___ Abnormal craving for certain foods

83. ___ Eats unusually large amounts of food

84. ___ Covers ears at many sounds

85. ___ Only certain sounds seem painful to him

86. ___ Fails to blink at bright lights

87. ___ Skin color lighter or darker than others in family
(which: lighter_____ darker_____)

88. ___ Prefers inanimate (nonliving) things

89. ___ Avoids people

90. ___ Insists on keeping certain object with him

91. ___ Always frightened or very anxious

92. ___ Inconsolable crying

93. ___ Notices changes or imperfections and tries to correct them

94. ___ Tidy (neat, avoids messy things)

95. ___ Has collected a particular thing (toy horses, bits of glass, etc.)

96. ___ After delay, repeats *phrases* he has heard

97. ___ After delay, repeats *whole sentences* he has heard

98. ___ Repeats *questions* or *conversations* he has heard, over and over, without variation

99. ___ Gets "hooked" or fixated on one topic (like cars, mops, death)

100. ___ Examines surfaces with fingers

101. ___ Holds bizarre pose or posture

102. ___ Chews or swallows nonfood objects

103. ___ Dislikes being touched or held

104. ___ Intensely aware of odors

105. ___ Hides skill or knowledge, so you are surprised later on

106. ___ Seems not to feel pain

107. ___ Terrified at unusual happenings

108. ___ Learned words useless to himself

109. ___ Learned certain words, then stopped using them

Use the rest of this sheet for supplying additional information that you think may lead to understanding the cause or diagnosis of the child's illness.

CARS: Childhood Autism Rating Scale (sample)

The following items are a sample of the questions found on the Childhood Autism Rating Scale (Eric Schopler, Robert Reichler, MD, and Barbara Rochen Renner, Western Psychological Services, Los Angeles: 1993), also known as the CARS. This instrument is often used to evaluate young children who may have autistic-spectrum disorders.

Evaluators using the CARS rate the child on a scale from one to four in each of fifteen areas. Children with a probable diagnosis of PDD-NOS or atypical PDD generally (but not always) fall between 30 and 37 on the complete CARS scale, which indicates a mild or moderate degree of autistic behavior.

Relating to People

Rating	Behavior
1	No evidence of difficulty or abnormality in relating to people. The child's behavior is appropriate for his or her age. Some shyness, fussiness, or annoyance at being told what to do may be observed, but not to an atypical degree.
1.5	(if between these points)
2	Mildly abnormal relationships. The child may avoid looking the adult in the eye, avoid the adult or become fussy if interaction is forced, be excessively shy, not be as responsive to the adult as is typical, or cling to parents somewhat more than most children of the same age.
2.5	(if between these points)
3	Moderately abnormal relationships. The child shows aloofness (seems unaware of adult) at times. Persistent and forceful attempts are necessary to get the child's attention at times. Minimal contact is initiated by the child.
3.5	(if between these points)
4	Severely abnormal relationships. The child is consistently aloof or unaware of what the adult is doing. He or she almost never responds or initiates contact with the adult. Only the most persistent attempts to get the child's attention have any effect.

Body Use

Rating	Behavior
1	Age-appropriate body use. The child moves with the same ease, agility, and coordination of a normal child of the same age.
1.5	(if between these points)
2	Mildly abnormal body use. Some minor peculiarities may be present, such as clumsiness, repetitive movements, poor coordination, or the rare appearance of more unusual movements.
2.5	(if between these points)
3	Moderately abnormal body use. Behaviors that are clearly strange or unusual for a child of this age may include strange finger movements, peculiar finger or body posturing, staring or picking at the body, self-directed aggression, rocking, spinning, finger-wiggling, or toe-walking.
3.5	(if between these points)
4	Severely abnormal body use. Intense or frequent movements of the type listed above are signs of severely abnormal body use. These behaviors may persist despite attempts to discourage them or involve the child in other activities.

Adaptation to Change

Rating	Behavior
1	Age-appropriate response to change. While the child may notice or comment on changes in routine, he or she accepts these changes without undue distress.
1.5	(if between these points)
2	Mildly abnormal adaptation to change. When an adult tries to change tasks, the child may continue the same activity or use the same materials.
2.5	(if between these points)
3	Moderately abnormal adaptation to change. The child actively resists changes in routine, tries to continue the old activity, and is difficult to distract. He or she may become angry and unhappy when an established routine is altered.
3.5	(if between these points)
4	Severely abnormal adaptation to change. The child shows severe reactions to change. If a change is forced, he or she may become extremely angry or uncooperative and respond with tantrums.

Listening Response

Rating	Behavior
1	Age-appropriate listening response. The child's listening behavior is normal and appropriate for age. Listening is used together with other senses.
1.5	(if between these points)
2	Mildly abnormal listening response. There may be some lack of response, or mild overreaction to certain sounds. Responses to sounds may be delayed, and sounds may need repetition to catch the child's attention. The child may be distracted by extraneous sounds.
2.5	(if between these points)
3	Moderately abnormal listening response. The child's responses to sounds vary; often ignores a sound the first few times it is made; may be startled or cover ears when hearing some everyday sounds.
3.5	(if between these points)
4	Severely abnormal listening response. The child overreacts and/or under reacts to sounds to an extremely marked degree, regardless of the type of sound.

Verbal Communication

Rating	Behavior
1	Normal verbal communication, age and situation appropriate.
1.5	(if between these points)
2	Mildly abnormal verbal communication. Speech shows overall retardation. Most speech is meaningful; however, some echolalia or pronoun reversal may occur. Some peculiar words or jargon may be used occasionally.
2.5	(if between these points)
3	Moderately abnormal verbal communication. Speech may be absent. When present, verbal communication may be a mixture of some meaningful speech and some peculiar speech such as jargon, echolalia, or pronoun reversal. Peculiarities in meaningful speech include excessive questioning or preoccupation with particular topics.
3.5	(if between these points)
4	Severely abnormal verbal communication. Meaningful speech is not used. The child may make infantile squeals, weird or animal-like sounds, complex noises approximating speech, or may show persistent, bizarre use of some recognizable words or phrases.

This sample was used with permission from Western Psychological Services and the authors.

The complete Childhood Autism Rating Scale is available to qualified professionals. Please write to:

Western Psychological Services
12031 Wilshire Boulevard.
Los Angeles, CA 90025

Notes

Chapter 1, *The Medical Facts About PDDs*

1. Dr. Bernard Rimland, "Plain Talk About PDD and the Diagnosis of Autism,"*Autism Research Review International* 7, no. 2 (Autism Research Institute, 1993).
2. Dr. Bernard Rimland, *Autism Research Review International* 11, no. 3 (Autism Research Institute, 1997).
3. P. Bolton and P. Griffiths, "Association of tuberous sclerosis of temporal lobes with autism and atypical autism," *Lancet* 349 (December 1997): 392-395.
4. A. J. Allan, MD, "Group A Streptococcal Infections and Childhood Neuropsychiatric Disorders—Relationships and Therapeutic Implications," *CNS Drugs* (October 1997).
5. V. K. Singh, MD, et al., "Serological Association of Measles Virus and Human Herpesvirus-6 with Brain Autoantibodies in Autism," *Clinical Immunology and Immunopathology* 89 (October 1998): 105-108.
6. Andrew Makefield, MD, et al., "Ileal-Lymphoid-Nodular Hyperplasia, Non-specific Colitis, and Pervasive Developmental Disorder in Children," *Lancet 351* (February 1998): 637-41.

Chapter 3, *Getting a Diagnosis*

1. Elizabeth Costello et al., "The Great Smoky Mountains Study of Youth: Functional Impairment and Serious Emotional Disturbance (SED)," *Archives of General Psychiatry* (1988): 1107-1116.

Chapter 5, *Medical Interventions*

1. *The Pill Book: 18th Edition* (New York: Bantam Books, 1988).
2. Susan Swedo, MD, et al., "Identification of Children with Pediatric Autoimmune Neuropsychiatric Disorders Associated with Streptococcal Infections by a Marker Associated with Rheumatic Fever," *American Journal of Psychiatry* 154 (January 1997): 110-112.
3. A. Weizman, MD, et al., "Abnormal Immune Response to Brain Tissue Antigen in the Syndrome of Autism," *American Journal of Psychiatry* 139, no. 11 (November 1982): 1462-1465. Eric Hollander et al., "B Lymphocyte Antigen D8/17 and Repetitive Behaviors in Autism," *American Journal of Psychiatry* 156, no. 2 (February 1999): 317-20. V. K. Singh, MD, et al., "Antibodies to Myelin Basic Protein in Children with Autistic Behavior," *Brain, Behavior and Immunity* 7, no. 1 (March 1993): 97-103.

4. Sidney Baker, MD, and Dr. Jon Pangborn, *Clinical Assessment Options for Children with Autism and Related Disorders: A Biomedical Approach* (San Diego: Autism Research Institute, 1998). This text is better known as the *DAN! Clinical Options Manual*.

5. Defeat Autism Now! Practitioner List, Autism Research Institute, *http://www.autism.com/ari/danlist.html*.

6. Andrew Wakefield, MD, et al., "Ileal-Lymphoid-Nodular Hyperplasia, Non-Specific Colitis, and Pervasive Developmental Disorder in Children," *The Lancet* 351: 9103 (February 1998).

7. Dr. Bernard Rimland, "Dimethylglycine (DMG) for Autism," (1996), *http://www.autism.com/ari/dmg2.html*.

8. Terence Monmaney, "St. John's wort: Regulatory vacuum leaves doubt about potency, effects of herb used for depression," *Los Angeles Times* (August 31, 1998).

Chapter 7, *Other Interventions*

1. R. Sandefur and E. Adams, "The Effects of Chiropractic Adjustments on the Behavior of Autistic Children: A Case Review," *Journal of the American Chiropractic Association* 21, no. 5 (December 1987).

2. Dr. Bernard Rimland, "Vitamin C in the Prevention and Treatment of Autism," 1998, Autism Research Institute (*http://www.autism.com/ari/editorials/vitaminc.html*).

3. Dr. Rosemary Waring, "Biochemical Parameters in Autistic Subgroups," October 1995 presentation to 4th Consensus Conference on Biological Basis and Clinical Perspectives in Autism, Troina, Sicily, based on ongoing studies at the University of Birmingham (UK) Biochemistry Department.

4. Dr. Robert J. Sinaiko, "The Biochemistry of Attentional/Behavioral Problems," presentation to the 1996 Feingold Association Conference (*http://www.feingold.org/sinaiko.shtml*).

5. R. S. Chamberlain and B. H. Herman, "A Novel Biochemical Model Linking Dysfunction in the Brain, Melatonin, Proopiomelanocortin Peptides, and Serotonin in Autism," *Biological Psychiatry* 28 (1990): 773-793.

6. M. Fux et al., "Inositol Treatment of Obsessive-Compulsive Disorder," *American Journal of Psychiatry* 153 (1996): 1219-1221.

7. J. Levine, "Controlled Trials of Inositol in Psychiatry," *European Neuropsychopharmacology* 7 (May 1997): 147-155.

8. T. Field et al., "Brief Report: Autistic Children's Attentiveness and Responsivity Improve After Touch Therapy," *Journal of Autism and Developmental Disorders* 27 (1997): 333-338.

Chapter 13, *Living with PDDs*

1. Demetrious Haracopos and Lennart Pedersen, "Sexuality and Autism, Danish Report," *http://giraffe.rmplc.co.uk/eduweb/sites/autism/sexaut.html* (1992).

Appendix D, *Medication Reference*

1. G. M. Realmuto, G. J. August, and B. D. Garfinkel, "Clinical effect of buspirone in autistic children," *Journal of Clinical Psychopharmacology* 9 (1989): 122-125.
2. J. J. Ratey et al., "Buspirone therapy for maladaptive behavior and anxiety in developmentally disabled persons," *Journal of Clinical Psychiatry* 50 (1989): 382-384.
3. A. Gedye, "Buspirone alone or with serotonergic diet reduced aggression in a developmentally disabled adult," *Biological Psychiatry* 30 (1991): 88-91.
4. J. J. Ratey et al., "Buspirone treatment of aggression and anxiety in mentally retarded patients: A multiple baseline, placebo lead-in study," *Journal of Clinical Psychiatry* 52 (1991): 159-162.
5. R. W. Ricketts et al., "Clinical effects of buspirone on intractable self-injury in adults with mental retardation," *Journal of the American Academy of Child and Adolescent Psychiatry* 33 (1994): 270-276.
6. C. T. Gordon et al., "A double-blind comparison of clomipramine, desipramine, and placebo in the treatment of autistic disorder," *Archives of General Psychiatry* 50 (1993): 441-447.
7. C. J. McDougle et al., "Clomipramine in autism: Preliminary evidence of efficacy," *Journal of the American Academy of Child and Adolescent Psychiatry* 31 (1992): 746-750.
8. H. J. Garber et al., "Clomipramine treatment of stereotypic behaviors and self-injury in patients with developmental disabilities," *Journal of the American Academy of Child and Adolescent Psychiatry* 31 (1992): 1157-1160.
9. J. R. Brasic et al., "Clomipramine ameliorates adventitious movements and compulsions in prepubertal boys with autistic disorder and severe mental retardation," *Neurology* 44 (1994): 1309-1312.
10. E. S. Brodkin et al., "Clomipramine in adults with pervasive developmental disorders: A prospective open-label investigation," *Journal of Child and Adolescent Psychopharmacology* (1997).
11. L. E. Sanchez et al., "A pilot study of clomipramine in young autistic children," *Journal of the American Academy of Child and Adolescent Psychiatry* 35 (1996): 537-544.
12. C. J. McDougle et al., "Effects of tryptophan depletion in drug-free adults with autistic disorder," *Archives of General Psychiatry* 53 (1996): 993-1000.
13. E. H. Cook Jr. et al., "Fluoxetine treatment of children and adults with autistic disorder and mental retardation," *Journal of the American Academy of Child and Adolescent Psychiatry* 31 (1992): 739-745.
14. A. Zuddas et al., "Clinical effects of clozapine on autistic disorder" (letter), *American Journal of Psychiatry* 153 (1996): 738.
15. S. E. Purdon et al., "Risperidone in the treatment of pervasive developmental disorder," *Canadian Journal of Psychiatry* 39 (1994): 400-405.
16. C. J. McDougle et al., "Risperidone in adults with autism or pervasive developmental disorder," *Journal of Child and Adolescent Psychopharmacology* 5 (1995): 273-282.
17. J. G. Simeon et al., "Risperidone effects in treatment-resistant adolescents: Preliminary case reports," *Journal of Child and Adolescent Psychopharmacology* 5 (1995): 69-79.

18. S. Fisman et al., "Case study: Anorexia nervosa and autistic disorder in an adolescent girl," *Journal of the American Academy of Child and Adolescent Psychiatry* 35 (1996): 937-940.

19. H. B. Demb, "Risperidone in young children with pervasive developmental disorders and other developmental disabilities" (letter), *Journal of Child and Adolescent Psychopharmacology* 6 (1996):79-80.

20. S. Fisman and M. Steele, "Use of risperidone in pervasive developmental disorders: A case series," *Journal of Child and Adolescent Psychopharmacology* 6 (1996): 177-190.

21. A. Hardan et al., "Case study: Risperidone treatment of children and adolescents with developmental disorders," *Journal of the American Academy of Child and Adolescent Psychiatry* 35 (1996): 1551-1556.

22. M. Rubin, "Use of atypical antipsychotics in children with mental retardation, autism, and other developmental disabilities," *Psychiatric Annals* 27 (1997): 219-221.

Glossary of Acronyms

AA	arachidonic acid
AAC	augmentative and alternative communication
ABA	Applied Behavioral Analysis
ABC	Aberrant Behavior Checklist
ABC-ASIEP	Autism Behavior Checklist of the Autism Screening Instrument for Educational Planning
ABIC	Adaptive Behavior Inventory for Children
ABR/BSER	Auditory Brainstem Response/Brain Stem Evoked Response
ACAP	Autistic Children's Activity Program
ADA	Americans with Disabilities Act
ADD	attention deficit disorder
ADHD	attention deficit hyperactivity disorder
ADI-R	Autism Diagnostic Interview-Revised
ADOS	Autism Diagnostic Observation Schedule
AFDC	Aid to Families with Dependent Children
AGRE	Autism Genetic Resource Exchange
AIDS	autoimmune deficiency syndrome
AIT	Auditory Integration Training
ALPHA	Assessment Link Between Phonology and Articulation Test
AMCHP	Association of Maternal and Child Health Programs
ANA	anti-neuronal antibody
ANDI	Autism Network for Dietary Intervention
APA	American Psychological Association
ARC	Association of Retarded Citizens
ARI	Autism Research Institute
ARRI	*Autism Research Review International*
ASD	autistic spectrum disorder

ASO/ASLO	group A beta-hemolytic streptococcus
ASPEN	Asperger Syndrome Education Network of America, Inc.
BASC	Behavior Assessment System for Children
BNF	*The British National Formulary*
BOS	Behavior Observation Scale for Autism
BRIAC	Behavior Rating Instrument for Autistic and other Atypical Children
BUN	blood urea nitrogen
CAMP	cyclic adenosine monophosphate
CAN	Cure Autism Now Foundation
CAP	comprehensive central auditory processing
CAPD	central auditory processing deficit
CARS	Childhood Autism Rating Scale
CAT	computer-assisted tomography
CBC	Achenbach Child Behavior Checklist
CCPT	child-centered play therapy
CELF-3	Clinical Evaluation of Language Fundamentals–3
CFIDS	chronic fatigue immune deficiency syndrome
CHADD	Children and Adults with Attention Deficit Disorders
CMS	Children's Memory Scale
CMS	chronic mononucleosis syndrome
CMV	cytomegalovirus
CNS	central nervous system
CPA	conditioned play audiometry
CRS	Conner's Rating Scales
CSHCN	Children with Special Health Care Needs Program
DAN!	Defeat Autism Now!
DARAS	Disability Access Rights and Advice Service
DASI-II	Developmental Assessment Screening Inventory II
DDP	Designated Disabled Program
DETS	Department of Education, Training and Employment
DGLA	dihomogamma-linolenic acid
DLA	Disability Living Allowance
DMG	Dimethylglycine

DMSO	dimethylsulfoxide
DNA	deoxyribonucleic acid
DO	Doctor of Osteopathy (Chiropractor)
DSM-IV	*Diagnostic and Statistical Manual of Mental Disorders*
EASe	Electronic Auditory Stimulation effect
EBV	Epstein-Barr virus
EEG	electroencephalogram
EFA	essential fatty acid
EIC	Earned Income Credit
EKG	electrocardiogram
EmA IgA	Endomysial Antibodies
EPS	extrapyramidal side effects
ESY	extended school year
FAPE	free and appropriate public education
FBA	functional behavior assessment
FC	Facilitated Communication (a form of AAC)
FCND	Feldenkrais for Children with Neurological Disorders
FDA	Federal Drug Administration
FEAT	Families for Early Autism Treatment
FIP	functional intervention plan
FOLKS	Friends of Landau-Kleffner Syndrome
FRAXA	fragile X syndrome
GABA	gamma-aminobutyric acid
GAGs	glycosaminoglycans
GARS	Gilliam Autism Rating Scale
GI	gastrointestinal
GLA	gammalinolenic acid
GP	general practitioner
HFA	high-functioning autism
HHV6, HHV7, HHV8, HSV-1, HSV-2	
	human herpes viruses
HMO	health maintenance organization
HNTBC	Halstead-Reitan Neuropsychological Test Battery for Children
HUD	Housing and Urban Development

HVP	hydrolyzed vegetable protein
IEP	Individualized Education Plan
IFA	Individualized Functional Assessment
IFSP	Individualized Family Service Plan
Ig	immunoglobin
IgA AGA	immunoglobin A Gliadin Antibodies
IgA ARA,	R1 type immunoglobin A Reticulin Antibodies
IgE	immunoglobulin E
IgG	immunoglobulin G
IgG1, IgG2, IgG3, IgG4	
	immunoglobulin G subclass abnormalities
IgM	immunoglobulin M
InLv	Independent Living on the Autistic Spectrum list
IPSEA	Independent Panel for Special Education Advice
IQ	intelligence quotient
IRC	Internet Relay Chat
IVIg	intravenous immunoglobulin infusion
JABA	*The Journal of Applied Behavior Analysis*
Kaufman-ABC	Kaufman Assessment Battery for Children
LDA	Learning Disabilities Association of America
Leiter-R	Leiter International Performance Scale—Revised
LEA	Local Educational Authority
LRE	least restrictive environment
LNNB	Luria-Nebraska Neuropsychological Battery
LNNB-CR	Luria-Nebraska Neuropsychological Battery—Children's Revision
LPAD	Learning Potential Assessment Device
MA	mental age
MAO	monoamine oxidase
MAOIs	Monoamineoxidase Inhibitors
MBD	minimal brain dysfunction
anti-MBP	myelin basic protein antibodies
MCT	medium chain triglycerides
MLT	melatonin
measles-IgG	measles virus antibodies

MMR	measles, mumps, and rubella (vaccine)
MRI	magnetic resonance imagery
MSD	multisystem neurological disorder
MSM	sulfur methyl-sulphonyl-methane
MTH	methamphetamine
NA	nucleic acid
NAAR	National Alliance for Autism Research
NAC	N-Acetyl-Cysteine
NAFP	neuron-axon filament protein
NAIC	National Association of Insurance Commissioners
NARHA	North American Riding for the Handicapped Association
NAS	National Autistic Society
NaSSA	noradrenergic and specific serotonergic antidepressant
ND	licensed naturopath
NICHCY	National Information Center for Children and Youth with Disabilities
NIDS	neuro-immune dysfunction syndromes
NIH	National Institutes of Health
NK cells	natural killer cells
NLP	neurolinguistic programming
NMS	neuroleptic malignant syndrome
NORD	National Organization for Rare Disorders Inc.
NRI	Norepinephrine Reuptake Inhibitor
NSAID	non-steroidal anti-inflammatory drug
OCD	obsessive-compulsive disorder
OCR	Office of Civil Rights
OHI	other health impaired
ORS	Ongoing Resourcing Scheme
OT	occupational therapy/therapist
PANDAS	Pediatric Autoimmune Neuropsychiatric Disorders Associated with Streptococcus
PAPS	phosphoadenylyl sulphate
PAS-ADD	Psychiatric Assessment Schedule for Adults with Developmental Disability
PCP	primary care provider

PDD	pervasive developmental disorder
PDD-NOS	pervasive developmental disorders not otherwise specified
PDMS	Peabody Developmental and Motor Scales
PDR	*Physicians' Desk Reference*
PEACH	Parents for the Early Intervention of Autism in Children
PEATC	Parent Educational Advocacy Training Center
PECS	Picture Exchange Communication System
PET	positron emission tomography
PIA	Parent Interviews for Autism
PIAT	Peabody Individual Achievement Test
PIC	Private Industry Council
PKU	phenylketonuria
PPA	phenylpropanolamine
PPVT-R	Peabody Picture Vocabulary Test—Revised
PRT	pivotal response training
PSC	Pediatric Symptom Checklist
PST	phenolsulfotransferase
PT	physical therapy/therapist
RAST	radioallergosorbent test
RET	rapid eye therapy
RINTB	Reitan-Indiana Neuropsychological Test Battery
SAD	seasonal affective disorder
S-B IV	Stanford-Binet Intelligence Test Fourth Edition
SBOs	**Soil-based organisms**
SCSIT	Southern California Sensory Integration Test
SED	seriously emotionally disturbed
SI	sensory integration
SIB	self-injurious behavior
SICD-R	Sequenced Inventory of Communication Development—Revised
SII	Sensory Integration International
SIPT	Sensory Integration and Praxis Tests
SPECT	single photon emission computed tomography
SNP	Special Needs Program
SWS	Supported Wage System

TARF	The Autism Research Foundation
TBP	Targeted Behaviour Program
SLP	speech and language pathologist
SSI	Supplemental/Social Security Income
SSRIs	selective serotonin reuptake inhibitors
TEACCH	structured teaching
TLC	Test of Language Competence
TOLD	Test of Language Development
TONI	Test of Non-Verbal Intelligence
TPE	therapeutic plasma exchange
TS	Tourette syndrome
TVP	textured vegetable protein
UCP	United Cerebral Palsy
WAIS-R	Weschler Adult Intelligence Scale
WAO	World Autism Organisation
WISC	Weschler Intelligence Scale for Children
WJPEB	Woodcock-Johnson Psycho Educational Battery
WPPSI	Weschler Preschool and Prima Scale of Intelligence
WRAT	Wide Range of Assessment Test

Index

A

American Association of Naturopathic
    Physicians, 205
American Psychological Association, 263
Americans with Disabilities Act, 286
    and community involvement, 333-
        334
amino acid profile, in diagnosis of
        immune-system-linked
        PDDs, 144
analysis, 183
Angelman syndrome, 29
    organizations for, 424
Angelo, Christopher, on law and PDDs,
    241-244
anger, coping with, 82-83
animal-assisted therapy, 167-168
    resources on, 412
anti-anxiety drugs, 117
antibiotics
    herbal, 221
    prophylactic therapy with, 148
anti-*Candida* diet, 226-227
antidepressants, 110-116
    natural, 115-116
antifungals, 152-153
anti-hypertension medications, 126-127
anti-neuronal antibody screen, in
        diagnosis of immune-
        system-linked PDDs, 144
antioxidants, 211-212
antipsychotics, 124-126
antispasmodic medications, 117-120
    for aggression or SIB, 120
anxiety, drugs for, 117
aphasia, 187
appeal
    of insurance coverage denial, 250-
        251
    of SSI denial, 357
applied behavior analysis, 84, 162-167
    drawbacks of, 165-166
    Greenspan on, 175
    outcomes in, 164
    programs similar to, 166-167
    resources on, 164-165, 411-412
apraxia, in PDDs, 26
arbitration, 242-243

ARC, and legal issues, 241
art therapy, 173
    resources on, 412
Asian medicine, 157
Asperger's syndrome, 22
    versus atypical PDD, 32
Assessment Link between Phonology
        and Articulation Test, 65
assessment, medical, 98-105
asthma, and allergies, 230-231
asthma medications, and PDDs, 139
Atehli, Annabel, on auditory integration
        training, 168
atonic seizures, 102
Attendants Allowance, UK, 359
Attention Deficit Disorders Evaluation
        Scale, 58
attention-deficit/hyperactivity disorder,
        versus PDDs, 27
atypical neuroleptics, 125
atypical PDD, 1-2
    categorization of, 19
    description of, 31-33
    and qualification for services, 278
audiological tests, 54-55
audiologists, in evaluation, 49, 52
auditory brain-stem response/brain
        stem-evoked response, 54
auditory integration
    resources on, 412-413
    training, 168-170
augmentative and alternative
        communication, 170-172
Australia
    Early Intervention programs in, 43-
        44
    education in, 313-314
    financial support in, 360-361
    legal advocacy in, 431
    national healthcare in, 258-259
autism
    brain differences in, 7
    classification of, in school systems,
        277-278
    factors affecting, 14-15
    genetics and, 12
    homeopathic remedies for, 205

autism (*continued*)
    national organizations for, 420-423
    research facilities for, 432-434
    resources for children on, 402-403
Autism Diagnostic Interview-Revised, 56
Autism Diagnostic Observation
    Schedule, 56
Autism Genetic Resource Exchange
    project, 159
Autism Research Institute, 19, 519
    on auditory integration training,
    168
    database of, 159
    Form E-3, 56
    Form E-2: Diagnostic Checklist, 56,
    159, 519-532
    on secretin, 151
    on stimulants, 120
Autism Society of America
    on auditory integration training,
    170
    and insurance advocacy, 263
    and legal issues, 241
autistic disorder, 22-23
autistic-like behavior, 31
autistic-like features, conditions with,
    28-31
autistic-spectrum disorders, 4, 31
    misinformation on, 195-196
    resources on, 401-402
autistic tendencies, 31
autoimmune disorders, and PDDs, 15,
    134-135
automatisms, 101
Axline, Virginia M., on play therapy,
    181
Ayres, Jean, on sensory integration, 182
Ayurvedic medicine, 157, 206-207, 491

B

Barron, Sean, 392
baseline data, in therapeutic intervention
    programs, 196
bathing, tips for, 343
Battelle Developmental Inventory, 61
Beck, Victoria and Gary, on secretin,
    151

behavior
    problems with, 323-324
    in school setting, problems with,
    297-299
    speech disorders and, 191-192
behavioral tests, 57-60
Behavior Assessment System for
    Children, 58
behavior modification
    programs for, 172-173. *See also*
    applied behavior analysis
    for self-injurious behavior, 157
Behavior Observation Scale for Autism,
    56
Behavior Rating Instrument for Autistic
    and Other Atypical
    Children, 56
Bérard, Guy, on auditory integration
    training, 168
Berry-Buktenica Tests, 64
Bettelheim, Bruno, 5, 328
Betts, Ellen, on insurance companies,
    236-239
bewilderment, 79-80
bibliotherapy, 370
bipolar disorder
    versus PDDs, 27
    SSRIs and, 111-112
blame. *See* genetic blame
blood count, in diagnosis of immune-
    system-linked PDDs, 143
blood tests, 100-101
    in diagnosis of immune-system-
    linked PDDs, 143-145
    with lithium use, 114
blood-type diet, 229
Bluestone, Judith, 175
bodywork, 232-234
Bondy, Andrew, and PECS, 171
bone conduction, 54
Boston Naming Test, 65
Brachmann-de Lange syndrome, 29
brain, 5
    electrical system of, 11
    in PDDs, 7-8
    structure of, 6, 6-7
brain stem, 6
    in autism, 7

Bratt, Berneen, on scams, 199
breakthrough drugs, 108-109
Broughton v. CIGNA, 242
Bruiniks-Oseretsky Test of Motor
    Proficiency, 64
Bufo toad toxin, 205
burnout, 325-326

C

California
    psychological assessment in, 47
    state healthcare in, 255
Callahan, Mary
    on allergy-induced autism, 138
    on living with child with
        disabilities, 317
Canada
    Early Intervention programs in, 43-
        44
    education in, 310-311
    financial support in, 358-359
    referrals in, 43
CanadaRx, 372
Canadian Naturopathic Association, 205
Candida albicans
    autism caused by, 35
    and diaper rash, 344
    diet to eliminate, 226-227
    medication for, 152-153
    and PDDs, 142
    tests for, in diagnosis of immune-
        system-linked PDDs, 144-
        145
    web site on, 227
case management
case management services, 380
casein, 141-142
    of medications, 129-131
    transition planning for, 368-369
casein-free diet, 224-226
caseworkers, in Early Intervention, 45
Cattell Scales, 61
caveman diet, 229
celiac disease, 142
    diet for, 226
    tests for, in diagnosis of immune-
        system-linked PDDs, 144

Center for the Study of Autism, visual
    training section, 231
central nervous system, 5, 132
cerebellum, 6
cerebral allergy. *See* allergy-induced
    autism
cerebral palsy, versus PDDs, 27
chemistry panel, in diagnosis of
    immune-system-linked
    PDDs, 143
child-development centers, regional,
    testing at, 48
Childhood Autism Rating Scale, 56-57,
    174, 519, 532-535
childhood disintegrative disorder, 23-24
childproofing
    household and household items,
        346-348
    your possessions, 346-348
    resources on, 408-409
Children's Memory Scale, 61
Chinese medicine, 206-207, 491
chiropractic, 157, 204
chronic fatigue immune deficiency
        syndrome
    and autism, 35
    and PDDs, 136
chronic mononucleosis syndrome, tests
        for, 144
classrooms
    diagnostic, 274
    in Early Intervention, 270-274
    successful, 287-292
        characteristics of, 287
    tips for, 292
classwork systems, 292
Clinical Evaluation of Language
        Fundamentals—3, 66
clothing
    special-needs, resources on, 409-
        410
    tips for, 343-344
cluttering, 187
COBRA plan, 247
coexisting conditions, medications and,
        153
cognitive-behavioral therapy, 181

college
    for students with PDDs, 90
    transition to, 310
College of Optometrists for Vision
        Development, 156
coloscopy, in diagnosis of immune-
        system-linked PDDs, 145
colostrum, 216
communication
    resources on, 418-419
    and support groups, 379
communication disorders
    versus PDDs, 26
    support organization for, 424
communication goals, 86-87
communications notebook, 276
community activities, 381-385
community isolation, and parents, 332-
        334
Community Trust associations for
        autism, 262
compassionate care exception, 245
complex partial seizure disorder,
        diagnosis of, 104
comprehensive central auditory
        processing testing, 54-55
Conner's Rating Scales, 58
Consent for Assessment form, 48
consolida/consound, 497
consultation appointment, 40-42
    preparation for, 38-39
Consumer Legal Remedies Act, 242
Continental Care Force, 365
Continental Pharmacy, 372
coping
    with diagnosis of PDDs, 76-83
    with seizures, 104-105
    with self-injurious behavior, 156-
        157
coprolalia, 189
Cornelia de Lange syndrome, 29
Corporate Angel, 365
Costello, Elizabeth, on pediatrician
        knowledge, 38
counseling, 181
court proceedings, 304-305
craniosacral therapy, 206, 233
creative coding, 245

Creutzfeldt-Jakob disease
    in IVIG, 146
    and PDDs, 136
cytomegalovirus, tests for, 144

D

D'Adamo, Peter J., 229
daily diary
    in diagnosis process, 39
    of therapeutic interventions, 196
daily life, tips for, 341-351
daily record keeping, 353-354
daily report form, for monitoring EI
        progress, 276
Dake, Lorelei, on speech therapy, 190
dance therapy, 173
day treatment centers, 274
decoration, tips for, 345-346
Defeat Autism Now! conference, 135
    protocol of, 234-235
dental care, and PDDs, 154-155
depression, with PDDs, 71
Designated Disabled Program, 311
Developmental Assessment Screening
        Inventory II, 61
developmental history, 68
developmental pediatrician
    on evaluation team, 49
    referral to, 42
Developmental Profile II, 61-62
Developmental Test of Visual-Motor
        Integration, 64
developmental tests, 60-63
diagnosis, 36-75
    disagreement with, 74-75
    personnel in, 36-37
    problems in, 41-42, 73-74
Diagnostic and Statistical Manual of
        Mental Disorders, fourth
        edition, on PDDs, 4
diagnostic classroom, 274
diagnostic tools, 519-535
diapers, 344
diarrhea, and PDDs, 14
diet, 224-230
    anti-Candida, 226-227
    blood-type, 229

Europe
    Early Intervention programs in, 43
    inclusion regulations in, 334
    referrals in, 43
    residential placement in, 388
evaluation facility, choice of, 48-49
evaluation instruments, 53-68
evaluation report, 69-71
    disagreement with, 74-75
evaluation team
    choice of, 49-51
    leader of, 50
expulsion, 299-300
extended school year services, 297
extrapyramidal side effects, of
            neuroleptics, 126
eye therapies, 231-232

F

facilitated communication, 171-172
    resources on, 414
family, 316-351. *See also* parents
    and ABA program, 165
    and IEP meeting, 279
    multigenerational, 337-338
    and picture communication, 171
    strife in, 317-318
    support from, 382
        lack of, 331-332
    and therapeutic interventions, 192-
            194
    tips for, 341-351
family counseling, 181
family dynamics, and PDDs, 5
family history, 68
family stories, 393-399
    about adoption and foster care,
            339-340
    about alternative interventions,
            201-203
    about atypical PDD, 32-33
    about autism, 23
    with childhood disintegrative
            disorder, 24
    about diagnosis, 2-3, 20-21, 37, 75
    about dreams, 16, 96
    about Early Intervention, 272-274

    about Epsom salt baths, 214
    about feelings, 77-82
    about fighting the system, 304
    about finances, 356, 358, 366
    about fragile X syndrome, 24-25
    about insurance, 261
    about insurance coverage, 239,
            243-246
    about living with a child with PDD,
            317-319, 322-329, 331-
            332, 334-335, 337
    about medical causes, 100
    about medications, 105, 118, 121,
            127-131, 150
    about metabolic disorders, 14, 140
    about misdiagnosis, 73-74
    about national healthcare, 255-259
    about natural antidepressants, 116
    about PDD-NOS diagnosis, 32
    about planning, 95
    about research, 158-159
    about Rett syndrome, 25-26
    about schooling, 289-291, 311,
            313-314
    about schools and diagnosis, 45-46
    about social opportunities, 285-286
    about speech disorders, 192
    about speech therapy, 190
    about strep infections, 133
    about supplements, 209-210, 216-
            217
    about support, 377, 381-385
    about therapeutic interventions,
            164-165, 173-174, 177-
            179, 185
    about therapeutic practitioners,
            196-197
    about transition planning, 368-369
    about vaccine-related PDDs, 137
family therapy, 334-335
Farmacia Rex S.R.L., 372
FastFoward program, 169-170, 413
fear, coping with, 77-79
Feingold diet, 227
Feldenkrais for Children with
            Neurological Disorders,
            233
Feldenkrais method, 233

insurance (*continued*)
and referral, 42
resources on, 404-405
schools and, 194
insurance companies, on PDDs, 236-239
insurance coverage
advocacy for, 263
compassionate care exception in, 245
educational services exemption in, 243-244
learning about, 249
mental health exemption in, 243
for new treatments, 245-246
intelligence tests, 60-63
International Chiropractic Pediatric Association, 204
Internet resources, on ABA, 165
intravenous immunoglobulin G, 146-147, 487
iridology, 232
Irlen lenses, 156, 231
resources on, 415
isolation
coping with, 375
and parents, 332-334

J

Jellinek, Michael S., 40

K

Kane, Patricia, on metabolic disorders, 140
Kanner's syndrome. *See* autism; autistic disorder
Katie Beckett waiver, 254
applying for, 254-255
Kaufman Assessment Battery for Children, 62
Kaufman, Barry Neil, on Son-Rise method, 178-179
Kaufman, Raun, 178-179
Ketchum, Caroline, on insurance advocacy, 263

ketogenic diet, 228-229
for seizures, 119
kidney stones, 211
Kinetic Family Drawing System for Family and School, 58-59
Kingsley, Emily Perl, on living with children with disabilities, 316-317
Kirkman Sales, 210
knitbone, 497
Koegel, Robert L., and pivotal response training, 180
Kozloff, Martin A., on behavior modification, 166-167
Kranowitz, Carol Stock, on sensory integration, 184
Kunin v. Benefit Trust Life Insurance Co., 240
kuru, and PDDs, 136

L

labels
information on, 18-20
problems with, 3-4
Landau-Kleffner syndrome, 29-30
language disorders, 188-189
law, and insurance coverage of PDD treatments, 240-243
leadership, and support groups, 378
leaky gut, 141-142
Learning Potential Assessment Device, 62
least restrictive environment, 287
Leiter International Performance Scale—Revised, 62
Lesch-Nyhan syndrome, and autistic features, 14
letter of medical necessity, 246
Lewis, Lisa, on casein-free/gluten-free diet, 226
Linwood method, 176-177
liquid medications, dosage and administration, 106-107
liver function test, 100
living with PDDs, 387-400
Local Educational Authority, UK, 312

multigenerational living, 337-338
multihandicapped, 277
multisystem neurological disorder, 34
music therapy, 173
    resources on, 412-413
mutism, selective, versus PDDs, 26-27
myoclonic seizures, 102

N

National Alliance for the Mentally Ill,
        drug study information,
        110
National Association of Hospitality
        Houses, 365
National Autistic Society, 257
national healthcare, 253-261
National Institutes of Health
    on secretin, 151
    on viruses, 146
National Institutes of Mental Health, on
        PANDAS treatment, 145-
        146
National Parks Service, 364
Natural Language Paradigm, 180
natural stimulants, 124
naturopathy, 157, 204-205
neighborhood activities, 383-385
nervines, 219
Neuro-Immune Dysfunction Syndromes
        Medical Research
        Advisory Board, 136
neuroleptic malignant syndrome, 113
neuroleptics, 124-126
    atypical, 125
    side effects of, 125-126
neurological disorders, combined, 28
neurologists
    definition of, 5
    and diagnosis of PDDs, 36
    in evaluation, 52
    on evaluation team, 49
neurology, 5-11
neurons, 7
    in autism, 7
    structure of, 8, 9
neuropsychiatric problems, of parents,
        327-328
neuropsychiatric tests, 57-60

NeuroSPECT, in diagnosis of immune-
        system-linked PDDs, 144
neurotransmitter(s), 8-11
    medications and, 110
    in transit, 10
Newman, Russ, on insurance coverage,
        263
New Zealand
    Early Intervention programs in, 44
    education in, 314-315
    financial support in, 361
    legal advocacy in, 431
    national healthcare in, 260-261
No Frills Pharmacy, 373
No Milk Page, 226
non-custodial parents, 338-339
noradrenergic and specific serotonergic
        antidepressant, 115

O

obsessive-compulsive disorder, 14
    versus PDDs, 27
    with PDDs, 71
    strep infection and, 133
occipital lobe, 6
occupational therapists
    in diagnosis of PDDs, 46
    in evaluation, 52
    on evaluation team, 49
occupational therapy, 177-178
    resources on, 417
    tests in, 63-64
Ongoing Resourcing Scheme, New
        Zealand, 314
online support groups, 377, 423-424
opiates, and leaky gut, 141-142
opioid blockers, 127
Opportunities Industrialization
        Commission, 309
Options Institute method, 178-179
Optometric Extension Program, 156
oral-motor apraxia, 188
oral tactile dysfunction, 186-187
organization, 183
orthomolecular medicine, 205-206
osteopathy, 206
otitis media, and PDDs, 135
overinvolvement, 324

over-the-counter stimulants, 123-124
Oxydess, 121, 452

P

PacifiCare Health Systems, Inc., 236-239
Paleolithic diet, 229
palilalia, 189
Parent Interviews for Autism, 57
parenting
    classes on, 322-323
    resources on, 405-406
parents. *See also* family
    and diagnosis, 37
    and discipline, 319-321
    and evaluation team, 50
    involvement with school, 296
    isolation and, 333, 375
    neuropsychiatric problems of, 327-328
    non-custodial, 338-339
    with PDDs, 396-399
    single, 336-337
    and special education assessment, 47-48
    and standardized test results, 53-54
    and testing, 67-68
parietal lobe, 6
partial seizures, 102
pathological demand avoidance
        syndrome, 35
Pauling, Linus, on orthomolecular
        medicine, 205-206
PDD-NOS, 1-2
    categorization of, 19
    description of, 31-32
    and qualification for services, 278
Peabody Developmental and Motor
        Scales, 62
Peabody Individual Achievement Test,
        62
Peabody Picture Vocabulary Test—
        Revised, 66
Pediatric Autoimmune Neuropsychiatric
        Disorder Associated with
        Streptococcus (PANDAS),
        133-134
    treatment of, 145-146

Pediatric Symptom Checklist, 40, 59
pediatricians
    and diagnosis of PDDs, 36-43
    problems with, 41-42
Peoples Pharmacy, 373
perseveration, 188
pervasive developmental disorders
    brain differences in, 7-8
    categories of, 18-35
    causes of, 5
    definition of, 4-5
    factors affecting, 14-15
    future with, 16-17
    genetics and, 12-13
    getting started after diagnosis of,
        76-97
    immune-system-linked, 132-153
        diagnosis in, 143-145
        treatment of, 145-153
    incidence of, 16
    insurance company's perspective
        on, 236-239
    as label, problems with, 3-4
    living with, 387-400
    medical facts about, 1-17
    national organizations for, 420-423
    new classifications of, 33-35
    resources on, for children, 402-403
    taking action on, 83-93
    web sites on, 403-404
petit mal seizures, 101
pharmaceutical companies, contact
        numbers for, 362-363
Pharmaceutical Manufacturers
        Association, directory of
        programs for indigent,
        362
Pharmacy Direct, 373
The Pharmacy Shop, 373
phenols, removal from diet, 214-215
phenylketonuria
    and autistic features, 14
    research into, 139
physical therapists
    in evaluation, 52
    on evaluation team, 49
physical therapy, 179-180
Picture Exchange Communication
        System, 171

pivotal response training, 167, 180
plan
    for goal achievement, 94
    making it happen, 95
plasmapheresis, 147-148
play therapy, 180-181
police, and disabled people, 350
Polygam (intravenous immunoglobulin
        G), 146-147, 487
Porcari, Damian, 165
Portwood, Madeleine, on sensory
        integration, 182
positron emission tomography, of brain,
        103-104
Potenza, Marc, on drug studies, 105,
        110
practitioners
    and adult diagnosis, 72
    as allies, 250
    and diagnosis of PDDs, 36
    in therapeutic interventions,
        evaluation of, 195-196
Prader-Willi syndrome, 30
    organizations for, 426-427
Preferred Prescription Plan, 373
prenatal infection, and PDDs, 15
Preschool Language Scale, 66
pressured speech, 112
primary care provider, 37
primary handicapping condition, 277
Private Industry Council, 309
private schools, 305-306
proanthocyanidins, 212, 510
probiotics, 217-218, 511
problem behaviors, 323-324
processing, 183
professional support, 379-381
projective tests, 57
prophylactic antibiotic therapy, 148
proprioceptive sense, 184
    sensory integration techniques for,
        186
Psychiatric Assessment Schedule for
        Adults with
        Developmental Disability,
        59
psychiatric tests, 57-60

psychiatrists
    in diagnosis of PDDs, 46
    in evaluation, 52
    on evaluation team, 49
psychoanalysis, 181
psychologists
    in diagnosis of PDDs, 46
    in evaluation, 52
    on evaluation team, 49
public advocacy, 304
Pugliese, Maria A., on addiction, 123

Q–R

radioallergosorbent test, 230
rapid eye therapy, 232
Rapp, Doris J., on allergy-induced
        PDDs, 138
rebound effect, 117, 121
record keeping, 352-354
    daily, 353-354
    school, 354
Record of Needs, 311-312
records, release of, 39
Recovery Zone site, 165
referral(s), 38
    for medication, 131-132
    problems in getting, 41-42
    roadblocks to, 42-43
referral forms, 250
regular classroom, 288
regular preschool classroom, EI in, 271
regulatory disorders, 34
Rehabilitation Act of 1973, Section 504,
        300-301
Reitan-Indiana Neuropsychological Test
        Battery, 59
relaxation techniques, 182
relief, 79
religious activities, 382-383
research on PDDs, 158-160
    facilities for, 432-434
resentment, 326-327
residential placement
    Linwood method in, 177
    options in, 387-388
    schooling in, 289
    for young children, 274-275

withdrawal
    from medications, 107-108
    social, 324
withdrawal dyskinesias, 125
Woodcock-Johnson Psycho Educational
                Battery—Revised, 63
work
    and PDDs, 389
    transition to, 309
World Health Organization, definition
                of autism, 56

X–Z
yeast infection. *See Candida albicans*
yogurt, 218

About the Author

 Mitzi Waltz, the author of *Pervasive Developmental Disorders: Finding a Diagnosis and Getting Help*, has been a professional journalist, writer, and editor for ten years, covering a range of topics from computers to domestic spy operations. She is the parent of a seven-year-old boy diagnosed with PDD-NOS and other neurological problems. Seven years of trying to solve the puzzle of her son's illness has called on all her research skills and has brought her into contact with top researchers in the field. She has been heavily involved in parent support work, both face-to-face and online, and has done a great deal of advocacy work in the medical, insurance, and education systems.

"I know from my advocacy work that there are thousands of families like mine out there, looking for answers but finding only a few pages in a neurology text, or perhaps a paragraph or two in a book about autism. Most parents are not trained researchers, and most would be afraid to cold-call a researcher at the National Institutes of Health or to challenge a school psychiatrist's incorrect assessment. I hope that my willingness to do so can help others better understand these disorders and how to treat them," says Mitzi.

Colophon

Patient-Centered Guides are about the experience of illness. They contain personal stories as well as a combination of practical and medical information. The faces on the covers of our Guides reflect the human side of the information we offer.

The cover of *Pervasive Developmental Disorders: Finding a Diagnosis and Getting Help* was designed by Edie Freedman using Adobe Photoshop 5.0 and QuarkXPress 3.32 with Onyx BT and Berkeley fonts from Bitstream. The cover photo is from Rubberball Productions and is used with their permission. The cover mechanical was prepared by Kathleen Wilson. The interior layout for the book was designed by Nancy Priest, Edie Freedman, and Alicia Cech. The interior fonts are Berkeley and Franklin Gothic. The text was prepared by Mike Sierra using FrameMaker 5.5. The book was copyedited by Lunaea Hougland and proofread by Phyllis Lindsay. Abigail Myers, Anna Snow, and Jane Ellin conducted quality assurance checks. The index was written by Jennifer Rushing-Schurr. The illustrations that appear in this book were produced by Robert Romano and Rhon Porter using Macromedia Freehand 8 and Adobe Photoshop 5. Interior composition for the book was done by Claire Cloutier LeBlanc, Sebastian Banker, Abigail Myers, and Anna Snow. Whenever possible, our books use RepKover™ lay-flat binding. If the page count exceeds the limit for lay-flat binding, perfect binding is used.

Patient-Centered Guides™

Questions Answered
Experiences Shared

We are committed to empowering individuals to evolve into informed consumers armed with the latest information and heartfelt support for their journey.

When your life is turned upside down, your need for information is great. You have to make critical medical decisions, often with what seems little to go on. Plus you have to break the news to family, quiet your own fears, cope with symptoms or treatment side effects, figure out how you're going to pay for things, and sometimes still get to work or get dinner on the table.

Patient-Centered Guides provide authoritative information for intelligent information seekers who want to become advocates of their own health. They cover the whole impact of illness on your life. In each book, there's a mix of:

- **Medical background for treatment decisions**
  We can give you information that can help you to intelligently work with your doctor to come to a decision. We start from the viewpoint that modern medicine has much to offer and also discuss complementary treatments. Where there are treatment controversies we present differing points of view.

- **Practical information**
  Once you've decided what to do about your illness, you still have to deal with treatments and changes to your life. We cover day-to-day practicalities, such as those you'd hear from a good nurse or a knowledgeable support group.

- **Emotional support**
  It's normal to have strong reactions to a condition that threatens your life or changes how you live. It's normal that the whole family is affected. We cover issues like the shock of diagnosis, living with uncertainty, and communicating with loved ones.

Each book also contains stories from both patients and doctors — medical "frequent fliers" who share, in their own words, the lessons and strategies they have learned when maneuvering through the often complicated maze of medical information that's available.

We provide information online, including updated listings of the resources that appear in this book. This is freely available for you to print out and copy to share with others, as long as you retain the copyright notice on the print-outs.

http://www.patientcenters.com

Other Books in the Series

Advanced Breast Cancer
A Guide to Living with Metastatic Disease
By Musa Mayer
ISBN 1-56592-522-X, Paperback 6" x 9", 542 pages, $19.95

"An excellent book...if knowledge is power, this book will be good medicine."
—David Spiegel, M.D.
Stanford University
Author,
Living Beyond Limits

Working with Your Doctor
Getting the Healthcare You Deserve
By Nancy Keene
ISBN 1-56592-273-5, Paperback, 6" x 9", 382 pages, $15.95

"Working with Your Doctor fills a genuine need for patients and their family members caught up in this new and intimidating age of impersonal, economically-driven health care delivery."
—James Dougherty, M.D.
Emeritus Professor of Surgery,
Albany Medical College

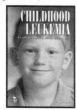

Childhood Leukemia
A Guide for Families, Friends & Caregivers
By Nancy Keene
ISBN 1-56592-191-7, Paperback, 6" x 9", 566 pages, $24.95

"What's so compelling about Childhood Leukemia *is the amount of useful medical information and practical advice it contains. Keene avoids jargon and lays out what's needed to deal with the medical system."*
—The Washington Post

Hydrocephalus
A Guide for Patients, Families & Friends
By Chuck Toporek and Kellie Robinson
ISBN 1-56592-410-X, Paperback, 6" x 9", 384 pages, $19.95

"In this book, the authors have provided a wonderful entry into the world of hydrocephalus to begin to remedy the neglect of this important condition. We are immensely grateful to them for their groundbreaking effort."
—Peter M. Black, M.D., Ph.D.
Franc D. Ingraham Professor of Neurosurgery,
Harvard Medical School
Neurosurgeon-in-Chief,
Brigham and Women's Hospital, Children's Hospital,
Boston, Massachusetts

Patient-Centered Guides
Published by O'Reilly & Associates, Inc.
Our products are available at a bookstore near you.
For information: **800-998-9938 • 707-829-0515 • info@oreilly.com**
101 Morris Street • Sebastopol • CA • 95472-9902

Your Child in the Hospital, Second Edition
A Practical Guide for Parents
By Nancy Keene and Rachel Prentice
ISBN 1-56592-573-4, Paperback, 5" x 8", 176 pages, $11.95

"When your child is ill or injured, the hospital setting can be overwhelming. Here is a terrific 'road map' to help keep families 'on track.'"

—James B. Fahner, M.D.
Division Chief,
Pediatric Hematology/Oncology,
DeVos Children's Hospital,
Grand Rapids, Michigan

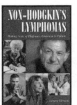

Choosing a Wheelchair
A Guide for Optimal Independence
By Gary Karp
ISBN 1-56592-411-8, Paperback, 5" x 8", 192 pages, $9.95

"I love the idea of putting knowledge often possessed only by professionals into the hands of new consumers. Gary Karp has done it. This book will empower people with disabilities to make informed equipment choices."

—Barry Corbet
Editor,
New Mobility Magazine

Non-Hodgkin's Lymphomas
Making Sense of Diagnosis, Treatment & Options
By Lorraine Johnston
ISBN 1-56592-444-4, Paperback, 6" x 9", 584 pages, $24.95

"When I gave this book to one of our patients, there was an instant, electric connection. A sense of enlightenment came over her while she absorbed the information. It was thrilling to see her so sparked with new energy and focus."

—Susan Weisberg, LCSW
Clinical Social Worker,
Stanford University Medical Center

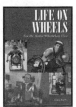

Life on Wheels
For the Active Wheelchair User
By Gary Karp
ISBN 1-56592-253-0, Paperback, 6" x 9", 576 pages, $24.95

"I think a book like this should be given to everyone in the rehab hospital ... it offers the broadest perspective of life on wheels that I've ever seen."

—Michelle Gittler, M.D.
Director,
Resident Training Program,
Schwab Rehab Hospital

Patient-Centered Guides
Published by O'Reilly & Associates, Inc.
Our products are available at a bookstore near you.
For information: **800-998-9938** • **707-829-0515** • **info@oreilly.com**
101 Morris Street • Sebastopol • CA • 95472-9902

Ten Patient Rights

1. Receive considerate and respectful care.

2. Obtain complete information on illness and treatment.

3. Participate in treatment decisions.

4. Give informed consent.

5. Refuse any treatment.

6. Receive reasonable medical care and skill.

7. Wait only a reasonable amount of time.

8. Have your records kept confidential.

9. Get copies of requested records.

10. Have an advocate with you.

Patient-Centered Guides
800-998-9938

We Care About What You Think

Which book did this card come from?

_____

Why did you purchase this book?

☐ I am directly impacted

☐ A family member or friend is directly impacted

☐ I am a health-care practitioner looking for information to recommend to patients and their families

☐ Other _____

How did you first find out about the book?

☐ Recommended by a friend/colleague/family member

☐ Recommended by a doctor/nurse

☐ Saw it in a bookstore

☐ Online

☐ Other _____

☐ *Please send me the Patient-Centered Guides catalog.*

What sources do you use to gather your medical information?

☐ Friends/family   ☐ A library

☐ Your doctor   ☐ Your nurse(s)

☐ Television (which shows?) _____

☐ Newspapers (which newspapers?) _____

☐ Magazines (which magazines?) _____

☐ Newsletters (which newsletters) _____

☐ The Internet (which newsgroups, mailing lists or Web sites?) _____

☐ Support Groups (which groups?) _____

☐ Other _____

What other medical conditions are of concern to you, your family, and community?

_____

Name _____ Company/Organization (Optional)

Address _____

City _____ State _____ Zip/Postal Code Country

Telephone _____ Internet or other email address (specify network)

BUSINESS REPLY MAIL

FIRST CLASS MAIL   PERMIT NO. 80   SEBASTOPOL, CA

Postage will be paid by addressee

O'Reilly & Associates, Inc.

101 Morris Street

Sebastopol, CA 95472-9902

Attn: Patient-Centered Guides